Praise for Visual Studio Tools for Office

"With the application development community so focused on the Smart Client revolution, a book that covers VSTO from A to Z is both important and necessary. This book lives up to big expectations. It is thorough, has tons of example code, and covers Office programming in general terms—topics that can be foreign to the seasoned .NET developer who has focused on ASP.NET applications for years. Congratulations to Eric Lippert and Eric Carter for such a valuable work!"
> —Tim Huckaby, CEO, InterKnowlogy, Microsoft regional director

"This book covers all of the ins and outs of programming with Visual Studio Tools for Office in a clear and concise way. Given the authors' exhaustive experiences with this subject, you can't get a more authoritative description of VSTO than this book!"
> —Paul Vick, technical lead, Visual Basic .NET, Microsoft Corporation

"Eric and Eric really get it. Professional programmers will love the rich power of Visual Studio and .NET, along with the ability to tap into Office programmability. This book walks you through programming Excel, Word, InfoPath, and Outlook solutions."
> —Vernon W. Hui, test lead, Microsoft Corporation

"This book is an in-depth, expert, and definitive guide to programming using Visual Studio Tools for Office 2005. It is a must-have book for anyone doing Office development."
> —Siew Moi Khor, programmer/writer, Microsoft Corporation

"We don't buy technical books for light reading, we buy them as a resource for developing a solution. This book is an excellent resource for someone getting started with Smart Client development. For example, it is common to hear a comment along the lines of, 'It is easy to manipulate the Task Pane in Office 2003 using VSTO 2005,' but until you see something like the example at the start of Chapter 15, it is hard to put 'easy' into perspective.
This is a thorough book that covers everything from calling Office applications from your application, to building applications that are Smart Documents. It allows the traditional Windows developer to really leverage the power of Office 2003."

—Bill Sheldon, principal engineer, InterKnowlogy, MVP

"Eric Carter and Eric Lippert have been the driving force behind Office development and Visual Studio Tools for Office 2005. The depth of their knowledge and understanding of VSTO and Office is evident in this book. Professional developers architecting enterprise solutions using VSTO 2005 and Office System 2003 now have a new weapon in their technical arsenal."

—Paul Stubbs, program manager, Microsoft Corporation

"This book is both a learning tool and a reference book, with a richness of tables containing object model objects and their properties, methods, and events. I would recommend it to anyone considering doing Office development using the .NET framework; especially people interested in VSTO programming."

—Rufus Littlefield, software design engineer/tester, Microsoft Corporation

Visual Studio Tools for Office

Microsoft .NET Development Series

John Montgomery, *Series Advisor*
Don Box, *Series Advisor*
Martin Heller, *Series Editor*

The **Microsoft .NET Development Series** is supported and developed by the leaders and experts of Microsoft development technologies including Microsoft architects and DevelopMentor instructors. The books in this series provide a core resource of information and understanding every developer needs in order to write effective applications and managed code. Learn from the leaders how to maximize your use of the .NET Framework and its programming languages.

Titles in the Series

Brad Abrams, *.NET Framework Standard Library Annotated Reference Volume 1: Base Class Library and Extended Numerics Library*, 0-321-15489-4

Brad Abrams and Tamara Abrams, *.NET Framework Standard Library Annotated Reference, Volume 2: Networking Library, Reflection Library, and XML Library*, 0-321-19445-4

Keith Ballinger, *.NET Web Services: Architecture and Implementation*, 0-321-11359-4

Bob Beauchemin, Niels Berglund, Dan Sullivan, *A First Look at SQL Server 2005 for Developers*, 0-321-18059-3

Don Box with Chris Sells, *Essential .NET, Volume 1: The Common Language Runtime*, 0-201-73411-7

Keith Brown, *The .NET Developer's Guide to Windows Security*, 0-321-22835-9

Eric Carter and Eric Lippert, *Visual Studio Tools for Office: Using C# with Excel, Word, Outlook, and InfoPath*, 0-321-33488-4

Mahesh Chand, *Graphics Programming with GDI+*, 0-321-16077-0

Krzysztof Cwalina and Brad Abrams, *Framework Design Guidelines: Conventions, Idioms, and Patterns for Reusable .NET Libraries*, 0-321-24675-6

Anders Hejlsberg, Scott Wiltamuth, Peter Golde, *The C# Programming Language*, 0-321-15491-6

Alex Homer, Dave Sussman, Mark Fussell, *ADO.NET and System.Xml v. 2.0—The Beta Version*, 0-321-24712-4

Alex Homer, Dave Sussman, Rob Howard, *ASP.NET v. 2.0—The Beta Version*, 0-321-25727-8

James S. Miller and Susann Ragsdale, *The Common Language Infrastructure Annotated Standard*, 0-321-15493-2

Christian Nagel, *Enterprise Services with the .NET Framework: Developing Distributed Business Solutions with .NET Enterprise Services*, 0-321-24673-X

Fritz Onion, *Essential ASP.NET with Examples in C#*, 0-201-76040-1

Fritz Onion, *Essential ASP.NET with Examples in Visual Basic .NET*, 0-201-76039-8

Ted Pattison and Dr. Joe Hummel, *Building Applications and Components with Visual Basic .NET*, 0-201-73495-8

Dr. Neil Roodyn, *eXtreme .NET: Introducing eXtreme Programming Techniques to .NET Developers*, 0-321-30363-6

Chris Sells, *Windows Forms Programming in C#*, 0-321-11620-8

Chris Sells and Justin Gehtland, *Windows Forms Programming in Visual Basic .NET*, 0-321-12519-3

Paul Vick, *The Visual Basic .NET Programming Language*, 0-321-16951-4

Damien Watkins, Mark Hammond, Brad Abrams, *Programming in the .NET Environment*, 0-201-77018-0

Shawn Wildermuth, *Pragmatic ADO.NET: Data Access for the Internet World*, 0-201-74568-2

Paul Yao and David Durant, *.NET Compact Framework Programming with C#*, 0-321-17403-8

Paul Yao and David Durant, *.NET Compact Framework Programming with Visual Basic .NET*, 0-321-17404-6

For more information go to www.awprofessional.com/msdotnetseries/

Visual Studio Tools for Office

Using C# with Excel, Word, Outlook, and InfoPath

- Eric Carter
- Eric Lippert

▲▼ **Addison-Wesley**

Upper Saddle River, NJ • Boston • Indianapolis • San Francisco

New York • Toronto • Montreal • London • Munich • Paris

Madrid • Capetown • Sydney • Tokyo • Singapore • Mexico City

Library of Congress
Cataloging-in-Publication Data

Carter, Eric.
  Visual studio tools for office: using C# with Excel, Word, Outlook, and InfoPath / Eric Carter, Eric Lippert.
    p. cm.
  ISBN 0-321-33488-4
  1. C# (Computer program language) 2. Microsoft Excel (Computer file) 3. Microsoft Office. I. Lippert, Eric. II. Title.

  QA76.73.C154C37 2005
  005.13′3—dc22
          2005016456

ISBN 0-321-33488-4
Text printed in the United States on recycled paper at R. R. Donnelley in Crawfordsville, Indiana.
First printing, September 2005

To my wife Tamsyn and our children Jason, Hayley,
Camilla, Rand, and Elizabeth.

—Eric Carter

To Leah Lippert, for embarking with me on a fabulous adventure. And to
David Lippert, who taught me to expect the unexpected along the way.

—Eric Lippert

Contents

About the Authors

E RIC CARTER is a lead developer on the Visual Studio Tools for Office (VSTO) team at Microsoft. He helped invent, design, and implement many of the features that are in VSTO today. Previously at Microsoft he worked on Visual Studio for Applications, the Visual Studio Macros IDE, and Visual Basic for Applications for Office 2000 and Office 2003.

E RIC LIPPERT'S primary focus during his nine years at Microsoft has been on improving the lives of developers by designing and implementing useful programming languages and development tools. He has worked on the Windows Scripting family of technologies and, most recently, Visual Studio Tools for Office.

Foreword

Monday, May 23, 2005

I FACE THE CHALLENGE OF COMPOSING a foreword to this particular book with some amount of trepidation. Let's face it: The names on the cover of this book inspire some amount of awe. It is humbling to know that one's words will introduce what one believes is to be the seminal work on a given topic, and believe me, I'm relatively sure that this one will meet those lofty goals. When approached with the invitation to grace the front matter of the book, my first response was to wonder what I could possibly add—couldn't they find some luminary at Microsoft to preface the book? It seems, however, that an outside voice adds some credence to the proceedings, so, dear reader, I speak meekly in the presence of greatness.

First, a little about me (it's the last chance I'm going to get in this short piece): I've been lurking about, programming Office in its various guises, for upward of 10 years. I've written a lot about the wonders, and gotchas, of Office development, and survived the glory years surrounding Office 2000, when it looked like Office might finally make a successful, integrated development platform. Around 2001, it became clear that no matter how hard I and like-minded folks wanted Office to become a respected development standard, it just wasn't going to make it with VBA as the programming language.

With the release of Visual Studio Tools for Office 2003, it finally looked like we had made some progress—no longer relegated to the 1990s, Office developers could embrace .NET and all its goodness, taking advantage of managed code, code-access security, xcopy deployment, and all the rest that .NET supplied. I loved this product, but it never really reached critical mass with the developer community. Most likely, the fact that you could only use COM-based controls on documents, and the fact that the product supplied no design-time experience at all, made it a slow starter.

Around that time, I remember very clearly sitting down at some Microsoft event and meeting Eric Carter. I didn't really know who he was at the time (and he certainly didn't know anything about me), but he seemed nice enough, and we chatted for several hours about Office development in general, and about VSTO in specific. Only later did I learn that he was high up in the development side of the product. (I spent hours worrying that I had said something really stupid while we were chatting. Hope not.) We began a long correspondence, in which I've more often than not made it clear that I've got a lot to learn about how .NET and Office interact. I've spent many hours learning from Eric's blog, and Eric Lippert's blog is just as meaty. If you are spending time doing Office development, make sure you drop by both:

http://blogs.msdn.com/ericlippert/

http://blogs.msdn.com/eric_carter/

I spent some measurable hours perusing the draft copy of this book, and in each chapter attempted to find some trick, some little nugget, that I had figured out on my own, that didn't appear in the book. I figured that if I was going to review the book, I should add something. The result: I was simply unable to find anything missing. Oh, I'm sure you'll find some little tidbit that you've figured out that won't appear here, but in my quick pass, I wasn't able to. I thought for sure I would catch them on something. Alas, I failed. And, I suppose, that's a good thing, right? Every time I thought I had them in a missing trick, there it was, right there in print. What that means is that you'll have the best possible reference book at your fingertips. Of course, you need to get your expectations set correctly—it's simply not possible, even in a 60-page chapter, to describe the entirety of the Excel or Word object model. But E&E have done an excellent job of pointing out the bits that make the biggest impact on .NET development.

If you're reading this foreword before purchasing the book, just do it. Buy the thing. If you've already bought it, why are you reading this? Get to the heart of the matter—skip ahead, and get going. You can always read this stuff later. There's a considerable hill ahead of you, and it's worth the climb. Office development using managed code has hit new strides with the release of Visual Studio 2005, and personally, I can't wait to take advantage of the answers I find in this book to build great applications.

—Ken Getz, *senior consultant for MCW Technologies*

Preface

I N 2002 THE FIRST RELEASE OF Visual Studio .NET and the .NET Framework was nearing completion. A few of us at Microsoft realized that Office programming was going to miss the .NET wave unless we did something about it.

What had come before was Visual Basic for Applications (VBA), a simple development environment integrated into all the Office applications. Each Office application had a rich object model that was accessed via a technology known as COM. Millions of developers identified themselves as "Office developers" and used VBA and the Office COM object models to do everything from automating repetitive tasks to creating complete business solutions that leveraged the rich features and user interface of Office. These developers realized that their users were spending their days in Office. By building solutions that ran inside of Office, they not only made their users happy, they were also able to create solutions that did more and cost less by reusing functionality already available in the Office applications.

Unfortunately, because of some limitations of VBA, Office programming was starting to get a bad rap. Solutions developed in VBA by small workgroups or individuals would gain momentum and a professional developer would have to take them over and start supporting them. To a professional developer, the VBA environment felt simple and limited, and of course, it enforced a single language: Visual Basic. VBA embedded code in every customized document, which made it hard to fix bugs and update solutions because a bug would get replicated in documents across the enterprise. Security weaknesses in the VBA model led to a rash of worms and macro viruses that made enterprises turn VBA off.

Visual Studio .NET and the .NET Framework provided a way to address all these problems. A huge opportunity existed to not only combine the richness of the new .NET Framework and developer tools with the powerful platform that Office has always provided for developers but to also solve the problems that were plaguing VBA. The result of this realization was Visual Studio Tools for Office (VSTO).

The first version of VSTO was simple, but it accomplished the key goal of letting professional developers use the full power of Visual Studio .NET and the .NET Framework to put code behind Excel 2003 and Word 2003 documents and templates. It let professional developers develop Office solutions in VB.NET and C#. It solved the problem of embedded code by linking a document to a .NET assembly instead of embedding it in the document. It also introduced a new security model that used .NET code-access security to prevent worms and macro viruses.

The second version of VSTO, known as VSTO 2005, the version of VSTO covered by this book, is even more ambitious. It brings with it functionality never available to the Office developer before, such as data binding and data/view separation, design-time views of Excel and Word documents inside Visual Studio, rich support for Windows Forms controls in the document, the ability to create custom Office task panes, server-side programming support against Office—and that's just scratching the surface. Although the primary target of VSTO is the professional developer, that does not mean that building an Office solution with VSTO is rocket science. VSTO makes it possible to create very rich applications with just a few lines of code.

This book tries to put into one place all the information you need to succeed using VSTO to program against Word 2003, Excel 2003, Outlook 2003, and InfoPath 2003. It introduces the Office object models and covers the most commonly used objects in those object models. In addition, this book will help you avoid some pitfalls that result from the COM origins of the Office object models.

This book also provides an insider view of all the rich features of VSTO. We participated in the design and implementation of many of these features. We can therefore speak from the unique perspective of living and breathing VSTO for the past three years. Programming Office using VSTO is powerful and fun. We hope you enjoy using VSTO as much as we enjoyed writing about it and creating it.

—Eric Carter
—Eric Lippert
May 2005

Acknowledgments

THOUGH THERE ARE ONLY TWO names on the cover, no book of this magnitude gets written without the efforts of many dedicated individuals.

Eric Carter would like to thank his entire family for the patience they showed while "Dad" was working on his book: Jason, Hayley, Camilla, Rand, and Elizabeth. Extreme thanks are due to his wife Tamsyn who was ever supportive and kept everything together somehow during this effort.

Eric Lippert would like to thank his excellent wife Leah for her support and tremendous patience over the many months that it took to put this together.

Many thanks to everyone at Addison-Wesley who made this book possible. Joan Murray, Jessica D'Amico, and Elizabeth Zdunich provided expertise, guidance, encouragement, and feedback through every step of the process. Stephane Thomas cajoled us for *years* to get a book proposal together. Thanks are also due to the production and marketing teams at Addison-Wesley, especially Gina Kanouse, Marie McKinley, and Curt Johnson.

A huge thank-you to everyone at Microsoft who over the last three years contributed to Visual Studio Tools for Office. Many people from different disciplines—design, development, education, evangelism, management, marketing and testing—dedicated their passion and energy toward bringing Office development into the managed code world. We could not have written this book without the efforts of all of them. One could not ask for a better group of people to have as colleagues.

A considerable number of industry experts gave the VSTO team valuable feedback over the years. Many thanks to everyone who came so far to give so much of their time and expertise by participating in Software Design Reviews and using early versions of the product. Their suggestions made VSTO a better product than the one we originally envisioned.

We especially thank Andrew Clinick and Hagen Green for their important contributions to this book.

Many thanks to our technical reviewers, whose always-constructive criticism was a huge help. They helped us remove a huge number of errors in the text; those that remain are our own. Thank you, Rufus Littlefield, Siew Moi Khor, Stephen Styrchak, Paul Vick, Paul Stubbs, Kathleen McGrath, Misha Shneerson, Mohit Gupta, and Vernon Hui. And finally, we'd also like to thank KD Hallman, Ken Getz, Mike Hernandez, BJ Holtgrewe, and Martin Heller for their ongoing insight and support.

■ Part One ■

An Introduction to VSTO

T HE FIRST PART OF THIS BOOK INTRODUCES the Office object models and the Office primary interop assemblies (PIAs). You also learn how to use Visual Studio to build automation executables, add-ins, and code behind the document using features of Visual Studio 2005 Tools for Office (VSTO).

- Chapter 1, "An Introduction to Office Programming," introduces the Office object models and examines their basic structure. The chapter describes how to work with objects, collections, and enumerations—the basic types found in all Office object models. You also learn how to use properties, methods, and events exposed by objects and collections in the Office object models. Chapter 1 also introduces the PIAs, which expose the Office object models to .NET code, and describes how to use and reference Office PIAs in a VSTO project.

- Chapter 2, "Introduction to Office Solutions," covers the main ways Office applications are customized and extended. The chapter describes the various kinds of Office solutions you can create using VSTO.

The Other Parts of This Book

Part Two: Office Programming in .NET

Part Two of this book covers the Office object models in more depth. Chapters 3 through 5 cover Excel, Chapters 6 through 8 cover Word, Chapters 9 through 11

■
1

cover Outlook, and Chapter 12 covers InfoPath. There is also some discussion in these chapters about application-specific features and issues. For example, Chapter 3 talks about how to build custom formulas in .NET for Excel. Chapter 5 discusses the Excel-specific "locale" issue in some detail. You can select which chapters of Part Two to read—if you are only interested in Excel development, you can read Chapters 3 through 5 and then skip to Part Three of this book.

Part Three: Office Programming in VSTO

Part Three of this book, comprised of Chapters 13 through 20, describes the features that Visual Studio 2005 Tools for Office brings to Office development. Part Three describes all the features of VSTO, including using Windows Forms controls in Excel and Word documents, using data binding against Office objects, building Smart Tags, and adding Windows Forms controls to Office's task pane.

Part Four: Advanced Office Programming

Finally, Part Four of this book covers advanced programming topics. Chapters 21 and 22 talk about working with XML in Word and Excel with VSTO. Chapter 23 covers how to build managed COM add-ins for Word and Excel. Chapter 24 describes how to develop Outlook add-ins in VSTO.

1.

An Introduction to Office Programming

Why Office Programming?

THE FAMILY OF OFFICE 2003 APPLICATIONS covered by this book (Excel 2003, Word 2003, Outlook 2003, and InfoPath 2003) represents an attractive platform on which to build solutions. You can customize and extend applications by developing solutions against their object models. By building a solution using the Office System, you can reuse some of the most feature-rich and popular applications available. A solution that analyzes or displays data can take advantage of the formatting, charting, calculation, and analysis features of Excel. A solution that creates documents can use the capability of Word to generate, format, and print documents. A solution that manipulates business information can present it in an Outlook folder or in an InfoPath form. It is far better to reuse the applications that you already know than to build these features from scratch.

Information workers use the Office environment on a daily basis. A solution built using Office can become a seamless part of that environment. Too frequently, users must go to a Web page or some other corporate application to get data that they want to cut and paste into an Excel workbook or a Word document anyway. Many users want to use Outlook as their business information portal. By integrating a solution with Office, you enable users to get the information they need without having to switch to another application.

Office Programming and the Professional Developer

Historically, most Office programming has been done via Visual Basic for Applications (VBA) and the macro recording features built in to some Office applications. Users would record a macro to automate a repetitive task within an Office application. Sometimes the code created by recording a macro would be further modified using VBA and turned into more complicated departmental solutions—often by users who were not trained as programmers and whose primary job was not programming. These solutions would sometimes make their way up the corporate food chain and get taken over by professional developers and turned into business solutions.

Unfortunately, VBA and its focus on macro recording sometimes resulted in Office solutions that were too limited for corporate and professional developers. It can be difficult for professional developers to make a VBA solution scale to an entire enterprise. VBA solutions were difficult to update after they were deployed. Often, the professional developer wanted to use a language other than VBA to continue to grow the solution. The ease of use of VBA, although a boon to users who were just getting started with coding, felt limiting to the professional developer who desired a richer programming environment.

Why .NET for Office?

The .NET Framework and its associated class libraries, technologies, and languages address many of the concerns that professional developers had with Office development. Today's Office development can be done using Visual Studio 2005, which is a rich programming environment for professional developers. Developers can use .NET languages such as Visual Basic .NET or C#. The PIAs allow .NET code to call the unmanaged object models that Office applications expose. The rich .NET class libraries enable developers to build Office solutions using technologies such as Windows Forms to show user interface (UI) and Web Services to connect to corporate data servers.

Why Visual Studio Tools for Office?

Visual Studio Tools 2005 for Office (VSTO) adds .NET support for Word, Excel, Outlook, and InfoPath programming to Visual Studio. VSTO turns the Word or Excel document being programmed against into a .NET class, replete with data binding support, controls that can be coded against much like a Windows Forms control, and other .NET features. It makes it easy to integrate .NET code into Outlook. It enables developers to put .NET code behind InfoPath forms. Developers can even program against key Office objects without having to traverse the entire Office object model.

How .NET Is It?

This book discusses many new .NET ways of programming against Office applications. However, some aspects of Office programming remain awkward using .NET. Most of these awkward areas are attributable to the fact that the Office object models were designed to work with a technology called COM. Although .NET code can talk to the Office object models via PIAs, the object models sometimes do not feel very .NET-friendly. Furthermore, the Office object models do not always follow the naming conventions or design patterns of classes that were designed for .NET.

In the future, many of the Office object models will likely be redesigned for .NET, and the object models will feel friendlier to a .NET developer. For now, developers must live in a transitional period in which some aspects of Office programming feel like they were designed for .NET, and others aspects do not. This book discusses some of the most difficult problems developers encounter when using .NET with Office and how to work around these problems.

Office Object Models

Almost all Office programming involves writing code that uses the object model of an Office application. The object model is the set of objects provided by the Office application that running code can use to control the Office application. The object model of each Office application is organized hierarchically with the object called Application forming the root of the hierarchy. From the Application object, other objects that make up the object model of the Office application can be accessed.

As an example of how object model objects are related in the object model hierarchy, Figure 1-1 shows some of the most important objects in the Word object model. The root object is the Application object. Also shown in this diagram are some other objects, including Documents, Document, Paragraphs, and Paragraph. The Application object and Documents object are related because the Documents object is returned via a property on the Application object. Other objects are not directly accessible from the root Application object, but are accessible by traversing a path. For example, the Paragraphs object is accessed by traversing the path from Application to Documents to Document to Paragraphs. Figure 1-2 shows a similar diagram for some major objects in the Excel object model hierarchy.

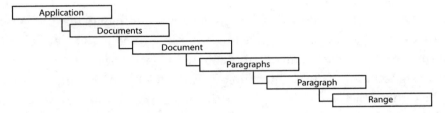

Figure 1-1 Hierarchy in the Word object model.

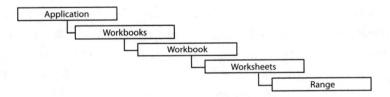

Figure 1-2 Hierarchy in the Excel object model.

Objects

Each Office application's object model consists of many objects that you can use to control the Office application. Word has 248 distinct objects, Excel has 196, and Outlook has 67. Objects tend to correspond to features and concepts in the application itself. For example, Word has objects such as Document, Bookmark, and Paragraph—all of which correspond to features of Word. Excel has objects such as Workbook, Worksheet, Font, Hyperlink, Chart, and Series—all of which correspond to features of Excel. As you might suppose, the most important and most used objects in the object models are the ones that correspond to the application itself, the document, and key elements in a document such as a range of text in Word. Most solutions use these key objects and only a small number of other objects in the object models. Table 1-1 lists some of the key objects in Word, Excel, and Outlook along with brief descriptions of what these objects do.

Table 1-1 Key Office Object Model Objects

Object Name	What It Does
All Office Applications	
Application	The root object of the object model. Provides properties that return other objects in the object model. Provides methods and properties to set application-wide settings. Raises application-level events.
CommandBars	Enables the developer to add, delete, and modify toolbars, buttons, menus, and menu items.
Window	Enables the developer to position windows and modify window-specific settings. In Outlook, the objects that perform this function are the Explorer and Inspector objects.
Word Objects	
Document	Represents the Word document. Is the root object of the content-specific part of the Word object model. Raises document-level events.
Paragraph	Enables the developer to access a paragraph in a Word document.
Range	Enables the developer to access and modify a range of text in a Word document. Provides methods and properties to set the text, set the formatting of the text, and perform other operations on the range of text.
Excel Objects	
Workbook	Represents the Excel workbook. Is the root object of the content-specific part of the Excel object model. Raises workbook-level events.
Worksheet	Enables the developer to work with a worksheet within an Excel workbook.
Range	Enables the developer to access and modify a cell or range of cells in an Excel workbook. Provides methods and properties to set the cell value, change the formatting, and perform other operations on the range of cells.

continues

Table 1-1 Continued

Outlook Objects	
`MAPIFolder`	Represents a folder within Outlook that can contain various Outlook items such as MailItem, ContactItem, and so on as well as other folders. Raises events at the folder level for selected actions that occur to the folder or items in the folder.
`MailItem`	Represents a mail item within Outlook. Provides methods and properties to access the subject and message body of the mail along with recipient and other information. Raises events when selected actions occur that involve the mail item.
`ContactItem`	Represents a contact within Outlook. Provides methods and properties to access the information in the contact. Raises events when selected actions occur that involve the contact.
`AppointmentItem`	Represents an appointment within Outlook. Provides methods and properties to access the information in the appointment. Raises events when selected actions occur that involve the appointment.

Where objects in an Office object model start to differ from typical .NET classes is that the vast majority of object model objects are not creatable or "new-able." In most Office object models, the number of objects that can be created by using the new keyword is on the order of one to five objects. In most Office solutions, new will never be used to create an Office object—instead, an already created Office object, typically the root Application object, is passed to the solution.

Because most Office object model objects cannot be created directly, they are instead accessed via the object model hierarchy. For example, Listing 1-1 shows how to get a Worksheet object in Excel starting from the Application object. This code is a bit of a long-winded way to navigate the hierarchy because it declares a variable to store each object as it traverses the hierarchy. The code assumes that the root Excel Application object has been passed to the code and assigned to a variable named app. It also uses C#'s as operator to cast the object returned from the Worksheets collection as a Worksheet, which is necessary because the Worksheet collection is a collection of `object` for reasons described in Chapter 3, "Programming Excel."

Listing 1-1 Navigating from the Application Object to a Worksheet in Excel

```
Excel.Workbooks myWorkbooks = app.Workbooks;
Excel.Workbook myWorkbook = myWorkbooks.get_Item(1);
Excel.Worksheets myWorksheets = myWorkbook.Worksheets;
Excel.Worksheet myWorksheet = myWorksheets.get_Item(1) as Excel.Worksheet;
```

If the code does not need to cache each object model object in a variable as it goes but only needs to get a Worksheet object, a more efficient way to write this code is as follows:

```
Excel.Worksheet myWorksheet2 = app.Workbooks.get_Item(1).
Worksheets.get_Item(1) as Excel.Worksheet;
```

Collections

Paragraphs and Documents are examples of a type of object called a collection. A collection is a specialized object that represents a group of objects. Typically, a collection is named so that its name is the plural of the type of the object it contains. For example, the Documents collection object is a collection of Document objects. Some collection objects may be collections of a value type such as a `string`.

Collections typically have a standard set of properties and methods. A collection has a Count property, which returns the number of objects in the collection. A collection also has an Item method, which takes a parameter, typically a number, to specify the index of the desired object in the collection. A collection may have other properties and methods in addition to these standard properties and methods.

Listing 1-2 shows iteration over a collection using the Count property of the collection and the Item method of the collection. Although this is not the preferred way of iterating over a collection (you typically use `foreach` instead), it does illustrate two key points. First, collections in Office object models are almost always 1-based, meaning they start at index 1 rather than index 0. Second, the parameter passed to the get_Item method is often passed as an `object` so you can either specify a numeric index as an `int` or the name of the object within the collection as a `string`.

Listing 1-2 Iterating Over a Collection Using the Count Property and the get_Item Method with Either an int or a string Index

```
Excel.Workbooks myWorkbooks = app.Workbooks;
int workbookCount = myWorkbooks.Count;

for (int i = 1; i <= workbookCount; i++)
{
  // Get the workbook by its int index
  Excel.Workbook myWorkbook = myWorkbooks.get_Item(i);

  // Get the workbook by its string index
  string workbookName = myWorkbook.Name;

  Excel.Workbook myWorkbook2 = myWorkbooks.get_Item(workbookName);
  MessageBox.Show(String.Format("Workbook {0}", myWorkbook2.Name));
}
```

If you were to look at the definition for the Workbooks collection's get_Item method, you would see that it takes an `object` parameter. Even though the get_Item method takes an `object` parameter, we pass an `int` value and a `string` value to it in Listing 1-2. This works because C# can automatically convert a value type such as an `int` or a `string` to an `object` when you pass the value type to a method that takes an `object`. This automatic conversion is called boxing. C# automatically creates an `object` instance known as a box to put the value type into when passing it to the method.

The preferred way of iterating over a collection is using the `foreach` syntax of C#, as shown in Listing 1-3.

Listing 1-3 Iterating over a Collection Using foreach

```
Excel.Workbooks myWorkbooks = app.Workbooks;

foreach (Excel.Workbook workbook in myWorkbooks)
{
  MessageBox.Show(String.Format("Workbook {0}", workbook.Name));
}
```

Sometimes you may want to iterate over a collection and delete objects from the collection by calling a Delete method on each object as you go. This is a risky practice because behavior of a collection in the Office object models is sometimes undefined if you are deleting items from it as you iterate over it. Instead, as you iterate over the Office object model collection, add the objects you want to delete to a .NET collection you have created, such as a list or an array. After you have iterated over the Office object model collection and added all the objects you want to delete to your collection, iterate over your collection and call the Delete method on each object.

Enumerations

An enumeration is a type defined in an object model that represents a fixed set of possible values. The Word object model contains 252 enumerations, Excel 195, and Outlook 55.

As an example of an enumeration, Word's object model contains an enumeration called WdWindowState. WdWindowState is an enumeration that has three possible values: wdWindowStateNormal, wdWindowStateMaximize, wdWindowStateMinimize. These are constants you can use directly in your code when testing for a value. Each value corresponds to an integer value. (For example, wdWindowStateNormal is equivalent to 0.) However, it is considered bad programming style to make comparisons to the integer values rather than the constant names themselves because it makes the code less readable.

Properties, Methods, and Events

Objects in an Office application's object model are .NET classes that have properties, methods, and events that can be accessed by solution code. An object in the object model is required to have at least one property, method, or event. Most of the objects in an Office application's object model have several properties, a few methods, and no events. The most important objects in the object model, such as Application and Document, are typically much more complex and have a much larger number of properties and methods as well as events. For example, Word's Application object has about 100 properties, 60 methods, and 20 events. Table 1-2 lists some of the properties, methods, and events on the Word Application object to give a sense of the types of functionality an object model object provides.

Table 1-2 Selected Properties, Methods, and Events from Word's Application Object

Name	What It Does
Properties	
ActiveDocument	Returns a Document object for the active document— the document that is currently being edited by the user.
ActivePrinter	Gets and sets the default printer.
Caption	Gets and sets the caption text for the application window—typically this is set to "Microsoft Word."
Documents	Returns a Documents collection that represents the collection of open Word documents.
Methods	
Activate	Brings Word to the front of other windows and makes it the active window.
NewWindow	Creates a new Word window that shows the same document as the currently active window and returns a Window object model object representing that new window.
Quit	Closes Word.
Events	
DocumentBeforeClose	An event that is raised before a document is closed. The Document object for the document being closed is passed as a parameter to the event along with a bool cancel parameter. If the code handling the event sets the cancel parameter to true, the document will not be closed.
DocumentOpen	An event that is raised when a document is opened. The Document object for the document being opened is passed as a parameter to the event.
WindowActivate	An event that is raised when a Word window is activated by the user, typically by clicking an inactive window thereby making it active. The Document object for the document being activated is passed as a parameter to the event along with a Window object for the window that was activated (because two windows could be showing the same document).

In Office object models, properties predominate, followed by methods, and trailed distantly by events. Figure 1-3 shows the distribution of properties, methods, and events in the Word, Excel, and Outlook object models. A couple of general statements can be made about the Office object models as shown by Figure 1-3. The Excel object model is the biggest of the Office object models in terms of total number of properties, methods, and events, followed closely by Word. Word has a very small number of events. We can also say that there are many more properties in Office object models than methods.

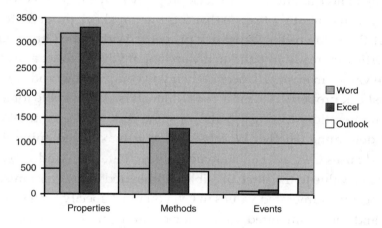

Figure 1-3 Distribution of properties, methods, and events in the Word, Excel, and Outlook object models.

Properties

Properties are simple methods which allow you to read or write particular named values associated with an object. For example, Word's Application object has a property called CapsLock, which returns a `bool` value. If the Caps Lock key is down, it will return `true`; if the Caps Lock key is up, it will return `false`. Listing 1-4 shows some code that examines this property. The code assumes that the root Application object of the Word object model has already been assigned to a variable called `app`.

Listing 1-4 A Property That Returns a Value Type—the bool CapsLock Property on Word's Application Object

```
if (app.CapsLock == true)
{
  MessageBox.Show("CapsLock key is down");
}
else
{
  MessageBox.Show("CapsLock key is up");
}
```

Another thing to note about the CapsLock property is that it is a read-only property. That is to say, you cannot write code that sets the CapsLock property to `false`; you can only get the value of the CapsLock property. Within the Office object model, many properties are read-only, and many are not. If you try to set a read-only property to some value, an error will occur when you compile your code.

The CapsLock property returns a `bool` value. It is also possible for a property to return an enumeration. Listing 1-5 shows some code that uses the WindowState property to determine whether Word's window is maximized, minimized, or normal. This code uses C#'s `switch` statement to evaluate the WindowState property and compare its value to the three possible enumerated value constants. Notice that when you specify enumerated values in C#, you must specify both the enumerated type name and the enumerated value—for example, if you just used `wdWindow-StateNormal` rather than `WdWindowState.wdWindowStateNormal` the code will not compile.

Listing 1-5 A Property That Returns an Enumeration—the WindowState Property on Word's Application Object

```
switch (app.WindowState)
{
  case Word.WdWindowState.wdWindowStateNormal:
    MessageBox.Show("Normal");
    break;

  case Word.WdWindowState.wdWindowStateMaximize:
    MessageBox.Show("Maximized");
    break;
```

```
case Word.WdWindowState.wdWindowStateMinimize:
  MessageBox.Show("Minimized");
  break;

default:
  break;
}
```

Properties can also return other object model objects. For example, Word's Application object has a property called ActiveDocument that returns the currently active document—the one the user is currently editing. The ActiveDocument property returns another object in the Word object model called Document. Document in turn also has properties, methods, and events. Listing 1-6 shows code that examines the ActiveDocument property and then displays the Name property of the Document object.

Listing 1-6 A Property That Returns Another Object Model Object—the ActiveDocument Property on Word's Application Object

```
Word.Document myDocument = app.ActiveDocument;
MessageBox.Show(myDocument.Name);
```

What happens if there is no active document—for example, if Word is running but no documents are opened? In the case of the ActiveDocument property, it throws an exception. So a safer version of the preceding code would catch the exception and report no active document was found. Listing 1-7 shows this safer version. An even better approach is to check the Count property of the Application object's Documents collection to see whether any documents are open before accessing the Active-Document property.

Listing 1-7 A Property That Might Throw an Exception—the ActiveDocument Property on Word's Application Object

```
Word.Document myDocument = null;
try
{
    myDocument = app.ActiveDocument;
    MessageBox.Show(myDocument.Name);
}
catch (Exception ex)
{
```

```
    MessageBox.Show(
        String.Format("No active document: {0}", ex.Message));
}
```

Object models sometimes behave differently in an error case in which the object you are asking for is not available or does not make sense in a particular context. The property can return a `null` value. The way to determine whether an object model property will throw an exception or return a `null` value is by consulting the object model documentation for the property in question. Excel's Application object uses this pattern for its ActiveWorkbook property. If no Excel workbook is open, it returns `null` instead of throwing an exception. Listing 1-8 shows how to write code that handles this pattern of behavior.

Listing 1-8 A Property That Might Return null—the ActiveWorkbook Property on Excel's Application Object

```
Excel.Workbook myWorkbook = app.ActiveWorkbook;

if (myWorkbook == null)
{
    MessageBox.Show("No active workbook");
}
else
{
    MessageBox.Show(myWorkbook.Name);
}
```

Parameterized Properties

The properties examined so far are parameterless. However, some properties require parameters. For example, Word's Application object has a property called FileDialog that returns a FileDialog object. The FileDialog property takes an enumeration parameter of type `MsoFileDialogType`, which is used to pick which FileDialog is returned. Its possible values are `msoFileDialogOpen`, `msoFileDialogSaveAs`, `msoFileDialogFilePicker`, and `msoFileDialogFolderPicker`.

C# does not support calling parameterized properties as properties. When you go to use the Word object model from C# and look for the FileDialog property on Word's Application object, it is nowhere to be seen. The FileDialog property is callable from C#, but only via a method—the method is named get_FileDialog. So when you are looking for a parameterized property in C#, be sure to look for the get_*Property* method (where *Property* is the name of the property you want to access). To set parameterized properties in C# (assuming they are not read-only properties), there is a separate method called set_*Property* (where *Property* is the name of the property you are going to set).

An exception to this is found when using VSTO. A handful of Word and Excel object model objects are extended by VSTO. These objects have been extended to give you a different way of accessing a parameterized property—via an indexer. An indexer enables you to access the property in the same way you would access an array—with the name of the property followed by a parameter list between the delimiters [and]. So for an object model object extended by VSTO, such as Worksheet, a parameterized property such as Range, which takes two parameters, can be called using the indexer syntax : Range[`parameter1`, `parameter2`] instead of get_Range(`parameter1`, `parameter2`).

The code in Listing 1-9 uses the FileDialog property called as a method and passes msoFileDialogFilePicker as a parameter to specify the type of FileDialog object to be returned. It then calls a method on the returned FileDialog object to show the dialog.

Listing 1-9 A Parameterized Property Called as a Method That Takes an Enumeration Parameter and Returns an Object Model Object—the FileDialog Property on Word's Application Object

```
Office.FileDialog dialog = app.get_FileDialog(
  Office.MsoFileDialogType.msoFileDialogFilePicker);
dialog.Show();
```

The Office object models also have properties that have optional parameters. Optional parameters are parameters that can be omitted and the Office application will fill in a default value for the parameter. Optional parameters are typically of type object because of how optional parameters are passed to the underlying COM API. In C#, you must pass a special value to optional parameters that are of type object if you do not want to specify the parameter. This special value is called Type.Missing, and it must be passed for optional parameters that you do not want to specify directly (unlike Visual Basic in which you can omit the parameter entirely). In VSTO projects, a "missing" variable is predeclared for you (that is, set to Type.Missing). Therefore, in VSTO code, you will often see missing passed rather than Type.Missing.

Occasionally, you will find an optional parameter is of some enumeration type rather than of type `object`. For this kind of optional parameter, you cannot pass `Type.Missing` and must instead pass a specific enumerated type value. You can find out what the default enumerated type value is for the optional parameter by consulting the documentation for the method or by using the object browser in a Visual Basic project—unfortunately, the C# object browser does not show the default value for an optional enumerated type parameter.

Listing 1-10 shows an example of calling a parameterized property called Range, which is found on Excel's Application object. The Range property is accessed via the get_Range method because parameterized properties can only be called via a method in C#. Calling the get_Range method on Excel's Application object returns the Range object in the active workbook as specified by the parameters passed to the method. The get_Range method takes two parameters. The first parameter is required, and the second parameter is optional. If you want to specify a single cell, you just pass the first parameter. If you want to specify multiple cells, you have to specify the top-left cell in the first parameter and the bottom-right cell in the second parameter.

Listing 1-10 A Parameterized Property Called as a Method with Optional Parameters—the Range Property on Excel's Application Object

```
// Calling a parameterized property with a missing optional parameter
Excel.Range myRange = app.get_Range("A1", Type.Missing);

// Calling a parameterized property without missing parameters
Excel.Range myRange2 = app.get_Range("A1", "B2");
```

In Word, optional parameters are handled differently than in the other Office applications. Word's object model requires that optional parameters be passed by reference. This means that you cannot pass `Type.Missing` directly as the code in Listing 1-10 did. Instead, you must declare a variable, set it to `Type.Missing`, and pass that variable by reference. You can reuse the same declared variable that has been set to `Type.Missing` if a parameter has multiple parameters you want to omit. In a VSTO project, you can just pass by reference the `missing` variable that is predeclared for you. Listing 1-11 shows how to specify optional parameters in Word. In this example, the code uses a parameterized property from Word's Application object called SynonymInfo, which has a required `string` parameter to specify a word you want a synonym for and an optional parameter to specify the language ID you want to use. The SynonymInfo property is accessed via the get_SynonymInfo method because parameterized properties can only be called via a method in C#. By omitting the optional language ID parameter and passing by reference a variable set to `Type.Missing`, Word will default to use the current language you have installed.

Listing 1-11 A Parameterized Property Called as a Method with Optional Parameters Passed by Reference—the SynonymInfo Property on Word's Application Object

```
object missing = Type.Missing;

// Calling a parameterized property in Word
// with a missing optional parameter
Word.SynonymInfo synonym = app.get_SynonymInfo(
    "happy", ref missing);
```

Properties Common to Most Objects

Because all the object model objects have `object` as their base class, you will always find the methods GetType, GetHashCode, Equals, and ToString on every object model object. You will also often find a property called Application that will return the Application object associated with the object. This is provided as a quick way to get back to the root of the object model. Many objects have a property called Creator, which gives you a code indicating which application the object was created in. Finally, you will often find a Parent property that returns the object that is the parent in the object model hierarchy.

Methods

A method is typically more complex than a property and represents a "verb" on the object that causes something to happen. It may or may not have a return value and is more likely to have parameters than a property.

The simplest form of a method has no return type and no parameters. Listing 1-12 shows the use of the Activate method from Word's Application object. This method activates the Word application, making its window the active window (the equivalent of clicking the Word window in the taskbar to activate it).

Listing 1-12   A Method with No Parameters and No Return Type—the Activate Method on Word's Application Object

```
MessageBox.Show("Activating the Word window.");

app.Activate();
```

Methods may also have parameters and no return type. Listing 1-13 shows an example of this kind of a method. The ChangeFileOpenDirectory method takes a `string` that is the name of the directory you want Word to default to when the Open dialog box is shown. For a method this simple, you might wonder why a property was not used instead—for example, you can imagine Word having a FileOpenDirectory property. In this case, the ChangeFileOpenDirectory only changes the default open directory temporarily—for the lifetime of the current Word session. When you exit Word and then restart Word, the default will no longer be what you set with this method. Perhaps for this reason, this functionality was exposed via a method rather than a property. A second reason why object models sometimes use a simple method such as this rather than a property is because some values exposed in an object model are "write-only"; that is, they can only be set but cannot be read. It is common to create a read-only property, but not common to create a write-only property. So when a write-only property is needed, a simple method is often used instead.

Listing 1-13   A Method with Parameters and No Return Type—the ChangeFileOpenDirectory Method on Word's Application Object

```
app.ChangeFileOpenDirectory(@"c:\temp");

MessageBox.Show("Will open out of temp for this session.");
```

Methods can have no parameters and a return type. Listing 1-14 shows an example of this kind of a method. The DefaultWebOptions method returns the Default-WebOptions object, which is then used to set options for Word's Web features. In this case, DefaultWebOptions really should have been implemented as a read-only property as opposed to a method.

Listing 1-14 A Method with No Parameters and A Return Type—the DefaultWebOptions Method on Word's Application Object

```
Word.DefaultWebOptions options = app.DefaultWebOptions();

MessageBox.Show(String.Format("Pixels per inch is {0}.",
    options.PixelsPerInch));
```

Methods can have parameters and a return type. Listing 1-15 shows an example of this kind of a method. The CentimetersToPoints method takes a centimeter value and converts it to points, which it returns as the return value of the method. Points is a unit often used by Word when specifying spacing in the document.

Listing 1-15 A Method with Parameters and a Return Type—the CentimetersToPoints Method on Word's Application Object

```
float centimeters = 15.0;

float points = app.CentimetersToPoints(centimeters);

MessageBox.Show(String.Format("{0} centimeters is {1} points.",
    centimeters, points));
```

Methods can also have optional parameters. Optional parameters do not need to be specified directly to call the method. For any parameters you do not want to specify, you pass a special value defined by .NET called `Type.Missing`. Listing 1-16 shows a method called CheckSpelling in Excel that has optional parameters. Listing 1-16 illustrates the syntax you use to omit parameters you do not want to specify. The CheckSpelling method takes a required `string`—the word you want to check the spelling of—along with two optional parameters. The first optional parameter enables you to pick a custom dictionary to check the spelling against. The second optional parameter enables you to tell the spell checker to ignore words in all upper-case—such as an acronym. In Listing 1-16, we check a phrase without specifying any of the optional parameters—we pass `Type.Missing` to each optional parameter. We also check a second phrase that has an acronym in all uppercase so we pass `Type.Missing` to the first optional parameter because we do not want to use a custom dictionary, but we specify the second optional parameter to be `true` so the spell checker will ignore the words in all uppercase.

Listing 1-16 A Method with Optional Parameters and a Return Type—the CheckSpelling Method on Excel's Application Object

```
string phrase1 = "Thes is spelled correctly. ";
string phrase2 = "This is spelled correctly AFAIK. ";

bool isCorrect1 = app.CheckSpelling(phrase1,
   Type.Missing, Type.Missing);

bool isCorrect2 = app.CheckSpelling(phrase2,
   Type.Missing, true);
```

Optional Parameters in Word

Optional parameters in Word can produce some strange looking C# code because the values passed to optional parameters must be passed by reference. For example, Listing 1-17 shows how to spell check a string using the Word object model in C#.

Listing 1-17 A Method with Optional Parameters Passed by Reference—the CheckSpelling Method on Word's Application Object

```
void SpellCheckString()
{
    string phrase1 = "Speling erors here.";
    object ignoreUpperCase = true;
    object missing = Type.Missing;

    bool spellingError = app.CheckSpelling(phrase1,
        ref missing, ref ignoreUpperCase, ref missing,
        ref missing, ref missing, ref missing,
        ref missing, ref missing, ref missing,
        ref missing, ref missing, ref missing);

    if (spellingError)
        MessageBox.Show("Spelling error found");
    else
        MessageBox.Show("No errors");
}
```

The first thing that probably comes to mind if you are a Visual Basic programmer and you have never seen code written against Word in C# is "Why is this so verbose?" Visual Basic does some special things for you when there are optional arguments in a method, so the Visual Basic version of this is much simpler, as shown in Listing 1-18.

Listing 1-18 A Method with Optional Parameters Passed by Reference Using Visual Basic—
the CheckSpelling Method on Word's Application Object

```
Public Sub SpellCheckString()
    Dim phrase1 As String = "Speling erors here."
    Dim spellingError As Boolean
    spellingError = app.CheckSpelling(myString, , True)

    If spellingError Then
      MsgBox("Spelling error found.")
    Else
      MsgBox("No error found.")
    End If
End Sub
```

In Visual Basic, you do not have to worry about passing a value for each optional argument—the language handles this for you. You can even use commas, as shown in Listing 1-18, to omit one particular variable you do not want to specify. In this case, we did not want to specify a custom dictionary, but we did want to pass a value for the parameter IgnoreUpperCase, so we omitted the custom dictionary argument by just leaving it out between the commas.

The first thing that probably comes to mind if you're a C# programmer and you have never seen code written against Word in C#, such as the code shown in Listing 1-17, is "Why is all that stuff passed by reference?" When you are talking to Office object model methods, properties, and events, you are talking to the object model through a .NET technology called COM interop (short for interoperate). The Office object models are all written in unmanaged code (C and C++) that is exposed via COM interfaces. You will read more detail later in this chapter about the technology called interop assemblies that allows managed code to call COM objects.

If you were to examine the COM definition for the CheckSpelling method used in Listing 1-17 as defined by Word's COM type library, you would see something like this:

```
HRESULT CheckSpelling(
    [in] BSTR Word,
    [in, optional] VARIANT* CustomDictionary,
    [in, optional] VARIANT* IgnoreUppercase,
    [in, optional] VARIANT* MainDictionary,
    [in, optional] VARIANT* CustomDictionary2,
    [in, optional] VARIANT* CustomDictionary3,
    [in, optional] VARIANT* CustomDictionary4,
```

```
[in, optional] VARIANT* CustomDictionary5,
[in, optional] VARIANT* CustomDictionary6,
[in, optional] VARIANT* CustomDictionary7,
[in, optional] VARIANT* CustomDictionary8,
[in, optional] VARIANT* CustomDictionary9,
[in, optional] VARIANT* CustomDictionary10,
[out, retval] VARIANT_BOOL* prop);
```

Note that any parameter that is marked as optional is specified as a pointer to a VARIANT in Word (VARIANT*). A VARIANT is a type in COM that is roughly equivalent to `object` in .NET—it can contain many different types of values. Excel does not typically use a pointer to a VARIANT for optional parameters, so you do not have this by ref issue for most of Excel. When the PIA is generated, the C# IntelliSense looks like this:

```
bool _Application.CheckSpelling(string Word,
   ref object CustomDictionary,
   ref object IgnoreUppercase,
   ref object MainDictionary,
   ref object CustomDictionary2,
   ref object CustomDictionary3,
   ref object CustomDictionary4,
   ref object CustomDictionary5,
   ref object CustomDictionary6,
   ref object CustomDictionary7,
   ref object CustomDictionary8,
   ref object CustomDictionary9,
   ref object CustomDictionary10)
```

Because of how Word defined optional parameters in its COM objects (as pointer to a VARIANT) and because of how that translates into .NET code (an object passed by reference), any optional argument in Word has to be passed by reference from C# and has to be declared as an `object`. Even though you would like to strongly type the `IgnoreUppercase` parameter to be a `bool` in the CheckSpelling example, you cannot. You have to type it as an object or you will get a compile error. This ends up being a little confusing because you can strongly type the first argument—the string you want to check. That's because in the CheckSpelling method, the `Word` argument (the string you are spell checking) is not an optional argument to CheckSpelling. Therefore, it is strongly typed and not passed by reference. Also note that optional arguments are always listed after all required arguments—that is, you will never find a situation where *argument1* is optional and *argument2* is not.

This brings us back to `Type.Missing`. In C# to omit an optional argument you pass an object by reference set to `Type.Missing`. In our example, we just declared one variable called `missing` and passed it in 11 times.

When you pass objects by reference to most managed functions, you do so because the managed function is telling you that it might change the value of that object you passed into the function. So it might seem bad to you that we are declaring one variable and passing it to all the parameters of CheckSpelling that we do not care about. After all, imagine you have a function that takes two parameters by reference. If you pass in the same variable set to `Type.Missing` to both parameters, what if the code evaluating the first parameter changes it from `Type.Missing` to some other value such as the `bool` value `true`? This would also affect both the first parameter and the second parameter, and the function might do something different when it looks at the second parameter that was originally set to `Type.Missing` because it is now set to `true` as well.

To avoid this, you might think we would have to declare a `missing1` through `missing11` variable because of the possibility that Word might go and change one of the by ref parameters on you and thereby make it so you are no longer passing `Type.Missing` but something else such as `true` that might cause unintended side effects.

Fortunately, you do not have to do this when working with Office object models. Remember that the underlying Word Application object is an unmanaged object, and you are talking to it through COM interop. The COM interop layer realizes that you are passing a `Type.Missing` to an optional argument on a COM object. So interop obliges and instead of passing a reference to your `missing` variable in some way, the interop layer passes a special COM value that indicates that the parameter was missing. Your `missing` variable that you passed by reference is safe because it was never really passed directly into Word. It is impossible for Word to mess with your variable, even though when you look at the syntax of the call it looks like it would be possible because it is passed by reference.

Therefore, the CheckSpelling code in Listing 1-17 is completely correct. Your `missing` variable is safe—it will not be changed on you by Word even though you pass it by reference. But remember, this is a special case that only applies when talking through COM interop to an unmanaged object model that has optional arguments. Do not let this special case make you sloppy when calling methods on objects outside the Office object model that require parameters to be passed by reference. When talking to non-Office object model methods, you have to be careful when passing parameters by reference because the managed method can change the variable you pass.

Events

You have now read about the use of properties and methods in some detail—these are both ways that your code controls the Office application. Events are the way the Office application talks back to your code and enables you to run additional code in response to some condition that occurred in the Office application.

In the Office object models, there are far fewer events than there are methods and properties—for example, there are 36 events in Word and 84 in Excel. Some of these events are duplicated on different objects. For example, when the user opens a Word document, both the Application object and the newly created Document object raise Open events. If you wanted to handle all Open events on all documents, you would handle the Open event on the Application object. If you had code associated with a particular document, you would handle the Open event on the corresponding Document object.

In most of the Office object models, events are raised by a handful of objects. The only objects that raise events in the Word object model are Application, Document, and OLEControl. The only objects that raise events in the Excel object model are Application, Workbook, Worksheet, Chart, OLEObject, and QueryTable. Outlook is a bit of an exception: About half of the objects in the Outlook object model raise events. However, most of these objects raise the same set of events, making the total number of unique events small in Outlook as well.

Table 1-3 shows all the events raised by Excel's Application object. This table represents almost all the events raised by Excel because events prefaced by Sheet are duplicated on Excel's Worksheet object and events prefaced by Workbook are duplicated on Excel's Workbook object. The only difference in these duplicated events is that the Application-level Sheet and Workbook events pass a parameter of type Sheet or Workbook to indicate which worksheet or workbook raised the event. Events raised by a Workbook object or Sheet object do not have to pass the `Sheet` or `Workbook` parameter because it is implicitly determined from which Workbook or Sheet object you are handling events for.

Table 1-3 Events Raised by Excel's Application Object

Event Name	When It Is Raised
NewWorkbook	When a new workbook is created
SheetActivate	When any worksheet is activated
SheetBeforeDoubleClick	When any worksheet is double-clicked
SheetBeforeRightClick	When any worksheet is right-clicked
SheetCalculate	After any worksheet is recalculated
SheetChange	When cells in any worksheet are changed by the user
SheetDeactivate	When any worksheet is deactivated
ShetFollowHyperlink	When the user clicks a hyperlink in any worksheet
SheetPivotTableUpdate	After the sheet of a PivotTable report has been updated
SheetSelectionChange	When the selection changes on any worksheet
WindowActivate	When any workbook window is activated
WindowDeactivate	When any workbook window is deactivated
WindowResize	When any workbook window is resized
WorkbookActivate	When any workbook is activated
WorkbookAddinInstall	When any workbook is installed as an add-in
WorkbookAddinUninstall	When any workbook is uninstalled as an add-in
WorkbookAfterXmlExport	After data in a workbook is exported as an XML data file
WorkbookAfterXmlImport	After data in a workbook is imported from an XML data file
WorkbookBeforeClose	Before any workbook is closed
WorkbookBeforePrint	Before any workbook is printed
WorkbookBeforeSave	Before any workbook is saved
WorkbookBeforeXmlExport	Before data in any workbook is exported as an XML data file

continues

Table 1-3 Continued

Event Name	When It Is Raised
WorkbookBeforeXmlImport	Before data in any workbook is imported from an XML data file
WorkbookDeactivate	When any workbook window is deactivated
WorkbookNewSheet	When a new worksheet is created in any workbook
WorkbookOpen	When any workbook is opened
WorkbookPivot TableCloseConnection	After a PivotTable report connection has been closed
WorkbookPivot TableOpenConnection	After a PivotTable report connection has been opened
WorkbookSync	When a workbook that is part of a document workspace is synchronized with a copy on the server

To handle the events raised by Office object models, you must first declare a callback method in your code that matches the signature expected by the event being raised. For example, the Open event on the Application object in Excel expects a callback method to match the signature of this delegate:

```
public delegate void AppEvents_WorkbookOpenEventHandler(Workbook wb);
```

To handle this event, you must declare a callback method that matches the expected signature. Note that we omit the `delegate` keyword shown in the signature above in our callback method because we are not defining a new delegate type, just implementing an existing one defined by the Office object model.

```
public void MyOpenHandler(Excel.Workbook wb)
{
   MessageBox.Show(wb.Name + " was opened. ");
}
```

Finally, you must connect your callback method up to the Excel Application object that raises this event. We create a new instance of the delegate object defined by the Excel object model called AppEvents_WorkbookOpenEventHandler. We pass to the constructor of this object our callback method. We then add this delegate object to the Excel Application WorkbookOpen event using the += operator.

```
app.WorkbookOpen +=
    new AppEvents_WorkbookOpenEventHandler(MyOpenHandler);
```

Although this seems complex, Visual Studio 2005 helps by auto-generating most of this line of code as well as the corresponding event handler automatically. If you were typing this line of code, after you type +=, Visual Studio displays a pop-up tooltip. If you press the Tab key twice then Visual Studio generates the rest of the line of code and the callback method automatically.

Listing 1-19 shows a complete implementation of a callback method and event hookup in a simple class. The callback method is called `MyOpenHandler` and is a member method of the class `SampleListener`. This code assumes that a client creates an instance of this class, passing the Excel Application object to the constructor of the class. The `ConnectEvents` method connects the callback method `MyOpen-Handler` to the Excel Application object's WorkbookOpen event. The `Disconnect-Events` method removes the callback method `MyOpenHandler` from the Excel Application object's WorkbookOpen event by using the -= operator on the delegate object. It might seem strange that we create a new instance of our delegate object when removing it, but this is the way C# supports removing delegates.

The result of this code is that any time a workbook is opened and `ConnectEvents` has been called, `MyOpenHandler` will handle the WorkbookOpen event raised by Excel's Application object and it will display a message box with the name of the workbook that was opened. `DisconnectEvents` can be called to stop `MyOpenHandler` from handling the WorkbookOpen event raised by Excel's Application object.

Listing 1-19 A Class That Listens to the Excel Application Object's WorkbookOpen Event

```
using Excel = Microsoft.Office.Interop.Excel;

class SampleListener
{
  private Excel.Application app;

  public SampleListener(Excel.Application application)
  {
    app = application;
```

```
  }

  public void ConnectEvents()
  {
    app.WorkbookOpen +=
      new AppEvents_WorkbookOpenEventHandler(this.MyOpenHandler);
  }

  public void DisconnectEvents()
  {
    app.WorkbookOpen -=
      new AppEvents_WorkbookOpenEventHandler(this.MyOpenHandler);
  }

  public void MyOpenHandler(Excel.Workbook workbook)
  {
    MessageBox.Show(String.Format("{0} was opened.",
      workbook.Name));
  }
}
```

The "My Button Stopped Working" Issue

One issue commonly encountered when beginning to program against Office events in .NET is known as the "my button stopped working" issue. A developer will write some code to handle a Click event raised by a CommandBarButton in the Office toolbar object model. This code will sometimes work temporarily but then stop. The user will click the button, but the Click event appears to have stopped working.

The cause of this issue is connecting an event callback to an object whose lifetime does not match the desired lifetime of the event. This typically occurs when the object to which you are connecting an event handler goes out of scope or gets set to null so that it gets garbage collected. Listing 1-20 shows an example of code that makes this mistake. In this case, an event handler is connected to a newly created CommandBarButton called btn. However, btn is declared as a local variable, so as soon as the ConnectEvents function exits and garbage collection occurs, btn gets garbage collected and the event connected to btn is not called.

The complete explanation of this behavior has to do with btn being associated with something called a Runtime Callable Wrapper (RCW), which is described in Chapter 24, "Creating Outlook Add-Ins with VSTO." Without going into too much depth, btn holds on to an RCW that is necessary for the event to propagate from the unmanaged Office COM object to the managed event handler. When btn goes out of scope and is garbage collected, the reference count on the RCW goes down, and the RCW is disposed—thereby breaking the event connection.

Listing 1-20 A Class That Fails to Handle the CommandBarButton Click Event

```
using Excel = Microsoft.Office.Interop.Excel;
using Office = Microsoft.Office.Core;

class SampleListener
{
  private Excel.Application app;

  public SampleListener(Excel.Application application)
  {
    app = application;
  }

  // This appears to connect to the Click event but
  // will fail because btn is not put in a more permanent
  // variable.
  public void ConnectEvents()
  {
    Office.CommandBar bar = Application.CommandBars["Standard"];

    Office.CommandBarButton myBtn = bar.Controls.Add(1,
      System.Type.Missing, System.Type.Missing,
      System.Type.Missing, System.Type.Missing) as
      Office.CommandBarButton;

    if (myBtn!= null)
    {
      myBtn.Caption = "My Button";
      myBtn.Tag = "SampleListener.btn";
      myBtn.Click += new  Office.
        _CommandBarButtonEvents_ClickEventHandler(
        myBtn_Click);
    }
  }

  // The Click event will never reach this handler.
  public void myBtn_Click(Office.CommandBarButton ctrl,
    ref bool cancelDefault)
  {
    MessageBox.Show("Button was clicked");
  }
}
```

Listing 1-21 shows a second example of a failed event listener class that is attempting to connect to Outlook's NewInspector event, which is raised by Outlook's Inspectors object. This event is raised whenever an inspector window opens (a window where you are viewing or editing an Outlook item). This code will also fail to get any events. In this case, it is more subtle because the event handler is connected to the Inspectors object, which is temporarily created in the line of code that begins with app.Inspectors. Because the Inspectors object returned by app.Inspectors is not stored in a permanent variable, the temporarily created Inspectors object is garbage collected, and the event connected to it will never get called.

Listing 1-21 A Class That Fails to Handle the Outlook Inspectors Object's NewInspector Event

```
using Outlook = Microsoft.Office.Interop.Outlook;

class SampleListener
{
  private Outlook.Application app;

  public SampleListener(Outlook.Application application)
  {
    app = application;
  }

  // This will appear to connect to the NewInspector event, but
  // will fail because Inspectors is not put in a more permanent
  // variable.
  public void ConnectEvents()
  {
    app.Inspectors.NewInspector += new Outlook.
      InspectorsEvents_NewInspectorEventHandler(
      MyNewInspectorHandler);
  }

  // The NewInspector event will never reach this handler.
  public void MyNewInspectorHandler(Outlook.Inspector inspector)
  {
    MessageBox.Show("New inspector.");
  }
}
```

The fix for this issue is to declare a variable whose lifetime matches the lifetime of your event handler and set it to the Office object for which you are handling the event. Listing 1-22 shows a rewritten class that successfully listens to the CommandBarButton Click event. This class works because instead of using the method-scoped variable btn, it uses a class-scoped member variable called myBtn. This ensures that the event handler will be connected for the lifetime of the class when ConnectEvents is called.

Listing 1-22 A Class That Succeeds in Handling the CommandBarButton Click Event Because It Stores the CommandBarButton Object in a Class Member Variable

```
using Excel = Microsoft.Office.Interop.Excel;
using Office = Microsoft.Office.Core;

class SampleListener
{
  private Excel.Application app;
  private Office.CommandBarButton myBtn;

  public SampleListener(Excel.Application application)
  {
    app = application;
  }

  public void ConnectEvents()
  {
    Office.CommandBar bar = Application.CommandBars["Standard"];

    myBtn = bar.Controls.Add(1,  System.Type.Missing,
      System.Type.Missing,  System.Type.Missing,
      System.Type.Missing) as Office.CommandBarButton;

    if (myBtn != null)
    {
      myBtn.Caption = "My Button";
      myBtn.Tag = "SampleListener.btn";
      myBtn.Click += new Office.
        _CommandBarButtonEvents_ClickEventHandler(
        myBtn_Click);
    }
  }

  public void myBtn_Click(Microsoft.Office.Core.CommandBarButton ctrl,
    ref bool cancelDefault)
  {
    MessageBox.Show("Button was clicked");
  }
}
```

Listing 1-23 shows a similar fix for our failed Outlook example. Here we declare a class-level variable called myInspectors that we assign to app.Inspectors. This ensures that our event handler will be connected for the lifetime of the class when ConnectEvents is called because the lifetime of myInspectors now matches the lifetime of the class.

Listing 1-23 A Class That Succeeds in Handling the Outlook Inspectors Object's NewInspector Event Because It Stores the Inspectors Object in a Class Member Variable

```
using Outlook = Microsoft.Office.Interop.Outlook;

class SampleListener
{
  private Outlook.Application app;
  private Outlook.Inspectors myInspectors;

  public SampleListener(Outlook.Application application)
  {
    app = application;
  }

  public void ConnectEvents()
  {
    this.myInspectors = myAplication.Inspectors;

    myInspectors.NewInspector += new Outlook.
        InspectorsEvents_NewInspectorEventHandler(
        MyNewInspectorHandler);
  }

  public void MyNewInspectorHandler(Outlook.Inspector inspector)
  {
    MessageBox.Show("New inspector.");
  }
}
```

When Method Names and Event Names Collide

In several cases in the Office object models, an object has an event and a method that have the same name. For example, Excel's Workbook object has an Activate event and an Activate method. Outlook's Inspector and Explorer objects have Close events and Close methods.

When using an Office object model object that has events such as Workbook, you are actually using an object that implements several interfaces. One of those interfaces has the definition of the Close method and a separate interface has the definition of the Close event. To handle an event for which a method name collides, you must cast your object to the interface that contains the event definitions. The interface that contains the event interfaces is named *ObjectName*Events_Event, where *ObjectName* is the name of the object such as Workbook or Inspector.

Listing 1-24 casts the Workbook object myWorkbook to Excel.WorkbookEvents_Event when adding the event handler. By casting myWorkbook to the WorkbookEvents_Event interface, we disambiguate between the Close method (which is on the Workbook interface) and the Close event (which is on the WorkbookEvents_Event interface).

Listing 1-24 A Class That Will Listen to the Excel Workbook Object's Activate Event by Casting to WorkbookEvents_Event

```
using Excel = Microsoft.Office.Interop.Excel;

class SampleListener
{
  private Excel.Workbook myWorkbook;

  public SampleListener(Excel.Workbook workbook)
  {
    myWorkbook = workbook;
  }

  public void ConnectEvents()
  {
    ((Excel.WorkbookEvents_Event)myWorkbook).Activate +=
      new Excel.WorkbookEvents_ActivateEventHandler(Activate)
  }

  public void Activate()
  {
    MessageBox.Show("Workbook Activated");
  }
}
```

The Office Primary Interop Assemblies (PIAs)

Before learning any more about how to build Office solutions, you need to understand in more detail the managed assemblies that you use to talk to the Office object model in .NET. The managed assemblies used to talk to Office are called the Office primary interop assemblies (PIAs).

As mentioned previously, when you are talking to an Office object model in .NET, you talk to it through a .NET technology called COM interop. The Office object models are all written in unmanaged code (C and C++) that exposes COM interfaces. To talk to these COM interfaces from managed code (C# or Visual Basic), you talk via a wrapper that allows managed code to talk to interoperate with the unmanaged COM interfaces of Office. This wrapper is a set of .NET classes compiled into an assembly called a Primary Interop Assembly, or PIA.

The word *primary* is used when describing these assemblies because they are the Office-approved wrappers for talking to the Office object models. This designation is needed because you could create your own wrapper for the Office COM object models by using a tool provided with .NET called TLBIMP. A wrapper you create on your own is called an interop assembly (IA) rather than a primary interop assembly. Even though you might be tempted to go play with TLBIMP and build your own interop assemblies, you should never use anything other than the Office-provided interop assemblies to do Office development. If every developer created his or her own sets of wrappers for Office development, then no Office solution could interoperate with anyone else's solution; each interop wrapper class of, say, Worksheet created by each developer would be considered a distinct type. Even though the interop assembly I created has a Worksheet object and the interop assembly you created has a Worksheet object, I cannot pass you my Worksheet object and you cannot pass me your Worksheet object. We need to both be using the same interop assembly: the primary interop assembly.

A second reason to not build your own interop assemblies is that Office has made special fixes to the PIAs to make them work better when doing Office development. If you generate your own then you are likely to run into issues that are fixed in the PIAs.

Installing the PIAs

The Office 2003 PIAs are available through the Office 2003 installer. The Office 2003 PIAs are also available as a Microsoft Windows Installer package that you can redistribute with your application. To install the Office 2003 PIAs through the Office 2003 Installer, when you do a setup, check the Choose advanced customization of applications check box in the first step of the Office 2003 Setup Wizard. Then in the tree control that appears in the next screen of the wizard, you will see a .NET Programmability Support node under each application for which PIAs are available, as shown in Figure 1-4. Click each of these .NET programmability support nodes and make sure that you set Run from my computer. Also, under the Office Tools node in the tree, you might want to turn on Microsoft Forms 2.0 .NET Programmability Support and Smart Tag .NET Programmability support. A second method to getting the Office 2003 PIAs is to do a Complete install of Office 2003—all the .NET programmability support will be turned on for you automatically.

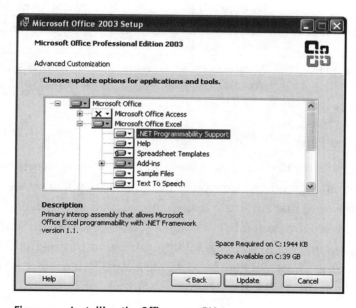

Figure 1-4 Installing the Office 2003 PIAs.

The Office PIAs get installed to the Global Assembly Cache (GAC). The GAC is usually in the Assembly subdirectory of the Windows directory.

A number of Office PIAs are available. Table 1-4 lists some of the most common ones. One PIA listed here that is of note is the Office.dll PIA, which is where common types that are shared between the Office applications such as CommandBar are found.

Table 1-4 Common Office PIAs

Description	Assembly Name	Namespace
Microsoft Excel 11.0 Object Library	Microsoft.Office.Interop. Excel.dll	Microsoft.Office.Interop. Excel
Microsoft Graph 11.0 Object Library	Microsoft.Office.Interop. Graph.dll	Microsoft.Office.Interop. Graph
Microsoft Office 11.0 Object Library	Office.dll	Microsoft.Office.Core
Microsoft Outlook 11.0 Object Library	Microsoft.Office.Interop. Outlook.dll	Microsoft.Office. Interop.Outlook
Microsoft SmartTags 2.0 Type Library	Microsoft.Office.Interop. SmartTag.dll	Microsoft.Office.Interop. SmartTag
Microsoft Word 11.0 Object Library	Microsoft.Office.Interop. Word.dll	Microsoft.Office. Interop.Word

Referencing the PIAs

Adding a reference to a PIA is not necessary for most VSTO projects because the reference is automatically added for you. The console application examples in this book, such as the ones that automate Excel, can be typed into a Visual Studio console project and compiled, but you must first add a reference to the necessary PIA. To add a reference, right-click the References folder under your project in the Visual Studio Solution Explorer, as shown in Figure 1-5. Choose Add Reference from the menu that pops up when you right-click the References folder.

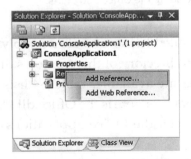

Figure 1-5 Adding a reference to a project.

Choose the COM tab of the Add Reference dialog that appears, as shown in Figure 1-6. The COM references are listed by component name, which matches the description column in Table 1-4. So, to add a reference to the Excel PIA, you choose the Microsoft Excel 11.0 Object Library and click the OK button to add the Excel 2003 PIA reference to your project, as shown in Figure 1-6.

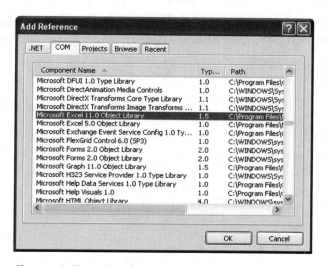

Figure 1-6 The Add Reference dialog.

Note in Figure 1-6 that the Path column in the COM tab of the Add References dialog displays the path to the COM library that the PIA wraps. For example, the Microsoft Excel 11.0 Object Library points to the location on your machine of the Excel.EXE executable. When you select these references and close the dialog, you can examine the properties of the actual references that were added by expanding the References folder in the project, right-clicking the references that you added, and choosing Properties. You will see that Visual Studio figures out the PIA managed object in the GAC that corresponds to the COM object you selected. In this case, you will not get a reference to the Excel.EXE executable but instead to the Microsoft.Office.Interop.Excel.dll in the GAC.

Finally, note that even though you did not explicitly add a reference to the Microsoft Office 11.0 Object Library (office.dll), a reference is added for you. This is because the Excel 11.0 Object Library uses types from the Microsoft Office 11.0 Object Library. Visual Studio detects this and adds the required Office PIA to your project references automatically.

Browsing the PIAs

When you look at the PIA you have referenced in the object browser in Visual Studio, you might find yourself very confused. The object browser shows many helper objects that are created as part of the interop wrapper. For example, consider what .NET Interop does to the seemingly simple Excel Application object. It turns it into a multiple-headed (8 heads to be exact, 36 if you count each delegate individually) monster. All of the following are public types that you see in the browser related to the Excel Application object:

Interfaces

- _Application
- AppEvents
- AppEvents_Event
- Application
- IAppEvents

Delegates

- AppEvents_*EventHandler (29 of them)

Classes

- AppEvents_SinkHelper (AppEvents)
- ApplicationClass (_Application, Application, AppEvents_Event)

This pattern repeats for Chart, OLEObject, QueryTable, Worksheet, and Workbook.

Let's try to untangle this mess by working our way backward from the original COM definition of the Excel Application object. The COM coclass for the Application object looks like this—it has two interfaces, a primary interface called _Application and an event interface called AppEvents. You can think of a coclass as something that defines the interfaces that a COM class implements.

```
coclass Application {
        [default] interface _Application;
        [default, source] dispinterface AppEvents;
};
```

TLBIMP (which is used to process the COM type library for Excel and make the PIA) directly imports the _Application and AppEvents interfaces, so this explains where two of the eight types come from. But the AppEvents interface is not very useful—it seems like an artifact of the TLBIMP conversion in some ways. It has to be processed further to create another interface described later called AppEvents_Event to be of any use.

When TLBIMP processes the COM coclass, it creates a .NET class called ApplicationClass, which is named by taking the coclass name and appending Class. It also creates a .NET interface with the same name as the coclass called Application for our example. If you look at Application in the browser, it has no properties and methods of its own, but it derives from the other two interfaces associated with the coclass: _Application and AppEvents_Event.

We have not yet explained where the AppEvents_Event interface comes from. When TLBIMP processes the AppEvents event interface on the coclass, it creates several helper types. First it creates AppEvents_Event, which looks like AppEvents but with events and delegate types replacing the methods in AppEvents. It also creates delegates named AppEvents_*EventHandler, where * is the method name for each method on the original AppEvents interface. Finally, it creates an AppEvents_SinkHelper, which can be ignored.

That leaves only the IAppEvents interface unexplained. TLBIMP imports this interface directly because it is a public type in the Excel type library. You can ignore this also. This is effectively a duplicate of AppEvents, except AppEvents is declared as a dispinterface in the type library, and IAppEvents is declared as a dual interface type.

So which of these do you really use? Basically, you should only use in your code the Application interface (which derives from _Application and AppEvents_Events) and the delegates. You can usually pretend the others do not exist. The one exception to this rule is when a method and event name collide, as described earlier in this chapter. To disambiguate between a method and an event you must cast to the _Application interface when you want to call the method or the AppEvents_Event interface when you want to connect to the event. Table 1-5 presents a summary.

Table 1-5 Interfaces, Delegates, and Events Associated with the Application Object in Excel

Name	Description
Interfaces	
_Application	Direct import from type library. (Ignore. Typically you do not use this directly unless a method and event name collide—Application interface derives from this.)
AppEvents	Direct import from type library. (Ignore—artifact that is not used in real coding.)
AppEvents_Event	Created while processing the AppEvents event interface (Ignore. Typically you do not use this directly unless a method and event name collide—Application interface derives from this.)
Application	Created while processing the Application coclass. (Use this interface.)
IAppEvents	Dual interface version of AppEvents in the type library (Ignore—artifact that is not use in real coding.)
Delegates	
AppEvents_*EventHandler (29 of them)	Created while processing the AppEvents event interface. (Use these. You use these when declaring delegates to handle events.)
Classes	
AppEvents_SinkHelper	Created while processing the AppEvents event interface (Ignore.)
ApplicationClass	Created while processing the Application coclass (Ignore. This is used behind the scenes to make it look like you can "new" an Application interface)

The Application interface that is created by TLBIMP for the coclass behaves in an interesting way. You can write code in C# that makes it look like you are creating an instance of the Application interface, which we all know is impossible:

```
Excel.Application myApp = new Excel.Application();
```

Really, this is syntactical sugar that is using the ApplicationClass behind the scenes (the Application interface is attributed to associate it with the ApplicationClass) to create an Excel Application object and return the appropriate interface.

Finally, we mentioned earlier that this pattern repeats for Chart, OLEObject, QueryTable, Worksheet, and Workbook. The mapping to Chart is straightforward—replace Application with Chart and AppEvents with ChartEvents and you'll get the general idea. Worksheet is a bit different. Its coclass looks like this:

```
coclass Worksheet {
        [default] interface _Worksheet;
        [default, source] dispinterface DocEvents;
    };
```

So for Worksheet, replace Application with Worksheet, but replace AppEvents with DocEvents—yielding DocEvents_*EventHandler as the delegates for WorkSheet events.

QueryTable is even weirder. Its coclass looks like this:

```
coclass QueryTable {
        [default] dispinterface _QueryTable;
        [default, source] dispinterface RefreshEvents;
    };
```

So for QueryTable, replace Application with QueryTable and replace AppEvents with RefreshEvents—yielding RefreshEvents_*EventHandler as the delegates for QueryTable events.

Dummy Methods

When you look at the Excel PIA in the object browser in Visual Studio, you might notice a slew of methods with the text *Dummy* in them. There's even an interface called IDummy.

No, this is not Excel's way of insulting your intelligence. Everything with Dummy in it is a test method that actually has a legitimate purpose and more descriptive names in Microsoft's internal "debug" version of Excel. For example, Application.Dummy6 is called Application.DebugMemory in the debug version of

Excel. Each method was renamed to Dummy in the retail version of Excel. All 508 of these Dummy methods actually do something in debug Excel, but in the retail version of Excel, they do nothing except raise an error when called.

Excel has marked these as "hidden," but the C# object browser shows hidden methods by default. When you view the PIA in the C# object browser, you will see these Dummy methods. If you create a Visual Basic project, the Visual Basic object browser will hide methods and properties with this attribute.

Conclusion

This chapter introduced the Office object models and examined the basic structure followed by object models. You learned how to work with objects, collections, and enumerations—the basic types found in any object model. You also learned how to use properties, methods, and events exposed by objects and collections in the Office object models.

This chapter introduced the Office primary interop assemblies that expose the Office object models to .NET code. You learned how to use and reference Office PIAs in a Visual Studio project. This chapter also described what you can ignore when viewing the PIA in the object browser.

The next chapter begins examining the basic patterns of development used in Office programming and provides examples of each.

■ 2 ■

Introduction to Office Solutions

The Three Basic Patterns of Office Solutions

N OW THAT YOU UNDERSTAND THE BASIC pattern of the Office object models, this chapter explains how developers pattern and build their Office solutions. Most solutions built using Office follow one of three patterns:

- Office automation executable
- Office add-in
- Code behind an Office document

An automation executable is a program separate from Office that controls and automates an Office application. An automation executable can be created with development tools such as Visual Studio. A typical example is a standalone console application or Windows Forms application that starts up an Office application and then automates it to perform some task. To start a solution built this way, the user of the solution starts the automation executable, which in turn starts up the Office application. Unlike the other two patterns, the automation code does not run in the Office process but runs in its own process and talks cross process to the Office process being automated.

An add-in is a class in an assembly (DLL) that Office loads and creates when needed. An add-in runs in process with the Office application instead of requiring its own process separate from the Office application process. To start a solution built this way, the user of the solution starts the Office application associated with the add-in. Office detects registered add-ins on startup and loads them. An add-in can customize an Office application in the same ways that code behind a document can. However, code behind a document unloads when the document associated with the code is closed—an add-in can remain loaded throughout the lifetime of the Office application.

The code behind pattern was popularized by Visual Basic for Applications (VBA)—a simple development environment that is included with Office that enables the developer to write Visual Basic code against the object model of a particular Office application and associate that code with a particular document or template. A document can be associated with C# or Visual Basic code behind using Visual Studio 2005 Tools for Office (VSTO). To start a solution built this way, the user of the solution opens a document that has code behind it or creates a new document from a template that has code behind it. The code behind the document will customize the Office application in some way while the document is open. For example, code behind the document might add menu items that are only present when the document is open or associate code with events that occur while the document is open.

We discuss two advanced patterns later in this book. The server document pattern involves running code on a server to manipulate data stored in an Office document without starting the Office application. VSTO makes this scenario possible through a feature called cached data. Chapter 18, "Server Data Scenarios," discusses this pattern. The XML and XSLT pattern is similar to the server document pattern and involves writing code to generate Word or Excel documents in WordprocessingML or SpreadsheetML format without starting the Office application. You can also generate these formats by applying an XSLT transform to some XML data. Chapters 21, "Working with XML in Excel," and 22, "Working with XML in Word," discuss these scenarios.

Hosted Code

The add-in and code behind patterns are sometimes called hosted code, which means that your code runs in the same process as the Office application.

Discovery of Hosted Code

For code to run in the Office application process, the Office application must be able to discover your code, load the code into its process space, and run your code. Office add-ins are registered in the Windows registry so that Office can find and start them. Using the registry seems a little non-.NET, but this is necessary because Office 2003 talks to add-ins as if they were COM objects through COM interop.

The code behind a document pattern does not require a registry entry. Instead, code is associated with a document by adding some special properties to the document file. Office reads these properties when the document opens, and then Office loads the code associated with the document.

Context Provided to Hosted Code

It is critical that your hosted code get context—it needs to get the Application object or Document object for the Office application into which it is loading. COM add-ins are provided with context through an interface implemented by the add-in class. Outlook add-ins in VSTO are provided with context through a class created in the project that represents the application being customized. Code behind a document in VSTO is provided with context through a class created in the project that represents the document being customized.

Entry Point for Hosted Code

At startup, Office calls into an entry point where your code can run for the first time and register for events that might occur later in the session. For a COM add-in, this entry point is the OnConnection method of the IDTExtensibility2 interface implemented by the COM add-in. For a VSTO Outlook add-in and VSTO code behind a document, this entry point is the Startup event handler.

How Code Gets Run After Startup

After hosted code starts up, code continues to run in one or more of the following ways.

Code Runs in Response to Events Raised by Office

The most common way that code runs after startup is in response to events that occur in the Office application. For example, Office raises events when a document opens or a cell in a spreadsheet changes. Listing 1-24 shows a simple class that listens to the Activate event that Excel's Worksheet object raises. Typically, you will hook up event listeners, such as the one shown in Listing 1-24, when the initial entry point of your code is called.

Interface Methods Called on Objects Provided to Office

Objects such as the startup class for a COM add-in implement an interface called IDTExtensibility2 that has methods that Office calls during the run of the Office application. For example, if the user turns off the COM add-in, Office calls the OnDisconnection method on the IDTExtensibility2 interface implemented by the COM add-in. In this way, additional code runs after the initial entry point has run.

Events Raised on Code Behind Classes

The classes generated in VSTO projects that represent the customized application or document handle the Startup and Shutdown events. After the constructor of the class executes, Office raises the Startup event. When the document is about to be closed, Office raises the Shutdown event.

How Code Gets Unloaded

Your code gets unloaded in a number of ways, depending on the development pattern you are using. If you are using the automation executable pattern, your code unloads when the automation executable you have written exits. If you are using the add-in pattern, your code unloads when the Office application exits or when the user turns off the add-in via an add-in management dialog. If you are using the code behind pattern, your code unloads when the document associated with your code is closed.

In the hosted patterns of running code, there is some method that is called or event that is raised notifying you that you are about to be unloaded. For COM add-ins, Office calls the OnDisconnection method. For VSTO code behind documents and Outlook add-ins, Office raises the Shutdown event before your code is unloaded.

Office Automation Executables

This section considers each of these three patterns of Office solutions in more detail. Office solutions that use the automation executable pattern start up an Office application in a very straightforward manner—by creating a new instance of the Application object associated with the Office application. Because the automation executable controls the Office application, the automation executable runs code at startup and any time thereafter when executing control returns to the automation executable.

When an automation executable uses `new` to create an Application object, the automation executable controls the lifetime of the application by holding the created Application object in a variable. The Office application determines whether it can shut down by determining the reference count or number of clients that are using its Application object.

In Listing 2-1, as soon as `new` is used to create the `myExcelApp` variable, Excel starts and adds one to its count of clients that it knows are holding a reference to Excel's Application object. When the `myExcelApp` variable goes out of scope (when Main exits), .NET garbage collection releases the object and Excel is notified that the console application no longer needs Excel's Application object. This causes Excel's count of clients holding a reference to Excel's Application object to go to zero, and Excel exits because no clients are using Excel anymore.

When you create an Office application by creating a new instance of the Application object, the application starts up without showing its window, which proves useful because you can automate the application without distracting the user by popping up windows. If you need to show the application window, you can set the Visible property of the Application object to `true`. If you make the main window visible, the user controls the lifetime of the application. In Excel, the application will not exit until the user quits the application and your variable holding the Excel Application object is garbage collected. Word behaves differently—the application exits when the user quits the application even if a variable is still holding an instance of the Word Application object.

Listing 2-1 sets the status bar of Excel to say "Hello World" and opens a new blank workbook in Excel by calling the Add method of Excel's Workbooks collection.

Chapters 3 through 5—"Programming Excel," "Working with Excel Events," and "Working with Excel Objects," respectively—cover the Excel object model in more detail.

Listing 2-1 Automation of Excel via a Console Application

```csharp
using System;
using Excel = Microsoft.Office.Interop.Excel;
using System.Windows.Forms;

namespace ConsoleApplication
{
  class Program
  {
    static bool exit = false;

    static void Main(string[] args)
    {
      Excel.Application myExcelApp = new Excel.Application();
      myExcelApp.Visible = true;
      myExcelApp.StatusBar = "Hello World";
      myExcelApp.Workbooks.Add(System.Type.Missing);

      myExcelApp.SheetBeforeDoubleClick +=
        new Excel.AppEvents_SheetBeforeDoubleClickEventHandler(
          myExcelApp_SheetBeforeDoubleClick);

      while (exit == false)
        System.Windows.Forms.Application.DoEvents();
    }

    static void myExcelApp_SheetBeforeDoubleClick(object sheet,
      Excel.Range target, ref bool cancel)
    {
      exit = true;
    }
  }
}
```

Listing 2-1 also illustrates how an automation executable can yield time back to the Office application. A reference to the System.Windows.Forms assembly must be added to the project. After event handlers are hooked up, System.Windows.Forms.Application.DoEvents() is called in a loop to allow the Excel application to run normally. If the user double-clicks a cell, Office yields time back to the event handler in the automation executable. In the handler for the Double-Click event, we set the static variable `exit` to `true`, which will cause the loop calling DoEvents to exit and the automation executable to exit.

You can see the lifetime management of Excel in action by running the automation executable in Listing 2-1 and exiting Excel without double-clicking a cell. Excel will continue to run in a hidden state, waiting for the console application to release its reference to Excel's Application object.

Creating a Console Application That Automates Word

This section walks you through the creation of a simple console application that automates Word to create a table specified in wiki text format. A wiki is a kind of online encyclopedia that users can contribute to. For an example, see http://www.officewiki.net for a wiki that documents the Office primary interop assemblies (PIAs). Wikis use simple, easy-to-edit text files that any visitor to the wiki can edit without having to know HTML. These text files have simple representations of even complex elements such as tables. Our console application will read a simple text file that specifies a table in wiki text format. It will then automate Word to create a Word table that matches the text file specification.

In the wiki text format, a table that looks like Table 2-1 is specified by the text in Listing 2-2.

Table 2-1 A Simple Table Showing the Properties and Methods of Word's Add-In Object

Property or Method	Name	Return Type
Property	Application	`Application`
Property	Autoload	`Boolean`
Property	Compiled	`Boolean`
Property	Creator	`Int32`
Method	Delete	`Void`
Property	Index	`Int32`

continues

Table 2-1 Continued

Property or Method	Name	Return Type
Property	Installed	Boolean
Property	Name	String
Property	Parent	Object
Property	Path	String

Listing 2-2 A Wiki Text Representation of Table 2-1

```
||Property or Method||Name||Return Type||
||Property||Application||Application||
||Property||Autoload||Boolean||
||Property||Compiled||Boolean||
||Property||Creator||Int32||
||Method||Delete||Void||
||Property||Index||Int32||
||Property||Installed||Boolean||
||Property||Name||String||
||Property||Parent||Object||
||Property||Path||String||
```

We will use Visual Studio 2005 to create a console application. After launching Visual Studio, choose New Project from the File menu. The New Project dialog box shows a variety of project types. Choose the Visual C# node from the list of project types, and choose the Windows node under the Visual C# node. This is slightly counterintuitive because there is an Office node available, too, but the Office node only shows VSTO code behind document projects and the VSTO Outlook add-in project.

After you choose the Windows node, you will see in the window to the right the available templates. Choose the Console Application template. Name your console application project, and then click the OK button to create your project. In Figure 2-1, we have created a console application called WordWiki. Note that the new project dialog can have a different appearance than the one shown in Figure 2-1 depending on the profile you are using. In this book, we assume you are using the Visual C# Development Settings profile. You can change your profile by choosing Import and Export Settings from the Tools menu.

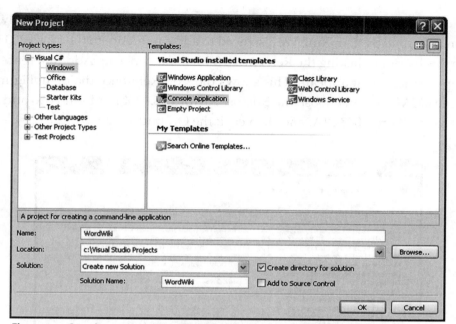

Figure 2-1 Creating a console application from the New Project dialog.

When you click the OK button, Visual Studio creates a console application project for you. Visual Studio displays the contents of the project in the Solution Explorer window, as shown in Figure 2-2.

Figure 2-2 The Console application project WordWiki shown in Solution Explorer.

By default, a newly created console application references the assemblies System, System.Data, and System.Xml. We also need to add a reference to the Word 2003 PIA. We do this by right-clicking the References folder and choosing Add Reference from the pop-up menu that appears. This shows the Add Reference dialog in Figure 2-3. Click the COM tab and choose the Microsoft Word 11.0 Object Library to add a reference to the Word 2003 PIA, and then click the OK button.

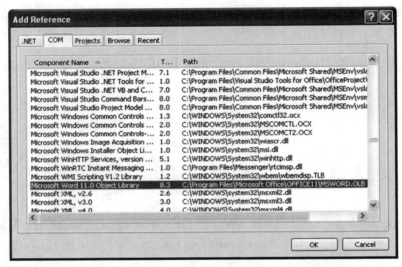

Figure 2-3 Adding a reference to the Microsoft Word 2003 PIA.

Visual Studio adds the reference to the Word 2003 PIA and adds additional references to the stdole, VBIDE, and Microsoft.Office.Core PIAs, as shown in Figure 2-4. These additional PIAs are ones that the Word PIA depends on. Stdole is a PIA that contains the definition of some of the types that COM object models need. VBIDE is the PIA for the object model associated with the VBA editor integrated into Office. Microsoft.Office.Core (office.dll) is the PIA for common functionality shared by all the Office applications, such as the object model for the toolbars and menus.

Now that the proper references have been added to the console application, let's start writing code. Double-click Program.cs in the Solution Explorer window to edit the main source code file for the console application. If you have outlining turned on, you will see the text "using ..." at the top of the Program.cs file with a + sign next to it. Click the + sign to expand out the code where the using directives are placed.

Add the following three using directives so that you can more easily use objects from the Word PIA and the Microsoft.Office.Core PIA as well as classes in the System.IO namespace.

```
using Office = Microsoft.Office.Core;
using Word = Microsoft.Office.Interop.Word;
using System.IO;
```

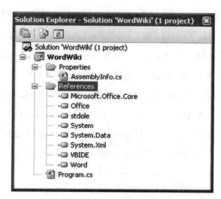

Figure 2-4 When you add the Word 2003 PIA, dependent PIA references are automatically added to the project.

We alias some of these namespaces so we do not have to type out the entire namespace, such as Microsoft.Office.Interop.Word, every time we want to declare a Word object. With the alias in place, we can just type Word to specify the namespace. We keep an alias namespace in place for Word and Office instead of just typing `using Microsoft.Office.Interop.Word` and importing all the types into global scope. This is because Word and Office define hundreds of types, and we do not want all these type names potentially colliding with types we define in our code or with other referenced types. Also for the purpose of this book, the code is clearer when it says Word.Application rather than Application, so you know what namespace the Application type is coming from.

We are now ready to write some code that automates Word to create a table after reading a text input file in the wiki table format. Listing 2-3 shows the entire listing of our program. Rather than explain every line of code in that listing, we focus on the lines of code that automate Word. We assume the reader has some knowledge of how to read a text file in .NET and parse a string via the Split method. We briefly touch on some objects in the Word object model here, but Chapters 6 through 8—"Programming Word," "Working with Word Events," and "Working with Word Objects," respectively—cover the Word object model in much more detail.

The first thing we do in Listing 2-3 is declare a new instance of the Word application object by adding this line of code to the Main method of our program class.

```
Word.Application theApplication = new Word.Application();
```

Although Word.Application is an interface, we are allowed to create a new instance of this interface because the compiler knows that the Word.Application interface is associated with a COM object that it knows how to start. When Word starts in response to an automation executable creating a new instance of its Application object, it starts up without showing any windows. You can automate Word in this invisible state when you want to automate Word without confusing the user by bringing up the Word window. For this example, we want to make Word show its main window, and we do so by adding this line of code:

```
theApplication.Visible = true;
```

Next, we want to create a new empty Word document into which we will generate our table. We do this by calling the Add method on the Documents collection returned by Word's Application object. The Add method takes four optional parameters that we want to omit. Optional parameters in Word methods are specified as omitted by passing by reference a variable containing the special value Type.Missing. We declare a variable called missing that we set to Type.Missing and pass it by reference to each parameter we want to omit, as shown here:

```
object missing = Type.Missing;
Word.Document theDocument = theApplication.Documents.Add(
    ref missing, ref missing, ref missing, ref missing);
```

With a document created, we want to read the input text file specified by the command-line argument passed to our console application. We want to parse that text file to calculate the number of columns and rows. When we know the number of columns and rows, we use the following line of code to get a Range object from the Document object. By passing our missing variable to the optional parameters, the Range method will return a range that includes the entire text of the document.

```
Word.Range range = theDocument.Range(ref missing, ref missing);
```

We then use our Range object to add a table by calling the Add method of the Tables collection returned by the Range object. We pass the Range object again as the first parameter to the Add method to specify that we want to replace the entire contents of the document with the table. We also specify the number of rows and columns we want:

```
Word.Table table = range.Tables.Add(range, rowCount,
    columnCount, ref missing, ref missing);
```

The Table object has a Cell method that takes a row and column and returns a Cell object. The Cell object has a Range property that returns a Range object for the cell in question that we can use to set the text and formatting of the cell. The code that sets the cells of the table is shown here. Note that as in most of the Office object models, the indices are 1-based, meaning they start with 1 as the minimum value rather than being 0-based and starting with 0 as the minimum value:

```
for (columnIndex = 1; columnIndex <= columnCount; columnIndex++)
{
    Word.Cell cell = table.Cell(rowIndex, columnIndex);
    cell.Range.Text = splitRow[columnIndex];
}
```

Code to set the formatting of the table by setting the table to size to fit contents and bolding the header row is shown below. We use the Row object returned by `table.Rows[1]`, which also has a Range property that returns a Range object for the row in question. Also, we encounter code that sets the first row of the table to be bolded. One would expect to be able to write the code `table.Rows[1].Range.Bold = true`, but Word's object model expects an `int` value (0 for false and 1 for true) rather than a `bool`. The Bold property doesn't return a `bool` because the range of text could be all bold, all not bold, or partially bold. Word uses the enumerated constant `WdConstants.WdUndefined` to specify the partially bold case.

```
// Format table
table.Rows[1].Range.Bold = 1;
table.AutoFitBehavior(Word.WdAutoFitBehavior.wdAutoFitContent);
```

Finally, some code at the end of the program forces Word to quit without saving changes:

```
// Quit without saving changes
object saveChanges = false;
theApplication.Quit(ref saveChanges, ref missing, ref missing);
```

If you do not write this code, Word will stay running even after the console application exits. When you show the Word window by setting the Application object's Visible property to `true`, Word puts the lifetime of the application in the hands of the end user rather than the automating program. So even when the automation executable exits, Word continues running. To force Word to exit, you must call the Quit method on Word's Application object. If this program didn't make the Word window visible—say for example, it created the document with the table and then saved it to a file all without showing the Word window—it would not have to call Quit because Word would exit when the program exited and released all its references to the Word objects.

To run the console application in Listing 2-3, you must create a text file that contains the text in Listing 2-2. Then pass the filename of the text file as a command-line argument to the console application. You can set up the debugger to do this by right-clicking the WordWiki project in Solution Explorer and choosing Properties. Then click the Debug tab and set the Command line arguments field to the name of your text file.

Listing 2-3 The Complete WordWiki Implementation

```csharp
using System;
using System.Collections.Generic;
using System.Text;
using System.IO;
using Office = Microsoft.Office.Core;
using Word = Microsoft.Office.Interop.Word;

namespace WordWiki
{
  class Program
  {
    static void Main(string[] args)
    {
      Word.Application theApplication = new Word.Application();
      theApplication.Visible = true;
```

```csharp
object missing = System.Type.Missing;
Word.Document theDocument = theApplication.Documents.Add(
  ref missing, ref missing, ref missing, ref missing);

TextReader reader = new System.IO.StreamReader(args[0]);

string[] separators = new string[1];
separators[0] = "||";
int rowCount = 0;
int columnCount = 0;

// Read rows and calculate number of rows and columns
System.Collections.Generic.List<string> rowList =
  new System.Collections.Generic.List<string>();

string row = reader.ReadLine();

while (row != null)
{
  rowCount++;
  rowList.Add(row);

  // If this is the first row,
  // calculate the number of columns
  if (rowCount == 1)
  {
    string[] splitHeaderRow = row.Split(
      separators, StringSplitOptions.None);

    // Ignore the first and last separator
    columnCount = splitHeaderRow.Length - 2;
  }

  row = reader.ReadLine();
}

// Create a table
Word.Range range = theDocument.Range(ref missing,
  ref missing);
Word.Table table = range.Tables.Add(range, rowCount,
  columnCount, ref missing, ref missing);

// Populate table
int columnIndex = 1;
int rowIndex = 1;

foreach (string r in rowList)
{
```

```csharp
        string[] splitRow = r.Split(separators,
          StringSplitOptions.None);

        for (columnIndex = 1; columnIndex <= columnCount;
          columnIndex++)
        {
          Word.Cell cell = table.Cell(rowIndex, columnIndex);
          cell.Range.Text = splitRow[columnIndex];
        }

        rowIndex++;
      }

      // Format table
      table.Rows[1].Range.Bold = 1;
      table.AutoFitBehavior(Word.WdAutoFitBehavior.
        wdAutoFitContent);

      // Wait for input from the command line before exiting
      System.Console.WriteLine("Table complete.");
      System.Console.ReadLine();

      // Quit without saving changes
      object saveChanges = false;
      theApplication.Quit(ref saveChanges, ref missing,
        ref missing);
    }
  }
}
```

Office Add-Ins

The second pattern used in Office development is the add-in pattern. This book covers several types of Office add-ins. These include VSTO add-ins for Outlook, COM add-ins for Excel and Word, and automation add-ins for Excel:

- **VSTO add-ins for Outlook**—This new VSTO feature makes it extremely easy to create an add-in for Outlook 2003. The model is the most ".NET" of all the add-in models and is very similar to the VSTO code behind model for documents. Chapter 24, "Creating Outlook Add-Ins with VSTO," describes this model in detail.

- **COM add-ins for Excel and Word**—A C# class in a class library project can implement the IDTExtensibility2 interface and register in the registry as a COM object and COM add-in. Through COM interop, Office creates the C# class and talks to it. Chapter 23, "Developing COM Add-Ins for Word and Excel," describes the creation of COM add-ins and some issues that make COM add-in development problematic.

- **Automation add-ins for Excel**—These managed classes expose public functions that Excel can use in formulas. The C# class must register in the registry as a COM object. Through COM interop, Excel can create an automation add-in and use its public methods in formulas. Automation add-ins and their use in Excel formulas are discussed in Chapter 3, "Programming Excel."

This book does not discuss some Office add-in technologies. Smart Documents add-ins are not discussed because VSTO provides a much easier way of accessing Smart Document functionality, albeit at the document or template level rather than at the application level. For more information on VSTO's support for Smart Documents, see Chapter 15, "Working with Actions Pane."

Creating an Outlook Add-In in VSTO

To create an Outlook add-in project in VSTO, choose Project from the New menu of the File menu in Visual Studio. Select the Visual C# node from the list of project types, and select the Office node under the Visual C# node. The Outlook add-in project appears in the list of templates. Type a name for your new Outlook add-in project, and pick a location for the project. Then click the OK button.

VSTO creates a project with references to the Outlook 2003 PIA, the core Office PIA, and other needed references, as shown in Figure 2-6. VSTO also adds a project item to the project called ThisApplication.cs. This project item contains a C# class that you will add to when implementing your Outlook add-in.

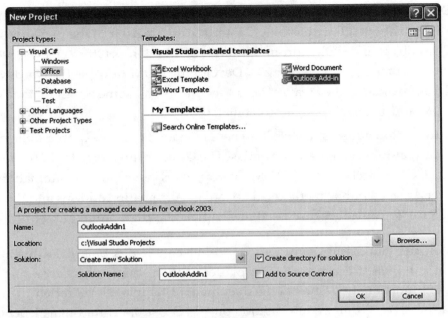

Figure 2-5 Creating a new Outlook add-in project.

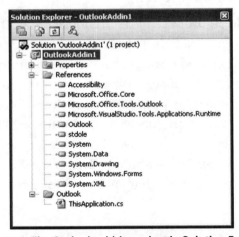

Figure 2-6 The Outlook add-in project in Solution Explorer.

If you double-click the ThisApplication.cs project item, you will see the code shown in Listing 2-4. There is a simple Startup and Shutdown event handler where you can write code that executes on the startup and shutdown of the add-in. The ThisApplication class derives from an aggregate of the Outlook Application object. This allows you to access properties and methods of the Outlook Application object by writing code such as this.Inspectors.Count in the ThisApplication class.

Listing 2-4 The Initial Code in the ThisApplication Class in an Outlook Add-In Project

```
using System;
using System.Windows.Forms;
using Microsoft.VisualStudio.Tools.Applications.Runtime;
using Outlook = Microsoft.Office.Interop.Outlook;

namespace OutlookAddin1
{
  public partial class ThisApplication
  {
    private void ThisApplication_Startup(object sender, EventArgs e)
    {
    }

    private void ThisApplication_Shutdown(object sender, EventArgs e)
    {
    }

    #region VSTO Designer generated code
    private void InternalStartup()
    {
      this.Startup += new System.
        EventHandler(ThisApplication_Startup);
      this.Shutdown += new System.
        EventHandler(ThisApplication_Shutdown);
    }
    #endregion
  }
}
```

Looking at Listing 2-4, you might wonder about the use of partial in the class definition. VSTO uses partial classes, which are a new feature of .NET that enables you to define part of a class in one file and another part of a class in a second file and then compile them together as one class. VSTO uses this feature to hide some additional generated code associated with the ThisApplication class from you to reduce the complexity of the class where you write your code. The final ThisApplication class will be compiled from the partial class in Listing 2-4 and additional code in a partial class generated by VSTO that is hidden from you.

The InternalStartup method is generated by VSTO and used to hook up any event handlers generated by VSTO. This is where the Startup and Shutdown event handlers are hooked up. You should not edit this section of the code. We may omit this block of code in some of the listings in this book, but the block of code must be in the class—otherwise, the class will fail to compile.

We are going to add to the code in Listing 2-4 to create an add-in that will solve an annoying problem—people replying inadvertently to an e-mail sent out to a mailing alias that contains a large number of people. Unless you have "Vice President" in your title, you probably do not want to be sending e-mail to more than, say, 25 people at any given time. We are going to create an add-in that will warn you if you do this and give you the "This is a potentially career-limiting move. Are you sure you want to send this e-mail to 25,000 people?" message.

Outlook's Application object has an ItemSend event that is raised whenever a user sends an e-mail. We will add additional code to the Startup method of the ThisApplication class to connect an event handler for the ItemSend event, as shown in Listing 2-5. Because the ThisApplication class derives from an aggregate of Outlook's Application object, we can write the code `this.ItemSend` because ItemSend is an event raised by the ThisApplication base class. The ItemSend event handler takes an `object` parameter called `item`, which is the Outlook item being sent. Because `item` could be any of a number of things, such as a meeting request or an e-mail message, `item` is passed as an `object` rather than as a specific type. The ItemSend event handler also has a `bool` parameter passed by reference called `cancel` that can be set to `true` to prevent the Outlook item from being sent.

In our ItemSend event handler, we need to check to see whether the `item` parameter which is passed as an `object` is actually an e-mail. The easiest way to achieve this is to use the `as` keyword to try to cast the `item` parameter to an Outlook.MailItem. If the cast succeeds, the resulting value will be non-`null`, and we will know that the item being sent is an Outlook.MailItem and therefore an e-mail message. We can then iterate through the Recipients collection on the MailItem object and check to see whether we are sending to any recipient lists that include more than 25 people. Each Recipient object in the Recipients collection has an AddressEntry property that returns an AddressEntry object. The AddressEntry object has a Members property that returns a collection that we can check the count of. If we find the count to be more than 25, we will show a dialog and ask the user if she really wants to send the mail. If the user clicks the No button, we will set the `cancel` parameter of the ItemSend event to `true` to cancel the sending of career-limiting e-mail.

Listing 2-5 A VSTO Outlook Add-In That Handles the ItemSend Event and Checks for More Than 25 Recipients

```csharp
using System;
using System.Windows.Forms;
using Microsoft.VisualStudio.Tools.Applications.Runtime;
using Outlook = Microsoft.Office.Interop.Outlook;

namespace OutlookAddin1
{
  public partial class ThisApplication
  {
    private void ThisApplication_Startup(object sender, EventArgs e)
    {
      this.ItemSend += new
        Outlook.ApplicationEvents_11_ItemSendEventHandler(
        ThisApplication_ItemSend);
    }

    void ThisApplication_ItemSend(object item, ref bool cancel)
    {
      Outlook.MailItem myItem = item as Outlook.MailItem;

      if (myItem != null)
      {
        foreach (Outlook.Recipient recip in myItem.Recipients)
        {
          if (recip.AddressEntry.Members.Count > 25)
          {
            // Ask the user if she really wants to send this e-mail
            string message = "Send mail to {0} with {1} people?";
            string caption = "More than 25 recipients";
            MessageBoxButtons buttons = MessageBoxButtons.YesNo;
            DialogResult result;

            result = MessageBox.Show(String.Format(message,
              recip.AddressEntry.Name,
              recip.AddressEntry.Members.Count),
              caption, buttons);
```

```
        if (result == DialogResult.No)
        {
          cancel = true;
          break;
        }
      }
    }
  }
}

private void ThisApplication_Shutdown(object sender, EventArgs e)
{
}

#region VSTO Designer generated code
private void InternalStartup()
{
  this.Startup += new System.
    EventHandler(ThisApplication_Startup);
  this.Shutdown += new System.
    EventHandler(ThisApplication_Shutdown);
}
#endregion
  }
}
```

When you run the project with the code shown in Listing 2-4, Outlook launches and the add-in loads. Try sending a mail to an alias that includes more than 25 people—you might want to go offline first in case you mistyped the code. If all works right, the add-in will display a dialog box warning you that you are sending an e-mail to more than 25 people, and you will be able to cancel the send of the e-mail. Exit Outlook to end your debugging session.

Chapter 24, "Creating Outlook Add-Ins with VSTO," discusses VSTO Outlook add-ins in more detail. Chapters 9 through 11—"Programming Outlook," "Working with Outlook Events," and "Working with Outlook Objects," respectively—discuss the Outlook object model.

Code Behind a Document

VSTO supports code behind a document by requiring that the developer use classes generated in a VSTO project that have pre-hooked-up context and pre-hooked-up events. These classes are sometimes called "code behind" classes because they are code associated with a particular document or worksheet. In Word, there is one code behind class corresponding to the document. In Excel, there are multiple code behind classes—one for the workbook and one for each worksheet or chart sheet in the workbook.

The first time your code runs in a VSTO code behind the document project is when Office raises the Startup event handled by any of the code behind classes created for you. VSTO provides context via the base class of the code behind class you are writing code in. A VSTO code behind class customizing an Excel worksheet derives from a base class that contains all the methods, properties, and events of an Excel worksheet. This enables you to write code such as this in the Startup method of a worksheet class.

```
MessageBox.Show(String.Format("{0} is the sheet name", this.Name));
```

By using `this.Name`, you are referring to the Name property of the Excel Worksheet object inherited from the base class. Listing 2-6 shows a VSTO code behind class for an Excel Worksheet. In addition to the Startup and Shutdown methods in the code behind class, there is also a generated method called InternalStartup. You should not put any of your code in this InternalStartup method because it is auto-generated by VSTO and modifying it can break Visual Studio's support for code behind classes. Instead, your startup code should go in the Startup event handler. VSTO code behind document classes also use partial classes to hide some additional code generated by VSTO.

Listing 2-6 A VSTO Excel Workbook Customization

```
using System;
using System.Data;
using System.Drawing;
using System.Windows.Forms;
using Microsoft.VisualStudio.Tools.Applications.Runtime;
using Excel = Microsoft.Office.Interop.Excel;
using Office = Microsoft.Office.Core;
```

```csharp
namespace ExcelWorkbook1
{
  public partial class Sheet1
  {
    private void Sheet1_Startup(object sender, EventArgs e)
    {
      // Initial entry point.
      // This code gets run first when the code behind is created
      // The context is implicit in the Sheet1 class
      MessageBox.Show("Code behind the document running.");
      MessageBox.Show(String.Format("{0} is the sheet name",
        this.Name));
    }

    private void Sheet1_Shutdown(object sender, EventArgs e)
    {
    }

    #region VSTO Designer generated code

    /// <summary>
    /// Required method for Designer support - do not modify
    /// the contents of this method with the code editor.
    /// </summary>
    private void InternalStartup()
    {
      this.Startup += new System.EventHandler(Sheet1_Startup);
      this.Shutdown += new System.EventHandler(Sheet1_Shutdown);
    }

    #endregion

  }
}
```

VSTO Code Behind a Document in Excel

In this section, we create some simple code behind a document in Excel using VSTO. First, start up VSTO and choose the File > New > Project menu item. As you have seen previously, navigate to the Office node under the Visual C# root.

We will create an Excel workbook project using C#. If you already have a workbook that you want to add VSTO customization code behind, you can specify its location in the dialog box shown in Figure 2-8 that appears after you click OK in the New Project dialog. This time we will just start from scratch, creating a new, blank workbook.

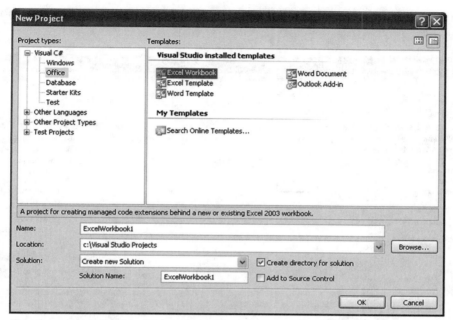

Figure 2-7 Using the New Project dialog to create an Excel Workbook project.

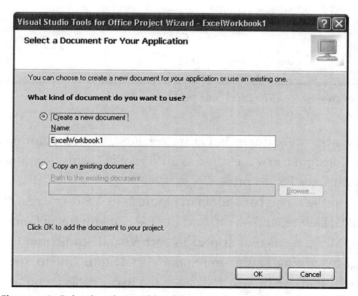

Figure 2-8 Selecting the workbook to associate with your code behind.

After we have created the project, the Designer view appears, as shown in Figure 2-9.

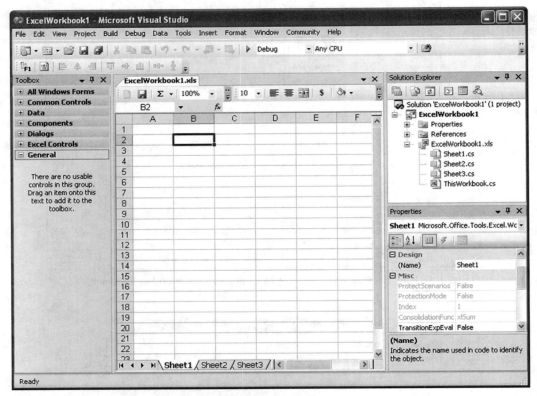

Figure 2-9 The design view for VSTO Excel code behind.

Notice a few interesting things in Figure 2-9. First, Excel is running inside Visual Studio 2005 as a designer, just the same as a Windows Forms designer would when developing a Windows Forms project.

Second, look at the menu bar shown in Figure 2-10. VSTO merges the Visual Studio menus (Build, Debug, and so on) and the Excel menu items (Format, Data, and so on) together. Menu items that appear in both Visual Studio and Excel (Tools, for example) merge by adding a submenu to the Visual Studio menu, such as Microsoft Office Excel Tools, that can be selected to see the Excel Tools menu.

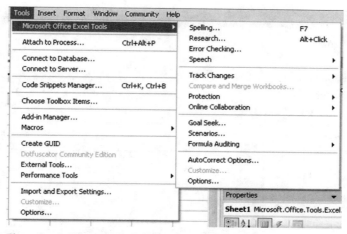

Figure 2-10 The merging of Visual Studio and Excel menus.

Third, notice in Figure 2-9 that the toolbox contains a new category: Excel Controls. When designing a document using Visual Studio, you can create named ranges and list objects using the Excel menu items familiar to Excel users, or the toolbox idiom familiar to Visual Studio users.

Fourth, notice that the Properties window shows the properties of the selected object—in this case, Sheet1. You can use the Properties window to edit properties of Excel's objects the same way that you would edit properties of controls and forms in a Windows Forms project.

Fifth, notice that the Solution Explorer has four classes in it already. Each underlying Excel Worksheet and Workbook object is represented by a .NET class that you can extend and customize. As you make changes to the document in the designer, the code behind updates automatically. For example, drag a list object from the toolbox onto the Sheet1 designer, and draw it to be 10 rows by 4 columns, as shown in Figure 2-11.

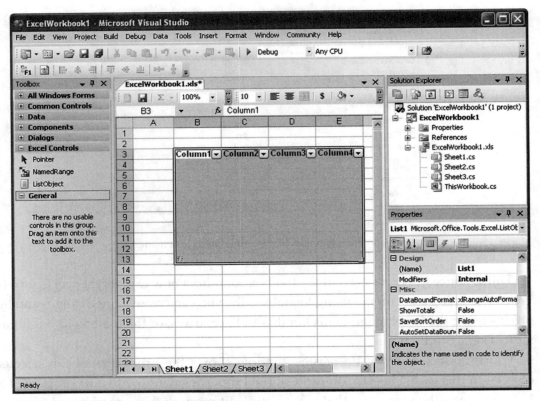

Figure 2-11 Creating a ListObject in the designer.

As you can see from the Properties window, the designer has chosen a default name for the new list object. We could edit it, but in this example, we will keep the default name List1.

Let's take a look at the code behind this worksheet and make some simple changes to it. Right-click Sheet1.cs in the Solution Explorer and choose View Code. We are going to briefly illustrate two VSTO features: ActionsPane and list object data binding. We will declare a Windows Forms button as a member variable of the class and call it myButton. In the Startup event, we will show that button in the Document Actions task pane of Excel by adding it to the ActionsPane's Controls collection. Doing so will cause Excel to show the Document Actions task pane and display our button. We will also handle the Click event of the button, and when the button is clicked we will data bind our list object to a randomly generated DataTable. Listing 2-7 shows this code.

Listing 2-7 A VSTO Customization That Adds a Control to the Document Actions Task Pane and Data Binds a ListObject Control to a DataTable

```
using System;
using System.Data;
using System.Drawing;
using System.Windows.Forms;
using Microsoft.VisualStudio.Tools.Applications.Runtime;
using Excel = Microsoft.Office.Interop.Excel;
using Office = Microsoft.Office.Core;

namespace ExcelWorkbook1
{
  public partial class Sheet1
  {
    Button myButton = new Button();
    DataTable table;

    private void Sheet1_Startup(object sender, EventArgs e)
    {
      myButton.Text = "Databind!";
      myButton.Click += new EventHandler(myButton_Click);
      Globals.ThisWorkbook.ActionsPane.Controls.Add(myButton);
    }

    void myButton_Click(object sender, EventArgs e)
    {
      List1.DataSource = null;
      table = new DataTable();
      Random r = new Random();

      for (int i = 0; i < 4; i++)
        table.Columns.Add("Col " + i.ToString());

      for (int i = 0; i < 20; i++)
        table.Rows.Add(r.NextDouble(), r.NextDouble(),
          r.NextDouble(), r.NextDouble());

      List1.DataSource = table;
    }
```

```
    private void Sheet1_Shutdown(object sender, EventArgs e)
    {
    }

    #region VSTO Designer generated code
    /// <summary>
    /// Required method for Designer support - do not modify
    /// the contents of this method with the code editor.
    /// </summary>
    private void InternalStartup()
    {
      this.Startup += new System.EventHandler(Sheet1_Startup);
      this.Shutdown += new System.EventHandler(Sheet1_Shutdown);
    }

    #endregion
  }
}
```

Build and run the code, and sure enough Excel starts up, the Startup event is raised for the sheet, and the button is added to the actions pane. Click the button and a random DataTable is generated and bound to the list object, as shown in Figure 2-12. Exit Excel to end your debugging session.

We have briefly illustrated VSTO's support for the Document Actions task pane and the ability to data bind that VSTO adds to Excel's list object. For more information on VSTO's support for the Document Actions task pane, see Chapter 15, "Working with Actions Pane." For more information on VSTO's support for data binding, see Chapter 17, "VSTO Data Programming."

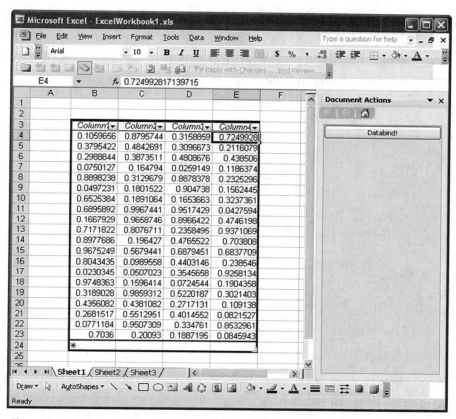

Figure 2-12   The result of running Listing 2-7 and clicking the button we added to the Document Actions task pane.

Conclusion

This chapter introduced the three basic patterns of Office solutions: an automation executable, an add-in, and code behind a document. The chapter also introduced how to build solutions following these three basic patterns using Visual Studio 2005 and Visual Studio 2005 Tools for Office.

Now that you know how to create a basic automation executable, add-in, and code behind the document solution, you will use these skills in the next chapters as the focus turns to specific functionality of Excel, Word, Outlook, and InfoPath that you can use in your solutions.

This chapter has only served as an introduction to add-ins and code behind documents. Chapter 24 covers VSTO add-ins for Outlook. Chapter 23 covers COM add-ins for Word and Excel. Chapter 3 covers automation add-ins for Excel. Chapters 13 through 17 cover the code behind document model of VSTO in detail.

Part Two
Office Programming in .NET

T he first two chapters of this book introduced Office object models and the Office PIAs. You have also seen how to use Visual Studio to build console applications, add-ins, and code behind the document using features of VSTO. The second part of this book covers the Office object models in more depth. If you are only interested in Excel development, read Chapters 3 through 5. If you are only interested in Word development, read Chapters 6 through 9. If you are only interested in Outlook development, read Chapters 7 through 11. If you are only interested in InfoPath development, read Chapter 12.

- Chapter 3, "Programming Excel," shows how you can customize Excel and in particular how you can create custom formulas for Excel.
- Chapter 4, "Working with Excel Events," covers the events that Excel raises that your code can handle.
- Chapter 5, "Working with Excel Objects," covers the object model of Excel in some detail, focusing on the most commonly used objects, properties, and methods.
- Chapter 6, "Programming Word," shows how you can customize Word and in particular how you can create research services for Word and other Office applications.
- Chapter 7, "Working with Word Events," covers the events that Word raises that your code can handle.

- Chapter 8, "Working with Word Objects," covers the object model of Word in some detail, focusing on the most commonly used objects, properties, and methods.
- Chapter 9, "Programming Outlook," shows how you can customize Outlook and in particular how you can create custom property pages for Outlook.
- Chapter 10, "Working with Outlook Events," covers the events that Outlook raises that your code can handle.
- Chapter 11, "Working with Outlook Objects," covers the object model of Outlook in some detail, focusing on the most commonly used objects, properties, and methods.
- Chapter 12, "Introduction to InfoPath," explores how to build InfoPath forms that use C# code.

■3■

Programming Excel

Ways to Customize Excel

EXCEL IS THE APPLICATION MOST FREQUENTLY programmed against in the Office family. Excel has a very rich object model with 196 objects that combined have more than 4,500 properties and methods. It supports several models for integrating your code, including add-ins and code behind documents. Most of these models were originally designed to allow the integration of COM components written in VB 6, VBA, C, or C++. However, through COM interop, managed objects written in C# or Visual Basic can masquerade as COM objects and participate in most of these models. This chapter briefly considers several of the ways that you can integrate your code with Excel and refers you to other chapters that discuss these approaches in more depth. This chapter also explores building user-defined functions for Excel and introduces the Excel object model.

Automation Executable

As mentioned in Chapter 2, "Introduction to Office Solutions," the simplest way to integrate with Excel is to start Excel from a console application or Windows Forms application and automate it from that external program. Chapter 2 provides a sample of an automation executable that automates Word.

COM Add-Ins

Excel can load a COM add-in that is a DLL that contains a class that implements IDTExtensibility2. The class that implements IDTExtensibility2 must be registered in the registry so that it can be discovered and talked to like other COM add-ins that extend Excel.

A COM add-in is typically written to add application-level functionality—functionality that is available to any workbook opened by Excel. For example, you might write a COM add-in that adds a menu item to convert a currency in the selected Excel worksheet cell to another currency based on current exchange rates.

Excel has a COM Add-Ins dialog box that enables users to turn COM add-ins on and off. Note that the dialog that is accessed by choosing Add-Ins from the Tools menu is *not* the COM Add-Ins dialog. That dialog is used to turn on and off automation add-ins and XLA add-ins, which are discussed later in this chapter. To access the COM Add-Ins dialog, you must perform the following steps:

1. Right-click a menu or toolbar in Excel and choose Customize from the pop-up menu, or from the Tools menu choose Customize to display the Customize dialog box.
2. Click the Commands tab of the Customize dialog.
3. Choose Tools from the list of Categories.
4. Scroll down the list of commands until you see a command that says COM Add-Ins.
5. Drag the COM Add-Ins command and drop it on a toolbar.
6. Close the Customize dialog box.

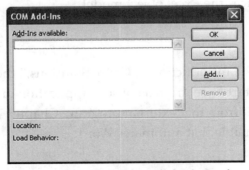

Figure 3-1 The COM Add-Ins dialog in Excel.

After completing these steps, click the COM Add-Ins toolbar button you added to a toolbar. Figure 3-1 shows the COM Add-Ins dialog.

You can add COM add-ins by using the Add button and remove them by using the Remove button. Typically, you will not have your users use this dialog to manage COM add-ins. Instead, you will install and remove a COM add-in by manipulating registry settings with the installer you create for your COM add-in.

Excel discovers the installed COM add-ins by reading from the registry. You can view the registry on your computer by going to the Windows Start menu and choosing Run. In the Run dialog box, type regedit for the program to run, and then click the OK button. Excel looks for COM add-ins in the registry keys under HKEY_CURRENT_USER\Software\Microsoft\Office\Excel\Addins. Excel also looks for COM add-ins in the registry keys under HKEY_LOCAL_MACHINE\ Software\Microsoft\Office\Excel\Addins. COM add-ins registered under HKEY_LOCAL_MACHINE are not shown in the COM Add-Ins dialog box and cannot be turned on or off by users. It is recommended you do not register your COM add-in under HKEY_LOCAL_MACHINE because it hides the COM add-in from the user.

COM add-ins are discussed in detail in Chapter 23, "Developing COM Add-Ins for Word and Excel."

Automation Add-Ins

Automation add-ins are classes that are registered in the registry as COM objects that expose public functions that can be used in Excel formulas. Automation add-ins that have been installed are shown in the Add-Ins dialog, which you can display by choosing Add-Ins from the Tools menu. This chapter examines automation add-ins in more detail during the discussion of how to create user-defined Excel functions for use in Excel formulas.

Visual Studio Tools for Office Code Behind

Visual Studio 2005 Tools for Office (VSTO) enables you to put C# or Visual Basic code behind Excel templates and workbooks. VSTO was designed from the ground up for C# and Visual Basic—so this model is the most ".NET" of all the models used to customize Excel. This model is used when you want to customize the behavior of a particular workbook or a particular set of workbooks created from a common template. For example, you might create a template for an expense reporting workbook that is used whenever anyone in your company creates an expense report. This template can add commands and functionality that are always available when the workbook created with it is opened.

VSTO's support for code behind a workbook is discussed in detail in Part Three of this book.

Smart Documents and XML Expansion Packs

Smart documents are another way to associate your code with an Excel template or workbook. Smart documents rely on attaching an XML schema to a workbook or template and associating your code with that schema. The combination of the schema and associated code is called an XML Expansion Pack. An XML Expansion Pack can be associated with an Excel workbook by choosing XML Expansion Packs from the XML menu in the Data menu. Figure 3-2 shows the XML Expansion Packs dialog.

Figure 3-2 The XML Expansion Packs dialog in Excel.

When an XML Expansion Pack is attached to a workbook, Excel loads the associated code and runs it while that workbook is opened. Smart document solutions can create a custom user interface in the Document Actions task pane. You can view the task pane in Excel by choosing Task Pane from the View menu. Figure 3-3 shows a custom Document Actions task pane in Excel.

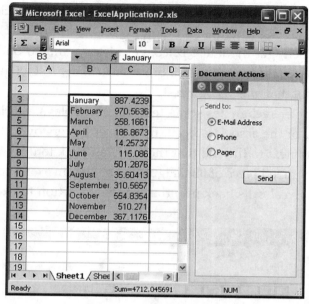

Figure 3-3 A custom Document Actions task pane in Excel.

It is possible to write smart document solutions "from scratch" in C# or Visual Basic. This book does not cover this approach. Instead, this book focuses on the VSTO approach, which was designed to make smart document development much easier and allow you to create a custom Document Actions task pane using Windows Forms. Chapter 15, "Working with Actions Pane," discusses this capability in more detail.

Smart Tags

Smart Tags enable a pop-up menu to be displayed containing actions relevant for a recognized piece of text in a workbook. You can control the text that Excel recognizes and the actions that are made available for that text by creating a Smart Tag DLL or by using VSTO code behind a document.

A Smart Tag DLL contains two types of components that are used by Excel: a recognizer and associated actions. A recognizer determines what text in the workbook is recognized as a Smart Tag. An action corresponds to a menu command displayed in the pop-up menu.

A recognizer could be created that tells Excel to recognize stock-ticker symbols (such as the MSFT stock symbol) and display a set of actions that can be taken for that symbol: buy, sell, get the latest price, get history, and so on. A "get history" action, for instance, could launch a Web browser to show a stock history Web page for the stock symbol that was recognized.

When a recognizer recognizes some text, Excel displays a little triangle in the lower-right corner of the associated cell. If the user hovers over the cell, a pop-up menu icon appears next to the cell that the user can click to drop down a menu of actions for the recognized piece of text. Figure 3-4 shows an example menu. When an action is selected, Excel calls back into the associated action to execute your code.

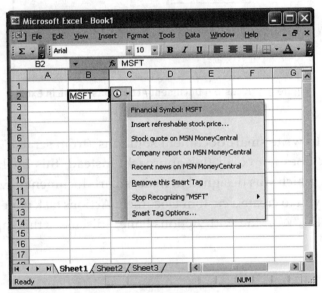

Figure 3-4 Smart Tags in Excel.

Smart Tags are managed from the Smart Tags page of the AutoCorrect dialog, as shown in Figure 3-5. You can display the Smart Tags page by choosing AutoCorrect Options from the Tools menu. Here the user can turn on and off individual recognizers as well as control other options relating to how Smart Tags display in the workbook.

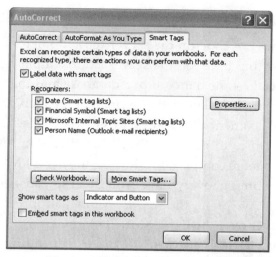

Figure 3-5 The Smart Tags page in the AutoCorrect dialog.

VSTO provides a simple model for creating a Smart Tag that works at the work-book or template level. Chapter 16, "Working with Smart Tags in VSTO," describes the VSTO model for working with Smart Tags in more detail.

It is possible to write Smart Tag recognizer and action classes in a DLL that work at the application level, but it is much more complex than the VSTO model. Chapter 16 also describes that approach.

XLA Add-Ins

Also found in the Add-Ins dialog (shown by selecting Add-Ins from the Tools menu) are XLA add-ins. An XLA add-in starts life as a workbook that has VBA code behind it. The developer can then save the workbook as an XLA or Excel add-in file by using Save As from the File menu and selecting XLA as the file format. An XLA file acts as an application-level add-in in the form of an invisible workbook that stays open for the lifetime of Excel. Although it is possible to save a workbook customized with VSTO as an XLA file, many of the features of VSTO do not work when the workbook is converted to an XLA file. Some of the features that do not work include VSTO's support for the Document Actions task pane and for Smart Tags. For this reason, Microsoft does not support or recommend saving a workbook customized with VSTO as an XLA file. Therefore, this book does not cover it further.

Server-Generated Documents

VSTO enables you to write code on the server that populates an Excel workbook with data without starting Excel on the server. For example, you might create an ASP.NET page that reads some data out of a database and then puts it in an Excel workbook and returns that workbook to the client of the Web page. VSTO provides a class called ServerDocument that makes it easy to do this. You can also use the XML file formats of Office to generate Excel documents in XML formats on the server, but this is much more complex. In addition, the Excel XML file format is lossy, meaning you cannot represent everything in an Excel spreadsheet in the Excel XML format. For this reason, we prefer the ServerDocument approach when generating documents on the server over the Excel XML file format.

Chapter 18, "Server Data Scenarios," describes generating documents on the server with ServerDocument.

Research Services

Excel has a task pane called the Research task pane that enables you to enter a search term and search various sources for that search term. Figure 3-6 shows the Research task pane.

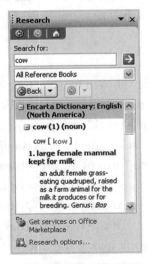

Figure 3-6 The Research task pane.

Excel enables developers to write a special Web service called a research service that implements a set of Web methods defined by Excel. A research service can be registered with Excel and used in Office's Research task pane. For example, you might write a research service that searches for a search term in a company database.

Chapter 6, "Programming Word," discusses creating a research service in more detail.

Programming User-Defined Functions

Excel enables the creation of user-defined functions that can be used in Excel formulas. A developer must create a special kind of DLL called an XLL. Excel also allows you to write custom functions in VBA that can be used in Excel formulas. Unfortunately, Excel does not support or recommend writing an XLL that uses managed code.

Building a Managed Automation Add-In That Provides User-Defined Functions

Fortunately, there is an easier way to create a user-defined function that does not require you to create an XLL. Excel 2003 supports a customization technology called an automation add-in that can easily be created in C# or Visual Basic.

First, launch Visual Studio and create a new C# class library project. Name the project AutomationAddin. In your Class1.cs file created for you in the new project, enter the code shown in Listing 3-1. This code defines a class called MyFunctions that implements a function called MultiplyNTimes. We will use this function as a custom formula. Our class also implements RegisterFunction and Unregister-Function, which are attributed with the ComRegisterFunction attribute and ComUnregisterFunction attribute respectively. The RegisterFunction will be called when the assembly is registered for COM interop. The UnregisterFunction will be called when the assembly is unregistered for COM interop. These functions put a necessary key in the registry that allow Excel to know that this class can be used as an automation add-in.

Listing 3-1 A C# Class Called MyFunctions That Exposes a User-Defined Function MultiplyNTimes

```csharp
using System;
using System.Runtime.InteropServices;
using Microsoft.Win32;

namespace AutomationAddin
{
  [ClassInterface(ClassInterfaceType.AutoDual)]
  public class MyFunctions
  {
    public MyFunctions()
    {
    }

    public double MultiplyNTimes(double number1,
      double number2, double timesToMultiply)
    {
      double result = number1;
      for (double i = 0; i < timesToMultiply; i++)
      {
        result = result * number2;
      }
      return result;
    }

    [ComRegisterFunctionAttribute]
    public static void RegisterFunction(Type type)
    {
      Registry.ClassesRoot.CreateSubKey(
        GetSubKeyName(type));
    }

    [ComUnregisterFunctionAttribute]
    public static void UnregisterFunction(Type type)
    {
      Registry.ClassesRoot.DeleteSubKey(
        GetSubKeyName(type),false);
    }

    private static string GetSubKeyName(Type type)
    {
      System.Text.StringBuilder s =
        new System.Text.StringBuilder();
      s.Append(@"CLSID\{");
      s.Append(type.GUID.ToString().ToUpper());
      s.Append(@"}\Programmable");
      return s.ToString();
```

```
      }
    }
  }
```

With this code written, you need to modify the project so that it will automatically register this class for COM interop when it is built. First, show the properties for the project by double-clicking the Properties node under the project node in Solution Explorer. In the properties designer that appears, click the Build tab and check the check box that says Register for COM Interop, as shown in Figure 3-7. Then choose Build Solution from the Build menu to build the class library project. Your actions will result in your class library project being built as well as registered in the registry as an automation add-in. Excel will now be able to see your C# class and use it.

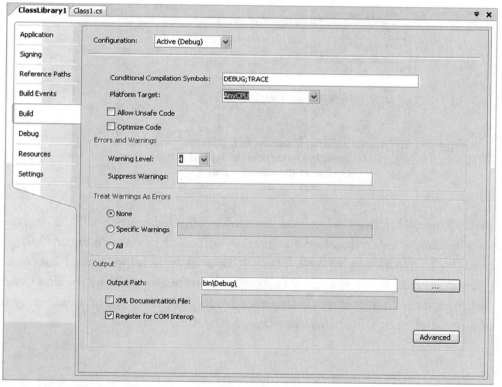

Figure 3-7 Setting Build options to register for COM interop.

Using Your Managed Automation Add-In in Excel

Launch Excel and choose Add-Ins from the Tools menu to display the Add-Ins dialog. In the Add-Ins dialog, click the Automation button. You can find the class you created by looking for `AutomationAddin.MyFunctions` in the list of automation servers, as shown in Figure 3-8.

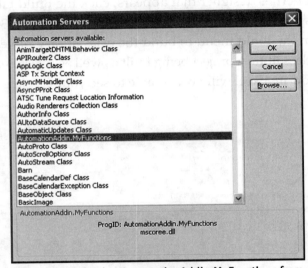

Figure 3-8 Selecting AutomationAddin.MyFunctions from the Automation Servers dialog.

By clicking OK in this dialog, you have added the `AutomationAddin.MyFunctions` class to the list of installed automation add-ins, as shown in Figure 3-9.

Now, try to use the function `MultiplyNTimes` in an Excel formula. First create a simple spreadsheet that has a number, a second number to multiply the first by, and a third number for how many times you want to multiply the first number by the second number. Figure 3-10 shows the spreadsheet.

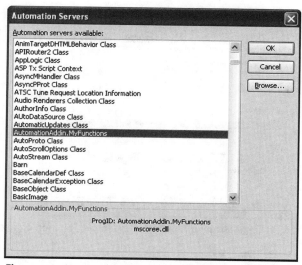

Figure 3-9 AutomationAddin.MyFunctions is now installed.

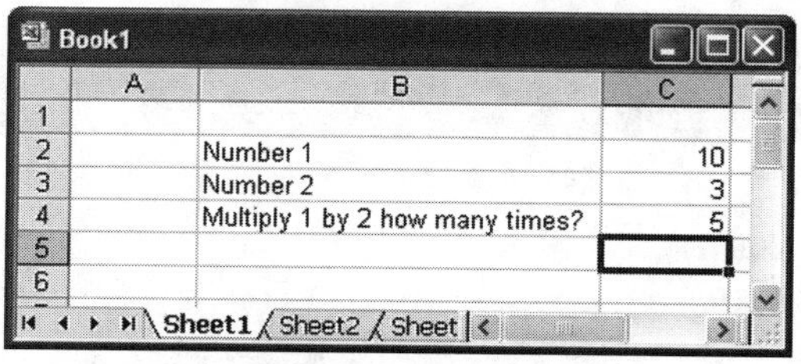

Figure 3-10 A simple spreadsheet to test the custom formula in.

Click an empty cell in the workbook below the numbers, and then click the Insert Function button (the button with the "fx" label) in the formula bar. From the dialog of available formulas, drop down the "Or select a category" drop-down box and choose AutomationAddin.MyFunctions. Then click the MultiplyNTimes function, as shown in Figure 3-11.

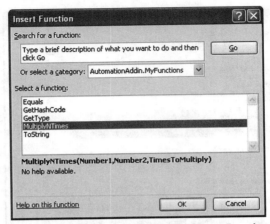

Figure 3-11 Picking MultiplyNTimes from the Insert Function dialog box.

When you click the OK button, Excel pops up a dialog to help select function arguments from cells in the spreadsheet, as shown in Figure 3-12.

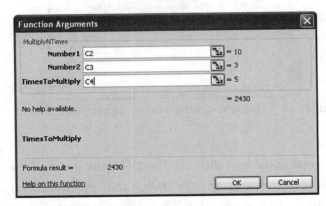

Figure 3-12 Setting the function arguments.

After you have selected function arguments from the appropriate cells, click OK to create the final spreadsheet, as shown in Figure 3-13, with the custom formula in cell C5.

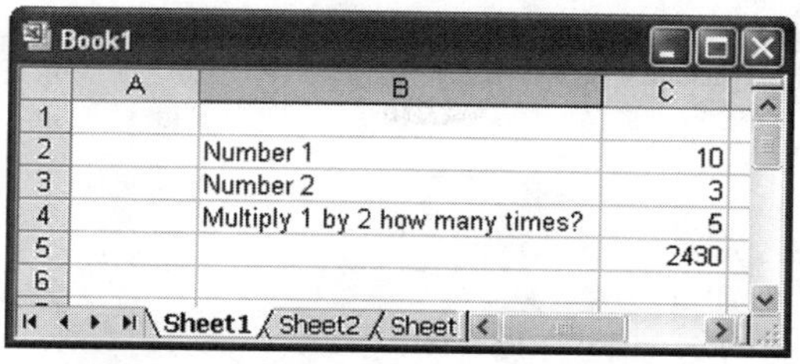

Figure 3-13 The final spreadsheet.

Some Additional User-Defined Functions

You might experiment with other functions that could be used in an Excel formula. For example, Listing 3-2 shows several other functions you could add to your `MyFunctions` class. To use Listing 3-2, you must add a reference to the Excel 11.0 Object Library and also add the code `using Excel = Microsoft.Office.Interop.Excel` to the top of your class file. Note in particular that when you declare a parameter as an object, Excel passes you a Range object. Also note how optional parameters are supported by the `AddNumbers` function. When a parameter is omitted, `System.Type.Missing` is passed as the value of the parameter.

Listing 3-2 Additional User-Defined Function That Could Be Added to the MyFunctions Class

```
public string GetStars(double number)
{
  System.Text.StringBuilder s =
    new System.Text.StringBuilder();
  s.Append('*', number);
  return s.ToString();
}

public double AddNumbers(double number1,
  [Optional] object number2, [Optional] object number3)
{
  double result = number1;

  if (number2 != System.Type.Missing)
  {
```

```csharp
      Excel.Range r2 = number2 as Excel.Range;
      double d2 = Convert.ToDouble(r2.Value2);
      result += d2;
    }

    if (number3 != System.Type.Missing)
    {
      Excel.Range r3 = number3 as Excel.Range;
      double d3 = Convert.ToDouble(r3.Value2);
      result += d3;
    }

    return result;
  }

public double CalculateArea(object range)
{
  Excel.Range r = range as Excel.Range;
  return Convert.ToDouble(r.Width) +
    Convert.ToDouble(r.Height);
}

public double NumberOfCells(object range)
{
  Excel.Range r = range as Excel.Range;
  return r.Cells.Count;
}

public string ToUpperCase(string input)
{
  return input.ToUpper();
}
```

Debugging User-defined Functions in a Managed Automation Add-Ins

You can debug a C# class library project that is acting as an automation add-in by setting Excel to be the program your class library project starts when you debug. Show the properties for the project by double-clicking the Properties node under the project node in Solution Explorer. In the properties designer that appears, click the Debug tab, and in the Start external program text box, type the full path to Excel.exe, as shown in Figure 3-14. Now, set a breakpoint on one of your user functions, press F5, and use the function in the spreadsheet. The debugger will stop in the implementation of your user function where the breakpoint was set.

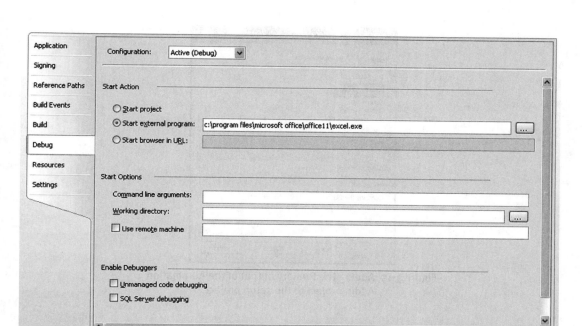

Figure 3-14 Setting Debug options to start Excel.

Deploying Managed Automation Add-Ins

To deploy an automation add-in, right-click your solution in Solution Explorer and choose New Project from the Add menu. From the Add New Project dialog, choose Setup Project from Other Project Types\Setup and Deployment in the Project Types tree.

Right-click the added setup project in Solution Explorer and choose Project Output from the Add menu. From the Add Project Output Group dialog box, choose the AutomationAddin project and select Primary Output, as shown in Figure 3-15.

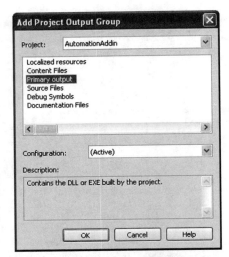

Figure 3-15 Adding the Primary output of the Automation Addin project to the setup project.

Because we told the project to register our managed object for COM interop, the setup project should already be set up correctly to register the managed object for COM interop at install time, too. To verify this, click the Primary output from AutomationAddin node in the setup project. In the Properties window for the primary output (our C# DLL), make sure that Register is set to vsdrpCOM.

Introduction to the Excel Object Model

Regardless of the approach you choose to integrate your code with Excel, you will eventually need to talk to the Excel object model to get things done. It is impossible to completely describe the Excel object model in this book, but we try to make you familiar with the most important objects in the Excel object model and show some of the most frequently used methods, properties, and events on these objects.

The Object Hierarchy

The first step in learning the Excel object model is getting an idea for the basic structure of the object model hierarchy. Figure 3-16 shows the most critical objects in the Excel object model and their hierarchical relationship.

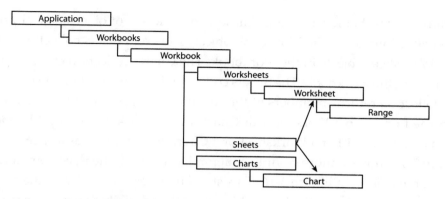

Figure 3-16 The basic hierarchy of the Excel object model.

A Workbook object has a collection called Sheets. The Sheets collection can contain objects of type Worksheet or Chart. A Chart is sometimes called a chart sheet because it covers the entire area that a worksheet would cover. You can insert a chart sheet into a workbook by right-clicking the worksheet tabs in the lower-left corner of the Excel workbook and choosing Insert. Figure 3-17 shows the dialog that appears. Note that two additional objects are found in the Sheets collection: MS Excel 4.0 macro sheets and MS Excel 5.0 dialog sheets. If you insert a macro sheet or dialog sheet into an Excel workbook, it is treated as a special kind of worksheet—there is not a special object model type corresponding to a macro sheet or a dialog sheet.

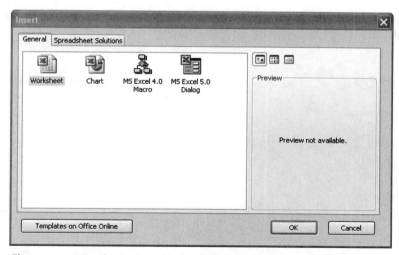

Figure 3-17 Inserting various kinds of "sheets" into an Excel Workbook.

Because a workbook can contain these various kinds of objects, Excel provides several collections off of the Workbook object. The Worksheets collection contains just the Worksheet objects in the workbook. The Charts collection contains just the chart sheets in the workbook. The Sheets collection is a mixed collection of both. The Sheets collection returns members of the collection as type object—you must cast the returned object to a Worksheet or Chart. In this book, when we talk about an object that could be either a Worksheet or a Chart, we refer to it as a sheet.

Figure 3-18 shows a more complete hierarchy tree with the major objects associated with the objects in Figure 3-16. This starts to give you an idea of the extensive hierarchy of objects that is the Excel object model, especially when you realize that this diagram shows less than half of the objects available. The objects shown in gray are coming from the Microsoft.Office.Core namespace, which is associated with the Microsoft Office 11.0 PIA (office.dll). These objects are shared by all the Office applications.

Figure 3-19 shows the object hierarchy associated with Range, a very important object in Excel that represents a range of cells you want to work with in your code. We have already used the Range object in Listing 3-2.

Figure 3-20 shows the object hierarchy associated with Shape—a Shape represents things that float on the worksheet that are not cells, such as embedded buttons, drawings, comment bubbles, and so on.

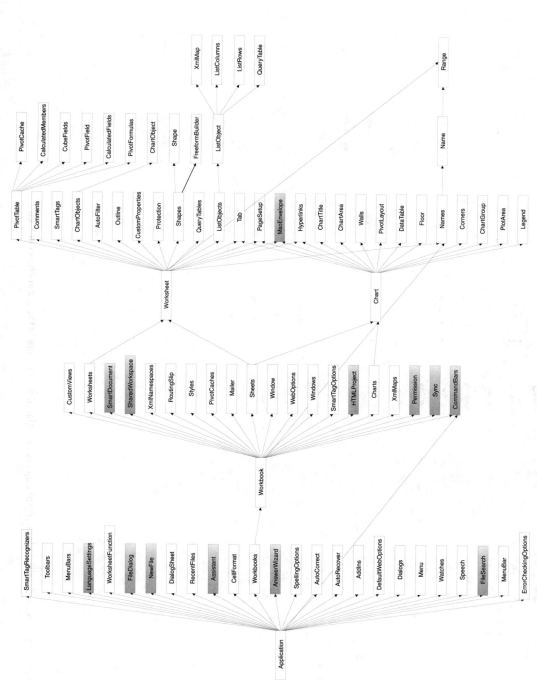

Figure 3-18 A more detailed hierarchy of some major objects in the Excel object model.

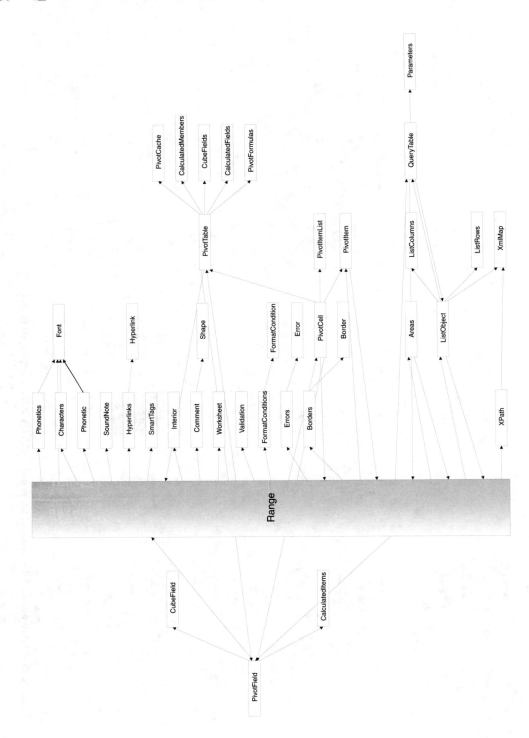

Figure 3-19 A more detailed hierarchy of objects associated with Range in the Excel object model.

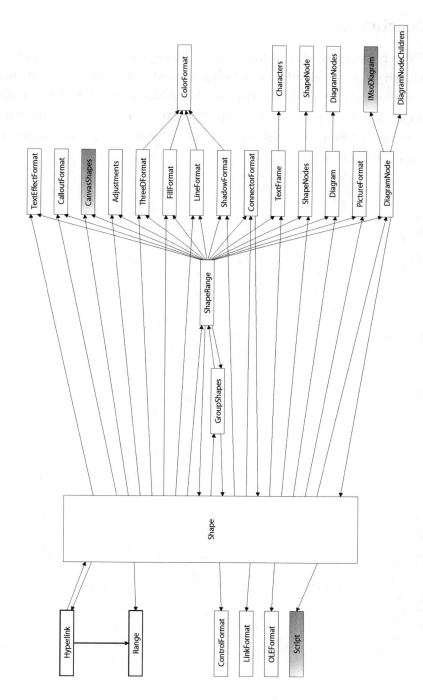

Figure 3-20 A more detailed hierarchy of objects associated with Shape in the Excel object model.

Conclusion

This chapter introduced the various ways you can integrate your code into Excel. The chapter described how to build automation add-ins to create user-defined functions for Excel. You also learned the basic hierarchy of the Excel object model. Chapter 4, "Working with Excel Events," discusses the events in the Excel object model. Chapter 5, "Working with Excel Objects," covers the most important objects in the Excel object model.

4. Working with Excel Events

Events in the Excel Object Model

UNDERSTANDING THE EVENTS IN THE Excel object model is critical because this is often the primary way that your code is run. This chapter examines all the events in the Excel object model, when they are raised, and the type of code you might associate with these events.

Many of the events in the Excel object model are repeated on the Application, Workbook, and Worksheet objects. This repetition allows you to decide whether you want to handle the event for all workbooks, for a particular workbook, or for a particular worksheet. For example, if you want to know when any worksheet in any open workbook is double-clicked, you would handle the Application object's Sheet-BeforeDoubleClick event. If you want to know when any worksheet in a particular workbook is double-clicked, you would handle the SheetBeforeDoubleClick event on that Workbook object. If you want to know when one particular sheet is double-clicked, you would handle the BeforeDoubleClick event on that Worksheet object. When an event is repeated on the Application, Workbook, and Worksheet object, it typically is raised first on Worksheet, then Workbook, and finally Application.

New Workbook and Worksheet Events

Excel's Application object raises a NewWorkbook event when a new blank workbook is created. This event is not raised when a new workbook is created from a template or an existing document. Excel also raises events when new worksheets are created in a particular workbook. Similarly, these events are only raised when a user first creates a new worksheet. They are never raised again on subsequent opens of the workbook.

This discussion now focuses on the various ways in which new workbook and worksheet events are raised:

- **Application.NewWorkbook** is raised when a new blank workbook is created. Excel passes the new Workbook object as a parameter to this event.

> NewWorkbook is the name of both a property and an event on the Application object. Because of this collision, you will not see the NewWorkbook event in Visual Studio's pop-up menu of properties, events, and methods associated with the Application object. Furthermore, a warning displays at compile time when you try to handle this event. To get Visual Studio's pop-up menus to work and the warning to go away, you can cast the Application object to the AppEvents_Event interface, as shown in Listing 4-1.

- **Application.WorkbookNewSheet** is raised when a new sheet is created in any open workbook. Excel passes the Workbook object that the new sheet was created in as a parameter to this event. It also passes the new sheet object. Because a workbook can contain both worksheets and chart sheets, the new sheet object is passed as an `object`. You can then cast it to either a Worksheet or a Chart.
- **Workbook.NewSheet** is raised on a workbook that has a new sheet created in it. Excel passes the new sheet object as a parameter to this event. The new sheet object is passed as an `object` that you can cast to either a Worksheet or a Chart.

Listing 4-1 shows a console application that handles the Application object's NewWorkbook and WorkbookNewSheet events. It also creates a new workbook and handles the NewSheet event for that newly created workbook. The console application handles the Close event for the workbook, so when you close the workbook the console application will exit and Excel will quit. Listing 4-1 shows several other common techniques. For the sheets passed as `object`, we use the `as` operator to cast the `object` to a Worksheet or a Chart. We then will check the result to verify it is not `null` to ascertain whether the cast succeeded. This method proves more efficient than using the `is` operator followed by the `as` operator, because the latter method requires two casts.

Listing 4-1 A Console Application That Handles New Workbook and Worksheet Events

```
using System;
using Excel = Microsoft.Office.Interop.Excel;
using System.Windows.Forms;

namespace ConsoleApplication
{
  class Program
  {
    static private Excel.Application app;
    static private Excel.Workbook workbook;
    static bool exit = false;

    static void Main(string[] args)
    {
      app = new Excel.Application();
      app.Visible = true;

      // We cast to AppEvents_Event because NewWorkbook
      // is the name of both a property and an event.
      ((Excel.AppEvents_Event)app).NewWorkbook +=
        new Excel.AppEvents_NewWorkbookEventHandler(
        App_NewWorkbook);

      app.WorkbookNewSheet +=
        new Excel.AppEvents_WorkbookNewSheetEventHandler(
        App_WorkbookNewSheet);

      workbook = app.Workbooks.Add(Type.Missing);
      workbook.NewSheet +=
        new Excel.WorkbookEvents_NewSheetEventHandler(
        Workbook_NewSheet);

      workbook.BeforeClose +=
        new Excel.WorkbookEvents_BeforeCloseEventHandler(
        Workbook_BeforeClose);

      while (exit == false)
```

```csharp
      System.Windows.Forms.Application.DoEvents();

   app.Quit();
}

static void App_NewWorkbook(Excel.Workbook workbook)
{
   Console.WriteLine(String.Format(
     "Application.NewWorkbook({0})", workbook.Name));
}

static void App_WorkbookNewSheet(Excel.Workbook workbook,
   object sheet)
{
   Excel.Worksheet worksheet = sheet as Excel.Worksheet;

   if (worksheet != null)
   {
     Console.WriteLine(String.Format(
       "Application.WorkbookNewSheet({0},{1})",
       workbook.Name, worksheet.Name));
   }

   Excel.Chart chart = sheet as Excel.Chart;

   if (chart != null)
   {
     Console.WriteLine(String.Format(
       "Application.WorkbookNewSheet({0},{1})",
       workbook.Name, chart.Name));
   }
}

static void Workbook_NewSheet(object sheet)
{
   Excel.Worksheet worksheet = sheet as Excel.Worksheet;

   if (worksheet != null)
   {
     Console.WriteLine(String.Format(
       "Workbook.NewSheet({0})", worksheet.Name));
   }

   Excel.Chart chart = sheet as Excel.Chart;

   if (chart != null)
   {
```

```
        Console.WriteLine(String.Format(
          "Workbook.NewSheet({0})", chart.Name));
      }
    }

    static void Workbook_BeforeClose(ref bool cancel)
    {
      exit = true;
    }
  }
}
```

As you consider the code in Listing 4-1, you might wonder how you will ever remember the syntax of complicated lines of code such as this one:

```
app.WorkbookNewSheet +=
  new Excel.AppEvents_WorkbookNewSheetEventHandler(
  App_WorkbookNewSheet);
```

Fortunately, Visual Studio 2005 helps by generating most of this line of code as well as the corresponding event handler automatically. If you were typing this line of code, after you type +=, Visual Studio displays a pop-up tooltip (see Figure 4-1). If you press the Tab key twice, Visual Studio generates the rest of the line of code and the event handler method automatically.

Figure 4-1 Visual Studio generates event handler code for you if you press the Tab key.

If you are using Visual Studio 2005 Tools for Office (VSTO), you can also use the Properties window to add event handlers to your workbook or worksheet classes. Double-click the project item for your workbook class (typically called ThisWorkbook.cs) or one of your worksheet classes (typically called Sheet1.cs, Sheet2.cs, and so on). Make sure the Properties window is visible. If it is not, choose Properties Window from the View menu to show the Properties window. Make sure that the workbook class (typically called ThisWorkbook) or a worksheet class (typically called Sheet1, Sheet2, and so on) is selected in the combo box at the top of the Properties window. Then click the lightning bolt icon to show events associated with the workbook or worksheet. Type the name of the method you want to use as an event handler in the edit box to the right of the event you want to handle.

Activation and Deactivation Events

Sixteen events in the Excel object model are raised when various objects are activated or deactivated. An object is considered activated when its window receives focus or it is made the selected or active object. For example, worksheets are activated and deactivated when you switch from one worksheet to another within a workbook. Clicking the tab for Sheet3 in a workbook that currently has Sheet1 selected raises a Deactivate event for Sheet1 (it is losing focus) and an Activate event for Sheet3 (it is getting focus). You can activate/deactive chart sheets in the same manner. Doing so raises Activate and Deactivate events on the Chart object corresponding to the chart sheet that was activated or deactivated.

You can also activate/deactivate worksheets. Consider the case where you have the workbooks Book1 and Book2 open at the same time. If you are currently editing Book1 and you switch from Book1 to Book2 by choosing Book2 from the Window menu, the Deactivate event for Book1 is raised and the Activate event for Book2 is raised.

Windows are another example of objects that are activated and deactivated. A workbook can have more than one window open that is showing the workbook. Consider the case where you have the workbook Book1 opened. If you choose New Window from the Window menu, two windows will open in Excel viewing Book1. One window has the caption Book1:1, and the other window has the caption Book1:2. As you switch between Book1:1 and Book1:2, the WindowActivate event is raised for the workbook. Switching between Book1:1 and Book1:2 does not raise the Workbook Activate or Deactivate events because Book1 remains the active workbook.

Note that Activate and Deactivate events are not raised when you switch to an application other than Excel and then switch back to Excel. You might expect that if you had Excel and Word open side by side on your monitor that switching focus by clicking from Excel to Word would raise Deactivate events inside Excel. This is not the case—Excel does not consider switching to another application a deactivation of any of its workbooks, sheets, or windows.

The discussion now turns to the various ways in which Activate and Deactivate events are raised:

- **Application.WorkbookActivate** is raised whenever a workbook is activated within Excel. Excel passes the Workbook object that was activated as a parameter to this event.
- **Workbook.Activate** is raised on a particular workbook that is activated. No parameter is passed to this event because the activated workbook is the Workbook object raising the event.

Activate is the name of both a method and an event on the Workbook object. Because of this collision, you will not see the Activate event in Visual Studio's pop-up menu of properties, events, and methods associated with the Application object. Furthermore, a warning displays at compile time when you try to handle this event.

To get Visual Studio's pop-up menus to work and to remove the warning, you can cast the Workbook object to the WorkbookEvents_Event interface, as shown in Listing 4-1.

- **Application.WorkbookDeactivate** is raised whenever any workbook is deactivated within Excel. Excel passes the Workbook object that was deactivated as a parameter to this event.
- **Workbook.Deactivate** is raised on a particular workbook that is deactivated. No parameter is passed to this event because the deactivated workbook is the Workbook object raising the event.
- **Application.SheetActivate** is raised whenever a worksheet is activated within Excel. Excel passes the sheet object that was activated as a parameter to this event. Because a workbook can contain both worksheets and chart sheets, the activated sheet is passed as an `object`. You can then cast it to either a Worksheet or a Chart.

- **Workbook.SheetActivate** is raised on a workbook that has a sheet that was activated. Excel passes the sheet object that was activated as a parameter to this event. Because a workbook can contain both worksheets and chart sheets, the activated sheet is passed as an `object`. You can then cast it to either a Worksheet or a Chart.

- **Worksheet.Activate** and **Chart.Activate** are raised on an activated worksheet or chart sheet. No parameter is passed to these events because the activated sheet is the Worksheet or Chart object raising this event.

Activate is the name of both a method and an event on the Worksheet and the Chart object. Because of this collision, you will not see the Activate event in Visual Studio's pop-up menu of properties, events, and methods associated with the Worksheet or Chart object. Furthermore, a warning displays at compile time when you try to handle this event. To get Visual Studio's pop-up menus to work and the warning to go away, you can cast the Worksheet object to the DocEvents_Event interface and cast the Chart object to the ChartEvents_Events interface, as shown in Listing 4-2.

It is strange that the interface you cast the Worksheet object to is called DocEvents_Event. This is due to the way the PIAs are generated—the event interface on the COM object Worksheet was called DocEvents rather than WorksheetEvents. The same inconsistency occurs with the Application object; it has an event interface called AppEvents rather than ApplicationEvents.

- **Application.SheetDeactivate** is raised whenever any worksheet is deactivated within Excel. Excel passes the sheet object that was deactivated as a parameter to this event. Because a workbook can contain both worksheets and chart sheets, the deactivated sheet is passed as an `object`. You can then cast it to either a Worksheet or a Chart.

- **Workbook.SheetDeactivate** is raised on a workbook that has a sheet that was deactivated. Excel passes the sheet object that was deactivated as a parameter to this event. Because a workbook can contain both worksheets and chart sheets, the deactivated sheet is passed as an `object`. You can then cast it to either a Worksheet or a Chart.

- **Worksheet.Deactivate** and **Chart.Deactivate** are raised on a deactivated worksheet or chart sheet. No parameters are passed to these events because the deactivated sheet is the Worksheet or Chart object raising this event.

- **Application.WindowActivate** is raised whenever a window is activated within Excel. Excel passes the Workbook object corresponding to the window that was activated as a parameter to this event. Excel also passes the Window object that was activated.

- **Workbook.WindowActivate** is raised on a workbook that has a window that was activated. Excel passes the Window object that was activated as a parameter to this event.

- **Application.WindowDeactivate** is raised whenever a window is deactivated within Excel. Excel passes the Workbook object corresponding to the window that was deactivated as a parameter to this event. Excel also passes the Window object that was deactivated.

- **Workbook.WindowDeactivate** is raised on a workbook that has a window that was deactivated. Excel passes the Window object that was deactivated as a parameter to this event.

Listing 4-2 shows a class that handles all of these events. It is passed an Excel Application object to its constructor. The constructor creates a new workbook and gets the first sheet in the workbook. Then it creates a chart sheet. It handles events raised on the Application object as well as the created workbook, the first worksheet in the workbook, and the chart sheet that it adds to the workbook. Because several events pass as a parameter a sheet as an `object`, a helper method called `ReportEvent-WithSheetParameter` is used to determine the type of sheet passed and display a message to the console.

Listing 4-2 A Class That Handles Activation and Deactivation Events

```csharp
using System;
using Excel = Microsoft.Office.Interop.Excel;

namespace ActivationAndDeactivation
{
  public class TestEventHandler
  {
    private Excel.Application app;
    private Excel.Workbook workbook;
    private Excel.Worksheet worksheet;
    private Excel.Chart chart;

    public TestEventHandler(Excel.Application application)
    {
      this.app = application;
      workbook = application.Workbooks.Add(Type.Missing);
      worksheet = workbook.Worksheets.get_Item(1)
        as Excel.Worksheet;

      chart = workbook.Charts.Add(Type.Missing, Type.Missing,
        Type.Missing, Type.Missing) as Excel.Chart;

      app.WorkbookActivate +=
        new Excel.AppEvents_WorkbookActivateEventHandler(
        App_WorkbookActivate);

      ((Excel.WorkbookEvents_Event)workbook).Activate +=
        new Excel.WorkbookEvents_ActivateEventHandler(
        Workbook_Activate);

      app.WorkbookDeactivate +=
        new Excel.AppEvents_WorkbookDeactivateEventHandler(
        App_WorkbookDeactivate);

      workbook.Deactivate +=
        new Excel.WorkbookEvents_DeactivateEventHandler(
        Workbook_Deactivate);

      app.SheetActivate +=
        new Excel.AppEvents_SheetActivateEventHandler(
        App_SheetActivate);

      workbook.SheetActivate +=
        new Excel.WorkbookEvents_SheetActivateEventHandler(
        Workbook_SheetActivate);
```

```csharp
      ((Excel.DocEvents_Event)worksheet).Activate +=
        new Excel.DocEvents_ActivateEventHandler(
        Worksheet_Activate);

      ((Excel.ChartEvents_Event)chart).Activate +=
        new Excel.ChartEvents_ActivateEventHandler(
        Chart_Activate);

    app.SheetDeactivate +=
      new Excel.AppEvents_SheetDeactivateEventHandler(
      App_SheetDeactivate);

    workbook.SheetDeactivate +=
      new Excel.WorkbookEvents_SheetDeactivateEventHandler(
      Workbook_SheetDeactivate);

    worksheet.Deactivate +=
      new Excel.DocEvents_DeactivateEventHandler(
      Worksheet_Deactivate);

    chart.Deactivate +=
      new Excel.ChartEvents_DeactivateEventHandler(
      Chart_Deactivate);

    app.WindowActivate +=
      new Excel.AppEvents_WindowActivateEventHandler(
      App_WindowActivate);

    workbook.WindowActivate +=
      new Excel.WorkbookEvents_WindowActivateEventHandler(
      Workbook_WindowActivate);

    app.WindowDeactivate +=
      new Excel.AppEvents_WindowDeactivateEventHandler(
      App_WindowDeactivate);

    workbook.WindowDeactivate +=
      new Excel.WorkbookEvents_WindowDeactivateEventHandler(
      Workbook_WindowDeactivate);
  }

void ReportEventWithSheetParameter(string eventName, object sheet)
{
  Excel.Worksheet worksheet = sheet as Excel.Worksheet;

  if (worksheet != null)
  {
    Console.WriteLine(String.Format("{0} ({1})",
```

```
      eventName, worksheet.Name));
  }

  Excel.Chart chart = sheet as Excel.Chart;

  if (chart != null)
  {
    Console.WriteLine(String.Format("{0} ({1})",
      eventName, chart.Name));
  }
}

void App_WorkbookActivate(Excel.Workbook workbook)
{
  Console.WriteLine(String.Format(
    "Application.WorkbookActivate({0})", workbook.Name));
}

void Workbook_Activate()
{
  Console.WriteLine("Workbook.Activate()");
}

void App_WorkbookDeactivate(Excel.Workbook workbook)
{
  Console.WriteLine(String.Format(
    "Application.WorkbookDeactivate({0})", workbook.Name));
}

void Workbook_Deactivate()
{
  Console.WriteLine("Workbook.Deactivate()");
}

void App_SheetActivate(object sheet)
{
  ReportEventWithSheetParameter(
    "Application.SheetActivate", sheet);
}

void Workbook_SheetActivate(object sheet)
{
  ReportEventWithSheetParameter(
    "Workbook.SheetActivate", sheet);
}

void Worksheet_Activate()
{
```

```csharp
    Console.WriteLine("Worksheet.Activate()");
}

void Chart_Activate()
{
    Console.WriteLine("Chart.Activate()");
}

void App_SheetDeactivate(object sheet)
{
    ReportEventWithSheetParameter(
        "Application.SheetDeactivate", sheet);
}

void Workbook_SheetDeactivate(object sheet)
{
    ReportEventWithSheetParameter(
        "Workbook.SheetDeactivate", sheet);
}

void Worksheet_Deactivate()
{
    Console.WriteLine("Worksheet.Deactivate()");
}

void Chart_Deactivate()
{
    Console.WriteLine("Chart.Deactivate()");
}

void App_WindowActivate(Excel.Workbook workbook,
    Excel.Window window)
{
    Console.WriteLine(String.Format(
        "Application.WindowActivate({0}, {1})",
        workbook.Name, window.Caption));
}

void Workbook_WindowActivate(Excel.Window window)
{
    Console.WriteLine(String.Format(
        "Workbook.WindowActivate({0})", window.Caption));
}

void App_WindowDeactivate(Excel.Workbook workbook,
    Excel.Window window)
{
    Console.WriteLine(String.Format(
```

```
        "Application.WindowDeactivate({0}, {1})",
        workbook.Name, window.Caption));
    }

    void Workbook_WindowDeactivate(Excel.Window window)
    {
      Console.WriteLine(String.Format(
        "Application.WindowActivate({1})",
        window.Caption));
    }
  }
}
```

Double-Click and Right-Click Events

Several events are raised when a worksheet or a chart sheet is double-clicked or right-clicked (clicked with the right mouse button). Double-click events occur when you double-click in the center of a cell in a worksheet or on a chart sheet. If you double-click the border of the cell, no events are raised. If you double-click column headers or row headers, no events are raised. If you double-click objects in a worksheet (Shape objects in the object model), such as an embedded chart, no events are raised. After you double-click a cell in Excel, Excel enters editing mode for that cell—a cursor displays in the cell allowing you to type into the cell. If you double-click a cell in editing mode, no events are raised.

The right-click events occur when you right-click a cell in a worksheet or on a chart sheet. A right-click event is also raised when you right-click column headers or row headers. If you right-click objects in a worksheet, such as an embedded chart, no events are raised.

The right-click and double-click events for a chart sheet do not raise events on the Application and Workbook objects. Instead, BeforeDoubleClick and BeforeRightClick events are raised directly on the Chart object.

All the right-click and double-click events have a "Before" in their names. This is because Excel is raising these events before Excel does its default behaviors for double-click and right-click—for example, displaying a context menu or going into edit mode for the cell you double-clicked. These events all have a `bool` parameter that is passed by a reference called `cancel` that allows you to cancel Excel's default behavior for the double-click or right-click that occurred by setting the `cancel` parameter to `true`.

Many of the right-click and double-click events pass a Range object as a parameter. A Range object represents a range of cells—it can represent a single cell or multiple cells. For example, if you select several cells and then right-click the selected cells, a Range object is passed to the right-click event that represents the selected cells.

Double-click and right-click events are raised in various ways, as follows:

- **Application.SheetBeforeDoubleClick** is raised whenever any cell in any worksheet within Excel is double-clicked. Excel passes as an `object` the Worksheet that was double-clicked, a Range for the range of cells that was double-clicked, and a `bool cancel` parameter passed by reference. The `cancel` parameter can be set to `true` by your event handler to prevent Excel from executing its default double-click behavior. This is a case where it really does not make sense that Worksheet is passed as `object` because a Chart is never passed. You will always have to cast the `object` to a Worksheet.

- **Workbook.SheetBeforeDoubleClick** is raised on a workbook that has a cell in a worksheet that was double-clicked. Excel passes the same parameters as the Application-level SheetBeforeDoubleClick.

- **Worksheet.BeforeDoubleClick** is raised on a worksheet that is double-clicked. Excel passes a Range for the range of cells that was double-clicked and a `bool cancel` parameter passed by reference. The `cancel` parameter can be set to `true` by your event handler to prevent Excel from executing its default double-click behavior.

- **Chart.BeforeDoubleClick** is raised on a chart sheet that is double-clicked. Excel passes as `int` an `elementID` and two parameters called `arg1` and `arg2`. The combination of these three parameters allows you to determine what element of the chart was double-clicked. Excel also passes a `bool cancel` parameter by reference. The `cancel` parameter can be set to `true` by your event handler to prevent Excel from executing its default double-click behavior.

- **Application.SheetBeforeRightClick** is raised whenever any cell in any worksheet within Excel is right-clicked. Excel passes as an `object` the Worksheet that was right-clicked, a Range for the range of cells that was right-clicked, and a `bool cancel` parameter passed by reference. The `cancel` parameter can be set to `true` by your event handler to prevent Excel from executing its default right-click behavior. This is a case where it really does not make sense that Worksheet is passed as an `object` because a Chart is never passed. You will always have to cast the `object` to a Worksheet.

- **Workbook.SheetBeforeRightClick** is raised on a workbook that has a cell in a worksheet that was right-clicked. Excel passes the same parameters as the Application-level SheetBeforeRightClick.

- **Worksheet.BeforeRightClick** is raised on a worksheet that is right-clicked. Excel passes a Range for the range of cells that was right-clicked and a `bool cancel` parameter passed by reference. The `cancel` parameter can be set to `true` by your event handler to prevent Excel from executing its default right-click behavior.

- **Chart.BeforeRightClick** is raised on a chart sheet that is right-clicked. Strangely enough, Excel does not pass any of the parameters that it passes to the Chart.BeforeDoubleClickEvent. Excel does pass a `bool cancel` parameter by reference. The `cancel` parameter can be set to `true` by your event handler to prevent Excel from executing its default right-click behavior.

Listing 4-3 shows a VSTO Workbook class that handles all of these events. This code assumes that you have added a chart sheet to the workbook and it is called Chart1. In VSTO, you do not have to keep a reference to the Workbook object or the Worksheet or Chart objects when handling events raised by these objects because they are already being kept by the project items generated in the VSTO project. You do need to keep a reference to the Application object when handling events raised by the Application object because it is not being kept anywhere in the VSTO project.

The `ThisWorkbook` class generated by VSTO derives from a class that has all the members of Excel's Workbook object, so we can add workbook event handlers by adding code that refers to `this`, as shown in Listing 4-3. We can get an Application object by using `this.Application` because Application is a property of Workbook. Because the returned application object is not being held as a reference by any other code, we must declare a class member variable to hold on to this Application object so that our events handlers will work. Chapter 1, "An Introduction to Office Programming," discusses this issue in more detail.

To get to the chart and the worksheet that are in our VSTO project, we use VSTO's Globals object, which lets us get to the classes `Chart1` and `Sheet1` that are declared in other project items. We do not have to hold these objects in a class member variable because they have lifetimes that match the lifetime of the VSTO code behind.

We also declare two helper functions in Listing 4-3. One casts the sheet that is passed as an `object` to a Worksheet and returns the name of the worksheet. The other gets the address of the Range that is passed to many of the events as the `target` parameter.

The handlers for the right-click events all set the `bool cancel` parameter that is passed by reference to `true`. This will make it so that Excel will not do its default behavior on right-click, which is typically to pop up a menu.

Listing 4-3 A VSTO Workbook Customization That Handles Double-Click and Right-Click Events

```
using System;
using System.Data;
using System.Drawing;
using System.Windows.Forms;
using Microsoft.VisualStudio.Tools.Applications.Runtime;
using Excel = Microsoft.Office.Interop.Excel;
using Office = Microsoft.Office.Core;

namespace ExcelWorkbook1
{
  public partial class ThisWorkbook
  {
    private Excel.Application app;

    private void ThisWorkbook_Startup(object sender, EventArgs e)
    {
      app = this.Application;

      app.SheetBeforeDoubleClick +=
        new Excel.AppEvents_SheetBeforeDoubleClickEventHandler(
        App_SheetBeforeDoubleClick);

      this.SheetBeforeDoubleClick +=
        new Excel.WorkbookEvents_SheetBeforeDoubleClickEventHandler(
        ThisWorkbook_SheetBeforeDoubleClick);

      Globals.Sheet1.BeforeDoubleClick +=
```

```
      new Excel.DocEvents_BeforeDoubleClickEventHandler(
      Sheet1_BeforeDoubleClick);

    Globals.Chart1.BeforeDoubleClick +=
      new Excel.ChartEvents_BeforeDoubleClickEventHandler(
      Chart1_BeforeDoubleClick);

    app.SheetBeforeRightClick +=
      new Excel.AppEvents_SheetBeforeRightClickEventHandler(
      App_SheetBeforeRightClick);

    this.SheetBeforeRightClick +=
      new Excel.WorkbookEvents_SheetBeforeRightClickEventHandler(
      ThisWorkbook_SheetBeforeRightClick);

    Globals.Sheet1.BeforeRightClick +=
      new Excel.DocEvents_BeforeRightClickEventHandler(
      Sheet1_BeforeRightClick);

    Globals.Chart1.BeforeRightClick +=
      new Excel.ChartEvents_BeforeRightClickEventHandler(
      Chart1_BeforeRightClick);
  }

private void ThisWorkbook_Shutdown(object sender, EventArgs e)
{
}

private string RangeAddress(Excel.Range target)
{
  return target.get_Address(missing, missing,
    Excel.XlReferenceStyle.xlA1, missing, missing);
}

private string SheetName(object sheet)
{
  Excel.Worksheet worksheet = sheet as Excel.Worksheet;
  if (worksheet != null)
    return worksheet.Name;
  else
    return String.Empty;
}

void App_SheetBeforeDoubleClick(object sheet,
  Excel.Range target, ref bool cancel)
{
  MessageBox.Show(String.Format(
    "Application.SheetBeforeDoubleClick({0},{1})",
```

```
      SheetName(sheet), RangeAddress(target)));
}

void ThisWorkbook_SheetBeforeDoubleClick(object sheet,
  Excel.Range target, ref bool cancel)
{
  MessageBox.Show(String.Format(
    "Workbook.SheetBeforeDoubleClick({0}, {1})",
    SheetName(sheet), RangeAddress(target)));
}

void Sheet1_BeforeDoubleClick(Excel.Range target,
  ref bool cancel)
{
  MessageBox.Show(String.Format(
    "Worksheet.SheetBeforeDoubleClick({0})",
    RangeAddress(target)));
}

void Chart1_BeforeDoubleClick(int elementID, int arg1,
  int arg2, ref bool cancel)
{
  MessageBox.Show(String.Format(
    "Chart.SheetBeforeDoubleClick({0}, {1}, {2})",
    elementID, arg1, arg2));
}

void App_SheetBeforeRightClick(object sheet,
  Excel.Range target, ref bool cancel)
{
  MessageBox.Show(String.Format(
    "Application.SheetBeforeRightClick({0},{1})",
    SheetName(sheet), RangeAddress(target)));
  cancel = true;
}

void ThisWorkbook_SheetBeforeRightClick(object sheet,
  Excel.Range target, ref bool cancel)
{
  MessageBox.Show(String.Format(
    "Workbook.SheetBeforeRightClick({0},{1})",
    SheetName(sheet), RangeAddress(target)));
  cancel = true;
}

void Sheet1_BeforeRightClick(Excel.Range target,
  ref bool cancel)
{
```

```
    MessageBox.Show(String.Format(
      "Worksheet.SheetBeforeRightClick({0})",
      RangeAddress(target)));
    cancel = true;
  }

  void Chart1_BeforeRightClick(ref bool cancel)
  {
    MessageBox.Show("Chart.SheetBeforeRightClick()");
    cancel = true;
  }

  #region VSTO Designer generated code

  /// <summary>
  /// Required method for Designer support - do not modify
  /// the contents of this method with the code editor.
  /// </summary>
  private void InternalStartup()
  {
    this.Startup += new System.EventHandler(ThisWorkbook_Startup);
    this.Shutdown += new System.EventHandler(ThisWorkbook_Shutdown);
  }

  #endregion

  }
}
```

Cancelable Events and Event Bubbling

Listing 4-3 raises an interesting question. What happens when multiple objects handle an event such as BeforeRightClick at multiple levels? Listing 4-3 handles the BeforeRightClick event at the Worksheet, Workbook, and Application level. Excel first raises the event at the Worksheet level for all code that has registered for the Worksheet-level event. Remember that other add-ins could be loaded in Excel handling Worksheet-level events as well. Your code might get the Worksheet.BeforeRightClick event first followed by some other add-in that also is handling the Worksheet.BeforeRightClick event. When multiple add-ins handle the same event on the same object, you cannot rely on any determinate order for who will get the event first. Therefore, do not write your code to rely on any particular ordering.

After events are raised at the Worksheet level, they are then raised at the Workbook level, and finally at the Application level. For a cancelable event, even if one event handler sets the `cancel` parameter to `true`, the events will continue to be raised to other event handlers. So even though the code in Listing 4-3 sets the `cancel` parameter to `true` in `Sheet1_BeforeRightClick`, Excel will continue to raise events on other handlers of the worksheet BeforeRightClick and then handlers of the Workbook.SheetBeforeRightClick followed by handlers of the Application.SheetBeforeRightClick.

Another thing you should know about cancelable events is that you can check the incoming `cancel` parameter in your event handler to see what the last event handler set it to. So in the `Sheet1_BeforeRightClick` handler, the incoming `cancel` parameter would be `false` assuming no other code is handling the event. In the `ThisWorkbook_SheetBeforeRightClick` handler, the incoming `cancel` parameter would be `true` because the last handler, `Sheet1_BeforeRightClick`, set it to `true`. This means that as an event bubbles through multiple handlers, each subsequent handler can override what the previous handlers did with respect to canceling the default right-click behavior in this example. Application-level handlers get the final say—although if multiple Application-level handlers exist for the same event, whether the event gets cancelled or not is indeterminate because no rules dictate which of multiple Application-level event handlers get an event first or last.

Calculate Events

Four events are raised when formulas in the worksheet are recalculated. The worksheet is recalculated whenever you change a cell that affects a formula referring to that cell or when you add or modify a formula:

- **Application.SheetCalculate** is raised whenever any sheet within Excel is recalculated. Excel passes the sheet as an `object` that was recalculated as a parameter to this event. The sheet object can be cast to a Worksheet or a Chart.

- **Workbook.SheetCalculate** is raised on a workbook that has a sheet that was recalculated. Excel passes the sheet as an `object` that was recalculated as a parameter to this event. The sheet object can be cast to a Worksheet or a Chart.

- **Worksheet.Calculate** is raised on a worksheet that was recalculated.

> Calculate is the name of both a method and an event on the Worksheet object. Because of this collision, you will not see the Calculate event in Visual Studio's pop-up menu of properties, events, and methods associated with the Worksheet object. Furthermore, a warning displays at compile time when you try to handle this event. To get Visual Studio's pop-up menus to work and the warning to go away, you can cast the Worksheet object to the DocEvents_Event interface, as shown in Listing 4-4.

- **Chart.Calculate** is raised on a chart sheet that was updated because data it referenced changed. This event does not occur until the chart is forced to redraw—so if the chart is not currently visible because it is not selected or displayed in its own window, the event will not be raised until the chart is visible.

Listing 4-4 shows a console application that handles all the calculation events. The console application creates a new workbook, gets the first worksheet in the workbook, and creates a chart in the workbook. The console application also handles the Close event for the created workbook to cause the console application to exit when the workbook is closed. To get Excel to raise worksheet and workbook Calculate events, add some values and formulas to the first worksheet in the workbook. To raise the Chart object's Calculate event, you can right-click the chart sheet that you are handling the event for and choose Source Data from the pop-up menu. Then, click the button to the right of the Data Range text box, switch to the first worksheet, and select a range of values for the chart sheet to display. When you change those values and switch back to the chart sheet, the Chart's Calculate event will be raised.

Listing 4-4 A Console Application That Handles Calculate Events

```csharp
using System;
using Excel = Microsoft.Office.Interop.Excel;

namespace ConsoleApplication
{
  class Program
  {
    static private Excel.Application app;
    static private Excel.Workbook workbook;
    static private Excel.Worksheet worksheet;
    static private Excel.Chart chart;
    static bool exit = false;

    static void Main(string[] args)
    {
      app = new Excel.Application();
      app.Visible = true;

      workbook = app.Workbooks.Add(Type.Missing);
      worksheet = workbook.Sheets.get_Item(1) as Excel.Worksheet;
      chart = workbook.Charts.Add(Type.Missing, Type.Missing,
        Type.Missing, Type.Missing) as Excel.Chart;

      app.SheetCalculate +=
        new Excel.AppEvents_SheetCalculateEventHandler(
        App_SheetCalculate);

      workbook.SheetCalculate +=
        new Excel.WorkbookEvents_SheetCalculateEventHandler(
        Workbook_SheetCalculate);

      ((Excel.DocEvents_Event)worksheet).Calculate +=
        new Excel.DocEvents_CalculateEventHandler(
        Worksheet_Calculate);

      chart.Calculate +=
        new Excel.ChartEvents_CalculateEventHandler(
        Chart_Calculate);

      workbook.BeforeClose +=
        new Excel.WorkbookEvents_BeforeCloseEventHandler(
        Workbook_BeforeClose);

      while (exit == false)
        System.Windows.Forms.Application.DoEvents();
```

```csharp
    app.Quit();
}

static void Workbook_BeforeClose(ref bool cancel)
{
  exit = true;
}

static string SheetName(object sheet)
{
  Excel.Worksheet worksheet = sheet as Excel.Worksheet;

  if (worksheet != null)
  {
    return worksheet.Name;
  }

  Excel.Chart chart = sheet as Excel.Chart;
  if (chart != null)
  {
    return chart.Name;
  }

  return String.Empty;
}

static void App_SheetCalculate(object sheet)
{
  Console.WriteLine(String.Format(
    "Application.SheetCalculate({0})",
    SheetName(sheet)));
}

static void Workbook_SheetCalculate(object sheet)
{
  Console.WriteLine(String.Format(
    "Workbook.SheetCalculate({0})", SheetName(sheet)));
}

static void Worksheet_Calculate()
{
  Console.WriteLine("Worksheet.Calculate()");
}

static void Chart_Calculate()
{
```

```
            Console.WriteLine("Chart.Calculate()");
        }
    }
}
```

Change Events

Excel raises several events when a cell or range of cells is changed in a worksheet. The cells must be changed by a user editing the cell for change events to be raised. Change events can also be raised when a cell is linked to external data and is changed as a result of refreshing the cell from the external data. Change events are not raised when a cell is changed because of a recalculation. They are not raised when the user changes formatting of the cell without changing the value of the cell. When a user is editing a cell and is in cell edit mode, the change events are not raised until the user exits cell edit mode by leaving that cell or pressing the Enter key:

- **Application.SheetChange** is raised when a cell or range of cells in any workbook is changed by the user or updated from external data. Excel passes the sheet as an `object` where the change occurred as a parameter to this event. You can always cast the sheet parameter to a Worksheet because the Change event is not raised for chart sheets. Excel also passes a Range as a parameter for the range of cells that was changed.

- **Workbook.SheetChange** is raised on a workbook when a cell or range of cells in that workbook is changed by the user or updated from external data. Excel passes the sheet as an `object` where the change occurred as a parameter to this event. You can always cast the sheet parameter to a Worksheet because the Change event is not raised for chart sheets. Excel also passes a Range as a parameter for the range of cells that was changed.

- **Worksheet.Change** is raised on a worksheet when a cell or range of cells in that worksheet is changed by the user or updated from external data. Excel passes a Range as a parameter for the range of cells that was changed.

Listing 4-5 shows a class that handles all the Change events. It is passed an Excel Application object to its constructor. The constructor creates a new workbook and gets the first worksheet in the workbook. It handles events raised on the Application object, the workbook, and the first worksheet in the workbook.

Listing 4-5 A Class That Handles Change Events

```
using System;
using Excel = Microsoft.Office.Interop.Excel;

namespace ChangeEvents
{
  public class ChangeEventHandler
  {
    private Excel.Application app;
    private Excel.Workbook workbook;
    private Excel.Worksheet worksheet;
    object missing = System.Type.Missing;

    public ChangeEventHandler(Excel.Application application)
    {
      this.app = application;
      workbook = app.Workbooks.Add(missing);
      worksheet = workbook.Worksheets.get_Item(1) as Excel.Worksheet;

      app.SheetChange +=
        new Excel.AppEvents_SheetChangeEventHandler(
        App_SheetChange);

      workbook.SheetChange +=
        new Excel.WorkbookEvents_SheetChangeEventHandler(
        Workbook_SheetChange);

      worksheet.Change +=
        new Excel.DocEvents_ChangeEventHandler(
        Worksheet_Change);
    }

    // Change events only pass worksheets, never charts.
    private string SheetName(object sheet)
    {
      Excel.Worksheet worksheet = sheet as Excel.Worksheet;
      return worksheet.Name;
    }

    private string RangeAddress(Excel.Range target)
    {
```

```
      return target.get_Address(missing, missing,
        Excel.XlReferenceStyle.xlA1, missing, missing);
  }

  void App_SheetChange(object sheet, Excel.Range target)
  {
    Console.WriteLine(String.Format(
      "Application.SheetChange({0},{1})",
      SheetName(sheet), RangeAddress(target)));
  }

  void Workbook_SheetChange(object sheet, Excel.Range target)
  {
    Console.WriteLine(String.Format(
      "Workbook.SheetChange({0},{1})",
      SheetName(sheet), RangeAddress(target)));
  }

  void Worksheet_Change(Excel.Range target)
  {
    Console.WriteLine(String.Format(
      "Worksheet.Change({0})",
      RangeAddress(target)));
  }
  }
}
```

Follow Hyperlink Events

Excel raises several events when a hyperlink in a cell is clicked. You might think this event is not very interesting, but you can use it as a simple way to invoke an action in your customization. The trick is to create a hyperlink that does nothing, and then handle the FollowHyperlink event and execute your action in that event handler.

To create a hyperlink that does nothing, right-click the cell where you want to put your hyperlink and choose HyperLink. For our example, we select cell C3. In the dialog that appears, click the Place in This Document button to the left of the dialog (see Figure 4-2). In the Type the cell reference text box, type **C3** or the reference of the cell to which you are adding a hyperlink. The logic behind doing this is that Excel will select the cell that C3 is linked to after the hyperlink is clicked and after your event handler runs. If you select a cell other than the cell the user clicked, the selection will move, which is confusing. So we effectively link the cell to itself, creating a do nothing link. In the Text to display text box, type the name of your command—the name you want displayed in the cell. In this example, we name the command Print.

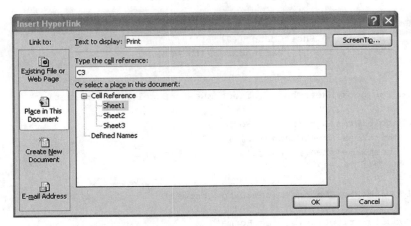

Figure 4-2 The Insert Hyperlink dialog.

The following events are raised when a hyperlink is clicked:

- **Application.SheetFollowHyperlink** is raised when a hyperlink is clicked in any workbook open in Excel. Excel passes a Hyperlink object as a parameter to this event. The Hyperlink object gives you information about the hyperlink that was clicked.

- **Workbook.SheetFollowHyperlink** is raised on a workbook when a hyperlink is clicked in that workbook. Excel passes a Hyperlink object as a parameter to this event. The Hyperlink object gives you information about the hyperlink that was clicked.

- **Worksheet.FollowHyperlink** is raised on a worksheet when a hyperlink is clicked in that worksheet. Excel passes a Hyperlink object as a parameter to this event. The Hyperlink object gives you information about the hyperlink that was clicked.

Listing 4-6 shows a VSTO customization class for the workbook project item. This class assumes a workbook that has a Print hyperlink in it, created as shown in Figure

4-2. The customization does nothing in the handlers of the Application or Workbook-level hyperlink events but log to the console window. The Worksheet-level handler detects that a hyperlink named Print was clicked and invokes the PrintOut method on the Workbook object to print the workbook.

Listing 4-6 A VSTO Workbook Customization That Handles Hyperlink Events

```
using System;
using System.Data;
using System.Drawing;
using System.Windows.Forms;
using Microsoft.VisualStudio.Tools.Applications.Runtime;
using Excel = Microsoft.Office.Interop.Excel;
using Office = Microsoft.Office.Core;

namespace ExcelWorkbook1
{
  public partial class ThisWorkbook
  {
    private Excel.Application app;

    private void ThisWorkbook_Startup(object sender, EventArgs e)
    {
      app = this.Application;

      app.SheetFollowHyperlink +=
        new Excel.AppEvents_SheetFollowHyperlinkEventHandler(
        App_SheetFollowHyperlink);

      this.SheetFollowHyperlink +=
        new Excel.WorkbookEvents_SheetFollowHyperlinkEventHandler(
        Workbook_SheetFollowHyperlink);

      Globals.Sheet1.FollowHyperlink +=
        new Excel.DocEvents_FollowHyperlinkEventHandler(
        Sheet_FollowHyperlink);
    }

    private string SheetName(object sheet)
    {
      Excel.Worksheet worksheet = sheet as Excel.Worksheet;
      if (worksheet != null)
        return worksheet.Name;
      else
        return String.Empty;
    }
```

```csharp
void App_SheetFollowHyperlink(object sheet, Excel.Hyperlink target)
{
  MessageBox.Show(String.Format(
    "Application.SheetFollowHyperlink({0},{1})",
    SheetName(sheet), target.Name));
}

void Workbook_SheetFollowHyperlink(object sheet, Excel.Hyperlink target)
{
  MessageBox.Show(String.Format(
    "Workbook.SheetFollowHyperlink({0},{1})",
    SheetName(sheet), target.Name));
}

void Sheet_FollowHyperlink(Excel.Hyperlink target)
{
  if (target.Name == "Print")
  {
    this.PrintOut(missing, missing, missing, missing,
      missing, missing, missing, missing);
  }
}

private void ThisWorkbook_Shutdown(object sender, EventArgs e)
{
}

#region VSTO Designer generated code

/// <summary>
/// Required method for Designer support - do not modify
/// the contents of this method with the code editor.
/// </summary>
private void InternalStartup()
{
  this.Startup += new System.EventHandler(ThisWorkbook_Startup);
  this.Shutdown += new System.EventHandler(ThisWorkbook_Shutdown);
}

#endregion

  }
}
```

Selection Change Events

Selection change events occur when the selected cell or cells change, or in the case of the Chart.Select event, when the selected chart element within a chart sheet changes:

- **Application.SheetSelectionChange** is raised whenever the selected cell or cells in any worksheet within Excel change. Excel passes the sheet upon which the selection changed to the event handler. However, the event handler's parameter is typed as `object`, so it must be cast to a Worksheet if you want to use the properties or methods of the Worksheet. You are guaranteed to always be able to cast the argument to Worksheet because the SheetSelectionChange event is not raised when selection changes on a Chart. Excel also passes the range of cells that is the new selection.

- **Workbook.SheetSelectionChange** is raised on a Workbook whenever the selected cell or cells in that workbook change. Excel passes as an `object` the sheet where the selection changed. You can always cast the sheet object to a Worksheet because this event is not raised for selection changes on a chart sheet. Excel also passes a Range for the range of cells that is the new selection.

- **Worksheet.SelectionChange** is raised on a Worksheet whenever the selected cell or cells in that worksheet change. Excel passes a Range for the range of cells that is the new selection.

- **Chart.Select** is raised on a Chart when the selected element within that chart sheet changes. Excel passes as `int` an `elementID` and two parameters called `arg1` and `arg2`. The combination of these three parameters allows you to determine what element of the chart was selected.

> Select is the name of both a method and an event on the Chart object. Because of this collision, you will not see the Select event in Visual Studio's pop-up menu of properties, events, and methods associated with the Chart object. Furthermore, a warning displays at compile time when you try to handle this event. To get Visual Studio's pop-up menus to work and the warning to go away, you can cast the Chart object to the ChartEvents_Events interface, as shown in Listing 4-2.

WindowResize Events

The WindowResize events are raised when a workbook window is resized. These events are only raised if the workbook window is not maximized to fill Excel's outer application window (see Figure 4-3). Events are raised if you resize a nonmaximized workbook window or minimize the workbook window. No resize events occur when you resize and minimize the outer Excel application window.

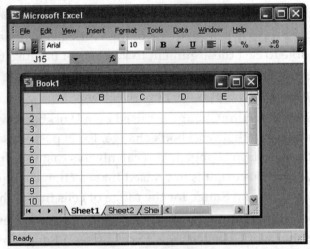

Figure 4-3 Window Resize events are only raised if the workbook window is not maximized to fill the application window.

- **Application.WindowResize** is raised when any nonmaximized workbook window is resized or minimized. Excel passes the Window object corresponding to the window that was resized or minimized as a parameter to this event. Excel also passes the Workbook object that was affected as a parameter to this event.
- **Workbook.WindowResize** is raised on a Workbook when a nonmaximized window associated with that workbook is resized or minimized. Excel passes the Window that was resized or minimized as a parameter to this event.

Add-In Install and Uninstall Events

A workbook can be saved into a special add-in format (XLA file) by selecting Save As from the File menu and then picking Microsoft Office Excel Add-in as the desired format. The workbook will then be saved to the Application Data\Microsoft\AddIns directory found under the user's document and settings directory. It will appear in the list of available add-ins that displays when you choose Add-Ins from the Tools menu. When you click the check box to enable the add-in, the workbook loads in a hidden state, and the Application.AddinInstall event is raised. When the user clicks the check box to disable the add-in, the Application.AddinUninstall event is raised.

Although you can theoretically save a workbook customized by VSTO as an XLA file, Microsoft does not support this scenario, because many VSTO features such as support for the Document Actions task pane and Smart Tags do not work when a workbook is saved as an XLA file.

XML Import and Export Events

Excel supports the import and export of custom XML data files by allowing you to take an XML schema and map it to cells in a workbook. It is then possible to export or import those cells to an XML data file that conforms to the mapped schema. Excel raises events on the Application and Workbook object before and after an XML file is imported or exported, allowing the developer to further customize and control this feature. Chapter 21, "Working with XML in Excel," discusses in detail the XML mapping features of Excel.

Before Close Events

Excel raises events before a workbook is closed. These events are to give your code a chance to prevent the closing of the workbook. Excel passes a `bool cancel` parameter to the event. If your event handler sets the `cancel` parameter to `true`, the pending close of the workbook is cancelled and the workbook remains open.

These events cannot be used to determine whether the workbook is actually going to close. Another event handler might run after your event handler—for example, an event handler in another add-in—and that event handler might set the `cancel` parameter to `true` preventing the close of the workbook. Furthermore, if the user has changed the workbook and is prompted to save changes when the workbook is closed, the user can click the Cancel button, causing the workbook to remain open.

If you need to run code only when the workbook is actually going to close, VSTO provides a Shutdown event that is not raised until all other event handlers and the user has allowed the close of the workbook.

- **Application.WorkbookBeforeClose** is raised before any workbook is closed, giving the event handler the chance to prevent the closing of the workbook. Excel passes the Workbook object that is about to be closed. Excel also passes by reference a `bool cancel` parameter. The `cancel` parameter can be set to `true` by your event handler to prevent Excel from closing the workbook.

- **Workbook.BeforeClose** is raised on a workbook that is about to be closed, giving the event handler the chance to prevent the closing of the workbook. Excel passes by reference a `bool cancel` parameter. The `cancel` parameter can be set to `true` by your event handler to prevent Excel from closing the workbook.

Before Print Events

Excel raises events before a workbook is printed. These events are raised when the user chooses Print or Print Preview from the File menu or presses the print toolbar button. Excel passes a `bool cancel` parameter to the event. If your event handler sets the `cancel` parameter to `true`, the pending print of the workbook will be cancelled and the print dialog or print preview view will not be shown. You might want to do this because you want to replace Excel's default printing behavior with some custom printing behavior of your own.

These events cannot be used to determine whether the workbook is actually going to be printed. Another event handler might run after your event handler and prevent the printing of the workbook. The user can also press the Cancel button in the Print dialog to stop the printing from occurring.

- **Application.WorkbookBeforePrint** is raised before any workbook is printed or print previewed, giving the event handler a chance to change the workbook before it is printed or change the default print behavior. Excel passes as a parameter the Workbook that is about to be printed. Excel also passes by reference a `bool cancel` parameter. The `cancel` parameter can be set to `true` by your event handler to prevent Excel from performing its default print behavior.

- **Workbook.BeforePrint** is raised on a workbook that is about to be printed or print previewed, giving the event handler a chance to change the workbook before it is printed or change the default print behavior. Excel passes by reference a `bool cancel` parameter. The `cancel` parameter can be set to `true` by your event handler to prevent performing its default print behavior.

Before Save Events

Excel raises cancelable events before a workbook is saved, allowing you to perform some custom action before the document is saved. These events are raised when the user chooses Save, Save As, or Save As Web Page commands. They are also raised when the user closes a workbook that has been modified and chooses to save when prompted. Excel passes a `bool cancel` parameter to the event. If your event handler sets the `cancel` parameter to `true`, the save will be cancelled and the save dialog will not be shown. You might want to do this because you want to replace Excel's default saving behavior with some custom saving behavior of your own.

These events cannot be used to determine whether the workbook is actually going to be saved. Another event handler might run after your event handler and prevent the save of the workbook. The user can also press Cancel in the Save dialog to stop the save of the workbook.

- **Application.WorkbookBeforeSave** is raised before any workbook is saved, giving the event handler a chance to prevent or override the saving of the workbook. Excel passes as a parameter the Workbook that is about to be saved. Excel also passes a `bool saveAsUI` parameter that tells the event handler whether Save or Save As was selected. Excel also passes by reference a `bool cancel` parameter. The `cancel` parameter can be set to `true` by your event handler to prevent Excel from performing its default save behavior.

- **Workbook.BeforeSave** is raised on a workbook that is about to be saved, giving the event handler a chance to prevent or override the saving of the workbook. Excel passes a `bool saveAsUI` parameter that tells the event handler whether Save or Save As was selected. Excel passes by reference a `bool cancel` parameter. The `cancel` parameter can be set to `true` by your event handler to prevent Excel from performing its default save behavior.

Open Events

Excel raises events when a workbook is opened or when a new workbook is created from a template or an existing document. If a new blank workbook is created, the Application.WorkbookNew event is raised.

- **Application.WorkbookOpen** is raised when any workbook is opened. Excel passes the Workbook that is opened as a parameter to this event. This event is not raised when a new blank workbook is created. The Application.WorkbookNew event is raised instead.

- **Workbook.Open** is raised on a workbook when it is opened.

Listing 4-7 shows a console application that handles the BeforeClose, BeforePrint, BeforeSave, and Open events. It sets the `cancel` parameter to `true` in the BeforeSave and BeforePrint handlers to prevent the saving and printing of the workbook.

Listing 4-7 A Console Application That Handles Close, Print, Save, and Open Events

```
using System;
using Excel = Microsoft.Office.Interop.Excel;

namespace ConsoleApplication
{
  class Program
  {
    static private Excel.Application app;
    static private Excel.Workbook workbook;
    static private bool exit = false;

    static void Main(string[] args)
    {
      app = new Excel.Application();
```

```
      app.Visible = true;

      workbook = app.Workbooks.Add(Type.Missing);

      app.WorkbookBeforeClose +=
        new Excel.AppEvents_WorkbookBeforeCloseEventHandler(
        App_WorkbookBeforeClose);

      workbook.BeforeClose +=
        new Excel.WorkbookEvents_BeforeCloseEventHandler(
        Workbook_BeforeClose);

      app.WorkbookBeforePrint +=
        new Excel.AppEvents_WorkbookBeforePrintEventHandler(
        App_WorkbookBeforePrint);

      workbook.BeforePrint +=
        new Excel.WorkbookEvents_BeforePrintEventHandler(
        Workbook_BeforePrint);

      app.WorkbookBeforeSave +=
        new Excel.AppEvents_WorkbookBeforeSaveEventHandler(
        App_WorkbookBeforeSave);

      workbook.BeforeSave +=
        new Excel.WorkbookEvents_BeforeSaveEventHandler(
        Workbook_BeforeSave);

      app.WorkbookOpen +=
        new Excel.AppEvents_WorkbookOpenEventHandler(
        App_WorkbookOpen);

      while (exit == false)
        System.Windows.Forms.Application.DoEvents();

      app.Quit();
    }

    static void App_WorkbookBeforeClose(Excel.Workbook workbook,
      ref bool cancel)
    {
      Console.WriteLine(String.Format(
        "Application.WorkbookBeforeClose({0})",
        workbook.Name));
    }

    static void Workbook_BeforeClose(ref bool cancel)
    {
```

```
      Console.WriteLine("Workbook.BeforeClose()");
      exit = true;
    }

    static void App_WorkbookBeforePrint(Excel.Workbook workbook,
      ref bool cancel)
    {
      Console.WriteLine(String.Format(
        "Application.WorkbookBeforePrint({0})",
        workbook.Name));
      cancel = true; // Don't allow printing
    }

    static void Workbook_BeforePrint(ref bool cancel)
    {
      Console.WriteLine("Workbook.BeforePrint()");
      cancel = true; // Don't allow printing
    }

    static void App_WorkbookBeforeSave(Excel.Workbook workbook,
      bool saveAsUI, ref bool cancel)
    {
      Console.WriteLine(String.Format(
        "Application.WorkbookBeforeSave({0},{1})",
        workbook.Name, saveAsUI));
      cancel = true; // Don't allow saving
    }

    static void Workbook_BeforeSave(bool saveAsUI, ref bool cancel)
    {
      Console.WriteLine(String.Format(
        "Workbook.BeforePrint({0})",
        saveAsUI));
      cancel = true; // Don't allow saving
    }

    static void App_WorkbookOpen(Excel.Workbook workbook)
    {
      Console.WriteLine(String.Format(
        "Appplication.WorkbookOpen({0})",
        workbook.Name));
    }
  }
}
```

Toolbar and Menu Events

A common way to run your code is by adding a custom toolbar button or menu item to Excel and handling the click event raised by that button or menu item. Both a toolbar and a menu bar are represented by the same object in the Office object model, an object called CommandBar. Figure 4-4 shows the hierarchy of CommandBar-related objects. The Application object has a collection of CommandBars that represent the main menu bar and all the available toolbars in Excel. You can see all the available toolbars in Excel by choosing Customize from the Tools menu.

The CommandBar objects are made available to your application by adding a reference to the Microsoft Office 11.0 Object Library PIA (office.dll). The CommandBar objects are found in the Microsoft.Office.Core namespace.

A CommandBar has a collection of CommandBarControls that contains objects of type CommandBarControl. A CommandBarControl can often be cast to a CommandBarButton, CommandBarPopup, or CommandBarComboBox. It is also possible to have a CommandBarControl that cannot be cast to one of these other types—for example, it is just a CommandBarControl and cannot be cast to a CommandBarButton, CommandBarPopup, or CommandBarComboxBox.

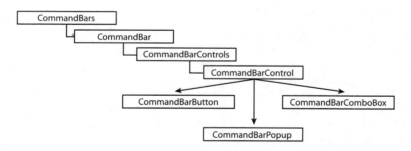

Figure 4-4 The hierarchy of CommandBar objects.

Listing 4-8 shows some code that iterates over all of the CommandBars available in Excel. The code displays the name or caption of each CommandBar and associated CommandBarControls. When Listing 4-8 gets to a CommandBarControl, it first checks whether it is a CommandBarButton, a CommandBarComboBox, or a CommandBarPopup, and then casts to the corresponding object. If it is not any of these object types, the code uses the CommandBarControl properties. Note that a

CommandBarPopup has a Controls property that returns a CommandBarControls collection. Our code uses recursion to iterate the CommandBarControls collection associated with a CommandBarPopup control.

Listing 4-8 A Console Application That Iterates Over All the CommandBars and CommandBarControls in Excel

```csharp
using System;
using Excel = Microsoft.Office.Interop.Excel;
using Office = Microsoft.Office.Core;
using System.Text;

namespace ConsoleApplication
{
  class Program
  {
    static private Excel.Application app;

    static void Main(string[] args)
    {
      app = new Excel.Application();
      Office.CommandBars bars = app.CommandBars;

      foreach (Office.CommandBar bar in bars)
      {
        Console.WriteLine(String.Format(
          "CommandBar: {0}", bar.Name));
        DisplayControls(bar.Controls, 1);
      }

      Console.ReadLine();
    }

    static void DisplayControls(Office.CommandBarControls ctls,
      int indentNumber)
    {
      System.Text.StringBuilder sb = new System.Text.StringBuilder();
      sb.Append(' ', indentNumber);

      foreach (Office.CommandBarControl ctl in ctls)
      {
        Office.CommandBarButton btn = ctl as Office.CommandBarButton;
        Office.CommandBarComboBox box = ctl as Office.CommandBarComboBox;
        Office.CommandBarPopup pop = ctl as Office.CommandBarPopup;

        if (btn != null)
        {
```

```
            sb.Append("CommandBarButton: ");
            sb.Append(btn.Caption);
            Console.WriteLine(sb.ToString());
        }
        else if (box != null)
        {
            sb.Append("CommandBarComboBox: ");
            sb.Append(box.Caption);
            Console.WriteLine(sb.ToString());
        }
        else if (pop != null)
        {
            DisplayControls(pop.Controls, indentNumber + 1);
        }
        else
        {
            sb.Append("CommandBarControl: ");
            sb.Append(ctl.Caption);
            Console.WriteLine(sb.ToString());
        }
    }
  }
 }
}
```

Excel raises several events on CommandBar, CommandBarButton, and Command-BarComboBox objects:

- **CommandBar.OnUpdate** is raised when any change occurs to a Command-Bar or associated CommandBarControls. This event is raised frequently and can even raise when selection changes in Excel. Handling this event could slow down Excel, so you should handle this event with caution.

- **CommandBarButton.Click** is raised on a CommandBarButton that is clicked. Excel passes the CommandBarButton that was clicked as a parameter to this event. It also passes by reference a `bool cancelDefault` parameter. The `cancelDefault` parameter can be set to `true` by your event handler to prevent Excel from executing the default action associated with the button. For example, you could handle this event for an existing button such as the Print button. By setting `cancelDefault` to `true`, you can prevent Excel from doing its default print behavior when the user clicks the button and instead replace that behavior with your own.

- **CommandBarComboBox.Change** is raised on a CommandBarComboBox that had its text value changed—either because the user chose an option from the drop-down or because the user typed a new value directly into the combo box. Excel passes the CommandBarComboBox that changed as a parameter to this event.

Listing 4-9 shows a console application that creates a CommandBar, a Command-BarButton, and a CommandBarComboBox. It handles the CommandBarButton.Click event to exit the application. It also displays changes made to the CommandBar-ComboBox in the console window. The CommandBar, CommandBarButton, and CommandBarComboBox are added temporarily; Excel will delete them automatically when the application exits. This is done by passing `true` to the last parameter of the CommandBarControls.Add method.

Listing 4-9 A Console Application That Adds a CommandBar and a CommandBarButton

```
using System;
using Office = Microsoft.Office.Core;
using Excel = Microsoft.Office.Interop.Excel;

namespace ConsoleApplication
{
  class Program
  {
    static private Excel.Application app;
    static bool close = false;
    static Office.CommandBarButton btn;
    static Office.CommandBarComboBox box;
    static object missing = Type.Missing;

    static void Main(string[] args)
    {
      app = new Excel.Application();
      app.Visible = true;

      Office.CommandBars bars = app.CommandBars;
      Office.CommandBar bar = bars.Add("My Custom Bar", missing,
        missing, true);
      bar.Visible = true;

      btn = bar.Controls.Add(Office.MsoControlType.msoControlButton,
        missing, missing, missing, true) as Office.CommandBarButton;
      btn.Click +=
```

```
        new Office._CommandBarButtonEvents_ClickEventHandler(
        Btn_Click);

      btn.Caption = "Stop Console Application";
      btn.Tag = "ConsoleApplication.btn";
      btn.Style = Office.MsoButtonStyle.msoButtonCaption;

      box = bar.Controls.Add(
        Office.MsoControlType.msoControlComboBox, missing,
        missing, missing, true) as Office.CommandBarComboBox;
      box.AddItem("Choice 1", 1);
      box.AddItem("Choice 2", 2);
      box.AddItem("Choice 3", 3);
      box.Tag = "ConsoleApplication.box";
      box.Change +=
        new Office._CommandBarComboBoxEvents_ChangeEventHandler(
        Box_Change);

      while (close == false)
        System.Windows.Forms.Application.DoEvents();
    }

    static void Btn_Click(Office.CommandBarButton ctrl,
      ref bool cancelDefault)
    {
      close = true;
    }

    static void Box_Change(Office.CommandBarComboBox ctrl)
    {
      Console.WriteLine("Selected " + ctrl.Text);
    }
  }
}
```

Additional Events

Several other less commonly used events in the Excel object model are listed in table 4-1. Figure 4-17 shows the envelope UI that is referred to in this table.

Table 4-1 Additional Excel Events

Events	Description
Application.SheetPivotTableUpdate Workbook.SheetPivotTableUpdate Worksheet.PivotTableUpdate	Raised when a sheet of a Pivot Table report has been updated.
Application.WorkbookPivotTable-CloseConnection Workbook.PivotTableCloseConnection	Raised when a PivotTable report connection is closed.
Application.WorkbookPivotTable-OpenConnection Workbook.PivotTableOpenConnection	Raised when a PivotTable report connection is opened.
Application.WorkbookSync Workbook.Sync	Raised when a workbook that is part of a document workspace is synchronized with the server.
Chart.DragOver	Raised when a range of cells is dragged over a chart.
Chart.DragPlot	Raised when a range of cells is dragged and dropped on a chart.
Chart.MouseDown	Raised when the user clicks the mouse button while the cursor is over a chart.
Chart.MouseMove	Raised when the user moves the mouse cursor within the bounds of a chart.
Chart.MouseUp	Raised when the user releases the mouse button while the cursor is over a chart.
Chart.Resize	Raised when the chart is resized.
Chart.SeriesChange	Raised when the user changes the data being displayed by the chart.

Events	Description
MsoEnvelop.EnvelopeShow	Raised when the envelope UI is shown inside Excel (see Figure 4-5).
MsoEnvelope.EnvelopeHide	Raised when the envelope UI is hidden (see Figure 4-5).
OLEObject.GotFocus	Raised when an OLEObject—an embedded ActiveX control or OLE object—gets the focus.
OLEObject.LostFocus	Raised when an OLEObject—an embedded ActiveX control or OLE object—loses focus.
QueryTable.AfterRefresh	Raised after a QueryTable is refreshed.
QueryTable.BeforeRefresh	Raised before a QueryTable is refreshed.

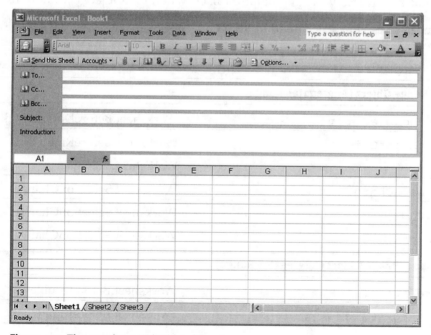

Figure 4-5 The envelope UI inside of Excel.

Events in Visual Studio 2005 Tools for Office

Several events are found in Visual Studio 2005 Tools for Office objects that are not found when using the Excel PIA alone. Table 4-2 lists these events. Almost all of these are events from the Excel PIA that are re-raised on different objects. For example, in the Excel PIA, there is no BeforeDoubleClick event on a Range object—in fact, there are no events on the Range object at all. In VSTO, the two objects that VSTO defines that represent a Range (NamedRange and XMLMappedRange) have a BeforeDoubleClick event. VSTO adds the BeforeDoubleClick event to these objects and raises the event whenever the Worksheet.BeforeDoubleClick event is raised and passed a Range object that matches the given NamedRange or XMLMappedRange object.

Another case where VSTO changes events is in the naming of the Activate event and the Select event on the Worksheet object. Both of these event names conflict with method names on Worksheet. To avoid this conflict, VSTO renames these events to ActivateEvent and SelectEvent.

There are also some new events such as the Startup and Shutdown events raised on VSTO project host items such as Workbook, Worksheet, and ChartSheet. ListObject also has several new events that are raised when ListObject is data bound.

Table 4-2 Events That Are Added in VSTO

Events	Re-Raised From
NamedRange Object (Aggregates Range)	
BeforeDoubleClick	Worksheet.BeforeDoubleClick
BeforeRightClick	Worksheet.BeforeRightClick
Change	Worksheet.Change
SelectionChange	Worksheet.SelectionChange
Selected	Worksheet.SelectionChange
Deselected	Worksheet.SelectionChange
XmlMappedRange Object (Aggregates Range)	
BeforeDoubleClick	Worksheet.BeforeDoubleClick
BeforeRightClick	Worksheet.BeforeRightClick

Events	Re-Raised From
Change	Worksheet.Change
SelectionChange	Worksheet.SelectionChange
Selected	Worksheet.SelectionChange
Deselected	Worksheet.SelectionChange
Workbook	
New	Application.NewWorkbook
Startup	New event
Shutdown	New event
ChartSheet (Aggregates Chart)	
Startup	New event
Shutdown	New event
Worksheet	
Startup	New event
Shutdown	New event
ListObject	
BeforeAddDataBoundRow	New event
BeforeDoubleClick	Worksheet.BeforeDoubleClick
BeforeRightClick	Worksheet.BeforeRightClick
Change	Worksheet.Change
DataBindingFailure	New event
DataMemberChanged	New event
DataSourceChanged	New event
Deselected	Worksheet.SelectionChange
ErrorAddDataBoundRow	New event
OriginalDataRestored	New event

continues

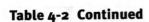

Table 4-2 Continued

Events	Re-Raised From
Selected	Worksheet.SelectionChange
SelectedIndexChanged	New event
SelectionChange	Worksheet.SelectionChange

Conclusion

This chapter has examined the various events raised by objects in the Excel object model. The chapter also introduced some of the major objects in the Excel object model such as Application, Workbook, and Document. You have also learned the additional events that are raised by VSTO objects in Excel.

Chapter 5, "Working with Excel Objects," discusses in more detail how to use the major objects in the Excel object model.

▪5▪
Working with Excel Objects

Working with the Application Object

THIS CHAPTER COVERS SOME OF THE MAJOR objects in the Excel object model starting with the Application object. The major objects in the Excel object model have many methods and properties, and it is beyond the scope of this book to completely describe these objects. Instead, this chapter focuses on the most commonly used methods and properties.

The Application object has the largest number of methods, properties, and events of any object in the Excel object model. The Application object is also the root object in the Excel object model hierarchy. You can access all the other objects in the object model by starting at the Application object and accessing its properties and the properties of objects it returns. The Application object also has a number of useful application-level settings.

Controlling Excel's Screen Updating Behavior

When your code is performing a set of changes to a workbook, you may want to set the ScreenUpdating property to `false` to prevent Excel from updating the screen while your code runs. Setting it back to `true` will refresh the screen and allow Excel to continue updating the screen.

Beyond the cosmetic benefit of not forcing the user to watch Excel change cells while your code runs, the ScreenUpdating property proves very useful for speeding up your code. Repainting the screen after each operation can be quite costly. Be sure to set this property back to `true` when your code is finished—otherwise, the user will be left with an Excel that does not paint. As you will see below, a `try-finally` block is a handy way to ensure that the property is reset even if an exception is thrown.

An even better convention to follow than just setting the ScreenUpdating property back to `true` is to save the value of the ScreenUpdating property before you change it and set it back to that value when you are done. An important thing to remember when doing Office development is that your code is not going to be the only code running inside of a particular Office application. Add-ins might be running, as well as other code behind other documents, and so on. You need to think about how your code might affect other code also running inside of Excel.

As an example, another add-in might be running a long operation of its own, and that add-in might have set the ScreenUpdating property to `false` to accelerate that operation. That add-in does an operation that triggers an event that is handled by your code. If your code sets the ScreenUpdating property to `false`, does something, and then sets it to `true` when it is done, you have now defeated the add-in's attempt to accelerate its own long operation because you have now turned screen updating back on. If instead you store the value of ScreenUpdating before you set it to `false` and later set ScreenUpdating back to its original value, you coexist better with the other code running inside of Excel.

Listing 5-1 shows an example of using the ScreenUpdating property with VSTO.

Because it is important that you set ScreenUpdating back to its original value after your code runs, you should use C#'s support for exception handling to ensure that even if an exception occurs in your code, ScreenUpdating will be set back to its original value.

C# supports `try`, `catch`, and `finally` blocks to deal with exceptions. You should put the code to set ScreenUpdating back to its original value in your `finally` block because this code will run both when an exception occurs or when no exception occurs.

Listing 5-1 A VSTO Customization That Sets the ScreenUpdating Property

```
private void Sheet1_Startup(object sender, System.EventArgs e)
{
  bool oldScreenUpdatingSetting = this.Application.ScreenUpdating;

  try
  {
    this.Application.ScreenUpdating = false;
    Random r = new Random();

    for (int i = 1; i < 1000; i++)
    {
      string address = String.Format("A{0}", i);
      Excel.Range range = Range[address, missing];
      range.Value2 = r.Next();
    }
  }
  finally
  {
    this.Application.ScreenUpdating = oldScreenUpdatingSetting;
  }
}
```

Controlling the Dialogs and Alerts that Excel Displays

Occasionally the code you write will cause Excel to display dialogs prompting the user to make a decision or alerting the user that something is about to occur. If you find this happening while a section of your code runs, you might want to prevent these dialog boxes from being displayed.

You can set the DisplayAlerts property to `false` to prevent Excel from displaying dialog boxes and messages when your code is running. Setting this property to `false` causes Excel to choose the default response to any dialog boxes or messages that might be shown. Be sure to get the original value of this property and set the property back to its original value after your code runs. Use `try`, `catch`, and `finally` blocks to ensure that you always set the property back to its original value, as shown in Listing 5-1.

Changing the Mouse Pointer

During a large operation, you might want to change the appearance of Excel's mouse pointer to an hourglass to let users know that they are waiting for something to complete. The Cursor property is a property of type `XlMousePointer` that allows you to change the appearance of Excel's mouse pointer. It can be set to the following values: `xlDefault`, `xlIBeam`, `xlNorthwestArrow`, and `xlWait`.

Be sure to get the original value of Cursor before changing it and set it back to its original value using `try`, `catch`, and `finally` blocks. Listing 5-2 shows use of the Cursor property.

Listing 5-2 A VSTO Customization That Sets the Cursor Property

```
private void Sheet1_Startup(object sender, System.EventArgs e)
{
  XlMousePointer originalCursor = this.Application.Cursor;

  try
  {
    this.Application.Cursor = XlMousePointer.xlWait;
    Random r = new Random();

    for (int i = 1; i < 2000; i++)
    {
      string address = String.Format("A{0}", i);
      Excel.Range range = this.Range[address, missing];
      range.Value2 = r.Next();
    }
  }
  finally
  {
    this.Application.Cursor = originalCursor;
  }
}
```

Displaying a Message in Excel's Status Bar

StatusBar is a property that allows you to set the message displayed in Excel's status bar, found at the lower-left corner of the Excel window. You can set the Status-Bar property to a `string` representing the message you want to display in the status bar. You can also set StatusBar to `false` to display Excel's default status bar message. If Excel is displaying the default status bar message, the StatusBar property returns a `false` value.

As with the other application properties in this section, you want to save the original value of the StatusBar property before changing it and be sure to set it back to its original value using `try`, `catch`, and `finally` blocks. Remember to save the value of the StatusBar property to an `object` variable because it can return a `string` or a `bool` value. Listing 5-3 shows an example.

Listing 5-3 A VSTO Customization That Uses the StatusBar Property to Show Progress

```
private void Sheet1_Startup(object sender, System.EventArgs e)
{
  object oldValue = this.Application.StatusBar;

  try
  {
    Random r = new Random();

    for (int i = 1; i < 2000; i++)
    {
      string address = String.Format("A{0}", i);
      Excel.Range range = this.Range[address, missing];
      range.Value2 = r.Next();

      string status = String.Format("Updating {0} of 2000...", i);
      this.Application.StatusBar = status;
    }
  }
  finally
  {
    this.Application.StatusBar = oldValue;
  }
}
```

A Property You Should Never Use

Excel provides a property called EnableEvents that can be set to `false` to prevent Excel from raising any of its events. Although you might be tempted to use this property, *don't* do it. Think again about the fact that your code is almost never going to be running by itself in Excel. Other developers will be creating add-ins and code behind documents that will also be running inside Excel. By setting this property to `false`, you effectively break all the other code that is loaded inside of Excel until you set it back to `true`.

The problem that this property is trying to fix is the problem of your code calling a method that in turn raises an event on your code. You might not want that event to be raised because you called the method and you therefore do not want your code to be notified of something it already knows.

For example, your code might call a method such as Close on Workbook that will cause Excel to raise the BeforeClose event. If you want to prevent your BeforeClose event handler from running in this case, you have several options that are better than using EnableEvents. The first option is to stop listening to the BeforeClose event before you call the Close method. A second option is to create a guard variable that you can set before you call Close. Your event handler for BeforeClose can check that guard variable and return immediately if the guard variable is set.

Controlling the Editing Experience in Excel

Excel provides a number of properties that you can use to control the editing experience in Excel. To understand the part of the Excel editing experience that these properties control, launch an instance of Excel and create a blank worksheet. Click a cell in that worksheet and type in a number. Notice that Excel lets you type in the cell or it lets you type in the formula bar, which is shown at the top of the window. You can move the insertion point inside of the cell to further edit the contents of the cell. When you press the Enter key after editing the cell, Excel moves to the next cell down. (Your editing settings might differ, but this explanation represents the default behavior of Excel 2003.)

Excel enables you to control whether the contents of the cell can be edited directly inside the cell through the Edit Directly in Cell option in the Edit tab in the Options dialog. The EditDirectlyInCell property lets you change this setting in your code.

Setting this property to `false` makes it so the user can only edit the contents of a cell using the formula bar.

When you press Enter after editing a cell, Excel typically moves to the cell below the cell you were editing. You can control this behavior in the Edit tab of the Options dialog. The MoveAfterReturn property and MoveAfterReturnDirection property enable you to control this behavior in your code. By setting MoveAfterReturn to `true`, you tell Excel to change the selected cell after the user presses Enter. MoveAfterReturnDirection controls the cell Excel moves to after the user presses Enter if MoveAfterReturn is set to `true`. MoveAfterReturnDirection can be set to a member of the `XlDirection` enumeration: `xlDown`, `xlToLeft`, `xlToRight`, or `xlUp`.

Controlling the Look of Excel

You can control the look of Excel through the properties listed in Table 5-1.

Table 5-1 Properties That Control Elements of the Excel User Interface

Property Name	Type	What It Does
DisplayFormulaBar	`bool`	Controls whether Excel displays the formula bar.
DisplayFullScreen	`bool`	Shows Excel in full-screen mode.
DisplayScrollBars	`bool`	Controls whether Excel displays the horizontal and vertical scroll bars for workbooks.
DisplayStatusBar	`bool`	Controls whether Excel displays the status bar at the lower-left corner of the Excel window.
Height	`double`	Sets the height in pixels of the main Excel window when WindowState is set to `XlWindowState.xlNormal`.
Left	`double`	Sets the left position in pixels of the main Excel window when WindowState is set to `XlWindowState.xlNormal`.
ShowToolTips	`bool`	Controls whether Excel shows tooltips for toolbar buttons.
ShowWindows InTaskbar	`bool`	Controls whether Excel shows open Excel windows with one taskbar button in the Windows taskbar for each open window.

continues

Table 5-1 Continued

Property Name	Type	What It Does
Top	double	Sets the top position in pixels of the main Excel window when WindowState is set to XlWindowState.xlNormal.
Visible	bool	Sets whether the Excel application window is visible.
Width	double	Sets the width in pixels of the main Excel window when WindowState is set to XlWindowState.xlNormal.
WindowState	XlWindowState	Sets whether the main Excel window is minimized (xlMinimized), maximized (xlMaximized), or normal (xlNormal). The Width, Height, Top, and Left settings only work when WindowState is set to XlWindowState.xlNormal.

Controlling File and Printer Settings

You can configure the behavior when a new blank workbook is created through the SheetsInNewWorkbook property. This property takes an int value for the number of blank worksheets that should be created in a new workbook. The default is three blank worksheets. As with most of these settings, you can also set this in the General page of Excel's Options dialog.

The DefaultFilePath property corresponds to the default file location setting in the General page of Excel's Options dialog. You can set this to a string representing the file path that you want Excel to use by default when opening and saving files.

You can set the default file format you want Excel to use when saving files by using the DefaultSaveFormat property. This property is of type XlFileFormat—an enumeration that has values for the various file formats Excel supports. For example, to save Excel files by default in Excel 5 format, you set this property to xlExcel5.

Another useful property when dealing with files is the RecentFiles property, which returns a collection of strings containing the names of all the recently opened files.

Properties That Return Active or Selected Objects

The Application object has a number of properties that return active objects—objects representing things that are active or selected within Excel. Table 5-2 shows some of these properties.

Table 5-2 Application Properties That Return Active Objects

Property Name	Type	What It Does
ActiveCell	Range	Returns the top-left cell of the active selection in the active window. If there isn't a worksheet with an active cell or if no workbooks are open, this property throws an exception.
ActiveChart	Chart	Returns the active chart sheet. If no chart sheet is active, this property returns `null`.
ActiveSheet	object	Returns the active worksheet or a chart sheet. The `object` returned can be cast to either a Worksheet or a Chart.
ActiveWindow	Window	Returns the active Window. If no windows are open, this property returns `null`.
ActiveWorkbook	Workbook	Returns the workbook that is associated with the active window. If no workbooks are open, this property returns `null`.
Charts	Sheets	Returns all the chart sheets in the active workbook. If no workbooks are open, this property returns `null`.
Names	Names	Returns all the names associated with the active workbook.
Selection	object	Returns the current selection in the active window. This can return a Range when cells are selected. If other elements are selected (such as a chart or an autoshape), it can return other types. You can use the `is` and `as` operators in C# to determine the returned type.
Sheets	Sheets	Returns all the sheets in the active workbook. This collection can contain both worksheets and chart sheets. Objects returned from this collection can be cast to either a Worksheet or a Chart.

Properties That Return Important Collections

The Application object is the root object of the object model and has properties that return several important collections. The Workbooks property returns the collection of open workbooks in Excel. The Windows property returns a collection representing the open windows in Excel. Both the Workbooks and Windows collections are discussed in more detail later in this chapter.

Controlling the Calculation of Workbooks

Excel provides a number of settings and methods that correspond to some of the options in the Calculation page of the Options dialog. The Application object provides a Calculation property of type `XlCalculation` that you can use to set Excel's calculation behavior. By default, Calculation is set to automatic calculation or `xlCalculationAutomatic`. You can also set Calculation to `xlCalculationSemiautomatic`, which means to calculate all dependent formulas except data tables. Finally, Calculation can be set to `xlCalculationManual`, which means Excel only recalculates the workbook when the user or your code forces a calculation.

If you have set Calculation to `xlCalculationManual` or `xlCalculationSemiautomatic`, you can force a complete recalculation of all open workbooks with the Calculate method. Using manual calculation may be another way to speed up your code if you are updating a large number of cells that are referred to by formulas. As with other application-level properties, you should restore the original value of the property in a `finally` block, as shown earlier in this chapter.

Using Built-In Excel Functions in Your Code

The WorksheetFunction property returns a WorksheetFunction object that enables you to call the built-in Excel formulas from your code. It provides access to more than 180 formulas. Listing 5-4 illustrates three of them.

Listing 5-4 A VSTO Customization That Uses the WorksheetFunction Object

```
private void Sheet1_Startup(object sender, System.EventArgs e)
{
  Excel.WorksheetFunction func = this.Application.WorksheetFunction;
  double result = func.Acos(.1);
  double result2 = func.Atan2(.1, .2);
  double result3 = func.Atanh(.1);
}
```

Selecting and Activating a Range of Cells

Goto is a method that causes Excel to select a range of cells and activate the workbook associated with that range of cells. It takes an optional object parameter that can be either a string containing cell reference (in "Sheet1!R1C1" format) or a Range object. We talk more about cell reference formats such as "Sheet1!R1C1" in the section "Working with the Range Object" later in this chapter. It also takes an optional object parameter that can be set to true to tell Excel to scroll the window so that the selection is at the upper-left corner of the window. Listing 5-5 shows some examples of calling the Goto method.

Listing 5-5 A VSTO Customization That Uses the Goto Method

```
private void Sheet1_Startup(object sender, System.EventArgs e)
{
  Excel.Application app = this.Application;

  app.Goto("R3C3", missing);
  app.Goto("Sheet2!R10C5", true);
  app.Goto("[BOOK1.XLS]Sheet1!R4C4", true);
  app.Goto(this.get_Range("R8C2", missing), true);
  app.Goto(this.get_Range("R1C1", "R20C3"), true);
}
```

Spell Checking

Excel provides a method called CheckSpelling that you can use to check the spelling of a single word. It takes a required string parameter containing the word to check. It also takes an optional object parameter that can be set to a string for the filename of the custom dictionary to use. Finally, it takes an optional object parameter that can be set to `true` to ignore uppercase words when spell checking. CheckSpelling returns `false` if the word passed to it is misspelled. Listing 5-6 shows an example of calling the CheckSpelling method.

Listing 5-6 A VSTO Customization That Uses the CheckSpelling Method

```
private void Sheet1_Startup(object sender, System.EventArgs e)
{
  Excel.Application app = this.Application;

  if (!app.CheckSpelling("funtastic", missing, missing))
  {
    MessageBox.Show("Funtastic was not spelled correctly".);
  }

  if (!app.CheckSpelling("fantastic", missing, missing))
  {
    MessageBox.Show("Fantastic was not spelled correctly.");
  }

  if (!app.CheckSpelling("FUNTASTIC", missing, true))
  {
    MessageBox.Show("FUNTASTIC was not spelled correctly.");
  }
}
```

Sending a Workbook in E-mail

Excel provides a simple way to send a workbook as an e-mail message using three methods called MailLogon, Workbook.SendMail, and MailLogoff. MailLogon logs on to the mail system and takes the username as a `string`, the user's password as a `string`, and whether to download new mail immediately as a `bool`. It is also important to check the MailSession property to make sure that a mail session is not already established. If MailSession is not `null`, you do not need to call the MailLogon method. Workbook's SendMail method takes the recipients as a required `string` if there is only one recipient or as an array of strings if there are multiple recipients. It also takes a subject for the message as a `string` and whether to request a read receipt as a `bool`. Listing 5-7 shows a simple example that mails a workbook.

Listing 5-7 A VSTO Customization That Mails a Workbook

```
private void ThisWorkbook_Startup(object sender, EventArgs e)
{
  Excel.Application app = this.Application;

  if (app.MailSession == null)
  {
    app.MailLogon(@"DOMAIN\JOHN", @"JOHN", missing);
  }

  this.SendMail(@"bar@domain.com", "Test message", missing);
  app.MailLogoff();
}
```

Quitting Excel

You can use the Quit method to exit Excel. If any unsaved workbooks are open, Excel prompts the user to save each unsaved workbook. You can suppress the prompts by setting the DisplayAlerts property to `false`, which causes Excel to quit without saving workbooks. You can also check the Workbook.Saved property on each workbook and call Workbook.Save to save each unsaved workbook. Remember that when users are prompted to save, they get a dialog box that looks like the one shown in Figure 5-1. If the user clicks the Cancel button or if any code is running that handles the BeforeClose event and sets the `cancel` parameter to `true`, Excel will not quit.

Figure 5-1 Excel prompts when you call Quit and a
workbook needs to be saved.

Undo in Excel

Excel has an Undo method that can be used to undo the last few actions taken by the user. However, Excel does not support undoing actions taken by your code. As soon as your code touches the object model, Excel clears the undo history and it does not add any of the actions your code performs to the undo history.

Sending Keyboard Commands to Excel

Excel provides a method called SendKeys that you can use as a last resort when you cannot find a way to accomplish a command through the object model but you know how to accomplish it through a keyboard command. It takes the keys you want to send to the application as a string and a `Wait` parameter that if set to `true` causes Excel to wait for the keystrokes to be processed by Excel before returning control to your code. You can specify modifier keys like Alt, Ctrl, and Shift by prefacing the keystroke you want to send by another character. For example, to send an Alt+T key command, you call `SendKeys("%t", Type.Missing)`, because % is the symbol SendKeys recognizes as Alt. The symbol SendKeys recognizes as Ctrl is ^ and Shift is +. In addition, special strings correspond to keys such as the down arrow. To send a down-arrow keystroke to Excel, you call `SendKeys("{DOWN}", Type.Missing)`. Table 5-3 lists the other special strings that correspond to common keys.

Table 5-3 Codes Used by SendKeys

Key	Key Code	Key	Key Code
Backspace	{BACKSPACE} or {BS}	Home	{HOME}
Break	{BREAK}	Ins	{INSERT}
Caps Lock	{CAPSLOCK}	Left arrow	{LEFT}
Clear	{CLEAR}	Num Lock	{NUMLOCK}
Delete or Del	{DELETE} or {DEL}	Page down	{PGDN}
Down arrow	{DOWN}	Page up	{PGUP}
End	{END}	Return	{RETURN}
Enter	~ (tilde)	Right arrow	{RIGHT}
Enter (numeric keypad)	{ENTER}	Scroll Lock	{SCROLLLOCK}
Esc	{ESCAPE} or {ESC}	Tab	{TAB}
F1 through F15	{F1} through {F15}	Up arrow	{UP}
Help	{HELP}		

Working with the Workbooks Collection

The Workbooks collection, available from the Application object's Workbooks property, contains a collection of the Workbook objects currently open in the application. It also has methods used to manage open workbooks, create new workbooks, and open existing workbook files.

Iterating over the Open Workbooks

Collections implement a special method called GetEnumerator that allows them to be iterated over. You do not ever have to call the GetEnumerator method directly because the `foreach` keyword in C# uses this method to iterate over a collection of Workbooks. See Listing 5-8 for an example of using `foreach`.

Listing 5-8 A VSTO Customization That Iterates over the Workbooks Collection Using foreach

```
private void Sheet1_Startup(object sender, System.EventArgs e)
{
  Excel.Workbooks workbooks = this.Application.Workbooks;

  foreach (Excel.Workbook workbook in workbooks)
  {
    MessageBox.Show(workbook.Name);
  }
}
```

Accessing a Workbook in the Workbooks Collection

To access a Workbook in the Workbooks collection, you use the get_Item method, which returns a Workbook object. The get_Item method has an Index parameter that is of type `object`. You can pass an `int` representing the one-based index of the Workbook in the collection you want to access. (Almost all collections in the Office object models are one-based.)

Alternatively, you can pass a `string` representing the name of the Workbook you want to access. The name for a workbook is the name of the file if it has been saved (for example, `"Book1.xls"`). If the workbook has not yet been saved, it will be the temporary name that Excel creates for a new workbook, typically Book1 with no file extension. Listing 5-9 shows an example of calling get_Item with both kinds of indexing.

Listing 5-9 A VSTO Customization That Gets a Workbook Using get_Item with an int and string Index

```
private void Sheet1_Startup(object sender, System.EventArgs e)
{
  Excel.Workbooks workbooks = this.Application.Workbooks;

  if (workbooks.Count > 0)
  {
    // Get the first workbook in the collection (1-based)
    Excel.Workbook wb = workbooks.get_Item(1);
    MessageBox.Show(wb.Name);

    // Get the same workbook by passing the name of the workbook.
    Excel.Workbook wb2 = workbooks.get_Item(wb.Name);
    MessageBox.Show(wb2.Name);
  }
}
```

You can also use the Workbooks collection's Count property to determine the number of open workbooks. You should check the Count property before accessing a workbook by index to make sure your index is within the bounds of the collection.

Creating a New Workbook

To create a new workbook, you can use the Workbooks collection's Add method. The Add method returns the newly created Workbook object. It takes as an optional parameter an `object` that can be set to a `string` specifying the filename of an existing workbook to use as a template. Alternatively, you can pass a member of the XlWBATemplate enumeration (`xlWBATChart` or `xlWBATWorksheet`) to specify that Excel should create a workbook with a single chart sheet or a single worksheet. If you omit the parameter by passing `Type.Missing`, Excel will create a new blank workbook with the number of worksheets specified by Application.SheetsInNew-Workbook property. Listing 5-10 shows several ways to create a new workbook.

Listing 5-10 A VSTO Customization That Creates New Workbooks Using Workbooks.Add

```
private void Sheet1_Startup(object sender, System.EventArgs e)
{
  Excel.Workbooks workbooks = this.Application.Workbooks;

  // Create a new workbook using mytemplate.xls as a template
  Excel.Workbook workbook1 = workbooks.Add(
    @"c:\mytemplate.xls");

  // Create a new workbook with one chart sheet
  Excel.Workbook workbook2 = workbooks.Add(
    Excel.XlWBATemplate.xlWBATChart);

  // Set default number of new sheets to create in a
  // new blank workbook to 10
  this.Application.SheetsInNewWorkbook = 10;

  // Create a blank workbook with 10 worksheets
  Excel.Workbook workbook3 = workbooks.Add(missing);
}
```

Opening an Existing Workbook

To open an existing workbook, you can use the Workbooks collection's Open method, which returns the opened Workbook object. Open has one required parameter—a `string` representing the filename of the workbook to open. It also has 14 optional parameters for which you can pass `Type.Missing` if you do not want to use any of these parameters. Listing 5-11 shows the simplest possible way of calling the Open method.

Listing 5-11 A VSTO Customization That Opens a Workbook Using the Workbooks.Open Method

```
private void ThisWorkbook_Startup(object sender, EventArgs e)
{
  Excel.Workbook workbook = this.Application.Workbooks.Open(
    @"c:\myworkbook.xls", missing, missing, missing,
    missing, missing, missing, missing, missing,
    missing, missing, missing, missing, missing, missing);

  MessageBox.Show(workbook.Name);
}
```

Closing All the Open Workbooks

Excel provides a Close method on the Workbooks collection to close all the open workbooks. The user is prompted to save any unsaved workbooks unless Application.DisplayAlerts is set to `false`. As with Application.Quit, you cannot be guaranteed that all the workbooks will actually be closed because the user can press the Cancel button when prompted to save a workbook and other event handlers that are loaded in Excel from other add-ins can handle the BeforeClose event and set the cancel parameter to `true`.

Working with the Workbook Object

The Workbook object represents an open workbook in Excel. The workbook has a Name property that returns the name of the workbook as a `string` (for example `"book1.xls"`). If the workbook has not yet been saved, this property returns the temporary name of the document, typically Book1. This name can be passed to get_Item on the Workbooks collection to access the workbook by name from that collection. Workbook also has a FullName property that returns the full filename of the workbook if the workbook has been saved (for example, `"c:\my documents \book1.xls"`). For a new unsaved workbook, it returns the default name Excel gave to the workbook, such as Book1.

Properties That Return Active or Selected Objects

The Workbook object has a number of properties that return active objects—objects representing things that are selected within the Excel workbook. Table 5-4 shows two of these properties.

Table 5-4 Workbook Properties That Return Active Objects

Property Name	Type	What It Does
ActiveChart	Chart	Returns the currently selected chart sheet in the workbook. If the currently selected sheet is not a chart sheet, this property returns `null`.
ActiveSheet	object	Returns the currently selected sheet in the workbook, which can be either a worksheet or a chart sheet. You can cast this to either a Worksheet or a Chart.

Properties That Return Important Collections

The Workbook object has a number of properties that return collections that you will frequently use. Table 5-5 shows some of these properties

Table 5-5 Workbook Properties That Return Important Collections

Property Name	Type	What It Does
Charts	Charts	Returns the Charts collection, which contains all the chart sheets in the workbook. The Charts collection has methods and properties to access a particular chart or to add a new chart sheet.
Sheets	Sheets	Returns the Sheets collection, which contains all the sheets in the workbook (both worksheets and chart sheets). The Sheets collection has methods and properties to access a particular sheet or to add a new sheet.
Windows	Windows	Returns the Windows collection, which contains all the open windows that are showing the workbook. The Windows collection has methods and properties to arrange and access windows.
Worksheets	Sheets	Returns the Worksheets collection, which contains all the worksheets in the workbook in a Sheets collection. The Worksheets collection has methods and properties to access a particular worksheet or to add a new worksheet.

Accessing Document Properties

Workbook has a BuiltinDocumentProperties property that returns an `object` that can be cast to a Microsoft.Office.Core.DocumentProperties collection representing the built-in document properties associated with the workbook. These are the properties that you see when you choose Properties from the File menu and click the Summary tab, including properties such as Title, Subject, Author, and Company. Table 5-6 shows the names of the built-in document properties associated with a workbook.

Workbook also has a CustomDocumentProperties that returns an `object` that can be cast to a Microsoft.Office.Core.DocumentProperties collection representing any custom document properties associated with the workbook. These are the custom properties that you see when you choose Properties from the File menu and click the Custom tab. Custom properties can be created by your code and used to store name and value pairs in the workbook. The DocumentProperties collection is discussed in more detail in the section "Working with Document Properties" later in this chapter.

Table 5-6 The Names of the Built-In Document Properties in Excel

Application name	Author	Category
Comments	Company	Creation date
Format	Hyperlink base	Keywords
Last author	Last print date	Last save time
Manager	Number of bytes	Number of characters
Number of characters (with spaces)	Number of hidden slides	Number of lines
Number of multimedia clips	Number of notes	Number of pages
Number of paragraphs	Number of slides	Number of words
Revision number	Security	Subject
Template	Title	Total editing time

Saving an Excel Workbook

The Workbook object has a number of properties and methods that are used to save a workbook, detect whether a workbook has been saved, and get the path and filename of a workbook.

The Saved property returns a `bool` value that tells you whether the latest changes to the workbook have been saved. If closing the document will cause Excel to prompt the user to save, the Saved property will return `false`. If the user creates a blank new workbook and does not modify it, the Saved property will return `true` until the user or your code makes a change to the document. You can set the Saved property to `true` to prevent a workbook from being saved, but be careful: any changes made in that document may be lost because the user will not be prompted to save when the document is closed.

A more common use of the Saved property is to try to keep the state of the Saved property the same as before your code ran. For example, your code might set or create some custom document properties, but if the user does not make any changes to the document while it is open, you might not want the user to be prompted to save. Your code can get the value of the Saved property, make the changes to the document properties, and then set the value of Saved back to the value before your code changed the workbook. This way the changes your code made will only be saved if the user makes an additional change to the document that requires a save. Listing 5-12 shows this approach.

Listing 5-12 A VSTO Customization That Manipulates Document Properties Without Affecting the Saved Property

```
private void ThisWorkbook_Startup(object sender, EventArgs e)
{
  bool oldSaved = this.Saved;

  try
  {
    Office.DocumentProperties props = this.
      BuiltinDocumentProperties as Office.DocumentProperties;

    props["Author"].Value = "Mark Twain";
  }
  finally
  {
    this.Saved = oldSaved;
  }
}
```

To save a workbook, you can use the Save method. If the workbook has already been saved, Excel just overwrites the file from the previous save. If the workbook is newly created and has not been saved yet, Excel tries to create a filename (such as Book2.xls if the new workbook was called Book2) and save it to the default file path set by Application.DefaultFilePath.

If you want to specify a filename to save the workbook to, you must use the SaveAs method. SaveAs takes the filename as a `string` parameter. It also takes a number of optional parameters that you can omit by passing `Type.Missing`.

If you want to save a copy of the workbook, use the SaveCopyAs method and pass it the copy's filename as a `string` parameter. SaveCopyAs creates a backup copy of the workbook. It does not affect the filename or save location of the Workbook it is called on.

You can also save the workbook while closing it using the Close method. If you omit all the optional parameters, the user will be prompted to save the workbook if it has been changed since it was created or opened. If you pass `false` to the SaveChanges parameter, it will close the workbook without saving changes. If you set the SaveChanges parameter to `true` and pass a file name as a `string` for the `Filename` parameter, it will save the workbook to the filename you specified.

Several additional properties are used to access the filename and location of the Workbook, as shown in Table 5-7.

Table 5-7 Workbook Properties That Return Filename and Path Information

Property Name	Type	What It Does
FullName	string	Returns the full name of the workbook, including the path. For a saved workbook, it returns the full filename of the workbook. For a new unsaved workbook, it returns the default name Excel gave to the workbook, such as Book1.
FullName-URLEncoded	string	Returns as a URL-encoded string the full name of the workbook, including the path.
Path	string	Returns the full path to the workbook (for example, `"C:\Documents and Settings\Eric Carter\My Documents"`). If the workbook has not yet been saved, this property returns an empty string.
Name	string	Returns the name of the workbook (for example, `"book1.xls"`). If the workbook has not yet been saved, this property returns the temporary name of the document, typically Book1. This can be passed to get_Item on the Workbooks collection to access this workbook.

Table 5-8 shows a number of other properties related to saving.

Table 5-8 Workbook Properties Related to Saving an Excel Workbook

Property Name	Type	What It Does
CreateBackup	`bool`	Sets whether a backup is created when the workbook is saved.
EnableAuto Recover	`bool`	Sets whether the auto-save feature of Excel is enabled. If enabled, Excel saves the workbook on a timed interval so if Excel should crash or the system should fail, a backed-up file is available.
FileFormat	`XlFile Format`	Returns the file format this workbook is saved as.
ReadOnly	`bool`	Returns `true` if the file was opened as read-only.

Naming Ranges of Cells

Excel enables you to associate a name (a `string` identifier) with any range of cells. You can define a name for a range of cells by writing code or by using the Define Name dialog box that is shown when you choose Insert > Name > Define from the Excel menu bar. You can also select a cell or range of cells you want to associate a name with and then type the name into the Name Box to the left of the formula bar, as shown in Figure 5-2. When you type the name into the Name Box, you need to press the Enter key after typing the name to set the name.

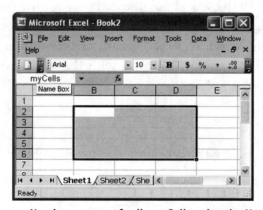

Figure 5-2 Naming a range of cells myCells using the Name Box.

The Names property returns the Names collection that can be used to access any ranges you have named within the workbook. The Names collection also enables you to create new named ranges. The Names collection is discussed in more detail in the section "Working with the Names Collection and the Name Object" later in this chapter.

When Excel Is Embedded in Another Application

CommandBars, Container, and IsInPlace are properties used when the workbook is opened inside another application such as Internet Explorer or Word. IsInPlace is a property that returns a `bool` value that tells you whether the workbook has been opened inside another application. The CommandBars property returns the Microsoft.Office.Core.CommandBars collection that is used when a document is in-place. The Container property returns an `object` that can be used to access the object model of the containing application.

Creating and Activating Windows

The Workbook class has a NewWindow method that you can use to create a new window on the workbook. Although you might expect the way to create new windows would involve calling Add on the Windows collection, it does not. The only way to create a new window is by using this method.

There is also an Activate method that activates the workbook by making the first window associated with the workbook the active window. You can activate a window other than the first window associated with the workbook by using the Windows collection and the Window object. For more information on the Windows and Window objects, see the section "Working with the Window Object" later in this chapter.

Printing a Workbook

The PrintOut method prints the workbook. It takes eight optional parameters, as shown in Table 5-9.

Table 5-9 The Optional Parameters of the PrintOut Method

Parameter Name	Type	What It Does
From	`object`	Sets the page number at which to start printing.
To	`object`	Sets the last page number to print.
Copies	`object`	Sets how many copies to print.
Preview	`object`	Set to `true` to show print preview.
ActivePrinter	`object`	Set to a `string` representing the printer to print to.
PrintToFile	`object`	Set to `true` to print to a file.
Collate	`object`	Set to `true` to collate multiple copies.
PrintToFileName	`object`	Set to a `string` representing the file name to print to if PrintToFile is set to `true`.

Protecting a Workbook

Excel enables you to protect two things at the workbook level: the order of the work-sheets in a workbook, and the size and positioning of the windows associated with a workbook. The Protect method takes three optional parameters: `Password`, `Structure`, and `Windows`. `Password` is an optional parameter that you can pass a `string` for the password for the workbook. `Structure` is an optional parameter that can be set to `true` to protect the sheet order so that the user cannot rearrange the order of the sheets in the workbook.

`Windows` is an optional parameter that can be set to `true` to protect the windows associated with the workbook from being moved or resized. For example, you could have two "tiled" windows showing a workbook; locking them prevents the user from moving them from the tiled positions. (See the section "Arranging Windows" later in this chapter for more information about tiling windows.)

Although all these parameters are optional, workbook protection does not really do anything unless you set the `Structure` or `Windows` parameter to `true`. If you want to protect cells in the workbook from being edited, you must use the Work-sheet.Protect method.

Working with the Worksheets, Charts, and Sheets Collections

The Worksheets, Charts, and Sheets collections are all very similar, so this section covers them together. They differ mainly in whether they contain worksheets (Worksheets) or chart sheets (Charts) or both (Sheets). In this section, as in the rest of the chapter, we use the word *sheet* to refer to either a chart sheet or a worksheet.

Iterating over the Open Sheets

These collections have a GetEnumerator method that allows them to be iterated over using the foreach keyword in C#, as shown in Listing 5-13.

Listing 5-13 A VSTO Customization That Iterates over the Worksheets, Charts, and Sheets Collections

```
private void ThisWorkbook_Startup(object sender, EventArgs e)
{
  Excel.Application app = this.Application;
  this.Charts.Add(missing, missing, missing, missing);

  foreach (Excel.Worksheet sheet in this.Worksheets)
  {
    MessageBox.Show(String.Format(
      "Worksheet {0}", sheet.Name));
  }

  foreach (Excel.Chart chart in this.Charts)
  {
    MessageBox.Show(String.Format(
      "Chart {0}", chart.Name));
  }

  foreach (object sheet in this.Sheets)
  {
    Excel.Worksheet worksheet = sheet as Excel.Worksheet;

    if (worksheet != null)
    {
      MessageBox.Show(String.Format(
        "Worksheet {0}", worksheet.Name));
    }

    Excel.Chart chart = sheet as Excel.Chart;
```

```
    if (chart != null)
    {
      MessageBox.Show(String.Format(
        "Chart {0}", chart.Name));
    }
  }
}
```

Accessing a Sheet in the Collection

To access a sheet in the Worksheets, Charts, and Sheets collections, you use a method called get_Item, which returns an `object`. You need to cast the returned `object` to a Worksheet or Chart. Objects returned from the Worksheets collection can always be cast to Worksheet. Objects returned from the Charts collection can always be cast to Chart. Objects returned from the Sheets collection should be tested using the `is` operator to determine whether the object returned is a Worksheet or a Chart. It can then be cast to the appropriate object.

The get_Item method takes an `Index` parameter of type `object`. You can pass a `string` representing the name of the worksheet or chart sheet or you can pass a 1-based index into the collection. You can check how many items are in a given collection by using the Count property.

Adding a Worksheet or Chart Sheet

To add a worksheet or chart sheet to a workbook, you use the Add method. The Add method on the Sheets and Worksheets collection takes four optional parameters of type `object`: `Before`, `After`, `Count`, and `Type`. The Charts collection Add method only takes the first three parameters.

The `Before` parameter can be set to a Worksheet or Chart representing the sheet before which the new sheet is to be added. The `After` parameter can be set to the Worksheet or Chart representing the sheet after which the new sheet is to be added. The `Count` parameter can be set to the number of new sheets you want to add. The `Type` parameter is set to `XlSheetType.xlWorksheet` to add a worksheet or `XlSheetType.xlChart` to add a chart sheet. Note that if you try to use `xlChart` as the `Type` parameter when using Worksheets.Add, Excel will throw an exception because Worksheets is a collection of only Worksheet objects. You can specify either Before or After, but not both parameters. If you omit the Before and After parameters, Excel adds the new sheet after all the existing sheets.

Listing 5-14 shows several different ways of using the Add method on the various collections.

Listing 5-14 A VSTO Customization That Uses the Add Method on the Charts, Sheets, and Worksheets Collections

```
private void ThisWorkbook_Startup(object sender, EventArgs e)
{
  Excel.Chart chart1 = this.Charts.Add(missing,
    missing, missing, missing) as Excel.Chart;

  Excel.Chart chart2 = this.Sheets.Add(missing,
    missing, missing, Excel.XlSheetType.xlChart) as Excel.Chart;

  Excel.Worksheet sheet1 = this.Sheets.Add(chart1,
    missing, 3, missing) as Excel.Worksheet;

  Excel.Worksheet sheet2 = this.Worksheets.Add(missing,
    chart2, missing, missing) as Excel.Worksheet;
}
```

Copying a Sheet

You can make a copy of a sheet by using the Copy method, which takes two optional parameters: Before and After. You can specify either Before or After, but not both parameters.

The Before parameter can be set to a Worksheet or Chart representing the sheet before which the sheet should be copied to. The After parameter can be set to a Worksheet or Chart representing the sheet after which the new sheet should be copied to. If you omit the Before and After parameters, Excel creates a new workbook and copies the sheet to the new workbook.

Moving a Sheet

The Move method moves the sheet to a different location in the workbook (that is, it moves it to a different tab location in the worksheet tabs) and has two optional parameters: `Before` and `After`. You can specify either `Before` or `After`, but not both parameters. If you omit both parameters, Excel creates a new workbook and moves the sheet to the new workbook.

Working with Document Properties

The DocumentProperties collection and DocumentProperty object are found in the Microsoft Office 11.0 Object Library (office.dll), which contains objects shared by all the Office applications. These objects are in the Microsoft.Office.Core namespace and are typically brought into your code in an Office namespace alias as shown here:

```
using Office = Microsoft.Office.Core;
```

Iterating over the DocumentProperties Collection

Listing 5-15 shows an example of iterating over the DocumentProperties collection returned by Workbook.CustomDocumentProperties and Workbook.BuiltInDocumentProperties.

Listing 5-15 A VSTO Customization That Iterates over DocumentProperties Collection

```
private void ThisWorkbook_Startup(object sender, EventArgs e)
{
  Office.DocumentProperties customProps = this.
    CustomDocumentProperties as Office.DocumentProperties;

  Office.DocumentProperties builtinProps = this.
    BuiltinDocumentProperties as Office.DocumentProperties;

  foreach (Office.DocumentProperty builtinProp in builtinProps)
  {
    MessageBox.Show(String.Format(
      "{0} - {1}", builtinProp.Name, builtinProp.Value));
  }

  foreach (Office.DocumentProperty customProp in customProps)
  {
    MessageBox.Show(String.Format(
      "{0} - {1}", customProp.Name, customProp.Value));
  }
}
```

Accessing a DocumentProperty in the DocumentProperties Collection

To access a DocumentProperty in a DocumentProperties collection, you use the C# indexing syntax `docProperty[object]`, which returns a DocumentProperty object. The indexer takes an `Index` parameter of type `object`. You can pass an `int` representing the 1-based index of the DocumentProperty in the collection you want to access. Alternatively, you can pass a `string` representing the name of the DocumentProperty you want to access. As with other collections, the Count property returns how many DocumentProperty objects are in the collection.

A DocumentProperty object has a Name property that returns a `string` containing the name of the property. It also has a Value property of type `object` that returns the value of the property. You can check what the type is of Value by using the Type property that returns a member of the `MsoDocProperties` enumeration: `msoProp-ertyTypeBoolean`, `msoPropertyTypeDate`, `msoPropertyTypeFloat`, `msoProp-ertyTypeNumber`, or `msoPropertyTypeString`.

Listing 5-16 shows how a DocumentProperty is accessed.

Listing 5-16 A VSTO Customization That Accesses a DocumentProperty Using an Indexer

```
private void ThisWorkbook_Startup(object sender, EventArgs e)
{
  Office.DocumentProperties builtinProps = this.
    BuiltinDocumentProperties as Office.DocumentProperties;

  Office.DocumentProperty authorProp = builtinProps["Author"];

  MessageBox.Show(String.Format(
    "Property {0} is {1}", authorProp.Name, authorProp.Value));

  Office.DocumentProperty thirdProp = builtinProps[3];

  MessageBox.Show(String.Format(
    "Property {0} is {1}", thirdProp.Name, thirdProp.Value));
}
```

Adding a DocumentProperty

You can add a custom DocumentProperty using the Add method. The Add method takes the parameters shown in Table 5-10.

Table 5-10 Parameters for the DocumentProperties Collection's Add Method

Parameter Name	Type	What It Does
Name	`string`	Sets the name of the new DocumentProperty.
LinkToContent	`bool`	Sets whether the property is linked to the contents of the container document.
Type	optional `object`	Sets the data type of the property. Can be one of the following `MsoDocProperties` enumerated values: `msoPropertyTypeBoolean`, `msoPropertyType-Date`, `msoPropertyTypeFloat`, `msoProperty-TypeNumber`, or `msoPropertyTypeString`.
Value	optional `object`	Sets the value of the property if LinkToContent is `false`.
LinkSource	optional `object`	Sets the source of the linked property if LinkToContent is `true`.

Listing 5-17 shows an example of adding a custom DocumentProperty of type `mso-PropertyTypeString`. Note that Excel will let you set the value to a long string, but it will truncate it to 255 characters. Fortunately, VSTO provides developers with a way to store larger amounts of data in a document through a feature called cached data. For more information on the cached data feature of VSTO, see Chapter 18, "Server Data Scenarios."

Listing 5-17 A VSTO Customization That Adds a Custom DocumentProperty

```
private void ThisWorkbook_Startup(object sender, EventArgs e)
{
  Office.DocumentProperties props = this.
    CustomDocumentProperties as Office.DocumentProperties;

  Office.DocumentProperty prop = props.Add("My Property",
    false, Office.MsoDocProperties.msoPropertyTypeString,
    "My Value", missing);
```

```
MessageBox.Show(String.Format(
    "Property {0} has value {1}.", prop.Name, prop.Value));
}
```

Working with the Windows Collections

The Application.Windows property returns a Windows collection that lets you iterate and access all the windows that are open in Excel. Similarly, the Workbook.Windows property lets you access windows that are associated with a particular workbook. These collections provide methods to arrange the open windows. Windows collections do not have a method to add a new window. Instead, you must call the Workbook.NewWindow method.

Iterating over the Open Windows

The Windows collection has a GetEnumerator method that allows it to be iterated over using the `foreach` keyword in C#, as shown in Listing 5-18.

Listing 5-18 A VSTO Customization That Iterates over the Windows Collection

```
private void ThisWorkbook_Startup(object sender, EventArgs e)
{
    Excel.Workbooks workbooks = this.Application.Workbooks;

    Excel.Workbook workbook1 = workbooks.Add(missing);
    Excel.Workbook workbook2 = workbooks.Add(missing);

    for (int i = 0; i < 10; i++)
    {
        workbook1.NewWindow();
        workbook2.NewWindow();
    }

    foreach (Excel.Window window in workbook1.Windows)
    {
        MessageBox.Show(String.Format(
            "Workbook1 Window: {0}", window.Caption));
    }

    foreach (Excel.Window window in this.Application.Windows)
```

```
      {
        MessageBox.Show(String.Format(
          "Application Window: {0}", window.Caption));
      }
    }
```

Accessing a Window in the Collection

To access a Window in the Windows collection, you use a method called get_Item, which returns a Window. The get_Item method takes an `Index` parameter that is of type `object`. You can pass a `string` representing the caption of the Window or you can pass a 1-based index into the Windows collection. You can check how many items are in a given collection by using the Count property. Listing 5-19 shows both getting a window by a 1-based index and by passing in the caption of the window.

Listing 5-19 A VSTO Customization That Gets a Window from the Windows Collection Using get_Item

```
private void ThisWorkbook_Startup(object sender, EventArgs e)
{
  string caption = "";
  Excel.Windows windows = this.Windows;

  if (windows.Count >= 1)
  {
    Excel.Window window = windows.get_Item(1);
    caption = window.Caption as string;
    MessageBox.Show(caption);
  }

  if (!String.IsNullOrEmpty(caption))
  {
    Excel.Window window2 = windows.get_Item(caption);
    string caption2 = window2.Caption as string;
    MessageBox.Show(caption2);
  }
}
```

Arranging Windows

Excel has various ways of arranging windows and synchronizing those windows so that when one window scrolls, the others scroll as well. The Arrange method lets you arrange a collection of windows as tiled, horizontal, vertical, or cascaded. This method also lets you synchronize two or more windows that are showing the same workbook so that when one window scrolls, the other windows scroll the same amount. Table 5-11 shows the optional parameters passed to the Arrange method.

Table 5-11 Optional Parameters for the Arrange Method

Property Name	Type	What It Does
ArrangeStyle	XlArrange-Style	Sets the style to use when arranging the windows: xlArrangeStyleCascade, xlArrangeStyleTiled, xlArrangeStyleHorizontal, xlArrangeStyleVertical.
ActiveWorkbook	bool	If set to true, only arranges the windows for the active workbook. If set to false, arranges all open windows.
SyncHorizontal	object	If set to true, when one window associated with a workbook scrolls horizontally, the other windows associated with the workbook will also scroll.
SyncVertical	object	If set to true, when one window associated with a workbook scrolls vertically, the other windows associated with the workbook will also scroll.

The CompareSideBySideWith method allows you to synchronize the scrolling of two windows showing the same workbook or two windows showing different workbooks. This method takes a string that represents the caption of the window to compare the currently active window with. The window you want to compare to the currently active window must be a member of the Windows collection you are using—so to be safe, you should use the Application.Windows collection because it contains all open windows.

As Listing 5-20 shows, it is important to activate the workbook whose windows you want to arrange. If you do not do this, the windows of the active workbook will be arranged rather than the workbook associated with the Windows collection. Listing 5-20 also illustrates the issue where the Activate method and the Activate event collide on the Workbook object. To get the compiler to not complain and IntelliSense to work, we cast the Workbook to an Excel._Workbook interface to let the compiler know we want the method and not the event.

Listing 5-20 A VSTO Customization That Arranges and Synchronizes Windows

```
private void ThisWorkbook_Startup(object sender, EventArgs e)
{
  Excel.Workbooks workbooks = this.Application.Workbooks;

  Excel.Workbook workbook1 = workbooks.Add(missing);
  Excel.Workbook workbook2 = workbooks.Add(missing);

  Excel.Window workbook1Window = workbook1.NewWindow();
  workbook2.NewWindow();

  ((Excel._Workbook)workbook1).Activate();

  workbook1.Windows.Arrange(
    Excel.XlArrangeStyle.xlArrangeStyleTiled,
    true, true, true);

  MessageBox.Show(String.Format(
    "Workbook {0} has its windows arranged tiled.",
    workbook1.Name));

  ((Excel._Workbook)workbook2).Activate();

  this.Application.Windows.CompareSideBySideWith(
    workbook1Window.Caption);

  MessageBox.Show(String.Format(
    "The windows {0} and {1} are synchronized",
    this.Application.ActiveWindow.Caption,
    workbook1Window.Caption));
}
```

Working with the Window Object

The Window object represents an Excel window. You can use the Window object to position a window associated with a workbook. You can also use the Window object to set display settings for a workbook such as whether to display gridlines and headings.

Positioning a Window

The Window object lets you position and change the way Excel displays a workbook within a window. Window has a WindowState property of type `XlWindowState` that can be used to set the window to `xlMaximized`, `xlMinimized`, or `xlNormal`.

When the WindowState is set to `xlNormal`, you can position the window using the Left, Top, Width, and Height properties. These properties are `double` values that represent points, not screen pixels. You can use the Window's PointsToScreenPixelsX and PointsToScreenPixelsY methods to convert points to pixels.

Display Settings Associated with a Window

A number of additional properties allow you to control the display of a window. Table 5-12 lists some of the most commonly used ones.

Table 5-12 Window Properties That Control the Display of a Window

Property Name	Type	What It Does
DisplayGridline	bool	If set to `false`, Excel won't display gridlines around cells.
DisplayHeadings	bool	If set to `false`, Excel won't display the row and column headers.
Display HorizontalScrollBar	bool	If set to `false`, Excel won't display the horizontal scroll bar.
Display VerticalScrollBar	bool	If set to `false`, Excel won't display the vertical scroll bar.
Display WorkbookTabs	bool	If set to `false`, Excel won't display the tabs to allow the user to switch to another worksheet.
EnableResize	bool	If set to `false`, Excel won't let the user resize the window when WindowState is set to `xlNormal`.
GridlineColor	int	Set to the color of the gridlines. Add a reference to your project to System.Drawing.dll and use the System.Drawing.ColorTranslator.ToOle method to generate a color Excel understands from a .NET color.

Property Name	Type	What It Does
ScrollColumn	int	Sets the left column that the window should scroll to.
ScrollRow	int	Sets the top row that the window should scroll to.
SplitColumn	double	Sets the column number where the window will be split into vertical panes.
SplitRow	double	Sets the row number where the window will be split into horizontal panes.
Visible	bool	Sets whether the window is visible.
Zoom	object	Zooms the window; set to 100 to zoom to 100%, 200 to zoom to 200%, and so on.

Listing 5-21 shows an example of using many of these properties. Note that we add a reference to System.Drawing.dll so that we can use the ColorTranslator object to set the GridlineColor property. The ColorTranslator object provides a method called ToOle, which takes a System.Drawing color and converts it to an Ole color format—the kind of color format that Office methods and properties that take colors expect.

Listing 5-21 A VSTO Customization That Controls the Display Options for a Window

```
private void ThisWorkbook_Startup(object sender, EventArgs e)
{
  Excel.Window win = this.NewWindow();

  win.WindowState = Excel.XlWindowState.xlNormal;
  win.Width = 200;
  win.Height = 200;
  win.Top = 8;
  win.Left = 8;
  win.DisplayGridlines = true;
  win.DisplayHeadings = false;
  win.DisplayHorizontalScrollBar = false;
  win.DisplayVerticalScrollBar = false;
  win.DisplayWorkbookTabs = false;
  win.EnableResize = false;

  win.GridlineColor = System.Drawing.ColorTranslator.
    ToOle(System.Drawing.Color.Blue);

  win.ScrollColumn = 10;
```

```
    win.ScrollRow = 20;
    win.Visible = true;
    win.Zoom = 150;
}
```

Working with the Names Collection and Name Object

The Names collection represents a set of ranges in the workbook that have been given names so that the range can be accessed by a name in a formula or by your code accessing the Names collection. The user can create and edit names using the Name Box, as shown in Figure 5-2, or by using the Name menu in the Insert menu. Also, names are sometimes automatically created by features of Excel. For example, when the user defines a custom print area, Excel creates a named range with the name Print_Area.

Iterating over the Names Collection

The Names collection has a GetEnumerator method that allows it to be iterated over using the `foreach` keyword in C#. For example, the following snippet iterates the Names collection associated with a workbook and displays the name of each Name object as well as the address of the range it refers to in standard format (for instance, `"=Sheet1!$A$5"`).

```
foreach (Excel.Name name in workbook.Names)
{
   Console.WriteLine(String.Format(
      "{0} refers to {1}", name.Name, name.RefersTo));
}
```

Accessing a Name in the Names Collection

To access a Name in the Names collection, you use a method called Item, which takes three optional parameters, as shown in Table 5-13.

Table 5-13 Optional Parameters for the Item Method

Parameter Name	Type	What It Does
Index	object	Pass the name of the Name or the index of the Name in the Names collection.
IndexLocal	object	Pass the localized name of the Name. A localized name typically exists when an Excel feature has created the name.
RefersTo	object	Pass the standard format refers to address (=Sheet1!$A$5) to get back the Name object that refers to that address.

Listing 5-22 shows some code that creates a Name and then accesses it in several ways. It creates the Name using the Add method that takes the name to be used for the Name object and the standard format address string (such as "=Sheet1!$A$5") that the newly created name will refer to.

Listing 5-22 A VSTO Customization That Creates a Name Object and Accesses It

```
private void ThisWorkbook_Startup(object sender, EventArgs e)
{
  Excel.Names names = this.Names;

  names.Add("MyName", "=Sheet1!$A$5", missing, missing,
    missing, missing, missing, missing, missing,
    missing, missing);

  Excel.Name name1 = names.Item(missing, missing,
    "=Sheet1!$A$5");

  MessageBox.Show(String.Format(
    "Name: {0} RefersTo: {1} RefersToR1C1: {2} Count: {3}",
    name1.Name, name1.RefersTo, name1.RefersToR1C1,
    name1.RefersToRange.Cells.Count));

  Excel.Name name2 = names.Item("MyName", missing, missing);
```

```
    MessageBox.Show(String.Format(
      "Name: {0} RefersTo: {1} RefersToR1C1: {2} Count: {3}",
      name2.Name, name2.RefersTo, name2.RefersToR1C1,
      name2.RefersToRange.Cells.Count));
  }
```

The Name Object

Given a Name object, you will commonly use several properties. The Name returns the name as a `string`. The RefersTo property returns the standard format address as a `string` that the Name refers to. The RefersToR1C1 returns the "rows and columns" format address as a `string` (such as `"=Sheet1!R26C9"`) that the Name refers to. Most importantly, the RefersToRange property returns an Excel Range object representing the range of cells that the name was assigned to.

To hide the name from the Define Name dialog and the Name Box drop-down, you can set the Visible property to `false`. To delete a Name, use the Delete method.

Working with the Worksheet Object

The Worksheet object represents a worksheet inside an Excel workbook. The Worksheet has a Name property that returns the name of the worksheet (for example `"Sheet1"`).

Worksheet Management

The Worksheet object has an Index property that gives a 1-based tab position for the worksheet in the tabbed worksheet tabs shown at the lower-left corner of a workbook window. You can move a worksheet to a different tab position by using the Move method. The Move method takes two optional parameters: a `Before` parameter that you can pass the sheet you want to move the worksheet before, and an `After` parameter that you can pass the sheet that you want to come after the moved worksheet. If you omit both optional parameters, Excel creates a new workbook and moves the worksheet to the new workbook.

It is also possible to make a copy of a worksheet using the Copy method. Like the Move method, it takes two optional parameters: a `Before` and `After` parameter that specify where the copied worksheet should go relative to other sheets. You can specify either `Before` or `After`, but not both parameters. If you omit both optional parameters, Excel creates a new workbook and copies the worksheet to the new workbook.

To activate a particular worksheet, use the Activate method. This method activates the sheet by making the first window associated with the worksheet the active window. It also selects the tab corresponding to the worksheet and displays that worksheet in the active window.

The equivalent of right-clicking a worksheet tab and choosing Delete from the pop-up menu is provided by the Delete method. When you use this method, Excel shows a warning dialog. You can prevent this warning dialog from appearing by using the Application object's DisplayAlerts property, which is discussed in the section "Controlling the Dialogs and Alerts that Excel Displays" earlier in this chapter.

You can hide a worksheet so that its tab is not shown at all by using the Visible property. The Visible property is of type `XlSheetVisibility` and can be set to `xlSheetVisible`, `xlSheetHidden`, and the `xlSheetVeryHidden`. The last value hides the worksheet so that it can only be shown again by setting the Visible property to `xlSheetVisible`. Setting the Visible property to `xlSheetHidden` hides the sheet, but the user can still unhide the sheet by going to the Format menu and choosing Sheet and then Unhide.

Sometimes a sheet is hidden using the Visible property so that the sheet can be used to store additional data that an application uses in a "scratch" worksheet that the user will not see. A better way to do this is provided by VSTO's cached data feature, described in Chapter 18. It has the added benefit that you can manipulate your hidden data in the Excel spreadsheet without starting up Excel. This lets you prefill an Excel worksheet with custom data on the server.

Note that a workbook must contain at least one visible worksheet. So when using the Delete method and the Visible property, you must keep this restriction in mind. If your code tries to hide or delete the last visible sheet in a workbook, an exception is thrown.

Listing 5-23 illustrates the usage of several of these properties and methods.

Listing 5-23 A VSTO Customization That Works with the Worksheets Collection

```
private void ThisWorkbook_Startup(object sender, EventArgs e)
{
  Excel.Worksheet sheetA = this.Worksheets.Add(
    missing, missing, missing, missing) as Excel.Worksheet;
  sheetA.Name = "SheetA";

  Excel.Worksheet sheetB = this.Worksheets.Add(
    missing, missing, missing, missing) as Excel.Worksheet;
  sheetB.Name = "SheetB";

  Excel.Worksheet sheetC = this.Worksheets.Add(
    missing, missing, missing, missing) as Excel.Worksheet;
  sheetC.Name = "SheetC";

  // Tab indexes
  string msg = "{0} is at tab index {1}";
  MessageBox.Show(String.Format(msg, sheetA.Name, sheetA.Index));
  MessageBox.Show(String.Format(msg, sheetB.Name, sheetB.Index));
  MessageBox.Show(String.Format(msg, sheetC.Name, sheetC.Index));

  sheetC.Move(sheetA, missing);
  MessageBox.Show("Moved SheetC in front of SheetA");

  // Tab indexes
  MessageBox.Show(String.Format(msg, sheetA.Name, sheetA.Index));
  MessageBox.Show(String.Format(msg, sheetB.Name, sheetB.Index));
  MessageBox.Show(String.Format(msg, sheetC.Name, sheetC.Index));

  sheetB.Copy(sheetA, missing);
  Excel.Worksheet sheetD = this.Worksheets.get_Item(
    sheetA.Index - 1) as Excel.Worksheet;

  ((Excel._Worksheet)sheetA).Activate();

  MessageBox.Show(String.Format(
    "Copied SheetB to create {0} at tab index {1}",
    sheetD.Name, sheetD.Index));

  sheetD.Delete();
  sheetA.Visible = Excel.XlSheetVisibility.xlSheetHidden;
  MessageBox.Show("Deleted SheetD and hid SheetA.");
}
```

Working with Names

As previously discussed, you can define named ranges at the workbook level by using Workbook.Names. You can also define named ranges that are scoped to a particular worksheet by using the Names property associated with a Worksheet object. The Names property returns a Names collection with only the names that are scoped to the Worksheet. For more information on the Names collection, see the section "Working with the Names Collection and the Name Object" earlier in this chapter.

Working with Worksheet Custom Properties

You can add custom properties that have a name and a value to the worksheet. Custom properties are a convenient way to associate additional hidden information with a worksheet that you do not want to put in a cell. Custom properties are not shown anywhere in the Excel user interface, unlike the document properties associated with a workbook. Custom properties at the worksheet level do not have the 256-character limit that document properties have for their value. You can store much larger chunks of data in a worksheet custom property.

The CustomProperties property returns a collection of custom properties associated with the worksheet. You can add a custom property by using the CustomProperties collection's Add method and passing a `string` for the name of the custom property you want to create and an `object` for the value you want to associate with the custom property. To get to a particular custom property, use the CustomProperties.Item method and pass the index of the property you want to get. Unfortunately, the Item method only takes a 1-based index and not the name of a custom property you have added. Therefore, you must iterate over the collection and check each returned CustomProperty object's Name property to determine whether you have found the custom property you want. Listing 5-24 shows an example of creating a custom property, then accessing it again.

Listing 5-24 A VSTO Customization That Accesses Custom DocumentProperty Objects

```
private void ThisWorkbook_Startup(object sender, EventArgs e)
{
  Excel.Worksheet sheet = this.Worksheets.Add(missing,
    missing, missing, missing) as Excel.Worksheet;

  // Add a custom property
```

```
Excel.CustomProperties props = sheet.CustomProperties;

props.Add("myProperty", "Some random value");
props.Add("otherProperty", 1);

// Now, enumerate the collection to find myProperty again.
foreach (Excel.CustomProperty prop in props)
{
  if (prop.Name == "myProperty")
  {
    MessageBox.Show(String.Format(
      "{0} property is set to {1}.",
      prop.Name, prop.Value));
    break;
  }
}
}
```

If you are using VSTO to associate code with a workbook, it is usually better to use cached data rather than custom properties. The cached data feature lets you put data sets and any XML serializable type into a data island in the document. This data island can also be accessed on the server without starting Excel. For more information on the cached data feature of VSTO, see Chapter 18.

Protecting a Worksheet

The Protect method protects the worksheet so that users cannot modify the worksheet. When a worksheet is protected using the Protect method, all the cells in the workbook are automatically locked. The Protect method corresponds to the Protect Sheet dialog shown in Figure 5-3. You can access this dialog by choosing Tools > Protection > Protect Sheet.

A number of optional parameters passed to the Protect method control exactly what can be modified, as shown in Table 5-14. Many of these options correspond to the checked list shown in Figure 5-3.

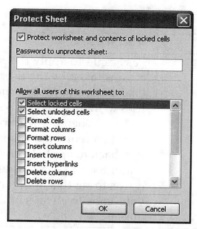

Figure 5-3 The Protect Sheet dialog.

Table 5-14 Optional Parameters for the Protect Method

Parameter Name	Type	What It Does
Password	object	You can pass the password as a `string` that you want to use to protect the document. You must pass this same password to the Unprotect method when you want to unprotect the document (or type the password when you choose to unprotect the document using Excel's protection menu in the Tools menu). If you omit this parameter, the worksheet can be unprotected without requiring a password.
DrawingObjects	object	Pass `true` to protect any shapes that are in the worksheet. The default value is `false`.
Contents	object	Pass `true` to protect the values of cells that have been locked (Range.Locked is `true`) and are not in the AllowEditRange collection (Range.AllowEdit is `false`). The default value is `true`.
Scenarios	object	Pass `true` to prevent scenarios from being edited. The default value is `true`.

continues

Table 5-14 Continued

Parameter Name	Type	What It Does
UserInterfaceOnly	object	Pass true to apply the protection settings to the actions taken by the user using the user interface. Pass false to protect the worksheet from code that tries to modify the worksheet. The default is false. When the workbook is saved and closed and then reopened at a later time, Excel sets protection back to apply to both user interface and code. You must run some code each time the workbook opens to set this option back to true if you want your code to always be able to modify protected objects.
AllowFormatting-Cells	object	Pass true to allow the user to format cells in the worksheet. The default value is false.
AllowFormatting-Columns	object	Pass true to allow users to format columns in the worksheet. The default value is false.
AllowFormatting-Rows	object	Pass true to allow users to format rows in the worksheet. The default value is false.
AllowInserting-Columns	object	Pass true to allow users to insert columns in the worksheet. The default value is false.
AllowInserting-Rows	object	Pass true to allow users to insert rows in the worksheet. The default value is false.
AllowInserting-Hyperlinks	object	Pass true to allow the user to insert hyperlinks in the worksheet. The default value is false.
AllowDeleting-Columns	object	Pass true to allow the user to delete columns in the worksheet. The default value is false. If you pass true, the user can only delete a column that has no locked cells. (Range.Locked for all the cells in the column is false.)
AllowDeleting-Rows	object	Pass true to allow the user to delete rows in the worksheet. The default value is false. If you pass true, the user can only delete a row that has no locked cells in it. (Range.Locked for all the cells in the row is false.)
AllowSorting	object	Pass true to allow the user to sort in the worksheet. The default value is false. If you pass true, the user can only sort a range of cells that has no locked cells in it (Range.Locked is false) or that has cells that have been added to the AllowEdit-Ranges collection (Range.AllowEdit is true).

Parameter Name	Type	What It Does
AllowFiltering	object	Pass true to allow the user to modify filters in the worksheet. The default value is false.
AllowUsingPivot-Tables	object	Pass true to allow the user to use pivot table reports in the worksheet. The default value is false.

You have two ways to exclude certain ranges of cells from being locked when the worksheet is protected. The first way is to add exclusions to protection using the AllowEditRanges collection that is returned from Worksheet.Protection.AllowEdit-Ranges. The AllowEditRanges collection corresponds to the Allow Users to Edit Ranges dialog shown in Figure 5-4. You can access this dialog by choosing Tools > Protection > Allow Users to Edit Ranges.

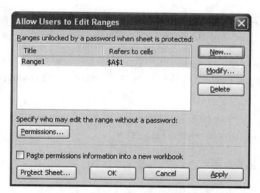

Figure 5-4 The Allow Users to Edit Ranges dialog.

Exclusions you make using the AllowEditRanges collection must be made before you use the Protect method to protect the worksheet. After you have protected the worksheet, no changes can be made to the AllowEditRanges collection until you unprotect the worksheet again. Exclusions you make in this way can be given a title and will display in the Allow Users to Edit Range dialog. A Range that is excluded from protection in this way will return true from its Range.AllowEdit property. Listing 5-25 shows a VSTO customization that creates two exclusions to protection using AllowEditRanges and then protects the worksheet using the Protect method.

Listing 5-25 A VSTO Customization That Adds Exclusions to Protection Using AllowEditRanges

```
private void ThisWorkbook_Startup(object sender, EventArgs e)
{
  Excel.Worksheet sheet = this.Worksheets.Add(missing,
    missing, missing, missing) as Excel.Worksheet;

  Excel.AllowEditRanges allowEdits = sheet.Protection.
    AllowEditRanges;

  allowEdits.Add("Editable Cell",
    sheet.get_Range("A1", missing), missing);

  sheet.Protect(missing, missing, missing, missing,
    missing, missing, missing, missing, missing,
    missing, missing, missing, missing, missing,
    missing, missing);

  Excel.Range protectedRange = sheet.get_Range("A2", missing);


  MessageBox.Show(String.Format(
    "A2's Locked is set to {0}", protectedRange.Locked));

  MessageBox.Show(String.Format(
    "A2's AllowEdit is set to {0}", protectedRange.AllowEdit));

  try
  {
    protectedRange.Value2 = "Should fail";
  }
  catch (Exception ex)
  {
    MessageBox.Show(ex.Message);
  }

  try
  {
    allowEdits.Add("This should fail",
      sheet.get_Range("A2", missing), missing);
  }
  catch (Exception ex)
  {
    // You can't add to the AllowEditRanges collection
    // when the worksheet is protected
    MessageBox.Show(ex.Message);
  }
```

```
  Excel.Range allowEditRange = sheet.get_Range("A1", missing);

  MessageBox.Show(String.Format(
    "A1's Locked is set to {0}", allowEditRange.Locked));

  MessageBox.Show(String.Format(
    "A1's AllowEdit is set to {0}", allowEditRange.AllowEdit));

  allowEditRange.Value2 = "Should succeed";
}
```

The second way to exclude certain ranges of cells from being locked when the worksheet is protected is by using the Range.Locked property. Cells you exclude in this way do not show up in the Allow Users to Edit Ranges dialog. Listing 5-26 shows adding exclusions to protection using the Range.Locked property.

Listing 5-26 A VSTO Customization That Adds Exclusions to Protection Using Range.Locked

```
private void ThisWorkbook_Startup(object sender, EventArgs e)
{
  Excel.Worksheet sheet = this.Worksheets.Add(missing,
    missing, missing, missing) as Excel.Worksheet;

  Excel.Range range1 = sheet.get_Range("A2", missing);
  range1.Locked = false;

  sheet.Protect(missing, missing, missing, missing,
    missing, missing, missing, missing, missing,
    missing, missing, missing, missing, missing,
    missing, missing);

  MessageBox.Show(String.Format(
    "A2's Locked is set to {0}", range1.Locked));

  MessageBox.Show(String.Format(
    "A2's AllowEdit is set to {0}", range1.AllowEdit));

  range1.Value2 = "Should succeed";
}
```

After a worksheet is protected, a number of properties let you examine the protection settings of the document and further modify protection options, as shown in Table 5-15.

Table 5-15 Properties That Let You Examine and Further Modify Document Protection

Property Name	Type	What It Does
EnableAutoFilter	bool	If set to `false`, Excel won't display the AutoFilter arrows when the worksheet is protected.
EnableOutlining	bool	If set to `false`, Excel won't display outlining symbols when the worksheet is protected.
EnablePivotTable	bool	If set to `false`, Excel won't display the pivot table controls and commands when the worksheet is protected.
EnableSelection	XlEnable-Selection	If set to `xlNoSelection`, Excel won't allow anything to be selected on a protected worksheet. If set to `xlUnlocked`, Excel will only allow unlocked cells (Range.Locked is set to `false`) to be selected. If set to `xlNoRestrictions`, any cell can be selected on a protected worksheet.
ProtectContents	bool	Read-only property that returns `false` if locked cells can be edited in the worksheet.
ProtectDrawing Objects	bool	Read-only property that returns `false` if shapes in the worksheet can be edited.
Protection	Protection	Returns a Protection object which has read-only properties corresponding to most of the optional parameters passed to the Protect method.
Protection.Allow-EditRanges	AllowEdit-Ranges	Returns an AllowEditRanges collection that lets you work with the ranges that users are allowed to edit.
ProtectionMode	bool	Read-only property that returns `true` if the worksheet is protected.
ProtectScenarios	bool	Read-only property that returns `false` if scenarios in the worksheet can be edited.

Working with OLEObjects

In addition to containing cells, a worksheet can contain embedded objects from other programs (such as an embedded Word document) and ActiveX controls. To work with these objects, you can use the OLEObjects method on the Worksheet object. The OLEObjects method takes an optional `Index` parameter of type `object` that you can pass the name of the OLEObject or the 1-based index of the OLEObject in the collection. The OLEObjects method also doubles as a way to get to the OLEObjects collection, which can be quite confusing. If you pass it a `string` that represents as a name or a 1-based index as an `int`, it returns the specified OLEObject. If you pass it `Type.Missing`, it returns the OLEObjects collection.

Any time you add an OLEObject to a worksheet, Excel also includes that object in the Shapes collection that is returned from the Shapes property on the Worksheet object. To get to the properties unique to an OLEObject, you use the Shape.OLEFormat property.

It is possible to write C# code that adds ActiveX controls to a worksheet and talks to them through casting OLEObject.Object or Shape.OLEFormat.Object to the appropriate type. You have to add a reference in your C# project for the COM library associated with the ActiveX control you want to use. Doing so causes Visual Studio to generate an interop assembly and add it to your project. Alternatively, if a primary interop assembly is registered for the COM library, Visual Studio automatically adds a reference to the pre-generated primary interop assembly. You can then cast OLEObject.Object or Shape.OLEFormat.Object to the correct type added by Visual Studio for the COM library object corresponding to the ActiveX control.

VSTO enables you to add Windows Forms controls to the worksheet—a much more powerful and .NET-centric way of working with controls. For this reason, we do not consider using ActiveX controls in any more detail in this book. For more information on VSTO's support for Windows Forms controls, see Chapter 14, "Using Windows Forms in VSTO."

Working with Shapes

The Shapes property returns a Shapes collection—a collection of Shape objects. A Shape object represents various objects that can be inserted into an Excel spreadsheet, including a drawing, an AutoShape, WordArt, an embedded object or ActiveX control, or a picture.

The Shapes collection has a Count property to determine how many shapes are in the Worksheet. It also has an Item method that takes a 1-based index to get a particular Shape out of the collection. You can also enumerate over the Shapes collection using `foreach`.

Several methods on the Shapes collection let you add various objects that can be represented as a Shape. These methods include AddCallout, AddConnector, AddCurve, AddDiagram, AddLabel, AddLine, AddOLEObject, AddPicture, AddPolyline, AddShape, AddTextbox, and AddTextEffect.

The Shape object has properties and methods to position the Shape on the worksheet. It also has properties and methods that let you format and modify the Shape object. Some of the objects returned by properties on the Shape object were shown in Figure 3-20.

Working with ChartObjects

In this book, we have used the phrase *chart sheet* when referring to a chart that is a sheet in the workbook. Figure 5-5 shows the last page of the Chart Wizard that is shown when you insert a new chart. Excel enables you to insert a chart as a new sheet—what we have called a chart sheet—and it allows you to add a chart as an object in a sheet. The object model calls a chart that is added as an object in a sheet a ChartObject.

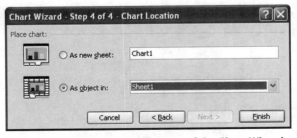

Figure 5-5 The Chart Location step of the Chart Wizard.

What complicates the matter is that the object in the object model for a chart sheet is a Chart, but a ChartObject also has a property that returns a Chart. A ChartObject has its own set of properties that control the placement of the chart in a worksheet. But the properties and methods to actually manipulate the chart contents are found on the Chart object returned by the ChartObject.Chart property.

To work with ChartObjects, you can use the ChartObjects method on the Worksheet object. The ChartObjects method takes an optional `Index` parameter of type `object` that you can pass the name of the ChartObject or the 1-based index of the ChartObject in the collection. The ChartObjects method also doubles as a way to get to the ChartObjects collection, which can be quite confusing. If you pass it a `string` that represents as a name or a 1-based index, it returns the specified ChartObject. If you pass it `Type.Missing`, it returns the ChartObjects collection.

To add a ChartObject to a worksheet, you use the ChartObjects.Add method, which takes `Left`, `Top`, `Width`, and `Height` as `double` values in points. Any time you add a ChartObject to a worksheet, Excel also includes that object in the Shapes collection that is returned from the Shapes property on the Worksheet object.

Working with Lists

Excel 2003 introduced the ability to create a list from a range of cells. Just select a range of cells, right-click the selection, and choose Create List. A list has column headers with drop-down options that make it easy for the user to sort and apply filters to the data in the list. It has a totals row that can automatically sum and perform other operations on a column of data. It has an insert row marked with an asterisk at the bottom of the list that allows users to add additional rows to the list. Figure 5-6 shows an example of a list in Excel.

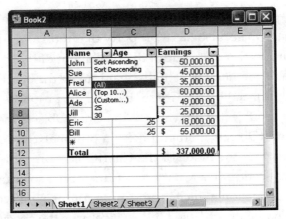

Figure 5-6 A list in Excel.

You can access the lists in a worksheet by using the ListObjects property. The ListObjects property returns the ListObjects collection. The ListObjects collection has a Count property to determine how many lists are in the Worksheet. It also has an Item method that takes a 1-based index or the name of the list object as a `string` to get a ListObject object out of the collection. You can also enumerate over the ListObjects collection using `foreach`.

Table 5-16 shows some of the most commonly used properties for the ListObject object. You will read more about ListObject in the discussion of VSTO's support for data in Chapter 17, "VSTO Data Programming."

Table 5-16 Key Properties of ListObject

Property Name	Type	What It Does
DataBodyRange	Range	Returns a Range representing the cells containing the data—the cells between the headers and the insert row.
HeaderRowRange	Range	Returns a Range representing the header cells.
InsertRowRange	Range	Returns a Range representing the cells in the insert row.
ShowAutoFilter	bool	If set to `false`, the drop-down filtering and sorting menus associated with the column headers won't be shown.
ShowTotals	bool	If set to `false`, the totals row won't be shown.
TotalsRowRange	Range	Returns a Range representing the cells in the totals row.

Working with the Range Object

The Range object represents a range of cells in a spreadsheet. A range can contain one cell, multiple contiguous cells, and even multiple discontiguous cells. You can select multiple discontiguous cells by holding down the Ctrl key as you select in Excel.

Getting a Range Object for a Particular Cell or Range of Cells

Excel provides a variety of ways to get a Range object. The Range object is the object you use when you want to work with a cell or range of cells in an Excel worksheet. Two ways to get a Range object were mentioned in the description of the Application object. Application.ActiveCell returns the top-left cell of the active selection in the active window. Application.Selection returns an `object` that represents the active selection in the active window. If the active selection is a range of cells, you can cast Application.Selection to a Range object. If something else is selected in the active window, such as a shape or a chart, Application.Selection returns that selected object instead.

Worksheet also provides several ways to get a Range object. The Worksheet.get_Range method is the most common way to get a Range object from a Worksheet. This method takes a required `object` parameter to which you can pass a `string`. It has a second optional parameter to which you can pass a second `string`. The strings you pass are in what is called A1-style reference format. The easiest way to explain the A1-style reference format is to give several examples.

The reference A1 specifies the cell at row 1, column A. The reference D22 specifies the cell at row 22, column D. The reference AA11 specifies the cell at row 11, column AA (column 27).

The reference $A$1 also refers to the cell at row 1, column A. If you use $ signs in an A1-style reference, they are ignored.

You can use the range operator (:) to specify a range of cells where the first A1-style reference is the top-left corner of the range followed by a colon operator followed by a second A1-style reference for the bottom-right corner of the range. The reference A1:B1 refers to the two cells at row 1, column A and row 1, column B. The reference A1:AA11 refers to all 297 cells in the block whose top-left corner is at row 1, column A and bottom-right corner is at row 11, column AA (column 27).

You can use the union operator (`,`) to specify multiple cells that could be discontiguous. For example, the reference `A1,C4` specifies a range of two cells where the first cell is at row 1, column A and the second cell is at row 4, column C. Users can select discontiguous ranges of cells by holding down the Ctrl key as they select various cells. The reference `A1,C4,C8,C10` is another valid A1-style reference that specifies four different cells.

The intersection operator (a space) lets you specify the intersection of cells. For example, the reference `A1:A10 A5:A15` resolves to the intersecting six cells starting at row 5, column A and ending at row 10, column A. The reference `A1:A10 A5:A15 A5` resolves to the single cell at row 5, column A.

You can also use any names you have defined in the worksheet in your A1-style reference. For example, suppose that you defined a named range called `foo` that refers to the cell A1. Some valid A1-style references using your name would include `foo:A2`, which refers to the cells at row 1, column A and row 2, column A. The reference `foo,A5:A6` refers to the cells at row 1, column A; row 5, column A; and row 6, column A.

As mentioned earlier, the get_Range method takes a second optional parameter to which you can pass a second A1-style reference string. The first parameter and the second parameter are effectively combined using the range operator. So the range that get_Range returns when you call `get_Range("A1", "A2")` is equivalent to the range you get when you call `get_Range("A1:A2", Type.Missing)`.

A second way to get a Range object is by using the Worksheet.Cells property, which returns a Range for all the cells in the worksheet. You can then use the same get_Range method on the returned Range object and pass A1-style references to select cells in the same way you do using get_Range from the Worksheet object. So `Cells.get_Range("A1:A2", Type.Missing)` is equivalent to `get_Range("A1:A2", Type.Missing)`. A more common use of the Cells property is to use it in conjunction with Range's get_Item property, which takes a row index and an optional column index. Using get_Item is a way to get to a particular cell without using the A1-style reference. So `Cells.get_Item(1,1)` is equivalent to `get_Range("A1", Type.Missing)`.

Another way to get a Range object is by using the Worksheet.Rows or Worksheet.Columns properties. These return a Range that acts differently than other

Range objects. For example, if you take the Range returned by Columns and display the count of cells in the range, it returns 256—the number of columns. But if you call the Select method on the returned Range, Excel selects all 16,772,216 cells in the worksheet. The easiest way to think of the ranges returned by Rows and Columns is that they behave similarly to how column and row headings behave in Excel.

Listing 5-27 shows several examples of using the get_Range method and the Cells, Rows, and Columns properties. We use the Value2 property of range to set every cell in the range to the string value specified. Figure 5-7 shows the result of running the program in Listing 5-27.

Listing 5-27 A VSTO Customization That Gets Range Objects

```
private void Sheet1_Startup(object sender, System.EventArgs e)
{
  Excel.Range r1 = this.get_Range("A1", missing);
  r1.Value2 = "r1";

  Excel.Range r2 = this.get_Range("B7:C9", missing);
  r2.Value2 = "r2";

  Excel.Range r3 = this.get_Range("C1,C3,C5", missing);
  r3.Value2 = "r3";

  Excel.Range r4 = this.get_Range("A1:A10 A5:A15", missing);
  r4.Value2 = "r4";

  Excel.Range r5 = this.get_Range("F4", "G8"); •
  r5.Value2 = "r5";

  Excel.Range r6 = this.Rows.get_Item(12, missing)
    as Excel.Range;

  r6.Value2 = "r6";

  Excel.Range r7 = this.Columns.get_Item(5, missing)
    as Excel.Range;

  r7.Value2 = "r7";
}
```

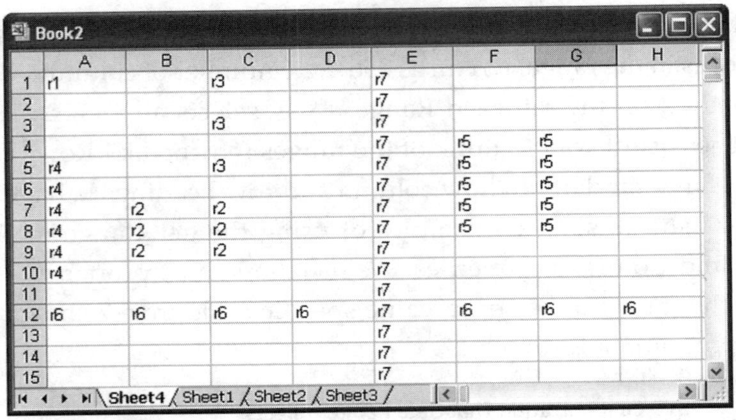

Figure 5-7 Result of running Listing 5-27.

Working with Addresses

Given a Range object, you often need to determine what cells it refers to. The get_Address method returns an address for the range in either A1 style or R1C1 style. You have already learned about A1-style references. R1C1-style references support all the same operators as discussed with A1-style references (colon for range, comma for union, and space for intersection). R1C1-style references have row and column numbers prefaced by R and C respectively. So cell A4 in R1C1 style would be R4C1. Figure 5-8 shows a range that consists of three areas that we consider in this section.

The address for the range in Figure 5-8 is shown here in A1 style and in R1C1 style:

```
$A$15:$F$28,$H$3:$J$9,$L$1
R15C1:R28C6,R3C8:R9C10,R1C12
```

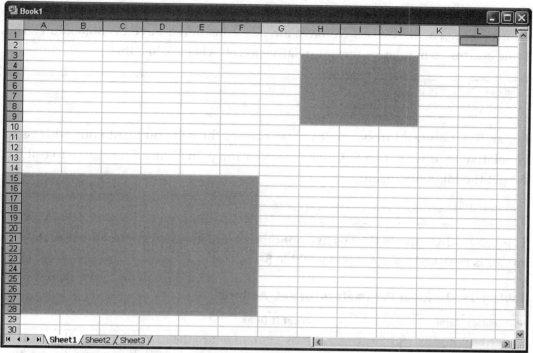

Figure 5-8 A range with three discontiguous areas.

Another option when getting an address is whether to get an external reference or a local reference. The addresses we have already shown for Figure 5-8 are local references. An external reference includes the name of the workbook and sheet where the range is. Here is the same range in Figure 5-8 expressed as an external reference in A1 style and R1C1 style.

```
[Book1]Sheet1!$A$15:$F$28,$H$3:$J$9,$L$1
[Book1]Sheet1!R15C1:R28C6,R3C8:R9C10,R1C12
```

For our example, the workbook we created the range in was not saved. When we save it as Book1.xls, the addresses look like this:

```
[Book1.xls]Sheet1!$A$15:$F$28,$H$3:$J$9,$L$1
[Book1.xls]Sheet1!R15C1:R28C6,R3C8:R9C10,R1C12
```

Another option when getting an address is whether to use an absolute address or a relative one. The addresses we have already considered have been absolute. The same addresses in relative format (relative to cell A1) look like this:

```
R[14]C:R[27]C[5],R[2]C[7]:R[8]C[9],RC[11]
A15:F28,H3:J9,L1
```

For an R1C1-style address, you can also specify the cell you want your address to be relative to. If we get an R1C1-style for our range in Figure 5-4 relative to cell B2, we get the following result:

```
R[13]C[-1]:R[26]C[4],R[1]C[6]:R[7]C[8],R[-1]C[10]
```

The get_Address method takes five optional parameters that control the way the reference is returned, as described in Table 5-17.

Table 5-17 Optional Parameters for get_Address

Parameter Name	Type	What It Does
RowAbsolute	object	Pass true to return the row part of the address as an absolute reference ($A$1). If you pass false, the row reference will not be absolute ($A1). The default is true.
ColumnAbsolute	object	Pass true to return the column part of the address as an absolute reference ($A$1). If you pass false, the column reference will not be absolute (A$1). The default is true.
ReferenceStyle	XlReferenceStyle	Pass xlA1 to return an A1-style reference. Pass xlR1C1 to return an R1C1-style reference.
External	object	Pass true to return an external reference. The default is false.
RelativeTo	object	Pass a Range object representing the cell that you want an R1C1-style reference to be relative to. Has no effect when used with A1-style references.

Listing 5-28 shows several examples of using get_Address with our example range.

Listing 5-28 A VSTO Customization That Uses get_Address

```
private void Sheet1_Startup(object sender, System.EventArgs e)
{
  Excel.Range range1 = this.get_Range(
    "$A$15:$F$28,$H$3:$J$9,$L$1", missing);

  System.Text.StringBuilder sb = new System.Text.StringBuilder();
  sb.AppendLine("A1-Style Addresses:");
  sb.AppendFormat("Default: {0}\n", range1.get_Address(
    missing, missing, Excel.XlReferenceStyle.xlA1,
    missing, missing));

  sb.AppendFormat("Relative rows: {0}\n",
    range1.get_Address(false, missing,
    Excel.XlReferenceStyle.xlA1, missing, missing));

  sb.AppendFormat("Row & Column Relative: {0}\n",
    range1.get_Address(false, false,
    Excel.XlReferenceStyle.xlA1, missing, missing));

  sb.AppendFormat("External: {0}\n", range1.get_Address(
    missing, missing, Excel.XlReferenceStyle.xlA1,
    true, missing));

  sb.AppendLine();
  sb.AppendLine("R1C1-Style Addresses:");
  sb.AppendFormat("Default: {0}\n", range1.get_Address(
    missing, missing, Excel.XlReferenceStyle.xlR1C1,
    missing, missing));

  sb.AppendFormat("Row & Column Relative to C5: {0}\n",
    range1.get_Address(false, false,
    Excel.XlReferenceStyle.xlR1C1, missing,
    this.get_Range("C5", missing)));

  sb.AppendFormat("External: {0}", range1.get_Address(
    missing, missing, Excel.XlReferenceStyle.xlR1C1,
    true, missing));

  MessageBox.Show(sb.ToString());
}
```

Creating New Ranges Using Operator Methods

We have discussed several "operators" that can be used in address strings, including the union operator (a comma) and the intersection operator (a space). You can also apply these operators through the Application.Union and Application.Intersection methods.

It is also possible to take a Range and get a new Range that is offset from it by some number of rows and columns by using the get_Offset method. This method takes a row and column value to offset the given range by and returns the newly off-set range. So calling get_Offset(5, 5) on the example range in Figure 5-8 returns a range with this A1-style address:

```
"$F$20:$K$33,$M$8:$O$14,$Q$6"
```

Listing 5-29 shows an example of using these operators. Note that Union and Inter-section take a lot of optional parameters, allowing you to union or intersect more than just two ranges.

Listing 5-29 A VSTO Customization That Uses Union, Intersection, and get_Offset

```
private void Sheet1_Startup(object sender, System.EventArgs e)
{
  Excel.Application app = this.Application;

  Excel.Range range1 = this.get_Range("$A$15:$F$28", missing);
  Excel.Range range2 = this.get_Range("$H$3:$J$9", missing);
  Excel.Range range3 = this.get_Range("$L$1", missing);
  Excel.Range range4 = this.get_Range("$A$11:$G$30", missing);

  Excel.Range rangeUnion = app.Union(range1, range2,
    range3, missing, missing, missing, missing, missing,
    missing, missing, missing, missing, missing, missing,
    missing, missing, missing, missing, missing, missing,
    missing, missing, missing, missing, missing, missing,
    missing, missing, missing, missing);

  Excel.Range rangeIntersection = app.Intersect(range1,
    range4, missing, missing, missing, missing, missing,
    missing, missing, missing, missing, missing, missing,
    missing, missing, missing, missing, missing, missing,
    missing, missing, missing, missing, missing, missing,
    missing, missing, missing, missing, missing);
```

```
    Excel.Range rangeOffset = rangeUnion.get_Offset(5, 5);

  MessageBox.Show(String.Format("Union: {0}",
    rangeUnion.get_Address(missing, missing,
    Excel.XlReferenceStyle.xlA1, missing, missing)));

  MessageBox.Show(String.Format("Intersection: {0}",
    rangeIntersection.get_Address(missing, missing,
    Excel.XlReferenceStyle.xlA1, missing, missing)));

  MessageBox.Show(String.Format("Offset: {0}",
    rangeOffset.get_Address(missing, missing,
    Excel.XlReferenceStyle.xlA1, missing, missing)));
}
```

Working with Areas

When there are multiple discontiguous ranges of cells in one Range, each discontiguous range is called an area. If there are multiple discontiguous areas in the Range, use the Areas property to access the each area (as a Range) via the Areas collection. The Areas collection has an Areas.Count property, and an Areas.get_Item method that takes an `int` parameter representing the 1-based index into the array. Listing 5-30 shows an example of iterating over our example range (which has three areas) and printing the address of each area.

Listing 5-30 A VSTO Customization That Works with Areas

```
private void Sheet1_Startup(object sender, System.EventArgs e)
{
  Excel.Range range1 = this.get_Range(
    "$A$15:$F$28,$H$3:$J$9,$L$1", missing);

  MessageBox.Show(String.Format("There are {0} areas",
    range1.Areas.Count));

  foreach (Excel.Range area in range1.Areas)
  {
    MessageBox.Show(String.Format("Area address is {0}",
      area.get_Address(missing, missing,
      Excel.XlReferenceStyle.xlA1, missing, missing)));
  }
}
```

Working with Cells

The Count property returns the number of cells in a given Range. You can get to a specific single-cell Range within a Range by using the get_Item method. The get_Item method takes a required row index and an optional column index. The column index can be omitted when the range is a one-dimensional array of cells because it only has cells from one column or one row—in this case, the parameter called RowIndex really acts like an array index. If the Range has multiple areas, you must get the area you want to work with first—otherwise, get_Item only returns cells out of the first area in the Range.

Listing 5-31 shows an example of using get_Item.

Listing 5-31 A VSTO Customization That Uses get_Item

```
private void Sheet1_Startup(object sender, System.EventArgs e)
{
  Excel.Range range1 = this.get_Range("$A$15:$F$28", missing);

  int rowCount = range1.Rows.Count;
  int columnCount = range1.Columns.Count;

  for (int i = 1; i <= rowCount; i++)
  {
    for (int j = 1; j <= columnCount; j++)
    {
      Excel.Range cell = range1.get_Item(i, j) as Excel.Range;
      string address = cell.get_Address(missing,
        missing, Excel.XlReferenceStyle.xlA1,
        missing, missing);

      cell.Value2 = String.Format("get_Item({0},{1})", i, j);
    }
  }
}
```

Working with Rows and Columns

Given a Range object, you can determine the row and column number of the top-left corner of its first area using the Row and Column properties. The row and column number are returned as int values.

You can also determine the total number of rows and columns in the first area using the Rows and Columns properties. These properties return special ranges that you can think of as corresponding to the row or column headers associated with the range. When we get Rows.Count from our example range in Figure 5-8, it returns 14, and Columns.Count returns 6. This makes sense because the first area in our selection (A15:F28) spans 6 columns and 14 rows.

To get the row and column position of the bottom-right corner of the first area, you can use the rather awkward expressions shown in Listing 5-32. Listing 5-32 also illustrates the use of get_Item, which takes the row and column index (relative to the top of the given range) and returns the cell (as a Range) at that row and column index. When you get a Rows or a Columns range, these ranges are one-dimensional—hence the parameter called RowIndex acts like an array index in this case.

Listing 5-32 A VSTO Customization That Gets Row and Column Positions

```
private void Sheet1_Startup(object sender, System.EventArgs e)
{
  Excel.Range range1 = this.get_Range(
    "$A$15:$F$28,$H$3:$J$9,$L$1", missing);
  Excel.Range area = range1.Areas.get_Item(1);

  int topLeftColumn = area.Column;
  int topLeftRow = area.Row;
  int bottomRightColumn = ((Excel.Range)area.Columns.
    get_Item(area.Columns.Count, missing)).Column;

  int bottomRightRow = ((Excel.Range)area.Rows.
    get_Item(area.Rows.Count, missing)).Row;

  MessageBox.Show(String.Format(
    "Area Top Left Column {0} and Row {1}",
    topLeftColumn, topLeftRow));
  MessageBox.Show(String.Format(
    "Area Bottom Right Column {0} and Row {1}",
    bottomRightColumn, bottomRightRow));

  MessageBox.Show(String.Format(
    "Total Rows in Area = {0}", area.Rows));
  MessageBox.Show(String.Format(
    "Total Columns in Area = {0}", area.Columns));
}
```

Working with Regions

The CurrentRegion property returns a Range that is expanded to include all cells up to a blank row and blank column. This expanded Range is called a region. So, for example, you might have a Range that includes several cells in a table—to get a Range that encompasses the entire table (assuming the table is bordered by blank rows and columns) you would use the CurrentRegion property on the smaller Range to return the entire table.

The get_End method is a method that works against the region associated with a Range. The get_End method takes a member of the `XlDirection` enumeration: either `xlDown`, `xlUp`, `xlToLeft`, or `xlToRight`. This method when passed `xlUp` returns the topmost cell in the region in the same column as the top-left cell of the Range. When passed `xlDown`, it returns the bottom-most cell in the region in the same column as the top left cell of the Range. When passed `xlToLeft`, it returns the leftmost cell in the region in the same row as the top-left cell of the Range. And when passed `xlToRight`, it returns the rightmost cell in the region in the same row as the top-left cell of the Range.

Selecting a Range

You can make a range the current selection using the Select method on a Range. Remember that calling Select changes the user's current selection, which is not a very nice thing to do without good reason. In some cases, however, you want to draw the user's attention to something, and in those cases selecting a Range is reasonable to do.

Editing the Values in a Range

Two methods are typically used to get and set the values in a range. The first way is to use the methods get_Value and set_Value. The second way is to use the property Value2. Value2 and get_Value differ in that the Value2 property returns cells that are currency or dates as a `double` value. Also, get_Value takes an optional parameter of type `XlRangeValueDataType`. If you pass `XlRangeValueData.xlRangeValueDefault`, you will get back an `object` representing the value of the cell for a single cell Range. For both Value2 and get_Value, if the Range contains multiple cells, you will get back an array of objects corresponding to the cells in the Range.

Listing 5-33 shows several examples of using Value2 including an example of passing an array of values to Value2. Setting the values of the cells in a Range all at once via an array is more efficient than making multiple calls to set each cell individually.

Listing 5-33 A VSTO Customization That Uses Value2

```
private void Sheet1_Startup(object sender, System.EventArgs e)
{
  Excel.Range range1 = this.get_Range("$A$15:$F$28", missing);
  range1.Value2 = "Test";

  int rowCount = range1.Rows.Count;
  int columnCount = range1.Columns.Count;

  object[,] array = new object[rowCount, columnCount];

  for (int i = 0; i < rowCount; i++)
  {
    for (int j = 0; j < columnCount; j++)
    {
      array[i, j] = i * j;
    }
  }

  range1.Value2 = array;
}
```

Copying, Clearing, and Deleting Ranges

Excel provides a number of methods to copy, clear, and delete a Range. The Copy method takes a Destination parameter that you can pass the destination of the copied range. The Clear method clears the content and formatting of the cells in the range. ClearContents clears just the values of the cells in the range, and ClearFormats clears just the formatting. The Delete method deletes the range of cells and takes as a parameter the direction in which to shift cells to replace deleted cells. The direction is passed as a member of the XlDeleteShiftDirection enumeration: xlShift-ToLeft or xlShiftUp.

Finding Text in a Range

The Find method allows you to find text in a Range and return the cell within the Range where the text is found. The Find method corresponds to the Find and Replace dialog shown in Figure 5-9. If you omit parameters when calling the Find method, it uses whatever settings were set by the user the last time the Find dialog was used. Furthermore, when you specify the parameters, the settings you specified appear in the Find dialog the next time the user opens it.

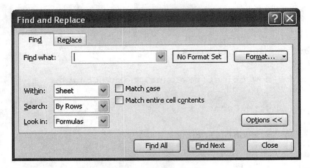

Figure 5-9 The Find and Replace dialog.

The Find method takes a number of parameters described in Table 5-18. Find returns a Range object if it succeeds and `null` if it fails to find anything. You can find the next cell that matches your find criteria by using the FindNext method. FindNext takes an optional `After` parameter to which you need to pass the last found Range to ensure you do not just keep finding the same cell over and over again. Listing 5-34 shows an example of using the Find and FindNext method where we search for any cells containing the character "2" and bold those cells.

Table 5-18 Parameters for the Find Method

Parameter Name	Type	What It Does
What	object	Pass the data to search for as a required string.
After	object	Pass a single cell after which you want the search to begin as a Range. The default is the top-left cell if this omitted.
LookIn	object	Pass the type to search.
LookAt	XlLookAt	Pass xlWhole to match the whole cell contents, xlPart to match parts of the cell contents.
SearchOrder	XlSearchOrder	Pass xlByRows to search by rows, xlBy-Columns to search by columns.
SearchDirection	XlSearch-Direction	Pass xlNext to search forward, xlPrevious to search backward.
MatchCase	object	Pass true to match case.
MatchByte	object	Pass true to have double-byte characters match only double-byte characters.
SearchFormat	object	Set to true if you want the search to respect the FindFormat options. You can change the FindFormat options by using the Application.FindFormat.

Listing 5-34 A VSTO Customization That Uses Find and FindNext

```
private void Sheet1_Startup(object sender, System.EventArgs e)
{
  Excel.Range range1 = this.get_Range("$A$15:$F$28", missing);

  int rowCount = range1.Rows.Count;
  int columnCount = range1.Columns.Count;

  object[,] array = new object[rowCount, columnCount];

  for (int i = 0; i < rowCount; i++)
  {
    for (int j = 0; j < columnCount; j++)
    {
      array[i, j] = i * j;
    }
  }
  range1.Value2 = array;
```

```
Excel.Range foundRange = range1.Find("2",
  range1.get_Item(1, 1), missing,
  Excel.XlLookAt.xlPart, missing,
  Excel.XlSearchDirection.xlNext,
  missing, missing, missing);

while (foundRange != null)
{
  foundRange.Font.Bold = true;
  foundRange = range1.FindNext(foundRange);
}
}
```

Formatting a Range of Cells

Excel provides several methods and properties to format a range of cells. Among the most useful is the NumberFormat property that you can set to format strings corresponding to the strings in the Custom category of the Format Cells dialog. For example, you can set NumberFormat to General to set no specific number format. Setting NumberFormat to m/d/yyyy sets a date format, and 0% sets the format to a percentage format. When using NumberFormat, be sure to consider the locale issue discussed in the section "Special Excel Issues" later in this chapter if you are building a console application or an add-in, because reading and setting this string can cause problems when running in different locales. If you are using a VSTO code behind a workbook or template project, you do not have to worry about the locale issue.

The Font property returns a Font object that can be used to set the Font to various sizes and styles. Listing 5-34 showed an example of the Font object used to bold the font of a cell.

Excel also enables you to create styles associated with a Workbook and apply those styles to a Range. You can create styles using Workbook.Styles. Listing 5-35 shows an example of creating a style and applying it to a Range.

Listing 5-35 A VSTO Customization That Creates and Applies Styles

```
private void Sheet1_Startup(object sender, System.EventArgs e)
{
  Excel.Range range1 = this.get_Range("$A$15:$F$28", missing);
  range1.Value2 = "Hello";

  Excel.Style style = Globals.ThisWorkbook.Styles.Add(
```

```
   "My Style", missing);

  style.Font.Bold = true;
  style.Borders.LineStyle = Excel.XlLineStyle.xlDash;
  style.Borders.ColorIndex = 3;
  style.NumberFormat = "General";

  range1.Style = "My Style";
}
```

Special Excel Issues

You need to be aware of several special considerations when using the Excel object model with .NET. This section examines two of the most important: working with multiple locales and working with Excel dates.

The Excel Locale Issue for Automation Executables and COM Add-Ins

When you program against the Excel object model using managed code in an automation executable or a COM add-in, Excel methods and properties can behave differently depending on the locale of the current thread. *Note that this problem does not occur in code behind the document solutions built with VSTO.* For example, if you want to set a formula for a Range and you are in the French locale, Excel requires you to use the localized French formula names and formatting:

```
sheet.get_Range("A1", Type.Missing).Formula = "=SOMME(3; 4)";
```

This behavior differs from VBA and VSTO code behind solutions that work independent of locale. VBA and VSTO always tell Excel that the locale is US English (locale id 1033). In VBA and VSTO code behind solutions, you do not have to think about locale when talking to Excel. You can write this code and have it work even in a French locale:

```
sheet.get_Range("A1", Type.Missing).Formula = "=SUM(3, 4)";
```

When managed code calls into the Excel object model, it tells Excel the locale it is running under (the locale of the current thread), which causes Excel to expect that you will provide formulas and other values in the localized format of that locale.

Excel will also return formulas and other values in the localized format of that locale. Excel expects localized strings for such things as date formats, NumberFormat strings associated with a Range, color names associated with NumberFormat strings, and formula names.

Using DateTime for Dates

As an example of the badness that can ensue if you do not think about this issue, consider what the following code does:

```
sheet.get_Range("A1", Type.Missing).Value2 = "03/11/02";
```

This value may be interpreted by Excel as March 11, 2002, November 3, 2002, or November 2, 2003 depending on the locale of the current thread.

For dates, you have a clear workaround. Do *not* pass dates as literal strings to Excel. Instead, construct a date using the System.DateTime object and pass it to Excel using DateTime's ToOADate method, as shown in Listing 5-36. The ToOADate method converts a DateTime to an OLE Automation date, which is the kind of date format that the Excel object model expects.

Listing 5-36 A VSTO Customization That Properly Passes a Date to Excel

```
private void Sheet1_Startup(object sender, System.EventArgs e)
{
   Excel.Range range1 = this.get_Range("$A$1", missing);

   // March 11, 2002
   System.DateTime date = new System.DateTime(2002, 3, 11);
   range1.Value2 = date.ToOADate();
}
```

Switching the Thread Locale to English and Back Is Not Recommended

You might think that a solution to the problems associated with setting or getting Range.NumberFormat and Range.Formula is to save the locale of the thread, temporarily switch the locale of the thread to English (locale id 1033), execute code that sets or gets a locale affected property such as NumberFormat or Formula, and then switch back to the saved locale. This approach is not recommended because it affects other add-ins that will not be expecting the locale switch.

Consider the following example. Your add-in is running on a French machine. Your add-in switches the locale to 1033 and sets a formula value. Another add-in is handling the Change event and displays a dialog box. That dialog box displays in English rather than French. So by changing the thread locale, you have changed the behavior of another add-in and been a bad Office citizen in general.

Using Reflection to Work Around the Locale Issue

The recommended workaround for COM add-ins or automation executables encountering the locale issue (when they access properties affected by the current locale such as the NumberFormat or Formula property) is to access these properties via reflection. Reflection enables you to specify an English locale to Excel and write code that will work regardless of the current thread locale. Listing 5-37 illustrates how to use reflection to set the NumberFormat and Formula properties.

Listing 5-37 Using Reflection to Work Around the Locale Issue in Excel

```
static void Main(string[] args)
{
  Excel.Application application = new Excel.Application();
  application.Visible = true;
  object missing = Type.Missing;

  Excel.Workbook workbook = application.Workbooks.Add(missing);
  Excel.Worksheet sheet = (Excel.Worksheet)workbook.Worksheets.Add(missing,
missing, missing, missing);
  Excel.Range range1 = sheet.get_Range("$A$1", missing);

  // Set Formula in English (US) using reflection
  typeof(Excel.Range).InvokeMember("Formula",
    System.Reflection.BindingFlags.Public |
    System.Reflection.BindingFlags.Instance |
    System.Reflection.BindingFlags.SetProperty,
    null, range1,
    new object[] { "=SUM(12, 34)" },
    System.Globalization.CultureInfo.GetCultureInfo(1033));

  // Set NumberFormat in English (US) using reflection
  typeof(Excel.Range).InvokeMember("NumberFormat",
    System.Reflection.BindingFlags.Public |
    System.Reflection.BindingFlags.Instance |
    System.Reflection.BindingFlags.SetProperty,
    null, range1,
```

```
        new object[] { "General" },
        System.Globalization.CultureInfo.GetCultureInfo(1033));
    }
```

Old Format or Invalid Type Library Error

A second issue that further complicates the Excel locale issue is that you can get an "Old format or invalid type library" error when using the Excel object model in an English Excel installation on a machine where the locale is set to a non-English locale. Excel is looking for a file called xllex.dll in Program Files\Microsoft Office\OFFICE11\1033 that it cannot find. The solution to this problem is to install the xllex.dll file or install the MUI language packs for Office. You can also make a copy of excel.exe, rename it to xllex.dll, and copy it to the 1033 directory.

VSTO and the Excel Locale Issue

VSTO code behind the document solutions solve the Excel locale issue by using a transparent proxy object that sits between you and the Excel object model. This proxy always tells Excel that the locale is US English (locale id 1033), which effectively makes VSTO match VBA behavior. If you are using VSTO code behind the document solutions, the Excel locale issue is solved for you and you do not have to worry about it further. If you are building a managed COM add-in for Excel or an automation executable, the issue still exists.

There are some caveats to VSTO's solution to the Excel locale issue. The VSTO transparent proxy can slow down your code slightly. It also causes Excel objects to display slightly differently when inspected in the debugger. Finally, if you compare a proxied Excel object such as Application to an unproxied Application object using the Equals operator, they will not evaluate to be equal.

If you want to bypass VSTO's transparent proxy for a particular object, you can use the Microsoft.Office.Tools.Excel.ExcelLocale1033Proxy.Unwrap method and pass the Excel object that you want to bypass the proxy for. This method removes the proxy and returns the raw PIA object which exposes you once again to the locale issue. You can also set the assembly level attribute ExcelLocale1033 in a VSTO project's AssemblyInfo.cs file to false to turn the transparent proxy off for the entire Excel solution.

If you navigate to objects from another PIA and then navigate back again to the Excel PIA, you can lose the transparent proxy. For example, if you get a Command-Bar object from the Microsoft.Office.Core PIA namespace from the Application.CommandBars collection and then use the CommandBar.Application property to get back to the Excel Application object, you have now lost the proxy and the locale issue will occur again.

Finally, if you create a new instance of Excel from a Word VSTO code behind solution, you are talking directly to the Excel PIA with no transparent proxy object, and the locale issue will continue to be in effect.

Converting Excel Dates to DateTime

Excel can represent dates in two formats: the 1900 format or the 1904 format. The 1900 format is based on a system where when converted to a number, it represents the number of elapsed days since January 1, 1900. The 1904 format is based on a system where when converted to a number, it represents the number of elapsed days since January 1, 1904. The 1904 format was introduced by early Macintosh computers because of a problem with the 1900 format that we describe later. You can determine which format a workbook is using by checking the Workbook.Date1904 property, which returns `true` if the workbook is using the 1904 format.

If an Excel workbook is using the 1904 format, and you convert a date from that workbook into a DateTime directly, you will get the wrong value. It will be off by 4 years and 2 leap days because DateTime is expecting the 1900 format where the value of the Excel date represented by a number is the number of elapsed days since January 1, 1900, not January 1, 1904. So this code would give bad date-times if you are using the 1904 format in your workbook.

```
object excelDate = myRange.get_value(Type.Missing);
DateTime possiblyBadDateIfExcelIsIn1904Mode = (DateTime)excelDate;
```

To get a 1904 format date into a DateTime format, you must add to the 1904 format date 4 years and 2 leap days (to make up for the fact that the 1904 has its 0 in 1904 rather than 1900). So if you write this code instead and use the function Convert-ExcelDateToDate in Listing 5-38, you will get the right result if the 1904 date system is used.

```
object excelDate = myRange.get_value(Type.Missing);
DateTime goodDate = ConvertExcelDateToDate(excelDate);
```

Listing 5-38 Converting Excel Dates to DateTime and Back Again

```
static readonly DateTime march1st1900 = new DateTime(1900, 03, 01);
static readonly DateTime december31st1899 = new DateTime(1899, 12, 31);
static readonly DateTime january1st1904 = new DateTime(1904, 01, 01);
static readonly TimeSpan date1904adjustment = new TimeSpan(4 * 365 + 2, 0, 0,
0, 0);
static readonly TimeSpan before1stMarchAdjustment = new TimeSpan(1, 0, 0, 0);
bool date1904 = ActiveWorkbook.Date1904;

object ConvertDateToExcelDate(DateTime date)
{
    LanguageSettings languageSettings = Application.LanguageSettings;
    int lcid = languageSettings.get_LanguageID(
      MsoAppLanguageID.msoLanguageIDUI);
    CultureInfo officeUICulture = new CultureInfo(lcid);
    DateTimeFormatInfo dateFormatProvider = officeUICulture.
      DateTimeFormat;
    string dateFormat = dateFormatProvider.ShortDatePattern;

    if (date1904)
    {
        if (date >= january1st1904)
            return date - date1904adjustment;
        else
            return date.ToString(dateFormat, dateFormatProvider);
    }
    if (date >= march1st1900)
        return date;
    if (date < march1st1900 && date > december31st1899)
        return date - before1stMarchAdjustment;
    return date.ToString(dateFormat, dateFormatProvider);
}


DateTime ConvertExcelDateToDate(object excelDate)
{
    DateTime date = (DateTime)excelDate;
    if (date1904)
        return date + date1904adjustment;
    if (date < march1st1900)
        return date + before1stMarchAdjustment;
    return date;
}
```

Listing 5-38 also has a correction for 1900 format dates. It turns out that when Lotus 1-2-3 was written, the programmers incorrectly thought that 1900 was a leap year. When Microsoft wrote Excel, they wanted to make sure they kept compatibility with existing Lotus 1-2-3 spreadsheets by making it so that they calculated the number of days elapsed since December 31, 1899, rather than January 1, 1900. When Date-Time was written, its creators did not try to back up to December 31, 1899—they calculated from January 1, 1900. So to get an Excel date in 1900 format that is before March 1, 1900 into a DateTime properly, you have to add one day.

Finally, Excel cannot represent days before January 1, 1900 when in 1900 format or days before January 1, 1904 when in 1904 format. Therefore, when you are converting a DateTime to an Excel date, you have to pass a string rather than a number representing the date—because these dates cannot be represented as dates in Excel (only as strings).

Conclusion

This chapter explored some of the most important objects in the Excel object model. We use many of these objects in the Excel examples in subsequent chapters. We also consider some additional Excel object model objects used to work with XML in Excel in Chapter 21, "Working with XML in Excel."

This chapter has described these objects as defined by the primary interop assemblies for Excel. You should be aware that VSTO extends some of these objects (Workbook, Worksheet, Range, Chart, ChartObject, and ListObject) to add some additional functionality such as data binding support. Part Three of this book examines those extensions.

6.

Programming Word

Ways to Customize Word

WORD HAS A VERY RICH OBJECT MODEL that consists of 248 objects that combined have more than 4,200 properties and methods. Word also supports several models for integrating your code, including add-ins and code behind documents. Most of these models were originally designed to allow the integration of COM components written in VB 6, VBA, C, or C++. However, through COM interop, managed objects written in C# or Visual Basic can masquerade as COM objects and participate in most of these models. This chapter briefly considers several of the ways that you can integrate your code with Word and refers you to other chapters that discuss these approaches in more depth. This chapter also explores building research services and introduces the Word object model.

Automation Executable

As mentioned in Chapter 2, "Introduction to Office Solutions," the simplest way to integrate with Word is to start Word from a console application or Windows Forms application and automate it from that external program. Chapter 2 provides a sample of an automation executable that automates Word.

COM Add-Ins

Word can load add-ins—in particular COM add-ins. A COM add-in is a DLL that contains a class that implements IDExtensibility2. The class that implements IDExtensibility2 must be registered in the registry so that it looks like a COM object to Word. A COM add-in is typically written to add application-level functionality—functionality that is available to any document opened by Word.

Word has a COM Add-Ins dialog box that enables users to turn COM add-ins on and off. To access the COM Add-Ins dialog, you must perform the following steps:

1. Right-click a menu or toolbar in Word and choose Customize from the pop-up menu, or from the Tools menu choose Customize to display the Customize dialog box.
2. Click the Commands tab of the Customize dialog.
3. Choose Tools from the list of Categories.
4. Scroll down the list of commands until you see a command that says COM Add-Ins.
5. Drag the COM Add-Ins command and drop it on a toolbar.
6. Close the Customize dialog box.

After you have completed these steps, click the COM Add-Ins toolbar button you added to a toolbar. Figure 6-1 shows the COM Add-Ins dialog.

Figure 6-1 The COM Add-Ins dialog box in Word.

You can add COM add-ins by using the Add button and remove them by using the Remove button. Typically, you will not have your users use this dialog to manage

COM add-ins. Instead, you will install and remove a COM add-in by manipulating registry settings with the installer you create for your COM add-in.

Word discovers the installed COM add-ins by reading from the registry. You can view the registry on your computer by going to the Windows Start menu and choosing Run. In the Run dialog box, type `regedit` for the program to run, and then click the OK button. Word looks for COM add-ins in the registry keys under HKEY_CURRENT_USER\Software\Microsoft\Office\Word\Addins. Word also looks for COM add-ins in the registry keys under HKEY_LOCAL_MACHINE\ Software\Microsoft\Office\Word\Addins. COM add-ins registered under HKEY_LOCAL_MACHINE are not shown in the COM Add-Ins dialog box and cannot be turned on or off by users. It is recommended you do not register your COM add-in under HKEY_LOCAL_MACHINE because it hides the COM add-in from the user.

COM add-ins are discussed in detail in Chapter 23, "Developing COM Add-Ins for Word and Excel."

Visual Studio Tools for Office Code Behind

Visual Studio 2005 Tools for Office (VSTO) enables you to put C# or Visual Basic code behind Word templates and documents. VSTO was designed from the ground up for C# and Visual Basic—so this model is the most ".NET" of all the models used to customize Word. This model is used when you want to customize the behavior of a particular document or a particular set of documents created from a common template. For example, you might want to create a template that is used whenever anyone in your company creates an invoice. This template can add commands and functionality that are always available when the document created with it is opened.

Note that Word templates in VSTO do not behave in the same way that templates behave in VBA. In VBA, both the code associated with the template and the code associated with the document run concurrently. In VSTO, the code associated with the template is associated with the document when a new document is created, and only the code associated with the document runs.

VSTO's support for code behind a document is discussed in detail in Part Three of this book.

Smart Documents and XML Expansion Packs

Smart documents are another way to associate your code with a Word template or document. Smart documents rely on attaching an XML schema to a document or template and associating your code with that schema. The combination of the schema and associated code is called an XML Expansion Pack. An XML Expansion Pack can be associated with a Word document by choosing Templates and Add-Ins from the Tools menu and clicking the XML Expansion Packs tab. Figure 6-2 shows the Templates and Add-Ins dialog.

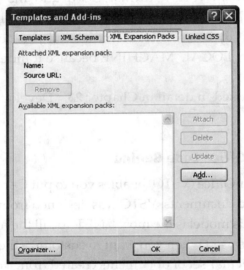

Figure 6-2 The XML Expansion Packs tab of
the Templates and Add-Ins dialog.

When an XML Expansion Pack is attached to a document, Word loads the associated code and runs it while that document is opened. Smart document solutions can create a custom user interface in the Document Actions task pane that can be brought up in Word by choosing Task Pane from the View menu.

It is possible to write smart document solutions from scratch in C# or Visual Basic. This book does not cover this approach. Instead, this book focuses on the VSTO approach, which was designed to make smart document development much easier and allow you to create a custom Document Actions task pane using Windows Forms. Chapter 15, "Working with Actions Pane," discusses this capability in more detail.

Smart Tags

Smart Tags enable a pop-up menu to be displayed containing actions relevant for a recognized piece of text in a document. You can control the text that Word recognizes and the actions that are made available for that text by creating a Smart Tag DLL or by using VSTO code behind a document.

A Smart Tag DLL contains two types of components that are used by Word: a recognizer and associated actions. A recognizer determines what text in the document is recognized as a Smart Tag. An action corresponds to a menu command displayed in the pop-up menu.

A recognizer could be created that tells Word to recognize stock-ticker symbols (such as the MSFT stock symbol) and display a set of actions that can be taken for that symbol: buy, sell, get the latest price, get history, and so on. A "get history" action, for instance, could launch a Web browser to show a stock history Web page for the stock symbol that was recognized.

When a recognizer recognizes some text, Word displays red-dotted underlining under the recognized text, as shown in Figure 6-3. If the user hovers over the text, a pop-up menu icon appears next to the text that the user can click to drop down a menu of actions for the recognized piece of text. Figure 6-4 shows an example menu. When an action is selected, Word calls back into the associated action to execute your code.

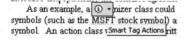

Figure 6-3 Some recognized text.

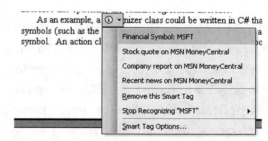

Figure 6-4 Dropping down the Smart Tag menu.

Smart Tags are managed from the Smart Tags page of the AutoCorrect dialog shown in Figure 6-5. To display the Smart Tags page, you choose the AutoCorrect Options from the Tools menu. Here the user can turn on and off individual recognizers as well as control other options relating to how Smart Tags display in the document.

Figure 6-5   The Smart Tags page in the AutoCorrect dialog.

VSTO provides a simple model for creating a Smart Tag that works at the workbook or template level. Chapter 16, "Working with Smart Tags in VSTO," describes the VSTO model for working with Smart Tags in more detail.

It is possible to write Smart Tag recognizer and action classes in a DLL that works at the application level, but it is much more complex than the VSTO model. Chapter 16 also describes that approach.

Server-Generated Documents

VSTO enables you to write code on the server that populates a Word document with data without starting Word on the server. For example, you might create an ASP.NET page that reads some data out of a database and then puts it in a Word document and returns that document to the client of the Web page. VSTO provides a class called ServerDocument that makes it easy to do this. Chapter 18, "Server Data Scenarios," describes generating documents on the server using the ServerDocument class.

You can also use the XML file formats of Office to generate Word documents in XML formats on the server, but this is much more complex. Chapter 22, "Working with XML in Word," discusses VSTO support for this scenario.

Programming Research Services

This section examines how to build research services for Word and other Office applications. Word has a task pane called the Research task pane that enables you to enter a search term and search various sources for that search term. Figure 6-6 shows the Research task pane.

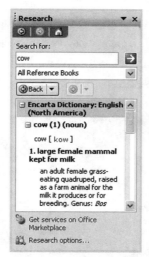

Figure 6-6 The Research task pane.

Office enables developers to write a special Web service called a research service that implements two Web methods defined by Office: Registration and Query. Both Web methods take a `string` and return a `string`. A research service can be registered with Office and used in Office's Research task pane. For example, you might write a research service that searches for the search term in a corporate database.

Although the signatures of the two Web methods you must declare are simple, the actual implementation of these methods is somewhat complex because Word has four separate XML schemas that must be used for the request passed to Registration, the response returned by Registration, the request passed to Query, and the response returned by Query.

The simplest way to build research services is by using the Research Service Development Extras Toolkit for Office that is available for download at http://www.microsoft.com/downloads/details.aspx?FamilyID=8b0a4427-9cfd-493e-82a7-16f8d88ebdc7. This toolkit provides helper classes to assist in parsing the requests and forming responses. Note that this example uses Visual Studio 2003 because the Research Service Development Toolkit was not available for Visual Studio 2005 at the time of this writing.

Getting Started with Research Services

After you have downloaded and installed the Research Service Development Extras Toolkit, launch Visual Studio 2003 and choose New Project from the File menu. Select Visual C# Projects in the Project Types window and click the Research Service Wrapper in the Templates window, as shown in Figure 6-7.

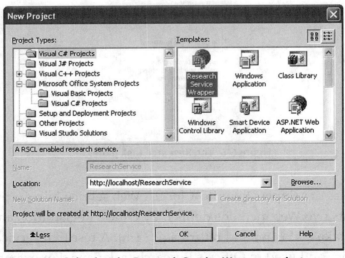

Figure 6-7 Selecting the Research Service Wrapper project.

When you click OK, a wizard appears that in Step 1 prompts you for the information needed to create your research service, as shown in Figure 6-8. The first step of the wizard prompts you for provider information and an ID for the provider. You can think of a provider as being like a Web site that potentially provides multiple services. For example, the ACME corporation might provide a number of different research services. You can click the New Guid button to automatically generate a unique ID for the provider.

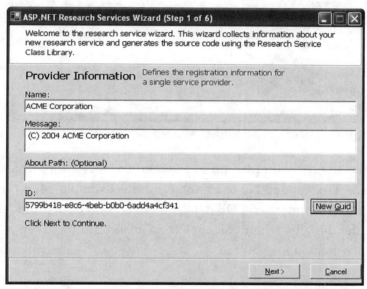

Figure 6-8 Step 1 of the ASP.NET Research Services Wizard.

Figure 6-9 shows Step 2 of the wizard. Here you specify the name of the service, a description of the service, and you assign the service a category from a list of categories that are predefined by Office. You also must have a unique ID for your service.

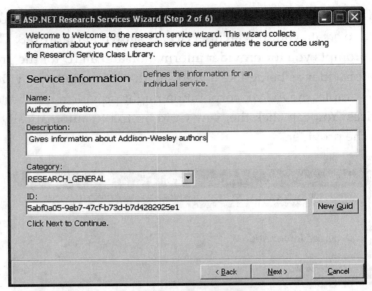

Figure 6-9 Step 2 of the ASP.NET Research Services Wizard.

Step 3 of the wizard prompts you as to whether you require licensing for your research service. We respond No to this step for this example. Step 4 lets you specify an OleDB data provider, a SqlDB data provider, or no data provider. We choose no data provider. Finally, when you click the Finish button in Step 5, the research service project is created for you.

A Simple Research Service

The wizard has created a project for our Author Information research service. Within the project is a file called ResearchService.asmx.cs. Edit this file to produce the result shown in Listing 6-1. If the user searches for the strings "Eric Carter" or "Eric Lippert," the service will send back information listing all the authors of this book.

Listing 6-1 The ResearchService.asmx.cs File

```
using System;
using Microsoft.Samples.Office.ResearchService;
using Microsoft.Samples.Office.ResearchService.Registration;
using Microsoft.Samples.Office.ResearchService.Query;

namespace ResearchService
{
```

```
public class ResearchService : ResearchWebService
{
  public override RegistrationResponse Registration(
    RegistrationRequest request)
  {
    return new RegistrationResponse();
  }

  public override QueryResponse Query(QueryRequest request)
  {
    QueryResponse response = new QueryResponse();
    if (request.QueryText == "Eric Carter" ||
      request.QueryText == "Eric Lippert")
    {
      DocumentResponseWriter responseWriter;

      responseWriter = new DocumentResponseWriter();
      responseWriter.WriteItem("Eric Carter", "One of the authors of this
book, a Lead Developer at Microsoft Corporation.");
      responseWriter.WriteItem("Eric Lippert", "One of the authors of this
book, a Developer at Microsoft Corporation.");

      response.WriteResponse(responseWriter);
    }
    return response;
  }
}
}
```

Registering the Research Service with Word

After building the project, the next step is to register it with Word. First, launch Word. Then, bring up Word's Research task pane by choosing Task Pane from the View menu. Drop down the available task panes from the pop-up menu at the top of the task pane and choose Research. At the very bottom of the Research task pane is some text that says Research options. Click that text to get the dialog shown in Figure 6-13. Then click the Add Services button. The dialog shown in Figure 6-10 appears. In this dialog, type the address to the Web service .asmx file. Then click the Add button.

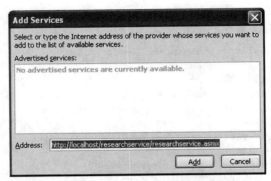

Figure 6-10 Word's Add Services dialog.

When you click the Add button, Word displays a dialog announcing the provider of the research service, as shown in Figure 6-11.

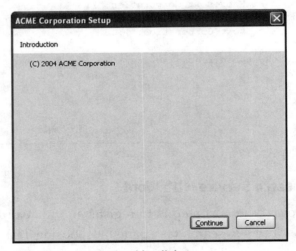

Figure 6-11 Word's Provider dialog.

Clicking Continue brings up a dialog showing details about the research service shown in Figure 6-12. Click Install to install the research service.

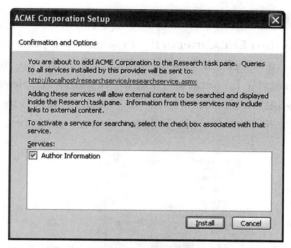

Figure 6-12 Research Service confirmation dialog.

Clicking Install returns to the Research Options dialog shown in Figure 6-13, which now has our Author Information research site installed in the Research Sites category. Click OK to continue.

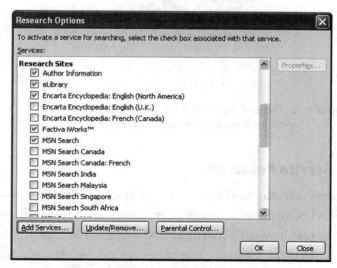

Figure 6-13 Research Options dialog.

Using the Research Service

Now, you can type the text **Eric Carter** in the Research task pane and drop down the list of sites to search to select All Research Sites. Click the green arrow button to search. The research service is contacted, and the response displays in the task pane, as shown in Figure 6-14. An alternative way to search for text is to type it in the document, select it, and then click it while holding down the Alt key.

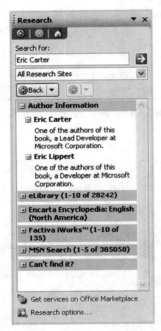

Figure 6-14 The Research task pane shows results from
the new Author Information research service.

More Research Service Resources

This has been a brief introduction to how to get started creating research service in C# using Visual Studio. You can do many more things with research services, including returning richer results with hyperlinks and images. For more information about creating research services, search http://msdn.microsoft.com for the phrase "research services."

Introduction to the Word Object Model

Regardless of the approach you choose to integrate your code with Word, you will eventually need to talk to the Word object model to get things done. It is impossible to completely describe the Word object model in this book, but we try to make you familiar with the most important objects in the Word object model and show some of the most frequently used methods, properties, and events on these objects.

The Object Hierarchy

The first step in learning the Word object model is to get an idea of the basic structure of the object model hierarchy. Figure 6-15 shows the most critical objects in the Word object model and their hierarchical relationship.

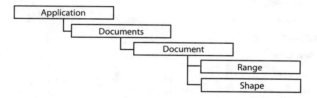

Figure 6-15 The basic hierarchy of the Word object model.

The Application object is used to access application-level settings and options. It also is the root object of the object model and provides access to the other objects in the object model. Figure 6-16 shows some of the object model objects associated with the Application object.

The Document object represents a Word document. Figure 6-17 shows some of the object model objects associated with the Document object.

The Range object represents a range of text within a document. Figure 6-18 shows some of the object model objects associated with the Range object.

The Shape object represents a figure, chart, picture, or other object that is embedded in a Word document. Figure 6-19 shows some of the object model objects associated with the Shape object.

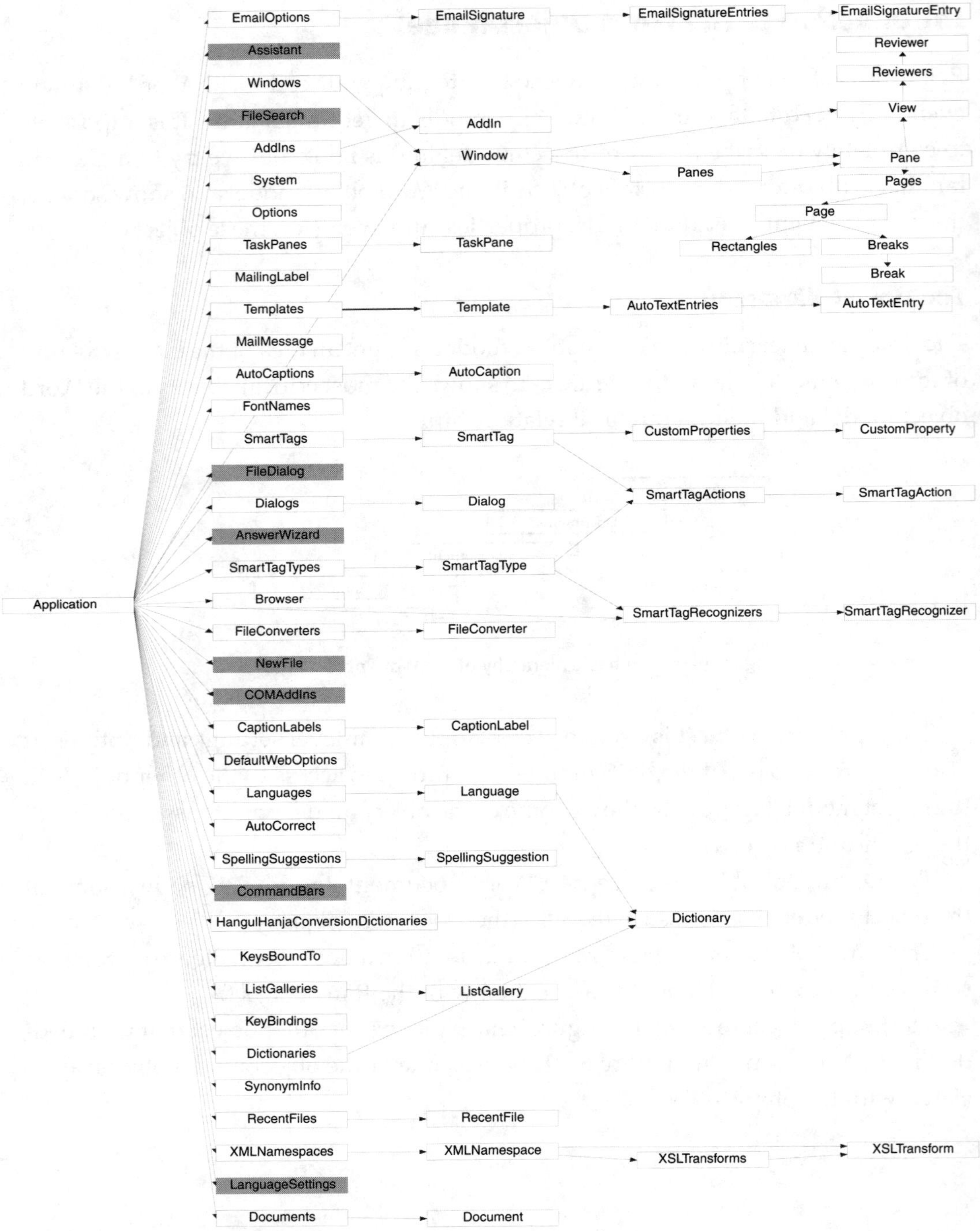

Figure 6-16 Objects associated with Word's Application object.

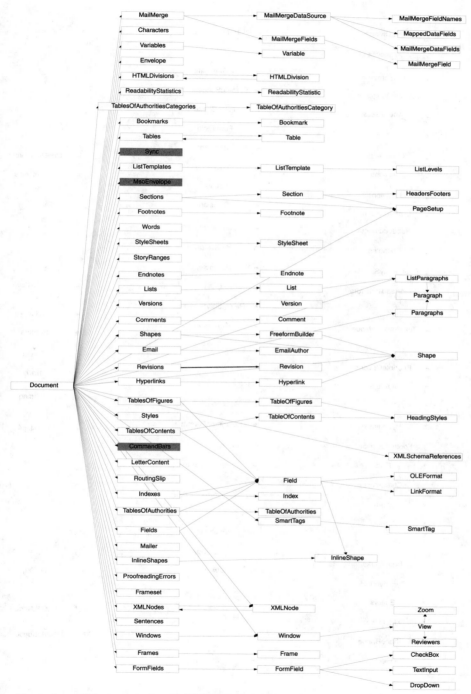

Figure 6-17 Objects associated with Word's Document object.

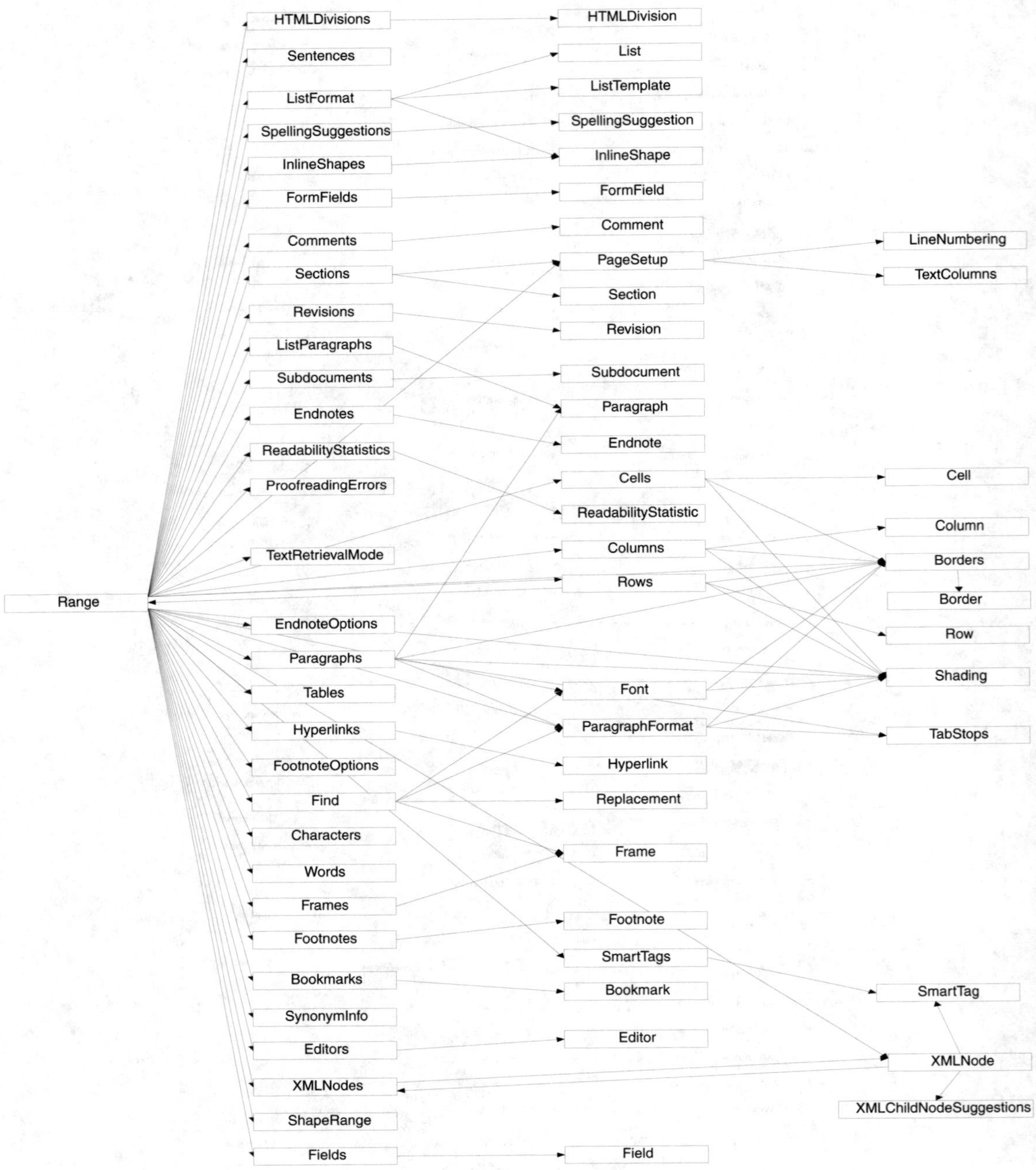

Figure 6-18　Objects associated with Word's Range object.

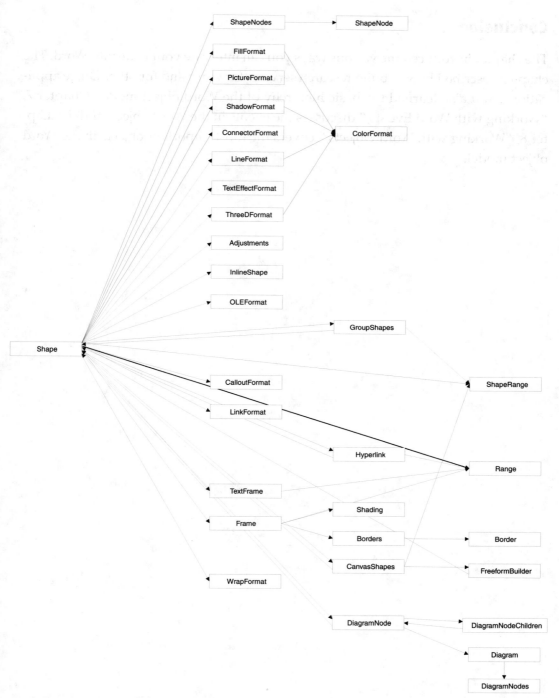

Figure 6-19 Objects associated with Word's Shape object.

Conclusion

The chapter introduced the various ways you can integrate your code into Word. The chapter described how to build research services for Word and for other Office applications. You also learned the basic hierarchy of the Word object model. Chapter 7, "Working with Word Events," discusses the events in the Word object model. Chapter 8, "Working with Word Objects," covers the most important objects in the Word object model.

7

Working with Word Events

Events in the Word Object Model

UNDERSTANDING THE EVENTS IN THE Word object model is critical because this is often the primary way that your code is run. This chapter covers all the events in the Word object model, when they are raised, and the type of code you might associate with these events.

Some of the events in the Word object model are repeated on the Application and Document objects. This repetition allows you to decide whether you want to handle the event for all documents or for a particular document. For example, if you want to know when any document is closed, you would handle the Application object's DocumentBeforeClose event. If you want to know when a particular document is closed, you would handle the Close event on a particular Document object. When an event is repeated on the Application and Document object, it is raised first on the Document object and then the Application object.

Why Are There Multiple Application and Document Event Interfaces?

When you work with the Word Object model, you will quickly notice multiple public interfaces, classes, and delegates that contain the text "ApplicationEvents" and "DocumentEvents":

- ApplicationEvents Interface
- ApplicationEvents_Event Interface
- ApplicationEvents_SinkHelper class
- ApplicationEvents2 Interface
- ApplicationsEvents2_Event Interface
- ApplicationEvents2_* Delegates
- ApplicationEvents2_SinkHelper class
- ApplicationEvents3 Interface
- ApplicationsEvents3_Event Interface
- ApplicationEvents3_* Delegates
- ApplicationEvents3_SinkHelper class
- ApplicationEvents4 Interface
- **ApplicationsEvents4_Event Interface**
- **ApplicationEvents4_* Delegates**
- ApplicationEvents4_SinkHelper class
- DocumentEvents Interface
- DocumentEvents_Event Interface
- DocumentEvents_* Delegates
- DocumentEvents_SinkHelper class
- DocumentEvents2 Interface
- **DocumentEvents2_Event Interface**
- **DocumentEvents2_* Delegates**
- DocumentEvents2_SinkHelper class

The only items from this list that you should ever use in your code are the ones in bold: ApplicationEvents4_Event interface, the ApplicationEvents4_* delegates, the DocumentEvents2_Event interface, and the DocumentEvents2_* delegates. You should only use the ApplicationEvents4_Event interface and the DocumentEvents2_Event interface when you have to cast an object declared as Application or Document to the corresponding event interface because a method name and event name collide. An example of this is the Document object that has both a Close method and a Close event. To disambiguate between the two, you will have to cast the Document object to the DocumentEvents2_Event interface when you want to handle the Close event.

The reason for the other items in this list is partially explained in Chapter 1, "An Introduction to Office Programming." However, this explanation only covers the existence of the SinkHelper class and why there is both an ApplicationEvents/DocumentEvents interface and an ApplicationEvents_Event/DocumentEvents_Event interface. The reason there are multiple numbered event interfaces goes back to the original COM implementation of the Word object model.

The Word Application and Document COM objects are defined by the IDL definition shown in Listing 7-1. Note that the Application object has four event interfaces, and Document has two. ApplicationEvents4 is the default event interface for Word's Application object, and DocumentEvents2 is the default event interface for Word's Document object. ApplicationEvents, ApplicationEvents2, ApplicationEvents3, and DocumentEvents are supported for legacy purposes. Word had to keep these older interfaces in place for backward-compatibility reasons because older versions of Word used these interfaces.

Listing 7-1 The IDL Definition of Word's Application and Document Objects

```
[
  uuid(000209FF-0000-0000-C000-000000000046),
]
coclass Application {
  [default] interface _Application;
  [source] dispinterface ApplicationEvents;
  [source] dispinterface ApplicationEvents2;
  [source] dispinterface ApplicationEvents3;
  [default, source] dispinterface ApplicationEvents4;
};

[
  uuid(00020906-0000-0000-C000-000000000046),
]
coclass Document {
  [default] interface _Document;
  [source] dispinterface DocumentEvents;
```

```
[default, source] dispinterface DocumentEvents2;
};
```

Visual Studio Generation of Event Handlers

As you consider the code in some of the listings in this chapter, you might wonder how you will ever remember the syntax of complicated lines of code such as this one:

```
application.DocumentBeforeClose +=
    new Word.ApplicationEvents4_DocumentBeforeCloseEventHandler(
    app_DocumentBeforeClose);
```

Fortunately, Visual Studio helps by generating most of this line of code as well as the corresponding event handler automatically. If you were typing this line of code, after you type +=, Visual Studio displays a pop-up tooltip, as shown in Figure 7-1. If you press the Tab key twice, Visual Studio generates the rest of the line of code and the event handler method (app_DocumentBeforeClose) automatically.

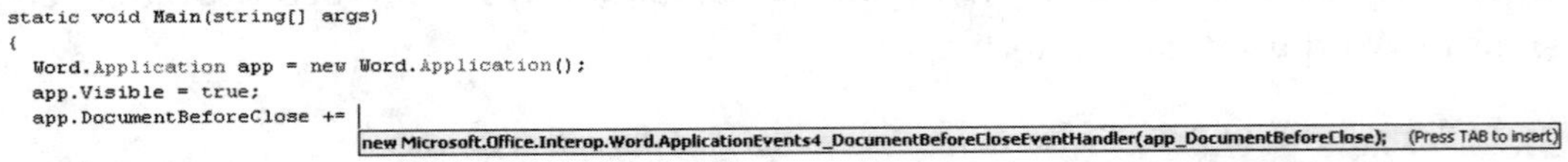

```
static void Main(string[] args)
{
  Word.Application app = new Word.Application();
  app.Visible = true;
  app.DocumentBeforeClose +=
      new Microsoft.Office.Interop.Word.ApplicationEvents4_DocumentBeforeCloseEventHandler(app_DocumentBeforeClose);    (Press TAB to insert)
```

Figure 7-1 Visual Studio generates event handler code for you if you press the Tab key.

If you are using Visual Studio Tools for Office (VSTO), you can also use the Properties window to add event handlers to your document class. Double-click the project item for your document class. Make sure the Properties window is visible. If it is not, choose Properties Window from the View menu to show the Properties window. Make sure that the document class (typically called ThisDocument) is selected in the combo box at the top of the Properties window. Then click the lightning bolt icon to show events associated with the document. Type the name of the method you want to use as an event handler in the edit box to the right of the event you want to handle.

Figure 7-2 shows the Properties window and an event handler we have added by typing the text "ThisDocument_New" in the edit box next to the New event. This will cause the New event to be handled by a method called ThisDocument_New in the document class. If the method does not already exist, Visual Studio will add the method for you.

Figure 7-2 Adding a Document event handler using the Property window in VSTO.

Startup and Shutdown Events

Several events are raised when the application is started and shut down. The Word Application object has a Startup event that is raised when the application is started up before any documents are loaded. However, this event is marked as "restricted" in the COM object model and probably should not be used at all. The only kind of customization that can handle this event is an add-in. The event is raised before documents are loaded and before an automation executable can establish an event handler. Even add-ins do not need to use this event because they already implement OnConnection, which serves the same purpose. Our recommendation is not to use the Application object's Startup event.

For VSTO customizations, we recommend that you use the Startup and Shutdown events raised by VSTO on a document project item. Startup is raised when the document is opened or created from a template. Shutdown is raised when the document is closed. In the project item created for you by VSTO, these events are already connected for you, as shown in Listing 7-2. The InternalStartup method shown in

Listing 7-2 is used by VSTO to connect the Startup and Shutdown event handlers as well as other events you might add using VSTO.

Listing 7-2 A VSTO Customization That Handles the Startup and Shutdown Events

```
public partial class ThisDocument
{
  private void ThisDocument_Startup(object sender, EventArgs e)
  {
  }

  private void ThisDocument_Shutdown(object sender, EventArgs e)
  {
  }

  private void InternalStartup()
  {
    this.Startup += new System.EventHandler(ThisDocument_Startup);
    this.Shutdown += new System.EventHandler(ThisDocument_Shutdown);
  }
}
```

Word raises the Quit event when the application shuts down. Listing 7-3 shows an example of handling the Quit event. Quit is the name of both a method and an event on Word's Application object. Because of this collision, you will not see the Quit event in Visual Studio's pop-up menu of properties, events, and methods associated with the Application object. Furthermore, a warning displays at compile time when you try to handle this event. To get Visual Studio's pop-up menus to work and the warning to go away, you can cast the Application object to the Application-Events4_Event interface, as shown in Listing 7-3.

Listing 7-3 A VSTO Customization That Handles the Quit Event

```
public partial class ThisDocument
{
  Word.Application app;

  private void ThisDocument_Startup(object sender, EventArgs e)
  {
    app = this.Application;
    ((Word.ApplicationEvents4_Event)app).Quit +=
      new Word.ApplicationEvents4_QuitEventHandler(
      App_Quit);
  }
```

```
void App_Quit()
{
  MessageBox.Show("Quit Event Raised");
}

private void InternalStartup()
{
  this.Startup += new System.EventHandler(ThisDocument_Startup);
}
}
```

New and Open Document Events

Word raises a NewDocument event on the Application object and a New event on a Document object when a new document is first created by the user either as a blank document or from a template or existing document. These events are never raised again on subsequent opens of the document. Word also raises a DocumentOpen event on the Application object and an Open event on a Document object when an existing document is opened:

- **Application.NewDocument** is raised whenever a document is created. Word passes the Document that was created as a parameter to this event.

- **Document.New** is raised on a template or a new blank document. So for example, when a document is first created from a template, you can handle the New event to set up the document for the first time. For subsequent opens of the document, you can handle the Open event or the Startup event raised by VSTO.

- **Application.DocumentOpen** is raised whenever an existing document is opened. Word passes the Document that was opened as a parameter to this event.

- **Document.Open** is raised on an existing document when it is opened.

Listing 7-4 shows a VSTO customization that handles the Application object's New-Document event and puts into the footer of every new document created in Word the date the document was created and the name of the user who created the document.

It also handles the Application object's DocumentOpen event to put into the header of an existing document that is opened the date the document was opened and the name of the user who opened the document.

Listing 7-4 A VSTO Customization That Handles the Application Object's NewDocument and Docu- mentOpen Events

```
public partial class ThisDocument
{
  Word.Application app;

  private void ThisDocument_Startup(object sender, EventArgs e)
  {
    app = this.Application;

    ((Word.ApplicationEvents4_Event)app).NewDocument +=
      new Word.ApplicationEvents4_NewDocumentEventHandler(
      App_NewDocument);

    app.DocumentOpen +=
      new Word.ApplicationEvents4_DocumentOpenEventHandler(
      App_DocumentOpen);
  }

  void App_NewDocument(Word.Document document)
  {
    MessageBox.Show(String.Format(
      "NewDocument event on {0}", document.Name));

    Word.Range range = document.Sections[1].Footers[
      Word.WdHeaderFooterIndex.wdHeaderFooterPrimary].Range;

    range.Text = String.Format("Created on {0} by {1}.",
      System.DateTime.Now, app.UserName);
  }

  void App_DocumentOpen(Word.Document document)
  {
    MessageBox.Show(String.Format(
      "NewDocument event on {0}", document.Name));

    Word.Range range = document.Sections[1].Headers[
      Word.WdHeaderFooterIndex.wdHeaderFooterPrimary].Range;

    range.Text = String.Format("Last opened on {0} by {1}.",
      System.DateTime.Now, app.UserName);
  }
```

```
  private void InternalStartup()
  {
    this.Startup += new System.EventHandler(ThisDocument_Startup);
  }
}
```

Listing 7-5 shows VSTO code behind a template that handles the Document object's New event to display the time in the footer when the document is first created from a template. It also handles the Document object's Open event to put into the header the date and user who last opened the document each time the document is opened.

To understand this listing, it is important to understand how Word templates work in VSTO. You should only write handlers for the Document object's New event in a template project. When a user creates a new document from that template, the code associated with the template will be associated with the newly created document, and the New event will be raised on the newly created document.

Listing 7-5 A VSTO Customization That Handles the Document Object's New and Open Events

```
public partial class ThisDocument
{
  private void ThisDocument_New()
  {
    MessageBox.Show("New event");
    Word.Range range = this.Sections[1].Footers[
      Word.WdHeaderFooterIndex.wdHeaderFooterPrimary].Range;

    range.Text = String.Format("Created on {0} by {1}.",
      System.DateTime.Now, this.Application.UserName);
  }

  private void ThisDocument_Open()
  {
    MessageBox.Show("Open event");
    Word.Range range = this.Sections[1].Headers[
      Word.WdHeaderFooterIndex.wdHeaderFooterPrimary].Range;

    range.Text = String.Format("Opened on {0} by {1}.",
      System.DateTime.Now, this.Application.UserName);
  }

  private void InternalStartup()
  {
    this.New += new Word.DocumentEvents2_NewEventHandler(
```

```
        this.ThisDocument_New);
      this.Open += new Word.DocumentEvents2_OpenEventHandler(
        this.ThisDocument_Open);
    }
  }
```

Document Close Events

Word raises events when a document is closed. The DocumentBeforeClose event is raised on the Application object before the document closes, which allows the handler to cancel the closing of the document. The Close event raised on the Document object does not allow canceling the closing of the document.

Unfortunately, the Close event is raised even in cases where the document is not really going to close. The event is raised before a dialog is shown to the user prompting the user to save the document. Users are asked whether they want to save with a Yes, No, and Cancel button. If the user selects Cancel, the document remains open even though a Close event was raised. It is also possible for another add-in to handle the DocumentBeforeClose event and cancel the close of the document. For this reason, it is better to use VSTO's Shutdown event on the document, which is not raised until after the user and any handlers of the DocumentBeforeClose event have been given a chance to cancel the closing of the document.

- **Application.DocumentBeforeClose** is raised before a document is closed. Word passes the Document that is about to close as a parameter to this event. It also passes by reference a `bool` `cancel` parameter. The `cancel` parameter can be set to `true` by your event handler to prevent Word from closing the document.

- **Document.Close** is raised when a document is about to be closed. However, as discussed earlier, the user can still cancel the closing of the document, so you cannot trust this event to tell you whether the document is going to close. Use VSTO's Shutdown event instead.

Close is the name of both a method and an event on the Document object. Because of this collision, you will not see the Close event in Visual Studio's pop-up menu of properties, events, and methods associated with the Document object. Furthermore, a warning displays at compile time when you try to handle this event. To get Visual Studio's pop-up menus to work and the warning to go away, you can cast the Document object to the DocumentEvents2_Event interface, as shown in Listing 7-6.

Listing 7-6 shows a VSTO customization that handles the Application object's DocumentBeforeClose event and the Document object's Close event. In the handler of the DocumentBeforeClose event, the code checks to see if the document contains any spelling errors. If it does, a dialog displays with the number of spelling errors, and the user is told to correct them before closing the document. The `cancel` parameter is set to `true` to prevent the document from closing. Another thing to try when running this code is to press the Cancel button when you are prompted to save and observe that the Document object's Close event fires in this case.

Listing 7-6 A VSTO Customization That Handles the Application Object's DocumentBeforeClose Event and the Document Object's Close Event

```
public partial class ThisDocument
{
  Word.Application app;
  Word.Document doc;

  void ThisDocument_Startup(object sender, EventArgs e)
  {
    app = this.Application;
    doc = app.Documents.Add(ref missing, ref missing,
      ref missing, ref missing);

    doc.Range(ref missing, ref missing).Text =
      "Lawts uf spellin errers!";

    app.DocumentBeforeClose += new
      Word.ApplicationEvents4_DocumentBeforeCloseEventHandler(
      App_DocumentBeforeClose);

    ((Word.DocumentEvents2_Event)doc).Close += new
```

```
        Word.DocumentEvents2_CloseEventHandler(
        Doc_Close);
    }

    void Doc_Close()
    {
      MessageBox.Show("Thanks for fixing the spelling errors.");
    }

    void App_DocumentBeforeClose(Word.Document document,
      ref bool cancel)
    {
      int spellingErrors = document.SpellingErrors.Count;
      if (spellingErrors > 0)
      {
        MessageBox.Show(String.Format(
          "There are still {0} spelling errors in this document.",
            spellingErrors));
        cancel = true;
      }
    }

    private void InternalStartup()
    {
      this.Startup += new EventHandler(ThisDocument_Startup);
    }
  }
```

Document Save Events

Word raises the DocumentBeforeSave event on the Application object before any document is saved. Word passes the Document that is about to be saved as a parameter to this event. It also passes by reference a `bool saveAsUI` parameter and a `bool cancel` parameter. If you set `saveAsUI` to `true`, the Save As dialog displays for the document. If you set the `cancel` parameter to `true`, the save will be canceled. Often this event is handled to implement a custom save routine—for example, you might cancel the DocumentBeforeSave event but call the SaveAs method on Document to enforce a particular file format.

Note that the DocumentBeforeSave event is also raised when Word does an AutoSave on a document. You should be careful that you test your code to make sure that it works properly when AutoSave is triggered.

Listing 7-7 shows a VSTO customization that handles the DocumentBeforeSave event. If the document contains any spelling errors, it cancels the save by setting the `cancel` parameter to `true`. It also sets the `saveAsUI` parameter to `true` to force a Save As dialog to be shown for every save. When the DocumentBeforeSave event is triggered for an AutoSave, the dialog shown in Figure 7-3 displays.

Listing 7-7 A VSTO Customization That Handles the Application Object's DocumentBeforeSave Event

```csharp
public partial class ThisDocument
{
  Word.Application app;

  void ThisDocument_Startup(object sender, EventArgs e)
  {
    app = this.Application;

    app.DocumentBeforeSave += new Word.
      ApplicationEvents4_DocumentBeforeSaveEventHandler(
      App_DocumentBeforeSave);
  }

  void App_DocumentBeforeSave(Word.Document document,
    ref bool saveAsUI, ref bool cancel)
  {
    saveAsUI = true;

    if (document.SpellingErrors.Count > 0)
    {
      MessageBox.Show(
        "You shouldn't save a document with spelling errors.");
      cancel = true;
    }
  }

  private void InternalStartup()
  {
    this.Startup += new EventHandler(ThisDocument_Startup);
  }
}
```

Figure 7-3 The message displayed by Word when an automatic save is cancelled.

Document Activation Events

Word raises several events on the Application object when the active document changes. One such event is the DocumentChange event. The name DocumentChange makes you think that maybe this event would tell you when the contents of the document change—unfortunately, Word does not have a general event that tells you this.

The active document changes when you create a new document—the new document becomes the active document. The active document changes when you open an existing document—the document you opened becomes the active document. The active document changes when you switch between open documents by clicking a document that is not currently active or selecting a document using the Window menu or the Windows taskbar.

It is also possible to have multiple windows viewing the same document—for example, because the user chose New Window from the Window menu. Word raises an event called WindowActivate that tells you when a particular window becomes the active window and an event called WindowDeactivate when a particular window is deactivated. Unlike Excel, switching to another application causes Word's WindowDeactivate event to be raised, and switching back to Word causes the WindowActivate event to be raised.

- **Application.DocumentChange** is raised when the active document changes (not when the contents of the document change). Word passes no parameters to this event. To determine the new active document, you must use the Application object's ActiveDocument property.

- **Application.WindowActivate** is raised when a Word window is activated. This can occur when the user switches between windows within Word or when the user switches to another application and then switches back to

Word. Word passes the Document associated with the window that was activated as a parameter to this event. Word also passes the Window that was activated as a parameter to this event.

- **Application.WindowDeactivate** is raised when a Word window is deactivated. This can occur when the user switches between windows within Word or when the user switches to another application. Word passes the Document associated with the window that was deactivated as a parameter to this event. Word also passes the Window that was deactivated as a parameter to this event.

Listing 7-8 shows a VSTO customization that handles the DocumentChange, WindowActivate, and WindowDeactivate events and displays a message box when these events are raised.

Listing 7-8 A VSTO Customization That Handles the Application Object's WindowActivate, WindowDeactivate, and DocumentChange Events

```
public partial class ThisDocument
{
  Word.Application app;

  void ThisDocument_Startup(object sender, EventArgs e)
  {
    app = this.Application;

    app.WindowActivate += new Word.
      ApplicationEvents4_WindowActivateEventHandler(
      App_WindowActivate);

    app.WindowDeactivate += new Word.
      ApplicationEvents4_WindowDeactivateEventHandler(
      App_WindowDeactivate);

    app.DocumentChange += new Word.
      ApplicationEvents4_DocumentChangeEventHandler(
      App_DocumentChange);
  }

  void App_WindowActivate(Word.Document document,
    Word.Window window)
  {
    MessageBox.Show(String.Format(
      "Window {0} was activated.", window.Caption));
```

```
    }

    void App_WindowDeactivate(Word.Document document,
      Word.Window window)
    {
      MessageBox.Show(String.Format(
        "Window {0} was deactivated.", window.Caption));
    }

    void App_DocumentChange()
    {
      MessageBox.Show(String.Format(
        "The active document is now {0}.",
        app.ActiveDocument.Name));
    }

    private void InternalStartup()
    {
      this.Startup += new EventHandler(ThisDocument_Startup);
    }
  }
```

Document Print Events

Word raises a DocumentBeforePrint event on the Application object before a document is printed. Word passes the Document that is about to be printed as a parameter to this event. It also passes by reference a `bool cancel` parameter. If you set the `cancel` parameter to `true`, the default printing of the document will be canceled. Often this event is handled to implement a custom print routine—for example, you might cancel Word's default print behavior and use the PrintOut method on Document to enforce a certain print format.

Listing 7-9 shows a VSTO customization that handles the DocumentBeforePrint event to enforce some custom print settings. It forces two copies to be printed and collation to be turned on when the user prints the document.

Listing 7-9 A VSTO Customization That Handles the Application Object's DocumentBeforePrint Event

```
public partial class ThisDocument
{
  Word.Application app;

  void ThisDocument_Startup(object sender, EventArgs e)
```

```
  {
    app = this.Application;

    app.DocumentBeforePrint += new Word.
      ApplicationEvents4_DocumentBeforePrintEventHandler(
      app_DocumentBeforePrint);
  }

  void app_DocumentBeforePrint(Word.Document document,
    ref bool cancel)
  {
    // Print 2 copies and collate.
    object copies = 2;
    object collate = true;

    document.PrintOut(ref missing, ref missing, ref missing,
      ref missing, ref missing, ref missing, ref missing,
      ref copies, ref missing, ref missing, ref missing,
      ref collate, ref missing, ref missing, ref missing,
      ref missing, ref missing, ref missing);

    // Cancel because we printed already
    // and don't want Word to print again.
    cancel = true;
  }

  private void InternalStartup()
  {
    this.Startup += new EventHandler(ThisDocument_Startup);
  }
}
```

Mouse Events

Word raises events when the user right-clicks or double-clicks in the document area of a window. If the user right-clicks or double-clicks in an area of the window such as the ruler or the scrollbar, no events are raised.

- **Application.WindowBeforeDoubleClick** is raised when the document area of a window is double-clicked. Word passes the selection that was double-clicked. This can be a range of text or other objects in the document such as a shape. Word also passes by reference a `bool cancel` parameter. The `cancel` parameter can be set to `true` by your event handler to prevent Word from doing the default action associated with a double-click.

- **Application.WindowBeforeRightClick** is raised when the document area of a window is right-clicked. Word passes the selection that was right-clicked. This can be a range of text or other objects in the document such as a shape. Word also passes by reference a `bool cancel` parameter. The `cancel` parameter can be set to `true` by your event handler to prevent Word from doing the default action associated with a right-click.

Listing 7-10 shows a VSTO customization that handles the WindowBefore-DoubleClick and WindowBeforeRightClick events. When the document is double-clicked, this application sets the selected range of text to be all caps. The range of text that is selected depends on where the user double-clicked. If the user double-clicks a word, the selection changes to be the word. If the user triple-clicks, the selection changes to be a paragraph. If the user double-clicks the page margin, the selection changes to be the line next to where the user double-clicked.

When a range of text is right-clicked, this customization sets the range of text to be title case. Finally, if you double-click a shape in the document, the color is set to a dark red. We also set `cancel` to `true` to prevent the shape Properties dialog from being shown when a shape is double-clicked and to prevent the right-click menu from appearing when a range of text is right-clicked.

Listing 7-10 A VSTO Customization That Handles the Application Object's WindowBefore-DoubleClick and WindowBeforeRightClick Events

```
public partial class ThisDocument
{
  Word.Application app;

  void ThisDocument_Startup(object sender, EventArgs e)
  {
    app = this.Application;

    app.WindowBeforeDoubleClick += new Word.
      ApplicationEvents4_WindowBeforeDoubleClickEventHandler(
      App_WindowBeforeDoubleClick);

    app.WindowBeforeRightClick += new Word.
      ApplicationEvents4_WindowBeforeRightClickEventHandler(
      App_WindowBeforeRightClick);
```

```
  }

  void App_WindowBeforeRightClick(Word.Selection selection,
    ref bool cancel)
  {
    if (selection.Type == Word.WdSelectionType.wdSelectionNormal)
    {
      selection.Range.Case = Word.WdCharacterCase.wdTitleWord;
      cancel = true;
    }
  }

  void App_WindowBeforeDoubleClick(Word.Selection selection,
    ref bool cancel)
  {
    if (selection.Type == Word.WdSelectionType.wdSelectionNormal)
    {
      selection.Range.Case = Word.WdCharacterCase.wdUpperCase;
    }
    else if (selection.Type == Word.WdSelectionType.wdSelectionShape)
    {
      selection.ShapeRange.Fill.ForeColor.RGB = 3000;
      cancel = true;
    }
  }

  private void InternalStartup()
  {
    this.Startup += new EventHandler(ThisDocument_Startup);
  }
}
```

Selection Events

Word raises several events when the selection changes in the active document.

- **Application.WindowSelectionChange** is raised when the selection in a document changes. This event is also raised when the location of the insertion point changes within the document because of clicking with the mouse or moving via navigation keys (such as page up and page down). This event is not raised when the insertion point is moved as a result of typing new text into the document. Word passes a Selection object representing the new selection as a parameter to this event. If only the insertion point has moved and no range of text is selected, the Selection object will be passed as a one-character-long Range object containing the character after the current location of the insertion point, and the Type property of the Selection object will return `WdSelectionType.wdSelectionIP`.

- **Application.XMLSelectionChange** is raised when the selected XML element changes in a document with XML mappings. Chapter 22, "Working with XML in Word," discusses using XML mappings in Word. Word passes the new Selection object as a parameter to this event. It also passes the old XMLNode object that was selected previously and the XMLNode object that is now selected. It also passes a reason for the selection change of type `WdXMLSelectionChange`, which can be `wdXMLSelectionChangeReasonDelete`, `wdXMLSelectionChangeReasonInsert`, or `wdXMLSelectionChangeReasonMove`.

Listing 7-11 shows a VSTO customization that uses the Range.Start and Range.End properties to display the start and end location of the selection. The code first checks whether the selection type is `wdSelectionIP` or `wdSelectionNormal`. It also prints the selection type using a helpful feature of Visual Studio—when you use the ToString() method associated with an enumerated type, it displays the string name of the enumeration instead of just displaying a number.

Listing 7-11 A VSTO Customization That Handles the Application Object's WindowSelectionChange Event

```
public partial class ThisDocument
{
  Word.Application app;

  void ThisDocument_Startup(object sender, EventArgs e)
  {
    app = this.Application;

    app.WindowSelectionChange += new Word.
      ApplicationEvents4_WindowSelectionChangeEventHandler(
      App_WindowSelectionChange);
  }

  void App_WindowSelectionChange(Word.Selection selection)
  {
    Word.WdSelectionType selType = selection.Type;
```

```
    MessageBox.Show(String.Format(
      "Selection type is {0}.", selType.ToString()));

    if (selType == Word.WdSelectionType.wdSelectionIP ||
      selType == Word.WdSelectionType.wdSelectionNormal)
    {
      MessageBox.Show(String.Format(
        "Start is {0} and End is {1}.",
        selection.Range.Start, selection.Range.End));
    }
  }

  private void InternalStartup()
  {
    this.Startup += new EventHandler(ThisDocument_Startup);
  }
}
```

Window Sizing Events

Word raises a WindowSize event on the Application object when a window associated with a document is resized. Once again, the behavior of this event is different than the window sizing event in Excel. The WindowSize event in Word is raised even when the document window is maximized to fill the Word application window and the Word application window is resized. The event is not raised for the Word application window when it is resized and no documents are opened.

Word passes the Document object associated with the window that was resized as a parameter to this event. Word also passes the Window object for the window that was resized.

XML Events

Word raises several events when XML elements have been mapped into the document using the XML Structure feature of Word. You have already learned about the Application object's XMLSelectionChange that is raised when the selection changes from one XML element to another. Chapter 22, "Working with XML in Word," considers Word's XML features in more detail.

- **Application.XMLValidationError** is raised when the XML in the document is not valid when compared to the schema associated with the document. Word passes the XMLNode object corresponding to the invalid element as a parameter to this event.

- **Document.XMLAfterInsert** is raised after the user adds a new XML element to the document. If multiple XML elements are added at the same time, the event will be raised for each element that was added. Word passes the XMLNode object for the newly added element as a parameter to this event. It also passes an `inUndoRedo bool` parameter that indicates whether the XML element was added because undo or redo was invoked.

- **Document.XMLBeforeDelete** is raised when the user deletes an XML element from the document. If multiple XML elements are removed at the same time, the event will be raised for each element that was removed. Word passes a Range object representing the range of text that was deleted. If an element was deleted without deleting any text, the Range will be passed as `null`. Word also passes the XMLNode object that was deleted and a `bool` `inUndoRedo` parameter that indicates whether the XML element was deleted because undo or redo was invoked.

Sync Events

Word raises the Document object's Sync event when a local document is synchronized with a copy on the server using Word's document workspace feature. Word passes a parameter of type `MsoSyncEventType` that gives additional information on the status of the document synchronization.

EPostage Events

Word supports a feature called electronic postage, which enables you to create an envelope or label with printed postage that is printed on an envelope or package along with the address. Figure 7-4 shows the Envelopes and Labels dialog box, which has an Add electronic postage check box and an E-postage Properties button that are used to configure electronic postage. Word provides three events to allow third parties to create an e-postage add-in: EPostageInsert, EPostageInsertEx, and

EPostagePropertyDialog. An e-postage add-in is distinguished from other Word add-ins by a special registry key. There can only be one active e-postage add-in installed in Word. This book does not consider these events further because it is unlikely that you will ever need to create your own electronic postage add-in. You can read more about e-postage add-ins by downloading the E-postage SDK at http://support.microsoft.com/?kbid=304095.

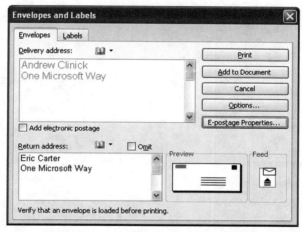

Figure 7-4 The Envelopes and Labels dialog with electronic postage options.

Mail Merge Events

Word raises eight events associated with the mail merge feature. To understand these events, you must first understand how mail merge works and when and why each of these events is raised.

The user starts a mail merge by choosing Mail Merge from the Letters and Mailings menu of the Tools menu. This causes the Application object's MailMergeWizardStateChange event to be raised, notifying us that we are moving from Step 0 to Step 1 of the Mail Merge Wizard. The Mail Merge task pane shown in Figure 7-5 then displays. The Mail Merge task pane is a wizard that can move back and forth through six steps. Whenever you move from step to step, the MailMergeWizardStateChange event is raised. When you close the document, the MailMergeWizardStateChange event is raised, moving from Step 6 back to Step 0.

Step 2 is not shown here—it prompts you as to whether you want to start from the current document or from a template or existing document on disk. In Step 2, we will choose to use the current document. When we get to Step 3 of the Mail Merge Wizard, the user is prompted to select a data source for the mail merge. Figure 7-6 shows Step 3.

Figure 7-5 Step 1 of the Mail Merge Wizard.

Figure 7-6 Step 3 of the Mail Merge Wizard.

We choose Use an existing list and click the Browse link to locate an Access database we have previously created called Authors.mdb. Figure 7-7 shows the dialog to pick a data source.

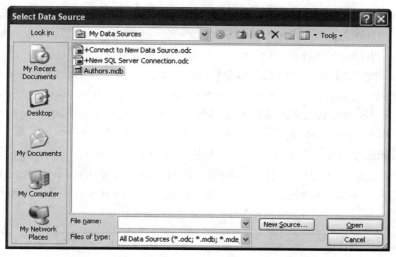

Figure 7-7 Selecting a data source.

After we select the data source and choose Open, the Application object's MailMergeDataSourceLoad event is raised. This event lets us know that a data source has been chosen and we can now examine the data source through the OM. After the MergeDataSourceLoad event has been raised, the Mail Merge Recipients dialog appears, as shown in Figure 7-8. This dialog shows each record in the data source and lets you further control which records you want to use for the mail merge.

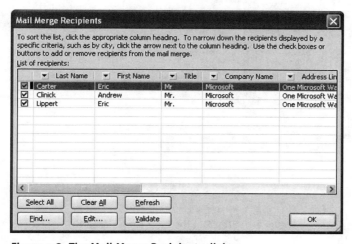

Figure 7-8 The Mail Merge Recipients dialog.

The Mail Merge Recipients dialog has a button called Validate. When clicked, this button raises the Application object's DataSourceValidate event. However, it only raises this event for the special e-postage add-in described earlier.

Step 4 of the Mail Merge Wizard lets you insert address blocks, greeting blocks, and other fields into the body of your document. Step 5 lets you preview the final look of your document when Word loads the data from your data source into the blocks you have defined.

Step 6 displays two actions you can take to complete the mail merge. The first is to print the generated letters. The second is to create a new document and insert each letter into the new document. You can also specify a third action by writing a line of code such as the following before Step 6 of the wizard is shown:

```
document.MailMerge.ShowSendToCustom = "My Custom Action...";
```

The MailMerge object's ShowSendToCustom property takes a `string` value and allows you to add a third custom action defined by your code to do at the end of a mail merge. When the user clicks this custom action, the Application object's MailMergeWizardSendToCustom event is raised. Figure 7-9 shows Step 6 of the Mail Merge Wizard with a custom action called My Custom Action.

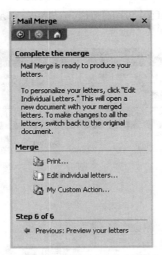

Figure 7-9 Step 6 of the Mail Merge Wizard.

When the user chooses Print or Edit individual letters, the Application object's MailMergeBeforeMerge event is raised. Word passes the start record and the end record that will be merged as int parameters. The default is to merge all the records. When all the records are going to be merged, Word passes 1 for the start record and −16 for the end record. Word also passes by reference a bool cancel parameter. If you set the cancel parameter to true, the mail merge will be canceled.

After the MailMergeBeforeMerge event is raised, Word shows a dialog letting the user change the records to merge, as shown in Figure 7-10. Unfortunately, if the user changes the records to be merged, Word does not re-raise the MailMergeBefore-Merge event. The next time the user does a mail merge, the user's last selection in the dialog will be reflected in the parameters passed to MailMergeBeforeMerge.

Figure 7-10 Selecting the records to merge.

When the user clicks the OK button in the dialog shown in Figure 7-10, the mail merge begins in earnest. Before Word merges a record from the data source to create a letter, it first raises the Application object's MailMergeBeforeRecordMerge event. It then creates the letter from the record and raises the Application object's MailMergeAfterRecordMerge event when the letter for the record has been generated. This sequence of MailMergeBeforeRecordMerge followed by MailMergeAfter-RecordMerge repeats for each record that is going to be merged. When all the records have been merged, Word raises the Application object's MailMergeAfterMerge event and passes the newly created Document object as a parameter if the user chose to Edit individual letters in Figure 7-9. If the user chose Print, null will be passed for the newly created document.

Listing 7-12 shows a VSTO customization that handles all the mail merge events.

Listing 7-12 A VSTO Customization That Handles Mail Merge Events

```
public partial class ThisDocument
{
  Word.Application app;

  void ThisDocument_Startup(object sender, EventArgs e)
  {
    app = this.Application;

    // Have to set ShowSendToCustom so that there is a custom command
    // that can be clicked to raise the MailMergeWizardSendToCustom event
    this.MailMerge.ShowSendToCustom = "My Custom Command";

    app.MailMergeAfterMerge += new Word.
      ApplicationEvents4_MailMergeAfterMergeEventHandler(
      App_MailMergeAfterMerge);

    app.MailMergeAfterRecordMerge += new Word.
      ApplicationEvents4_MailMergeAfterRecordMergeEventHandler(
      App_MailMergeAfterRecordMerge);

    app.MailMergeBeforeMerge += new Word.
      ApplicationEvents4_MailMergeBeforeMergeEventHandler(
      App_MailMergeBeforeMerge);

    app.MailMergeBeforeRecordMerge += new Word.
      ApplicationEvents4_MailMergeBeforeRecordMergeEventHandler(
      App_MailMergeBeforeRecordMerge);

    app.MailMergeDataSourceLoad += new Word.
      ApplicationEvents4_MailMergeDataSourceLoadEventHandler(
      App_MailMergeDataSourceLoad);

    app.MailMergeDataSourceValidate += new Word.
      ApplicationEvents4_MailMergeDataSourceValidateEventHandler(
      App_MailMergeDataSourceValidate);

    app.MailMergeWizardSendToCustom += new Word.
      ApplicationEvents4_MailMergeWizardSendToCustomEventHandler(
      App_MailMergeWizardSendToCustom);

    app.MailMergeWizardStateChange += new Word.
      ApplicationEvents4_MailMergeWizardStateChangeEventHandler(
      App_MailMergeWizardStateChange);
  }

  void App_MailMergeAfterMerge(Word.Document document,
```

```
    Word.Document documentResult)
{
  MessageBox.Show(String.Format(
    "MailMergeAfterMerge: Source = {0}, Result = {1}",
    document.Name, documentResult.Name));
}


void App_MailMergeAfterRecordMerge(Word.Document document)
{
  MessageBox.Show(String.Format(
    "MailMergeAfterRecordMerge for {0}",
    document.Name));
}


void App_MailMergeBeforeMerge(Word.Document document,
  int startRecord, int endRecord, ref bool cancel)
{
  MessageBox.Show(String.Format(
    "MailMergeBeforeMerge for {0}", document.Name));

  // Word passes -16 as the EndRecord if the user
  // chose to merge all records.
  if (endRecord == -16)
  {
    endRecord = document.MailMerge.DataSource.RecordCount;
  }

  MessageBox.Show(String.Format(
    "Merging records from record {0} to record {1}."
    , startRecord, endRecord));
}


void App_MailMergeBeforeRecordMerge(Word.Document document,
  ref bool cancel)
{
  MessageBox.Show(String.Format(
    "MailMergeBeforeRecordMerge for {0}.",
    document.Name));
}


void App_MailMergeDataSourceLoad(Word.Document document)
{
  MessageBox.Show(String.Format(
    "MailMergeDataSourceLoad for {0}.",
    document.Name));

  MessageBox.Show(String.Format(
    "The data source is {0}.",
```

```
      document.MailMerge.DataSource.Name));
  }

  // This event won't fire except for an e-postage add-in
  void App_MailMergeDataSourceValidate(Word.Document document,
    ref bool handled)
  {
    MessageBox.Show(String.Format(
      "MailMergeDataSourceValidate for {0}.",
      document.Name));
  }

  void App_MailMergeWizardSendToCustom(Word.Document document)
  {
    MessageBox.Show(String.Format(
      "MailMergeWizardSendToCustom for {0}.",
      document.Name));
  }

  void App_MailMergeWizardStateChange(Word.Document document,
    ref int fromState, ref int toState, ref bool handled)
  {
    MessageBox.Show(String.Format(
      "MailMergeWizardStateChange for {0}.",
      document.Name));
  }

  private void InternalStartup()
  {
    this.Startup += new EventHandler(ThisDocument_Startup);
  }
}
```

CommandBar Events

A common way to run your code is by adding a custom toolbar button or menu item to Word and handling the click event raised by that button or menu item. Word uses the same object model as Excel to add toolbar buttons and menu items. Chapter 4, "Working with Excel Events," discussed this model in more detail.

One difference between Excel and Word is that Word can save an added toolbar or menu item in a template or a document. The default location that a new toolbar or menu item is saved to is the Normal template (normal.dot). You can specify that the new toolbar or menu item be associated with another template or with a document by using the Application object's CustomizationContext property. The Customization-Context property takes an `object` that is either a Template object or a Document object. Subsequent calls to add toolbars or buttons (for example, a CommandBar-Button) will be saved in the template or document you set using the Customiza-tionContext property.

Listing 7-13 shows a listing similar to the Excel example in Listing 4-9, with two significant differences. First, we use the CustomizationContext property to make it so the toolbar we add will be associated with a particular document. Second, we pass `true` as the last parameter to the various Add methods so that the CommandBar, CommandBarButton, and CommandBarComboBox are added permanently rather than temporarily.

Listing 7-13 A VSTO Customization That Adds a Custom Command Bar

```
public partial class ThisDocument
{
  Word.Application app;
  Office.CommandBarButton btn;
  Office.CommandBarComboBox box;

  void ThisDocument_Startup(object sender, EventArgs e)
  {
    app = this.Application;

    // Store the new command bar in this document.
    app.CustomizationContext = this;

    Office.CommandBars bars = this.CommandBars;
    Office.CommandBar bar = bars.Add("My Custom Bar",
      missing, missing, true);
    bar.Visible = true;

    btn = bar.Controls.Add(
      Office.MsoControlType.msoControlButton,
      missing, missing, missing, true) as Office.CommandBarButton;

    btn.Click += new Office.
      _CommandBarButtonEvents_ClickEventHandler(
      Btn_Click);

    btn.Caption = "Display Message";
    btn.Tag = "WordDocument1.btn";
    btn.Style = Office.MsoButtonStyle.msoButtonCaption;
```

```
    box = bar.Controls.Add(
       Office.MsoControlType.msoControlComboBox,
       missing, missing, missing, true) as Office.CommandBarComboBox;
    box.Tag = "WordDocument1.box";

    box.AddItem("Choice 1", 1);
    box.AddItem("Choice 2", 2);
    box.AddItem("Choice 3", 3);
    box.Change += new Office.
       _CommandBarComboBoxEvents_ChangeEventHandler(
       Box_Change);
}

static void Btn_Click(Office.CommandBarButton ctrl,
    ref bool cancelDefault)
{
    MessageBox.Show("You clicked the button.");
}

static void Box_Change(Office.CommandBarComboBox ctrl)
{
    MessageBox.Show(String.Format(
       "You selected {0}.", ctrl.Text));
}

private void InternalStartup()
{
    this.Startup += new EventHandler(ThisDocument_Startup);
}
}
```

Events in Visual Studio Tools for Office

Several events are found on VSTO objects that are not found when using the Word PIA alone. Table 7-1 lists these events. Almost all of these are events from the Word PIA that are re-raised on different objects. For example, in the Word PIA, there is no BeforeSave event on the Document. However, there is a DocumentBeforeSave event on the Application object that passes as a parameter the Document that is about to be saved. VSTO adds a BeforeSave event to the Document object for Word. The Document object's BeforeSave event is raised whenever the Application object's DocumentBeforeSave event is raised with the given Document object as a parameter.

Another case where VSTO changes events is in the naming of the Close event and the Sync event on the Document object. Both of these event names conflict with method names on Document. To avoid this conflict, VSTO renames these events to CloseEvent and SyncEvent.

VSTO adds events to some objects that have no events at all in the Word PIA. These objects include Bookmark, XMLNode, and XMLNodes. Table 7-1 lists the events added to these objects. You can determine what a particular event does by reading the documentation for the event from which it is re-raised.

Table 7-1 Events That Are Added in VSTO

Events	Re-Raised From
Document Object	
ActivateEvent	Application.WindowActivate
BeforeClose	Application.DocumentBeforeClose
BeforeDoubleClick	Application.WindowBeforeDoubleClick
BeforePrint	Application.DocumentBeforePrint
BeforeRightClick	Application.WindowBeforeRightClick
BeforeSave	Application.DocumentBeforeSave
CloseEvent	Renamed Document.Close event to avoid collisions
Deactivate	Application.WindowDeactivate
MailMergeAfterMerge	Application.MailMergeAfterMerge
MailMergeAfterRecordMerge	Application.MailMergeAfterRecordMerge
MailMergeBeforeMerge	Application.MailMergeBeforeMerge
MailMergeBeforeRecordMerge	Application.MailMergeBeforeRecordMerge
MailMergeDataSourceLoad	Application.MailMergeDataSourceLoad
MailMergeWizardSendToCustom	Application.MailMergeWizardSendToCustom
MailMergeWizardStateChange	Application.MailMergeWizardStateChange
SelectionChange	Application.WindowSelectionChange

continues

Table 7-1 Continued

Events	Re-Raised From
Startup	New event raised by VSTO
Shutdown	New event raised by VSTO
SyncEvent	Renamed Document.Sync event to avoid collisions
WindowSize	Application.WindowSize
Bookmark Object	
BeforeDoubleClick	Application.WindowBeforeDoubleClick
BeforeRightClick	Application.WindowBeforeRightClick
Deselected	Application.WindowSelectionChange
Selected	Application.WindowSelectionChange
SelectionChange	Application.WindowSelectionChange
XMLNode Object	
AfterInsert	Document.XMLAfterInsert
BeforeDelete	Document.XMLBeforeDelete
ContextEnter	Application.XMLSelectionChange
ContextLeave	Application.XMLSelectionChange
Deselect	Application.WindowSelectionChange
Select	Application.WindowSelectionChange
ValidationError	Application.XMLValidationError

Events	Re-Raised From
XMLNodes Object	
AfterInsert	Document.XMLAfterInsert
BeforeDelete	Document.XMLBeforeDelete
ContextEnter	Application.XMLSelectionChange
ContextLeave	Application.XMLSelectionChange
Deselect	Application.WindowSelectionChange
Select	Application.WindowSelectionChange
ValidationError	Application.XMLValidationError

Conclusion

This chapter covered the various events raised by objects in the Word object model. The chapter also examined how VSTO adds some new events to Word objects. Chapter 8, "Working with Word Objects," discusses in more detail the most important objects in the Word object model and how to use them in your code.

▌8▐

Working with Word Objects

Working with the Application Object

THIS CHAPTER EXAMINES SOME OF THE major objects in the Word object
model, starting with the Application object. Many of the objects in the Word
object model are very large, and it is beyond the scope of this book to completely
describe these objects. Instead, this discussion focuses on the most commonly used
methods and properties associated with these objects.

This chapter describes these objects as defined by the primary interop assemblies
for Word. You should be aware that VSTO extends some of these objects (Document,
Bookmark, XMLNodes, and XMLNode) to add some additional functionality such
as data binding support. Part Three of this book, starting with Chapter 13, "The
VSTO Programming Model," covers those extensions.

The Application object is the largest object in the Word object model. The Application
object is also the root object in the Word object model hierarchy. You can access
all the other objects in the object model by starting at Application object and accessing
its properties and the properties of objects it returns. The Application object also
has a number of application-level settings that prove useful when automating Word.

Controlling Word's Screen Updating Behavior

When your code is performing a set of changes to a document, you might want to set the Application object's ScreenUpdating property to `false` to prevent Word from updating the screen while your code runs. Turning off screen updating can also improve the performance of a long operation. Setting the property back to `true` refreshes the screen and allows Word to continue updating the screen.

When changing an application-level property such as ScreenUpdating, always save the value of the property before you change it and set it back to that value when you have finished. Doing so is important because your code will almost never be running by itself inside the Word process—it will usually run along side other code loaded into the Word process.

For example, another add-in might be running a long operation on the document, and that add-in might have set the ScreenUpdating property to `false` to accelerate that operation. That add-in might change the document in some way that triggers an event handled by your code. If your event handler sets the ScreenUpdating property to `false` and then sets it back to `true` when you have finished, you have now defeated the add-in's attempt to accelerate its own long operation. If instead you save the value of ScreenUpdating before you change it, set ScreenUpdating to `false`, and then set ScreenUpdating back to its original value, your code will coexist better with other code running inside of Word.

The best way to do this is to use C#'s support for exception handling to ensure that even if an exception occurs in your code, the application-level property you are changing will be set back to its original value. You should put the code to set the application-level property back to its original value in a `finally` block because this code will run both when no exception occurs and when an exception occurs. Listing 8-1 shows an example of saving the state of the ScreenUpdating property, setting the property to `false`, and then restoring the original value of the property in a `finally` block. VSTO declares a class variable called `missing` of type `object` that is set to `System.Type.Missing`. We pass this class variable by reference to all the optional parameters.

Listing 8-1 A VSTO Customization That Uses the ScreenUpdating Property

```
private void ThisDocument_Startup(object sender, EventArgs e)
{
  Word.Application app = this.Application;
  bool oldScreenUpdateSetting = app.ScreenUpdating;
  Word.Range range = this.Range(ref missing, ref missing);

  try
  {
    app.ScreenUpdating = false;
    Random r = new Random();
    for (int i = 1; i < 1000; i++)
    {
      range.Text = range.Text + r.NextDouble().ToString();
      if (i % 333 == 0)
        app.ScreenRefresh():
    }
  }
  finally
  {
    app.ScreenUpdating = oldScreenUpdateSetting;
  }
}
```

In addition to the ScreenUpdating property, Word's Application object has a Screen-Refresh method. You can call this method to force a refresh of the screen—typically during an operation when you have set ScreenUpdating to `false`. For example, you might do the first few steps of an operation and then refresh the screen to show the user the new state of the document and then perform additional steps and refresh the screen again.

Controlling the Dialogs and Alerts That Word Displays

Occasionally, the code you write will cause Word to display dialogs prompting the user to make a decision or alerting the user that something is about to occur. If you find this happening in a section of your code, you might want to prevent these dialog boxes from being displayed so that your code can run without requiring intervention from the user.

You can set the DisplayAlerts property to a member of the `WdAlertLevel` enumeration. If set to `wdAlertsNone`, this prevents Word from displaying dialog boxes and messages when your code is running and causes Word to choose the default response to any dialog boxes or messages that might display. You can also set the property to `wdAlertsMessageBox` to only let Word display message boxes and not alerts. Setting the property to `wdAlertsAll` restores Word's default behavior.

Be sure to get the original value of this property and set the property back to its original value after your code runs. Use `try` and `finally` blocks to ensure that you set the property back to its original value even when an exception occurs.

Changing the Mouse Pointer

During a long operation, you might want to change the appearance of Word's mouse pointer to an hourglass to let users know that they are waiting for some operation to complete. Word's Application object has a System property that returns a System object. The System object has a Cursor property of type `WdCursorType` that enables you to change the appearance of Word's mouse pointer. You can set it to the following values: `wdCursorIBeam`, `wdCursorNormal`, `wdCursorNorthwestArrow`, or `wdCursorWait`. Listing 8-2 shows the use of the Cursor property.

Listing 8-2 A VSTO Customization That Sets the Cursor Property

```
private void ThisDocument_Startup(object sender, EventArgs e)
{
  Word.Application app = this.Application;
  Word.WdCursorType oldCursor = app.System.Cursor;
  Word.Range range = this.Range(ref missing, ref missing);

  try
  {
    app.System.Cursor = Word.WdCursorType.wdCursorWait;
    Random r = new Random();
    for (int i = 1; i < 1000; i++)
    {
      range.Text = range.Text + r.NextDouble().ToString();
    }
  }
  finally
  {
    app.System.Cursor = oldCursor;
  }
}
```

Displaying a Message in Word's Status Bar or Window Caption

Word lets you set a custom message in the Word status bar, which is at the lower-left corner of Word's window. StatusBar is a property that can be set to a `string` value representing the message you want to display in Word's status bar. Unlike most of the other properties in this section, you cannot save the original value of the StatusBar property and set it back after you have changed it. StatusBar is a write-only property and cannot be read.

You can control the text shown in Word's window caption using the Caption property. Caption is a property that can be set to a `string` value representing the text you want to display in Word's window caption.

Listing 8-3 shows an example of setting the StatusBar property to inform the user of the progress of a long operation. The operation has 1,000 steps, and after every 100 steps the code appends an additional period (.) to the status bar message to indicate to the user that the operation is still in progress.

Listing 8-3 A VSTO Customization That Sets the StatusBar Property

```
private void ThisDocument_Startup(object sender, EventArgs e)
{
    Word.Application app = this.Application;
    string status = "Creating Document...";
    app.StatusBar = status;
    Word.Range range = this.Range(ref missing, ref missing);

    try
    {
        app.System.Cursor = Word.WdCursorType.wdCursorWait;
        Random r = new Random();
        for (int i = 1; i < 1000; i++)
        {
            range.Text = range.Text + r.NextDouble().ToString();
            if (i % 100 == 0)
            {
                status += ".";
                app.StatusBar = status;
            }
        }
    }
    finally
    {
        app.StatusBar = String.Empty;
    }
}
```

Controlling the Look of Word

Word enables you to control the Word user interface through other properties, such as those listed in Table 8-1. Listing 8-4 shows code behind a VSTO Word document that sets many of these properties.

Table 8-1 Properties That Control Elements of the Word User Interface

Property Name	Type	What It Does
DisplayAuto-CompleteTips	bool	Controls whether Word displays auto-complete tips for completing words, phrases, and dates as you type.
DisplayRecentFiles	bool	Controls whether Word displays recently open files in the File menu. You can control how many files Word displays by using the Recent-Files object associated with the Application object and setting the RecentFiles object's Maximum property to a number between 0 and 9.
DisplayScreenTips	bool	Controls whether Word displays pop-up tooltips for text having comments, for foot-notes and end notes, and for hyperlinked text.
DisplayScrollBars	bool	Controls whether Word displays the horizontal and vertical scroll bars for all open documents.
DisplayStatusBar	bool	Controls whether Word displays the status bar for the active document. The value of this property can change when the active document changes.
Height	int	Sets the height in points of the main Word window when WindowState is set to wdWindowStateNormal.
Left	int	Sets the left position in points of the main Word window when WindowState is set to wdWindowStateNormal.
ShowWindowsInTaskbar	bool	Sets whether Word creates a window and task bar button for each open document (true) also called SDI mode or uses one window that contains all open document windows (false), which is also called MDI mode.
Top	int	Sets the top position in points of the main Word window when WindowState is set to wdWindowStateNormal.

Property Name	Type	What It Does
Visible	bool	Sets whether the Word application window is visible.
Width	int	Sets the width in points of the main Word window when WindowState is set to WdWindowState.wdWindowStateNormal.
WindowState	WdWin- dowState	Sets whether the main Word window is mini- mized (wdWindowStateMinimize), maxi- mized (wdWindowStateMaximize) or normal (wdWindowStateNormal). The Width, Height, Left, and Top settings only have an effect when WindowState is set to wdWindowStateNormal.

Listing 8-4 A VSTO Customization and Helper Function That Modifies the Word User Interface

```
private void ThisDocument_Startup(object sender, EventArgs e)
{
  Word.Application app = this.Application;

  app.DisplayAutoCompleteTips = GetBool("Auto complete tips?");
  app.DisplayRecentFiles = GetBool("Display recent files?");
  app.DisplayScreenTips = GetBool("Display screen tips?");
  app.DisplayScrollBars = GetBool("Display scroll bars?");
  app.DisplayStatusBar =
    GetBool("Display status bar for active document?");

  app.ShowWindowsInTaskbar = GetBool("Multiple windows?");
  app.Visible = GetBool("Visible application window?");

  app.WindowState = Word.WdWindowState.wdWindowStateNormal;
  app.Width = 200;
  app.Height = 300;
  app.Top = 50;
  app.Left = 100;
}

private bool GetBool(string message)
{
  return MessageBox.Show(message, "Word UI Demo",
    MessageBoxButtons.YesNo) == DialogResult.Yes;
}
```

Properties That Return Active or Selected Objects

The Application object has a number of properties that return active objects—objects representing things that are active or selected within Word. Table 8-2 shows some of these properties. Listing 8-5 shows code behind a VSTO Word document that examines these properties.

Table 8-2 Application Properties That Return Active Objects

Property Name	Type	What It Does
ActiveDocument	Document	Returns the active Document—the document that currently has focus within Word. If there are no open documents, an exception is thrown.
ActivePrinter	string	Returns a string for the active printer (for example, "Epson Stylus COLOR 860 ESC/P 2 on LPT1:").
ActiveWindow	Window	Returns the active Window. If no windows are open, an exception is thrown.
NormalTemplate	Template	Returns a Template object representing the Normal template (normal.dot).
Selection	Selection	Returns a Selection object that represents the current selection or insertion point in the document.

Listing 8-5 A VSTO Customization and Helper Function That Examine Active Objects

```
private void ThisDocument_Startup(object sender, EventArgs e)
{
  Word.Application app = this.Application;
  ShowItem("ActiveDocument", app.ActiveDocument.Name);
  ShowItem("ActivePrinter", app.ActivePrinter);
  ShowItem("ActiveWindow", app.ActiveWindow.Caption);
  ShowItem("NormalTemplate", app.NormalTemplate.Name);
  ShowItem("Selection", app.Selection.Start.ToString());
}

private void ShowItem(string name, string status)
{
  MessageBox.Show(status, name);
}
```

Properties That Return Important Collections

The Application object has a number of properties that return collections that you will frequently use. Table 8-3 shows several of these properties. Listing 8-6 shows code behind a VSTO Word document that gets the count of these collections and the first item out of each collection.

Table 8-3 Application Properties That Return Important Collections

Property Name	Type	What It Does
CommandBars	Command-Bars	Returns the CommandBars collection, which lets you modify or add to Word's toolbars and menus. Changes made to toolbars and menus are saved in a template or in a document—use the CustomizationContext property to set where changes are stored.
Dialogs	Dialogs	Returns the Dialogs collection, which lets you access the built-in Word dialog boxes (of which there are more than 240). You can show a particular dialog box using this collection.
Documents	Documents	Returns the Documents collection, which contains all the documents currently open in Word.
FontNames	FontNames	Returns the FontNames collection, which contains all the fonts that are currently installed and available for use.
KeyBindings	KeyBind-ings	Returns the KeyBindings collection, which lets you examine, modify, and add key shortcuts that are assigned to Word commands.
RecentFiles	Recent-Files	Returns the RecentFiles collection, which lets you examine and re-open any of the 9 most recently opened files.
TaskPanes	TaskPanes	Returns the TaskPanes collection, which allows you to show or detect which of the 14 built-in task panes are visible.
Templates	Templates	Returns the Templates collection, which lets you examine the installed templates and their properties.
Windows	Windows	Returns the Windows collection, which represents the windows currently open in Word.

Listing 8-6 A VSTO Customization and Helper Function That Examines Collection

```csharp
private void ThisDocument_Startup(object sender, EventArgs e)
{
  Word.Application app = this.Application;

  Show(String.Format("There are {0} command bars.",
    app.CommandBars.Count));

  Show(String.Format("CommandBar 1 is {0}.",
    app.CommandBars[1].Name));

  Show(String.Format("There are {0} dialog boxes.",
    app.Dialogs.Count));

  Show("Click OK to invoke the About dialog...");

  app.Dialogs[Word.WdWordDialog.wdDialogHelpAbout].
    Show(ref missing);

  Show(String.Format("There are {0} open documents.",
    app.Documents.Count));

  object i = 1;
  Word.Document doc = app.Documents.get_Item(ref i);

  Show(String.Format("Document 1 is {0}.",
    doc.Name));

  Show(String.Format("There are {0} fonts.",
    app.FontNames.Count));

  Show(String.Format("FontName 1 is {0}.",
    app.FontNames[1]));

  Show(String.Format("There are {0} key bindings.",
    app.KeyBindings.Count));

  if (app.KeyBindings.Count > 0)
  {
    Show(String.Format("KeyBinding 1 is {0}.",
      app.KeyBindings[1].Command));
  }

  Show(String.Format("There are {0} recent files.",
    app.RecentFiles.Count));

  Show(String.Format("RecentFile 1 is {0}.",
```

```
        app.RecentFiles[1].Name));

    Show(String.Format("There are {0} task panes.",
        app.TaskPanes.Count));

    Show("Click OK to activate the help task pane.");

    app.TaskPanes[Word.WdTaskPanes.wdTaskPaneHelp].
        Visible = true;

    Show(String.Format("There are {0} templates.",
        app.Templates.Count));

    Show(String.Format("Template 1 is {0}.",
        app.Templates.get_Item(ref i).FullName));

    Show(String.Format("There are {0} windows.",
        app.Windows.Count));

    Show(String.Format("Window 1 is {0}.",
        Application.Windows.get_Item(ref i).Caption));
}

private void Show(string text)
{
    MessageBox.Show(text, "Active Objects");
}
```

Accessing Items in Collections

As you might have noticed in Listing 8-6, items in a Word collection are accessed in two different ways depending on whether the index into the collection is strongly typed or weakly typed. In the case of the KeyBindings collection, the index is strongly typed as an integer. As such, you can use the index operator ([]) to get to an item in a collection. The code looks like this:

```
Word.KeyBinding k = Application.KeyBindings[1];
```

For a collection for which the index into the collection is typed as an object passed by reference, you must use the get_Item method of the collection. The Templates collection is an example of this. It has an index of type object passed by reference. This is because you can either pass a string if you know the name of the template in the collection or you can pass an `int` for the index of the template in the collection. To get a Template from the Templates collection by `int` index, you can write this code:

```
object index = 1;
Word.Template t = Application.Templates.get_Item(ref index);
```

To get a Template from the Templates collection by `string` name, you can write this code:

```
object index = "Normal.dot";
Word.Template t = Application.Templates.get_Item(ref index);
```

Note that in both cases, you must declare an `object` first and then pass a reference to the `object`. When passing parameters by reference, you must always declare an `object` variable first and then pass that declared variable by reference.

Visual Studio is not much help when trying to figure this out. It encourages you to use the index operator even on a collection such as Templates, as shown in Figure 8-1. If you try to use the index operator when the index is passed by reference, however, you receive a compile error.

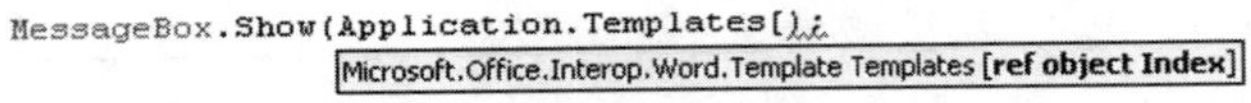

```
MessageBox.Show(Application.Templates[);
```
Microsoft.Office.Interop.Word.Template Templates **[ref object Index]**

Figure 8-1 Visual Studio IntelliSense leads you down the wrong path of using the index operator with an object parameter passed by reference.

Furthermore, Visual Studio IntelliSense doesn't display get_Item as a method you can call on the collection in the popup IntelliSense as shown in Figure 8-2 unless you change your settings to show advanced members. To do this, go to the Options dialog by choosing Options… from the Tools menu. In the tree of options, navigate to Text Editor\C#\General and uncheck the "Hide Advanced Members" check box.

`MessageBox.Show(Application.Templates.);`

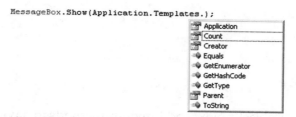

Figure 8-2 Visual Studio IntelliSense does not show the get_Item method when Hide Advanced Members is checked in the Options dialog.

Navigating a Document

The Browser property returns the Browser object, which gives you access to the same functionality available in the browser control that is shown directly below Word's vertical scroll bar, as shown in Figure 8-3.

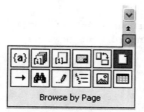

Figure 8-3 Word's browser control.

To use the Browser object, first set the Browser object's Target property to a member of the `WdBrowseTarget` enumeration as shown here:

- `wdBrowseComment`
- `wdBrowseEdit`
- `wdBrowseEndnote`
- `wdBrowseField`
- `wdBrowseFind`
- `wdBrowseFootnote`
- `wdBrowseGoTo`
- `wdBrowseGraphic`

- wdBrowseHeading
- wdBrowsePage
- wdBrowseSection
- wdBrowseTable

Then use the Browser object's Next and Previous methods to navigate from element to element. Listing 8-7 shows an example of this.

Listing 8-7 A VSTO Customization That Uses the Browser Object

```
private void ThisDocument_Startup(object sender, EventArgs e)
{
  // Generate some random text in the document.
  Word.Range r = Range(ref missing, ref missing);
  System.Text.StringBuilder builder = new System.Text.StringBuilder();
  Random rand = new Random();

  for (int i = 0; i < 1000; i++)
  {
    builder.Append(rand.NextDouble().ToString());
    builder.Append(System.Environment.NewLine);
  }

  r.Text = builder.ToString();

  // Browse by page
  Application.Browser.Target = Word.WdBrowseTarget.wdBrowsePage;

  for (int j = 0; j < 10; j++)
  {
    Application.Browser.Next();
    Application.Selection.Text =
      String.Format("<<<<<< PAGE {0} >>>>>>\n", j);
  }
}
```

Note that using this approach also changes the selection in the document, which you often do not want to do. Later in this chapter, you learn about the Range object and the various ways you manipulate text with the Range object without changing the selection. The Range object's Goto, GotoNext, and GotoPrevious methods provide the same kind of navigation control that the Browser object provides, without changing the selection.

Working with Word's Options

The Options property provides access to options you might set via the Options dialog. The Options property returns an Options object that has more than 200 properties that you can set.

Listing 8-8 shows an example that gets and then prompts the user to decide whether to change several of the properties on the Options object. The properties set are options from the Save page of Word's Options dialog. Listing 8-8 also shows the Save page in the Options dialog after prompting the user to change options associated with that page.

Listing 8-8 A VSTO Customization That Uses the Options Object and Shows a Built-In Dialog

```
private void ThisDocument_Startup(object sender, EventArgs e)
{
  Word.Options o = Application.Options;

  o.CreateBackup = DisplayAndSet(
    "Always create backup copy", o.CreateBackup);
  o.AllowFastSave = DisplayAndSet(
    "Allow fast saves", o.AllowFastSave);
  o.BackgroundSave = DisplayAndSet(
    "Allow background saves", o.BackgroundSave);
  o.SavePropertiesPrompt = DisplayAndSet(
    "Prompt for document properties", o.SavePropertiesPrompt);
  o.SaveNormalPrompt = DisplayAndSet(
    "Prompt to save Normal template", o.SaveNormalPrompt);

  Application.Dialogs[Word.
    WdWordDialog.wdDialogToolsOptionsSave].
    Show(ref missing);
}

private bool DisplayAndSet(string settingName, bool settingValue)
{
  string title = "Options Demo";
  string checkState = "unchecked.";
  string action = "check";

  if (settingValue == true)
  {
    checkState = "checked.";
    action = "uncheck";
  }
```

```csharp
    string message = String.Format(
      "{0} is {1}.\nDo you want to {2} it?",
      settingName, checkState, action);

    DialogResult r = MessageBox.Show(message,
      title, MessageBoxButtons.YesNo);

    if (r == DialogResult.Yes)
    {
      return !settingValue;
    }
    else
    {
      return settingValue;
    }
  }
```

Working with the New and Getting Started Document Task Panes

The NewDocument property returns a NewFile object that lets you customize the New Document and Getting Started task panes. The NewFile object is a shared object in the office.dll PIA that defines types in the Microsoft.Office.Core namespace. The NewFile object is also used by Excel because it shares the same task pane infrastructure. To get to the NewFile object in Excel, use the Excel Application object's NewWorkbook property.

In four sections of the New Document task pane, you can add your own documents, templates, or web addresses. These four sections are the New section, the Templates section, the Recently used templates section, and the Other files section. Figure 8-4 shows the New Document task pane and these four sections. You can also add your own document, template, or web address to the Open section of the Getting Started task pane.

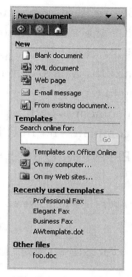

Figure 8-4 The New Document task pane.

The NewDocument property returns a NewFile object that has two methods of interest: Add and Remove. These methods take a file name as a `string`, a member of the `Office.MsoFileNewSection` enumeration to specify the section you want to add or remove from, the display name as a `string` that you want displayed in the task pane, and the action to take when the user clicks the link in the task pane.

The action is specified using a member of the `Office.MsoFileNewAction` enumeration. Possible actions include `msoOpenFile`, which opens the document or URL using Internet Explorer; `msoCreateNewFile`, which creates a new document based on the existing document or template; and `msoEditFile`, which opens an existing document for editing in Word.

Listing 8-9 shows some code that adds a document or hyperlink to each of the four sections in the New Document task pane. It also adds a document to the Getting Started task pane. To show the New Document task pane, the code uses an unusual technique—it finds the command bar control for the File > New command (that has an ID of 18) and executes that command. This is done because the New Document task pane cannot be shown in any other way—it is not accessible through the TaskPanes object as you would expect.

The code in Listing 8-9 also handles the Document object's BeforeClose event to remove the added commands from the task pane. As you saw in Chapter 7,

"Working with Word Events," the BeforeClose event can be raised multiple times for the same document if the user cancels the save or close of the document or if other BeforeClose event handlers cancel the close. In this case, even if the code in the BeforeClose event runs multiple times, the calls to NewFile.Remove do not raise any exceptions if the item you are trying to remove does not exist.

Note that in Listing 8-9 NewDocument is both a property name and an event name. To get the compiler to not complain and IntelliSense to work, we cast the Application object to the Word._Application interface to let the compiler know we want the property and not the event.

Listing 8-9 A VSTO Customization That Adds Links to the New Document Task Pane

```
public partial class ThisDocument
{
  private void ThisDocument_Startup(object sender, EventArgs e)
  {
    Office.NewFile newFile =
      ((Word._Application)Application).NewDocument;

    newFile.Add(@"c:\foo.doc",
      Office.MsoFileNewSection.msoNew,
      "msoNew msoEdit",
      Office.MsoFileNewAction.msoEditFile);

    newFile.Add(@"c:\foo.doc",
      Office.MsoFileNewSection.msoNewfromTemplate,
      "msoNewFromTemplate msoCreateNewFile",
      Office.MsoFileNewAction.msoCreateNewFile);

    newFile.Add(@"c:\foo.doc",
      Office.MsoFileNewSection.msoNewfromExistingFile,
      "msoNewFromExistingFile msoCreateNewFile",
      Office.MsoFileNewAction.msoCreateNewFile);

    newFile.Add(@"http://www.microsoft.com",
      Office.MsoFileNewSection.msoBottomSection,
      "msoBottomSection msoOpenFile",
      Office.MsoFileNewAction.msoOpenFile);

    newFile.Add(@"c:\foo.doc",
      Office.MsoFileNewSection.msoOpenDocument,
      "msoOpenDocument msoEdit",
      Office.MsoFileNewAction.msoEditFile);

    // Execute the "New" command found
```

```
      // in the File menu to show
      // the new document task pane.
      Application.CommandBars.FindControl(
        1, 18, missing, missing).Execute();
    }

  private void ThisDocument_BeforeClose(object sender,
    System.ComponentModel.CancelEventArgs e)
  {
    Office.NewFile newFile =
      ((Word._Application)Application).NewDocument;

    newFile.Remove(@"c:\foo.doc",
      Office.MsoFileNewSection.msoNew,
      "msoNew msoEdit",
      Office.MsoFileNewAction.msoEditFile);

    newFile.Remove(@"c:\foo.doc",
      Office.MsoFileNewSection.msoNewfromTemplate,
      "msoNewFromTemplate msoCreateNewFile",
      Office.MsoFileNewAction.msoCreateNewFile);

    newFile.Remove(@"c:\foo.doc",
      Office.MsoFileNewSection.msoNewfromExistingFile,
      "msoNewFromExistingFile msoCreateNewFile",
      Office.MsoFileNewAction.msoCreateNewFile);

    newFile.Remove(@"http://www.microsoft.com",
      Office.MsoFileNewSection.msoBottomSection,
      "msoBottomSection msoOpenFile",
      Office.MsoFileNewAction.msoOpenFile);

    newFile.Remove(@"c:\foo.doc",
      Office.MsoFileNewSection.msoOpenDocument,
      "msoOpenDocument msoEdit",
      Office.MsoFileNewAction.msoEditFile);
  }

  private void InternalStartup()
  {
    this.Startup += new EventHandler(ThisDocument_Startup);
    this.BeforeClose +=
      new System.ComponentModel.CancelEventHandler(
      this.ThisDocument_BeforeClose);
  }
}
```

Working with the File Save Format Options

The DefaultSaveFormat property enables you to change the default format that Word saves in when the user creates a new document and then saves it. For example, setting DefaultSaveFormat to `"Text"` will cause Word to save new files in a text only format. Setting DefaultSaveFormat to an empty string will cause Word to save in the default file format.

You can also specify that one of the installed file converters be used as the default save format. The FileConverters property returns a collection of available file converters that save in formats such as Works format. Each FileConverter object in the FileConverters collection has a ClassName property that returns a `string`. You can set the DefaultSaveFormat property to the `string` returned by the ClassName property of the FileConverter you want to use as the default save format. For example, the Works 6.0 & 7.0 FileConverter object has a ClassName property that returns `"wks632"`. Setting DefaultSaveFormat to `"wks632"` will make Works 6.0 & 7.0 the default save format.

Working with File Dialogs

Word provides several properties and methods that enable you to change the directory that the Open and Save dialog default to. The ChangeFileOpenDirectory method takes a `string` parameter that is the new path that you want the Open and Save dialog to default to. A change made using this method only lasts until the user exits the application or ChangeFileOpenDirectory is called again during the run of the application.

To permanently change the directory that the Open and Save dialog default to, you can use the Options object's DefaultFilePath property. Prompt the user if you permanently change a setting like this. Users usually do not appreciate it when programs change their settings without asking their permission first.

If you need to display a customized file dialog, you can use the get_FileDialog method, which returns a FileDialog object you can customize and show to the user. The get_FileDialog method takes a required parameter of type `Office.MsoFileDialogType`, which can be one of the following enumerated values: `msoFileDialogOpen`, `msoFileDialogSaveAs`, `msoFileDialogFilePicker`, or `msoFileDialogFolderPicker`.

Listing 8-10 shows an example that gets a FileDialog of type `msoFileDialog-FilePicker` and modifies it to let the user select files from the desktop to copy to their C:\ directory. There are several things to observe in this example. First, the File-Dialog object has several properties that enable you to customize the dialog, including AllowMultiSelect, ButtonName, InitialFileName, InitialView, and Title.

Listing 8-10 also illustrates that showing the FileDialog using the Show method does not do any Word action such as opening files when the user clicks the default button. Instead, it returns an integer value that is –1 if the user clicked the default button and 0 if the user clicked the Cancel button. If the user clicks the default button and Show returns a –1, the code iterates over the FileDialog's SelectedItems collection to get the files that the user selected to copy.

Listing 8-10 A VSTO Customization That Modifies Word's File Dialog

```
private void ThisDocument_Startup(object sender, EventArgs e)
{
  Office.FileDialog f = Application.get_FileDialog(
    Office.MsoFileDialogType.msoFileDialogFilePicker);

  f.AllowMultiSelect = true;
  f.ButtonName = @"Copy to C:\";
  f.InitialFileName = System.Environment.
   GetFolderPath(Environment.SpecialFolder.Desktop);
  f.InitialView = Office.MsoFileDialogView.msoFileDialogViewList;
  f.Title = @"Select files to copy to c:\";
  int result = f.Show();

  if (result == -1)
  {
    foreach (string s in f.SelectedItems)
    {
      System.IO.FileInfo fileName = new System.IO.FileInfo(s);
      System.IO.File.Copy(fileName.FullName, @"c:\" + fileName.Name);
    }
  }
}
```

User Information

Word's Application object has several properties that return user information including UserName, UserAddress, and UserInitials. These `string` properties return the user information the user entered when installing the product. The user can also edit this information by going to Word's Options dialog and editing the fields under the User Information tab.

Checking Grammar and Spelling

Word provides some application-level methods that enable you to use Word's grammar and spelling engine to check arbitrary strings. CheckGrammar is a method that takes a `string` and returns a `bool` value. It returns `true` if the string is deemed grammatically correct by Word's grammar checker and `false` if it is not. Check-Spelling is a method that that takes a `string` and returns `true` if the string is spelled correctly, `false` if the string is not spelled correctly.

The GetSpellingSuggestions method can take a single word that is misspelled and suggest possible correct spellings for the word. It takes a required `string` that is the word to check. It also takes a number of optional parameters. It returns a Spelling-Suggestions collection that contains possible correct spellings.

Listing 8-11 shows a VSTO customization that uses these application-level grammar and spelling checking functions. In Listing 8-11 optional arguments cause the code to get a little verbose. The CheckSpelling and GetSpellingSuggestions methods have multiple optional parameters—many of which are used to specify additional dictionaries to consult.

Listing 8-11 A VSTO Customization That Checks Grammar and Spelling

```
private void ThisDocument_Startup(object sender, EventArgs e)
{
  string badString = "This are grammatically incorrect.";
  string goodString = "This is grammatically correct.";
  string badString2 = "I cain't spel.";
  string goodString2 = "I can spell.";
  string singleWord = "spel";

  MessageBox.Show(String.Format(
    "{0}\nCheckGrammar returns {1}.",
    badString, Application.CheckGrammar(badString)));

  MessageBox.Show(String.Format(
    "{0}\nCheckGrammar returns {1}.",
    goodString, Application.CheckGrammar(goodString)));
```

```
      MessageBox.Show(SpellingHelper(badString2));
      MessageBox.Show(SpellingHelper(goodString2));

      MessageBox.Show(String.Format(
        "Getting spelling suggestions for {0}.", singleWord));

      Word.SpellingSuggestions suggestions =
        Application.GetSpellingSuggestions(
        singleWord, ref missing, ref missing, ref missing,
        ref missing, ref missing, ref missing, ref missing,
        ref missing, ref missing, ref missing, ref missing,
        ref missing, ref missing);

      foreach (Word.SpellingSuggestion s in suggestions)
      {
        MessageBox.Show(s.Name);
      }
    }

    private string SpellingHelper(string phrase)
    {
      bool correctSpelling = Application.CheckSpelling(
        phrase, ref missing, ref missing, ref missing,
        ref missing, ref missing, ref missing, ref missing,
        ref missing, ref missing, ref missing, ref missing,
        ref missing);

      if (correctSpelling)
        return String.Format("{0} is spelled correctly.", phrase);
      else
        return String.Format("{0} is spelled incorrectly.", phrase);
    }
```

Exiting Word

The Quit method can be used to exit Word. If any unsaved documents are open, Word prompts the user to save each unsaved document. When users are prompted to save, they get a dialog box that has a Cancel button. If the user clicks Cancel, or if any code is running that is handling the Application.DocumentBeforeClose event sets the `cancel` parameter to `true`, Word does not quit.

Setting the DisplayAlerts property to `wdAlertsNone` will not suppress Word prompting the user to save. Fortunately, the Quit method takes three optional parameters that can control whether Word prompts the user to save. The first optional parameter, called `SaveChanges`, is of type `object` and can be passed a member of the `WdSaveOptions` enumeration: `wdDoNotSaveChanges`, `wdPrompt-ToSaveChanges`, or `wdSaveChanges`. The second optional parameter, called `OriginalFormat`, is of type `object` and can be passed a member of the `WdOriginalFormat` enumeration: `wdOriginalDocumentFormat`, `wdPromptUser`, or `wdWordDocument`. This parameter controls Word's behavior when saving a changed document whose original format was not Word document format. The final optional parameter is called `RouteDocument` and is of type `object`. Passing `true` for this parameter routes the document to the next recipient if a routing slip is attached.

Listing 8-12 shows a VSTO application that calls Quit without saving changes. It also illustrates an issue where the Quit method and the Quit event collide on the Application object. To get the compiler to not complain and IntelliSense to work, the code casts the Application object to a Word._Application interface to let the compiler know to invoke the method and not the event.

Listing 8-12 A VSTO Customization That Calls Quit

```
private void ThisDocument_Startup(object sender, EventArgs e)
{
  Range(ref missing, ref missing).Text = "Sample text";
  object saveChanges = false;
  ((Word._Application)Application).Quit(
    ref saveChanges, ref missing, ref missing);
}
```

Working with the Dialog Object

This chapter has briefly considered the Dialogs collection returned by the Application object's Dialogs property. You have also learned about the FileDialog object. You now learn in more detail how you can use and display Word's built-in dialogs by using the Dialog object.

Showing the Dialog and Letting Word Execute Actions

After you have a Dialog object, typically by using the Dialog collection's index operator, you can show the dialog in a variety of ways. The simplest way to show the dialog associated with a Dialog object is to call the Show method, which displays the dialog and lets Word execute any action the user takes in the dialog box. The Show method has an optional `TimeOut` parameter of type `object` that takes the number of milliseconds Word will wait before closing the dialog box automatically. If you omit the parameter, Word waits until the user closes the dialog box.

The Show method returns an `int` value that tells you what button the user chose to close the dialog box. If the return value is -1, the user clicked the OK button. If the return value is -2, the user clicked the Close button. If the return value is 0, the user clicked the Cancel button.

Selecting the Tab on a Dialog box

For tabbed dialog boxes, such as the Options dialog, the Dialog object provides a DefaultTab property of type `WdWordDialogTab`. The DefaultTab property can be set before showing the dialog to ensure the dialog comes up with a particular tab selected. `WdWordDialogType` is an enumeration that contains values for the various tabs found in Word's built-in dialogs.

Showing the Dialog and Preventing Word from Executing Actions

Sometimes you will want to show a dialog without letting Word actually execute the action associated with the dialog box. For example, you might want to show the Print dialog box but execute your own custom actions when the user clicks OK in the Print dialog.

The Dialog object has a Display method that will show the dialog while preventing Word from executing the action associated with the dialog. Just as with the Show method, the Display method takes an optional `TimeOut` parameter of type `object` and returns an `int` value that tells you which button the user pressed to close the dialog box.

After you use the Display method to show a dialog, you can use the Execute method to apply the action the user took in the dialog that was shown using the Display method. As an example (one that would likely annoy a Word user), you might show the Print dialog and detect that a user clicked OK. But you might then prompt again to ask whether they are sure they want to print. If the user clicks Yes, you would call the Execute method on the dialog to print the document, as shown in Listing 8-13.

Listing 8-13 A VSTO Customization That Uses Display and Execute to Confirm Printing

```
private void ThisDocument_Startup(object sender, EventArgs e)
{
  Range(ref missing, ref missing).InsertAfter("Test text");
  Word.Dialog d = Application.Dialogs[
    Word.WdWordDialog.wdDialogFilePrint];

  int result = d.Display(ref missing);

  if (result == -1)
  {
    DialogResult r = MessageBox.Show(
      "Are you sure you want to print?",
      "Annoying confirmation",
      MessageBoxButtons.YesNoCancel);

    if (r == DialogResult.Yes)
    {
      d.Execute();
    }
  }
}
```

Getting and Setting Fields in a Dialog

It is possible to prefill fields in a dialog box before showing it and to get fields from a dialog box after showing it. Unfortunately, it is rather difficult and inconsistent in availability and relies on some obscure functionality that originated from the original programming language for Word called Word Basic.

The Dialog object you are working with may have several late-bound properties that can be get and set. A late-bound property does not appear in the type definition for the Dialog object, and so it cannot be seen using IntelliSense. In C#, a late-bound property cannot be called directly; it must be called through reflection. To use a late-bound property, you must first determine what the late-bound property names and types are for a particular dialog box. Then you must use the .NET framework reflection APIs to get and set the property.

The available late-bound properties change depending on the type of dialog that you got from the Dialogs collection. So when you get a wdDialogXMLOptions dialog box, it will have one set of late-bound properties, and when you get a wdDialogFilePrint dialog box, it will have a different set of late-bound properties.

Determining what the late-bound property names are for a particular dialog box involves some searching in older Word Basic help files. To get the Word Basic help files, search the Web for "wrdbasic.exe" to find an installer from Microsoft that installs Word Basic help. After you have installed the Word Basic help file, you can try to find a Word Basic function in the help file that corresponds to the dialog you are using.

The Word Basic function is typically named as a concatenation of the menu name and command name. For example, the Word Basic function for the Print dialog in the File menu is FilePrint. By looking in the Word Basic help file for the FilePrint method, you will find that it has 14 parameters. Table 8-4 shows some of the late-bound properties documented in the Word Basic help file for the FilePrint (and hence the Print dialog box).

Table 8-4 Some Late-Bound Properties Associated with the Print Dialog

Property Name	Type	What It Does
Range	Selected int values	If 1, prints the selection. If 2, prints the current page. If 3, prints the range of pages specified by From and To. If 4, prints the range of pages specified by Pages.
NumCopies	int	The number of copies to print.
Pages	string	The page numbers and page ranges to print, such as "1-10, 15" which would print pages 1 through 10 and page 15.

For newer dialogs that were not around in Word 95 and are not listed in the Word Basic help file, you can try to figure out how to get to a particular dialog option by trial and error. For example, in the XML Options dialog, which is new to Word 2003 (WdWordDialog.wdDialogXMLOptions), you can determine some of the properties by writing reflection code to try to invoke names that seem reasonable based on the names of the controls in the dialog box. If the code fails, you know you guessed the wrong property name. If the code succeeds, you have found a property name. In this way you would discover that AutomaticValidation, IgnoreMixedContent,

ShowAdvancedXMLErrors, and ShowPlaceholderText are some of the properties associated with the XML Options dialog. At this point, however, you are really out there on your own. A search on the Web for "ShowAdvancedXMLErrors," for example, returned no hits—you might be the first person and the last person in the world to use this late-bound property.

Listing 8-14 shows a VSTO customization that prepopulates the Print dialog box with a page range and number of copies to print. It uses reflection to set the Range, NumCopies, and Pages properties on the Dialog object. The helper method Set-PropertyHelper uses reflection to set a late-bound property. The helper method Get-PropertyHelper uses reflection to get the value of a late-bound property. The code in Listing 8-14 will display the Print dialog without allowing Word to execute any actions. The user can change values in the dialog. The code then shows the values of Range, NumCopies, and Pages after the dialog has been displayed.

Listing 8-14 A VSTO Customization That Accesses Late-Bound Properties on a Dialog

```
private void ThisDocument_Startup(object sender, EventArgs e)
{
  // Create 20 pages
  Word.Range r = Range(ref missing, ref missing);
  for (int i = 1; i < 20; i++)
  {
    object pageBreak = Word.WdBreakType.wdPageBreak;
    r.InsertBreak(ref pageBreak);
  }

  Word.Dialog d = Application.Dialogs[
    Word.WdWordDialog.wdDialogFilePrint];

  // Set late-bound properties
  SetPropertyHelper(d, "Range", 4);
  SetPropertyHelper(d, "NumCopies", 2);
  SetPropertyHelper(d, "Pages", "1-10, 15");

  int result = d.Display(ref missing);

  // Get late-bound properties
  MessageBox.Show(String.Format(
    "Range is {0}.",
    GetPropertyHelper(d, "Range")));

  MessageBox.Show(String.Format(
    "NumCopies is {0}.",
```

```
      GetPropertyHelper(d, "NumCopies")));

    MessageBox.Show(String.Format(
      "Pages is {0}.",
      GetPropertyHelper(d, "Pages")));
  }

  private void SetPropertyHelper(object targetObject,
    string propertyName, object propertyValue)
  {
    targetObject.GetType().InvokeMember(propertyName,
      System.Reflection.BindingFlags.Public |
      System.Reflection.BindingFlags.Instance |
      System.Reflection.BindingFlags.SetProperty,
      null,
      targetObject,
      new object[] { propertyValue },
      System.Globalization.CultureInfo.CurrentCulture);
  }

  private object GetPropertyHelper(object targetObject, string propertyName)
  {
    return targetObject.GetType().InvokeMember(propertyName,
      System.Reflection.BindingFlags.Public |
      System.Reflection.BindingFlags.Instance |
      System.Reflection.BindingFlags.GetProperty,
      null,
      targetObject,
      null,
      System.Globalization.CultureInfo.CurrentCulture);
  }
```

Working with Windows

The Application object has several properties that are used to control Word's windows. We have already considered several properties including Width, Height, WindowState, Top, Left, Windows, ActiveWindow, and ShowWindowsInTaskBar.

Word provides some additional methods on the Application object that prove useful for managing windows. The Application object's Activate method is used to make Word the active application when another application has focus. The Application object's Move method is used to move the active window when the WindowState is set to wdWindowStateNormal and takes a Top and Left parameter in pixels. The Application object's Resize method is used to resize the active window when the WindowState is set to `wdWindowStateNormal` and takes a `Width` and `Height` parameter in pixels.

Creating New Windows

The Application object's NewWindow method creates a new window for the active document and returns the newly created Window. This is the equivalent of choosing New Window from the Window menu.

You can also create a new window using the Windows collection's Add method. This method takes an optional `Window` parameter by reference, which tells Word which document to create a new Window for. If you omit the `Window` parameter, Word will create a new window for the active document.

Iterating over the Open Windows

The Windows collection returned by the Windows property of the Application object has a GetEnumerator method that allows it to be iterated over using the `foreach` keyword in C#, as shown in Listing 8-15.

Listing 8-15 A VSTO Customization That Iterates over the Open Windows

```
private void ThisDocument_Startup(object sender, EventArgs e)
{
  // Create 20 windows
  for (int i = 0; i < 20; i++)
  {
    Application.NewWindow();
  }

  foreach (Word.Window w in Application.Windows)
  {
    MessageBox.Show(w.Caption);
  }
}
```

Accessing a Window in the Collection

To access a Window in the Windows collection, you use a method called get_Item, which returns a Window. The get_Item method takes an `Index` parameter by reference that is of type object. You can pass a string representing the caption of the Window or you can pass a 1-based index into the Windows collection. You can check how many items are in a given collection by using the Count property. Listing 8-16 shows both getting a window using a 1-based index and using the caption of a window.

Listing 8-16 A VSTO Customization That Uses get_Item to Get a Window

```
private void ThisDocument_Startup(object sender, EventArgs e)
{
  Word.Application app = this.Application;

  // Create some windows
  app.NewWindow();
  app.NewWindow();
  object stringIndex = app.NewWindow().Caption;

  MessageBox.Show(String.Format(
    "There are {0} windows.",
    app.Windows.Count));

  object index = 1;
  Word.Window w = app.Windows.get_Item(ref index);
  MessageBox.Show(w.Caption);

  Word.Window w2 = app.Windows.get_Item(ref stringIndex);
  MessageBox.Show(w2.Caption);
}
```

Arranging Windows

Word has various ways of arranging windows and synchronizing those windows so that when one window scrolls, other windows scroll as well. The Arrange method enables you to arrange a collection of windows and is the equivalent of selecting Arrange All from the Windows menu. This method takes an optional object parameter by reference that can be passed a member of the WdArrangeStyle enumeration: wdIcons or wdTiled. Passing wdTiled only makes sense when you have put Word into MDI mode by setting the Application object's ShowWindowsInTaskbar to false. You also have to set the WindowState of each Window object to wdWindowStateMinimize if Arrange is to do anything when passed wdTiled.

The CompareSideBySideWith method enables you to synchronize the scrolling of two windows showing two different documents. This method is the equivalent of choosing Compare Side by Side With from the Window menu when you have multiple documents open in Word. The CompareSideBySideWith method takes a Document parameter that is the document you want to compare to the currently active document. To change the currently active document before you call this method, you can use the Document object's Activate method.

After you have established side-by-side mode, you can further control it by calling the ResetSideBySideWith method, which takes a Document parameter that is the document you want to reset side by side with against the currently active document. The SyncScrollingSideBySide property tells you whether you are in side-by-side mode and lets you temporarily disable the synchronization of scrolling. The BreakSideBySide method turns side-by-side mode off.

Listing 8-17 shows an example of first arranging two document windows and then establishing side-by-side mode.

Listing 8-17 A VSTO Customization That Uses the Arrange and CompareSideBySideWith Methods

```csharp
private void ThisDocument_Startup(object sender, EventArgs e)
{
  // Create a second document
  Word.Document doc2 = Application.Documents.Add(
    ref missing, ref missing, ref missing, ref missing);
  Word.Range r1 = this.Range(ref missing, ref missing);
  Word.Range r2 = doc2.Range(ref missing, ref missing);

  // Fill both documents with random text
  Random rand = new Random();
  for (int i = 0; i < 1000; i++)
  {
    string randomNumber = rand.NextDouble().ToString();
    r1.InsertAfter(randomNumber + System.Environment.NewLine);
    r2.InsertAfter(randomNumber + System.Environment.NewLine);
  }

  // Arrange windows
  Application.Windows.Arrange(ref missing);
  MessageBox.Show("Windows are tiled.");

  // Activate this document and synchronize with doc2
  this.Activate();
```

```
    object docObject = doc2;
    Application.Windows.CompareSideBySideWith(ref docObject);
    MessageBox.Show("Windows are in side by side mode.");
}
```

Working with Templates

The Templates property on the Application object returns the Templates collection. The Templates collection provides you with access to the templates available in Word. Like most other collections in Word, you can use `foreach` to iterate over each Template in the Templates collection. You can also use the Templates collection's get_Item method to get to a particular template in the collection, passing by reference an `object` set to a `string` for the name of the template or an `int` for the 1-based index into the collection.

You can also get to a Template object by using the Application object's Normal-Template property, which returns a Template object for normal.dot—the global template that is always open and associated with a document when you have not specified a different template. If you have a Document object and you want to determine what template is associated with it, you can use the Document object's AttachedTemplate. When you get the value of AttachedTemplate, it returns an `object` that you can cast to a Template object. When you set the value of AttachedTemplate, you can pass either a Template object or a `string` containing the filename of the template.

The Template object's OpenAsDocument method enables you to open a template as a document and edit it. The Name property is a `string` property that returns the name of the template, such as `"Template.dot"`. FullName is a `string` property that returns the complete filename of the template, such as `"c:\my templates\Template.dot"`. Path is a `string` property that returns the folder the template is in, such as `"c:\my templates"`.

Types of Templates

The Template object's Type property returns a member of the `WdTemplateType` enumeration that designates the type of the template. A template can be one of three types. Figure 8-5 shows the Templates and Add-ins dialog which illustrates two of the three types. A template can be attached to a document—in this case the template AWTemplate.dot is attached to the active document. A template attached to a document has a type of `wdAttachedTemplate`. The Templates collection will contain an attached template only while the document the template is attached to is opened. When the document associated with the template is closed, the Template object attached to that document will no longer be in the Templates collection (unless of course it is attached to another document that is still open).

A template can also be installed as a global template or add-in. In Figure 8-5, the template SnagIt Add-in.dot is a global add-in template. A global template has a type of `wdGlobalTemplate`. Templates installed in this way are often acting as a simple add-in, providing toolbars or additional menu commands to Word. A template of this type will always be in the Templates collection until it is uninstalled or removed using the Templates and Add-ins dialog.

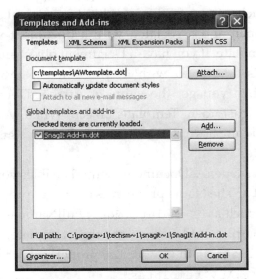

Figure 8-5　The Templates and Add-ins dialog showing the attached template and global templates.

The third type of template is not shown in this dialog. The normal.dot template is always open in Word and is of type `wdNormalTemplate`. This template is always present in the Templates collection.

The Templates collection does not have an Add method. Templates are added indirectly through actions you take with other objects. For example, setting the Document's AttachedTemplate property to change the template attached to a document adds the template to the Templates collection if it is not already there. Opening a document that has an attached template not already in the Templates collection adds the attached template to the Templates collection. Templates with type `wdAttachedTemplate` are removed from the Templates collection when all documents are closed that are using the attached template. You can also add templates of type `wdGlobalTemplate` to the Templates collection using the Add method of the AddIns collection.

Working with Documents

The Documents collection, available from the Application object's Documents property, contains a collection of Document objects currently open in Word. It also has methods used to access a Document in the collection, create a new document, open an existing document, close all the documents, and save all the documents.

Iterating over the Open Documents

The documents collection can be iterated over using the `foreach` keyword in C#. Listing 8-18 shows a simple example of iterating over the open documents in Word and printing the name of each document to the console.

Listing 8-18 Iterating over the Documents Collection Using foreach

```
foreach (Word.Document doc in Application.Documents)
{
  Console.WriteLine(doc.Name);
}
```

Accessing a Document in the Documents Collection

To access a Document in the Documents collection, you use the get_Item method, which returns a Document object. The get_Item method has an `Index` parameter passed by reference that is of type `object`. You can pass an `int` representing the 1-based index of the document in the collection you want to access.

Alternatively, you can pass a `string` representing the name of the document you want to access. The name you pass for a document is the full name of the file if it has been saved (for example, `"c:\Documents and Settings\John\Desktop \Doc1.doc"`). If the document has not yet been saved, the name to pass is the temporary name that Word creates for a new document. This temporary name is typically something like Document1, with no file extension. Listing 8-19 shows an example of calling get_Item with a 1-based index and a `string` index.

Listing 8-19 A VSTO Customization That Uses get_Item to Get a Document

```
private void ThisDocument_Startup(object sender, EventArgs e)
{
  // Add 5 documents
  for (int i = 0; i < 5; i++)
  {
    Application.Documents.Add(ref missing,
      ref missing, ref missing, ref missing);
  }

  // Iterate over the open documents using foreach
  foreach (Word.Document doc in Application.Documents)
  {
    MessageBox.Show(doc.Name);
  }

  // Get a document by 1-based index.
  object index = 2;
  Word.Document doc1 = Application.Documents.get_Item(ref index);
  MessageBox.Show(String.Format(
    "The document at index {0} is {1}.",
    index, doc1.FullName));

  // Get a document by full name
  object stringIndex = doc1.FullName;
  Word.Document doc2 = Application.Documents.get_Item(ref index);
  MessageBox.Show(String.Format(
```

```
        "The document at string index {0} is {1}.",
        stringIndex, doc2.FullName));
}
```

You can also use the Count property to determine the number of open documents. You should check the Count property before accessing a document by index.

Creating a New Document

To create a new document, you can use the Documents collection's Add method. The Add method returns the newly created Document object. It takes four optional by reference parameters of type `object`, as described in Table 8-5.

Table 8-5 Optional Parameters for the Documents Collection's Add Method

Parameter Name	What It Does
Template	Pass the short name of the template to be used (for example, `"mytemplate.dot"`) if the template is in the Templates collection. If the template is not in the Templates collection, pass the full filename to the template (for example, `"c:\mytemplates\template1.dot"`). If you omit this parameter, Word uses the Normal template.
NewTemplate	Pass the `bool` value `true` if the document should be opened as a template. The default is `false`.
DocumentType	Pass a member of the `WdNewDocumentType` enumeration: `wdNewBlankDocument`, `wdNewEmailMessage`, `wdNewFrameset`, or `wdNewWebPage`. The default is `wdNewBlankDocument`.
Visible	Pass the `bool` value `true` if the document should be opened in a visible window. The default is `true`.

Opening an Existing Document

To open an existing document, use the Documents collection's Open method, which returns the opened Document object. The Open method takes one required `object` parameter to which you pass the `string` representing the filename to open. The Open method also takes 15 optional by reference parameters of type `object`, as described in Table 8-6.

Table 8-6 Optional Parameters for the Documents Collection's Open Method

Parameter Name	What It Does
ConfirmConversions	Pass `true` to display the Convert File dialog box if the filename passed to Open is not in Microsoft Word format.
ReadOnly	Pass `true` to open the document as read-only. If the document is already set to read-only on disk, passing `false` will not affect the read-only status of the document. The default is `false`.
AddToRecentFiles	Pass `true` to add the file name to the list of recently used files in the File menu. The default is `true`.
PasswordDocument	Pass a `string` representing the password for opening the document if the document is password protected.
PasswordTemplate	Pass a `string` representing the password for opening the template if the template is password protected.
Revert	If the document you are opening with the Open method is already opened in Word, pass `true` to discard any unsaved changes in the already open document. Pass `false` to activate the already open document.
WritePasswordDocument	Pass a `string` representing the password for saving changes to the document if the document is password protected.
WritePasswordTemplate	Pass a `string` representing the password for saving changes to the template if the template is password protected.
Format	Pass a member of the `WdOpenFormat` enumeration specifying the file conversion to be used when opening the document.

Parameter Name	What It Does
Encoding	Pass a member of the `Office.MsoEncoding` enumeration specifying the code page or character set to be used when you open the document.
Visible	Pass `true` to open the document in a visible window. The default is `true`.
OpenConflictDocument	Pass `true` to open the conflict file for a document that has offline conflicts.
OpenAndRepair	Pass `true` to try to repair a corrupted document.
DocumentDirection	Pass a member of the `WdDocumentDirection` enumeration specifying the horizontal flow of text in the opened document.
NoEncodingDialog	Pass `true` to prevent Word from displaying the Encoding dialog box if the text encoding of the document cannot be determined.

Listing 8-20 shows the simplest possible way to call the Open method to open a document. The code omits all the parameters by passing by reference the `missing` class member variable in VSTO, which is of type `object` and has been set to `System.Type.Missing`.

Listing 8-20 A VSTO Customization That Uses the Open Method to Open a Document

```
private void ThisDocument_Startup(object sender, EventArgs e)
{
  object fileName = "c:\test.doc";

  Word.Document doc = Application.Documents.Open(ref fileName,
    ref missing, ref missing, ref missing,
    ref missing, ref missing, ref missing,
    ref missing, ref missing, ref missing,
    ref missing, ref missing, ref missing,
    ref missing, ref missing, ref missing);

  MessageBox.Show(String.Format(
    "Just opened {0}.", doc.Name));
}
```

Closing All Open Documents

The Close method on the Documents collection closes all the open documents in Word. It takes three optional parameters of type `object` by reference. The first optional parameter, called `SaveChanges`, is of type `object` and can be passed a member of the `WdSaveOptions` enumeration—either `wdDoNotSaveChanges`, `wdPromptToSaveChanges`, or `wdSaveChanges`. The second optional parameter, called `OriginalFormat`, is of type `object` and can be passed a member of the `WdOriginalFormat` enumeration. The second parameter controls Word's behavior when saving a changed document whose original format was not Word document format. This parameter can be passed `wdOriginalDocumentFormat`, `wdPromptUser`, or `wdWordDocument`. The final optional parameter is called `RouteDocument` and is of type `object`. Passing `true` for this parameter routes the document to the next recipient if a routing slip is attached.

It is also possible to close an individual document using the Document object's Close method, as discussed later in this chapter. You have already learned how to use the Application object's Quit method as a third way to close all open documents and quit Word. The Quit method takes the same parameters as Documents.Close and Document.Close.

Saving All Open Documents

The Save method on the Documents collection saves all the open documents in Word. It takes two optional parameters. The first optional parameter, called `NoPrompt`, is of type `object` and can be set to `true` to have Word automatically save all open documents without prompting the user. The second optional parameter, called `OriginalFormat`, is of type `object` and can be passed a member of the `WdOriginalFormat` enumeration. The second parameter controls Word's behavior when saving a changed document whose original format was not Word document format.

It is also possible to save an individual document using the Document object's Save or SaveAs methods, as discussed later in this chapter.

Working with a Document

The Document object represents an open document in Word. The Document object has a Name property that returns a `string` representing the name of the document (for example, `"doc1.doc"`). If the document has not yet been saved, this property returns the temporary name of the document, typically something like Document1.

Document also has a FullName property that returns a `string` representing the full filename of the document if the document has been saved. Once again, if the document has not been saved, this property returns the temporary name of the document, such as Document1. The FullName of the document can be passed to the get_Item method of the Documents collection to access the document by name from that collection. The Path property returns a `string` representing the path to the folder where the document is stored. For example, a document with FullName `"c:\mydocuments\doc1.doc"` returns `"c:\mydocuments"` for the Path property. If the document has not yet been saved, the Path returns an empty string.

The Type property is of type `WdDocumentType` and can be used to determine whether the document is a Word document or a Word template file. A Word document returns the enumerated value `wdTypeDocument`. A template returns the value `wdTypeTemplate`.

Preserving the Dirty State of a Document

Saved is a `bool` property that tells you whether a document needs to be saved. A document that has not been changed, such as a brand new document that has not been typed in yet or a document that has been opened but not edited, returns `true` for Saved. A document that has been changed returns `false` until the user or code saves the document and thereby resets the Saved property to `true`. A document that has been changed but not saved is often referred to as a "dirty" document.

You can also set the value of the Saved property so that a change made by your code does not dirty the document. For example, you might make a change through code to a document but you do not want to actually save the change made by your code unless the user makes some additional change to the document. This is often desirable because when users open a document and do not edit it, they are confused when they are prompted to save because code associated with the document changed the state of the document in some way. You can get the value of the Saved property, make the change to the document, and then set the value of Saved back, as shown in Listing 8-21.

Listing 8-21 A VSTO Customization That Preserves the Dirty State of the Document by Using the Saved Property

```
private void ThisDocument_Startup(object sender, EventArgs e)
{
  bool oldSaved = this.Saved;

  try
  {
    Office.DocumentProperties props = this.
      CustomDocumentProperties as Office.DocumentProperties;

    Office.DocumentProperty prop = props.Add(
      "My Property", false,
      Office.MsoDocProperties.msoPropertyTypeString,
      "My Value", missing);
  }
  finally
  {
    this.Saved = oldSaved;
  }
}
```

Closing and Saving a Document

The Close method enables you to close a document. The Close method takes three optional `object` parameters passed by reference. The first optional parameter, called `SaveChanges`, is of type `object` and can be passed a member of the `WdSaveOptions` enumeration—either `wdDoNotSaveChanges`, `wdPromptToSaveChanges`, or `wdSaveChanges`. The second optional parameter, called `OriginalFormat`, is of type `object` and can be passed a member of the `WdOriginalFormat` enumeration. The second parameter controls Word's behavior when saving a changed document whose original format was not Word document format. This parameter can be passed `wdOriginalDocumentFormat`, `wdPromptUser`, or `wdWordDocument`. The final optional parameter is called `RouteDocument` and is of type `object`. Passing `true` for this parameter routes the document to the next recipient if a routing slip is attached.

The Save method saves the document and does the same thing that choosing Save from the File menu would do. If the document has already been saved, it saves the document to the location it was last saved to. If the document has not yet been saved, it brings up the Save As dialog so that the user can select a place to save the document.

The SaveAs method takes 16 optional `object` parameters passed by reference. It gives you full control over the filename to save to as well as the file format and several other options. Table 8-7 lists the optional parameters of type `object` that are passed by reference to the SaveAs method.

Table 8-7 Optional Parameters for the Document Object's SaveAs Method

Parameter Name	What It Does
FileName	Pass a `string` representing the file name to use for the document. The default is the current FullName of the document.
FileFormat	Pass a member of the `WdSaveFormat` enumeration to specify the file format to save as.
LockComments	Pass `true` to lock the document for comments. The default is `false`.
Password	Pass the password for opening the document as a `string`.
AddToRecentFiles	Pass `true` to add the file name to the list of recently used files in the File menu. The default is `true`.
WritePassword	Pass the password for saving changes to the document as a `string`.
ReadOnlyRecommended	Pass `true` to have Word always suggest the document be opened as read only. The default is `false`.
EmbedTrueTypeFonts	Pass `true` to save TrueType fonts in the document. If omitted, Word will use the value of Document.EmbedTrueTypeFonts.
SaveNativePictureFormat	Pass `true` to save pictures imported from the Mac in their Windows version.
SaveFormsData	Pass `true` to save the data entered by the user entered in a form as a data record.
SaveAsAOCELetter	Pass `true` to save the document as an AOCE letter if the document has an attached mailer.

continues

Table 8-7 Continued

Parameter Name	What It Does
Encoding	Pass a member of the `Office.MsoEncoding` enumeration specifying the code page or character set to be used when you save the document.
InsertLineBreaks	If the document is saved in a text format (for example you passed `WdSaveFormat.wdFormatText` to the FileFormat parameter) pass `true` to insert line breaks at the end of each line of text.
AllowSubstitutions	If the document is saved in a text format, pass `true` to convert some symbols with text that looks similar—for example replace the symbol © with (c).
LineEnding	If the document is saved in a text format, pass a member of the `WdLineEndingType` enumeration to specify the way Word marks line and paragraph breaks.
AddBiDiMarks	If you pass `true`, Word adds control characters to the file to preserve the bidirectional layout of the document.

Working with Windows Associated with a Document

A particular document can have one or more windows associated with it. Even when a document is opened with `false` passed to the `Visible` parameter of the Documents collection's Open method, it still has a window associated with it, albeit a window whose Visible property is `false`. When a document has multiple windows associated with it, you can use the Windows property to return the collection of windows associated with that document. You can determine which of the windows will have the focus when the document is active by using the ActiveWindow property. To activate a particular document and make its ActiveWindow the one with focus, use the Activate method.

Changing the Template Attached to a Document

A document always has a template associated with it. By default, the template is the Normal template (normal.dot), also available from the Application object's Normal-Template property. A document might be associated with some other template, usually because it was created from a particular template.

If you have a Document object and you want to determine what template is associated with it, you can use the AttachedTemplate property. When you get the value of AttachedTemplate, it returns an `object` that you can cast to a Template object. When you set the value of AttachedTemplate, you can pass either a Template object or a `string` containing the filename of the template.

Important Collections Associated with Both Document and Range

The Document and Range objects share a number of properties that return collections you will frequently use. Rather than consider these properties in both this section and the section later in this chapter on Range, they are both covered here only. Table 8-8 shows these properties associated with both Range and Document that return important collection objects.

Table 8-8 Properties Associated with Both Document and Range That Return Important Collections

Property Name	Type	What It Does
Bookmarks	`Bookmarks`	Returns the Bookmarks collection. Bookmarks can be used to mark certain areas of a document and then return easily to those areas of the document. Bookmarks are discussed in more detail in the section "Working with Bookmarks" later in this chapter.
Characters	`Characters`	Returns the Characters collection, which enables you to work with a Document or Range at the level of an individual character. The Characters collection returns one-character long Range objects.
Comments	`Comments`	Returns the Comments collection, which enables you to access comments made by reviewers in the Document or Range.
Endnotes	`Endnotes`	Returns the Endnotes collection, which enables you to access the endnotes associated with a Document or Range.
Fields	`Fields`	Returns the Fields collection, which enables you to access the fields used in a Document or Range.

continues

Table 8-8 Continued

Property Name	Type	What It Does
Footnotes	Footnotes	Returns the Footnotes collection, which enables you to access the footnotes used in a Document or Range.
Hyperlinks	Hyperlinks	Returns the Hyperlinks collection, which enables you to access hyperlinks in a Document or Range.
InlineShapes	Inline-Shapes	Returns the InlineShapes collection, which enables you to access an InlineShape (an InlineShape can include a drawing, an ActiveX control, and many other types of objects enumerated in the Office.MsoShapeType enumeration) that has been inserted inline with the text in a Document or Range.
Paragraphs	Paragraphs	Returns the Paragraphs collection, which enables you to access individual Paragraph objects associated with the Document or Range.
Revisions	Revisions	Returns the Revisions collection, which enables you to access a Revision made in the Document or Range.
Sections	Sections	Returns the Sections collection, which enables you to access a Section within the Document or Range. A new Section can be added using the Break command from the Insert menu.
Sentences	Sentences	Returns the Sentences collection, which enables you to work with a Document or Range at the level of an individual sentence. The Sentences collection returns a Range object for each sentence.
Tables	Tables	Returns the Tables collection, which enables you to access a Table within the Document or Range.
Words	Words	Returns the Words collection, which enables you to work with a Document or Range at the level of an individual word. The Words collection returns a Range object for each word.

Note that the Characters, Sentences, and Words collections are special collections that return Range objects when you iterate over them. Listing 8-22 shows a VSTO customization that uses these collections as well as the Paragraphs collection. It creates a document with some text in it and then a second document to output information about the first document.

Listing 8-22 A VSTO Customization That Uses the Characters, Paragraphs, Sentences, and Words Collections

```
public partial class ThisDocument
{
  private void ThisDocument_Startup(object sender, EventArgs e)
  {
    Word.Range r = this.Range(ref missing, ref missing);
    r.Text = "Whether I shall turn out to be the hero of my own life, or
whether that station will be held by anybody else, these pages must show. To
begin my life with the beginning of my life, I record that I was born (as I
have been informed and believe) on a Friday, at twelve o'clock at night. It
was remarked that the clock began to strike, and I began to cry, simultane-
ously.";

    Word.Document reportDoc = this.Application.Documents.
      Add(ref missing, ref missing, ref missing, ref missing);

    Word.Range report = reportDoc.Range(ref missing, ref missing);

    report.InsertAfter(String.Format(
      "There are {0} paragraphs.\n",
      this.Paragraphs.Count));

    foreach (Word.Paragraph paragraph in this.Paragraphs)
    {
      report.InsertAfter(String.Format(
        "{0}\n", paragraph.Range.Text));
    }

    report.InsertAfter(String.Format(
      "There are {0} sentences.\n",
      this.Sentences.Count));

    foreach (Word.Range sentence in this.Sentences)
    {
      report.InsertAfter(String.Format(
        "{0}\n", sentence.Text));
    }
```

```csharp
    report.InsertAfter(String.Format(
      "There are {0} words.\n",
      this.Words.Count));

    foreach (Word.Range word in this.Words)
    {
      report.InsertAfter(String.Format(
        "{0}\n", word.Text));
    }

    report.InsertAfter(String.Format(
      "There are {0} characters.\n",
      this.Characters.Count));

    foreach (Word.Range character in this.Characters)
    {
      report.InsertAfter(String.Format(
        "{0}\n", character.Text));
    }
  }

  private void InternalStartup()
  {
    this.Startup += new EventHandler(ThisDocument_Startup);
  }
}
```

Important Collections Associated with Document Only

Some properties return collections only associated with Document and not with Range. Table 8-9 shows several of these properties.

Table 8-9 Properties Associated with Document That Return Important Collections

Property Name	Type	What It Does
CommandBars	CommandBars	Returns the CommandBars collection. The CommandBars collection is used to add new toolbars, buttons, and menus to Word.
Shapes	Shapes	Returns the Shapes collection. The Shapes collection contains Shape objects (a Shape can include a drawing, an ActiveX control, and many other types of objects enumerated in the Office.MsoShapeType enumeration) that are not inline with text but are free floating in the document.
StoryRanges	StoryRanges	Returns the StoryRanges collection. The StoryRanges collection provides a way to access ranges of text that are not part of the main body of the document, including headers, footers, footnotes, and so on. The StoryRanges collection's get_Item method is passed a member of the enumeration WdStoryType.
Versions	Versions	Returns information about the different versions of the document if the document is being checked in and out of a workspace.

Working with Document Properties

Document has a BuiltinDocumentProperties property that returns an `object` that can be cast to an Office.DocumentProperties collection representing the built-in document properties associated with the document. These are the properties that you see when you choose Properties from the File menu and click the Summary tab. These include properties such as Title, Subject, Author, and Company. Table 8-10 shows the names of all the document properties associated with a document.

Table 8-10 The Names of the Built-In Document Properties in Word

Application name	Author	Category
Comments	Company	Creation date
Format	Hyperlink base	Keywords

continues

Table 8-10 Continued

Last author	Last print date	Last save time
Manager	Number of bytes	Number of characters
Number of characters (with spaces)	Number of hidden slides	Number of lines
Number of multimedia clips	Number of notes	Number of pages
Number of paragraphs	Number of slides	Number of words
Revision number	Security	Subject
Template	Title	Total editing time

Document also has a CustomDocumentProperties property that returns an `object` that can be cast to an Office.DocumentProperties collection representing any custom document properties associated with the document. These are the custom properties that you see when you choose Properties from the File menu and click the Custom tab. Custom properties can be created by your code and used to store name and value pairs in the document.

The DocumentProperties collection and DocumentProperty object are found in the Microsoft Office 11.0 Object Library (office.dll), which contains objects shared by all the Office applications. These objects are in the Microsoft.Office.Core namespace and are typically brought into Office projects in an Office namespace as shown here:

```
using Office = Microsoft.Office.Core;
```

Listing 8-23 shows an example of iterating over the DocumentProperties collection returned by the CustomDocumentProperties and BuiltInDocumentProperties properties. We get the value of the built-in properties in a `try`/`catch` block because some built-in properties throw exceptions when their value is accessed.

Listing 8-23 A VSTO Customization That Iterates over DocumentProperties Collections

```
private void ThisDocument_Startup(object sender, EventArgs e)
{
  Office.DocumentProperties cProps =
    this.CustomDocumentProperties as Office.DocumentProperties;
```

```
    Office.DocumentProperties bProps =
        this.BuiltInDocumentProperties as Office.DocumentProperties;

    Word.Document doc = this.Application.Documents.Add(
        ref missing, ref missing, ref missing, ref missing);

    Word.Range range = doc.Range(ref missing, ref missing);
    range.InsertAfter("Built-in Document Properties\n\n");

    foreach (Office.DocumentProperty bProp in bProps)
    {
      string name = bProp.Name;
      object value = null;
      try
      {
        value = bProp.Value;
      }
      catch (Exception ex)
      {
        value = ex.Message;
      }

      range.InsertAfter(String.Format(
        "{0} - {1}\n",
        name,
        value));
    }

    range.InsertAfter("Custom Document Properties\n\n");
    foreach (Office.DocumentProperty cProp in cProps)
    {
      range.InsertAfter(String.Format(
        "{0} - {1}\n",
        cProp.Name,
        cProp.Value));
    }
  }
```

To access a DocumentProperty in a DocumentProperties collection, you use the C# indexing syntax (`docProperties[object]`), which returns a DocumentProperty object. The indexer takes an `Index` parameter of type `object`. You can pass an `int` representing the 1-based index of the DocumentProperty in the collection you want to access. Alternatively, you can pass a `string` representing the name of the DocumentProperty you want to access. As with other collections, the Count property returns how many DocumentProperty objects are in the collection.

A DocumentProperty object has a Name property that returns a `string` containing the name of the property. It also has a Value property of type `object` that returns the value of the property. You can check what the type is of `Value` by using the Type property that returns a member of the `Office.MsoDocProperties` enumeration: `msoPropertyTypeBoolean`, `msoPropertyTypeDate`, `msoPropertyTypeFloat`, `msoPropertyTypeNumber`, or `msoPropertyTypeString`.

Listing 8-24 shows how a DocumentProperty is accessed.

Listing 8-24 A VSTO Customization That Accesses a DocumentProperty Using an Indexer

```
private void ThisDocument_Startup(object sender, EventArgs e)
{
  Office.DocumentProperties bProps =
    this.BuiltInDocumentProperties as Office.DocumentProperties;

  Office.DocumentProperty author = bProps["Author"];

  MessageBox.Show(String.Format(
    "Property {0} is set to {1}.",
    author.Name, author.Value));

  Office.DocumentProperty third = bProps[3];

  MessageBox.Show(String.Format(
    "Property {0} is set to {1}.",
    third.Name, third.Value));
}
```

You can add a custom DocumentProperty to a DocumentProperties collection by using the Add method. The Add method takes the parameters shown in Table 8-11.

Table 8-11 The DocumentProperties Collection's Add Method Parameters

Parameter Name	Type	What It Does
Name	`string`	Sets the name of the new property.
LinkToContent	`bool`	Sets whether the property is linked to the contents of the container document.
Type	optional object	Sets the data type of the property. Can be one of the following `Office.MsoDocProperties` enumerated values: `msoPropertyType-Boolean`, `msoPropertyTypeDate`, `msoProp-ertyTypeFloat`, `msoPropertyTypeNumber`, or `msoPropertyTypeString`.

Parameter Name	Type	What It Does
Value	optional object	Sets the value of the property if LinkToContent is `false`.
LinkSource	optional object	Sets the source of the linked property if LinkTo-Content is `true`.

Listing 8-25 shows an example of adding a custom DocumentProperty of type `mso-PropertyTypeString`. Note that Word will let you set the value to a long `string`, but it will truncate it to 255 characters. Fortunately, VSTO enables developers to store larger amounts of data in a document through a feature called cached data. For more information on the cached data feature of VSTO, see Chapter 18, "Server Data Scenarios."

Listing 8-25 A VSTO Customization That Adds a Custom DocumentProperty

```
private void ThisDocument_Startup(object sender, EventArgs e)
{
  Office.DocumentProperties props =
    this.CustomDocumentProperties as Office.DocumentProperties;

  Office.DocumentProperty prop =
    props.Add("My Property", false,
    Office.MsoDocProperties.msoPropertyTypeString,
    "My Value", missing);

  MessageBox.Show(String.Format(
    "Property {0} is set to {1}.",
    prop.Name, prop.Value));
}
```

Checking Spelling and Grammar in Documents and Ranges

You can control the grammar checking in a Document or Range by using the following methods and properties. GrammarChecked is a `bool` property that returns `true` if the grammar in the document or range has been checked. If the grammar has not yet been checked, you can force a grammar check by calling the CheckGrammar method. You can control whether Word shows the grammatical errors in the document by setting the ShowGrammaticalErrors property to `true` or `false`. The

GrammaticalErrors property returns a ProofreadingErrors collection, which is a collection of Range objects containing the ranges of grammatically incorrect text.

A similar set of methods and properties exist for checking spelling. SpellingChecked is a `bool` property that returns `true` if the spelling in the document or range has been checked. If the spelling has not yet been checked, you can force a spelling check by calling the CheckSpelling method. The CheckSpelling takes 12 optional `object` parameters passed by reference that you can omit unless you want to specify additional custom dictionaries to check the spelling against.

You can control whether Word shows the spelling errors in the document by setting the ShowSpellingErrors property to `true` or `false`. The SpellingErrors property returns a ProofreadingErrors collection, which is a collection of Range objects containing the ranges of incorrectly spelled text.

Listing 8-26 shows an example that uses many of these properties and methods.

Listing 8-26 A VSTO Customization That Checks Grammar and Spelling

```
private void ThisDocument_Startup(object sender, EventArgs e)
{
  this.Range(ref missing, ref missing).Text =
    "This are a test of the emegency broadcastin system.";

  if (this.GrammarChecked == false)
    this.CheckGrammar();

  if (this.SpellingChecked == false)
  {
    this.CheckSpelling(ref missing, ref missing,
      ref missing, ref missing, ref missing, ref missing,
      ref missing, ref missing, ref missing, ref missing,
      ref missing, ref missing);
  }

  this.ShowGrammaticalErrors = true;
  this.ShowSpellingErrors = true;

  foreach (Word.Range range in this.GrammaticalErrors)
  {
    MessageBox.Show(String.Format(
      "Grammatical error: {0}",
      range.Text));
  }

  foreach (Word.Range range in this.SpellingErrors)
  {
```

```
    MessageBox.Show(String.Format(
        "Spelling error: {0}",
        range.Text));
    }
  }
```

Printing a Document

The Document object has a PageSetup property that returns a PageSetup object that has several properties for configuring the printing of a document. The PrintOut method can be used to print a document. It has 18 optional `object` parameters passed by reference. Table 8-12 lists some of the most commonly used optional parameters for PrintOut.

Table 8-12 Some of the Optional Parameters for PrintOut

Parameter Name	What It Does
Background	Pass `true` to have PrintOut return immediately and let the code continue while Word prints in the background.
Range	Pass a member of the `WdPrintOutRange` enumeration: `wdPrintAllDocument`, `wdPrintCurrentPage`, `wdPrint-FromTo`, `wdPrintRangeOfPages`, or `wdPrintSelection`.
OutputFileName	Pass the full filename of the file you want to print to when PrintToFile is passed `true`.
From	Pass the starting page number to print from when Range is set to `wdPrintFromTo`.
To	Pass the ending page number to print to when Range is set to `wdPrintFromTo`.
Copies	Pass the number of copies to print.
Pages	When Range is set to `wdPrintRangeOfPages`, pass a `string` representing the page numbers and page ranges to print (for example, "1-5, 15").
PageType	Pass a member of the `WdPrintOutPages` enumeration: `wdPrintAllPages`, `wdPrintEvenPagesOnly`, or `wdPrintOddPagesOnly`.
PrintToFile	Pass `true` to print to a file. Used in conjuction with the OutputFileName parameter.
Collate	Pass `true` to collate.

Listing 8-27 shows a simple example that sets some page margin options using the PageSetup property and then calls PrintOut specifying that two copies be printed.

Listing 8-27 A VSTO Customization That Uses the PrintOut Method

```
private void ThisDocument_Startup(object sender, EventArgs e)
{
  this.Range(ref missing, ref missing).Text =
    "This is a test of printing.";

  // Margins are specified in points.
  PageSetup.LeftMargin = 72F;
  PageSetup.RightMargin = 72F;

  object copies = 2;
  this.PrintOut(ref missing, ref missing, ref missing, ref missing,
    ref missing, ref missing, ref missing, ref copies,
    ref missing, ref missing, ref missing, ref missing,
    ref missing, ref missing, ref missing, ref missing,
    ref missing, ref missing);
}
```

Working with Document Protection

Document protection enables you to protect a Word document so the document can only be edited in certain ways by certain people. Document protection in Word works on the principle of exclusions—you first protect the whole document as read-only, and then mark certain areas of the document as exclusions. This allows your users to edit only the parts of the document that you specify as exclusions.

Figure 8-6 shows the Protect Document task pane that is shown when you choose Protect Document from the Tools menu. The Allow only this type of editing in the document check box has been checked and the drop-down set to not allow any changes. You can optionally allow users to make comments in the document, fill out forms, or make tracked changes to the document.

Given a basic protection level for the document, you can then add some exceptions by selecting the parts of the document that should be editable and checking either a Groups or Individuals check box to allow that group or individual to edit the selection. Word always provides an Everyone group, but you can add groups and individuals by clicking the More users link in the task pane. Clicking this link brings up a dialog that lets you enter a Windows username (DOMAIN\username), Windows user group (DOMAIN\usergroup), or e-mail address.

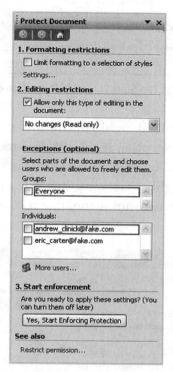

Figure 8-6 The Protect Document task pane.

After you have selected the parts of the document you want to be exceptions and checked the check box next to the groups or individuals you want to be able to edit those parts of the document, click the Yes, Start Enforcing Protection button to protect the document to bring up the Start Enforcing Protection dialog shown in Figure 8-7. Word prompts you for an optional password if you want to require a password to remove the document protection. Word can also use user authentication to protect and encrypt the document to further protect it.

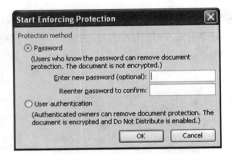

Figure 8-7 The Start Enforcing Protection dialog.

With protection enforced, Word highlights the area of the document that you are allowed to edit based on the exception set for the document. Figure 8-8 shows a document that has been protected but has the first sentence as an editing exception for the Everyone group. Word highlights the regions that you are allowed to edit in the document and provides a task pane for navigating between regions you are allowed to edit.

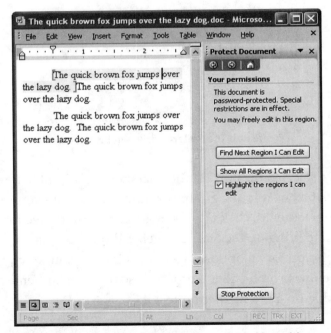

Figure 8-8 A document with protection enforced but with an
exception to allow editing of the first sentence.

Document protection settings apply to code that is talking to the Word object model, too. If the user is not allowed to edit any sentence but the first sentence, code is also restricted to only being able to change the first sentence. If you run code that tries to change protected parts of the document, an exception is raised.

Word provides several properties and methods that enable you to programmatically protect the document and examine protection settings, as listed in Table 8-13.

Table 8-13 Properties and Methods Used with Document Protection

Name	Type	What It Does
ProtectionType	WdProtectionType	Returns the protection type for the document: `wdAllowOnlyComments`, `wdAllowOnlyFormFields`, `wdAllowOnlyReading`, `wdAllowOnlyRevisions`, or `wdNoProtection`.
Permission	Permission	The Permission object lets you work with IRM (Information Rights Management) permissions. This type of protection via IRM permissions is more secure than simple document protection because it involves more validation of identity and encryption of the document.
Protect(…)		The Protect method lets you apply protection programmatically.
Unprotect(…)		The Unprotect method lets you remove protection programmatically.
Range.Editors	Editors	Given a Range that is an exclusion, Range.Editors will return an Editors collection, which lets you inspect the groups and individuals allowed to edit that Range.

Working with Password Protection

In addition to a password that may be associated with document protection, a Word document can have a password that must be entered to open the document. It can also have a second password associated with it that must be entered to modify or write to the document. These passwords can be set by choosing the Tools menu in the Save As Dialog and picking Security Options. Figure 8-9 shows the Security dialog.

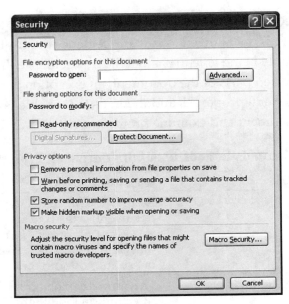

Figure 8-9 The Security dialog.

The Document object's HasPassword property returns `true` if the document has been protected with a password that must be entered to open the document. The Password property is a write-only property that can be set to a `string` value representing the password for the document. Word also has the notion of a password to allow the user to modify or write to the document. If the WriteReserved property returns `true`, the document has been protected with a password that must be entered to modify or write to the document. The WritePassword property is a write-only property that can be set to a `string` value representing the write and modify password for the document.

Undo and Redo

Unlike Excel, Word adds the changes you make with your code to the undo stack. You can undo and redo actions your code or a user has taken using the Document object's Undo and Redo methods. Both methods take by reference an optional object parameter that you can set to the number of undo steps or redo steps you want to take. The UndoClear method clears the undo stack making it so the user can neither undo nor redo any recent actions.

Working with the Range Object

The Range object in the Word object model is the primary way to interact with the content of the document. A Range represents a range of contiguous text and provides a way to interact with that range of text along with any additional elements that are contained in that range of text such as tables, shapes, lists, and bookmarks. You can get and use as many Range objects as you need in your code.

Working with a Range does not change the selection in the document unless you use Range's Select method, which will make the Range you have defined into the active selection. If you are interested in working with the active selection, you can use the Selection object, which shares many properties and methods with the Range object.

A Range has a start and end that are specified in units of characters in the document and include characters that do not print, such as the carriage return between paragraphs. A Range whose start and end are the same is sometimes called a collapsed Range and can be thought of as the equivalent of an insertion point at a particular location in the document.

Word also has the concept of a "story," which is the part of the document that the Range comes from. Most commonly, you work with the main text story, which is the main body of the document. You might also want to get to other text elements in the document such as headers, footers, comments, footnotes and endnotes. These other text elements are different stories from the main text story.

Getting a Range

You have several ways to get a Range. We have already considered several document-level collections such as Sentences, Words, and Characters that return Range objects. The most common way to get a Range is to use the Range method on the Document object. The Range method takes two optional `object` parameters passed by reference—a `Start` and an `End` position. You can pass an `int` value to `Start` and `End` representing the start and end position of the Range you want to get within the document. If you omit the `Start` parameter, it defaults to 0, which is the first position in the document. If you omit the `End` parameter, it defaults to the last position in the document.

Listing 8-28 shows an example of getting a Range object using the Document object's Range method. The Range retrieved has a start index of 0 and an end index of 9. As Figure 8-10 shows, the retrieved Range includes nonprinting paragraph marks.

Listing 8-28 A VSTO Customization That Works with a Range Object

```
private void ThisDocument_Startup(object sender, EventArgs e)
{
  Word.Range r = this.Range(ref missing, ref missing);

  r.Text = "This\nis\na\ntest.";

  object startIndex = 0;
  object endIndex = 9;

  Word.Range r2 = this.Range(ref startIndex, ref endIndex);
  r2.Select();
  string result = r2.Text;

  MessageBox.Show(result.Length.ToString());
  MessageBox.Show(r2.Text);
}
```

Figure 8-10 The result of running Listing 8-28—a range of length 9, including nonprinting paragraph characters.

Another way to get a Range is by using the Document object's StoryRanges collection. The StoryRanges collection enables you to get a Range that is not part of the main document, such as a Range within headers, footers, or endnotes. This collection has an index operator that takes a member of the WdStoryType enumeration that specifies what StoryRange you want to access. Listing 8-29 shows some code that iterates over the StoryRanges in the document and displays the type of each StoryRange.

Listing 8-29 A VSTO Customization That Iterates over the StoryRanges in the Document

```
private void ThisDocument_Startup(object sender, EventArgs e)
{
  Word.Range mainTextStory = this.StoryRanges[
    Word.WdStoryType.wdMainTextStory];

  foreach (Word.Range range in this.StoryRanges)
  {
    MessageBox.Show(String.Format(
      "Story range {0} has length {1}.",
      range.StoryType.ToString(), range.StoryLength));
  }
}
```

Another way to a get a Range is by getting it from the current selection. The Application object's Selection property returns the active selection in the active document as a Selection object. The Selection object has a Range property that returns a Range object that you can work with without affecting the selection (unless you change the Range in some way that forces the selection to reset such as by replacing the text in the selection). Before getting a Range from a Selection object, verify that the Selection contains a valid Range by checking the Selection object's Type property. For example, the user could have selected a shape in the document, in which case the Range would not be applicable when retrieved from Selection.Range. Listing 8-30 shows an example that checks the Selection.Type property before using Selection.Range. It also checks whether Selection is null, which is a bit of overkill for this example. This case would only arise if no documents are open.

Listing 8-30 A VSTO Customization That Gets a Range Object from a Selection Object

```
private void ThisDocument_Startup(object sender, EventArgs e)
{
  Word.Selection s = this.Application.Selection;

  if (s != null)
  {
    if (s.Type == Word.WdSelectionType.wdSelectionNormal)
    {
      Word.Range r = s.Range;
      MessageBox(r.Text);
    }
  }
}
```

Identifying a Range

A Range has several properties to help identify it. The Start and End property return the start and end character index of the Range. The Document property returns the document object the Range is associated with. The StoryType property returns a member of the WdStoryType enumeration identifying the StoryRange with which the Range is associated.

The get_Information method takes a parameter of type WdInformation and returns information as an object about the Range depending on the enumerated value that is passed to the method. Listing 8-31 shows an example of getting the information associated with a range. If you call get_Information on a Range with an enumerated type that is not applicable, get_Information will return –1 as a return value.

Listing 8-31 A VSTO Customization That Gets Information About a Range

```
private void ThisDocument_Startup(object sender, EventArgs e)
{
  Word.Range r = this.Range(ref missing, ref missing);

  r.Text = "This\nis\na\ntest.";

  object startIndex = 0;
  object endIndex = 9;

  Word.Range r2 = this.Range(ref startIndex, ref endIndex);
  r2.InsertAfter("\n");

  for (int i = 1; i < 27; i++)
  {
    GetInfo(r2, (Word.WdInformation)i);
  }
}

private void GetInfo(Word.Range r, Word.WdInformation info)
{
  string result = String.Format(
    "Range.Information({0}) returns {1}.\n",
    info.ToString(), r.get_Information(info));
  r.InsertAfter(result);
}
```

Changing a Range

Given a Range object, a number of properties and methods enable you to change what a Range refers to. A simple way to modify a Range object is to set the values of the Start and End properties. In addition, you can use several methods to change the Range in other ways.

The Expand method expands a Range so that it encompasses the units of the enumeration WdUnits: wdCharacter, wdWord, wdSentence, wdParagraph, wdSection, wdStory, wdCell, wdColumn, wdRow, or wdTable. The Expand method takes a range that only partially covers one of these units and expands it so that the range includes the unit specified.

For example, consider Figure 8-11. For this and subsequent figures, we have turned on Word's formatting marks (Tools > Options > View > Formatting Marks > All) so that you can see clearly the spaces and any paragraph marks in the text. The original Range is shown in white text on a black background. The expanded Range after calling Expand with wdWord is shown by the larger border. The original Range only contained e qui—the last part of the word *The* and the first part of the word *quick*. Calling Expand with wdWord expands the range so that it covers complete words. The expanded Range after calling Expand contains The quick as well as the space after the word *quick*.

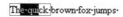

Figure 8-11 Result of calling Expand(WdUnits.wdWord) on a Range.

Figure 8-12 shows another example where only three characters of a word are selected. Calling Expand with wdWord expands the Range so that it covers the complete word *quick* as well as the space after the word *quick*.

Figure 8-12 Result of calling Expand(WdUnits.wdWord) on a Range.

Note that calling Expand repeatedly on a Range passing `wdWord` does not expand the Range to cover additional words. After a Range no longer contains any partial words, calling Expand with `wdWord` has no effect. It also follows that a Range that does not start or end with any partial words to start with will not be changed when you call Expand and pass `wdWord`. This applies to the other members of the WdUnits enumeration. For example, when a Range does not contain any partial sentences, calling Expand with `wdSentence` has no effect.

Figure 8-13 shows an example of calling Expand passing `wdSentence`. The original Range contains parts of two sentences. The result of calling Expand is that two complete sentences are made part of the Range.

Figure 8-13 Result of calling Expand(WdUnits.wdSentence) on a Range.

Figure 8-14 shows another example of calling Expand passing `wdSentence`. The original Range contains just `dog`. Expanding the Range adds the rest of the sentence plus the spaces after the sentence.

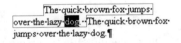

Figure 8-14 Result of calling Expand(WdUnits.wdSentence) on a Range.

The Expand method can change both the start and the end of a Range. The EndOf method works in a similar way to the Expand method but only changes the end of a Range. The EndOf method takes by reference two optional parameters of type `object`: `Unit` and `Extend`. The `Unit` parameter can be passed a member of the `WdUnits` enumeration. The `Extend` parameter can be passed a member of the `WdMovementType` enumeration: `wdMove` or `wdExtend`. If you pass `wdExtend`, the EndOf method acts like the Expand method would if it were not allowed to change the start of a Range. Figure 8-15 shows an example of calling EndOf passing `wdWord` and `wdExtend`. It expands the Range to cover the partial word at the end of the Range but does not expand to cover the partial word at the beginning of the Range.

The·quick·brown·fox·jumps·

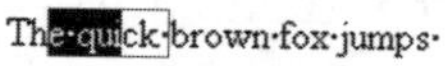

Figure 8-15 Result of calling EndOf(WdUnits.wdWord, WdMovementType.wdExtend) on a Range.

If you pass wdMove for the second parameter (which is the default if you omit the parameter), EndOf returns a Range whose start and end is equal—effectively returning you an insertion point at the end of the expansion. Figure 8-16 shows a Range that initially partially covers two words. Calling EndOf on this Range and passing wdMove for the second parameter yields a Range whose start and end is 10—at the end of the second word.

The·quick·brown·fox·jumps·

Figure 8-16 Result of calling EndOf(WdUnits.wdWord, WdMovementType.wdMove) on a Range.

The StartOf method works like the EndOf method but only changes the start of the range. The StartOf method takes by reference two optional parameters of type `object`: `Unit` and `Extend`. The `Unit` parameter can be passed a member of the `WdUnits` enumeration. The Extend parameter can be passed a member of the `WdMovementType` enumeration: `wdMove` or `wdExtend`. If you pass `wdExtend`, the StartOf method acts like the Expand method would if it were not allowed to change the end of a range. Figure 8-17 shows an example of calling StartOf passing `wdWord` and `wdExtend`. It expands the Range to cover the partial word at the beginning of the Range but does not expand to cover the partial word at the end of the Range.

The·quick·brown·fox·jumps·

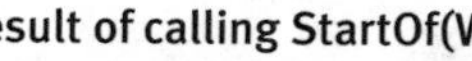

Figure 8-17 Result of calling StartOf(WdUnits.wdWord, WdMovementType.wdExtend) on a Range.

As with EndOf, the StartOf method when passed `wdMove` for the second parameter returns a Range whose start and end is equal—effectively returning you an insertion point at the beginning of the expansion. Figure 8-18 shows a Range containing a word at the end of a sentence. Calling StartOf and passing `wdSentence` and `wdMove` yields a Range where start and end are 0—effectively an insertion point at the beginning of the sentence.

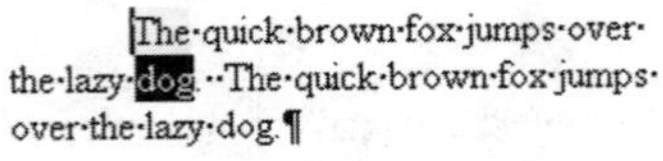

The·quick·brown·fox·jumps·over·the·lazy·dog.···The·quick·brown·fox·jumps·over·the·lazy·dog.¶

Figure 8-18 Result of calling StartOf(WdUnits.wdSentence, WdMovementType.wdMove) on a Range.

Moving a Range

The Move method can be called repeatedly to move a Range by WdUnit through the document. It does not expand the Range, but instead moves the Range, creating a Range whose start and end are equal. The Move method takes by reference optional `Unit` and `Count` parameters of type `object`. For `Unit`, you pass the member of the `WdUnit` enumeration that you want to move by. The default value of `Unit` is `wdCharacter`. For Count, you pass a positive or negative `int` specifying how many units you want to move forward or backward. The Move method returns the number of units by which the Range was moved or returns 0 if the Range was not moved. Figure 8-19 shows an example of calling Move passing `wdWord` and 1. Figure 8-20 shows an example of calling Move passing `wdWord` and −1. In the first case, the Range moves to the start of the next word. In the latter case, the Range moves to the beginning of the partially selected word.

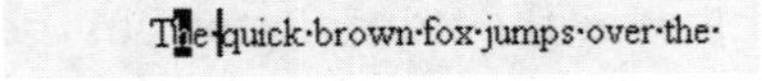

The·quick·brown·fox·jumps·over·the·

Figure 8-19 Result of calling Move(WdUnits.wdWord, 1) on a Range containing *h* from *The*.

The·quick·brown·fox·jumps·over·the·

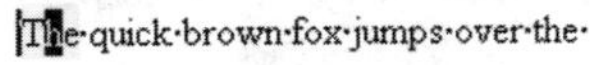

Figure 8-20 Result of calling Move(WdUnits.wdWord, -1) on a Range containing *h* from *The*.

The Next method works like Move when passed a positive count. Instead of modifying the Range directly, it returns a new Range that would be the result after calling Move. The Previous method works like Move when passed a negative count and also returns a new Range instead of modifying the existing Range. In the case where the Move method would have returned 0 because the Move was not possible, Next and Previous return a `null` Range.

The MoveUntil method takes a required `object` by reference parameter to which you can pass a `string` containing the characters that you want to find. It takes a second optional `object` parameter by reference to which you can pass the number of characters after the Range to search. If MoveUntil cannot find a specified character within the number of characters you pass, it will not change the Range. You can pass a negative number of characters to search the characters before the range. You can also pass to the second optional `object` parameter the constant `WdConstants.wdForward` or `WdConstants.wdBackward` to specify to search forward or backward without specifying a limit on the number of characters to search.

Figure 8-21 shows the result of calling MoveUntil passing `"abc"` as the `string` and `WdConstants.wdForward` for the second parameter. It searches forward until it finds either character *a*, *b*, or *c*. The first of those it finds is the *c* in the word *quick*. It sets the start and end of the Range to 7.

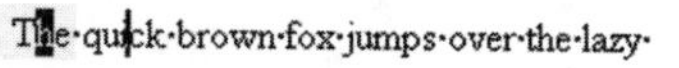

The·quick·brown·fox·jumps·over·the·lazy·

Figure 8-21 Result of calling MoveUntil("abc", WdConstants.wdForward) on a Range containing *h* from *The*.

Range has a MoveStart and MoveUntilStart method that work like Move and MoveUntil but only affect the start position of the Range unless the start is moved forward to a position beyond the end, in which case Start and End are set to the same value. Similarly, Range has a MoveEnd and MoveUntilEnd method that work like Move and MoveUntil but only affect the end position of the Range.

The SetRange method takes a `Start` and `End` parameter as an `int` to set the start and end position of the Range in characters. Using the SetRange is the equivalent of setting the Start and End properties on Range.

Ranges and Stories

Given a Range, you can expand the range to include the full story associated with the Range using the WholeStory method. Some stories are split into multiple linked text elements in a document (text box stories can be linked, and header and footer stories can be linked), so calling WholeStory cannot give you each of the multiple linked text elements. For these cases, you can use the NextStoryRange property to get the next linked story of the same type.

Navigating a Range

Earlier in this chapter, you read about the Browser object, which lets you access the same functionality that is available in the browser control shown in Figure 8-3. The Browser object enables you to easily go to the next element of a particular type in a document such as the next bookmark, comment, or field. However, the Browser object affects the selection in the document, which is often undesirable.

To go to the next element of a particular type without affecting the selection, you can use the GoTo method of the Range object. GoTo does not affect the Range object it is called on but instead returns a new Range object that represents the resulting Range after calling GoTo. The GoTo method takes by reference four optional object parameters. The first parameter, the What parameter, can be passed a member of the WdGoToItem enumeration:

- wdGoToBookmark
- wdGoToComment
- wdGoToEndnote
- wdGoToEquation
- wdGoToField
- wdGoToFootnote
- wdGoToGrammaticalError
- wdGoToGraphic
- wdGoToHeading
- wdGoToLine
- wdGoToObject

- wdGoToPage
- wdGoToPercent
- wdGoToProofreadingError
- wdGoToRevision
- wdGoToSection
- wdGoToTable

The second parameter, the `Which` parameter, can be passed a member of the `WdGo-ToDirection` enumeration: `wdGoToAbsolute`, `wdGoToFirst`, `wdGoToLast`, `wdGo-ToNext`, `wdGoToPrevious`, or `wdGoToRelative`. The `wdGoToAbsolute` value can be used to go to the n-th item of the type specified by the `What` parameter.

The third parameter, the `Count` parameter, is passed the number of the item to get and is affected by the second parameter. For example, if `What` is passed `wdGoToLine` and `Count` is passed 1, then depending on the `Which` parameter, GoTo could go to the next line after the Range (`wdGoToNext`) or the first line in the document (`wdGo-ToAbsolute`) or the line previous to the current Range (`wdGoToPrevious`).

The fourth parameter, the `Name` parameter, can be passed a name if the `What` argument specifies an element identifiable by name: `wdGoToBookmark`, `wdGoToComment`, or `wdGoToField`.

GoToNext and GoToPrevious are simpler versions of the GoTo method that only take the `What` parameter and go to the next or previous instance of the type of object specified by the `What` parameter.

Listing 8-32 shows an example of using the GoTo method on a Range to navigate through the pages in a document and display the first sentence on each page. We also use get_Information to get the page count and Expand to expand the collapsed Range returned by GoTo to include the first sentence on the page.

Listing 8-32 A VSTO Customization That Uses the GoTo Method

```
private void ThisDocument_Startup(object sender, EventArgs e)
{
  // Generate some random text in the document.
  Word.Range r = Range(ref missing, ref missing);
  System.Text.StringBuilder builder = new
    System.Text.StringBuilder();
  Random rand = new Random();
```

```
for (int i = 0; i < 200; i++)
{
  builder.AppendLine(rand.NextDouble().ToString());
}

r.Text = builder.ToString();
int maxPage = (int)r.get_Information(
  Word.WdInformation.wdNumberOfPagesInDocument);

// GoTo to navigate the pages
for (int page = 1; page <= maxPage; page++)
{
  object what = Word.WdGoToItem.wdGoToPage;
  object which = Word.WdGoToDirection.wdGoToAbsolute;
  object count = page;
  object sentence = Word.WdUnits.wdSentence;

  Word.Range r2 = r.GoTo(ref what, ref which,
    ref count, ref missing);
  r2.Expand(ref sentence);

  MessageBox.Show(String.Format(
    "First sentence is {0} starting at position {1}.",
    r2.Text, r2.Start));
}
}
```

Collapsing a Range

We have already mentioned several times the concept of a collapsed Range—a Range whose start and end is equal. The Collapse method takes a Range and collapses it. It takes by reference an optional parameter Direction of type object. You can pass a member of the WdCollapseDirection enumeration: wdCollapseEnd, which makes Start equal to End; or wdCollapseStart, which makes End equal to Start. If you omit the Direction parameter, the default is wdCollapseStart.

Getting Text from a Range

The Text property returns a string containing the text in the Range. The behavior of the Text property can be changed by using the TextRetrievalMode property, which returns a TextRetrievalMode object. Setting the TextRetrievalMode object's Include-FieldCodes property to true makes it so the Text property returns field codes. The default is the setting of the Field Codes check box in the View page of the Options dialog.

Setting the TextRetrievalMode object's IncludeHiddenText property to `true` makes it so the Text property returns hidden text in the document. The default is the setting of the Hidden Text check box in the View page of the Options dialog.

The TextRetrievalMode object's ViewType property can also affect what the Text property returns. The ViewType property can be set to a member of the `WdViewType` enumeration: `wdMasterView`, `wdNormalView`, `wdOutlineView`, `wdPrintPreview`, `wdPrintView`, `wdReadingView`, or `wdWebView`. When set to `wdOutlineView`, for example, Text only returns the text visible in outline view.

Listing 8-33 shows the creation of some text in a document that includes a field and some hidden text. The Text property is then used in several ways, showing the effect of changing TextRetrievalMode settings.

Listing 8-33 A VSTO Customization That Modifies TextRetrievalMode Settings

```
private void ThisDocument_Startup(object sender, EventArgs e)
{
  // Generate some random text in the document.
  Word.Range r = Range(ref missing, ref missing);
  r.Text = "Hello ";
  object collapseDirection = Word.WdCollapseDirection.wdCollapseEnd;
  object date = Word.WdFieldType.wdFieldDate;

  // Add a field
  r.Collapse(ref collapseDirection);
  r.Fields.Add(r, ref date, ref missing, ref missing);

  // Hide some text
  r.SetRange(1,2);
  r.Font.Hidden = 1;

  r = Range(ref missing, ref missing);
  r.TextRetrievalMode.IncludeFieldCodes = false;
  r.TextRetrievalMode.IncludeHiddenText = false;

  MessageBox.Show(r.Text);
  r.TextRetrievalMode.IncludeFieldCodes = true;
  MessageBox.Show(r.Text);
  r.TextRetrievalMode.IncludeHiddenText = true;
  MessageBox.Show(r.Text);
}
```

Setting the Text in a Range

Setting the Text property to a string value is the most basic way to set text in a Range. Setting the Text property replaces the text in the Range with the string value and changes the end of the Range so the start and end cover the length of the new string. If the Range is collapsed, setting the Text property does not replace any existing text, but it inserts the new string at the location of the Range and changes the end of the Range so that the start and end cover the length of the new string.

Setting the Text property only changes the characters of the Range, not the formatting. If you have one Range formatted a particular way and a second Range you want to copy both the text of the first Range and its formatting to, you can use the FormattedText property, which takes a Range. Listing 8-34 shows an example of using the FormattedText property to take one Range that is formatted and set the text and formatting of a second Range to the first.

Listing 8-34 A VSTO Customization That Uses FormattedText to Set Text and Formatting

```
private void ThisDocument_Startup(object sender, EventArgs e)
{
  Word.Range r = Range(ref missing, ref missing);
  r.Text = "Hello Hello Happy";
  object start1 = 0;
  object end1 = 5;
  r = Range(ref start1, ref end1);
  r.Bold = 1;

  object start2 = 12;
  object end2 = 17;
  Word.Range r2 = Range(ref start2, ref end2);
  r2.FormattedText = r;
}
```

Each time you set the Text property, it replaces the existing Range and changes the end of the Range so that the start and end cover the new string. The InsertAfter method lets you add text immediately after the Range without replacing the existing Range. The InsertAfter method takes a `string` for the text you want to insert after the Range. InsertAfter changes the end of the Range so that the start and end cover the old Range and the string you have added after the Range.

The InsertBefore method lets you add text immediately before the Range without replacing the existing Range. The InsertBefore method takes a `string` for the text you want to insert before the Range. InsertBefore changes the end of the Range so that the start and end cover the old Range and the string you have added before the Range.

Inserting Nonprinting Characters and Breaks

You have several ways to insert nonprinting characters such as tabs and paragraph marks. A simple way is to use escaped string literals. In a C# string, you can specify a tab with the character sequence \t. You can specify a paragraph mark (a new line) by using either \n or \r. Listing 8-35 shows some examples of using escaped string literals to insert nonprinting characters. Figure 8-22 shows the result of running Listing 8-35 with nonprinting characters showing.

Listing 8-35 A VSTO Customization That Uses Escaped String Literals and the Text Property

```
private void ThisDocument_Startup(object sender, EventArgs e)
{
  Word.Range r = Range(ref missing, ref missing);
  r.Text = "Item\tName\n";
  r.InsertAfter("111\t1/4\" pipe\n");
  r.InsertAfter("112\t1/2\" pipe\n");
  r.InsertAfter("\n\n");
  r.InsertAfter("File path: c:\\Temp\\Doc1.doc");
}
```

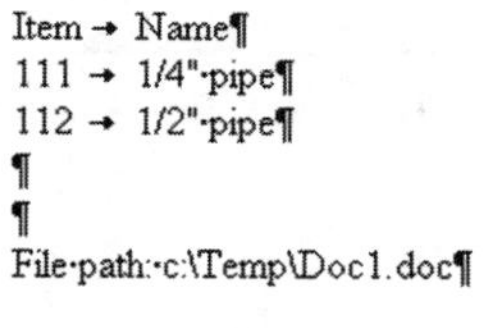

Item → Name¶
111 → 1/4"·pipe¶
112 → 1/2"·pipe¶
¶
¶
File·path:·c:\Temp\Doc1.doc¶

Figure 8-22 Result of running Listing 8-35.

It is also possible to insert paragraphs using the InsertParagraph method. The InsertParagraph method inserts a new paragraph at the start position of the Range, replacing the current Range. It changes the Range so that it covers the start position and the newly inserted paragraph mark. InsertParagraph is the equivalent of setting the Text property to /n. InsertParagraphBefore inserts a new paragraph at the start position of the Range and changes the end of the Range to expand it to cover the old Range and the newly inserted paragraph mark. InsertParagraphBefore is the equivalent of calling the InsertBefore method and passing /n. InsertParagraphAfter is the equivalent of calling the InsertAfter method and passing /n.

Figure 8-23 shows some additional kinds of breaks that a user can insert into a document using the Break command from the Insert menu. These types of breaks can be inserted programmatically using Range's InsertBreak method. The Insert-Break method takes by reference an optional parameter of type object to which you can pass a member of the WdBreakType enumeration. The members of the WdBreak-Type enumeration correspond to the breaks in Figure 8-23: wdPageBreak, wdColumnBreak, wdTextWrappingBreak, wdSectionBreakNextPage, wdSec-tionBreakContinuous, wdSectionBreakEvenPage, or wdSectionBreakOddPage. InsertBreak works like setting the Text property would—the current Range is replaced with the break, or if the Range is collapsed, the break is inserted at the position of the Range.

Figure 8-23 The Insert Break dialog.

Working with Formatting

The Font property returns a Font object that controls font settings for the Range. Many of the properties associated with Font, such as the Bold property, that you would expect to be of type bool are instead of type int. This is because a particular Range could be all bold, partially bold, or not bold, for example. If the Range is partially bold, it returns WdConstants.wdUndefined. If the Range is not bold, it returns a 0. If the Range is all bold, it returns a –1; this is another example where the COM implementation of the Word OM peeks through because –1 corresponds to a true value in COM object models. This can cause confusion because the bool value for true in .NET when cast to an integer is 1, not –1. So when checking the value of these properties, remember to not make the mistake of comparing to 1 or the bool value of `true` cast to an `int` because this will cause your code to fail to detect the state properly. Instead, always compare to 0 or the `bool` value of `false` cast to an `int`.

Table 8-14 lists several of the most frequently used properties associated with the Font object.

Table 8-14 Frequently Used Properties Associated with the Font Object

Property Name	Type	What It Does
AllCaps	int	Set to –1 to format the font as all capital letters.
Bold	int	Set to –1 to format the font as bold.
Color	WdColor	Set to a member of the `WdColor` enumeration to set the color of the font.
ColorIndex	WdColor-Index	Set to a member of the `WdColorIndex` enumeration to set the color of the font.
Hidden	int	Set to –1 to hide the text of the Range.
Italic	int	Set to –1 to format the font as italic.
Name	string	Set to a `string` representing the name of the font.
Size	float	Set to a size in points.
SmallCaps	int	Set to –1 to format the font as small caps.
Underline	WdUnderline	Set to a member of the `WdUnderline` enumeration to set the underline format of the font.

Another way to set the formatting of a Range is to use the set_Style method. The set_Style method takes by reference an `object` parameter. You can pass a `string` representing the name of the style you want to use to format the Range.

Listing 8-36 shows some formatting of a Range using Font properties and the set_Style method. Figure 8-24 shows the document created by Listing 8-36.

Listing 8-36 A VSTO Customization That Formats a Range

```
private void ThisDocument_Startup(object sender, EventArgs e)
{
  object collapseEnd = Word.WdCollapseDirection.wdCollapseEnd;
```

```
Word.Range r = Range(ref missing, ref missing);
r.Text = "Item\tName\n";
r.Font.Name = "Verdana";
r.Font.Size = 20.0F;

r.Collapse(ref collapseEnd);
r.InsertAfter("111\t1/4\" pipe\n");
r.HighlightColorIndex = Word.WdColorIndex.wdGray25;
r.Italic = -1;
r.Font.Size = 10.0F;
r.Font.Name = "Times New Roman";

r.Collapse(ref collapseEnd);
r.InsertAfter("112\t1/2\" pipe\n");
r.Shading.BackgroundPatternColor = Word.WdColor.wdColorBlack;
r.Font.Color = Word.WdColor.wdColorWhite;
r.Font.Size = 10.0F;
r.Font.SmallCaps = -1;
r.Font.Name = "Verdana";

r.Collapse(ref collapseEnd);
r.InsertAfter("This should be a heading.");
object style = "Heading 1";
r.set_Style(ref style);
}
```

Figure 8-24 Result of running Listing 8-36.

Find and Replace

The Find property returns a Find object that you can use to search a Range. The Find object allows you to set options similar to the ones you find in Word's Find dialog. The Find object's Text property can be set to the string you want to search for. The Find object's MatchWholeWord property can be set to false to allow matching of the string against a partial word in the Range. After the find options have been set up, the Find object's Execute method executes the find against the Range. Execute takes a number of optional parameters by reference—some of which correspond to properties on the Find object. So you have an option of either presetting Find properties and then calling Execute and omitting the optional parameters by passing `ref missing`, or you can skip presetting Find properties and pass optional parameters to the Execute method. In Listing 8-36, we take the former approach. Execute returns `true` if it is able to find the text specified and modifies the Range so that it covers the found text. In Listing 8-37, calling Execute modifies the Range to have a start of 20 and an end of 24.

Listing 8-37 A VSTO Customization That Uses the Find Object

```
private void ThisDocument_Startup(object sender, EventArgs e)
{
  Word.Range r = Range(ref missing, ref missing);
  r.Text = "The quick brown fox jumped over the lazy dog.";

  Word.Find f = r.Find;
  f.Text = "jump";
  f.MatchWholeWord = false;

  if (f.Execute(ref missing, ref missing, ref missing,
        ref missing, ref missing, ref missing, ref missing,
        ref missing, ref missing, ref missing, ref missing,
        ref missing, ref missing, ref missing, ref missing))
  {
    MessageBox.Show(String.Format(
      "Found {0} at position {1},{2}.",
      f.Text, r.Start, r.End));
  }
}
```

It is also possible to iterate over multiple found items using the Find object's Found property instead of checking the return value of Execute each time. Listing 8-38 shows an example of iterating over every occurrence of the string `"jump"` in a document. This example bolds every instance of *jump* that it finds in the document.

Listing 8-38 A VSTO Customization That Uses the Find Object's Found Property to Iterate over Found Items

```
private void ThisDocument_Startup(object sender, EventArgs e)
{
  Word.Range r = Range(ref missing, ref missing);
  r.Text = "Jumping lizards!  Jump on down to Mr. Jumpkin's jumpin' trampoline
store.";

  Word.Find f = r.Find;
  f.Text = "jump";
  f.MatchWholeWord = false;

  f.Execute(ref missing, ref missing, ref missing,
    ref missing, ref missing, ref missing, ref missing,
    ref missing, ref missing, ref missing, ref missing,
    ref missing, ref missing,ref missing, ref missing);

  while (f.Found)
  {
    MessageBox.Show(String.Format(
      "Found {0} at position {1},{2}.",
      f.Text, r.Start, r.End));

    r.Font.Bold = -1;

    f.Execute(ref missing, ref missing, ref missing,
      ref missing, ref missing, ref missing, ref missing,
      ref missing, ref missing, ref missing, ref missing,
      ref missing, ref missing, ref missing, ref missing);
  }
}
```

The Find object has a Replacement property that returns a Replacement object, which allows you to set options for doing a find and replace. The Replacement object's Text property lets you set the text you want to use to replace found text with. In addition, to perform a replacement, you must pass a member of the WdReplace enumeration to the Replace parameter of the Execute method (the eleventh optional parameter). You can pass wdReplaceAll to replace all found occurrences or wdReplaceOne to replace the first found occurrence. In Listing 8-39, we use the Replacement.Text property to set the replace string, and then call Execute passing wdReplaceAll to the Replace parameter.

Listing 8-39 A VSTO Customization That Performs a Replace

```
private void ThisDocument_Startup(object sender, EventArgs e)
{
  Word.Range r = Range(ref missing, ref missing);
  r.Text = "The quick brown fox jumped over the lazy dog.";

  Word.Find f = r.Find;
  f.Text = "jump";
  f.MatchWholeWord = false;
  f.Replacement.Text = "leap";

  object replace = Word.WdReplace.wdReplaceAll;
  if (f.Execute(ref missing, ref missing, ref missing,
    ref missing, ref missing, ref missing, ref missing,
    ref missing, ref missing, ref missing, ref replace,
    ref missing, ref missing, ref missing, ref missing))
  {
    MessageBox.Show(String.Format(
      "Replaced {0} at position {1},{2}.",
      f.Text, r.Start, r.End));
  }
}
```

Working with Bookmarks

Bookmarks provide you a way to name and keep track of a particular Range. The user can even edit the Range and the modified Range will still be accessible by its name unless the user completely deletes the Range.

To create and manage bookmarks, you can use Word's Bookmark dialog. You can select some text in the document, choose Bookmark from the Insert menu, and give the range of text a name then click the Add button to add a bookmark, as shown in Figure 8-25. Existing bookmarks can be selected and navigated to using the Go To button. They can also be removed using the Delete button.

Figure 8-25 The Bookmark dialog.

VSTO provides some additional tools for creating bookmarks. For example, you can drag a bookmark control from the Visual Studio control toolbox to the Word document to create a bookmark. VSTO also adds any bookmarks in the document as named class member variables of the ThisDocument class. VSTO support for bookmarks is described in more detail in Chapter 13.

If you check the Bookmarks check box in the View page of Word's Options dialog, Word shows gray brackets around any bookmarks defined in your document. Figure 8-26 shows the brackets Word displays. Here we have created a bookmark that includes the word *brown* and the space after *brown*.

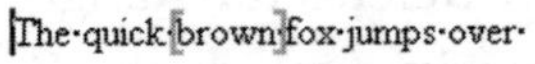

The·quick·brown·fox·jumps·over·

**Figure 8-26 Result of checking the Bookmarks check box in
the View page of Word's Options dialog.**

To programmatically create and manage bookmarks, you can use the Document object's Bookmarks property or the Range object's Bookmarks property. Both return a Bookmarks collection; the former returns all the bookmarks defined in the document, the latter returns just the bookmarks defined within the Range you are working with.

The Bookmarks collection's Add method adds a bookmark. It takes a required Name parameter to which you pass a string representing the name you want to use for the bookmark. The name parameter must be one word. The Add method also takes by reference an optional object parameter to which you pass the Range you want to create a bookmark for. The method returns the newly added Bookmark object.

The Bookmarks collection's Exists method takes a string representing the name of a bookmark and returns a bool value indicating whether the bookmark exists in the document. The get_Item method allows you to get to a bookmark given its name or 1-based index in the Bookmarks collection. The get_Item method takes by reference an object parameter that can be set to a string representing the name of the bookmark or the 1-based index. Given a Bookmark object, you can get the Range it refers to by using the Bookmark object's Range property.

Listing 8-40 shows an example of working with bookmarks. It first creates several bookmarks, and then gets them again using the get_Item method.

Listing 8-40 A VSTO Customization That Works with Bookmarks

```
private void ThisDocument_Startup(object sender, EventArgs e)
{
  object collapseEnd = Word.WdCollapseDirection.wdCollapseEnd;
  Word.Range r = Range(ref missing, ref missing);
  r.Text = "The quick brown fox ";
  object range1 = r;
  this.Bookmarks.Add("FirstHalf", ref range1);

  r.Collapse(ref collapseEnd);
  r.Text = "jumped over the lazy dog.";
  object range2 = r;
  this.Bookmarks.Add("SecondHalf", ref range2);

  if (this.Bookmarks.Exists("FirstHalf") == true)
  {
    MessageBox.Show("FirstHalf exists");
  }

  object firstHalfName = "FirstHalf";
  Word.Bookmark b = this.Bookmarks.get_Item(ref firstHalfName);
  MessageBox.Show(String.Format(
    "FirstHalf starts at {0} and ends at {1}.",
    b.Range.Start, b.Range.End));
}
```

Bookmarks are easily deleted from the document. For example, setting the Text property of the Range associated with a bookmark replaces the Range and in the process deletes the bookmark associated with the Range. VSTO extends Bookmark and adds some additional functionality to preserve the bookmark even when you set the Text property. For more information on VSTO's support for bookmarks and the bookmark control, see Chapter 13.

Working with Tables

As previously mentioned, both the Document and Range object have a Tables property that returns the Tables collection, which contains tables in the Document or Range. To add a Table, you can use the Tables collection's Add method, which takes a Range where you want to add the table, the number of rows and number of columns in the table, and two optional object parameters passed by reference that specify the auto-fit behavior of the table. The Add method returns the newly added table.

Listing 8-41 shows code that adds and populates a small table. It uses the returned Table object's Rows property to get the Rows collection. It uses the index operator on the Rows collection to get an individual Row object. It then uses the Row object's Cells property to get the Cells collection. It uses the index operator on the Cells collection to get to an individual Cell object. Finally, it uses the Cell object's Range property to get a Range corresponding to the Cell object and uses the Range object's Text to property set the value of the cell.

Listing 8-41 A VSTO Customization That Creates and Populates a Simple Table

```
private void ThisDocument_Startup(object sender, EventArgs e)
{
  Word.Range r = Range(ref missing, ref missing);
  Word.Table t = r.Tables.Add(r, 5, 5, ref missing, ref missing);

  for (int i = 1; i <= 5; i++)
  {
    for (int j = 1; j <= 5; j++)
    {
      t.Rows[i].Cells[j].Range.Text = String.Format(
```

```
                "{0}, {1}", i, j);
        }
    }
}
```

The Table object's Cell method provides an easier way of getting to a Cell. The Cell method takes an `int` row and column parameter and returns a Cell object. Listing 8-42 shows the use of the Cell method along with the use of several auto-formatting techniques as we create a simple multiplication table. The Columns object's AutoFit method is used to resize the column widths to fit the contents of the cells. The Table object's set_Style method takes an `object` by reference that is set to the name of a table style as found in the Table AutoFormat dialog. The Table object's ApplyStyle-LastRow and ApplyStyleLastColumn properties are set to `false` in Listing 8-42 to specify that no special style be applied to the last row or last column in the table.

Listing 8-42 A VSTO Customization That Creates a Multiplication Table

```
private void ThisDocument_Startup(object sender, EventArgs e)
{
  Word.Range r = Range(ref missing, ref missing);
  Word.Table t = r.Tables.Add(r, 12, 12, ref missing,
    ref missing);

  for (int i = 1; i <= 12; i++)
  {
    for (int j = 1; j <= 12; j++)
    {
      Word.Cell c = t.Cell(i,j);
      if (i == 1 && j == 1)
      {
        c.Range.Text = "X";
      }
      else if (i == 1)
      {
        c.Range.Text = j.ToString();
      }
      else if (j == 1)
      {
        c.Range.Text = i.ToString();
      }
      else
      {
```

```
        int result = i * j;
        c.Range.Text = result.ToString();
      }
    }
  }

  t.Columns.AutoFit();
  object styleString = "Table Classic 2";
  t.set_Style(ref styleString);
  t.ApplyStyleLastRow = false;
  t.ApplyStyleLastColumn = false;
}
```

Conclusion

This chapter has explored some of the most important objects in the Word object model. We use many of these objects in the Word examples in subsequent chapters. We also consider some additional Word object model objects used to work with XML in Word in Chapter 22, "Working with XML in Word."

This chapter has described these objects as defined by the primary interop assemblies for Word. Be aware, however, that VSTO extends some of these objects (Document, Bookmark, XMLNodes, and XMLNode) to add some additional functionality, such as data binding support. Part Three of this book, starting with Chapter 13, covers those extensions.

▪9▪

Programming Outlook

Ways to Customize Outlook

OUTLOOK HAS AN OBJECT MODEL THAT consists of 67 objects that combined have more than 1,700 properties and methods. The Outlook object model is about a third as big as the Excel and Word object models and tends to give you less control over Outlook than you would expect. Outlook does have a larger number of events compared to the Word and Excel object models—more than 300 events. However, the large number of events is mainly due to 16 events that are duplicated on 15 Outlook objects.

The main way that you will integrate your code into Outlook is via add-ins. This model was originally designed to allow the integration of COM components written in VB6, VBA, C, or C++. However, through COM interop, a managed object can masquerade as a COM object and participate in the Outlook add-in model.

Automation Executable

As mentioned in Chapter 2, "Introduction to Office Solutions," you can start Outlook from a console application or Windows application and automate it from that external program. The problem with this approach is that you cannot add your automation executable to the exclusion list of the Outlook object model security guard.

The Outlook object model security guard prevents code from accessing sensitive parts of the Outlook object model such as the address book or the send mail functionality. Its purpose is to protect Outlook from code that might spread as an e-mail worm virus. Outlook has a mechanism to trust a particular installed add-in and let it bypass the Outlook object model guard that is discussed in Chapter 11. It does not have a mechanism to trust an automation executable and let an automation executable bypass the guard.

Add-Ins

When building add-ins for Outlook, you have two choices: You can either build a COM add-in or a VSTO Outlook add-in. A VSTO Outlook add-in solves many of the problems associated with COM add-in development and is the preferred model for Outlook 2003 add-in development. You can read about this model for Outlook add-ins in Chapter 24, "Creating Outlook Add-Ins with VSTO." The only time you would want to consider building a COM add-in instead is if you need to target versions of Outlook that are older than Outlook 2003. You can read about building COM add-ins in Chapter 23, "Developing COM Add-Ins for Word and Excel."

Outlook has a COM add-ins dialog box that enables users to enable and disable add-ins. Both VSTO add-ins and COM add-ins appear in the COM Add-Ins dialog box. This dialog box is very well hidden. To access the COM Add-Ins dialog, you must follow these steps:

1. Choose Options from the Tools menu to bring up the Options dialog.
2. Click the Other tab of the Options dialog.
3. Click the Advanced Options button to bring up the Advanced Options dialog.
4. Click the COM Add-Ins button to bring up the COM Add-Ins dialog.

Figure 9-1 shows the COM Add-Ins dialog.

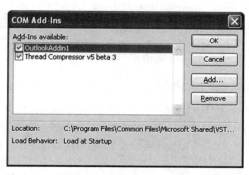

Figure 9-1 The COM Add-Ins dialog in Outlook.

COM add-ins can be added and removed from the dialog by using the Add and Remove buttons. VSTO add-ins cannot be added using the Add button, but can be removed using the Remove button. Each add-in has a check box that can be checked and unchecked to enable or disable the add-in while still leaving it in the list of available add-ins. Typically, you will not use this dialog to add and remove add-ins—only to disable and enable available add-ins. The addition and removal of add-ins is handled by the installer of your COM add-in or VSTO add-in.

Outlook discovers the add-ins that are installed by reading the registry keys under My Computer\HKEY_CURRENT_USER\Software\Microsoft\Office\Outlook\Addins in the registry. You can view the registry on your computer by going to the Windows Start menu and choosing Run. In the Run dialog box, type **regedit** for the program to run then click the OK button. You can also register add-ins for Outlook under My Computer\HKEY_LOCAL_MACHINE\Software\Microsoft\Office\Outlook\Addins. Add-ins registered under HKEY_LOCAL_MACHINE do not appear in the COM Add-Ins dialog box and cannot be enabled or disabled by users.

Smart Tags

Smart Tags are a feature that enables the display of a pop-up menu with actions for a given piece of text on the screen. Outlook supports Smart Tags in several ways.

Smart Tags When Word Is the E-mail Editor

First, if Word is used as the e-mail editor in Outlook, Smart Tags appear when you edit e-mail messages. To set Word as the e-mail editor, you can use the Options command from the Tools menu to display Outlook's Options dialog. On the Mail Format page, check the Use Microsoft Office Word 2003 to edit e-mail messages, as shown in Figure 9-2.

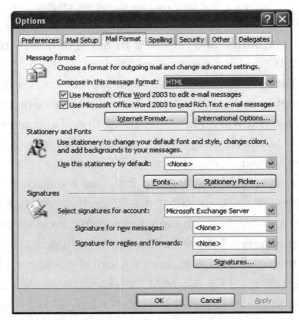

Figure 9-2 Specifying Word as the e-mail editor.

In addition to specifying Word as the e-mail editor, you must also configure Word's Smart Tag options as described in Chapter 6, "Programming Word." Then, when you create a new e-mail message, you will be able to see Smart Tags in your message, as shown in Figure 9-3.

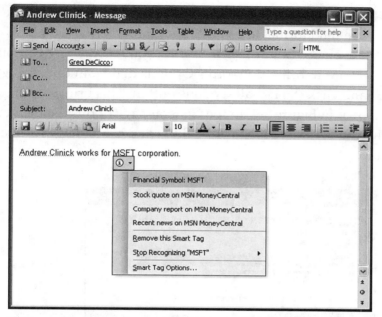

Figure 9-3 Smart Tags in an e-mail message when Word is the e-mail editor.

Smart Tags in the Research Task Pane When Word Is the E-mail Editor

You can register Smart Tags to recognize text in the Research task pane. If Word is being used as the e-mail editor, the user can select some text in the e-mail, right-click the text, and choose Look Up to bring up the Research task pane. Results in the Research task pane may include text that is tagged by Smart Tags.

Smart Tags Embedded in HTML Format E-mail and Displayed in the Reading Pane

A third way Smart Tags are supported in Outlook is if you use Word as the e-mail editor and send e-mail in HTML format. If Word's send format is configured appropriately, Smart Tags can be embedded in the HTML formatted message. Users who read the messages that have the Smart Tag installed and have Outlook's security settings set to allow it will be able to see Smart Tags display in Outlook's reading pane. Outlook's reading pane is effectively an HTML Web browser.

To configure this use of Smart Tags, you must first specify Word as the e-mail editor and choose the send format to be HTML, as shown in Figure 9-2. To configure Word to be able to embed Smart Tags in HTML, you must choose Options from the Tools menu of Word to bring up Word's Options dialog. In this dialog, select the General page and click the E-mail Options button. This brings up the E-mail Options dialog shown in Figure 9-4. In the General page of this dialog, you must set the HTML filtering options to None or Medium and check the Save Smart Tags in e-mail check box.

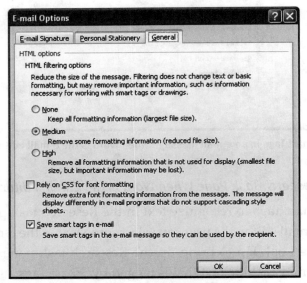

Figure 9-4 E-mail options to enable the embedding of
Smart Tags in HTML e-mail messages.

Finally, you must ensure that security settings of Outlook will allow Smart Tags to appear. In Outlook's Options dialog box, select the Security page and make sure the Zone is set to the Internet Zone, as shown in Figure 9-5.

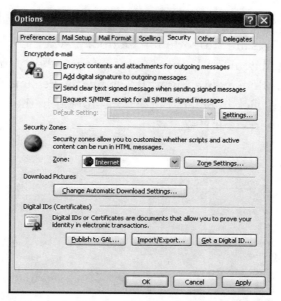

Figure 9-5 Internet zone security required to allow Smart Tags to be
displayed in e-mail messages.

With all these settings configured, you should be able to type an e-mail message, send it, and when it is received, you can see the Smart Tag appear in the reading pane, as shown in Figure 9-6. The Smart Tag looks a little different because the reading pane uses Internet Explorer's menu style rather than the Office menu style.

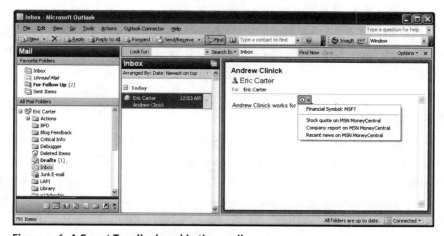

Figure 9-6 A Smart Tag displayed in the reading pane.

Persona Menu Smart Tags

The final way Smart Tags are supported in Outlook is via the Persona menu. This menu appears on e-mail items and other Outlook items when you click the Persona icon shown in many Outlook views. Figure 9-7 shows the Persona icon and the menu that appears when you click it. Smart Tag actions appear in the Additional Actions submenu that is shown in Figure 9-7.

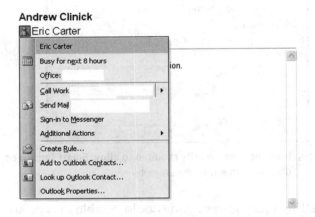

Figure 9-7 The Persona menu in Outlook—Smart Tag actions appear under the Additional Actions submenu.

VSTO cannot be used to provide Smart Tags for Outlook because VSTO only supports Smart Tags for code behind a document. The Outlook uses of Smart Tags are not at the document level but at the application level. Chapter 16, "Working with Smart Tags in VSTO," describes how to create an application-level Smart Tag in C# that could be used in e-mail when Word is your e-mail editor.

Custom Property Pages

An Outlook add-in can add a custom property page to the Properties dialog box for a folder or to Outlook's Options dialog. We walk through how this is done using a VSTO Outlook add-in. First, create a VSTO Outlook add-in project in VSTO by following the instructions in Chapter 24.

After you have created a basic VSTO Outlook add-in project, you need to add a user control project item to the project. A user control is a special kind of Windows Forms control that is useful for inserting into another window. To add a user control to your project, click the project node in the Solution Explorer, and then choose Add User Control from the Project menu. When you double-click the newly added user control project item, you will see the user control designer shown in Figure 9-8. You can resize the user control using the drag handle in the lower-right corner. Resize it to about 410×355 pixels, which is the size of a property page in Outlook. With the user control resized, use the controls toolbox (choose Toolbox from the View menu if it is not already showing) to add controls to your user control surface. In Figure 9-8, we have added several check boxes, radio buttons, and buttons to the user control surface.

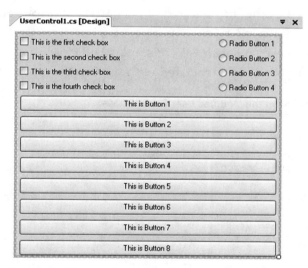

Figure 9-8 The user control designer.

To use this user control as a custom property page, we must make some modifications to the code behind it. Right-click the user control project item in the Solution Explorer and choose View Code. We first must implement an interface required by Outlook called PropertyPage. The PropertyPage interface has two methods and a property. The Apply method is called on our PropertyPage implementation when the user clicks the Apply button in the Outlook Options or Folder Properties dialog. The GetPageInfo method gets a help filename and help context so that you can provide help for your custom property page. The Dirty property is a bool property that you can use to let Outlook know whether the user has changed any settings in your custom property page. When Dirty returns true, Outlook knows to enable the Apply button in the dialog so that the user can apply changes made in the custom property page.

Second, we must add a property that Outlook will call to get the caption for the property page tab. This property must be marked with a DispId attribute that Outlook uses to identify which property will return the caption for the property page tab. The name of the property does not matter as long as it returns a string; in Listing 9-1, we name the property PageCaption.

Listing 9-1 shows what your class should look like after you have made these modifications. Because user controls use the partial class feature in Visual Studio, all the code that is specific to how many buttons or controls you added should not show up in this file but in the other hidden part of the partial class. Note that the code uses the System.Runtime.InteropServices namespace for the DispID attribute on the Caption property. The code also declares a constant called captionDispID that is set to the ID Outlook expects will be associated with the Caption property.

Listing 9-1 First Version of the Modified User Control Class

```
using System;
using System.Windows.Forms;
using Outlook = Microsoft.Office.Interop.Outlook;
using System.Runtime.InteropServices;

namespace OutlookAddin1
{
  public partial class UserControl1 :
    UserControl, Outlook.PropertyPage
  {
    const int captionDispID = -518;
    bool isDirty = false;

    public UserControl1()
    {
      InitializeComponent();
    }

    void Outlook.PropertyPage.Apply()
    {
      MessageBox.Show("The user clicked the Apply button.");
    }

    bool Outlook.PropertyPage.Dirty
```

```
    {
      get
      {
        return isDirty;
      }
    }

    void Outlook.PropertyPage.GetPageInfo(ref string helpFile,
      ref int helpContext)
    {

    }

    [DispId(captionDispID)]
    public string PageCaption
    {
      get
      {
        return "Test Page";
      }
    }
  }
}
```

With the user control created, two event handlers must be added. The first event handler is for the Application object's OptionsPagesAdd event. This event is raised when Outlook is ready to add custom property pages to the Outlook Options dialog, which is shown when the user chooses Options from the Tools menu. The event handler is passed a `pages` parameter of type `PropertyPages` that has an Add method that can be used to add a user control as a custom property page.

The second event handler is for the NameSpace object's OptionsPagesAdd event. This event is raised when Outlook is ready to add custom property pages when a properties dialog box for a folder is displayed. The properties dialog box for a folder is shown when the user right-clicks a folder and chooses Properties from the pop-up menu. The event handler is passed a `pages` parameter of type `PropertyPages` that has an Add method that can be used to add a user control as a custom property page. The event handler is also passed a folder parameter of type `MAPIFolder` that specifies the folder for which the properties dialog box will be shown.

Listing 9-2 shows an implementation of a VSTO `ThisApplication` class that handles these two events. In the event handlers for the Application object's OptionsPagesAdd event and the NameSpace object's OptionsPagesAdd event, an instance of the user control in Listing 9-1 is created and passed as the first parameter to the PropertyPages.Add method. The second property is passed an empty string because the caption for the custom property page is retrieved by Outlook calling the `PageCaption` property on the user control that has been attributed with a `DispID` known to Outlook.

Listing 9-2 A VSTO Outlook Add-In That Handles the OptionsPagesAdd Event on Application and Namespace

```
using System;
using System.Windows.Forms;
using Microsoft.VisualStudio.Tools.Applications.Runtime;
using Outlook = Microsoft.Office.Interop.Outlook;

namespace OutlookAddin1
{
  public partial class ThisApplication
  {
    Outlook.NameSpace nameSpace;

    private void ThisApplication_Startup(object sender, EventArgs e)
    {
      this.OptionsPageAdd += new
        Outlook.ApplicationEvents_11_OptionsPagesAddEventHandler(
        ThisApplication_OptionsPagesAdd);

      nameSpace = this.Session;
      nameSpace.OptionsPagesAdd += new
        Outlook.NameSpaceEvents_OptionsPagesAddEventHandler(
        NameSpace_OptionsPagesAdd);
    }

    private void ThisApplication_Shutdown(object sender, EventArgs e)
    {
    }

    void ThisApplication_OptionsPagesAdd(Outlook.PropertyPages pages)
    {
      pages.Add(new UserControl1(), "");
    }

    void NameSpace_OptionsPagesAdd(Outlook.PropertyPages pages,
      Outlook.MAPIFolder folder)
    {
      pages.Add(new UserControl1(), "");
    }
```

```
    #region VSTO Designer generated code
    private void InternalStartup()
    {
      this.Startup += new EventHandler(ThisApplication_Startup);
      this.Shutdown += new EventHandler(ThisApplication_Shutdown);
    }
    #endregion
  }
}
```

If you compile and run this VSTO add-in, you will get the result shown in Figure 9-9 when you show Outlook's Options dialog and click the Test Page tab.

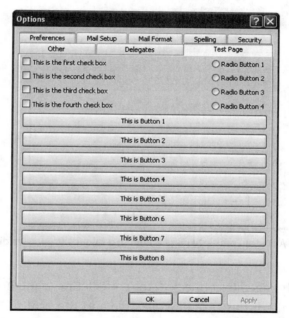

Figure 9-9 A custom property page added to Outlook's Options dialog.

If you right-click a folder and choose Properties, you can also see that the custom property page is added to the folder's Properties dialog, as shown in Figure 9-10.

If you play with these dialogs a bit, you will notice that the Apply button never gets enabled when you change the check boxes or radio buttons in the custom property page. Also note that the Apply method that was implemented as part of implementing the PropertyPage interface is never called. To fix this, the implementation of the user control is modified as shown in Listing 9-3 so that when a check box or radio button is changed, it changes the value of the class variable isDirty to true. In addition, the code notifies Outlook that the property page state has changed by connecting to Outlook's PropertyPageSite object. The code declares a propertyPage-Site class member variable and sets it by calling the InitializePropertyPageSite method in the Load event handler. The Load event handler must use reflection to get the PropertyPageSite object.

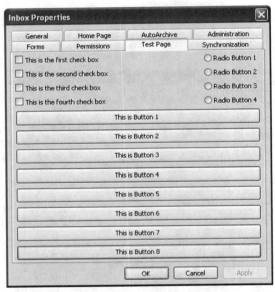

Figure 9-10 A custom property page added to a folder's Properties dialog.

With the PropertyPageSite connected, the code defines a method called SetIsDirty that changes the state of the isDirty variable and then calls Outlook's Property-PageSite.OnStatusChange method. This notifies Outlook that it needs to call into the PropertyPage interface to get the new state of the custom property page. A complete implementation would detect any changes made to the property page that could change the dirty state and potentially detect when a change is undone and clear the dirty state back to false.

Finally, the code raises the CheckedChanged event of the first check box on the custom property page. When the changed state changes, the code calls SetIsDirty to set the dirty state to true and notifies Outlook that the state has changed.

Listing 9-3 Second Version of a User Control Class That Handles Dirty State Properly

```csharp
using System;
using System.Windows.Forms;
using Outlook = Microsoft.Office.Interop.Outlook;
using System.Runtime.InteropServices;

namespace OutlookAddin1
{
  public partial class UserControl1 : UserControl,
    Outlook.PropertyPage
  {
    const int captionDispID = -518;
    bool isDirty = false;
    private Outlook.PropertyPageSite propertyPageSite = null;

    public UserControl1()
    {
      InitializeComponent();

      this.Load += new EventHandler(UserControl1_Load);
      this.checkBox1.CheckedChanged += new
        System.EventHandler(this.OnCheckBox1Changed);
    }

    void Outlook.PropertyPage.Apply()
    {
      MessageBox.Show("The user clicked the Apply button.");
    }

    bool Outlook.PropertyPage.Dirty
    {
      get
      {
        return isDirty;
      }
    }

    void Outlook.PropertyPage.GetPageInfo(ref string helpFile,
      ref int helpContext) { }

    [DispId(captionDispID)]
    public string Caption
    {
      get
      {
        return "Test Page";
      }
    }
```

```
private void SetIsDirty(bool value)
{
  isDirty = value;
  propertyPageSite.OnStatusChange();
}

private void OnCheckBox1Changed(object sender, EventArgs e)
{
  SetIsDirty(true);
}

void UserControl1_Load(object sender, EventArgs e)
{
  InitializePropertyPageSite();
}

void InitializePropertyPageSite()
{
  string windowsFormsStrongName =
    typeof(System.Windows.Forms.Form).Assembly.FullName;

  Type oleObjectType = Type.GetType(
    System.Reflection.Assembly.CreateQualifiedName(
    windowsFormsStrongName,
    "System.Windows.Forms.UnsafeNativeMethods")).
    GetNestedType("IOleObject");

  System.Reflection.MethodInfo getClientSiteMethodInfo =
    oleObjectType.GetMethod("GetClientSite");

  propertyPageSite = (Outlook.PropertyPageSite)
    getClientSiteMethodInfo.Invoke(this, null);
  }
 }
}
```

Now when you run the add-in and change the checked state of the first check box in the custom property page, the dirty state is changed and Outlook's PropertyPage-Site is notified. The result is that the Apply button is enabled. Clicking the Apply button invokes the test dialog in Listing 9-3's implementation of the Apply method.

Introduction to the Outlook Object Model

Regardless of the approach you choose to integrate your code with Outlook, you will eventually need to talk to the Outlook object model to get things done. This section introduces the Outlook object model; Chapter 10, "Working with Outlook Events," and Chapter 11, "Working with Outlook Objects," describe some of the most frequently used properties, methods, and events. This chapter also briefly examines another object model you can use with Outlook called Collaboration Data Objects (CDO).

The Object Hierarchy of the Outlook Object Model

The first step in starting to learn the Outlook object model is getting an idea for the basic structure of the object model hierarchy. Figure 9-11 shows some of the most critical objects in the Outlook object model and their hierarchical relationship.

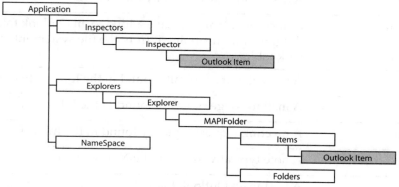

Figure 9-11 The basic hierarchy of the Outlook object model.

The Outlook object model has the notion of an Outlook item. An Outlook item is represented in the object model as an `object` and can be cast to one of 15 different Outlook item types shown in Table 9-1. Some objects in the object model, such as the MAPIFolder object, contain an Items collection that can contain instances of any of the 15 Outlook item types—therefore, the folder may contain a mixture of MailItem objects, TaskRequestItem objects, and so on. When you iterate over a collection of Items, Outlook returns each item to you as an `object` that you must cast to one of the 15 Outlook item types before using it.

Another example of an Outlook object model object that is associated with multiple Outlook item types is the Inspector object. The Inspector object represents a window providing a detail view for one of the 15 different Outlook item types. It could be providing a view on a NoteItem, a MeetingItem, and so forth. Inspector has a CurrentItem property that returns the Outlook item it is displaying as an `object`.

You must cast the `object` returned by CurrentItem to one of the Outlook item types in Table 9-1 before using it. Chapter 11 discusses Outlook items in more detail.

Figure 9-12 shows a more complete view of the Outlook object model. (All the objects considered Outlook items are colored gray.) Note in this diagram that the Inspector object and the Items object points to a gray circle, which represents any of the Outlook items colored gray.

Table 9-1 Outlook Item Types

Object	Description
ContactItem	A contact item typically found in the Contacts folder.
DistListItem	A distribution list typically found in the Contacts folder.
DocumentItem	A document that you have added to an Outlook folder by dragging and dropping it from the file system into the Outlook folder.
JournalItem	A journal entry typically found in the Journal folder.
MailItem	A mail message typically found in the Inbox folder.
MeetingItem	A meeting request typically found in the Inbox folder.
NoteItem	A note typically found in the Notes folder.
PostItem	A post in an Outlook folder.
RemoteItem	A mail message that has not yet been fully retrieved from the server but has the subject of the message, the received date and time, the sender, the size of the message, and the first 256 characters of the message body.
ReportItem	A mail delivery report such as a report when mail delivery failed typically found in the Inbox folder.
TaskItem	A task typically found in the Tasks folder.
TaskRequestAcceptItem	A response to a TaskRequestItem typically found in the Inbox folder.
TaskRequestDeclineItem	A response to a TaskRequestItem typically found in the Inbox folder.
TaskRequestItem	A task request sent to another user typically found in the Inbox folder.
TaskRequestUpdateItem	An update to a TaskRequestItem typically found in the Inbox folder.

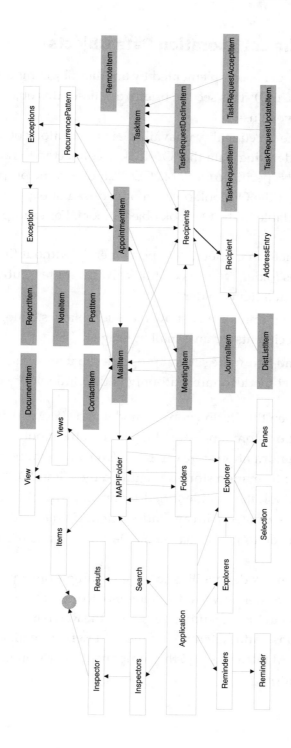

Figure 9-12 Some of the objects in the Outlook object model—gray objects are all "Outlook items."

Introduction to the Collaboration Data Objects

The Outlook object model is complemented by another object model called Collaboration Data Objects (CDO). This section briefly discusses this object model and the reasons you might have to use it.

CDO provides some functionality unavailable in the Outlook object model. CDO works against the underlying data that Outlook is connected to rather than working against UI elements specific to Outlook. CDO exposes some properties of folders and Outlook items that the Outlook object model does not expose. CDO also provides methods unavailable in the Outlook object model. For example:

- CDO lets you delete an Outlook item permanently without first routing it to the Deleted Items folder, whereas Outlook always routes Outlook items you delete to the Deleted Items folder.
- CDO lets you programmatically show the Select Names dialog that can be used to choose recipients for an e-mail message.
- CDO lets you read and write several properties that are either not available in the Outlook object model or are read-only in the Outlook object model.

The connection between the Outlook object model and CDO is that every Outlook item is in an information store represented in Outlook by a root folder in Outlook's Folder List view. An information store can be an Exchange mailbox on a server or a local PST file. Every information store is identified by a StoreID. Within that information store, an Outlook item is identified by an EntryID. So if you can get the StoreID and EntryID associated with an Outlook item via the Outlook object model, you can write CDO code to get to that same Outlook item using the StoreID and EntryID.

Before we show some code that illustrates navigating from an Outlook item to a CDO item, let's first consider how to add a reference to the CDO object model. Given that you have a project in Visual Studio, right-click the References folder in the Solution Explorer and choose Add Reference. In the Add Reference dialog shown in Figure 9-13, click the COM tab and select the component Microsoft CDO 1.21 Library. Then click the OK button.

The result of clicking OK in the dialog shown in Figure 9-13 is that a reference is added to the CDO library. The CDO library is contained in a namespace called MAPI. No pre-generated PIA for the CDO library exists—so Visual Studio creates an interop assembly (IA) for the CDO library.

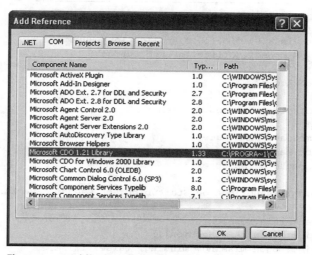

Figure 9-13 Adding a reference to CDO.

Listing 9-4 shows a VSTO Outlook add-in that navigates from an Outlook MailItem to the corresponding CDO Message object. It handles the Inspectors.New-Inspector event and displays a dialog showing the subject using both an Outlook Item object and CDO's Message object.

Also illustrated in this code is the use of CDO's root object called the Session object. In the Startup method, the code creates a new instance of the Session object and then calls the Session.Logon method to initialize the Session object. In the Shutdown method, the code calls Logoff on the Session object to clean it up properly.

The GetMessageFromOutlookItem method gets the CDO Message object that corresponds to an Outlook Item object. It uses a reflection helper method called Get-PropertyHelper to get property values in a late-bound way. It gets an EntryID and a StoreID, and then uses the GetMessage method on Session to get a CDO Message object. The GetOutlookItemFromMessage takes a CDO Message and gets the corresponding Outlook Item object. It gets an EntryID and StoreID using properties on CDO's Message object. It then uses the GetItemFromID method on Outlook's NameSpace object to get an Outlook Item object.

Listing 9-4 Getting from an Outlook MailItem to a CDO Message Object

```
using System;
using System.Windows.Forms;
using Microsoft.VisualStudio.Tools.Applications.Runtime;
using Outlook = Microsoft.Office.Interop.Outlook;

namespace OutlookAddin1
{
  public partial class ThisApplication
  {
    Outlook.NameSpace nameSpace;
    MAPI.Session mapiSession;
    Outlook.Inspectors inspectors;

    private void ThisApplication_Startup(object sender, EventArgs e)
    {
      nameSpace = this.Session;
      mapiSession = new MAPI.Session();
      mapiSession.Logon(missing, missing, false, false,
        missing, missing, missing);

      inspectors = this.Inspectors;
      inspectors.NewInspector += new
        Outlook.InspectorsEvents_NewInspectorEventHandler(
        Inspectors_NewInspector);
    }

    private void ThisApplication_Shutdown(object sender, EventArgs e)
    {
      mapiSession.Logoff();
    }

    MAPI.Message GetMessageFromOutlookItem(object outlookItem)
    {
      object entryID = GetPropertyHelper(outlookItem, "EntryID");
      object parentFolder = GetPropertyHelper(outlookItem, "Parent");
      object storeID = GetPropertyHelper(parentFolder, "StoreID");

      return (MAPI.Message)mapiSession.GetMessage(entryID, storeID);
    }
```

```csharp
object GetOutlookItemFromMessage(MAPI.Message message)
{
    string entryID = (string)message.ID;
    string storeID = (string)message.StoreID;
    return nameSpace.GetItemFromID(entryID, storeID);
}

private object GetPropertyHelper(object targetObject,
    string propertyName)
{
    return targetObject.GetType().InvokeMember(propertyName,
        System.Reflection.BindingFlags.Public |
        System.Reflection.BindingFlags.Instance |
        System.Reflection.BindingFlags.GetProperty,
        null,
        targetObject,
        null,
        System.Globalization.CultureInfo.CurrentCulture);
}

void Inspectors_NewInspector(Outlook.Inspector inspector)
{
    object inspectedItem = inspector.CurrentItem;

    MAPI.Message message = GetMessageFromOutlookItem(inspectedItem);
    MessageBox.Show(String.Format(
        "message.Subject={0}", message.Subject));

    object outlookItem = GetOutlookItemFromMessage(message);
    MessageBox.Show(String.Format(
        "outlookItem.Subject={0}",
        GetPropertyHelper(outlookItem, "Subject")));
}

#region VSTO Designer generated code
private void InternalStartup()
{
    this.Startup += new EventHandler(ThisApplication_Startup);
    this.Shutdown += new EventHandler(ThisApplication_Shutdown);
}
#endregion
    }
}
```

Figure 9-14 shows a diagram of the objects in the CDO object model. This book does not cover the CDO object model in any additional depth.

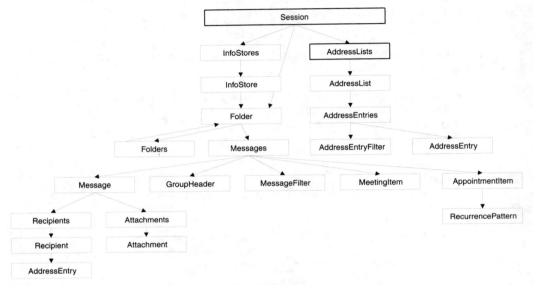

Figure 9-14 The Collaboration Data Objects (CDO) object model.

Conclusion

This chapter introduced the various ways you can integrate your code into Outlook. You learned about Outlook's ability to add a custom property page to the Outlook Option's dialog or to a folder's Properties dialog. This chapter also introduced the basic hierarchy of the Outlook object model and briefly considered the Collaboration Data Objects object model. Chapter 10 describes the events in the Outlook object model. Chapter 11 describes the most important objects in the Outlook object model. Chapter 24 describes building VSTO Outlook add-ins.

▉ 10 ▪

Working with Outlook Events

Events in the Outlook Object Model

U NDERSTANDING THE EVENTS IN THE Outlook object model is critical because this is often the primary way that your code is run. This chapter covers many of the events in the Outlook object model, when they are raised, and the type of code you might associate with these events.

Outlook associates the same set of events with all the Outlook item object types listed in Table 10-1. In this chapter, we will refer to Item events, but there is no Item object per se in the Outlook object model. Instead, you will find the same set of Item events (defined by ItemEvents_10_Event interface) on each of the 15 Outlook object model objects listed in Table 10-1.

Table 10-1 Outlook Item Objects

Object	Description
AppointmentItem	An appointment item typically found in the Calendar folder.
ContactItem	A contact item typically found in the Contacts folder.
DistListItem	A distribution list typically found in the Contacts folder.
DocumentItem	A document that you have added to an Outlook folder by dragging and dropping it from the file system into the Outlook folder.
JournalItem	A journal entry typically found in the Journal folder.
MailItem	A mail message typically found in the Inbox folder.
MeetingItem	A meeting request typically found in the Inbox folder.
NoteItem	A note typically found in the Notes folder.
PostItem	A post in an Outlook folder.
RemoteItem	A mail message that has not yet been fully retrieved from the server but has the subject of the message, the received date and time, the sender, the size of the message, and the first 256 characters of the message body.
ReportItem	A mail delivery report such as a report when mail delivery failed typically found in Outlook's Inbox folder.
TaskItem	A task typically found in the Tasks folder.
TaskRequestAcceptItem	A response to a TaskRequestItem typically found in the Inbox folder.
TaskRequestDeclineItem	A response to a TaskRequestItem typically found in the Inbox folder.
TaskRequestItem	A task request sent to another user typically found in the Inbox folder.
TaskRequestUpdateItem	An update to a TaskRequestItem typically found in the Inbox folder.

Why Are There Multiple Event Interfaces?

When you work with the Outlook object model, you will quickly notice multiple public interfaces, classes, and delegates associated with events:

- ApplicationEvents interface
- ApplicationEvents_Event interface
- ApplicationEvents_* delegates
- ApplicationEvents_SinkHelper class
- ApplicationEvents_10 interface
- ApplicationsEvents_10_Event interface
- ApplicationEvents_10_* delegates
- ApplicationEvents_10_SinkHelper class
- ApplicationEvents_11 interface
- **ApplicationsEvents_11_Event interface**
- **ApplicationEvents_11_* delegates**
- ApplicationEvents_11_SinkHelper class

- ExplorerEvents interface
- ExplorerEvents_Event interface
- ExplorerEvents_* delegates
- ExplorerEvents_SinkHelper class
- ExplorerEvents_10 interface
- **ExplorerEvents_10_Event interface**
- **ExplorerEvents_10_* delegates**
- ExplorerEvents10_SinkHelper class

- ExplorersEvents interface
- **ExplorersEvents_Event interface**
- **ExplorersEvents_* delegates**
- ExplorersEvents_SinkHelper class

- FoldersEvents interface
- **FoldersEvents_Event interface**
- **FoldersEvents_* delegates**
- FoldersEvents_SinkHelper class

- InspectorEvents interface
- InspectorEvents_Event interface
- InspectorEvents_* delegates
- InspectorEvents_SinkHelper class
- InspectorEvents_10 interface
- **InspectorEvents_10_Event interface**
- **InspectorEvents_10_* delegates**
- InspectorEvents_10_SinkHelper class

- ItemEvents interface
- ItemEvents_Event interface
- ItemEvents_* delegates
- ItemEvents_SinkHelper class
- ItemEvents_10 interface
- **ItemEvents_10_Event interface**
- **ItemEvents_10_* delegates**
- ItemEvents_10_SinkHelper class

- ItemsEvents interface
- **ItemsEvents_Event interface**
- **ItemsEvents_* delegates**
- ItemsEvents_SinkHelper class

- NameSpaceEvents interface
- **NameSpaceEvents_Event interface**

- **NameSpaceEvents_* delegates**
- NameSpaceEvents_SinkHelper class

- OutlookBarGroupsEvents interface
- **OutlookBarGroupsEvents_Event interface**
- **OutlookBarGroupsEvents_* delegates**
- OutlookBarGroupsEvents_SinkHelper class

- OutlookBarPaneEvents interface
- **OutlookBarPaneEvents_Event interface**
- **OutlookBarPaneEvents_* delegates**
- OutlookBarPaneEvents_SinkHelper class

- OutlookBarShortcutsEvents interface
- **OutlookBarShortcutsEvents_Event interface**
- **OutlookBarShortcutsEvents_* delegates**
- OutlookBarShortcutsEvents_SinkHelper class

- ReminderCollectionEvents interface
- **ReminderCollectionEvents_Event interface**
- **ReminderCollectionEvents_* delegates**
- ReminderCollectionEvents_SinkHelper class

- ResultsEvents interface
- **ResultsEvents_Event interface**
- **ResultsEvents_* delegates**
- ResultsEvents_SinkHelper class

- SyncObjectEvents interface
- **SyncObjectEvents_Event interface**
- **SyncObjectEvents_* delegates**
- SyncObjectEvents_SinkHelper class

- ViewsEvents interface
- **ViewsEvents_Event interface**
- **ViewsEvents_* delegates**
- ViewsEvents_SinkHelper class

The only elements from this list that you should ever use in your code are the ones in bold text. The *_Event interfaces in bold should only be used when you have to cast an object to its corresponding event interface because a method name and event name collide. An example of this is the Inspector object, which has both a Close method and a Close event. To disambiguate between the two, you have to cast the Inspector object to InspectorEvents_10_Event when you want to handle the Close event.

Chapter 1, "An Introduction to Office Programming," briefly explains the reason for the other items in this list. However, this explanation only explains the SinkHelper class and why there is both an *Object*Events interface and an *Object*Events_Event interface. The reason there are multiple numbered events associated with some objects goes back to the original COM implementation of the Outlook object model.

Outlook's Application, Explorer, Inspector, and Item COM objects have had their event interfaces defined over multiple versions. For example, consider the Application events. Events defined in Outlook XP for the Application object are on the interface named ApplicationEvents_Event. Events that were new in Outlook 2000 are on the interface named ApplicationEvents_10_Events. (Outlook 2000 was known internally at Microsoft as Outlook 10.) ApplicationEvents_10_Events also contains all the events that are in the ApplicationEvents_Event. Events that were new in Outlook 2003 are on the interface named ApplicationEvents_11_Events. (Outlook 2003 was known internally at Microsoft as Outlook 11.) The ApplicationEvents_11_Events interface includes all the events defined in Outlook XP and Outlook 2000. Because ApplicationEvents_11_Events contains all the events defined for Application, this is the only interface you should use for Outlook 2003 development.

Application-Level Events

This section covers events that occur at the Application level. This includes either events raised on the Application object or events that are raised on the main Outlook windows. The two primary windows displayed by Outlook are represented in the Outlook object model by the Explorer object and the Inspector object. An Explorer object represents the main Outlook window in which the contents of folders display. An Inspector object represents the Outlook window that appears when you double-click an Outlook item—for example, when you double-click a mail item in your inbox. Figure 10-1 shows representative Explorer and Inspector windows.

It is possible to have zero or more Explorer and zero or more Inspector windows open at any given time. For example, if you right-click a document in the My Documents folder and choose Mail Recipient from the Send To menu, Outlook launches with only an Inspector window open. If you launch Outlook by picking it from the Start menu, it typically starts up with just the main Outlook window open, which is an Explorer window. If you right-click a folder within Outlook and choose Open in New Window, doing so creates an additional Explorer window to display that folder. Outlook can also run in a mode with neither an Explorer nor an Inspector window running—for example, when it is started by the ActiveSync application shipped by Microsoft for syncing phones and PDAs to Outlook.

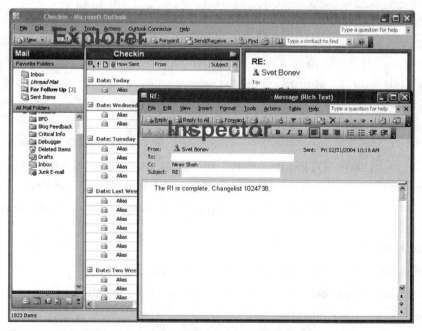

Figure 10-1 An Explorer window and an Inspector window.

Startup and Quit Events

Outlook raises several events during startup and shutdown:

- **Application.Startup** is raised when Outlook has completely started up. This event is raised after add-ins have been loaded so that an add-in can handle this event—that is, it is not raised before add-ins are loaded (as are some events in Word and Excel).
- **Application.MAPILogonComplete** is raised after Outlook has logged on to the mail services it is configured to connect to.
- **Application.Quit** is raised when Outlook is about to exit. This event is raised before add-ins have been unloaded so that an add-in can handle this event. A VSTO Outlook add-in is unloaded before the Quit event is raised and should use the Shutdown event instead.

> Quit is the name of both a method and an event on the Application object. Because of this collision, you will not see the Quit event in Visual Studio's pop-up menu of properties, events, and methods associated with the Application object. Furthermore, a warning displays at compile time when you try to handle this event. To get Visual Studio's pop-up menus to work and the warning to go away, you can cast the Application object to the ApplicationEvents_11_Event interface, as shown in Listing 10-1.

The order in which IDTExtensibility2 methods associated with a COM add-in (described in Chapter 23, "Developing COM Add-Ins for Word and Excel") and Outlook's Startup, Quit, and MAPILogonComplete events occur is shown here:

- **User launches Outlook.**

  OnConnection method of IDTExtensibility2 is called.

  OnStartupComplete method of IDTExtensibility2 is called.

  Startup event is raised.

  MAPILogonComplete event is raised.

- **User quits Outlook.**

  Quit event is raised.

  OnBeginShutdown of IDTExtensibility2 is called.

  OnDisconnection of IDTExtensibility2 is called.

Listing 10-1 shows an add-in that handles these three events. It also displays message boxes when the methods of IDTExtensibility2 are called.

> For simplicity, the COM add-in listings in this chapter do not include the fix described in Chapter 24, "Creating Outlook Add-Ins with VSTO," that is required to get Outlook to always shut down reliably when loading a COM add-in.
>
> Even though this book includes some COM add-in samples, our recommendation is that you create VSTO Outlook add-ins rather than COM add-ins to avoid the issues described in Chapter 24.

Listing 10-1 A COM Add-In That Handles the Application Object's Quit, Startup, and MAPILogonComplete Events

```
namespace MyAddin2
{
  using System;
  using Extensibility;
  using Outlook = Microsoft.Office.Interop.Outlook;
  using System.Windows.Forms;
  using System.Runtime.InteropServices;

  [GuidAttribute("FEC2B9E7-9366-4AD2-AD05-4CF0167AC9C6"),
    ProgId("MyAddin2.Connect")]
  public class Connect : Object, Extensibility.IDTExtensibility2
  {
    Outlook.Application applicationObject;

    public void OnConnection(object application,
      Extensibility.ext_ConnectMode connectMode,
      object addInInst, ref System.Array custom)
    {
      applicationObject = (Outlook.Application)application;

      applicationObject.Startup += new
        Outlook.ApplicationEvents_11_StartupEventHandler(
```

```
      ApplicationObject_Startup);

   ((Outlook.ApplicationEvents_11_Event)applicationObject).
      Quit += new
      Outlook.ApplicationEvents_11_QuitEventHandler(
      ApplicationObject_Quit);

   applicationObject.MAPILogonComplete += new
      Outlook.ApplicationEvents_11_MAPILogonCompleteEventHandler(
      ApplicationObject_MAPILogonComplete);

   MessageBox.Show("OnConnection");
}

public void OnDisconnection(
   Extensibility.ext_DisconnectMode disconnectMode,
   ref System.Array custom)
{
   MessageBox.Show("OnDisconnection");
}

public void OnAddInsUpdate(ref System.Array custom) { }
public void OnStartupComplete(ref System.Array custom)
{
   MessageBox.Show("OnStartupComplete");
}

public void OnBeginShutdown(ref System.Array custom)
{
   MessageBox.Show("OnBeginShutdown");
}

void ApplicationObject_Startup()
{
   MessageBox.Show("Startup Event");
}

void ApplicationObject_MAPILogonComplete()
{
   MessageBox.Show("MAPILogonComplete Event");
}

void ApplicationObject_Quit()
{
   MessageBox.Show("Quit Event");
}
   }
}
```

The order in which a VSTO Outlook add-in's Startup and Shutdown event handlers and Outlook's Startup, Quit, and MAPILogonComplete events occur is shown here:

- **User launches Outlook.**

  VSTO Startup event is raised.

  Outlook Application object's Startup event is raised.

  Outlook Application object's MAPILogonComplete event is raised.

- **User quits Outlook.**

  Outlook Application object's Quit event is raised—the VSTO add-in system uses this event to control how the add-in unloads so you may or may not see this event. Your code should handle the Shutdown event instead.

  VSTO Shutdown event is raised.

Activation Events

When an Explorer or Inspector window becomes the active window (activates) or loses focus to another window (deactivates), events are raised:

- **Explorer.Activate** is raised on an Explorer object when the window it corresponds to becomes the active window.

- **Inspector.Activate** is raised on an Inspector object when the window it corresponds to becomes the active window.

> Activate is the name of both a method and an event on the Explorer and Inspector object. Because of this collision, you will not see the Activate event in Visual Studio's pop-up menu of properties, events, and methods associated with the Explorer or Inspector object. Furthermore, a warning displays at compile time when you try to handle this event. To get Visual Studio's pop-up menus to work and the warning to go away, you can cast the Explorer object to the ExplorerEvents_10_Event interface and the Inspector object to the InspectorEvents_10_Event interface, as shown in Listing 10-2.

- **Explorer.Deactivate** is raised on an Explorer object when the window it corresponds to loses focus to another window.
- **Inspector.Deactivate** is raised on an Inspector object when the window it corresponds to loses focus to another window.

Listing 10-2 shows a VSTO Outlook add-in that handles Activate and Deactivate events for the Explorer object.

> For simplicity, future VSTO Outlook add-in listings in this chapter omit the using... lines of code at the beginning of the VSTO ThisApplication class, the region marked with #region VSTO generated code, and the Shutdown event handler.

Listing 10-2 A VSTO Add-In That Handles the Explorer Object's Activate and Deactivate Events

```
using System;
using System.Windows.Forms;
using Microsoft.VisualStudio.Tools.Applications.Runtime;
using Outlook = Microsoft.Office.Interop.Outlook;

namespace OutlookAddin1
{
  public partial class ThisApplication
  {
    Outlook.Explorer explorer;

    private void ThisApplication_Startup(object sender, EventArgs e)
    {
      explorer = this.ActiveExplorer();

      ((Outlook.ExplorerEvents_10_Event)explorer).Activate +=
        new Outlook.ExplorerEvents_10_ActivateEventHandler(
        Explorer_Activate);

      explorer.Deactivate += new
        Outlook.ExplorerEvents_10_DeactivateEventHandler(
        Explorer_Deactivate);
    }

    void Explorer_Activate()
    {
      MessageBox.Show(String.Format(
```

```
        "The explorer with caption {0} was activated.",
        explorer.Caption));
    }

    void Explorer_Deactivate()
    {
      MessageBox.Show(String.Format(
        "The explorer with caption {0} was deactivated.",
        explorer.Caption));
    }

    private void ThisApplication_Shutdown(object sender, EventArgs e)
    {
    }

    #region VSTO generated code
    private void InternalStartup()
    {
      this.Startup += new EventHandler(ThisApplication_Startup);
      this.Shutdown += new EventHandler(ThisApplication_Shutdown);
    }
    #endregion
  }
}
```

New Window Events

When a new Explorer or Inspector window is created, Outlook raises an event:

- **Explorers.NewExplorer** is raised when a new Explorer window is created. The newly created Explorer is passed as a parameter to this event.

- **Inspectors.NewInspector** is raised when a new Inspector window is created. The newly created Inspector is passed as a parameter to this event.

Listing 24-1 shows an example of handling these events.

Window Events

When an Explorer or Inspector window is maximized, minimized, moved, or resized, events are raised by Outlook. All of these events can be cancelled to prevent the change to the window from occurring:

- **Explorer.BeforeMaximize** is raised on an Explorer object when the window it corresponds to is about to be maximized. Outlook passes by reference a `bool` `cancel` parameter. The `cancel` parameter can be set to `true` by your event handler to prevent Outlook from maximizing the window.

- **Inspector.BeforeMaximize** is raised on an Inspector object when the window it corresponds to is about to be maximized. Outlook passes by reference a `bool cancel` parameter. The `cancel` parameter can be set to `true` by your event handler to prevent Outlook from maximizing the window.

- **Explorer.BeforeMinimize** is raised on an Explorer object when the window it corresponds to is about to be minimized. Outlook passes by reference a `bool` `cancel` parameter. The `cancel` parameter can be set to `true` by your event handler to prevent Outlook from minimizing the window.

- **Inspector.BeforeMinimize** is raised on an Inspector object when the window it corresponds to is about to be minimized. Outlook passes by reference a `bool cancel` parameter. The `cancel` parameter can be set to `true` by your event handler to prevent Outlook from minimizing the window.

- **Explorer.BeforeMove** is raised on an Explorer object when the window it corresponds to is about to be moved. Outlook passes by reference a `bool cancel` parameter. The `cancel` parameter can be set to `true` by your event handler to prevent Outlook from moving the window.

- **Inspector.BeforeMove** is raised on an Inspector object when the window it corresponds to is about to be moved. Outlook passes by reference a `bool` `cancel` parameter. The `cancel` parameter can be set to `true` by your event handler to prevent Outlook from moving the window.

- **Explorer.BeforeSize** is raised on an Explorer object when the window it corresponds to is about to be resized. Outlook passes by reference a `bool cancel` parameter. The `cancel` parameter can be set to `true` by your event handler to prevent Outlook from resizing the window.

- **Inspector.BeforeSize** is raised on an Inspector object when the window it corresponds to is about to be resized. Outlook passes by reference a `bool cancel` parameter. The `cancel` parameter can be set to `true` by your event handler to prevent Outlook from resizing the window.

Close Events

When an Explorer or Inspector window is closed, Outlook raises an event:

- **Explorer.Close** is raised on an Explorer object when the window it corresponds to has been closed.
- **Inspector.Close** is raised on an Inspector object when the window it corresponds to has been closed.

Close is the name of both a method and an event on the Explorer and Inspector object. Because of this collision, you will not see the Close event in Visual Studio's pop-up menu of properties, events, and methods associated with the Explorer or Inspector object. Furthermore, a warning displays at compile time when you try to handle this event. To get Visual Studio's pop-up menus to work and the warning to go away, you can cast the Explorer object to the ExplorerEvents_10_Event interface and the Inspector object to the InspectorEvents_10_Event interface, as shown in Listing 9-1.

Listing 24-1 shows an example of handling these events.

View and Selection Change Events

As you navigate from folder to folder in an Explorer window, Outlook displays a view of the items in the folder you have selected. The user can also change the view for a particular folder by using the View menu and choosing a different view from the Current View menu in the Arrange By menu. Outlook raises events when the view changes or the selection changes:

- **Explorer.BeforeViewSwitch** is raised on an Explorer object when the user changes the view for a particular folder by using the View menu. This event is not raised when the user simply switches from folder to folder thereby changing the view (but the ViewSwitch event is). Outlook passes a `newView` parameter that is of type `object`. This parameter can be cast to a `string` value representing the name of the view about to be switched to. Outlook also passes by reference a `bool cancel` parameter. The `cancel` parameter can be set to `true` by your event handler to prevent Outlook from switching to the view the user selected.

- **Explorer.ViewSwitch** is raised on an Explorer object when the view changes either because the user changed the view using the View menu or because the user selected another folder.

- **Inspector.SelectionChange** is raised on an Explorer object when the selection in the Explorer window changes.

- **Explorer.BeforeFolderSwitch** is raised on an Explorer object before the active folder changes. Outlook passes a `newFolder` parameter of type `object`. This parameter can be cast to a MAPIFolder that represents what the new active folder will be. Outlook also passes by reference a `bool cancel` parameter. The `cancel` parameter can be set to `true` by your event handler to prevent Outlook from switching to the folder the user selected.

- **Explorer.FolderSwitch** is raised on an Explorer object when the active folder changes.

Listing 10-3 shows a VSTO Outlook add-in that handles these events.

Listing 10-3 A VSTO Add-In That Handles View and Selection Change Events

```
namespace OutlookAddin1
{
  public partial class ThisApplication
  {
    Outlook.Explorer explorer;

    private void ThisApplication_Startup(object sender, EventArgs e)
    {
      explorer = this.ActiveExplorer();

      explorer.BeforeViewSwitch += new
        Outlook.ExplorerEvents_10_BeforeViewSwitchEventHandler(
        Explorer_BeforeViewSwitch);

      explorer.ViewSwitch += new
        Outlook.ExplorerEvents_10_ViewSwitchEventHandler(
        Explorer_ViewSwitch);

      explorer.SelectionChange +=new
```

```csharp
      Outlook.ExplorerEvents_10_SelectionChangeEventHandler(
      Explorer_SelectionChange);

  explorer.BeforeFolderSwitch += new
    Outlook.ExplorerEvents_10_BeforeFolderSwitchEventHandler(
    Explorer_BeforeFolderSwitch);

  explorer.FolderSwitch += new
    Outlook.ExplorerEvents_10_FolderSwitchEventHandler(
    Explorer_FolderSwitch);
}

void Explorer_BeforeViewSwitch(object newView,
  ref bool cancel)
{
  MessageBox.Show(String.Format(
    "About to switch to {0}.", newView));
}

void Explorer_ViewSwitch()
{
  Outlook.View view = explorer.CurrentView as Outlook.View;
  if (view != null)
  {
    MessageBox.Show(String.Format(
      "The view has been switched. Current view is now {0}.",
      view.Name));
  }
}

void Explorer_SelectionChange()
{
  MessageBox.Show(String.Format(
    "Selection changed. {0} items selected.",
    explorer.Selection.Count));
}

void Explorer_BeforeFolderSwitch(object newFolder,
  ref bool cancel)
{
  Outlook.MAPIFolder folder = (Outlook.MAPIFolder)newFolder;
  MessageBox.Show(String.Format(
    "The new folder will be {0}.",
    folder.Name));
}

void Explorer_FolderSwitch()
{
```

```
                MessageBox.Show("Folder switch");
            }
        }
    }
```

Folder Change Events

Given a collection of folders in Outlook, several events are raised when folders in that collection change:

- **Folders.FolderAdd** is raised on a Folders collection when a new folder is added. Outlook passes a `folder` parameter of type `MAPIFolder` representing the newly added folder.
- **Folders.FolderRemove** is raised on a Folders collection when a folder is deleted.
- **Folders.FolderChange** is raised on a Folders collection when a folder is changed. Examples of changes include when the folder is renamed or when the number of items in the folder changes. Outlook passes a `folder` parameter of type `MAPIFolder` representing the folder that has changed.

Listing 10-4 shows an add-in that handles folder change events for any subfolders under the Inbox folder. To get to a Folders collection, we first get a NameSpace object. The NameSpace object is accessed by calling the Application.Session property. The NameSpace object has a method called GetDefaultFolder that returns a MAPIFolder object to which you can pass a member of the enumeration `OlDefaultFolders` to get a standard Outlook folder. In Listing 10-4, we pass `olFolderInbox` to get a MAPIFolder for the Inbox. We then connect our event handlers to the Folders collection associated with the Inbox's MAPIFolder object.

Listing 10-4 A VSTO Add-In That Handles Folder Change Events

```
namespace OutlookAddin1
{
    public partial class ThisApplication
    {
        Outlook.Folders folders;
        private void ThisApplication_Startup(object sender, EventArgs e)
        {
```

```
    Outlook.NameSpace ns = this.Session;
    Outlook.MAPIFolder folder = ns.GetDefaultFolder(
      Outlook.OlDefaultFolders.olFolderInbox);
    folders = folder.Folders;

    folders.FolderAdd += new
      Outlook.FoldersEvents_FolderAddEventHandler(
      Folders_FolderAdd);

    folders.FolderChange += new
      Outlook.FoldersEvents_FolderChangeEventHandler(
      Folders_FolderChange);

    folders.FolderRemove += new
      Outlook.FoldersEvents_FolderRemoveEventHandler(
      Folders_FolderRemove);
  }

  void Folders_FolderAdd(Outlook.MAPIFolder folder)
  {
    MessageBox.Show(String.Format(
      "Added {0} folder.", folder.Name));
  }

  void Folders_FolderChange(Outlook.MAPIFolder folder)
  {
    MessageBox.Show(String.Format(
      "Changed {0} folder. ", folder.Name));
  }

  void Folders_FolderRemove()
  {
    MessageBox.Show("Removed a folder.");
  }
  }
 }
```

Outlook Item Events

Outlook has many events that occur at the Outlook item level. We refer to Item
events in this section, but there is no Item object per se in the Outlook object model.
Instead, you will find Item events on each of the 15 Outlook object model objects
listed in Table 10-1.

Item Addition, Deletion, and Change Events

Several events are raised when Outlook items are added, deleted, or changed:

- **Items.ItemRemove** is raised when an item is deleted from the Items collection associated with a folder—for example, when an item is deleted from the collection of items in the Inbox folder. It is raised once for each item removed from the collection. Unfortunately, the item removed from the collection is not passed as a parameter to this event and is difficult to determine unless you store the previous state of the items in the folder in some way. This event is also not raised if more than 16 items are deleted at once or when the last item in a folder is deleted if the folder is in a PST file. You can work around these limitations by using the FolderChange event described in the "Folder Change Events" section earlier in this chapter. For example, you could store the number of items in the folder in a variable and when handling the Folder-Change event determine whether the number of items in the folder have decreased.

- **Items.ItemChange** is raised when an item is changed in the Items collection associated with a folder—for example, when an item is changed in the collection of Outlook items in the Inbox folder. Outlook passes the Outlook item that has changed as an `object` parameter to this event.

- **Items.ItemAdd** is raised when an item is added to the Items collection associated with a folder—for example, when an item is added to the collection of Outlook items in the Inbox folder. It is raised once for each item that is added to the collection. Outlook passes the Outlook item that was added as an `object` parameter to this event. Unfortunately, this event is not raised if a large number of items are added at once. You can work around this limitation by using the FolderChange event described in the "Folder Change Events" section earlier in this chapter. For example, you could store the state of the items in the folder that you want to monitor for changes and when handling the FolderChange event determine whether the new state of the items in the folder matches the state you have stored.

- **Item.BeforeDelete** is raised on an Outlook item when the item is deleted. However, the item must be deleted from an Inspector window—the event is not raised if you just delete the item from a folder. Outlook passes by reference a `bool cancel` parameter. The `cancel` parameter can be set to `true` by your event handler to prevent Outlook from deleting the item

Listing 10-5 shows some VSTO Outlook add-in code that handles these events. To get to an individual MailItem to handle the Item.BeforeDelete event, the code first gets the NameSpace object. The NameSpace object is accessed by calling the Application.Session property. The NameSpace object has a method called GetDefaultFolder that returns a MAPIFolder to which you can pass a member of the enumeration `OlDefaultFolders` to get a standard Outlook folder. In Listing 10-5, we pass `olFolderInbox` to get a MAPIFolder for the Inbox. We then use the Items collection associated with the Inbox's MAPIFolder to connect our event handlers to as well as to get an individual MailItem to handle the Item.BeforeDelete event for.

Listing 10-5 A VSTO Add-In That Handles Item Addition, Change, and Delete Events

```csharp
namespace OutlookAddin1
{
  public partial class ThisApplication
  {
    Outlook.MailItem mailItem;
    Outlook.Items items;
    private void ThisApplication_Startup(object sender, EventArgs e)
    {
      Outlook.NameSpace ns = this.Session;
      Outlook.MAPIFolder inbox = ns.
        GetDefaultFolder(Outlook.OlDefaultFolders.olFolderInbox);

      foreach (object o in inbox.Items)
      {
        mailItem = o as Outlook.MailItem;
        if (mailItem != null)
        {
          break;
        }
      }

      if (mailItem == null)
      {
        MessageBox.Show("Couldn't find a mail item to connect to.");
      }
      else
      {
```

```csharp
      mailItem.BeforeDelete += new
        Outlook.ItemEvents_10_BeforeDeleteEventHandler(
        MailItem_BeforeDelete);

      MessageBox.Show(String.Format(
        "Connected to the mail item with subject {0}.",
        mailItem.Subject));
    }

  items = inbox.Items;
  items.ItemRemove += new
    Outlook.ItemsEvents_ItemRemoveEventHandler(
    Items_ItemRemove);

  items.ItemChange += new
    Outlook.ItemsEvents_ItemChangeEventHandler(
    Items_ItemChange);

  items.ItemAdd += new
    Outlook.ItemsEvents_ItemAddEventHandler(
    Items_ItemAdd);
  }

void MailItem_BeforeDelete(object item, ref bool cancel)
{
  MessageBox.Show(String.Format(
    "The mail item {0} cannot be deleted.",
    mailItem.Subject));
  cancel = true;
}

void Items_ItemRemove()
{
  MessageBox.Show("An item is about to be removed.");
}

void GenerateItemMessage(object item, string operation)
{
  Outlook.MailItem mailItem = item as Outlook.MailItem;
  if (mailItem != null)
  {
    MessageBox.Show(String.Format(
      "MailItem {0} was just {1}.",
      mailItem.Subject, operation));
  }
  else
  {
```

```
      MessageBox.Show(String.Format(
        "An Outlook item was just {0}.", operation));
    }
  }

  void Items_ItemChange(object item)
  {
    GenerateItemMessage(item, "changed");
  }

  void Items_ItemAdd(object item)
  {
    GenerateItemMessage(item, "added");
  }
 }
}
```

Copy, Paste, Cut, and Delete Events

Outlook raises several events when Outlook items are copied, cut, or pasted. These events are raised on an Explorer object. An Explorer object has a Selection property that returns the current selected items in the Explorer. Because many of the Explorer events telling you that a copy, cut, or paste is about to occur do not pass the items that are being acted upon, you must examine the Selection object to determine the items that are being acted upon:

- **Explorer.BeforeItemCopy** is raised before one or more Outlook items are copied. Outlook passes by reference a `bool cancel` parameter. The `cancel` parameter can be set to `true` by your event handler to prevent the item or items from being copied.

- **Explorer.BeforeItemCut** is raised before one or more Outlook items are cut. Outlook passes by reference a `bool cancel` parameter. The `cancel` parameter can be set to `true` by your event handler to prevent the item or items from being cut.

- **Explorer.BeforeItemPaste** is raised before one or more Outlook items are pasted. Outlook passes a `clipboardContent` parameter as an `object`. If the clipboard contains Outlook items that have been cut or copied, you can cast the `clipboardContent` parameter to a Selection object and examine what is about to be pasted. Outlook next passes a `target` parameter of type `MAPI-Folder`. This represents the destination folder to which the item or items will be pasted. Outlook also passes by reference a `bool cancel` parameter. The `cancel` parameter can be set to `true` by your event handler to prevent the item or items from being pasted.

Listing 10-6 shows a VSTO Outlook add-in that handles these events. It uses a helper function called `GenerateItemsMessage` that iterates over the items in a Selection object and displays a dialog with the subject of each MailItem selected.

Listing 10-6 A VSTO Add-In That Handles Copy, Cut, and Paste Events

```
namespace OutlookAddin1
{
  public partial class ThisApplication
  {
    Outlook.Explorer explorer;

    private void ThisApplication_Startup(object sender, EventArgs e)
    {
      explorer = this.ActiveExplorer();

      explorer.BeforeItemCopy += new
        Outlook.ExplorerEvents_10_BeforeItemCopyEventHandler(
        Explorer_BeforeItemCopy);

      explorer.BeforeItemCut += new
        Outlook.ExplorerEvents_10_BeforeItemCutEventHandler(
        Explorer_BeforeItemCut);

      explorer.BeforeItemPaste += new
        Outlook.ExplorerEvents_10_BeforeItemPasteEventHandler(
        Explorer_BeforeItemPaste);
    }

    void GenerateItemsMessage(Outlook.Selection selection,
      string operation)
    {
      System.Text.StringBuilder b = new System.Text.StringBuilder();
      b.AppendFormat("Items to be {0}:\n\n", operation);

      foreach (object o in selection)
      {
        Outlook.MailItem mi = o as Outlook.MailItem;
        if (mi != null)
```

```
      {
        b.AppendFormat("MailItem: {0}\n", mi.Subject);
      }
      else
      {
        b.AppendLine("Other Outlook item");
      }
    }
    MessageBox.Show(b.ToString());
  }

  void Explorer_BeforeItemCopy(ref bool cancel)
  {
    GenerateItemsMessage(explorer.Selection, "copied");
  }

  void Explorer_BeforeItemCut(ref bool cancel)
  {
    GenerateItemsMessage(explorer.Selection, "cut");
  }

  void Explorer_BeforeItemPaste(ref object clipboardContent,
    Outlook.MAPIFolder target, ref bool cancel)
  {
    if (clipboardContent is Outlook.Selection)
    {
      Outlook.Selection selection =
        clipboardContent as Outlook.Selection;

      GenerateItemsMessage(selection, "pasted");
    }
    else
    {
      MessageBox.Show("The clipboard is not a Selection object.");
    }
  }
}
}
```

Property Change Events

A typical Outlook item has many associated properties, such as CreationTime, Importance, LastModificationTime, and so on. All the properties associated with an Outlook item are contained by the ItemProperties property. When any of these properties are changed, Outlook raises the PropertyChange event. It is also possible to define additional custom properties and associate them with an Outlook item. When custom properties are changed, Outlook raises the CustomPropertyChange event:

- **Item.PropertyChange** is raised when a property of an Outlook item is changed. Outlook passes a `name` parameter as a `string` that represents the name of the property that was changed.

- **Item.CustomPropertyChange** is raised when a user-defined property of an Outlook item is changed. Outlook passes a `name` parameter as a `string` that represents the name of the user-defined property that was changed.

Open, Read, Write, and Close Events

Outlook raises events when an Outlook item is opened, written to, or closed:

- **Item.Read** is raised when an Outlook item is displayed from within either an Explorer or Inspector view. This event has nothing to do with the Read or Unread status of an item, just whether it is being displayed in a view.

- **Item.Open** is raised when an Outlook item is opened in an Inspector view. Outlook passes by reference a `bool cancel` parameter. The `cancel` parameter can be set to `true` by your event handler to prevent the item from being opened.

- **Item.Write** is raised when an Outlook item is saved after being modified. Outlook passes by reference a `bool cancel` parameter. The `cancel` parameter can be set to `true` by your event handler to prevent the item or items from being written to.

- **Item.Close** is raised when an Outlook item is closed after being opened in an Inspector view. Outlook passes by reference a `bool cancel` parameter. The `cancel` parameter can be set to `true` by your event handler to prevent the item or items from being closed.

Close is the name of both a method and an event on Outlook item objects. Because of this collision, you will not see the Close event in Visual Studio's pop-up menu of properties, events, and methods associated with an Outlook item. Furthermore, a warning displays at compile time when you try to handle this event. To get Visual Studio's pop-up menus to work and the warning to go away, you can cast the Explorer object to the ItemEvents_10_Event, as shown in Listing 10-7.

Listing 10-7 shows a VSTO Outlook add-in that handles these events.

Listing 10-7 A VSTO Add-In That Handles Open, Read, Write, and Close Events

```
namespace OutlookAddin1
{
  public partial class ThisApplication
  {
    Outlook.MailItem mailItem;

    private void ThisApplication_Startup(object sender, EventArgs e)
    {
      Outlook.NameSpace ns = this.Session;
      Outlook.MAPIFolder inbox =
        ns.GetDefaultFolder(
        Outlook.OlDefaultFolders.olFolderInbox);

      foreach (object o in inbox.Items)
      {
        mailItem = o as Outlook.MailItem;
        if (mailItem != null)
        {
          break;
        }
      }

      if (mailItem == null)
      {
        MessageBox.Show("Couldn't find a mail item to connect to.");
      }
      else
      {
        MessageBox.Show(String.Format(
          "Connected to the mail item with subject {0}.",
```

```
      mailItem.Subject);

    mailItem.Read += new
      Outlook.ItemEvents_10_ReadEventHandler(
      MailItem_Read);

    mailItem.Open += new
      Outlook.ItemEvents_10_OpenEventHandler(
      MailItem_Open);

    mailItem.Write += new
      Outlook.ItemEvents_10_WriteEventHandler(
      MailItem_Write);

    ((Outlook.ItemEvents_10_Event)mailItem).Close += new
      Outlook.ItemEvents_10_CloseEventHandler(
      MailItem_Close);
  }
}

void MailItem_Read()
{
  MessageBox.Show("Read");
}

void MailItem_Open(ref bool cancel)
{
  MessageBox.Show("Open");
}

void MailItem_Write(ref bool cancel)
{
  MessageBox.Show("Write");
}

void MailItem_Close(ref bool cancel)
{
  MessageBox.Show("Close");
}
  }
}
```

E-mail Events

Outlook raises several e-mail-related events when new mail is received, when an Outlook item is sent by e-mail, or when an Outlook item is forwarded or replied to:

- **Application.NewMail** is raised when new items are received in the Inbox, including mail messages, meeting requests, and task requests.

- **Application.NewMailEx** is raised when new items are received in the Inbox, including mail messages, meeting requests, and task requests. An `entryIDs` parameter is passed as a `string`. The `entryIDs` parameter contains a comma-delimited list of the entry IDs of the Outlook items that were received. An entry ID uniquely identifies an Outlook item.

- **Application.ItemSend** is raised when an Outlook item is sent—for example, when the user has an Outlook item open in an Inspector window and clicks the Send button. An `item` parameter is passed as an `object` that contains the Outlook item being sent. Outlook also passes by reference a `bool cancel` parameter. The `cancel` parameter can be set to `true` by your event handler to prevent the item from being sent.

- **Item.Send** is raised when an Outlook item is sent—for example, when the user has an Outlook item open in an Inspector window and clicks the Send button. Outlook passes by reference a `bool cancel` parameter. The `cancel` parameter can be set to `true` by your event handler to prevent the item from being sent.

- **Item.Reply** is raised when an Outlook item is replied to. A response parameter is passed as an `object` and represents the Outlook item that was created as a response to the original Outlook item. Outlook also passes by reference a `bool cancel` parameter. The `cancel` parameter can be set to `true` by your event handler to prevent the item from being replied to.

- **Item.ReplyAll** is raised when an Outlook item is replied to using the Reply All button. A response parameter is passed as an `object` and represents the Outlook item that was created as a response to the original Outlook item. Outlook also passes by reference a `bool cancel` parameter. The `cancel` parameter can be set to `true` by your event handler to prevent the item from being replied to.

- **Item.Forward** is raised when an Outlook item is forwarded. A response parameter is passed as an `object` and represents the Outlook item that was created to forward the original Outlook item. Outlook also passes by reference a `bool cancel` parameter. The `cancel` parameter can be set to `true` by your event handler to prevent the item from being forwarded.

Listing 10-8 shows a VSTO Outlook add-in that handles these events.

Listing 10-8 A VSTO Add-In That Handles E-mail Events

```
namespace OutlookAddin1
{
  public partial class ThisApplication
  {
    Outlook.MailItem mailItem;

    private void ThisApplication_Startup(object sender, EventArgs e)
    {
      this.NewMail += new
        Outlook.ApplicationEvents_11_NewMailEventHandler(
        ThisApplication_NewMail);

      this.NewMailEx += new
        Outlook.ApplicationEvents_11_NewMailExEventHandler(
        ThisApplication_NewMailEx);

      this.ItemSend += new
        Outlook.ApplicationEvents_11_ItemSendEventHandler(
        ThisApplication_ItemSend);

      Outlook.NameSpace ns = this.Session;
      Outlook.MAPIFolder inbox = ns.GetDefaultFolder(
        Outlook.OlDefaultFolders.olFolderInbox);

      foreach (object o in inbox.Items)
      {
        mailItem = o as Outlook.MailItem;
        if (mailItem != null)
        {
          break;
        }
      }

      if (mailItem == null)
      {
        MessageBox.Show("Couldn't find a mail item.");
```

```csharp
    }
    else
    {
      MessageBox.Show(String.Format(
        "Connected to the mail item {0}.",
        mailItem.Subject));

      ((Outlook.ItemEvents_10_Event)mailItem).Send += new
        Outlook.ItemEvents_10_SendEventHandler(
        MailItem_Send);

      ((Outlook.ItemEvents_10_Event)mailItem).Reply += new
        Outlook.ItemEvents_10_ReplyEventHandler(
        MailItem_Reply);

      ((Outlook.ItemEvents_10_Event)mailItem).ReplyAll += new
        Outlook.ItemEvents_10_ReplyAllEventHandler(
        MailItem_ReplyAll);

      ((Outlook.ItemEvents_10_Event)mailItem).Forward += new
        Outlook.ItemEvents_10_ForwardEventHandler(
        MailItem_Forward);
  }
}

void GenerateItemMessage(object item, string operation)
{
  Outlook.MailItem mi = item as Outlook.MailItem;
  if (mi != null)
  {
    MessageBox.Show(String.Format(
      "MailItem {0} will be {0].",
      mi.Subject, operation));
  }
  else
  {
    MessageBox.Show(String.Format(
      "An Outlook item will be {0}.",
      Operation));
  }
}

void ThisApplication_NewMail()
{
  MessageBox.Show("New mail was received");
}

void ThisApplication_NewMailEx(string entryIDCollection)
```

```
  {
    MessageBox.Show(String.Format(
      "NewMailEx: {0}.",
      entryIDCollection));
  }

  void ThisApplication_ItemSend(object item,
    ref bool cancel)
  {
    GenerateItemMessage(item, "sent");
  }

  void MailItem_Send(ref bool cancel)
  {
    MessageBox.Show("MailItem Send");
  }

  void MailItem_Reply(object response,
    ref bool cancel)
  {
    GenerateItemMessage(response, "generated as a reply");
  }

  void MailItem_ReplyAll(object response,
    ref bool cancel)
  {
    GenerateItemMessage(response,
      "generated as a reply to all");
  }

  void MailItem_Forward(object forward, ref bool cancel)
  {
    GenerateItemMessage(forward, "generated as a forward");
  }
  }
}
```

Attachment Events

Outlook raises events when attachments are added to an Outlook item and when attachments associated with an Outlook item are read or saved:

- **Item.AttachmentAdd** is raised when an attachment is added to an Outlook item. Outlook passes an attachment parameter that represents the attachment that was added.

- **Item.AttachmentRead** is raised when an attachment attached to an Outlook item is opened for reading. Outlook passes an `attachment` parameter that represents the attachment that was read.

- **Item.BeforeAttachmentSave** is raised when an attachment attached to an Outlook item is about to be saved. Outlook passes an `attachment` parameter that represents the attachment that is about to be saved. Outlook also passes by reference a `bool cancel` parameter. The `cancel` parameter can be set to `true` by your event handler to prevent the attachment from being saved.

Custom Action Events

Outlook enables you to associate custom actions with an Outlook item. A custom action is given a name and some default behavior—for example, you can create a custom action whose default behavior is to act on the original item or to create a new reply to the existing item. You can also set whether the action is shown as a button or a menu command or both. When the custom action is invoked from the menu or toolbar, the CustomAction event is raised on the associated Outlook item.

Figure 10-2 shows a custom action that has been associated with an Outlook mail item called My custom action. Outlook displays the custom action in the Action menu when an Inspector window is opened on the mail item. It also displays the custom action as a toolbar button.

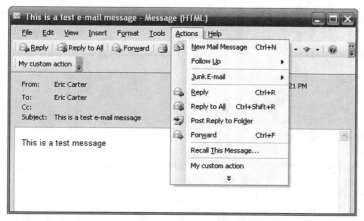

Figure 10-2 A custom action called My custom action.

- **Item.CustomAction** is raised when a custom action associated with an Outlook item is invoked. Outlook passes an `action` parameter as an `object` that represents the custom action that was invoked. This parameter can be cast to an Action object. Outlook passes a `response` parameter as an `object` that represents the Outlook item created because of the custom action. Outlook also passes by reference a `bool cancel` parameter. The `cancel` parameter can be set to `true` by your event handler to prevent the custom action from being invoked.

Listing 10-9 shows a VSTO Outlook add-in that creates a custom action called My custom action. The CustomAction event is handled to set the subject when the custom action is invoked.

Listing 10-9 A VSTO Add-In That Creates a Custom Action and Handles a Custom Action Event

```
namespace OutlookAddin1
{
  public partial class ThisApplication
  {
    Outlook.MailItem mailItem;

    private void ThisApplication_Startup(object sender, EventArgs e)
    {
      Outlook.NameSpace ns = this.Session;
      Outlook.MAPIFolder inbox = ns.GetDefaultFolder(
        Outlook.OlDefaultFolders.olFolderInbox);

      foreach (object o in inbox.Items)
      {
        mailItem = o as Outlook.MailItem;
        if (mailItem != null)
        {
          break;
        }
      }

      if (mailItem == null)
      {
        MessageBox.Show("Couldn't find a mail item.");
      }
      else
```

```
    {
        MessageBox.Show(String.Format(
          "Connected to the mail item {0}.",
          mailItem.Subject));

        mailItem.CustomAction += new
          Outlook.ItemEvents_10_CustomActionEventHandler(
          MailItem_CustomAction);

        Outlook.Action action = mailItem.Actions.Add();
        action.Name = "My custom action";
        action.ShowOn =
          Outlook.OlActionShowOn.olMenuAndToolbar;
        action.ReplyStyle =
          Outlook.OlActionReplyStyle.olLinkOriginalItem;
    }
}

void MailItem_CustomAction(object action,
  object response, ref bool cancel)
{
    Outlook.Action action = (Outlook.Action)action;
    Outlook.MailItem mailItem = (Outlook.MailItem)response;
    if (action.Name == "My custom action")
    {
        mailItem.Subject = "Created by my custom action";
    }
}
}
}
```

Other Events

Table 10-2 lists several other less commonly used events in the Outlook object model. Figure 10-3 shows the Shortcuts pane of the Outlook bar, with which several events in Table 10-2 are associated.

Table 10-2 Additional Outlook Events

Events	Description
Search Events	
Application.AdvancedSearchCompleted	When the AdvancedSearch method on the Application object is invoked programmatically, this event is raised when the search is complete.
Application.AdvancedSearchStopped	When the AdvancedSearch method on the Application object is invoked programmatically, this event is raised if the search is stopped by calling Stop on the Search object returned by the AdvancedSearch method.
Synchronization Events	
SyncObject.OnError	Raised when a synchronization error occurs while synchronizing the Send\Receive group corresponding to the SyncObject.
SyncObject.Progress	Raised periodically while synchronizing the Send\Receive group corresponding to the SyncObject.
SyncObject.SyncEnd	Raised when the synchronization is complete for the Send\Receive group corresponding to the SyncObject.
SyncObject.SyncStart	Raised when the synchronization starts for the Send\Receive group corresponding to the SyncObject.
Reminder Events	
Application.Reminder	Raised before a reminder is displayed.
Reminders.BeforeReminderShow	Raised before a reminder is displayed.
ReminderCollection.ReminderAdd	Raised when a reminder is added to the ReminderCollection.
ReminderCollection.ReminderChange	Raised when a reminder is changed in the ReminderCollection.
ReminderCollection.ReminderFire	Raised before a reminder in the ReminderCollection is displayed.

Events	Description
ReminderCollection.ReminderRemove	Raised when a reminder is removed from the ReminderCollection.
ReminderCollection.ReminderSnooze	Raised when a reminder in the Reminder-Collection is snoozed.
Outlook Bar Shortcuts Pane Events	
OutlookBarGroups.BeforeGroupAdd	Raised before a new group is added to the Shortcuts pane in the Outlook bar.
OutlookBarGroups.BeforeGroupRemove	Raised before a group is removed from the Shortcuts pane in the Outlook bar.
OutlookBarGroups.GroupAdd	Raised when a new group is added to the Shortcuts pane in the Outlook bar.
OutlookBarPane.BeforeGroupSwitch	Raised before the user switches to a different group in the Shortcuts pane in the Outlook bar.
OutlookBarPane.BeforeNavigate	Raised when the user clicks on a Shortcut in the Shortcuts pane in the Outlook bar.
OutlookBarShortcuts.BeforeShortcutAdd	Raised before a Shortcut is added to the Shortcuts pane in the Outlook bar.
OutlookBarShortcuts.BeforeShort-cutRemove	Raised before a shortcut is removed from the Shortcuts pane in the Outlook bar.
OutlookBarShortcuts.ShortcutAdd	Raised when a shortcut is added to the Shortcuts pane in the Outlook bar.

Figure 10-3 The Shortcuts pane showing two groups (Shortcuts and Group1) and two shortcuts (Outlook Today and Inbox).

Conclusion

This chapter covered the various events raised by objects in the Outlook object model. Chapter 11, "Working with Outlook Objects," discusses in more detail the most important objects in the Outlook object model and how to use them in your code.

■11 ■

Working with Outlook Objects

Working with the Application Object

THIS CHAPTER EXAMINES some of the major objects in the Outlook object model, starting with the Application object. Many of the objects in the Outlook object model are very large, and it is beyond the scope of this book to completely describe these objects. Instead, this chapter focuses on the most commonly used methods and properties associated with these objects.

The Application object is the root object in the Outlook object model hierarchy, meaning that you can access all the other objects in the object model by starting at the Application object and accessing its properties and methods and the properties and methods of objects it returns.

A companion object to the Application object is the NameSpace object, which is retrieved by using the Application object's Session property. Some confusion can arise because functionality that you would expect to be on the Application object is often found on the NameSpace object. For example, the way to get to the root folders that are open in Outlook is through the NameSpace object's Folders property. The Application object has no Folders property.

Methods and Properties That Return Active or Selected Objects

The Application object has a number of methods and properties that return active objects—objects representing things that are active or selected within Outlook. Table 11-1 shows some of these properties and methods.

Table 11-1 Application Properties and Methods That Return Active Objects

Name	Type	What It Does
ActiveExplorer()	`Explorer`	Returns the active Explorer object—the Explorer window that currently has focus within Outlook. If an Inspector window is active, this returns the Explorer window that is front-most in the stack of Outlook windows. If no Explorer windows are open, this method returns `null`.
ActiveInspector()	`Inspector`	Returns the active Inspector object—the Inspector window that currently has focus within Outlook. If an Explorer window is active, this returns the Inspector window that is front-most in the stack of Outlook windows. If no Inspector windows are open, this method returns `null`.
ActiveWindow()	`object`	Returns the active window as an `object`. If no windows are open, this method returns `null`. The returned `object` can be cast to either an Explorer or Inspector object.
Session	`Session`	A property that returns the NameSpace object.
GetNameSpace()	`Session`	A method that returns the NameSpace object. Takes the type of NameSpace to return as a string. However, the only string you can pass to GetNameSpace is the string `"MAPI"`. This is an older way to get the NameSpace object. The newer way to access the NameSpace object that is used in this book is through the Session property.

Properties That Return Important Collections

The Application object has a number of properties that return collections that you will frequently use. Table 11-2 shows several of these properties. Listing 11-1 shows some code from a VSTO Outlook add-in that works with the active object methods and properties shown in Table 11-1 and the collections shown in Table 11-2.

Table 11-2 Application Properties That Return Important Collections

Property Name	Type	What It Does
Explorers	`Explorers`	Returns the Explorers collection, which enables you to access any open Explorer windows.
Inspectors	`Inspectors`	Returns the Inspectors collection, which enables you to access any open Inspector windows.
Reminders	`Reminders`	Returns the Reminders collection, which enables you to access all the current reminders.

Listing 11-1 A VSTO Add-In That Works with Active Objects and Collections

```
private void ThisApplication_Startup(object sender, EventArgs e)
{
  Outlook.Explorer activeExplorer = this.ActiveExplorer();

  if (activeExplorer != null)
  {
    MessageBox.Show(String.Format(
      "The active explorer is {0}.",
      activeExplorer.Caption));
  }

  Outlook.Inspector activeInspector = this.ActiveInspector();
  if (activeInspector != null)
  {
    MessageBox.Show(String.Format(
      "The Active Inspector is {0}.",
      activeInspector.Caption));
  }

  object activeWindow = this.ActiveWindow();
  if (activeWindow != null)
  {
    Outlook.Explorer explorer = activeWindow
      as Outlook.Explorer;
    Outlook.Inspector inspector = activeWindow
```

```csharp
        as Outlook.Inspector;

    if (explorer != null)
    {
      MessageBox.Show(String.Format(
        "The active window is an Explorer: {0}.",
        explorer.Caption));
    }
    else if (inspector != null)
    {
      MessageBox.Show(String.Format(
        "The active window is an Inspector: {0}.",
        inspector.Caption));
    }
  }
  else
  {
    MessageBox.Show("No Outlook windows are open");
  }

Outlook.NameSpace ns = this.Session;
MessageBox.Show(String.Format(
  "There are {0} root folders.",
  ns.Folders.Count));

MessageBox.Show(String.Format(
  "There are {0} explorer windows.",
  this.Explorers.Count));

foreach (Outlook.Explorer explorer in this.Explorers)
{
  MessageBox.Show(explorer.Caption);
}

MessageBox.Show(String.Format(
  "There are {0} inspector windows.",
  this.Inspectors.Count));

foreach (Outlook.Inspector inspector in this.Inspectors)
{
  MessageBox.Show(inspector.Caption);
}

MessageBox.Show(String.Format(
  "There are {0} reminders.",
  this.Reminders.Count));

System.Text.StringBuilder reminders =
```

```
      new System.Text.StringBuilder();

   foreach (Outlook.Reminder reminder in this.Reminders)
   {
      reminders.AppendLine(reminder.Caption);
   }
   MessageBox.Show(reminders.ToString());
}
```

Performing a Search and Creating a Search Folder

Outlook provides an AdvancedSearch method on the Application object that allows you to perform a search in Outlook. The AdvancedSearch method works asynchronously and raises the AdvancedSearchComplete event when the search has completed. You can also save a search you perform using the AdvancedSearch method as an Outlook Search folder. AdvancedSearch takes four parameters, as shown in Table 11-3.

Table 11-3 Parameters for the AdvancedSearch Method

Parameter Name	Type	Description
Scope	string	Pass the name of the folder or folders that you want to search. For example, to search the Inbox, pass the string `"'Inbox'"`. To search the Inbox and Calendar, pass `"'Inbox', 'Calendar'"`. You can pass the full name of a folder, including the path to the folder, to search a folder within a folder. The scope string `"'Reference\Reviews'"` searches a folder called Reviews nested in a folder called Reference in the default Outlook Store. You can search a folder in another PST Outlook data file that is open inside of Outlook. The Scope string `"'\\Archive\Backup'"` searches a folder called Backup in a PST file called Archive that is open in Outlook.
Filter	optional object	Pass the filter string that specifies what you want to search for. You learn how to construct this string below.
SearchSub-Folders	optional object	Pass `true` to also search any subfolders under the folders specified in Scope.

Table 11-3 Continued

Parameter Name	Type	Description
Tag	optional object	Pass a `string` to uniquely name the search so that when you handle the Application.AdvancedSearchComplete event you can distinguish between a search created by you and other searches created by other loaded add-ins. This is critical—you cannot assume that you are the only add-in that is handling this event. You must carefully tag your searches with a unique string to ensure that your add-in does not act on an advanced search started by another add-in.

We now consider how to construct the filter string that was mentioned in Table 11-3. The easiest way to do this is to let Outlook's built-in UI for constructing filters build the string for you. To do this, first select the folder you want to search. From the Arrange By menu in the View menu, choose Custom to display the Customize View dialog (see Figure 11-1).

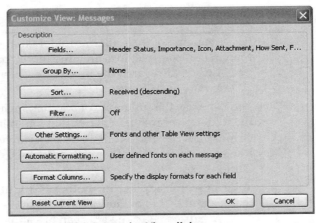

Figure 11-1 The Customize View dialog.

Click the Filter button to display the Filter dialog. You can use this dialog to create the filter you want. In Figure 11-2, we have simply set the filter to show messages where the word *review* is in the subject field.

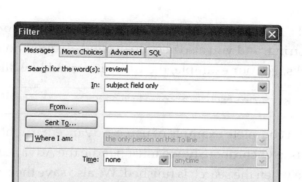

Figure 11-2 The Filter dialog.

After you have edited the filter to yield the results you want, click the SQL tab shown in Figure 11-3. Check the Edit these criteria directly check box. Doing so enables you to select the filter string and copy and paste it into your code. After you have copied the filter string onto the clipboard, you can cancel out of the Filter Dialog and the Customize View dialog.

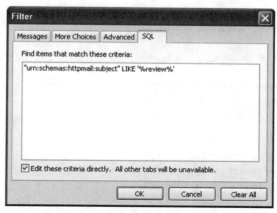

Figure 11-3 The SQL tab of the Filter dialog displays a filter string.

Finally, paste the filter string into your code. You will want to use C#'s @ operator to preface the string, and you also need to expand all quotation marks to be double quotation marks. For our example, the C# code would look like this:

```
string filter = @"""urn:schemas:httpmail:subject"" LIKE '%review%'";
```

Listing 11-2 shows a complete example of using AdvancedSearch. Note that because the search proceeds asynchronously, we must handle the AdvancedSearchComplete event to determine when the search is finished. We also save the completed search as a search folder by calling Save on the completed Search object.

Listing 11-2 A VSTO Add-In That Uses the AdvancedSearch Method

```
public partial class ThisApplication
{
  const string searchTag = "'review' Search In Inbox";

  private void ThisApplication_Startup(object sender,
    EventArgs e)
  {
    this.AdvancedSearchComplete += new
      Outlook.ApplicationEvents_11_AdvancedSearchCompleteEventHandler(
      ThisApplication_AdvancedSearchComplete);
    this.AdvancedSearchStopped += new
      Outlook.ApplicationEvents_11_AdvancedSearchStoppedEventHandler(
      ThisApplication_AdvancedSearchStopped);

    string scope = @"'Inbox'";
    string filter =
      @"""urn:schemas:httpmail:subject"" LIKE '%review%'";
    bool searchSubfolders = true;

    try
    {
      MessageBox.Show("Starting search");
      this.AdvancedSearch(scope, filter,
        searchSubfolders, searchTag);
    }
    catch (Exception ex)
    {
      MessageBox.Show(ex.Message);
    }
  }

  void ThisApplication_AdvancedSearchStopped(
```

```
  Outlook.Search searchObject)
{
  if (searchObject.Tag == searchTag)
  {
    MessageBox.Show(String.Format(
      "Search completed.  Found {0} results.",
      searchObject.Results.Count));

    // Save this search as a search folder
    searchObject.Save(searchTag);
  }
}

void ThisApplication_AdvancedSearchComplete(
  Outlook.Search searchObject)
{
  if (searchObject.Tag == searchTag)
  {
    MessageBox.Show(String.Format(
      "Search was stopped.  Found {0} results.",
      searchObject.Results.Count));
  }
}

#region VSTO Designer generated code
private void InternalStartup()
{
  this.Startup += new System.EventHandler(ThisApplication_Startup);
}
#endregion
}
```

Copying a File into an Outlook Folder

Outlook provides a method to copy an existing document such as a spreadsheet on your desktop to an Outlook folder. The Application object's CopyFile method takes as a parameter a FilePath as a `string`, which is the full path to the document you want to copy into the Outlook folder. It also takes a `DestFolderPath` parameter, which is the name of the Outlook folder you want to copy the document to. Listing 11-3 shows an example of using CopyFile to put a spreadsheet called mydoc.xls into the Inbox and a second spreadsheet called mydoc2.xls into a folder called Reviews nested within a folder called Reference.

Listing 11-3 A VSTO Add-In That Uses the CopyFile Method

```
private void ThisApplication_Startup(object sender, EventArgs e)
{
  this.CopyFile(@"c:\mydoc.xls", "Inbox");
  this.CopyFile(@"c:\mydoc2.xls", @"Reference\Reviews");
}
```

Quitting Outlook

The Quit method can be used to exit Outlook. If any unsaved Outlook items are opened, Outlook prompts the user to save each unsaved Outlook item. When users are prompted to save, they get a dialog box that gives them a Cancel button. If the user clicks Cancel, Outlook does not quit.

Working with the Explorers and Inspectors Collections

Listing 11-1 showed how to use C#'s `foreach` keyword to iterate over the Explorers and the Inspectors collections. It is also possible to get to an Explorer or Inspector using the index operator ([]) and passing an index as an `object`. That index can either be a 1-based index into the array of Explorers or Inspectors, or it can be a `string` index that is the caption of the Explorer or Inspector window in the array. Listing 11-4 illustrates using both types of indices with the Explorers and Inspectors collections.

Listing 11-4 also illustrates how to create a new Inspector and Explorer window. Both the Explorers and Inspectors collections have an Add method. The Explorers collection's Add method takes a Folder parameter of type MAPIFolder, which is the folder to display a new Explorer window for. It takes a second optional parameter of type `OlFolderDisplayMode` that enables you to set the initial display used in the newly created Explorer window. The Add method returns the newly created Explorer object. To show the newly created Explorer object, you must then call the Explorer object's Display method.

The Inspectors collection's Add method takes an `object` parameter, which is the Outlook item to display an Inspector window for. In Listing 11-4, we get an Outlook item out of the Inbox folder and create an Inspector window for it. To show the newly created Inspector object, you must then call the Inspector object's Display method, which takes an optional parameter called `Modal` of type `object` to which you can pass `true` to show the Inspector as a modal dialog, or `false` to show the Inspector as a modeless dialog. If you omit the parameter, it defaults to `false`.

Listing 11-4 A VSTO Add-In That Works with Explorer and Inspector Windows

```
private void ThisApplication_Startup(object sender, EventArgs e)
{
  Outlook.MAPIFolder folder = this.Session.
    GetDefaultFolder(Outlook.OlDefaultFolders.olFolderInbox);

  // Create a new explorer
  Outlook.Explorer newExplorer = this.Explorers.Add(
    folder, Outlook.OlFolderDisplayMode.olFolderDisplayNormal);

  newExplorer.Display();
  string explorerIndex = newExplorer.Caption;

  // Get an explorer by passing a string and by passing an index
  Outlook.Explorer exp = this.Explorers[explorerIndex];
  MessageBox.Show(String.Format(
    "Got explorer {0}.",
    exp.Caption));

  exp = this.Explorers[1];
  MessageBox.Show(String.Format(
    "Got explorer {0}.",
    exp.Caption));

  // Create a new inspector
  object item = folder.Items[1];
  Outlook.Inspector newInspector = this.Inspectors.Add(item);
  newInspector.Display(false);
  string inspectorIndex = newInspector.Caption;

  // Get an inspector by passing a string and by passing an index
  Outlook.Inspector inspector = this.Inspectors[inspectorIndex];
  MessageBox.Show(String.Format(
    "Got inspector {0}.",
    inspector.Caption));

  inspector = this.Inspectors[1];
  MessageBox.Show(String.Format(
    "Got inspector {0}.",
    inspector.Caption));
}
```

Working with the Explorer Object

The Explorer object represents an Outlook Explorer window—the main window in Outlook that displays views of folders. It is possible to open multiple Explorer windows—you can right-click a folder in one Explorer window and choose the option Open in New Window. Doing so creates a new Explorer window with the folder you selected to open in a new window as the active folder.

Working with the Selected Folder, View, and Items

The Explorer object has several methods and properties that enable you to work with the currently selected folder in the Explorer window, the view being used to display the list of items in that folder, and the currently selected items.

The CurrentFolder property returns a MAPIFolder object representing the folder selected in the Explorer window. An Explorer window always has a selected folder. To change the selected folder in an Explorer window, you can use the Explorer object's SelectFolder method, which takes as a parameter the MAPIFolder object you want to select. You can also determine whether a particular folder is currently selected by using the Explorer object's IsFolderSelected method, which takes as a parameter the MAPIFolder object you want to check to see whether it is selected. The IsFolderSelected method returns `true` if the folder is selected in the Explorer window and `false` if it is not.

Listing 11-5 shows some code that displays the name of the currently selected folder. It then checks to see whether the Contacts folder is selected. If it isn't selected, it selects it. Finally, it displays the name of the newly selected folder. Listing 11-5 uses the NameSpace object's GetDefaultFolder method to get a MAPIFolder object for the Contacts folder.

Listing 11-5 A VSTO Add-In That Selects the Contacts Folder

```
private void ThisApplication_Startup(object sender, EventArgs e)
{
  Outlook.Explorer exp = this.ActiveExplorer();

  if (exp != null)
  {
    MessageBox.Show(String.Format(
      "{0} is selected.",
      exp.CurrentFolder.Name));
```

```
Outlook.MAPIFolder folder = this.Session.GetDefaultFolder(
    Outlook.OlDefaultFolders.olFolderContacts);

if (!exp.IsFolderSelected(folder))
{
    exp.SelectFolder(folder);
}

MessageBox.Show(String.Format(
    "{0} is selected.",
    exp.CurrentFolder.Name));
  }
}
```

The CurrentView property returns a View object representing the view that is being used to display the items in the folder. A folder has a number of views that can be used to display its contents such as view by date, by conversation, by sender, and so on. It is also possible to define custom views. You can see the views that are defined for a given folder by selecting that folder in an Explorer window, then choosing View > Arrange By > Current View > Define Views to display the dialog shown in Figure 11-4.

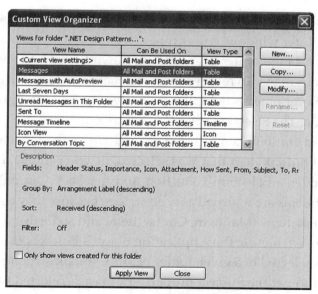

Figure 11-4 The Custom View Organizer dialog shows views associated with a folder.

You can change the view used by an Explorer window by setting the Explorer object's CurrentView property to a View object associated with the folder. Listing 11-6 demonstrates this by selecting the Inbox folder and then setting the view for the Inbox folder to one of the View objects associated with the folder.

Listing 11-6 A VSTO Add-In That Selects the Inbox Folder and Changes the View

```
private void ThisApplication_Startup(object sender, EventArgs e)
{
  Outlook.Explorer exp = this.ActiveExplorer();

  if (exp != null)
  {
    Outlook.MAPIFolder folder = this.Session.GetDefaultFolder(
      Outlook.OlDefaultFolders.olFolderInbox);
    exp.SelectFolder(folder);

    Outlook.View view = folder.Views[folder.Views.Count];
    exp.CurrentView = view;
    MessageBox.Show(String.Format(
      "The view is now {0}.",
      view.Name));
  }
}
```

In addition to a selected folder and selected view, there can also be Outlook items selected in an Explorer window. A user can select multiple items in a folder by Shift-clicking to select a range of items or holding down the Ctrl key while clicking to select discontiguous items. To retrieve the items that are selected in an Explorer window, use the Explorer object's Selection property. The Selection property returns a Selection collection. The Selection collection has a Count property that gives you the number of selected Outlook items. It also has an Item method that allows you to get to an individual Outlook item that was selected, or you can use the `foreach` keyword to iterate over a Selection collection and get back Outlook items that are selected. Outlook items are returned as type `object` because they could be any of the 15 types of Outlook items (MailItem, ContactItem, and so forth).

In Listing 11-6, we handle the Application object's BeforeFolderSwitch event to display the items selected in a given folder before Outlook switches to a new folder. We use reflection to get the Subject property from each selected Outlook item. We know that the Subject property exists on all 15 types of Outlook items, so this is a safe property to get for any Outlook item contained in the selection. This simplifies the code so it does not have to have a cast to all 15 Outlook item types before accessing the Subject property.

Listing 11-7 A VSTO Add-In That Iterates over the Selected Outlook Items in a Folder

```
public partial class ThisApplication
{
  Outlook.Explorer explorer;

  private void ThisApplication_Startup(object sender,
    EventArgs e)
  {
    Outlook.Explorer explorer = this.ActiveExplorer();

    if (explorer != null)
    {
      explorer.BeforeFolderSwitch += new
        Outlook.ExplorerEvents_10_BeforeFolderSwitchEventHandler(
        Explorer_BeforeFolderSwitch);
    }
  }

  private object GetPropertyHelper(object targetObject,
    string propertyName)
  {
    return targetObject.GetType().InvokeMember(propertyName,
      System.Reflection.BindingFlags.Public |
      System.Reflection.BindingFlags.Instance |
      System.Reflection.BindingFlags.GetProperty,
      null,
      targetObject,
      null,
      System.Globalization.CultureInfo.CurrentCulture);
  }

  void Explorer_BeforeFolderSwitch(object newFolder,
    ref bool cancel)
  {
    Outlook.Selection selection = explorer.Selection;
    foreach (object o in selection)
    {
      string subject = (string)GetPropertyHelper(o, "Subject");
      MessageBox.Show(String.Format(
        "An Outlook Item is selected with subject {0}.",
        subject));
    }
```

```
    }

    #region VSTO generated code
    private void InternalStartup()
    {
        this.Startup += new System.EventHandler(ThisApplication_Startup);
    }
    #endregion
}
```

Working with an Explorer Window

Table 11-4 lists several properties and methods used to set and get the position of an Explorer window as well as some other commonly used properties and methods related to the management of the window.

Table 11-4 Explorer Properties and Methods

Name	Type	Description
Activate()		Makes the Explorer window the active window with focus.
Caption	string	Read-only property that returns a `string` value containing the caption of the Explorer window.
Close()		Method that closes the Explorer window.
Height	int	Gets and sets the height of the Explorer window in pixels. This can only be set when the WindowState is set to `OlWindowState.olNormalWindow`.
Left	int	Gets and sets the left position of the Explorer window in pixels. This can only be set when the WindowState is set to `OlWindowState.olNormalWindow`.
Top	int	Gets and sets the top position of the Explorer window in pixels. This property can only be set when the WindowState is set to `OlWindowState.olNormalWindow`.
Width	int	Gets and sets the width of the Explorer window in pixels. This can only be set when the WindowState is set to `OlWindowState.olNormalWindow`.
WindowState	optional object	Gets and sets the window state of the Explorer window using the `OlWindowState` enumeration. Can be set to `olMaximized`, `olMinimized`, and `olNormalWindow`.

Adding Buttons and Menus to an Explorer Window

The CommandBars property returns a CommandBars object, which is defined in the Microsoft Office 11.0 Object Library PIA object. Outlook uses the same object model used by Word and Excel to work with buttons and menus in an Explorer window. Refer to Chapter 4, "Working with Excel Events," for more information on the CommandBars object hierarchy and examples of using the CommandBar objects. Listing 11-8 shows a VSTO add-in that creates a toolbar and a button and handles the click event for the newly added button.

Listing 11-8 A VSTO Add-In That Adds a Toolbar and Button to an Explorer Window

```
public partial class ThisApplication
{
  Office.CommandBarButton btn1;

  private void ThisApplication_Startup(object sender,
    EventArgs e)
  {
    Outlook.Explorer explorer = this.ActiveExplorer();

    if (explorer != null)
    {
      Office.CommandBar bar = explorer.CommandBars.Add(
        "My Command Bar", missing, missing, true);
      bar.Visible = true;

      btn1 = (Office.CommandBarButton)bar.Controls.Add(
        Office.MsoControlType.msoControlButton, missing,
        missing, missing, true);

      btn1.Click += new
        Office._CommandBarButtonEvents_ClickEventHandler(
        Btn1_Click);
      btn1.Caption = "My Custom Button";
      btn1.Tag = "OutlookAddin1.btn1";
      btn1.Style = Office.MsoButtonStyle.msoButtonCaption;
    }
  }

  void Btn1_Click(Office.CommandBarButton ctrl,
    ref bool cancelDefault)
  {
```

```
        MessageBox.Show("You clicked my button!");
    }

    #region VSTO Designer generated code
    private void InternalStartup()
    {
        this.Startup += new System.EventHandler(ThisApplication_Startup);
    }
    #endregion
}
```

Associating a Web View with a Folder

It is possible to associate with an Outlook folder an HTML Web page by right-clicking a folder, choosing Properties, and then clicking the Home Page tab of the dialog that appears. Figure 11-5 shows the Home Page tab of the Properties dialog. You can also associate a Web page with a Folder using the MAPIFolder object's WebViewURL property. If you check the Show home page by default for this folder or set the MAPIFolder object's WebViewOn property to `true`, users are shown the Web page when they select the folder rather than an Outlook view of the items in the folder.

You can get to the HTML document object model for the Web page displayed by a folder by using the Explorer object's HTMLDocument property. This property only returns a non-`null` value if the selected folder is associated with a Web page. Interacting with the HTML document object model of a Web page through this property is an advanced topic and is not covered further in this book.

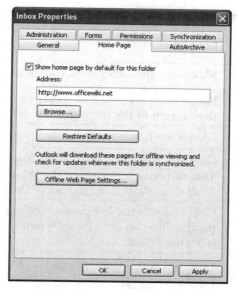

Figure 11-5 Associating an HTML page with a folder.

Working with the Inspector Object

The Inspector window is the window in Outlook that shows detailed information for a particular Outlook item. This is the window that displays when you double-click an item in an Outlook folder. You can have multiple Inspector windows open at any given time.

Working with the Outlook Item Associated with the Inspector

An Inspector window is always associated with 1 of the 15 Outlook item types listed in Table 10-1. To get to the Outlook item associated with an Inspector object, use the CurrentItem property which returns an Outlook item as an `object`. You can cast the returned `object` to 1 of the 15 Outlook item types.

Working with an Inspector Window

Table 11-5 lists several properties and methods that are used to set and get the position of an Inspector window as well as some other commonly used properties and methods related to the management of the window.

Table 11-5 Inspector Properties and Methods

Name	Type	Description
Activate()		Makes the Inspector window the active window with focus.
Caption	string	Read-only property that returns a `string` value containing the caption of the Inspector window.
Close()		Closes the Inspector window.
Height	int	Gets and sets the height of the Inspector window in pixels. This can only be set when the WindowState is set to `OlWindowState.olNormalWindow`.
Left	int	Gets and sets the left position of the Inspector window in pixels. This can only be set when the WindowState is set to `OlWindowState.olNormalWindow`.
Top	int	Gets and sets the top position of the Inspector window in pixels. This property can only be set when the WindowState is set to `OlWindowState.olNormalWindow`.
Width	int	Gets and sets the width of the Inspector window in pixels. This can only be set when the WindowState is set to `OlWindowState.olNormalWindow`.
WindowState	optional object	Gets and sets the window state of the Inspector window using the `OlWindowState` enumeration. Can be set to `olMaximized`, `olMinimized`, and `olNormalWindow`.

Working with Different Inspector Editor Types

In the Mail Format page of Outlook's Options dialog, users can set preferences for what kind of formats and editor they want to use when editing an Outlook item. The Options dialog can be accessed using the Options menu command in the Tools menu. Figure 11-6 shows this dialog. Two key options are what message format to use (HTML, Rich Text, or Plain Text) and whether to use Word as the editor of e-mail messages and rich text.

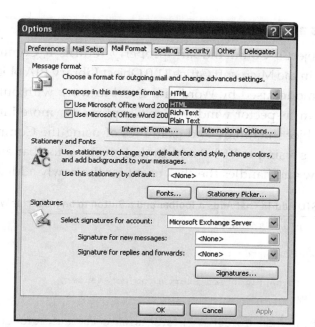

Figure 11-6 Picking formats and editor preferences in
the Options dialog.

These settings help to determine what the Inspector object's EditorType property returns. EditorType returns a member of the OlEditorType enumeration: olEditorHTML, olEditorRTF, olEditorText, or olEditorWord. If the EditorType returns olEditorHTML, you can get to the HTML document object model for the Inspector window by using the Inspector object's HTMLEditor property. Using the HTML document object model is an advanced topic and is not covered in this book.

If the user has chosen to use Word as his editor, the Inspector object's IsWordMail property returns true. This means that Outlook has started an instance of Word and is embedding the Word editor in the Inspector window. Outlook has also created a Word Document to edit the Outlook item in. You can access Word's Document object by using the WordEditor property. This property returns an object that you can cast to Word's Document object.

Adding Buttons and Menus to an Inspector Window

The Inspector object's CommandBars property returns a CommandBars object, which is defined in the Microsoft Office 11.0 Object Library PIA object. Outlook uses the same object model used by Word and Excel to work with buttons and menus associated with an Inspector window. See Chapter 4 for more information on the CommandBars object hierarchy and examples of using the CommandBar objects. Listing 11-9 shows a simple VSTO add-in that creates a toolbar and a button in an Inspector window and handles the click event for the newly added button.

Listing 11-9 A VSTO Add-In That Adds a Toolbar and a Button to an Inspector Window

```
public partial class ThisApplication
{
  Office.CommandBarButton btn1;

  private void ThisApplication_Startup(object sender,
    EventArgs e)
  {
    Outlook.MAPIFolder folder = this.Session.GetDefaultFolder(
      Outlook.OlDefaultFolders.olFolderInbox);
    Outlook.Inspector inspector = this.Inspectors.Add(
      folder.Items[1]);
    inspector.Display(missing);

    Office.CommandBar bar = inspector.CommandBars.Add(
      "My Command Bar", missing, missing, true);
    bar.Visible = true;

    btn1 = (Office.CommandBarButton)bar.Controls.Add(
      Office.MsoControlType.msoControlButton,
      missing, missing, missing, true);
    btn1.Click += new
      Office._CommandBarButtonEvents_ClickEventHandler(
      Btn1_Click);
    btn1.Caption = "My Custom Button";
    btn1.Tag = "OutlookAddin1.btn1";
    btn1.Style = Office.MsoButtonStyle.msoButtonCaption;
  }

  void Btn1_Click(Office.CommandBarButton ctrl,
    ref bool cancelDefault)
  {
    MessageBox.Show("You clicked my button!");
  }
```

```
#region VSTO Designer generated code
private void InternalStartup()
{
    this.Startup += new System.EventHandler(ThisApplication_Startup);
}
#endregion
}
```

Working with the NameSpace Object

A companion object to the Application object is the NameSpace object, which is retrieved by using the Application object's Session property. As noted earlier, some confusion can arise because functionality that you would expect to be on the Application object is actually often found on the NameSpace object. Further increasing the confusion is the Application.GetNameSpace method, which is an older way to get to a NameSpace object. This method takes a string for the type of NameSpace to return implying that you can get different types of NameSpace objects. In reality, the GetNameSpace method only accepts one string (`"MAPI"`). In this chapter, we use the Application object's Session property (added in Outlook 98) to get a NameSpace object rather than the older GetNameSpace method.

Working with the Root Folders of the Open Outlook Stores

The NameSpace object's Folders property returns a Folders collection, allowing you to iterate over all the root folders that are open within Outlook. Each root folder is the root of what is called a Store. A root folder could correspond to an Exchange account or some other e-mail account. It could also correspond to an Outlook data file, such as a .PST file. Every folder and Outlook item under a particular root folder share the same StoreID.

You can iterate over the Folders collection using C#'s `foreach` keyword. You can also get to a particular MAPIFolder in the Folders collection by using the index operator ([]). The index operator can be passed a `string` representing the name of the Folder in the Folders collection, or a 1-based index representing the index of the Folder within the Folders collection.

Although the Folders collection provides Add and Remove methods, these methods are not applicable to root folders because root folders represent accounts that are added and removed by adding and removing e-mail accounts or adding and removing Outlook data files. The following section discusses how a Store is added and removed programmatically.

Listing 11-10 illustrates iterating over the Folders collection using foreach. It also shows how to get a MAPIFolder using the index operator on the Folders collection. Finally, it shows adding a new Folder to an existing store using the Folders collection's Add method.

Listing 11-10 VSTO Add-In That Iterates over the Root Folders and Adds a New Folder

```
private void ThisApplication_Startup(object sender,
   EventArgs e)
{
   foreach (Outlook.MAPIFolder folder in this.Session.Folders)
   {
     MessageBox.Show(folder.Name);
   }

   Outlook.MAPIFolder rootFolder = this.Session.Folders[1];
   Outlook.MAPIFolder newFolder = rootFolder.Folders.Add(
     "Test Notes Folder",
     Outlook.OlDefaultFolders.olFolderNotes);

   MessageBox.Show(String.Format(
     "A new folder has been created in the store {0}.",
     rootFolder.Name));
}
```

Adding and Removing Outlook Stores

To programmatically add a Store, you can use the NameSpace object's AddStore or AddStoreEx methods. The AddStore method takes a Store parameter of type object. You can pass a string representing the complete filename of the PST file to add. If the PST file you provide does not exist, Outlook creates the file for you. AddStoreEx takes the same Store parameter of type object that AddStore does. It also takes a second Type parameter of type OlStoreType. To this parameter, you can pass a member of the `OlStoreType` enumeration, which will control the format in which the PST file will be created should you pass a PST file that does not exist. The possible values you can pass are `olStoreDefault`, `olStoreUnicode`, or `olStoreANSI`.

Use the NameSpace object's RemoveStore method to programmatically remove a Store. RemoveStore removes the Store from Outlook but does not delete the actual PST file or mailbox on the server associated with the Store. RemoveStore takes a `Folder` parameter of type MAPIFolder. This parameter must be one of the root folders in the NameSpace object's Folders collection.

Determining the Current User

The NameSpace object's CurrentUser property returns a Recipient object representing the logged-in user. Given a Recipient object, you can use the Recipient object's Name property to get the name of the logged-in user.

Checking Whether Outlook Is Offline

You can determine whether Outlook is offline by getting the value of the NameSpace object's Offline property. This property returns `true` if Outlook is offline and not connected to a server.

Getting Standard Folders Such As the Inbox Folder

A method already used in several examples in this chapter to get standard Outlook folders such as the Inbox folder is the NameSpace object's GetDefaultFolder method. This method takes a `FolderType` parameter of type `OlDefaultFolders` and returns a MAPIFolder object. Table 11-6 lists the members of the `OlDefaultFolders` enumeration that can be passed to GetDefaultFolder and the standard Outlook folder that is returned.

Table 11-6 Members of the OlDefaultFolders Enumeration That Can Be Passed to NameSpace Object's GetDefaultFolder Method

Enumeration Member	GetDefaultFolder Result
olFolderCalendars	Returns the Calendar folder
olFolderConflicts	Returns the Conflicts folder
olFolderContacts	Returns the Contacts folder
olFolderDeletedItems	Returns the Deleted Items folder
olFolderDrafts	Returns the Drafts folder
olFolderInbox	Returns the Inbox folder
olFolderJournal	Returns the Journal folder
olFolderJunk	Returns the Junk E-mail folder
olFolderLocalFailures	Returns the Local Sync Failures folder
olFolderNotes	Returns the Notes folder
olFolderOutbox	Returns the Outbox folder
olFolderSentMail	Returns the Sent Items folder
olFolderServerFailures	Returns the Server Sync Failures folder
olFolderSyncIssues	Returns the Sync Issues folder
olFolderTasks	Returns the Tasks folder
olPublicFoldersAllPublicFolders	Returns the Public Folders folder

Getting a Folder or Outlook Item by ID

All Outlook items and folders are uniquely identified by an EntryID and a StoreID. Each Outlook item and folder within a given Store share the same StoreID. The EntryID is unique within a given Store. So the combination of an EntryID and StoreID uniquely identifies a folder or an Outlook item. When you have created a new Outlook item by using the Items collection's Add method or the Application object's CreateItem method, the newly created Outlook item will not be assigned an EntryID until you call the Save method on the newly created item.

Both a MAPIFolder and the 15 Outlook item types have an EntryID property that returns the EntryID for the folder or item as a `string`. But only MAPIFolders have a StoreID property. To determine the StoreID that corresponds to a particular

Outlook item, you must get the parent MAPIFolder using the Parent property of an Outlook item and then determine the StoreID from the parent folder.

The NameSpace object's GetFolderFromID method takes an EntryID parameter as a `string` and an optional `StoreID` parameter as an `object` to which you can pass the StoreID as a `string`. If you omit the `StoreID` parameter by passing `Type.Missing`, Outlook assumes it should look in the default Store (the Store in which the default Inbox and Calendar are found). The GetFolderFromID method returns the MAPIFolder object identified by the EntryID and StoreID.

The NameSpace object's GetItemFromID method takes an `EntryID` parameter as a `string` and an optional `StoreID` parameter as an `object` to which you can pass the StoreID as a `string`. If you omit the `StoreID` parameter by passing `Type.Missing`, Outlook assumes it should look in the default Store. The GetItemFromID method returns the `object` for the Outlook item identified by the EntryID and StoreID. You can then cast the returned `object` to 1 of the 15 Outlook item types listed in Table 10-1.

Listing 11-11 illustrates getting a folder and an Outlook item by EntryID and StoreID.

Listing 11-11 A VSTO Add-In That Uses the NameSpace Object's GetFolderFromID and GetItemFromID Methods

```
private void ThisApplication_Startup(object sender, EventArgs e)
{
  Outlook.MAPIFolder inbox = this.Session.GetDefaultFolder(
    Outlook.OlDefaultFolders.olFolderInbox);
  string inboxStoreID = inbox.StoreID;
  string inboxEntryID = inbox.EntryID;

  object outlookItem = inbox.Items[1];
  string itemStoreID = inboxStoreID;
  string itemEntryID = (string)GetPropertyHelper(
    outlookItem, "EntryID");

  Outlook.MAPIFolder theFolder = this.Session.GetFolderFromID(
    inboxStoreID, inboxEntryID);
  MessageBox.Show(theFolder.Name);

  object theItem = this.Session.GetItemFromID(
    itemStoreID, itemEntryID);
  MessageBox.Show((string)GetPropertyHelper(
    theItem, "Subject"));
```

```
    }

    private object GetPropertyHelper(object targetObject,
      string propertyName)
    {
      return targetObject.GetType().InvokeMember(propertyName,
        System.Reflection.BindingFlags.Public |
        System.Reflection.BindingFlags.Instance |
        System.Reflection.BindingFlags.GetProperty,
        null,
        targetObject,
        null,
        System.Globalization.CultureInfo.CurrentCulture);
    }
```

Accessing Address Books and Address Entries

The NameSpace object's AddressLists property returns the AddressLists collection. The AddressLists collection is a collection containing all the available address books as AddressList objects. The AddressList object has an AddressEntries collection, which is a collection of AddressEntry objects. Each AddressEntry object represents an address in an address book.

Listing 11-12 iterates over the available address books and displays the name of each address book. It also displays the name of the first address entry in each address book.

Listing 11-12 A VSTO Add-In That Iterates over Available Address Books

```
private void ThisApplication_Startup(object sender, EventArgs e)
{
  Outlook.AddressLists lists = this.Session.AddressLists;
  foreach (Outlook.AddressList list in lists)
  {
    MessageBox.Show(String.Format(
      "{0} has {1} address entries.",
      list.Name, list.AddressEntries.Count));

    if (list.AddressEntries.Count > 0)
    {
      MessageBox.Show(String.Format(
        "The first address in this address book is {0}.",
        list.AddressEntries[1].Name));
    }
```

```
    }
  }
```

Displaying the Outlook Folder Picker Dialog

The NameSpace object provides a method that allows you to display Outlook's folder picker dialog shown in Figure 11-7. The folder picker dialog provides a way for the user to pick a folder as well as create a new folder. The NameSpace object's PickFolder method displays the folder picker dialog as a modal dialog box. The method returns the MAPIFolder object corresponding to the folder the user picked in the dialog. If the user cancels the dialog box, this method will return null.

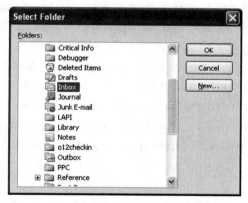

Figure 11-7 Outlook's Select Folder dialog.

Working with the MAPIFolder Object

This chapter has already covered how to iterate over Folders collections, how to get a MAPIFolder out of a Folders collection using the index operator, how to access Outlook's default folders, how to get a MAPIFolder by EntryID and StoreID, and how to use Outlook's folder picker dialog to get a MAPIFolder. This section now examines some additional properties and methods associated with the MAPIFolder object.

Other Identifiers for a Folder

The MAPIFolder object's Name property returns the display name of a folder as a `string`. For example, the default server sync failures folder identified by `OlDefaultFolders.olFolderServerFailures` returns the string `"Server Failures"` for its Name property.

The MAPIFolder object's FolderPath property returns the full name of the folder as a `string`, including the names of the containing folders. For example, the default server sync failures folder identified by `OlDefaultFolders.olFolderServer-Failures` returns the string `"\\Eric Carter\Sync Issues\Server Failures"` for its FolderPath property. For this example, the Server Failures folder is contained in a folder called Sync Issues in the Store called Eric Carter.

The MAPIFolder object's Description property returns a `string` containing the description of the folder. This is a read/write property that can be set to any `string` value. The MAPIFolder object's ShowItemCount property controls whether the folder shows the unread item count, total item count, or no count when displayed in the Outlook Navigation pane folder list. It can return or be set to a member of the `OlShowItemCount` enumeration: `olNoItemCount`, `olShowTotalItemCount`, or `olShowUnreadItemCount`. If you want to determine the number of unread items in a particular folder, use the MAPIFolder object's UnReadItemCount property, which returns an `int` value representing the unread item count.

Accessing Subfolders Contained in a Folder

A MAPIFolder may contain subfolders. The MAPIFolder object's Folders property returns a Folders collection, which contains any additional MAPIFolder objects that are subfolders of the given folder.

As described earlier, you can iterate over the subfolders contained in the Folders collection for a MAPIFolder using C#'s `foreach` keyword. You can also get to a particular MAPIFolder in the Folders collection by using the index operator ([]). The index operator can be passed a `string` representing the name of the Folder in the Folders collection, or a 1-based index representing the index of the Folder within the Folders collection.

The Folders collection's Add method enables you to add a new subfolder to the subfolders associated with a MAPIFolder. The Add method takes the name of the new folder as a `string` parameter. It also takes as an optional `object` parameter the Outlook folder type to use for the new folder. You can pass this parameter a subset of the `OlDefaultFolders` constants: `olFolderCalendar`, `olFolderContacts`, `olFolderDrafts`, `olFolderInbox`, `olFolderJournal`, `olFolderNotes`, `olPublicFoldersAllPublicFolders`, or `olFolderTasks`. If you omit this parameter by passing `Type.Missing`, the Outlook folder type of the newly created folder matches the folder type of the parent folder. Also note that a folder of type `olPublicFoldersAllPublicFolders` can only be added somewhere under the root public folder returned by the NameSpace object's GetDefaultFolder(olPublicFoldersAllPublicFolders).

The Folders collection's Remove method enables you to remove a subfolder by passing the 1-based index of the folder in the Folders collection. Figuring out what the 1-based index is can be a bit of a pain—it is usually easier to just call the Delete method on the MAPIFolder object representing the subfolder you want to remove.

Listing 11-13 shows a VSTO add-in that iterates over the subfolders of the Inbox folder, and then adds a new folder using the Folders collection's Add method. It then deletes the newly added folder using the MAPIFolder object's Delete method rather than the Folders collection's Remove method.

Listing 11-13 A VSTO Add-In That Iterates over Subfolders of the Inbox Folder, Adds a New Subfolder, and Then Deletes It

```
private void ThisApplication_Startup(object sender, EventArgs e)
{
  Outlook.MAPIFolder folder = this.Session.GetDefaultFolder(
    Outlook.OlDefaultFolders.olFolderInbox);
  MessageBox.Show(String.Format(
    "There are {0} subfolders in the Inbox.",
    folder.Folders.Count));

  foreach (Outlook.MAPIFolder subFolder in folder.Folders)
  {
    MessageBox.Show(String.Format(
      "Sub folder {0}.", subFolder.Name));
  }

  Outlook.MAPIFolder newSubFolder = folder.Folders.Add(
    "New Temporary Folder", missing);
  MessageBox.Show(
    "A new subfolder was just added under the Inbox folder");
```

```
    newSubFolder.Delete();
    MessageBox.Show("The new subfolder was just deleted.");
}
```

Accessing Items Contained in a Folder

A MAPIFolder's main purpose in life is to contain Outlook items. When you create a new folder, you have to specify the type of folder it is. This type constrains the types of Outlook items it can contain. Figure 11-8 shows Outlook's Create New Folder dialog, which appears when you right-click a folder or root folder (Store) in Outlook and choose New Folder. The Create New Folder dialog makes the user decide what kind of items the folder can contain: Calendar Items, Contact Items, Journal Items, Mail and Post Items, Note Items, or Task Items. This constraint is enforced by Outlook—if you try to drag a Mail item to a folder that was created to contain Calendar items, the item type will be changed to a Calendar item.

Figure 11-8 Outlook's Create New Folder dialog.

The MAPIFolder object's Items property returns an Items collection containing Outlook items in the folder. Each Outlook item in the folder is returned as an `object`. You can use the fact that folders are constrained to contain certain types of Outlook items when iterating over items in a folder. If you check the type of item that folder contains by looking at the DefaultItemType property, you can write code that only tries to cast the objects returned from the Items collection to the Outlook item types that are allowed in that folder. So for example, if you are iterating over items in a Folder whose DefaultItemType property returns `olContactItem`, objects returned from the Items collection can be cast to either a ContactItem or a DistListItem.

Table 11-7 shows how the member of the `OlDefaultFolders` enumeration you pass in when you create the folder using Folders.Add corresponds to the returned DefaultItemType and what possible Outlook item types could be found in that folder.

Table 11-7 Relationship Between Folders.Add Folder Type (OlDefaultFolders), DefaultItemType Value, and Outlook Item Types Found in a Folder

Folder Created with OlDefaultFolders Enumeration Member	DefaultItemType Returns OlItemType Enumeration Member	Possible Outlook Item Types in Folder
`olFolderCalendar`	`olAppointmentItem`	AppointmentItem
`olFolderContacts`	`olContactItem`	ContactItem, DistListItem
`olFolderJournal`	`olJournalItem`	JournalItem
`olFolderInbox` `olFolderDrafts`	`olMailItem`	MailItem, PostItem, MeetingItem, RemoteItem, ReportItem, DocumentItem, TaskRequestAcceptItem, TaskRequestDeclineItem, TaskRequestItem, TaskRequestUpdateItem
`olFolderNotes`	`olNoteItem`	NoteItem
`olPublicFolders-AllPublicFolders`	`olPostItem`	PostItem
`olFolderTasks`	`olTaskItem`	TaskItem

Listing 11-14 shows an add-in that iterates over the top-level folders in each open Store and iterates over the items in each of those folders. It uses the DefaultItemType property to determine which kinds of items a particular folder might have in it and casts the objects returned from the Items collection to one of the expected types in the folder. Note that there is a case where the expected cast might fail. An object that is a MailItem that has restricted permissions cannot be cast to a MailItem unless the item has been opened in Outlook in an Inspector window with security permissions verified.

Listing 11-14 A VSTO Add-In That Iterates over Items in Folders and Performs Appropriate Casts

```
private void ThisApplication_Startup(object sender, EventArgs e)
{
  Outlook.Folders rootFolders = this.Session.Folders;
  foreach (Outlook.MAPIFolder folder in rootFolders)
  {
    Outlook.Folders subFolders = folder.Folders;
    foreach (Outlook.MAPIFolder subfolder in subFolders)
    {
      IterateFolder(subfolder);
    }
  }
}

public void IterateFolder(Outlook.MAPIFolder folder)
{
  System.Text.StringBuilder subject = new
    System.Text.StringBuilder();

  subject.AppendLine(folder.Name);
  foreach (object item in folder.Items)
  {
    subject.AppendLine(GetSubject(item,
      folder.DefaultItemType));
  }
  MessageBox.Show(subject.ToString());
}

public string GetSubject(object item,
  Outlook.OlItemType type)
{
  switch (type)
  {
    case Outlook.OlItemType.olAppointmentItem:
```

```
  Outlook.AppointmentItem appointment = item
    as Outlook.AppointmentItem;
  if (appointment != null)
    return appointment.Subject;

  break;
case Outlook.OlItemType.olContactItem:
case Outlook.OlItemType.olDistributionListItem:

  Outlook.ContactItem contact = item as
    Outlook.ContactItem;
  if (contact != null)
    return contact.Subject;

  Outlook.DistListItem distlist = item as
    Outlook.DistListItem;
  if (distlist != null)
    return distlist.Subject;

  break;
case Outlook.OlItemType.olJournalItem:

  Outlook.JournalItem journal = item as
    Outlook.JournalItem;
  if (journal != null)
    return journal.Subject;

  break;
case Outlook.OlItemType.olMailItem:

  Outlook.MailItem mail = item as
    Outlook.MailItem;
  if (mail != null)
    return mail.Subject;

  Outlook.PostItem post = item as
    Outlook.PostItem;
  if (post != null)
    return post.Subject;

  Outlook.MeetingItem meeting = item as
    Outlook.MeetingItem;
  if (meeting != null)
    return meeting.Subject;

  Outlook.RemoteItem remote = item as
    Outlook.RemoteItem;
  if (remote != null)
```

```
        return remote.Subject;

    Outlook.ReportItem report = item as
      Outlook.ReportItem;
    if (report != null)
      return report.Subject;

    Outlook.DocumentItem doc = item as
      Outlook.DocumentItem;
    if (doc != null)
      return doc.Subject;

    Outlook.TaskRequestAcceptItem tra = item as
      Outlook.TaskRequestAcceptItem;
    if (tra != null)
      return tra.Subject;

    Outlook.TaskRequestDeclineItem trd = item as
      Outlook.TaskRequestDeclineItem;
    if (trd != null)
      return trd.Subject;

    Outlook.TaskRequestItem tr = item as
      Outlook.TaskRequestItem;
    if (tr != null)
      return tr.Subject;

    Outlook.TaskRequestUpdateItem tru = item as
      Outlook.TaskRequestUpdateItem;
    if (tru != null)
      return tru.Subject;

    break;
case Outlook.OlItemType.olNoteItem:

    Outlook.NoteItem note = item as Outlook.NoteItem;
    if (note != null)
      return note.Subject;

    break;
case Outlook.OlItemType.olPostItem:

    Outlook.PostItem post2 = item as Outlook.PostItem;
    if (post2 != null)
      return post2.Subject;

    break;
```

```
      case Outlook.OlItemType.olTaskItem:

        Outlook.TaskItem task = item as Outlook.TaskItem;
        if (task != null)
          return task.Subject;

        break;
    }

    MessageBox.Show(String.Format(
      "Couldn't cast item with subject {0} and class {1}.",
      (string)GetPropertyHelper(item, "Subject"),
      (string)GetPropertyHelper(item, "Class")));
    return "";
  }

  private object GetPropertyHelper(object targetObject,
    string propertyName)
  {
    return targetObject.GetType().InvokeMember(propertyName,
      System.Reflection.BindingFlags.Public |
      System.Reflection.BindingFlags.Instance |
      System.Reflection.BindingFlags.GetProperty,
      null,
      targetObject,
      null,
      System.Globalization.CultureInfo.CurrentCulture);
  }
```

Working with a Folder's View Settings

A MAPIFolder has a Views property that returns a Views collection. The Views collection contains all the available View objects for a folder that correspond to the views shown in the Custom View Organizer dialog in Figure 11-4. You can determine the view currently being used by the folder by accessing the MAPIFolder object's CurrentView property, which returns a View object. The CurrentView property is read-only—you cannot change the current view by setting the CurrentView property to another View object. Instead, you must access one of the View objects in the Views collection and call the View object's Apply method to make the view associated with the folder the active view.

Listing 11-15 shows add-in code that gets the name of the current view for the Inbox folder. It then iterates over the available views for the Inbox folder and applies each view.

Listing 11-15 A VSTO Add-In That Iterates over Available Views for the Inbox Folder and Applies Each View

```
private void ThisApplication_Startup(object sender, EventArgs e)
{
  Outlook.MAPIFolder inbox = this.Session.GetDefaultFolder(
    Outlook.OlDefaultFolders.olFolderInbox);
  this.ActiveExplorer().CurrentFolder = inbox;

  MessageBox.Show(String.Format(
    "Current inbox view is {0}.",
    inbox.CurrentView.Name));

  foreach (Outlook.View view in inbox.Views)
  {
    view.Apply();
    MessageBox.Show(String.Format(
      "Current inbox view is now {0}.",
      inbox.CurrentView.Name));
  }
}
```

Copying or Moving a Folder to a New Location

You can copy a folder and its dependent folders and items to a new location using the MAPIFolder object's CopyTo method. The CopyTo method takes a DestinationFolder parameter of type MAPIFolder, which will be the parent folder for the copied folder. It returns a MAPIFolder for the newly copied folder. The copy is a "deep copy" because all the items and subfolders rooted at the folder you call the CopyTo method on are copied to the new location.

You can move a folder and its dependent folders and items to a new location using the MAPIFolder's MoveTo method. The MoveTo method takes a DestinationFolder parameter of type MAPIFolder, which will be the parent folder for the moved folder. The folder is moved along with all dependent folders and items to the new location.

Displaying a Folder in an Explorer View

You can open a MAPIFolder in a new Explorer view by calling the MAPIFolder object's Display method. To use an existing Explorer view, you can set the Explorer object's CurrentFolder to the MAPIFolder you want to display in the existing Explorer view. Listing 11-15 uses this approach.

Working with the Items Collection

This chapter has already covered how to iterate over the Outlook items in a MAPI-Folder by using `foreach` with the Items collection. This section examines some additional methods that you can use when working with the Items collection.

Iterating over Outlook Items

The Items collection's SetColumns method enables you to tell Outlook to cache certain properties when you iterate over the Items collection so that access to those properties will be fast. An Outlook item has a number of properties associated with it—name value pairs that can be accessed by using an Outlook item's ItemProperties property. A typical MailItem has around 80 properties associated with it.

If you know that you are going to iterate using `foreach` over the Items collection and you are only going to be accessing the Subject and CreationTime properties of Outlook items in that collection, you can call the Items collection's SetColumns method before iterating the collection and pass the string `"Subject, Creation-Time"`. Some limitations apply to which properties can be cached (for example, properties which return objects cannot be cached)—check the documentation before using this method. After you have iterated over the collection, use the Items collection's ResetColumns method to clear the cache of properties Outlook created.

The Items collection's Sort method enables you to apply a sort order to the Items collection before you iterate over the collection using `foreach`. The method takes a `Property` parameter as a `string`, which gives the name of the property by which to sort. You pass the name of the property enclosed in square brackets. To sort by subject you would pass `"[Subject]"`. The Sort method also takes an optional `Descending` parameter that can be passed `true` to sort descending, `false` to sort ascending. The default value if you pass `Type.Missing` is `false`. Some limitations apply to which properties can sorted on—check the documentation before using this method.

Listing 11-16 illustrates using the SetColumns and Sort methods. It times the operation of iterating through all the items in the Inbox and examining the Subject property without calling SetColumns. It then times the operation again but calls Set-Columns first. Finally, Sort is illustrated, and the first item and last item in the sorted Items collection are accessed using the index operator. The Items collection's Count property is also used to get the index of the last item in the Items collection.

Listing 11-16 A VSTO Add-In That Uses the Items Collection's SetColumns and Sort Methods

```
private void ThisApplication_Startup(object sender, EventArgs e)
{
  Outlook.MAPIFolder inbox = this.Session.GetDefaultFolder(
    Outlook.OlDefaultFolders.olFolderInbox);

  Outlook.Items myItems = inbox.Items;

  MessageBox.Show("Click OK to start the test.");

  System.DateTime start = System.DateTime.Now;
  foreach (object item in myItems)
  {
    string subject = (string)GetPropertyHelper(item, "Subject");
  }
  System.DateTime end = System.DateTime.Now;
  System.TimeSpan result1 = end.Subtract(start);

  MessageBox.Show(String.Format(
    "Without calling SetColumns this took {0} ticks.",
    result1.Ticks));

  start = System.DateTime.Now;
  myItems.SetColumns("Subject");
  foreach (object item in myItems)
  {
    string subject = (string)GetPropertyHelper(item, "Subject");
  }
  end = System.DateTime.Now;
  System.TimeSpan result2 = end.Subtract(start);

  MessageBox.Show(String.Format(
    "With SetColumns this took {0} ticks.",
    result2.Ticks));
```

```
    myItems.ResetColumns();

    myItems.Sort("[Subject]", missing);
    object firstItem = myItems[1];
    object lastItem = myItems[myItems.Count];

    MessageBox.Show(String.Format(
        "First item is {0}.",
        (string)GetPropertyHelper(firstItem, "Subject")));
    MessageBox.Show(String.Format(
        "Last item is {0}." ,
        (string)GetPropertyHelper(lastItem, "Subject")));
}

private object GetPropertyHelper(object targetObject,
    string propertyName)
{
    return targetObject.GetType().InvokeMember(propertyName,
        System.Reflection.BindingFlags.Public |
        System.Reflection.BindingFlags.Instance |
        System.Reflection.BindingFlags.GetProperty,
        null,
        targetObject,
        null,
        System.Globalization.CultureInfo.CurrentCulture);
}
```

Finding an Outlook Item

The Items collection's Find method enables you to find an Outlook item in the Items collection by querying the value of one or more properties associated with the Outlook item. The Find method takes a `string`, which contains a filter to apply to find an Outlook item. For example, you might want to find an Outlook item in the items collection with its Subject property set to `"RE: Payroll"`. The way you would call Find would look like this:

```
object foundItem = myItems.Find(@"[Subject] = ""RE: Payroll""");
```

The query string has the name of the property in brackets. We use C#'s literal string syntax (@) to specify a string with quotation marks surrounding the value we are searching the Subject field for. Alternatively, you could call Find substituting apostrophes for the quotation marks used in the first example:

```
object foundItem = myItems.Find(@"[Subject] = 'RE: Payroll'";
```

If the Items collection does not contain an Outlook item whose Subject property is equal to `"RE: Payroll"`, the Find method returns `null`. If there are multiple Outlook items in the Items collection whose Subject property is equal to `"RE: Payroll"`, you can continue finding additional items by using the Items collection's FindNext method. The FindNext method finds the next Outlook item in the collection that matches the filter string passed to Find. You can continue to call FindNext until FindNext returns `null` indicating that no more items could be found, as shown in Listing 11-17.

Listing 11-17 A VSTO Add-In That Uses the Items Collection's Find and FindNext Methods

```
private void ThisApplication_Startup(object sender, EventArgs e)
{
  Outlook.MAPIFolder inbox = this.Session.GetDefaultFolder(
    Outlook.OlDefaultFolders.olFolderInbox);
  Outlook.Items myItems = inbox.Items;

  object foundItem = myItems.Find(@"[Subject] = ""RE: Payroll""");
  while (foundItem != null)
  {
    MessageBox.Show(String.Format(
      "Found item with EntryID {0}.",
      (string)GetPropertyHelper(foundItem, "EntryID")));
    foundItem = myItems.FindNext();
  }
}

private object GetPropertyHelper(object targetObject,
  string propertyName)
{
  return targetObject.GetType().InvokeMember(propertyName,
    System.Reflection.BindingFlags.Public |
    System.Reflection.BindingFlags.Instance |
    System.Reflection.BindingFlags.GetProperty,
    null,
    targetObject,
    null,
    System.Globalization.CultureInfo.CurrentCulture);
}
```

We have illustrated a rather simple filter string that just checks to see whether a text property called Subject matches a string. It is possible to use the logical operators AND, OR, and NOT to specify multiple criteria. For example, the following filter strings check both the property Subject and the property CompanyName. The first finds an Outlook item where the Subject is `"RE: Payroll"` and the CompanyName is `"Microsoft"`. The second finds an Outlook item where the Subject is `"RE: Payroll"` or the CompanyName is `"Microsoft"`. The third finds an Outlook item where the Subject is `"RE: Payroll"` and the CompanyName is not `"Microsoft"`.

```
object foundItem = myItems.Find(@"[Subject] = 'RE: Payroll' AND [CompanyName]
= 'Microsoft'");

object foundItem = myItems.Find(@"[Subject] = 'RE: Payroll' OR [CompanyName] =
'Microsoft'");

object foundItem = myItems.Find(@"[Subject] = 'RE: Payroll' AND NOT [Company-
Name] = 'Microsoft'");
```

When searching for a property that is an integer value, it is not necessary to enclose the integer value you are searching for in quotes. The same is true for a property that is a boolean property. This example searches for an Outlook item whose integer property OutlookInternalVersion is equal to 116359 and whose boolean property NoAging is set to False.

```
object foundItem = myItems.Find(@"[OutlookInternalVersion] = 116359
AND [NoAging] = False";
```

Some limitations apply to which properties you can use in a filter string. For example, properties that return objects cannot be examined in a filter string. Check the documentation of the Outlook object model for more information.

If you are working with an Items collection that has a large number of Outlook items in it, consider using the Items collection's Restrict method rather than Find and FindNext. The Restrict method is used in a similar way to how SetColumns and Sort are used. You call the Restrict method on the Items collection passing the same kind of filter string you provide to the Find method. You then can use `foreach` to iterate over the Items collection, and only the Outlook items that match the filter string will be iterated over. The Restrict method can be faster than Find and FindNext if you have a large number of items in the Items collection and you only expect to find a few items. Listing 11-18 illustrates using the Restrict method.

Listing 11-18 A VSTO Add-In That Uses the Items Collection's Restrict Method

```
private void ThisApplication_Startup(object sender, EventArgs e)
{
  Outlook.MAPIFolder inbox = this.Session.GetDefaultFolder(
    Outlook.OlDefaultFolders.olFolderInbox);
  Outlook.Items myItems = inbox.Items;

  myItems.Restrict(@"[Subject] = ""RE: Payroll""");
  foreach (object foundItem in myItems)
  {
    MessageBox.Show(String.Format(
      "Found item with EntryID {0}.",
      (string)GetPropertyHelper(foundItem, "EntryID")));
  }
}

private object GetPropertyHelper(object targetObject,
  string propertyName)
{
  return targetObject.GetType().InvokeMember(propertyName,
    System.Reflection.BindingFlags.Public |
    System.Reflection.BindingFlags.Instance |
    System.Reflection.BindingFlags.GetProperty,
    null,
    targetObject,
    null,
    System.Globalization.CultureInfo.CurrentCulture);
}
```

Adding an Outlook Item to an Items Collection

To add a new Outlook Item to an Items collection, use the Items collection's Add method. The Add method takes an optional Type parameter of type object to which you can pass a member of the OlItemType enumeration: olAppointmentItem, olContactItem, olDistributionListItem, olJournalItem, olMailItem, olNoteItem, olPostItem, or olTaskItem. If you omit the Type parameter by passing Type.Missing, the type of the item is determined by the type of folder (as determined by DefaultItemType) that you are adding the item to. The Add method returns an `object`, which can be cast to the Outlook item type corresponding to the `Type` parameter that was passed in.

You must remember that you can only add an Outlook item that is compatible with the folder type the Items collection came from—for example, it is not possible to add a ContactItem to an Items collection from a folder that is designated to hold MailItems and PostItems. For more information on the Outlook item types that can be contained by a particular folder type, see Table 11-6.

Listing 11-19 shows an example of using the Add method to add a PostItem and a MailItem to the Inbox folder. Note that using the Add method is not sufficient to get the PostItem and MailItem added to the Inbox folder. For the PostItem, we also have to call the Save method on the newly created Outlook item; otherwise, Outlook discards the PostItem when the variable `postItem` that refers to it goes out of scope. We also have to call Save on the newly created MailItem. In addition, we have to call the Move method to move the newly created MailItem into the Inbox folder. This is necessary because Outlook puts newly created MailItems into the Drafts folder by default—even though we called Add on the Items collection associated with the Inbox. Without the call to Move, the newly created MailItem remains in the Drafts folder.

Listing 11-19 A VSTO Add-In That Adds a MailItem and a PostItem

```
private void ThisApplication_Startup(object sender, EventArgs e)
{
  Outlook.MAPIFolder inbox = this.Session.GetDefaultFolder(
    Outlook.OlDefaultFolders.olFolderInbox);
  Outlook.Items myItems = inbox.Items;

  Outlook.PostItem postItem = myItems.Add(
    Outlook.OlItemType.olPostItem) as Outlook.PostItem;
  postItem.Subject = "Test1";
  postItem.Save();

  Outlook.MailItem mailItem = myItems.Add(
    Outlook.OlItemType.olMailItem) as Outlook.MailItem;
  mailItem.Subject = "Test2";
  mailItem.Save();
  mailItem.Move(inbox);
}
```

An alternate way to create an Outlook item is to use the Application object's CreateItem method. This method takes a `Type` parameter of type `OlItemType` that is passed a member of the `OlItemType` enumeration. It returns an `object` representing the newly created Outlook item. You must then save the created item and place it in the folder you want to store it in. Listing 11-20 shows code that uses CreateItem to do the same thing that Listing 11-19 does. In Listing 11-20, we must move the new MailItem and PostItem to the Inbox folder using the Move method on MailItem and PostItem.

Listing 11-20 A VSTO Add-In That Uses the Application Object's CreateItem Method to Add a MailItem and a PostItem

```
private void ThisApplication_Startup(object sender, EventArgs e)
{
  Outlook.MAPIFolder inbox = this.Session.GetDefaultFolder(
    Outlook.OlDefaultFolders.olFolderInbox);

  Outlook.MailItem mailItem = this.CreateItem(
    Outlook.OlItemType.olMailItem) as Outlook.MailItem;
  mailItem.Subject = "Test 1";
  mailItem.Save();
  mailItem.Move(inbox);

  Outlook.PostItem postItem = this.CreateItem(
    Outlook.OlItemType.olPostItem) as Outlook.PostItem;
  postItem.Subject = "Test 2";
  postItem.Save();
  postItem.Move(inbox);
}
```

Properties and Methods Common to Outlook Items

This chapter has discussed the 15 Outlook item types: ContactItem, DistListItem, DocumentItem, JournalItem, MailItem, MeetingItem, NoteItem, PostItem, RemoteItem, ReportItem, TaskItem, TaskRequestAcceptItem, TaskRequestDeclineItem, TaskRequestItem, and TaskRequestUpdateItem. We group these object model types together because all of these types share many common properties and methods listed in Table 11-8. The properties and methods in this table are found on all Outlook item types. The properties and methods marked in this table with an asterisk are found on all Outlook item types except NoteItem—NoteItem is a special case in the Outlook item family and has a subset of the properties and methods that the other Outlook item types share.

Table 11-8 Properties and Methods Common to all Outlook Items

Actions*	Application	Attachments*
AutoResolvedWinner	BillingInformation*	Body
Categories	Class	Close
Companies*	Conflicts	ConversationIndex*
ConversationTopic*	Copy	CreationTime
Delete	Display	DownloadState
EntryID	FormDescription*	GetInspector
Importance*	IsConflict	ItemProperties
LastModificationTime	Links	MarkForDownload
MessageClass	Mileage*	Move
NoAging*	InternalVersion*	OutlookVersion*
Parent	PrintOut	Save
SaveAs	Saved	Sensitivity*
Session	ShowCategoriesDialog*	Size
Subject	UnRead*	UserProperties*

We now consider several of these common properties and methods. Even though we talk about Outlook Items as if there were an OutlookItem type in the Outlook object model, there is no such type—the OutlookItem type is a conceptual way of talking about the properties and methods common to the 15 Outlook item types in the Outlook object model. So when we talk about the Save method, for example, that method is found on ContactItem, PostItem, MailItem, and all the other Outlook item types.

Given an object that you know is 1 of the 15 Outlook item types, you can either cast it to the correct Outlook item type or you can talk to the object via reflection if you are talking to a property common to all Outlook items. Some of the code listings in this section that use the GetPropertyHelper method have illustrated this point. Usually, it will be preferable to cast the object to the specific item type rather than use reflection.

Creating an Outlook Item

You have already learned the two primary ways in which you can create an Outlook item in the section "Adding an Outlook Item to an Items Collection." You can either call the Items collection's Add method or the Application object's CreateItem method. These methods take a member of the `OlItemType` enumeration and return an object that can be cast to the Outlook item type corresponding to the `OlItemType` enumeration, as shown in Table 11-9.

Table 11-9 Correspondence Between OlItemType and Outlook Item Types

OlItemType member	Outlook Item Type
olAppointmentItem	AppointmentItem
olContactItem	ContactItem
olDistributionListItem	DistListItem
olMailItem	MailItem
olNoteItem	NoteItem
olJournalItem	JournalItem
olPostItem	PostItem
olTaskItem	TaskItem

Notice that there are eight items in this table, which leaves out seven Outlook item types. How do you create the other seven remaining Outlook item types? The remaining types are created by Outlook or created as a result of other actions you take with an existing Outlook item type. Table 11-10 identifies how the other Outlook item types are created.

Table 11-10 How the Other Outlook Item Types Are Created

Outlook Item Type	How Created
DocumentItem	The Items collection's Add method also accepts a member of the `OlOfficeDocItemsType` enumeration: `olWord-DocumentItem`, `olExcelWorkSheetItem`, or `olPow-erPointShowItem`. Calling the Items collection's Add method with any of these constants returns an `object` that can be cast to a DocumentItem. You can also create a DocumentItem using the Application object's CopyFile method.
MeetingItem	Cannot be created directly. Created by Outlook when AppointmentItem.MeetingStatus is set to `olMeeting` and sent to one or more recipients.
RemoteItem	Cannot be created directly. Created by Outlook when you use a Remote Access System connection.
ReportItem	Cannot be created directly. Created by the mail transport system.
TaskRequestAcceptItem	Cannot be created directly. Created by Outlook as part of the task delegation feature.
TaskRequestDeclineItem	Cannot be created directly. Created by Outlook as part of the task delegation feature.
TaskRequestItem	Cannot be created directly. Created by Outlook as part of the task delegation feature.
TaskRequestUpdateItem	Cannot be created directly. Created by Outlook as part of the task delegation feature.

Identifying the Specific Type of an Outlook Item

You can determine the specific type of an Outlook item given to you as type `object` by using the as operator to cast it to the expected type, as shown in Listing 11-21. The code gets an Outlook item out of the Inbox and then uses the as operator to cast it to an Outlook MailItem. If the Outlook item is not a MailItem (for example, it might be a PostItem instead) the `mailItem` variable will be set to `null` because the as operator will be unable to cast it to a MailItem. If the casts succeeds, `mailItem` will be non-`null` and the code proceeds to display the subject of the mail message.

Listing 11-21 A VSTO Add-In That Uses the as Operator on an Outlook Item of Type object

```
private void ThisApplication_Startup(object sender, EventArgs e)
{
  Outlook.MAPIFolder inbox = this.Session.GetDefaultFolder(
    Outlook.OlDefaultFolders.olFolderInbox);
  object item = inbox.Items[1];

  Outlook.MailItem mailItem = item as Outlook.MailItem;
  if (mailItem != null)
    MessageBox.Show(mailItem.Subject);
}
```

You can also use the is operator to determine the specific type of an Outlook item. Listing 11-22 shows some code that uses the is operator and then the as operator to cast to either an Outlook.MailItem or an Outlook.PostItem. Using the is and as operators together is considered to be inefficient because this results in two type checks, which is more expensive than just using the as operator and checking whether the result is null, as shown in Listing 11-21.

Listing 11-22 A VSTO Add-In That Uses the is Operator on an Outlook Item of Type object

```
private void ThisApplication_Startup(object sender, EventArgs e)
{
  Outlook.MAPIFolder inbox = this.Session.GetDefaultFolder(
    Outlook.OlDefaultFolders.olFolderInbox);
  object item = inbox.Items[1];

  if (item is Outlook.MailItem)
  {
    Outlook.MailItem mailItem = item as Outlook.MailItem;
    MessageBox.Show(mailItem.Subject);
  }
  else if (item is Outlook.PostItem)
  {
    Outlook.PostItem postItem = item as Outlook.PostItem;
    MessageBox.Show(postItem.Subject);
  }
}
```

A final way to determine the type of an Outlook item of type object is to use reflection to invoke the Class property, which is found on every Outlook item type. The

Class property returns a member of the `OlObjectClass` enumeration. Table 11-11 shows the correspondence between the `OlObjectClass` enumerated values and each Outlook item types.

Table 11-11 Correspondence Between Outlook Item Type and OlObjectClass Enumerated Value

Outlook Item Type	OlObjectClass Enumeration Member
AppointmentItem	olAppointment
ContactItem	olContact
DistListItem	olDistributionList
DocumentItem	olDocument
JournalItem	olJournal
MailItem	olMail
MeetingItem	olMeetingRequest
NoteItem	olNote
PostItem	olPost
RemoteItem	olRemote
ReportItem	olReport
TaskItem	olTask
TaskRequestAcceptItem	olTaskRequestAccept
TaskRequestDeclineItem	olTaskRequestDecline
TaskRequestItem	olTaskRequest
TaskRequestUpdateItem	olTaskRequestUpdate

Listing 11-23 shows some add-in code that uses our helper method GetProperty-Helper to call the Class property on an Outlook item of type `object`. It then uses a `switch` statement, which for illustration purposes contains all the members of the `OlObjectClass` enumeration that correspond to Outlook item types. The code in Listing 11-23 would be more efficient than using the `as` operator if your code needs to cast to multiple specific Outlook item types given an Outlook item of type `object`. For example, the code in Listing 11-15 would be more efficient if it were rewritten to use the approach in Listing 11-23. The approach in Listing 11-23 only needs to make one reflection call to get the Class value and then one cast using the `as` operator to get the specific Outlook item type.

Listing 11-23 Add-In Code That Uses the Class Property to Determine the Outlook Item Type

```
private void ThisApplication_Startup(object sender, EventArgs e)
{
  Outlook.MAPIFolder inbox = this.Session.GetDefaultFolder(
    Outlook.OlDefaultFolders.olFolderInbox);
  object item = inbox.Items[1];

  Outlook.OlObjectClass objectClass = Outlook.OlObjectClass(
    GetPropertyHelper(item, "Class"));
  MessageBox.Show(String.Format(
    "Class is {0}.",
    objectClass.ToString()));

  switch (objectClass)
  {
    case Outlook.OlObjectClass.olAppointment:
      break;
    case Outlook.OlObjectClass.olContact:
      break;
    case Outlook.OlObjectClass.olDistributionList:
      break;
    case Outlook.OlObjectClass.olDocument:
      break;
    case Outlook.OlObjectClass.olJournal:
      break;
    case Outlook.OlObjectClass.olMail:
      Outlook.MailItem mail = item as Outlook.MailItem;
      if (mail != null)
      {
        MessageBox.Show(String.Format(
          "Found mail item with subject {0}.",
          mail.Subject));
      }
      break;
    case Outlook.OlObjectClass.olMeetingRequest:
      break;
    case Outlook.OlObjectClass.olNote:
      break;
    case Outlook.OlObjectClass.olPost:
```

```
      Outlook.PostItem post = item as Outlook.PostItem;
      if (post != null)
      {
        MessageBox.Show(String.Format(
          "Found post item with subject {0}.",
          post.Subject));
      }
      break;
    case Outlook.OlObjectClass.olRemote:
      break;
    case Outlook.OlObjectClass.olReport:
      break;
    case Outlook.OlObjectClass.olTask:
      break;
    case Outlook.OlObjectClass.olTaskRequest:
      break;
    case Outlook.OlObjectClass.olTaskRequestAccept:
      break;
    case Outlook.OlObjectClass.olTaskRequestDecline:
      break;
    case Outlook.OlObjectClass.olTaskRequestUpdate:
      break;
    default:
  }
}

private object GetPropertyHelper(object targetObject,
  string propertyName)
{
  return targetObject.GetType().InvokeMember(propertyName,
    System.Reflection.BindingFlags.Public |
    System.Reflection.BindingFlags.Instance |
    System.Reflection.BindingFlags.GetProperty,
    null,
    targetObject,
    null,
    System.Globalization.CultureInfo.CurrentCulture);
}
```

Other Properties Associated with All Outlook Items

This section covers several commonly used properties associated with all Outlook item types (with the possible exception of NoteItem). When we say *properties* in the context of Outlook items, some confusion can arise. Some properties are on the actual Outlook item type—for example, the Subject property is a callable property on all Outlook item object types. There is a MailItem.Subject property, PostItem.Subject, ContactItem.Subject, and so forth. Sometimes a property that is on an Outlook item object type is also accessible via the OutlookItem.ItemProperties collection. If you iterate over the ItemProperties collection, you will find an ItemProperty object where ItemProperty.Name returns `"Subject"`.

The creators of the Outlook object model exposed some of the properties in the ItemProperties collection as first-class properties on the object types themselves. So the Subject property can be accessed either by using OutlookItem.Subject or OutlookItem.ItemProperties["Subject"]. Other properties that are more obscure were not exposed out as properties on the objects themselves. For example, the EnableSharedAttachments property can only be accessed via OutlookItem.ItemProperties["EnableSharedAttachments"]. You will learn more about the ItemProperties collection later in this chapter.

Table 11-12 lists several properties callable on all Outlook item object types. Properties marked with an asterisk are not available on the NoteItem object.

Table 11-12 Properties Associated with All Outlook Items

Name	Type	What It Does
Body	`string`	Gets and sets the body text of the Outlook item.
Categories	`string`	Gets and sets the categories assigned to the Outlook item. For example, an Outlook item assigned to the Business and Favorites category would return the string `"Business, Favorites"`.
ConversationIndex*	`string`	Gets an identifier for the conversation index.
ConversationTopic*	`string`	Gets the conversation topic of the Outlook item.
Importance*	`OlImportance`	Gets and sets the importance as a member of the `OlImportance` enumeration: `olImportanceHigh`, `olImportanceLow`, or `olImportanceNormal`.
Sensitivity*	`OlSensitivity`	Gets and sets the sensitivity as a member of the `OlSensitivity` enumeration: `olConfidential`, `olNormal`, `olPersonal`, or `olPrivate`.

Name	Type	What It Does
CreationTime	`DateTime`	Gets the DateTime the Outlook item was created.
LastModification-Time	`DateTime`	Gets the DateTime the Outlook item was last modified.
Size	`int`	Gets the size in bytes of the Outlook item.
Subject	`string`	Gets and sets the subject of the Outlook item.
UnRead*	`bool`	Gets and sets whether the Outlook item has been open yet by the end user.

Copying or Moving an Outlook Item to a New Location

An Outlook item can be copied or moved from one folder to another. The Outlook item's Copy method creates a copy of the Outlook item and returns the newly created item as an `object`. The Outlook item's Move method moves an Outlook item from one folder to another. It takes a `DestFldr` parameter of type MAPIFolder to which you pass the folder to which you want to move the Outlook item.

Deleting an Outlook Item

To delete an Outlook item, call the Outlook item's Delete method. Doing so causes the Outlook item to be moved to the Deleted Items folder, where it stays until the user empties the Deleted Items folder. If you do not want the item to appear in the Deleted Items folder, you must call Delete twice—the first call moves the item to the Deleted Items folder, and the second call deletes it from the Deleted Items folder, as shown in Listing 11-24.

Listing 11-24 A VSTO Add-In That Deletes an Item, and Then Permanently Deletes It by Removing It from the Deleted Items Folder

```
private void ThisApplication_Startup(object sender, EventArgs e)
{
  Outlook.MAPIFolder inbox = this.Session.GetDefaultFolder(
    Outlook.OlDefaultFolders.olFolderInbox);

  Outlook.PostItem postItem = inbox.Items.Add(
    Outlook.OlItemType.olPostItem) as Outlook.PostItem;
  string subject = "Test Post To Be Deleted";
```

```
postItem.Subject = subject;
postItem.Save();

MessageBox.Show("New post item is in inbox");
string entryID1 = postItem.EntryID;

postItem.Delete();
MessageBox.Show("New post item is in deleted items");
Outlook.MAPIFolder deletedItems = this.Session.GetDefaultFolder(
  Outlook.OlDefaultFolders.olFolderDeletedItems);
Outlook.PostItem post = deletedItems.Items.Find(
  String.Format("[Subject] = '{0}'", subject)) as Outlook.PostItem;

if (post != null)
{
  string entryID2 = post.EntryID;
  if (entryID1 != entryID2)
  {
    MessageBox.Show(entryID1);
    MessageBox.Show(entryID2);
    MessageBox.Show(
      "When you delete an item its entry ID changes.");
  }
  post.Delete();
  MessageBox.Show("Removed post from deleted items folder.");
}
}
```

Note in Listing 11-24 that we cannot find the item we just deleted in the Deleted Items folder using the EntryID because the EntryID changes when you delete the Outlook item. Instead, we use the Subject, which is not ideal because the Subject is not guaranteed to be unique. A better approach to deleting an item permanently and preventing it from showing up in the Deleted Items folder is using the CDO object model that was briefly described in Chapter 9, "Programming Outlook." Listing 11-25 shows this approach. We assume the VSTO Outlook add-in has a reference to the CDO object model interop assembly that adds the MAPI NameSpace to the project. We use the GetMessageFromOutlookItem method and GetPropertyHelper methods previously introduced in Listing 9-4.

Listing 11-25 A VSTO Add-In That Uses CDO to Permanently Delete an Outlook Item

```csharp
public partial class ThisApplication
{
  MAPI.Session mapiSession;

  private void ThisApplication_Startup(object sender, EventArgs e)
  {
    mapiSession = new MAPI.Session();
    mapiSession.Logon(missing, missing, false, false,
      missing, missing, missing);

    Outlook.MAPIFolder inbox = this.Session.GetDefaultFolder(
      Outlook.OlDefaultFolders.olFolderInbox);

    Outlook.PostItem postItem = inbox.Items.Add(
      Outlook.OlItemType.olPostItem) as Outlook.PostItem;
    postItem.Subject = "Test Post To Be Deleted"; ;
    postItem.Save();
    MessageBox.Show("New post item is in inbox");

    MAPI.Message message = GetMessageFromOutlookItem(postItem);
    message.Delete(Type.Missing);
    MessageBox.Show("New post item was permanently deleted.");
  }

  MAPI.Message GetMessageFromOutlookItem(object OutlookItem)
  {
    object entryID = GetPropertyHelper(OutlookItem, "EntryID");
    object parentFolder = GetPropertyHelper(OutlookItem, "Parent");
    object storeID = GetPropertyHelper(parentFolder, "StoreID");
    return (MAPI.Message)mapiSession.GetMessage(entryID, storeID);
  }

  private object GetPropertyHelper(object targetObject,
    string propertyName)
  {
    return targetObject.GetType().InvokeMember(propertyName,
      System.Reflection.BindingFlags.Public |
      System.Reflection.BindingFlags.Instance |
      System.Reflection.BindingFlags.GetProperty,
      null,
      targetObject,
      null,
      System.Globalization.CultureInfo.CurrentCulture);
  }

  #region VSTO Designer generated code
```

```
  private void InternalStartup()
  {
    this.Startup += new System.EventHandler(ThisApplication_Startup);
  }
  #endregion
}
```

Displaying an Outlook Item in an Inspector View

The Outlook item's GetInspector method gives you an Inspector object to display an Outlook item. You can configure the Inspector before showing it by calling the Inspector object's Display method. The Display method takes an optional `Modal` parameter of type `object` to which you can pass `true` to show the inspector as a modal dialog or `false` to show it as a modeless dialog.

If you do not need to configure the Inspector first before you display it, you can just use the Display method on an Outlook item. The Display method displays an Inspector and takes an optional `Modal` parameter of type `object` to which you can pass `true` to show the inspector as a modal dialog or `false` to show it as a modeless dialog.

If an Inspector window is open for a given Outlook item, you can close the Inspector window by using the Close method on the Outlook item being displayed. The Close method takes a `SaveMode` parameter of type `OlInspectorClose`. You can pass a member of the `OlInspectorClose` enumeration to this parameter: `olDiscard` to discard changes made in the Inspector window, `olPromptForSave` to prompt the user to save if changes were made, and `olSave` to save without prompting.

Listing 11-26 creates a PostItem in the Inbox folder then calls the Display method to display an Inspector window for it. It then calls the Close method passing `OlInspectorClose.olDiscard` to close the Inspector window. Note that we have to cast the PostItem to the Outlook._PostItem interface to disambiguate between the Close method and the Close event, which collide on Outlook item objects.

Listing 11-26 A VSTO Add-In That Uses the Display and Close Method

```
private void ThisApplication_Startup(object sender, EventArgs e)
{
  Outlook.MAPIFolder inbox = this.Session.GetDefaultFolder(
```

```
      Outlook.OlDefaultFolders.olFolderInbox);

    Outlook.PostItem postItem = inbox.Items.Add(
      Outlook.OlItemType.olPostItem) as Outlook.PostItem;
    postItem.Subject = "Test to be shown in Inspector window.";
    postItem.Save();

    postItem.Display(false);
    MessageBox.Show("Post item is shown in inspector window.");
    ((Outlook._PostItem)postItem).Close(
      Outlook.OlInspectorClose.olDiscard);
}
```

Working with Built-In and Custom Properties Associated with an Outlook Item

The ItemProperties property returns the ItemProperties collection associated with an Outlook item. This collection contains ItemProperty objects for each property associated with the Outlook item. By *property*, we mean a name value pair that may or may not also have a get/set property on the Outlook item type. The ItemProperties collection can be iterated over using the `foreach` keyword. It also supports C#'s index operator ([]). You can pass a `string` as the index representing the name of the ItemProperty you want to access. You can also pass a 1-based index for the Item-Property you want to access in the collection.

Listing 11-27 shows code that gets an ItemProperty object associated with a newly created PostItem using the index operator with a `string` and numeric index. Listing 11-27 also illustrates iterating over all the ItemProperty objects in the ItemProperties collection using `foreach`.

Listing 11-27 A VSTO Add-In That Works with ItemProperty Objects

```
private void ThisApplication_Startup(object sender, EventArgs e)
{
  Outlook.MAPIFolder inbox = this.Session.GetDefaultFolder(
    Outlook.OlDefaultFolders.olFolderInbox);

  Outlook.PostItem postItem = inbox.Items.Add(
    Outlook.OlItemType.olPostItem) as Outlook.PostItem;

  MessageBox.Show(String.Format(
    "There are {0} properties associated with this post.",
```

```
     postItem.ItemProperties.Count));

  // Getting an ItemProperty with a string index
  Outlook.ItemProperty subject = postItem.
     ItemProperties["Subject"];
  MessageBox.Show(String.Format(
     "The property 'Subject' has value {0}.",
     subject.Value));

  // Getting an ItemProperty with a numeric index
  Outlook.ItemProperty firstProp = postItem.
     ItemProperties[1];
  MessageBox.Show(String.Format(
     "The first property has name {0} and value {1}.",
     firstProp.Name,
     firstProp.Value));

  // Iterating the ItemProperties collection with foreach
  System.Text.StringBuilder result = new
     System.Text.StringBuilder();

  foreach (Outlook.ItemProperty property
     in postItem.ItemProperties)
  {
     result.AppendFormat("{0} of type {1} has value {2}.\n",
        property.Name, property.Type.ToString(),
        property.Value);
  }
  MessageBox.Show(result.ToString());
}
```

You can add your own custom properties to an Outlook item. Custom properties that you have added are accessed by using the UserProperties property. An Outlook item's UserProperties property returns a UserProperties collection that contains UserProperty objects representing custom properties you have added to an Outlook item. Just as with the ItemProperties collection, the UserProperties collection can be iterated over using the `foreach` keyword. A particular UserProperty in the collection can be accessed using the index operator ([]) to which you pass a `string` representing the name of the UserProperty or the 1-based index of the UserProperty in the collection.

To add your own custom property, use the UserProperties collection's Add method. This method takes a required Name parameter of type `string` to which you pass the name of the new custom property. You must also specify the type of the new property by passing a member of the `OlUserPropertyType` enumeration. Common members of that enumeration you might use include `olDateTime`, `olNumber`, `olText`, and `olYesNo`. Other types are also supported—consult the Outlook object model documentation for more information. The Add method also takes two optional parameters that we omit: `AddToFolderFields` and `DisplayFormat`. Note that you can add custom properties to all Outlook item types except the NoteItem and DocumentItem types.

Listing 11-28 shows the creation of several custom properties using the User-Properties.Add method.

Listing 11-28 A VSTO Add-In That Works with Custom Properties

```
private void ThisApplication_Startup(object sender, EventArgs e)
{
  Outlook.MAPIFolder inbox = this.Session.GetDefaultFolder(
    Outlook.OlDefaultFolders.olFolderInbox);

  Outlook.PostItem postItem = inbox.Items.Add(
    Outlook.OlItemType.olPostItem) as Outlook.PostItem;
  postItem.Subject = "User Properties Test";
  postItem.Save();

  Outlook.UserProperties userProperties =
    postItem.UserProperties;

  Outlook.UserProperty dateProp = userProperties.Add(
    "DateProp", Outlook.OlUserPropertyType.olDateTime,
    missing, missing);
  dateProp.Value = System.DateTime.Now;

  Outlook.UserProperty numberProp = userProperties.Add(
    "NumberProp", Outlook.OlUserPropertyType.olNumber,
    missing, missing);
  numberProp.Value = 123;

  Outlook.UserProperty textProp = userProperties.Add(
    "TextProp", Outlook.OlUserPropertyType.olText,
    missing, missing);
  textProp.Value = "Hello world";

  Outlook.UserProperty boolProp = userProperties.Add(
    "BoolProp", Outlook.OlUserPropertyType.olYesNo,
    missing, missing);
  boolProp.Value = true;
```

```
MessageBox.Show(String.Format(
    "There are now {0} UserProperties.",
    userProperties.Count));

postItem.Save();
}
```

Saving an Outlook Item

As you have already seen, when you create an Outlook item you have to call the Save method or the newly created item gets discarded when your variable containing the newly created item goes out of scope. You can check whether an Outlook item needs to be saved by accessing the Saved property. For example, in Listing 11-28, if we examine the Saved property right before we call postItem.Save at the end of the function, Saved would return `false` because some changes were made to the Outlook item (user properties were added) after the Save method was earlier in the function.

The code in Listing 11-28 actually works even when you omit the last call to Save. Consider what happens, however, if we omit the last call to Save. If you examine the newly created item, its Saved state is still `false` after this function runs. If you double-click the newly created item to display an Inspector view and then close the Inspector view without making any changes, Outlook prompts users to save the changes made to the item, which is confusing to users because they did not make any changes. Outlook prompts to save because it still detects that it needs to save the changes made to the user properties by the add-in code. If you exit Outlook, Outlook will save the changes to the newly created item and on the next run of Outlook, the saved state of the new item will be back to `true`.

Showing the Categories Dialog for an Outlook Item

You can show the Categories dialog in Figure 11-9 by using the Outlook item's Show-CategoriesDialog method. This dialog allows the user to select categories to associate with an Outlook item. As described earlier, the Outlook item's Categories property enables you to examine what categories an Outlook item is associated with. The Categories property returns a `string` value with each category associated with the Outlook item in a comma-delimited list.

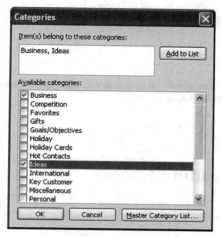

Figure 11-9 Outlook's Categories dialog.

Mail Properties and Methods

Several commonly used properties and methods are associated with items that would be found in a mail folder, such as a MailItem or a PostItem. The BodyFormat property tells you what format the body of a mail message is in. It sets or gets a member of the `OlBodyFormat` enumeration: `olFormatHTML`, `olFormatPlain`, `olFormatRichText`, or `olFormatUnspecified`. When a message is set to have its BodyFormat in `olFormatHTML`, the HTML for the body of the message can be set or get via the HTMLBody property. This property gets and sets the `string` value, which is the HTML content of the message.

Listing 11-29 shows add-in code that creates a PostItem using the BodyFormat and HTMLBody properties. Figure 11-10 shows the PostItem created by Listing 11-29.

Listing 11-29 A VSTO Add-In That Creates a PostItem with BodyFormat set to olFormatHTML

```
private void ThisApplication_Startup(object sender, EventArgs e)
{
  Outlook.MAPIFolder inbox = this.Session.GetDefaultFolder(
    Outlook.OlDefaultFolders.olFolderInbox);

  Outlook.PostItem postItem = inbox.Items.Add(
    Outlook.OlItemType.olPostItem) as Outlook.PostItem;
  postItem.Subject = "HTML Example";
  postItem.BodyFormat = Outlook.OlBodyFormat.olFormatHTML;
  postItem.HTMLBody =
```

```
  "<HTML><BODY><H1>Heading 1</H1><UL><LI>Item 1</LI><LI>Item
2</LI></UL></BODY></HTML>";
  postItem.Save();
}
```

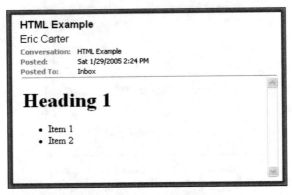

Figure 11-10 PostItem created by Listing 11-29.

The Forward method returns a new Outlook item that can be forwarded to a recipient. Given a MailItem, for example, the MailItem object's Forward method returns a new MailItem. This MailItem can then be given a recipient. Recipients of a MailItem are accessed via the Recipients property, which returns a Recipients collection. A new Recipient can be added by using the Recipients collection's Add method, which takes a `string` representing the display name of the recipient. When a recipient is added, the Outlook item can be sent in e-mail by calling the Outlook item's Send method.

Listing 11-30 illustrates working with the Forward method, the Recipients collection, and the Send method. It creates a PostItem that it then forwards as a MailItem to a recipient. Note that when calling the Forward method and the Send method, we have to cast to the _PostItem and _MailItem interfaces because Forward and Send are both method and event names.

Listing 11-30 A VSTO Add-In That Creates a PostItem and Then Forwards It as a MailItem

```
private void ThisApplication_Startup(object sender, EventArgs e)
{
  Outlook.MAPIFolder inbox = this.Session.GetDefaultFolder(
    Outlook.OlDefaultFolders.olFolderInbox);

  Outlook.PostItem postItem = inbox.Items.Add(
    Outlook.OlItemType.olPostItem) as Outlook.PostItem;
```

```
postItem.Subject = "HTML Example";
postItem.BodyFormat = Outlook.OlBodyFormat.olFormatHTML;
postItem.HTMLBody =
  "<HTML><BODY><H1>Hello World</H1></BODY></HTML>";
postItem.Save();

// Forward the PostItem to someone
Outlook.MailItem forwardedItem =
  ((Outlook._PostItem)postItem).Forward();
forwardedItem.Recipients.Add("Eric Carter");
((Outlook._MailItem)forwardedItem).Send();
}
```

An identical pattern is followed to reply or reply all to an Outlook item. The original item has its Reply or ReplyAll method called, which generates a new MailItem object. The Recipients collection of the new MailItem object is modified if needed. Finally, the new MailItem object's Send method is invoked to send the new MailItem.

Outlook Issues

This section examines two special issues relating to Outlook development. The first is the Outlook object model security dialog and how to prevent your add-in code from triggering it. The second Outlook-specific issue is a third object model, called Extended MAPI, that can be used in addition to the Outlook object model and the CDO object model. We briefly consider when you might need to resort to using it and how this is typically done.

Outlook Object Model Security

Occasionally as you develop Outlook 2003 add-ins, you might write code that causes the Outlook object model security dialog to display (see Figure 11-11). This dialog was added to prevent the spread of viruses and worms that accessed parts of the Outlook object model such as the address book to spread themselves.

Typically, you want to prevent this dialog from coming up because it can distress your users. When you understand why this dialog appears, you can refactor your code to avoid this dialog. If you write a COM add-in, you are passed an Application object to the OnConnection method of IDTExtensibility2. If you write a VSTO add-in, you can access the methods and properties of Outlook's application object through the base class of the ThisApplication class. The Application object passed to OnConnection and the base class of VSTO's ThisApplication class are trusted in Outlook 2003—as long as you obtain all other objects you use from these trusted objects, you never have to worry about the object model security dialog.

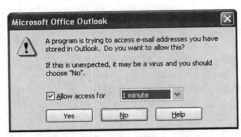

Figure 11-11 The Outlook object model security dialog.

If you create a new instance of the Application object, this new instance will not be trusted, and the objects you create or access from it will sometimes cause the Outlook object model security dialog to appear. Also, the objects passed into your event handlers as parameters are not trusted objects, and accessing restricted methods and properties on these objects can cause the Outlook object model security dialog to appear. If you trigger the Outlook object model security dialog by using these objects, you should find a way to get the same object through your trusted Application object.

A handful of restricted properties and methods of the Outlook object model can cause the security dialog to appear when you talk to an object that was not obtained from a trusted Application object. Table 11-13 shows the complete list of properties and methods in the Outlook object model that can cause the security dialog to appear when you call them on an object that was not obtained from a trusted Application object.

Table 11-13 Properties and Methods That Can Cause the Outlook Security Dialog to appear if Accessed from Objects Not Obtained from a Trusted Application Object

Object	Restricted Properties and Methods
Action	Execute()
AddressEntries	All properties and methods.
AddressEntry	All properties and methods.

Object	Restricted Properties and Methods
AppointmentItem	Body NetMeetingOrganizerAlias OptionalAttendees Organizer RequiredAttendees Resources Respond() SaveAs() Send()
ContactItem	Body Email1Address Email1AddressType Email1DisplayName Email1EntryID Email2Address Email2AddressType Email2DisplayName Email2EntryID Email3Address Email3AddressType Email3DisplayName Email3EntryID IMAddress NetMeetingAlias ReferredBy SaveAs()
DistListItem	Body GetMember() SaveAs()
Inspector	HTMLEditor WordEditor
ItemProperties	Any access of a restricted property associated with an Outlook item
JournalItem	Body ContactNames SaveAs()

continues

Table 11-13 Continued

Object	Restricted Properties and Methods
MailItem	Bcc Body Cc HTLMBody ReceivedByName ReceivedOnBehalfOfName ReplyRecipientNames SaveAs() Send() SenderEmailAddress SenderEmailType SenderName SentOnBehalfOfName To
MeetingItem	Body SaveAs() SenderName
NameSpace	CurrentUser GetRecipientFromID
PostItem	Body HTMLBody SaveAs() SenderName
Recipient	All properties and methods.
Recipients	All properties and methods.
TaskItem	Body ContactNames Contacts Delegator Owner SaveAs() Send() StatusUpdateRecipients StatusOnCompletionRecipients
UserProperties	Find()
UserProperty	Formula

Listing 11-31 illustrates a COM add-in that uses a trusted and an untrusted Application object. The first block of code gets a MailItem out of the Inbox using the Application object passed to OnConnection, which we have set to a class member variable called `trustedApplication`. It then tries to access the MailItem object's Body property (which is a restricted property) on the object obtained via the trustedApplication object. This action will not cause the object model security dialog to appear. The second block of code uses an Application object we have created using the new keyword. This Application object is not trusted, and the Outlook item we obtain via this `untrustedApplication` variable causes the object model security dialog to appear when we access the restricted Body property.

Listing 11-31 A COM Add-In That Accesses a MailItem's Body Property Through a Trusted Application Object and Through an Untrusted Application Object

```
public void OnConnection(object application,
   Extensibility.ext_ConnectMode connectMode,
   object addInInst,
   ref System.Array custom)
{
   trustedApplication = application as Outlook.Application;
   untrustedApplication = new Outlook.Application();

   // Using trusted application
   Outlook.MAPIFolder inbox = trustedApplication.Session.
     GetDefaultFolder(Outlook.OlDefaultFolders.olFolderInbox);

   Outlook.MailItem mailItem = inbox.Items[1] as Outlook.MailItem;
   if (mailItem != null)
     MessageBox.Show(mailItem.Body);

   // Using untrusted application causes dialog to appear
   Outlook.MAPIFolder inbox2 = untrustedApplication.Session.
     GetDefaultFolder(Outlook.OlDefaultFolders.olFolderInbox);
   Outlook.MailItem mailItem2 = inbox2.Items[1] as Outlook.MailItem;
   if (mailItem2 != null)
     MessageBox.Show(mailItem2.Body);
}
```

Listing 11-32 shows a VSTO add-in that has a similar problem because it tries to access a restricted property on an Outlook item passed into an event handler as a parameter. As mentioned earlier, parameters passed into event handlers are untrusted, and accessing properties on these parameters that are restricted causes the Outlook object model security dialog to appear.

Listing 11-32 A VSTO Add-In That Tries to Access the Body Property of a MailItem Obtained from an Untrusted Event Parameter

```
private void ThisApplication_Startup(object sender, EventArgs e)
{
  this.ItemSend += new
    Outlook.ApplicationEvents_11_ItemSendEventHandler(
    ThisApplication_ItemSend);
}

void ThisApplication_ItemSend(object Item, ref bool Cancel)
{
  Outlook.MailItem untrustedMailItem = Item as
    Outlook.MailItem;
  if (untrustedMailItem != null)
  {
    MessageBox.Show(String.Format(
      "Untrusted body {0}", untrustedMailItem.Body));
  }
}
```

If you are developing for a version of Outlook older than 2003, the Application object provided to an add-in is not trusted by default. Also, some installations of Outlook 2003 are configured to not trust any COM or VSTO add-ins by default. For these cases, you have to use the Outlook security administration tools, which rely on a public exchange folder and a form template (Outlooksecurit.oft) that can be installed and configured to provide specific add-ins with a trusted Application object. For VSTO Add-ins, you need to use the Outlook security administration tools to trust the AddinLoader.dll component that loads all VSTO add-ins. You also need to deploy appropriate .NET security policy as described in Chapter 19.

Extended MAPI

Occasionally, you will find a property in the Outlook object model that you really want to change but is read-only. Sometimes it is possible to change these properties using another API set called Extended MAPI. Extended MAPI is a C++-oriented API that talks directly to the MAPI store that backs Outlook folders and items. The way .NET developers typically use Extended MAPI is by creating an assembly written in managed C++. Your existing managed code can then call the managed C++ assembly, which can then call into Extended MAPI. This is an advanced scenario that is not covered further in this book.

Conclusion

This chapter examined some of the most important objects in the Outlook object model. The chapter covered the properties and methods common to all of the 15 Outlook item types. You have also learned about the Outlook object model security issue.

▗ 12 ▗

Introduction to InfoPath

What Is InfoPath?

I NFOPATH IS AN OFFICE APPLICATION THAT enables users to design and fill out rich, XML-based forms. When designing a form, you can start with a blank form or infer the form structure from an XML data file, an XML schema file, a database, or even a Web service.

Every form can be composed of one or more views. A view is what users see when they fill out the form. Each view consists of one or more controls that are data-bound to XML data nodes. A node is a field or group in the data source that represents an item of the XML data behind the form.

You can add features such as conditional formatting, spell checking, and auto-complete to forms using the form's designer, but more complex forms might require custom code to achieve the desired results. For example, you might write code behind a form to verify that an e-mail address is valid, to fetch a current stock quote from a Web service, or to restrict certain views to be available only to users with a particular role such as an administrator.

Before VSTO, code behind forms in InfoPath consisted solely of JScript and VBScript code developed with the Microsoft Script Editor. Although easy to use, the script languages lack some of the language features that make developing and maintaining larger, more complex customized forms easier, such as strong typing, IntelliSense, and access to the .NET framework.

This chapter discusses how to use VSTO to create InfoPath forms with managed code behind them. The chapter starts with a brief overview of what must be installed on your machine to develop managed code behind an InfoPath form with VSTO and shows how Visual Studio and InfoPath work together. Then the chapter covers the InfoPath security model, deployment model, and event-driven programming model. We consider the data events that you can handle in your code. We also consider the InfoPath form object model and how to handle form-related events.

Getting Started

Before you can use VSTO to put code behind InfoPath forms, you must ensure that the following things are installed on your development machine:

- Visual Studio 2005
- InfoPath 2003 Service Pack 1 or later
- The Microsoft Office InfoPath 2003 Toolkit for Visual Studio 2005

The toolkit must be installed last because it has an explicit dependency on both Visual Studio and InfoPath.

InfoPath Service Pack 1 contains the primary interop assemblies (PIAs) for InfoPath so that managed code can automate the InfoPath object model. Service Pack 1 also added the OnSave event, improved support for some offline scenarios, and digital signature support. You will read more about the details later in this chapter.

Creating a New Project

After you have the toolkit installed, open Visual Studio and choose New Project from the File Menu. Open up the Visual C# node in the tree view, choose Office, and then choose the InfoPath Form Template project as shown in Figure 12-1.

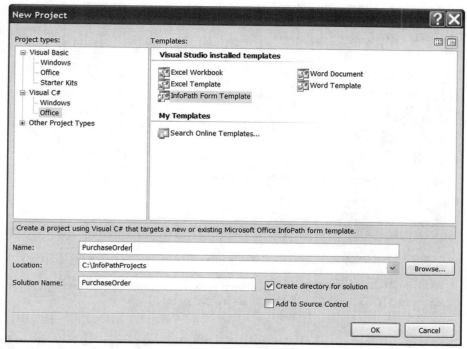

Figure 12-1 Creating an InfoPath project in Visual Studio.

The location is the location on the development machine, not the
final location from which the published form will be accessed by
your users.

After you click OK, the Project Wizard asks whether you want to create a new
form or open a form that you have already created with InfoPath as shown in
Figure 12-2.

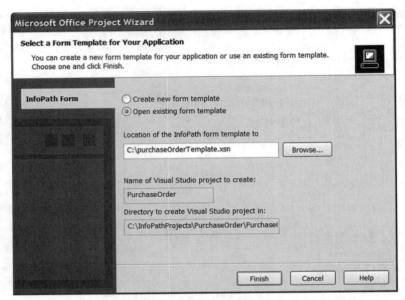

Figure 12-2 Creating the project based on a blank or existing form.

To create a new, blank form, keep the default selection of Create new form template and click Finish. To create a new form template based on an XML data file, XML schema, database connection, or Web service, create the form template in InfoPath first without using Visual Studio, and then open it as an existing form template. After you have a form template created in InfoPath, you can select the Open existing form template option and browse to the form template (.xsn) or form template definition (.xsf) file.

> JScript (.js) or VBScript (.vbs) files associated with an existing form template will also be imported but the script itself will be nonfunctional. Other scripts, such as scripts used for custom task pane extensibility for example, are not affected. If you select a form template that already has managed code, the associated code is not included in the import; rather, you should open the Visual Studio project associated with the form template.

After you have created your project, you can use Visual Studio as your code editor at the same time as you design the form using the InfoPath designer window, as shown in Figure 12-3. While developing for InfoPath, you will frequently switch between the InfoPath designer window and the Visual Studio window. In addition, when you press F5 in your project, InfoPath starts up another InfoPath window called a "preview" window to preview what your form would look like at runtime. This makes for three top-level windows you might be juggling at any given time. When you close the InfoPath preview window, Visual Studio stops debugging the project. If you accidentally close the InfoPath designer window, you can reopen it by choosing Open InfoPath from Visual Studio's Project menu.

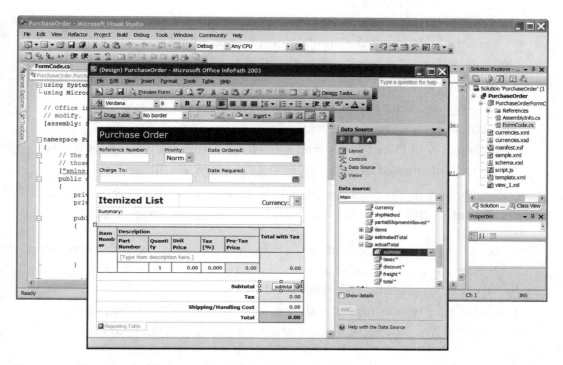

Figure 12-3 Visual Studio window and the InfoPath designer window run as two separate windows.

Take a look at the Solution Explorer window on the right side of Visual Studio. Behind the scenes, a form template consists of many files working together. By default, when working with just InfoPath, the XML template, XML schemas, XSL views, and so on are hidden unless you choose Extract Form Files from the File menu and then explore that folder in Windows Explorer. When designing the code behind a form in Visual Studio, you can see and edit all files in the InfoPath project directly. However, the InfoPath designer "locks" all the forms files. If you want to manually edit the files in Visual Studio, first close the InfoPath designer window to unlock the files.

Visual Studio adds the following new commands to facilitate the development of code behind an InfoPath form:

- Open InfoPath (opens the InfoPath designer window)
- Publish Form (the equivalent of choosing Publish from InfoPath's File menu)
- Preview > Default (previews the form you are designing in an InfoPath window—the equivalent of creating a new form from the template you have designed)
- Preview > With Data File (previews the form you are designing with a custom XML file passed in as the initial data the form is editing)
- Preview > With User Role (previews the form with a custom role defined using InfoPath's User Roles command in the InfoPath Tools menu)

These commands are available in the Visual Studio Project menu, the Tools menu, and in the context menu that displays when you right-click the InfoPath Project node in the Visual Studio Solution Explorer window.

The InfoPath Project Properties dialog, also accessible from the project's right-click menu, has two settings that prove useful when previewing your form as shown in Figure 12-4.

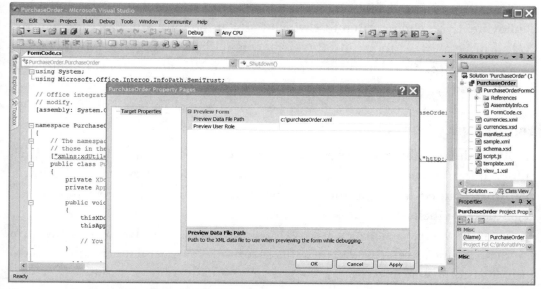

Figure 12-4 Setting InfoPath-specific project properties.

The first text box, called Preview Data File Path, takes a path to a custom XML file. Without a custom XML file, InfoPath previews with the default XML file used when filling out a new form. A custom XML file is useful for simulating what a user would experience if an existing form, saved from a previous editing session, were reopened. You can also use the Preview > With Data File command to achieve the same result.

The second text box, called Preview User Role, sets a "preview role." You can create forms that have different views depending on the "role" of the user filling out the form; an administrator might have a different view than an accountant. These roles are defined using InfoPath's User Roles command in the InfoPath Tools menu. You can also use the Preview > With User Role command to achieve the same result.

Form Security

Before delving into the specifics of how the InfoPath event-driven programming model works, you need to understand how the security model works.

InfoPath was designed to be "secure by default" to provide protection for the end users using InfoPath to fill out your forms. As an InfoPath developer, the burden is on you to ensure your form can be deployed without problems. The method of deployment you choose can affect which parts of the InfoPath object model your code will be allowed to use. To understand how the method of deployment you choose can affect decisions during form development, take a look at the InfoPath security model.

Form Security Levels

InfoPath defines three security levels: restricted, domain, and full trust. Each InfoPath form requires and is granted a certain level. If the granted level is lower than the required level, the form will not run. This security system is enforced regardless of whether there is code behind the form.

Forms in the restricted security level can only access resources within the form template itself. A form that requires this security level must not attempt to access local files, for instance.

Forms in the domain security level can use files and connect to resources on the machine hosting the form without asking the user. If a form in the domain security level attempts to read or write information from a different machine, InfoPath prompts the user to ensure that the cross-domain access is acceptable.

Forms in the full trust security level have complete and unrestricted access to every resource that the user running the form has access to. Only forms installed to trusted locations or digitally signed with a trusted signature are fully trusted. (Deployment location and security are discussed below.)

When running a form, you can see whether it was granted the restricted, domain, or full trust security level by looking at the icon in the status bar as shown in Figure 12-5.

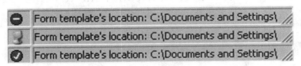

Figure 12-5 The form's security level and location are shown in the status bar when a user fills out a form. The icons shown are for the restricted, domain, and full trust security levels, respectively.

Automatically and Manually Setting the Required Security Level

InfoPath 2003 Service Pack 1 automatically sets the required security level as you design your form. It can do so by determining which features the form uses and the minimum security level the form needs to function properly.

For example, if a form on the local intranet (\\MyComputer\MyShare\Template1.xsn), posts to a Web server on the Internet (http://www.contoso.com), that is potentially dangerous. A malicious form might be attempting to trick you into entering sensitive information that would then be sent across the Internet. The form would require at a minimum the domain security level, not the restricted security level. If a user runs this form without sufficient evidence for InfoPath to grant the form the domain security level, the form will not run. Even if it is granted the domain security level, at runtime InfoPath warns the user when the form attempts to post the information to the new domain.

> InfoPath can automatically determine the required security level by looking at the properties of the form, but it does not look at the code behind the form, and therefore might set the required security level too low. For example, if you deploy a form that successfully requests domain trust but calls XDocument.SaveAs in an event handler, the form will load but will fail at runtime if the event handler is called. In this case, InfoPath shows an error to the end user explaining there is not sufficient permission to perform the operation.

To manually change the required security level of an InfoPath form, open the form template in design mode. Select the Form Options menu item located in the Tools menu, and click the Security tab as shown in Figure 12-6.

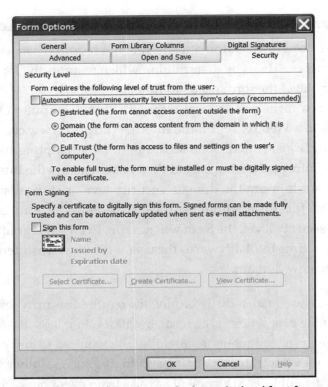

Figure 12-6 Specifying the required security level for a form.

Deployment Location and Security

You have many options when deploying forms, and covering them completely is beyond the scope of this chapter. For the purposes of this chapter, we discuss only the impact of deployment location on security level.

You can deploy a form in two ways: the "URL" and the "URN". URL deployment is used by default when you use Save or Save As from the InfoPath designer. Use URL deployment to publish the form to some shared location such as a Web server, SharePoint site, shared network directory, and so on.

InfoPath uses Internet Explorer security settings to determine what security level to grant to URL-deployed forms. If Internet Explorer would classify the form's location as an internet or local intranet site, InfoPath will grant the form the restricted security level. If Internet Explorer thinks that the form's location is a "trusted site" or the "my computer" domain, InfoPath will grant the domain security level. Forms from locations on Internet Explorer's "restricted sites" list are not allowed to run at all.

URN deployment is necessary (but not sufficient) to ensure that InfoPath grants a form full trust. Choose Publish from the File menu of InfoPath to deploy a form to a URN. A URN-published form can be installed to the local machine or digitally signed with a trusted certificate to ensure that InfoPath fully trusts the form.

Registering a Form Template to Grant Full Trust

After you have published a form using URN deployment, the easiest way to enable a form template to be granted full trust on your machine is to call the RegisterSolution method on the form. If called from within an InfoPath form itself, this would require the full trust security level. This presents somewhat of a chicken-and-egg problem: We need to be fully trusted to register a template as fully trusted.

Fortunately, InfoPath can be automated from an automation executable, much as we automated Word and Excel in Chapter 2, "Introduction to Office Solutions." We use automation to call the RegisterSolution method; because it is not an InfoPath form calling the method, but rather a fully trusted utility program, there is no chicken-and-egg problem.

Suppose we have a mortgage application form template that we want to be a full trust form template while we are developing and debugging it. There are two ways to register the form template: We can register the .XSF file or the .XSN file.

What's the difference? If you are registering the form template so that it is fully trusted on your development machine, it makes more sense just to register the .XSF file, which can be found in the InfoPath project folder. If you are registering a form template that is going to be published to a central location for end users to use, however, register the .XSN file after publishing the form.

Listing 12-1 shows a console application that registers an .XSF file so it can be granted full trust. To use this code, create a new console application and add a reference to the InfoPath PIA.

Listing 12-1 A Console Application That Registers an XSF file So That It Can Be Granted Full Trust

```
using System;
using System.XML;
using InfoPath = Microsoft.Office.Interop.InfoPath;
```

```
public class RegisterForm
{
  public static void Main(string[] args)
  {
    const string xsfLocation =
      @"C:\InfoPathProjects\MortgageApplication\manifest.xsf";

    // Remove the publishUrl
    XMLDocument xsfDom = new XMLDocument();
    xsfDom.PreserveWhitespace = true;
    xsfDom.Load(xsfLocation);
    XMLNamespaceManager xns =
      new XMLNamespaceManager(new NameTable());

    xns.AddNamespace("xsf", xsfDom.DocumentElement.NamespaceURI);

    XMLNode xDoc = xsfDom.SelectSingleNode(
      "/xsf:xDocumentClass", xns);

    xDoc.Attributes.RemoveNamedItem("publishUrl");
    xsfDom.Save(xsfLocation);

    // Register the file
    InfoPath.ExternalApplicationClass ip =
      new InfoPath.ExternalApplicationClass();

    ip.RegisterSolution(xsfLocation, "overwrite");
  }
}
```

When registering an InfoPath form to be fully trusted, it must not have a publishUrl. A publishUrl means the solution is URL-based. Remember that URN-based solutions cannot have a URL component and also be granted full trust. The console application in Listing 12-1 removes the publishUrl (if it exists) from the .XSF form template definition and then registers the .XSF file to enable this form to run with full trust permissions on your machine.

Do not forget to select the Full Trust option in the Security tab of the Form Options dialog when designing the form on which you are going to run this console application. After you have run the console application, running the form in full trust is as easy as double-clicking the manifest.xsf file.

More Information

A full discussion of the InfoPath security model and deployment system is beyond the scope of this book. For more information, refer to the InfoPath SDK documents titled "Security Guidelines for Developing InfoPath Forms" and "Form Security Model" available on MSDN at http://msdn.microsoft.com/library/en-us/ipsdk/html/ipsdkSecureAForm_HV01083590.asp and http://msdn.microsoft.com/library/en-us/ipsdk/html/ipsdkFormSecurityModel_HV01083562.asp.

For more information about digitally signing your form template, see the InfoPath Team Blog at http://blogs.msdn.com/infopath/archive/2004/05/10/129216.aspx. The InfoPath SDK, also available on MSDN, discusses using the RegForm tool to help form designers create installable form templates.

Programming InfoPath

InfoPath uses a declarative, per-form, event-driven approach to programming customized forms. That is, code consists of declarations that define which event handlers are to be invoked when form elements or data elements source events. Code in InfoPath is always written behind a *specific* form template; it is not possible to write "application-level" code that is executed for *all* form templates. Code runs when events are raised that have been declaratively handled by event handlers.

There are two "root" objects in the InfoPath object model. The Application object is the root of the runtime object model; every programmable object in InfoPath can be accessed through the Application object. The other "root" object is the ExternalApplication object. The ExternalApplication object is useful for automating InfoPath by an automation executable rather than from code behind a form, as shown in Listing 12-1. However, this chapter only discusses how to create code behind a form and does not cover automation executables further.

When you create an InfoPath form template project in VSTO, Visual Studio automatically generates a FormCode.cs file for you to add the code behind the form. It generates some "boilerplate" code for you to get started containing methods called when the InfoPath form starts up and shuts down, as shown in Listing 12-2.

Listing 12-2 The FormCode.cs File

```csharp
namespace PurchaseOrder
{
  //[Attribute omitted]
  public class PurchaseOrder
  {
    private XDocument thisXDocument;
    private Application  thisApplication;

    public void _Startup(Application app, XDocument doc)
    {
      thisXDocument = doc;
      thisApplication = app;
    }

    public void _Shutdown()
    {
    }
  }
}
```

When the InfoPath form starts up, InfoPath calls the _Startup method and passes in an Application and XDocument object. By default, the managed class that represents the InfoPath form stashes away references to these objects in thisApplication and thisXDocument so that your event handlers and other code can use them later. The same Application object is passed to all currently executing forms. The XDocument object is a specific instance that refers to the form to which it is passed.

Although you now have references to the Application and XDocument objects in the _Startup method, do not actually make any InfoPath object model calls yet. Calling the InfoPath object model is not allowed in either the _Startup or _Shutdown methods. During these method, calls to the object model are unavailable because the form is either still in the process of being created or is being terminated.

Event-Based Programming

While filling out the form, various user actions directly or indirectly trigger events. Take the OnLoad event, for example. To handle (that is, register an event handler to be called when the event occurs) the OnLoad event, select the InfoPath designer's Tools menu, then the Programming submenu, and then the On Load Event menu item. Notice that the InfoPath designer automatically creates a code stub and handles the event. Whenever you add an event handler to an InfoPath form, you always do it using the InfoPath designer window and its associated menus, never by using any commands within Visual Studio.

```
[InfoPathEventHandler(EventType=InfoPathEventType.OnLoad)]
public void OnLoad(DocReturnEvent e)
{
  // Write your code here
}
```

You will immediately notice that an InfoPath event is not hooked up in the traditional .NET way of creating a new delegate and adding that delegate to an object that raises the event using the += operator. Instead, InfoPath events are hooked up via attributes—the InfoPath runtime reflects on the attributing of methods in your code to determine events that are handled by your code and the methods to call when an event is raised. In this case, the attribute InfoPathEventHandler is added to your OnLoad event handler. This attribute is constructed with Event-Type=InfoPathEventType.OnLoad, which tells the InfoPath runtime to raise the OnLoad event on this attributed method.

Let's add some code to our OnLoad handler to restrict users from creating a new form if it is not presently business hours. (Note that this does not restrict editing existing forms, just creating new ones.) Listing 12-3 shows the new OnLoad handler.

Listing 12-3 On OnLoad Handler That Restricts Creation of New Forms to Be During Business Hours

```
[InfoPathEventHandler(EventType=InfoPathEventType.OnLoad)]
public void OnLoad(DocReturnEvent e)
{
  if ((DateTime.Now.Hour < 8 // earlier than 8am
    || DateTime.Now.Hour > 17 // later than 5pm
    || DateTime.Today.DayOfWeek == DayOfWeek.Saturday
    || DateTime.Today.DayOfWeek == DayOfWeek.Sunday)
    && thisXDocument.IsNew) // is a new form
  {
    thisXDocument.UI.Alert("You can only create a new" +
    " mortgage application 8am to 5pm, Monday through Friday.");
    e.ReturnStatus = false; // fail loading the form
```

```
        }
    }
```

The IsNew property and UI.Alert method both require the domain security level.

All form events in InfoPath are cancelable through code. In this OnLoad event example, setting the ReturnStatus property to `false` on the DocReturnEvent object e tells InfoPath to fail the OnLoad event (and thus fail loading the form) when the event handler has returned. The default value is `true`.

Previewing

Press F5 or choose Start from the Debug menu in Visual Studio and the code in Listing 12-3 will be compiled and start running in InfoPath's preview form mode. Depending on what time and day you run the code in Listing 12-3, you may or may not be able to fill out the form!

Suppose you are working late—later than 5 p.m. at least. The OnLoad handler will not allow you to create a new form because thisXDocument.IsNew always returns `true` when you press F5 or choose Start from the debug menu. How can you force the form to look like an already created form? If you double-click the template.xml file (located in the Visual Studio project folder), you will start InfoPath and cause InfoPath to think it is opening an already created form. The template.xml file is used internally by InfoPath when creating a new form after you double-click the .XSN form template. However, directly opening this file tricks InfoPath into thinking it is an existing or previously saved form.

Previewing is a very useful technique when designing and debugging a form, but it is important to realize that previewing a form causes the following side effects:

- If you choose the Tools menu, and then the Preview submenu, you will see that there is a With data file menu item. Previewing with a data file is never considered to be creating a new form. Instead, it is considered to be viewing an existing form.
- Previewing does not allow the user to save changes.

- InfoPath will not grant the full trust security level to a previewed form, only the domain or restricted security levels.

So in addition to previewing, you should also use your form in a production environment with InfoPath running by itself to verify that everything works properly.

Data Source Events

The InfoPath object model consists of objects that expose properties, methods, and events. InfoPath's programming model has two kinds of events: data source events, and form events. Because InfoPath's programming model emphasizes the role of events, let's take a look at the data source events first, and then some of the useful form events, properties, and methods of the various objects.

The number of data source events is small compared to the number of form events, but they are arguably the most powerful. Typically, most of the code behind a form involves sinking data source events.

Three data source events raise sequentially in the order listed here:

- OnBeforeChange
- OnValidate
- OnAfterChange

Each of these events can be raised on any data node (that is, element, attribute, or group of elements) in the data source.

Although the events are always raised in this order, InfoPath does not guarantee that the events will be raised one *immediately* after the other. For example, if you have a hierarchy and have event handlers for different levels in the hierarchy, you might not see the events handled immediately after each other for a given data source node. You might see OnBeforeChange raise for a group first, then OnBeforeChange handled next for a field, and then OnValidate for the group, and so on.

While learning about these events and their functions, keep in mind that a data source change could occur because the text in a data node was deleted, cut, pasted, dragged, dropped, or modified in some other way. Furthermore, changes are not limited to textual changes in single elements. Inserting, deleting, or replacing a section, and repeating table row or list item also trigger data source events.

For example, suppose that we are sinking these three events for a text node called FirstName, which is bound to a text box containing the text *Jogn*. If the user fixes the typo by changing the text box to *John*, each event for the node bound to this text box will be raised twice: once as a delete operation (the text *Jogn* was deleted) and once as an insert operation (the text *John* was inserted). You will learn how to handle these cases by examining the Operation property on the DataDOMEvent object.

Furthermore, the events will not just raise on the node that changed, but also "bubble up" on the parent node of the changed node, and on its parent, and so on, until the root of the data source tree is reached.

The following sections first take a look at two ways to create event handlers using InfoPath, and then describe exactly the purpose of each of these three events.

Creating an Event Handler

How do you create an event handler for a particular data node? For example, suppose you have a mortgage application form and you want to handle the OnBeforeChange event for the telephone number HomePhone. Using the InfoPath designer, click the drop-down button on the data node called HomePhone and choose Properties, and then the Validation and Event Handlers tab, as shown in Figure 12-7.

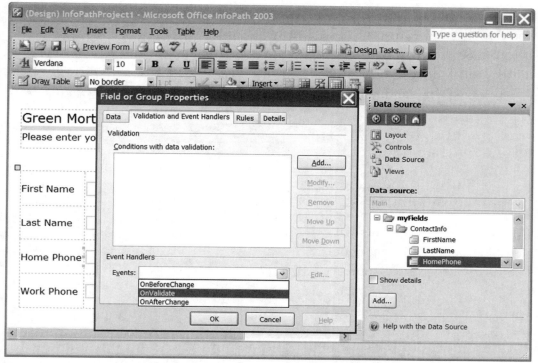

Figure 12-7 Selecting a data source node and showing the Properties dialog.

From the Events drop-down, select the OnBeforeChange event. Then click the Edit button. Visual Studio will automatically generate the appropriate event handler with the appropriate attributing. We sometimes omit the attributing in our example code in this chapter as we do here—but remember that the correct attributing must be in place for InfoPath to raise an event to a particular handler. These attributes are difficult to generate by hand—which is why you should use the dialogs of InfoPath to create these event handlers:

```
public void HomePhone_OnBeforeChange(DataDOMEvent e)
{
// Write your code here. Warning: Ensure that the constraint you
// are enforcing is compatible with the default value you set
// for this XML node.
}
```

You might want to start from a data-bound control to get to a data node for which you want to handle an event. If the data node is bound to a control, you can get to the same dialog shown in Figure 12-7 by first double-clicking the data-bound control in the view to get to its Properties dialog, as shown in Figure 12-8.

Click the Data Validation button to get to the dialog box shown in Figure 12-7.

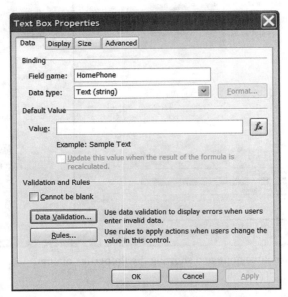

Figure 12-8 Selecting a control's properties to handle a data event.

The OnBeforeChange Event

The OnBeforeChange event fires before the change is made to the underlying XML data. If you want to abort the change, the OnBeforeChange event is your only chance; by the time the OnValidate event is raised, the change has already been made to the underlying data source.

To reject the change to the data, set the ReturnStatus property of the Data-DOMEvent argument e to `false`. When ReturnStatus is set to `false`, InfoPath will show an error dialog informing the user that the change is not allowed.

Several additional useful properties are associated with the DataDOMEvent object. The Operation property returns a `string` set to `"Delete"`, `"Update"`, or `"Insert"`. This tells you whether the user is deleting data, updating data, or inserting new data. The ReturnMessage property accepts a `string` that is shown in a dialog when the change is rejected. The NewValue property returns a `string` for the new value of the data node that was changed. The OldValue property returns a `string` for the value of the data node before it was changed.

Listing 12-4 shows an OnBeforeChange event handler that validates that an e-mail address is in a valid format. In Listing 12-4, we first check the DataDOMevent object's Operation property to make sure we are not in a delete operation. If we are in a delete operation, the NewValue property would be `null`. We then validate the e-mail address returned by the NewValue property by using a regular expression. If the change is not matched by our regular expression, we set ReturnStatus to `false` and set ReturnMessage to the message text we want InfoPath to use in the error dialog.

Listing 12-4 An OnBeforeChange Event Handler

```
public void Address_OnBeforeChange(DataDOMEvent e)
{
  if (e.Operation == "Delete") // only handle update and insert
    return;
  string newEmail = e.NewValue;
  if (newEmail.Length > 0)
  {
    Regex emailRegEx = new Regex(
      @"^[a-z][\w\.-]*[a-z0-9]@[a-z0-9][\w\.-]*" +
      @"[a-z0-9]\.[a-z][a-z\.]*[a-z]$",
      RegexOptions.IgnoreCase);
    e.ReturnStatus = emailRegEx.IsMatch(newEmail);
    e.ReturnMessage = "Please use a valid email address.";
  }
}
```

You cannot change the data source itself from within the event handler—for example, you cannot set the NewValue property to a different string. InfoPath "locks" the data source to make it read-only for the duration of the event, to prevent the scenario where one event handler attempts to change the data, triggering another change event handler, which might then trigger yet another change event handler, and so on. Making the data source read-only while the event sink runs prevents these "event storm" scenarios.

Data source change events are fired when the form loads and the data source is first created. If you set the DataDOMEvent object's ReturnStatus property to `false` during this data source creation phase, the form will fail to load. Use caution when writing an OnBeforeChange event handler.

The OnValidate Event

By the time the OnValidate event raises, the new value has already been written into the data source. The most common reason to sink an OnValidate event is to implement error handling.

A form error is typically shown in an InfoPath form by a red dashed "error visual" rectangle surrounding the control. For instance, if you require that a telephone number include the area code, you might use an error visual rectangle to indicate an improper format, as shown in Figure 12-9.

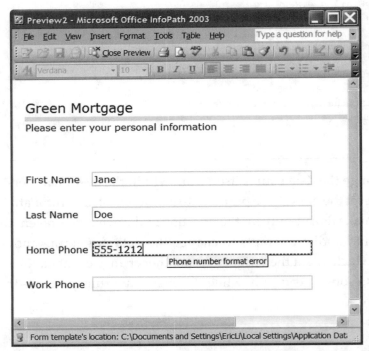

Figure 12-9　A data validation error shown in InfoPath with a red dashed rectangle.

Let's add error handling for telephone number data using the OnValidate event. Listing 12-5 shows an OnValidate handler that uses some additional features of the InfoPath object model. The code uses the DataDOMEvent object's ReportError method to report data validation errors. The ReportError method takes the parameters listed in Table 12-1.

Table 12-1 Parameters Passed to the DataDomEvent Object's ReportError Method

Parameter Name	Type	What It Does
varNode	`object`	The data node to associate with the error. If this data node is bound to one or more controls, the controls might display error visuals.
bstrShortError-Message	`string`	The short error message is the message shown in the tooltip when the user hovers over a control that is data-bound to the data node passed to varNode.
fSiteIndependent	optional `bool`	Set to `true` to tell InfoPath that the error applies to all potentially matching nodes, which proves useful when you add an error to a node that is repeating and you want to add an error to the collection of nodes instead of a particular node. If set to `false`, the error is associated with the specific node passed to varNode and no other.
bstrDetailed-ErrorMessage	optional `string`	The long error message typically has more information than the short error message and has additional troubleshooting options.
lErrorCode	optional `int`	An error code value; it is sometimes convenient to be able to give each error condition a number. Setting an error code proves particularly useful if you have an existing error reporting system whose numeric codes you want reuse.
bstrType	optional `string`	Tells InfoPath how to first reveal the error: If you pass the string `"modeless"`, InfoPath will passively alert the user via an error visual on the control. If you pass the string `"modal"`, InfoPath will show a dialog prompting the user with the long error message.

Listing 12-5 also illustrates the use of the XDocument object's Errors collection as an alternative way to report errors. Recall from Listing 12-2 that the code generated for the InfoPath form has cached away the XDocument object in the `thisXDocument` variable. The code uses the `thisXDocument` variable to access the XDocument object for the form. It accesses the XDocument object's Errors collection and uses the Errors collection's Add method to associate errors with the form. The arguments to the Errors.Add are very similar to those of ReportError, with three differences. First, Errors.Add has no "site-independent" option. Second, Errors.Add allows you to tag an error condition with a string parameter called `bstrConditionName` as well as with an error code. This condition string is for your internal use only does not display to the end user. Third, you can call Errors.Add at any time in any handler, but ReportError may only be called from within an OnValidate event handler.

Listing 12-5 An OnValidate Event Handler That Uses the DataDOMEvent Object's ReportError Method and the XDocument Object's Errors Collection

```
public void HomePhone_OnValidate(DataDOMEvent e)
{
  // Ensure that the format is "xxx-xxx-xxxx"
  if (e.NewValue == null)
    return;
  bool siteIndependent = false;
  int errorCode = 0;
  string modal = "modal";
  string newPhone = e.NewValue;
  if (newPhone.Length != 12)
  {
    // Tell InfoPath what node caused the error, whether the error
    // is associated with this node, what the short and long error
    // messages should be, and whether to produce a modal or
    // modeless error dialog:

    e.ReportError(e.Site, "Phone number format error",
      siteIndependent, "Phone number expected format is xxx-xxx-xxxx.",
      errorCode, "modeless");
  }
  else
  {
    int indexOfHyphen = newPhone.IndexOf('-');
    if (indexOfHyphen != 3)
    {
      thisXDocument.Errors.Add(e.Site, "NoExpectedHyphen",
        "No hyphen found", "Expected a hyphen after 3 digits.",
```

```
        errorCode, modal);
    }
    else
    {
      indexOfHyphen = newPhone.IndexOf('-', indexOfHyphen + 1);
      if (indexOfHyphen != 7)
      {
        thisXDocument.Errors.Add(e.Site, "NoExpectedHyphen",
          "Second hyphen not found",
          "Expected a hyphen after 6 digits.",
          errorCode, modal);
      }
    }
  }
}
```

Site Versus Source

Another thing to note in Listing 12-5 is the code passes the Site property of the Data-DOMEvent object to give ReportErrors and Errors.Add the data node where the error occurred. The Site property of the DataDOMEvent object refers to the data node currently processing the validation event (that is, the data node to which the event handler is listening). The DataDOMEvent object's Source property refers to the data node that changed and triggered validation. Remember that events can "bubble up" from child nodes to parent nodes; if you are sinking the OnValidate event of a parent node and the user changes a child node, the Site will refer to the parent node handling the event, and the Source will refer to the child node that triggered the event in the first place.

> The Site and Source properties and the Errors.Add and ReportError methods all require the domain security level.

The OnAfterChange Event

In OnBeforeChange and OnValidate events, the data source is read-only and cannot be modified by your event handler code. When can your code modify the data source? Code you write in an OnAfterChange event handler is allowed to edit the data source if InfoPath is not raising the OnAfterChange event for an undo or redo operation invoked by the user. Your OnAfterChange event handler can detect whether an undo or redo resulted in the event being raised by checking the Data-DOMEvent's IsUndoRedo property.

If you directly update the data node that your event handler corresponds to, use caution—otherwise you could create infinite recursion. Listing 12-6 shows a simple OnAfterChange event handler that directly changes the data node it is handling the event for by setting e.Site.text to a new value. It prevents recursion by first checking to see whether e.Site.text is already set to the new value. It also checks the IsUndoRedo property to make sure OnAfterChange was not raised as a result of an undo or redo.

Listing 12-6 An OnAfterChange Event Handler That Updates the Data in the Node for Which It Is Handling the OnAfterChange Event

```
[InfoPathEventHandler(MatchPath="/my:myFields/my:someField",
  EventType=InfoPathEventType.OnAfterChange)]
public void someField_OnAfterChange(DataDOMEvent e)
{
  if (e.IsUndoRedo)
    return;

  if (e.Site.text == "newFieldValue")
    return; // prevents recursion

  e.Site.text = "newFieldValue";
}
```

Form Events, Properties, and Methods

Data source events prove very useful for ensuring that data constraints are maintained and taking action when the user makes changes to data. InfoPath also provides a form object model that you can use to further customize the behavior of your form. Some of the scenarios the form object model enables are as follows:

- Consider the earlier example of a form that displays interest rate quotes to the user filling out the form. You might want to create an "Administrator" view of the form that allows authorized people to change the quoted interest rates.

- You might want to integrate context-sensitive help as the user navigates through your form.

- You might want a custom task pane to extend and further customize the experience of filling out the form.

- You might want to customize how your forms are saved and submitted. Instead of submitting via a data connection or allowing a user to save to any location, you could restrict where the form is saved.

The remainder of this chapter examines the form object model and discusses how to create a custom task pane for a form. The InfoPath forms object model contains many events, properties, and methods. This book discusses only some of the most commonly used parts of the InfoPath forms object model.

Button Events and View Switching

A view is a surface on which you insert controls and form content in the designer; it is what the user looks at while filling out the form. Lengthy forms are often composed of multiple views. In addition, data being edited can be displayed in multiple views—for example, you might have a timecard that can be viewed in a less-detailed view for someone who wants to quickly enter information. A more detailed view might also be available for a manager trying to generate end of payperiod reports. You can find a list of available views for the data being edited in InfoPath's View menu. A user can switch between various views at will.

Switching between views might not be the desired behavior, especially if your views are supposed to be sequential or have dependencies. While designing your form, you have an option to remove the name of a view from the View menu and to prevent users from choosing a particular view. The code behind the form can then switch views programmatically by using the XDocument.View.SwitchView method.

Suppose you have a mortgage application with two views. The first view allows the user to fill out contact information: name, phone numbers, and so on. When all the required contact information is filled out, the user can click Go to Mortgage Details button. You can add a button to the form by selecting the Controls task pane in the InfoPath form design view and dragging a button onto the form designer. If you right-click the button and choose Properties, you can then open the Properties dialog shown in Figure 12-10.

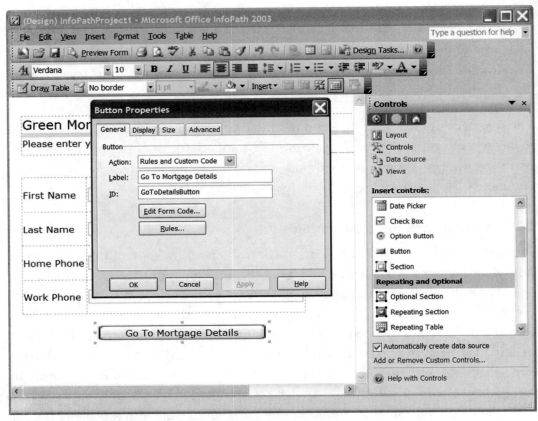

Figure 12-10 Creating a button with the Form Designer.

We want this button to switch to another view to display the mortgage details, but only if the first and last name text boxes are filled on the contact information view. We can do this by clicking the Edit Form Code button in the Properties dialog shown in Figure 12-10, which causes Visual Studio to emit an event handler for the OnClick event raised by the button.

Listing 12-7 shows code for the OnClick event handler that switches the view. Because this is not a data event but rather a forms event, the event argument object DocActionsEvent does not refer to the data nodes that we are interested in checking before we switch the view. The code gets to the data nodes by querying the XML data source using an XPATH query, and then verifies that the strings that come back are valid before changing views.

Listing 12-7 uses the XDocument object's DOM property to access an IXML-DOMDocument object. It then uses the IXMDOMDocument object's selectSingleNode method to get a node by passing the XPATH query strings to get to FirstName and LastName. Finally, it examines the retrieved node's text property to see whether the FirstName and LastName fields have been filled in.

Listing 12-7 also uses two other methods from XDocument. The XDocument object's UI property returns a UI object. The UI object's Alert method displays a simple message box within InfoPath. The XDocument object's View property returns a View object. The View object represents the currently active view in the form. Listing 12-7 use the View object's SwitchView method to change to another view if the FirstName and LastName data nodes have been entered.

Listing 12-7 An OnClick Event Handler for a Button That Switches the View

```
[InfoPathEventHandler(MatchPath="GoToDetailsButton",
  EventType=InfoPathEventType.OnClick)]
public void GoToDetailsButton_OnClick(DocActionEvent e)
{
  const string FirstNameXPath = "/my:myFields/my:FirstName";
  const string LastNameXPath = "/my:myFields/my:LastName";
  IXMLDOMDocument mainData = thisXDocument.DOM;
  if (string.IsNullOrEmpty(
    mainData.selectSingleNode(FirstNameXPath).text) ||
    string.IsNullOrEmpty(
    mainData.selectSingleNode(LastNameXPath).text))
  {
    thisXDocument.UI.Alert("Please fill in first and last name.");
  }
  else
  {
    thisXDocument.View.SwitchView("Mortgage Details");
  }
}
```

The OnContextChange Event and the Custom Task Pane

Another way to write code to handle form changes is to use the XDocument object's OnContextChange event. What exactly do we mean by "context"?

The user can only be interacting with one control at a time; mouse clicks or key presses are handled by the control that has the focus. The context of a form is the data source node bound to the control that presently has the focus.

Consider the example of a contact information form. Each text box is bound to a particular node in the data source. As the user filling out the form uses the mouse or keyboard to move the focus from one control to the next on the form, context changes to a different data node, and the XDocument object's OnContextChange event is raised.

You could have more than one control bound to the same data node. In that case, if the user were to change the focus from one control to another bound to the same data node, the context change event would not raise because context has not changed. In a repeating control, the OnContextChange event is raised when focus is changed from row to row. However, the OnContextChange event does not indicate the new row position.

Creating a Custom Task Pane

A common way to use OnContextChange event is to integrate a dynamic help system into a form. By detecting when the form is editing a different data node, we can provide help for the data node being edited in the task pane. The first thing we need to do is enable the custom task pane for this form. Choose Form Options from the Tools menu of the InfoPath designer and select the Advanced tab, as shown in Figure 12-11.

Using the Advanced tab of the Form Options dialog, you can enable the custom task pane and add HTML files as resource files that can be displayed in the task pane. Click the Resource Files button to bring up the Resource Files dialog box. Click the Add button to add HTML files as resources to the InfoPath form. For this example, we add three HTML files: one named `GeneralHelp.htm`, a second named `Name-Help.htm`, and a third named `PhoneHelp.htm`. Note that as you add the HTML files they display in the Solution Explorer in Visual Studio.

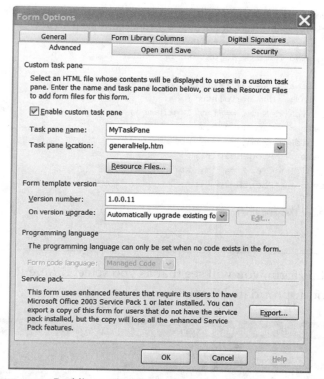

Figure 12-11 Enabling and adding resources to the custom task pane.

After you have added several HTML files to the form, you can handle the OnContextChange event to display the appropriate HTML file in the task pane for a particular context. To generate a handler for the OnContextChange event, choose the On Context Change Event command from the Programming menu in the Tools menu of the InfoPath designer. Listing 12-8 shows an OnContextChange event handler that switches between `GeneralHelp.htm`, `NameHelp.htm`, and `PhoneHelp.htm` in the task pane depending on the current data node.

Listing 12-8 An OnContextChange Event Handler That Switches the HTML Shown in the Task Pane

```
[InfoPathEventHandler(EventType=InfoPathEventType.OnContextChange)]
public void OnContextChange(DocContextChangeEvent e)
{
  if (e.Type == "ContextNode")
  {
```

```
        HTMLTaskPane helpTaskPane =
          (HTMLTaskPane)thisXDocument.View.Window.TaskPanes[0];
        string navigateTo = "GeneralHelp.htm";
        string thisNodeName = e.Context.nodeName;

        if (thisNodeName == "my:FirstName")
          navigateTo = "NameHelp.htm";
        else if (thisNodeName == "my:LastName")
          navigateTo = "NameHelp.htm";
        else if (thisNodeName == "my:HomePhone")
          navigateTo = "PhoneHelp.htm";
        else if (thisNodeName == "my:WorkPhone")
          navigateTo = "PhoneHelp.htm";

        helpTaskPane.Navigate(navigateTo);
    }
}
```

If you preview this form, you will see that as you select different text boxes the task pane displays the appropriate HTML files.

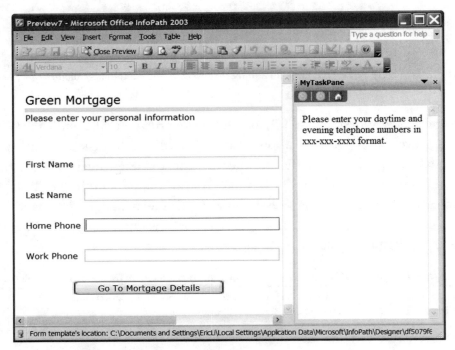

Figure 12-12 The custom task pane at runtime.

The code in Listing 12-8 checks the DocContextChangeEvent object's Type property to verify it is `"ContextNode"`. InfoPath only supports a type of `"ContextNode"` as of Service Pack 1 but other values may be introduced in future versions of InfoPath. As a result, the check for `"ContextNode"` is recommended for forward-compatibility reasons.

You probably noticed that the Infopath object model exposes an array of task panes. The custom task pane is always located at index 0. Other indices reference built-in task panes available while filling out a form. For example, index 4 is the Help task pane.

> Forms in the restricted security level can access the task panes collection, but reading the Context property requires at least the domain security level.

Focus Versus Selection

What if you want to determine the current context in some event handler other than an OnContextChange handler? The XDocument's View property returns a View object. The View object has a GetContextNodes method that can be called from any event handler. It returns a collection of all the XML nodes that are in context: not just the node bound to the control with the focus, but all of its parent nodes in the data source tree as well.

The View object also provides a GetSelectedNodes method that returns the collection of XML nodes bound to the currently selected controls. This is a subtle distinction: Only one control can have the focus at any one time, but a user can select multiple controls.

You might be tempted to use the GetSelectedNodes or GetContextNodes methods in a button click handler. Unfortunately, this does not work; as soon as the user clicks the button, the focus and selection change to the button itself.

> GetContextNodes and GetSelectedNodes both require at least the domain security level.

Setting Selection

Two other useful methods on the View object are the SelectNodes and SelectText methods. SelectText takes a single IXMLDOMNode, and SelectNodes takes two IXMLDOMNodes (to define the start and end of a range) to determine what to select. For example, consider the earlier example in which we wrote an OnClick event handler for a button to ensure that the FirstName and LastName fields were not blank before switching views. You could use the SelectText method to select the text box that was blank so that the user could simply start typing into the blank text box to fix the error.

Overriding Submit, Confirm, and Save

So far you have seen how to use data source and form events to ensure that data entered by users is valid, reacts to users navigating around the form, and so on. This chapter has not yet discussed what happens to the data in the form when all the information is entered and validated. Somehow, the data must be saved to disk or submitted to a server somewhere.

Suppose you want to prevent the user from specifying a destination for the saved data. Rather, when the user is done with the form, you want to ensure that the data is always saved to a particular shared directory on your intranet. You can accomplish this by handling the OnSubmitRequest event and writing code to force the data to be saved to that location.

The first thing you need to do is to disallow users from saving. Go to the Tools menu in the InfoPath designer, then Form Options, and then click the Open and Save tab. Uncheck the Save and Save As check box, as shown in Figure 12-13.

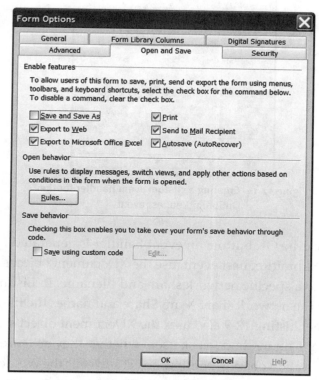

Figure 12-13 Disabling Save and Save As for a form.

The next step is to handle the OnSubmitRequest event. This event is raised when the Submit action is invoked when filling out the form. To handle this event, choose Submitting Forms from the InfoPath Tools menu. Select the Enable Submit commands and buttons radio button, and then pick Custom submit using form code from the Submit to: drop-down, as shown in Figure 12-14.

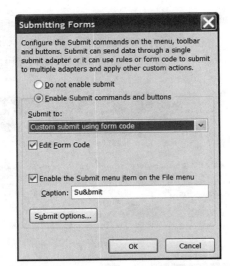

Figure 12-14 Creating a custom event handler for the OnSubmitRequest event.

When you click the OK button, an event handler is generated for you in Visual Studio. In the OnSubmitRequest event, use the XDocument object's SaveAs method to save the form to a specific network share and filename. In Listing 12-9, the code saves the form to the network share \\myShare and names the file using the user's first and last name. Listing 12-9 also uses the XDocument object's UI object. It calls the UI object's Confirm method to ask users whether they are sure want to save. It also uses the Application object's Window object and calls the Window object's Close method to close the window associated with the form after the form is saved.

Listing 12-9 An OnSubmitRequest Event Handler That Forces the Form to be Saved to a Particular Network Share

```
[InfoPathEventHandler(EventType=InfoPathEventType.OnSubmitRequest)]
public void OnSubmitRequest(DocReturnEvent e)
{
  XdConfirmChoice submitChoice;
  if (thisXDocument.Errors.Count > 0)
  {
    submitChoice = thisXDocument.UI.Confirm(
      "Errors exist on the form. Continue submitting?",
      XdConfirmButtons.xdYesNo);
  }
  else
```

```
    {
      submitChoice = thisXDocument.UI.Confirm(
        "Are you sure you want to submit?", XdConfirmButtons.xdYesNo);
    }

    if (submitChoice == XdConfirmChoice.xdYes)
    {
      string firstName = thisXDocument.DOM.selectSingleNode(
        "/my:myFields/my:FirstName").text;
      string lastName = thisXDocument.DOM.selectSingleNode(
        "/my:myFields/my:LastName").text;
      string fileName = firstName + "_" + lastName + ".XML";
      thisXDocument.SaveAs(@"\\myShare\forms$\" + fileName);
      thisXDocument.UI.Alert("Thank you, " +
        firstName + "! You will be contacted shortly.");
      thisApplication.ActiveWindow.Close(true /*force*/);
      // No need to set ReturnStatus because InfoPath closes
    }
    else
      e.ReturnStatus = false;
  }
```

InfoPath uses the ReturnStatus flag to determine whether the OnSubmitRequest event succeeded. It is not necessary to set the ReturnStatus flag to `true` in this example when closing the form window because the runtime is immediately shut down when the form window is closed.

> The call to Confirm requires the domain security level and the call to SaveAs requires the full trust security level. Therefore, we will need to either digitally sign or register the form template to get full trust permissions.

Conclusion

This chapter introduced InfoPath development with VSTO. You learned how to create a new VSTO InfoPath project based on a new form or an existing form. The chapter also covered key objects that you will code against, including InfoPath's Application object, the XDocument object (which represents a form), the View object, and objects passed as parameters to events such as the DataDOMEvent object.

This chapter also examined the InfoPath security model. You learned how a form is granted a particular security level, such as restricted, domain, or full trust. The chapter also covered InfoPath's data model and key data events such as OnBeforeChange, OnValidate, and OnAfterChange. You also read about the InfoPath's form object model and how to handle key events, including OnLoad, a button click handler, OnContextChange, and OnSubmitRequest.

As you have no doubt discovered while working through the examples in this chapter, InfoPath development differs quite a bit from the Excel, Word, and Outlook development experience. Whenever you add an event handler, you must do so using the menus and commands in InfoPath—you never use Visual Studio to add an event handler. Event handlers do not follow the traditional .NET event model of declaring new delegates and adding them to an event source using the += syntax of C#. Instead, methods that will handle InfoPath events are attributed. These attributes are somewhat difficult to create and edit—hence the need to have the InfoPath menus and dialogs generate these handlers for you. Finally, InfoPath development differs from Excel and Outlook because the "design view" of an InfoPath form is the InfoPath application window, not a designer that shows up in place within Visual Studio.

This book does not cover InfoPath in any additional detail. For more information on InfoPath programming, consult the MSDN page for InfoPath at http://msdn.microsoft.com/library/en-us/odc_2003_ta/html/odc_ancInfo.asp.

■ Part Three ■

Office Programming in VSTO

S O FAR YOU HAVE SEEN how to use Visual Studio to develop managed customizations and add-ins that can run in various Office applications. Clearly, it is possible to use the power of both managed code and the rich Office object models together. However, compare the development process for such solutions to, say, designing a Windows Forms-based application in Visual Studio. Developers of forms-based solutions get visual designers, powerful data binding, and a truly object-oriented programming model. These tools help professional developers manage the complexity of modern application construction.

Visual Studio Tools for Office (VSTO) takes the same approach to Word and Excel solution development. VSTO features include the following:

- Word and Excel run as designers inside Visual Studio.
- Workbooks, worksheets, and documents are represented by customizable, extensible classes in an object-oriented programming model.
- Managed controls can be hosted by worksheets and documents.
- Business process code can be logically separated from display code.
- Windows Forms data binding connects business data to controls.
- Business data can be cached in the document and manipulated as XML, enabling both offline client and server scenarios.

Part Three of this book explores these features:

- Chapter 13, "The VSTO Programming Model," shows how VSTO extends the Word and Excel object models.
- Chapter 14, "Using Windows Forms in VSTO," covers adding Windows Forms controls to VSTO-customized documents.
- Chapter 15, "Working with Actions Pane," shows how to add managed controls to Office's Document Actions task pane.
- Chapter 16, "Working with Smart Tags in VSTO," shows how to implement Smart Tags using managed code.
- Chapters 17, "VSTO Data Programming," and 18, "Server Data Scenarios," discuss ways to manipulate datasets associated with the document on the client and server.
- Chapter 19, ".NET Code Security," covers the VSTO security model.
- Chapter 20, "Deployment," shows how to deploy your customized documents.

Part Three also examines some advanced topics regarding using XML with Word and Excel, and creating managed application-level add-ins in Word, Excel, and Outlook.

13

The VSTO Programming Model

The VSTO Programming Model

I N WINDOWS FORMS PROGRAMMING, A FORM is a window that contains controls, such as buttons, combo boxes, and so on. To implement a form, you can drag and drop controls from the Visual Studio toolbox onto the form's designer. The form designer then generates a customized subclass of the Form class. Because each form is implemented by its own class, you can then further customize the form code by adding properties and methods of your own to the class. And because all the controls are added as properties on the form class, you can use IntelliSense to more rapidly program those custom methods.

VSTO's system of host items and host controls is directly analogous to Windows Forms. By *"host"* we mean the application—Word or Excel—which hosts the customization. Host items are like forms: programmable objects that contain user interface elements called host controls. The Workbook, Worksheet, and Chartsheet objects are host items in Excel; the Document object is the sole host item in Word. In Outlook, the Outlook Application object is exposed as a host item.

As we saw back in Chapter 2, "Introduction to Office Solutions," the Visual Studio Excel and Word designers create custom classes which extend the Worksheet and Document base classes. As you place host controls such as lists, named ranges, charts and buttons onto the worksheet they are exposed as fields on the customized subclass.

Separation of Data and View

Some people use spreadsheet software solely for its original purpose: to lay out financial data on a grid of cells that automatically recalculates sums, averages and other formulas as they update the data. For example, you might have a simple Excel spreadsheet that calculates the total expenses for a wedding given all the costs involved. Similarly, some people use word-processing software solely for its original purpose: to automatically typeset letters, memos, essays, books and other written material.

However, in a business setting spreadsheets and documents have evolved to have both high internal complexity and external dependencies. Unlike a wedding budget, a spreadsheet containing an expense report or a document containing an invoice is likely to be just one small part of a much larger business process. This fact has implications on the design of a programming model. Consider this VBA code that might be found in a spreadsheet that is part of a larger business process:

```
SendUpdateEmail ThisWorkbook.Sheets(1).Cells(12,15).Value2
```

Clearly, the unreadable snippet is sending an e-mail to someone, but because the Excel object model emphasizes how the *spreadsheet* represents the data, not what the *data* represent, it is hard to say what exactly this is doing. The code is not only hard to read, it is brittle; redesigning the spreadsheet layout could break the code. We could improve this code by using a named range rather than a hard-coded direct reference to a particular cell:

```
SendUpdateEmail ThisWorkbook.Names("ApproverEmail").RefersToRange.Value2
```

Better, but it would be even nicer if the particular range showed up in IntelliSense. VSTO builds a convenient custom object model for each worksheet, workbook, or document so that you can more easily access the named items contained therein:

```
SendUpdateEmail(ExpenseReportSheet.ApproverEmail.Value2);
```

A more readable, maintainable, and discoverable object model is a welcome addition. However, even in the preceding snippet, the VSTO programming model still does not address the more fundamental problem: We are manipulating the data via an object model that treats them as part of a spreadsheet. The spreadsheet is still the lens through which we see the data; instead of writing a program that manipulates ice cream sales records, we wrote a program that manipulates a list and a chart.

The crux of the matter is that Word and Excel are *editors*; they are for *designing documents that display data*. Therefore, their object models thoroughly conflate the data themselves with the "view," the information about how to display them. To mitigate this conflation, the VSTO programming model was designed to enable developers to logically separate view code from data code. Host items and host controls represent the "view" elements; host items and host controls can be data bound to classes that represent the business data.

Model-View-Controller

If you're familiar with design patterns, you will have already recognized this as based on the Model-View-Controller (MVC) design pattern. In the MVC pattern, the data model code represents the business data and the processes that manipulate it. The view code reads the data, listens to Change events from the data, and figures out how to display it. The controller code mediates between the view and the data code, updating the data based upon the gestures the user makes in the view (mouse clicks, key presses, and so on).

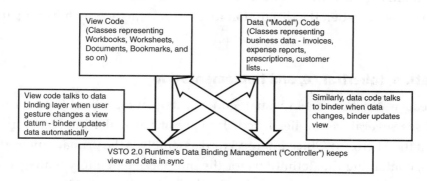

Figure 13-1 Model-View-Controller architecture.

Benefits of Separation

Logically separating the data code from the view code leads to a number of benefits when building more complex business documents on top of Word and Excel:

- Business data and rules can be encapsulated in ADO.NET datasets and reused in different applications.
- Changes to view code are less likely to unexpectedly break data code (and vice versa).
- Data code can cache local copies of database state for offline processing.
- Server-side code can manipulate cached data inside the document without starting up Word/Excel.

Now that you know some of the design philosophy behind VSTO, let's take a look at how the host items and host controls actually extend the Word and Excel object models. (The data side is covered in Chapter 17, "VSTO Data Programming," and server-side data manipulation is covered in Chapter 18, "Server Data Scenarios.")

VSTO Extensions to Word and Excel Objects

VSTO extends the Word and Excel object models in several ways. Although it is possible to use these features without understanding what is actually happening "behind the scenes," it is helpful to take a look back there. This section explains by what mechanisms host items and host controls extend the Word and Excel programming models. Then the discussion focuses on exactly which new features are available.

Aggregation, Inheritance, and Implementation

If you create a Word project in Visual Studio and open the Object Browser window, you will see several assemblies listed. Two are of particular interest. You already know that the Microsoft.Office.Interop.Word assembly is the primary interop assembly (PIA), containing the definitions for the interfaces that allow managed code to call the unmanaged Word object model. Similarly, the Microsoft.Office.Interop.Excel assembly is the PIA for the unmanaged Excel object model.

You can find the VSTO extensions to the Word and Excel object models in the Microsoft.Office.Tools.Word and Microsoft.Office.Tools.Excel assemblies; each contains a namespace of the same name.

From a VSTO Word document project, open the Object Browser and take a look at the Document host item class in the Tools namespace, as shown in Figure 13-2.

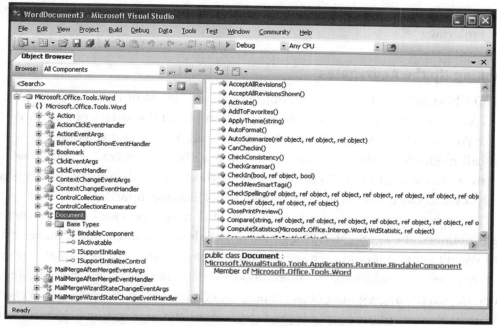

Figure 13-2 Examining the Document host item class in the Object Browser.

Notice that the host item class *implements* the properties, methods, and events defined by the Document interface from the PIA, and *extends* the BindableCompo-nent base class. Chapter 17 gets into the details of how data-bindable components work; for now, the fact that this class implements the properties, methods, and events from the PIA interface rather than extends a base class is important. It is important to notice that even though the Document host item class has all the methods, properties, and events of the Document interface from the PIA, the type definition does not actually say that it implements the Document *interface* itself. This is a subtle distinction that we will discuss in more detail later.

Conceptually, the difference between extending a base class and implementing the properties, methods, and events from an interface is that the former describes an "is a" relationship, whereas the latter describes a "can act like" relationship. A Microsoft.Office.Tools.Word.Document object *really is* a bindable component; it actually shares functionality—code—with its base class. But it merely *looks like* and *acts like* a Word Document object; it *is not* a Word document object as far as Word is concerned.

For example, the Sheet1 class in Excel has your event handlers and host controls. It extends the Microsoft.Office.Tools.Excel.Worksheet base class and implements the properties, methods, and events defined by the Microsoft.Office.Interop.Excel.Worksheet interface.

Hooking Up the Aggregates

VSTO's host item and host control objects *aggregate* some of the underlying Word and Excel document objects (such as the Document and Bookmark objects in Word, or the Worksheet and NamedRange objects in Excel). You have already seen how you can call methods on the document object in a VSTO customization. Suppose, for instance, that you call the CheckGrammar method on the document. If this is not really a Word Document object but merely looks like one, how does it work?

The aggregating object's implementation of that method checks to see whether it has obtained the aggregated Document object already. If it has not, it makes a call into Word to obtain it (and caches away the object so that it will be available immediately when you make a second method call). After it has the reference to the aggregated object, the aggregating object calls CheckGrammar on the aggregated object. The great majority of the properties and methods on the aggregating objects do nothing more than just pass the arguments along to the PIA code, which then passes them along to the unmanaged object model.

Events work in the analogous way; if your code listens to an event exposed by an aggregating object, the aggregating object listens to the event on the aggregated object on your behalf. When the event is raised by the aggregated object, the aggregating object's delegate is called, which then raises the aggregating object's event and calls your event handling delegate.

All the host controls are hooked up in a similar manner as the host items. For instance, if you have a NamedRange host control member of a worksheet, the aggregating Worksheet object itself creates an aggregating NamedRange object. The first time you call a method on the host control, the aggregating class obtains the underlying "real" object from Excel and passes the call along.

This might seem like a whole lot of rigmarole to go through just to add new functionality to the Word and Excel object models. The key benefit that this system of aggregates affords is that each host item class in each project can be customized. One spreadsheet can have an InvoiceSheet class with a CustomerNameRange property, another can have a MedicalHistorySheet class with a CholesterolLevelChart property, and so on.

In short, VSTO *extends* the Word and Excel object models by *aggregating* the unmanaged object models with managed objects. VSTO enables developers to further customize and extend some of those objects—those representing the workbook, worksheet, chart sheet, and document—through subclassing.

Obtaining the Aggregated Object

Much of the time, the foregoing details about how the aggregation model works are just that: implementation details. Whether the host item "is a" worksheet or merely "looks like" one seems to be an academic point. However, in some rare scenarios, it does matter.

Word's and Excel's object models were not written with the expectation that managed aggregates would implement their interfaces; when you call a method that takes a range, Excel expects that you are passing it a real range, not an aggregated range that acts like a range.

For instance, suppose you have a customized worksheet with two host controls: a NamedRange member called InvoiceTotals and a Chart object called InvoiceChart. You might want to write code something like this snippet:

```
this.InvoiceChart.SetSourceData(this.InvoiceTotals,
    Excel.XlRowCol.xlColumns);
```

This code will not compile because the SetSourceData method on the chart aggregate must be passed an object that implements the Range interface. It looks like at runtime the InvoiceChart aggregate will pass InvoiceTotals, an aggregated range, to the "real" aggregated chart. But Excel will expect that the object passed to SetSourceData *is a* range, whereas in fact it is the VSTO aggregate; it merely *looks like* an Excel range.

When just calling methods, reading or writing properties, and listening to events, the aggregate is more or less transparent; you can just use the object as though it really were the thing it is aggregating. If for any reason you need to pass the aggregate to an Excel object model method that requires the real Excel object, you can obtain the real Excel object via the InnerObject property. The code above will compile and work properly if you rewrite it to look like this:

```
this.InvoiceChart.SetSourceData(this.InvoiceTotals.InnerObject,
    Excel.XlRowCol.xlColumns);
```

Aggregation and Windows Forms Controls

If you drag and drop a Windows Forms button onto a worksheet or document, the button control is also aggregated. However, Windows Forms controls are aggregated slightly differently than the NamedRange, Bookmark, ListObject, and other controls built in to Word and Excel. There are two relevant differences between Windows Forms controls and Office's controls. First, Windows Forms controls are implemented by *extensible managed classes*, unlike the *unmanaged* Office controls, which only expose *interfaces* in their PIAs. Second, Word and Excel controls inherently know how they are situated in relation to their containing document or worksheet; non-Office controls on a worksheet do not know that they are in a worksheet.

Word and Excel overcome the second difference by aggregating an *extender* onto a control sited on a document or worksheet. Word's extender implements the properties, methods, and events of the _OLEControl interface that can be found in the Word PIA (but as with other aggregated VSTO controls, the type definition does not actually claim to implement the _OLEControl interface). It has five methods, all of which take no arguments and return no result: Activate, Copy, Cut, Delete, and Select. It also exposes floating-point read-write properties Top, Left, Height, and Width, string properties Name and AltHTML, and an Automation object. Excel's extender implements the properties, methods, and events of the _OLEObject interface that can be found in the Excel PIA.

When you drop a button onto a document or worksheet, the project system adds a new field to the host item class, but types it as `Microsoft.Office.Tools.Word.-Controls.Button` or `Excel.Controls.Button`, respectively. Because the underlying System.Windows.Forms.Button class is extensible, this time the aggregate actually is a subclass of the Windows Forms control. However, it still must aggregate the unmanaged extender interface provided by Word or Excel.

As a further convenience, the managed objects representing embedded Windows Forms controls also have read-only Right and Bottom properties aggregated onto them.

Improving C# Interoperability

The Word and Excel object models were originally designed with VBA in mind. Unfortunately, there are some language features which VBA and VB.NET support but C# does not, such as parameterized properties. In VBA, you could do something like this:

```
Set Up = ThisWorkbook.Names.Item("MyRange").RefersToRange.End(xlUp)
```

End is a read-only property that takes an argument, but C# does not support passing arguments to property getters; arguments can only be passed to methods and indexers in C#. Therefore, the PIA exposes the property getter as a function. You could talk to the PIA like this in C#:

```
Up = ThisWorkbook.Names.Item("MyRange", System.Type.Missing,
    System.Type.Missing).RefersToRange.get_End(
    Microsoft.Office.Interop.Excel.XlDirection.xlUp)
```

Note that the PIA interface calls out that this is a "getter" function; for writable properties there would be a corresponding set_ function that took the parameters and new value as arguments.

C# does, however, support something similar to parameterized property accessors: parameterized indexers. In a VSTO project with a host item or host item control that has been extended, you can accomplish the same task like this:

```
Up = MyRange.End[Excel.XlDirection.xlUp];
```

The get_End accessor function is implemented by the aggregate, so you can still use it if you want to. However, because it is no longer necessary and there is a more elegant solution, it is not displayed in the IntelliSense drop-down.

In several places in the VSTO object model, parameterized indexers have replaced parameterized properties; you will find a list of them all along with the rest of the changes to the object model at the end of this chapter.

The "Tag" Field

Every host item and host control now has a field called Tag, which can be set to any value. This field is entirely for you to use as you see fit; it is neither read nor written by any code other than your customization code. It is included because it is very common for developers to have auxiliary data associated with a particular control, but no field on the control itself in which to store the data. Having the object keep track of its own auxiliary data is, in many cases, more straightforward than building an external table mapping controls onto data.

Event Model Improvements

Like VBA, VSTO encourages an event-driven programming style. In traditional VBA programming, relatively few of the objects source events, which can make writing event-driven code cumbersome. For instance, in Word, the only way to detect when the user double-clicks a bookmark using the standard VBA object model is to declare an "events" class module with a member referring to the application:

```
Public WithEvents WordApp As Word.Application
```

Then sink the event and detect whether the clicked range overlaps the bookmark:

```
Private Sub App_WindowBeforeDoubleClick(ByVal Sel As Selection, _
  Cancel As Boolean)
  If Sel.Range.InRange(ThisDocument.Bookmarks(1).Range) Then
    MsgBox "Customer Clicked"
  End If
End Sub
```

And initialize the event module:

```
Dim WordEvents As New WordEventsModule
Sub InitializeEventHandlers
  Set WordEvents.WordApp = Word.Application
End Sub
```

And then add code that calls the initialization method. In short, this process requires a fair amount of work to detect when an application-level event refers to a specific document or control. The VSTO extensions to the Word and Excel object models were designed to mitigate difficulties in some tasks, such as sinking events on specific controls. In VSTO, the bookmark object itself sources events, so you can start listening to it as you would sink any other event:

```
MyBookmark.BeforeDoubleClick += new ClickEventHandler(OnDoubleClick);
```

In Chapter 2, you saw some of the new VSTO extensions to the view object model in action. You also read about events added by VSTO in Chapters 4, "Working with Excel Events," and 7, "Working with Word Events." At the end of this chapter, we describe all the additions to the event model in detail.

Dynamic Controls

In Chapter 2, you saw that VSTO allows developers to build customized document solutions by using Word and Excel as designers inside Visual Studio. The host item classes expose the host controls present at design time as custom properties on a class that aggregates the underlying unmanaged object.

But what about host controls not present at design time? What if you want to create new named ranges, bookmarks, buttons, or other controls at runtime? It would be nice to be able to use the new events and other extensions to the programming model on dynamically generated controls. As you will see, VSTO supports dynamically adding both host items and host controls, although the former is a little bit trickier to pull off.

Chapter 14 shows how to dynamically add Windows Forms controls to Word and Excel documents.

The Controls Collection

In a Windows Forms application, every form class has a property called Controls that refers to a collection of all the controls hosted by the form. In VSTO, each worksheet and document class contains a similarly named property; in Word, the document class contains an instance of `Microsoft.Office.Tools.Word.-ControlCollection`, in Excel each worksheet class contains an instance of `Microsoft.Office.Tools.Excel.ControlCollection`. They are quite similar; the following sections discuss their differences.

Enumerating and Searching the Collection

You can use the Controls collection to enumerate the set of aggregated controls and perform actions upon all of them. For instance, you could disable all the button controls on a sheet or document:

```
foreach (object control in this.Controls)
{
    Button button = control as Button;
    if (button != null)
        button.Enabled = false;
}
```

The Controls collection also has some of the indexing and searching methods you would expect. Both the Excel and Word flavors have methods with these signatures:

```
bool Contains(string name)
bool Contains(object control)
int IndexOf(string name)
int IndexOf(object control)
```

If the collection does not contain the searched-for control, then IndexOf returns −1. Both collections can be enumerated via the `foreach` loop; should you want to enumerate the collection yourself, you can call GetEnumerator. This method returns a ControlCollectionEnumerator object from the Microsoft.Office.Tools.Excel or Microsoft.Office.Tools.Word namespace, as appropriate. They are essentially identical functionally. Both classes have only three public methods:

- object get Current
- bool MoveNext()
- void Reset()

Current returns `null` when moved past the final element in the collection, MoveNext moves the enumerator to the next element, and Reset starts the enumerator over at the beginning of the collection.

Both collections also expose three index operators, which take a name `string`, `int index`, and `object` respectively. The indexers throw an ArgumentOutOfRangeException if there is no such control in the collection.

Adding New Word and Excel Host Controls Dynamically

The worksheet and document Controls collections provide methods to dynamically create host controls. In Word, you can dynamically create aggregated bookmarks:

```
Microsoft.Office.Tools.Word.Bookmark AddBookmark(
    Microsoft.Office.Interop.Word.Range range, string name)
```

This method creates a new bookmark on the given range and aggregates it with the VSTO host control class.

> XMLNode and XMLNodes host controls cannot be created dynamically in Word. The XMLMappedRange host control cannot be created dynamically in Excel.

In Excel, you can dynamically create aggregated NamedRanges, ListObjects, and Chart controls. Of those, only Chart controls can be positioned at arbitrary coordinates; the rest must all be positioned with a range object:

```
Microsoft.Office.Tools.Excel.Chart AddChart(
  Microsoft.Office.Interop.Excel.Range range, string name)
Microsoft.Office.Tools.Excel.Chart AddChart(
  double left, double top, double width, double height, string name)
Microsoft.Office.Tools.Excel.NamedRange AddNamedRange(
  Microsoft.Office.Interop.Excel.Range range, string name)
Microsoft.Office.Tools.Excel.ListObject AddListObject(
  Microsoft.Office.Interop.Excel.Range range, string name)
```

Removing Controls

The host controls added to a worksheet or document host item class at design time are exposed as properties on the host item class. If at runtime the user were to accidentally delete one, save the document, and then reload it, the customization code would be unable to find the aggregated control. This would likely result in an exception because eventually the customization would try to listen to an event or call a method on the missing aggregated control. If the customization detects this condition, it will throw a ControlNotFoundException.

Although it is difficult to prevent end users from accidentally or deliberately deleting controls without locking the document, the Controls collection can at least try to prevent *programmatic* destruction of controls added at design time. There are four equivalent ways to remove controls from the Controls collection; all will throw a CannotRemoveControlException if you attempt to remove a control that was not added dynamically.

The four ways to remove a dynamic control are to call Delete() on the control itself, or to call Remove(object control), Remove(string name), or RemoveAt(int index) on the Controls collection itself. All four of these remove the control from the collection, remove the control from the document or worksheet, and destroy the extender object.

Most collections have a Clear() method that removes every member from the collection. Because completely clearing a Controls collection would almost always result in an exception when a design-time control was removed, this method always throws a NotSupportedException, and is hidden from IntelliSense.

Dynamic Controls Information Is Not Persisted

What happens when you add one or more dynamic controls to a document, save it, and reload it later?

Dynamically created Windows Forms controls such as buttons and check boxes do not survive being saved and then loaded. They just disappear; your customization code can create them again afresh the next time the document is loaded.

Because "host" controls such as ranges and bookmarks are themselves part of the document, they will be persisted along with the rest of the document. However, the controls do not save any information about any aggregating objects you may have created around them. When the document is reloaded, the controls will still be there, but there will be no aggregates wrapping them. You will have to re-add the controls to the Controls collection to create new aggregates for the controls. The Controls collection provides Add methods that can reconnect an aggregate to an existing control in the document without creating a new control in the document.

Advanced Topic: Dynamic Host Items

As you have just seen, adding new aggregated host controls onto a host item is relatively straightforward: just call the appropriate method on the controls collection for the containing host item and the control is created, aggregated, and placed on the host item automatically.

But what if you should want to use some of the features of an aggregated host item class on a dynamically created worksheet? To do that, you need only three lines of code. Understanding those three lines will require us to delve somewhat deeper into how the VSTO runtime, the hosting application, and the aggregating class all work together.

Start by creating a helper method on an existing worksheet class that takes in the worksheet you want to be aggregated and returns an aggregated worksheet:

```
internal Microsoft.Office.Tools.Excel.Worksheet AggregateWorksheet(
    Microsoft.Office.Interop.Excel.Worksheet worksheet)
{
```

Recall that the aggregating object obtains the aggregated object "on demand." That is, it obtains the underlying object only when the first method is called that must be passed along to the underlying object. That means that the aggregating object must not require the aggregated object when the aggregating object is constructed, but it does need to be able to obtain that object at any time. Somehow the aggregating object must talk to the host and obtain the unique object is aggregating.

It does so by passing a string called "the cookie," which identifies the aggregated object to a special service object provided by the host. In the event that an error occurs when attempting to fetch the worksheet, the runtime will need to raise an error. It is possible that the cookie that uniquely identifies the aggregated object might contain control characters or be otherwise unsuitable for display. Therefore, the aggregate constructor also takes a "human-readable" name used in the event that the host is unable to find the object to be aggregated. In the case of Excel worksheets, we will use a cookie that is already created for each worksheet by VBA called the CodeName. To initialize that cookie, we must make a call into the VBA engine to force the cookie to be created.

How do we obtain a reference to the service that maps cookies onto unmanaged host objects? The already aggregated host item has a member variable called Run-timeCallback that contains a reference to the VSTO runtime library's service provider. *Service provider* is actually a bit of a misnomer; a service provider is an object that knows how to obtain objects that provide services, not necessarily one that provides those services itself. We identify services by the interface they implement.

Finally, to make data binding work properly, the aggregating class needs to know what object contains this worksheet; Chapter 17 covers data binding in more detail.

Let's put all this together. We need to obtain five things to create an aggregating worksheet:

- A host-provided service that can obtain the aggregated object
- The cookie that the host application uses to identify the worksheet
- A human-readable name for the worksheet
- The container of the worksheet
- The VSTO runtime service provider

We obtain the service that maps the name and container to the aggregated object by passing the appropriate interface type to the VSTO runtime service provider:

```
IHostItemProvider hostItemProvider = (IHostItemProvider)
    this.RuntimeCallBack.GetService(typeof(IHostItemProvider));
```

We next have to make a call into VBA to initialize the CodeName for the new worksheet. This line of code does nothing except force VBA to initialize. It does not add a VBA project to the workbook or anything else of that nature. However, it does access the VBProject object. For a solution that dynamically creates host items in Excel, you must make sure that users of your solution have Trust access to Visual Basic Project checked in the VBA Security dialog (Tools > Macro > Security). Otherwise, this line of code will fail:

```
this.VBProject.VBComponents.Item(1);
```

We will use the name of the new Worksheet object for the human-readable name and the CodeName as the host cookie. The container of the new worksheet is the same as the container of the current worksheet:

```
return new Microsoft.Office.Tools.Excel.Worksheet(hostItemProvider,
    this.RuntimeCallback, worksheet.CodeName, this.Container,
    worksheet.Name);
}
```

Just as dynamic host controls are not re-created when a document containing them is saved and then reloaded, dynamic host items are also not re-created.

Advanced Topic: Inspecting the Generated Code

Let's take a deeper look behind the scenes at what is going on when you customize a worksheet or document. Create a new Excel C# project, create a named range, and take a look at the code for Sheet1.cs.

Listing 13-1 The Developer's Customized Worksheet Class

```
namespace ExcelWorkbook1
{
  public partial class Sheet1
  {
    private void Sheet1_Startup(object sender, System.EventArgs e)
    {
      this.MyRange.Value2 = "Hello";
    }
    private void Sheet1_Shutdown(object sender, System.EventArgs e)
    {
    }
    #region VSTO Designer generated code
    /// <summary>
    /// Required method for Designer support - do not modify
    /// the contents of this method with the code editor.
    /// </summary>
    private void InternalStartup()
    {
      this.Startup += new System.EventHandler(Sheet1_Startup);
      this.Shutdown += new System.EventHandler(Sheet1_Shutdown);
    }
    #endregion
  }
}
```

Upon closer inspection, a few questions might come to mind. What does that partial mean in the class declaration? Where is the MyRange property declared and initialized? Didn't we say earlier that the customized worksheet class extends a base class? Where is the base class declaration?

It's the partial that is the key. C# and Visual Basic support a new syntax that allows a class declaration to be split up among several files. The portion that you see before you is the home of all your developer-customized code; the automatically generated code is hidden in another portion of the class not displayed by default.

Click the Show All Files button in the Solution Explorer and you will see that a number of normally hidden files make up the class, as shown in Figure 13-3.

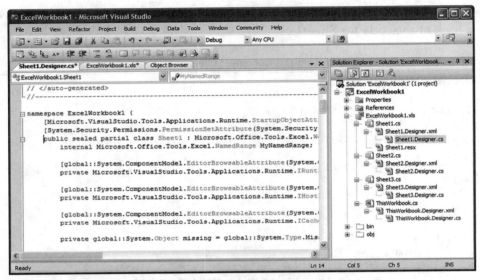

Figure 13-3 Using the Show All Files button to examine hidden code.

First, notice that behind every worksheet there is an XML file for the worksheet. If you look at the first few lines of the XML, you will see that it contains a description of the contents of the worksheet and how to represent it as a class. This "blueprint" contains information about what namespace the class should live in, what the name of the class should be, what controls are exposed on the class, how Excel identifies those controls, and so on.

Behind this language-independent representation of the class there is another C# file that contains the other half of the partial class, generated from the XML blueprint. It begins something like this:

```
namespace ExcelWorkbook1 {
    [Microsoft.VisualStudio.Tools.Applications.Runtime.
      StartupObjectAttribute(1)]
    [System.Security.Permissions.PermissionSetAttribute(
      System.Security.Permissions.SecurityAction.Demand,
      Name="FullTrust")]
    public sealed partial class Sheet1 :
      Microsoft.Office.Tools.Excel.Worksheet,
```

```
Microsoft.VisualStudio.Tools.Applications.Runtime.IStartup {
    internal Microsoft.Office.Tools.Excel.NamedRange MyRange;
```

As you can see, here is where the base classes are specified and the member variables declared. The class also specifies that it is one of the startup classes in your customization assembly, and that code that calls members of this class must be fully trusted.

There is plenty more code in the hidden portion of the partial class, most of which is devoted to initializing controls, starting up data binding, and handling data caching; Chapter 17 discusses data binding in more detail. The constructor, in particular, should look familiar:

```
public Sheet1(IRuntimeServiceProvider RuntimeCallback) :
    base(((IHostItemProvider)(RuntimeCallback.GetService(
    typeof(IHostItemProvider))))), RuntimeCallback, "Sheet1",
    null, "Sheet1")
{
    this.RuntimeCallback = RuntimeCallback;
}
```

This is functionally the same code as just discussed in the previous section on creating custom host items by calling the aggregate base class constructor.

If you ever want to debug through this code, ensure that Just My Code Debugging is turned off (via the Tools > Options > Debugging > General dialog); you can then put breakpoints on any portion of the hidden code, just like any other code.

Do not attempt to edit the hidden code. Every time you make a change in the designer that would result in a new control being added, or even change a control property, the hidden half of the partial class is completely regenerated. Any changes you have made to the hidden half will be lost; that is why it is hidden by default!

The Startup and Shutdown Sequences

You have probably noticed by now that we have been putting custom initialization code in an event handler:

```
private void Sheet1_Startup(object sender, System.EventArgs e) {
    this.MyRange.Value2 = "Hello";
}
```

But exactly what happens, in what order, as the startup classes are created and initialized? Excel customizations typically have many startup classes, one for each sheet and one for the workbook itself; which ones load first?

You already saw a clue that answers the latter question. In the hidden half of the partial class, each class declaration has an attribute:

```
[Microsoft.VisualStudio.Tools.Applications.Runtime.
   StartupObjectAttribute(1)]
```

The Workbook class has 0 for the argument, Sheet1 has 1, Sheet2 has 2, and so on. The workbook aggregate always has ordinal 0, and each worksheet is given its ordinal based on what order Excel enumerates its sheets. The startup sequence happens in four phases, and each phase is executed on each startup class in order of the given ordinal before the next phase begins.

In the first phase, each class is constructed using the constructor mentioned above. This simply constructs the classes and stores away the information that will be needed later to fetch the unmanaged aggregated objects from Excel or Word.

In the second phase, the Initialize method of each startup class is called—again, in multiclass customizations, starting with the workbook and then each worksheet by ordinal. If you look at the hidden half of the partial class, you will see the Initialize method:

```
[global::System.Diagnostics.DebuggerNonUserCodeAttribute()]
[global::System.ComponentModel.EditorBrowsableAttribute(
   System.ComponentModel.EditorBrowsableState.Never)]
public void Initialize() {
   this.HostItemHost = ((IHostItemProvider)
     (this.RuntimeCallback.GetService(typeof(IHostItemProvider))));
   this.DataHost = ((ICachedDataProvider)
     (this.RuntimeCallback.GetService(typeof(ICachedDataProvider))));
   Globals.Sheet1 = this;
   System.Windows.Forms.Application.EnableVisualStyles();
   this.InitializeCachedData();
   this.InitializeControls();
   this.InitializeComponents();
   this.InitializeData();
   this.BeginInitialization();
}
```

The attributes prevent the Initialize method from showing up in IntelliSense drop-downs and mark the method as being "not my code" for the Debug Just My Code feature. The initializer then fetches services from the host needed to initialize the view and data elements, sets up the global class (discussed in more detail later in this chapter), loads cached data, and initializes all the controls.

In the third phase, data binding code is activated. Data bindings must be activated after all the classes are initialized because a control on Sheet2 might be bound to a dataset on Sheet1.

Finally, in the fourth phase, after everything is constructed, initialized, and data bound, each startup class raises its Startup event, and the code in the developer's half of the partial class runs.

This multiphase startup sequence ensures that you can write handlers for the Startup event that can assume not just that the class itself is ready to go, but that every startup class in the customization is ready to go.

Ideally, it would be a good idea to write Startup event handlers for each class that do not depend on the order in which they are executed. If you must, however, you can always look at the startup attributes to see in what order the events will be executed.

The shutdown sequence is similar but simpler. As the host application, Word or Excel, shuts down, each host item class raises the Shutdown event. Shutdown events are raised in the same order as each phase in the startup sequence.

The Globals Class in Excel

Suppose you're writing code in the Sheet1 class that needs to set a property on a control hosted by Sheet2. You are probably going to need to obtain the instance of the *aggregated* Sheet2 class somehow. Instead of aggregating properties representing all the other sheets and the workbook aggregates onto each startup class, VSTO exposes all the sheets and the workbook as static members of the Globals class:

```
private void Sheet1_Startup(object sender, System.EventArgs e)
{
    Globals.Sheet2.MyRange.Value2 = "Hello";
}
```

Because at least the first three phases of the startup sequence have finished at this point, you know that the Globals class and Sheet2 have been initialized, although Sheet2's Startup event has probably not fired yet.

Notice that by default, controls aggregated onto the worksheet classes are given the `internal` visibility modifier. You can change the visibility modifier generated for a control by selecting the control in the designer and then selecting the Modifiers property in the Properties window. However, if you change the visibility of the control to `private`, you will be unable to access the control's field from the Globals class.

The Globals class is also constructed using partial classes, although by default there is no visible portion. Rather, each generated code file defines a portion of the Globals class. You can see this code at the bottom of the hidden file for each class. Should you for some reason want to add your own custom members to the Globals class, you can always create your own portion of the partial class.

VSTO Extensions to the Word and Excel Object Models

This chapter finishes up with a detailed list of every new property, event, and method aggregated onto the Word and Excel objects by the VSTO aggregates, with the exception of the new data binding features (which Chapter 17 covers). For Outlook, only the Application object is aggregated, and no new events, methods, or properties are added to that object.

As mentioned previously, every aggregated object now has a Tag property that you can use for any purpose you choose and an InnerObject property that you can use to access the aggregated object. In addition, each host control now has a Delete method that removes it (if it can be added dynamically at runtime) from its document or worksheet. Because every aggregating object has these properties and methods now, they are not mentioned again in the following topics.

The Word Document Class

VSTO Word projects have exactly one host item class. Every customized document class inherits from the aggregating class `Microsoft.Office.Tools.Word.Document` and implements the properties, methods, and events defined by the `Microsoft.Office.Interop.Word.Document` interface.

Document objects in VSTO source the following new events shown in Table 13-1, all of which are raised by the Document object when the Application object raises the identically named event.

Table 13-1 New Events on VSTO's Aggregated Document Object

Event Name	Delegate	Notes
ActivateEvent	WindowEventHandler	From Application, renamed from WindowActivate
BeforeClose	CancelEventHandler	From Application
BeforeDoubleClick	ClickEventHandler	From Application
BeforePrint	CancelEventHandler	From Application
BeforeRightClick	ClickEventHandler	From Application
BeforeSave	SaveEventHandler	From Application
CloseEvent	DocumentEvents2_CloseEventHandler	From Document, renamed
Deactivate	WindowEventHandler	From Application
EPostageInsert	EventHandler	From Application
EPostagePropertyDialog	EventHandler	From Application
MailMergeAfterMerge	MailMergeAfterMergeEventHandler	From Application
MailMergeAfterRecordMerge	EventHandler	From Application
MailMergeBeforeMerge	EventHandler	From Application
MailMergeBeforeRecordMerge	CancelEventHandler	From Application
MailMergeDataSourceLoad	EventHandler	From Application
MailMergeDataSourceValidate	HandledEventHandler	From Application
MailMergeWindowSendTo-Custom	EventHandler	From Application
MailMergeWizardStateChange	MailMergeWizardStateChangeEventHandler	From Application
New	DocumentEvents2_NewEventHandler	From Document, delayed

continues

Table 13-1 Continued

Event Name	Delegate	Notes
Open	DocumentEvents2_ OpenEventHandler	From Document, delayed
SelectionChange	SelectionEventHandler	From Application
Shutdown	EventHandler	
Startup	EventHandler	
SyncEvent	DocumentEvents2_ SyncEventHandler	From Application, renamed
WindowSize	WindowEventHandler	From Application
XMLAfterInsert	DocumentEvents2_ XMLAfterInsertHandler	From Document
XMLBeforeDelete	DocumentEvents2_ XMLBeforeDelete- Handler	From Document

Notice that the Sync and Close events have been renamed to avoid a naming conflict; C# does not allow a class to have an event and a method with the same name.

The Document class now has OnStartup and OnShutdown methods that force the Document object to source the Startup and Shutdown events.

The New and Open events are delayed so that they are not raised until the aggregate class is fully initialized. These events would normally be raised before any user-authored code could run. If user code does not run until after the event has been raised, however, how would you add an event handling delegate to listen to the event? Therefore, the events are delayed until after the customization's event binding code can run.

The event delegate types could use some additional explanation. All the event delegate types that begin with `DocumentEvents2_` are from the Word PIA. The `System.EventHandler`, `System.ComponentModel.CancelEventHandler` and `System.ComponentModel.HandledEventHandler` delegates are straightforward. The remaining delegate types are all defined in the Microsoft.Office.Tools.Word namespace and have signatures as follows:

```
delegate void ClickEventHandler(object sender, ClickEventArgs e);
delegate void MailMergeAfterMergeEventHandler(object sender,
  MailMergeAfterMergeEventArgs e);
delegate void MailMergeWizardStateChangeEventHandler(object sender,
  MailMergeWizardStateChangeEventArgs e);
delegate void SaveEventHandler(object sender, SaveEventArgs e);
delegate void SelectionEventHandler(object sender, SelectionEventArgs e)
delegate void WindowEventHandler(object sender, WindowEventArgs e);
```

The arguments classes of each are as follows:

- The ClickEventArgs class inherits from System.ComponentModel.CancelEventArgs and therefore has a Cancel property. It also exposes the selection that was clicked:

```
class ClickEventArgs : CancelEventArgs {
   ClickEventArgs (Interop.Word.Selection selection, bool cancel)
   Interop.Word.Selection Selection { get; }
}
```

- The MailMergeAfterMergeEventArgs class exposes the new document created:

```
class MailMergeAfterMergeEventArgs : EventArgs {
  MailMergeAfterMergeEventArgs(Interop.Word.Document newDocument)
  Interop.Word.Document NewDocument { get; }
}
```

- The MailMergeWizardStateChangeEventArgs class exposes the previous, current, and handled states:

```
class MailMergeWizardStateChangeEventArgs : EventArgs {
  MailMergeWizardStateChangeEventArgs (int fromState,
    int toState, bool handled)
  int FromState { get; }
  int ToState { get; }
  bool Handled { get; }
}
```

- The `SaveEventArgs` class allows the handler to instruct the event source whether the Save As dialog should display. This is also a cancelable event:

```
class SaveEventArgs : CancelEventArgs {
  SaveEventArgs (bool showSaveAsUI, bool cancel)
  bool ShowSaveAsDialog { get; set; }
}
```

- The `SelectionEventArgs` class provides the selection that was changed:

```
class SelectionEventArgs : EventArgs {
  SelectionEventArgs (Interop.Word.Selection selection)
  Interop.Word.Selection Selection{ get; }
}
```

- The `WindowEventArgs` class provides the window that was activated, deactivated, or resized:

```
class WindowEventArgs : EventArgs {
 WindowEventArgs(Interop.Word.Window window)
 Interop.Word.Window Window { get; }
}
```

In addition to the new events, the Document object also contains two new collections. First, as discussed earlier in this chapter, the Document object aggregate contains a collection of controls. Second, the Document object now contains a VSTOSmartTags collection (discussed further in Chapter 16, "Working with Smart Tags in VSTO").

C# does not support parameterized properties, but two methods in the `Document` interface use parameterized properties. To make it easier to call these methods from C#, both properties now return instances of helper classes that allow you to use parameterized indexers. They are as follows:

```
_ActiveWritingStyleType ActiveWritingStyle { get; }
_CompatibilityType Compatibility { get; }
```

> The helper classes are scoped to within the customized host item's base class itself, not to the Microsoft.Office.Tools.Word namespace.

The helper classes are as follows:

```
class _ActiveWritingStyleType : System.MarshalByRefObject {
  public string this[object languageID] { get; set; }
}
class _CompatibilityType : System.MarshalByRefObject {
  public string this[Interop.Word.WdCompatibility Type] { get; set; }
}
```

This means that you can access these properties by passing the parameter to the index to fetch or set the property:

```
style = this.ActiveWritingStyle[id];
```

The derived class can be further customized to add new events, methods, and properties. As you edit the document in the Word designer, any bookmarks or other host controls (such as buttons, check boxes, and so on) that you drop onto the design surface will be added as members of the document class. Similarly, any XML mappings added to the document will be added to the document class as either an XMLNode member (if the mapping is to a single node) or an XMLNodes member (if the mapping is to a repeatable node).

The document class has one additional new method, RemoveCustomization, which takes no arguments and has no return value. Calling this method on the aggregated document object removes the customization information from the document, so that after it is saved and reloaded, the customization code will no longer run.

Finally, the document class has a new property, ThisApplication, which refers to the Application object. This property exists to help migrate VSTO 2003 code that referred to a ThisApplication object. The document class also has an `ActionsPane` property, which is covered in detail in Chapter 15, "Working with Actions Pane."

The Word Bookmark Host Control

Bookmark objects in the Word object model do not source any events. The aggregated host control Bookmark in VSTO sources the following new events shown in Table 13-2:

Table 13-2 New Events on VSTO's Aggregated Bookmark Object

Event Name	Delegate
BeforeDoubleClick	ClickEventHandler
BeforeRightClick	ClickEventHandler
Deselected	SelectionEventHandler
Selected	SelectionEventHandler
SelectionChange	SelectionEventHandler

The delegate types and their corresponding argument classes are documented in the document class topic above.

As a convenience for both view programming and data binding, bookmark host controls also aggregate more than 150 methods and properties of the Range object that they represent. For example, these two lines of code are functionally identical:

```
columns = this.bookmark1.range.columns;
columns = this.bookmark1.columns;
```

The methods and properties of the Range object aggregated onto the Bookmark object are for the most part straightforward proxies that just call the method or property accessor on the aggregated range, so almost all of the methods will be functionally identical whether you call them from the Range or the Bookmark.

Three exceptions apply. First, setting the Text property on the Range object directly can sometimes result in the bookmark itself being deleted by Word. If you set the Text property by calling the new property added to the Bookmark aggregate, it ensures that the bookmark is not deleted.

Second and third, the Information and XML properties from the PIA interface are parameterized properties. Because C# does not support calling parameterized properties, the bookmark host control uses helper classes that enable you to use parameterized indexers from C#. The properties are now defined as follows:

```
_InformationType Information { get; }
_XMLType XML { get; }
```

The helper classes are scoped inside the Bookmark class itself:

```
class _InformationType : System.MarshalByRefObject {
  object this[Interop.Word.WdInformation Type] { get; }
}

class _XMLType : System.MarshalByRefObject {
  public string this[bool DataOnly] { get; }
}
```

You can then use the properties like this:

```
info = this.myBookmark.Information[WdInformation.wdCapsLock];
```

The Word XMLNode and XMLNodes Host Control Classes

When you map a schema into a Word document, element declarations that have a maxOccurs attribute in the schema equal to 1 are represented in the host item class as XMLNode objects. All others are represented as XMLNodes objects, because there could be more than one of them.

Table 13-3 shows the new events in VSTO that the XMLNode and XMLNodes objects source.

Table 13-3 New Events on VSTO's Aggregated XMLNode and XMLNodes Objects

Event Name	Delegate
AfterInsert	NodeInsertAndDeleteEventHandler
BeforeDelete	NodeInsertAndDeleteEventHandler
ContextEnter	ContextChangeEventHandler
ContextLeave	ContextChangeEventHandler
Deselect	ContextChangeEventHandler
Select	ContextChangeEventHandler
ValidationError	EventHandler

As you can see, we have two new delegate classes, and therefore two new event argument classes. These events are normally sourced by the application object.

The delegates and event argument classes are all in the Microsoft.Office.Tools.Word namespace. The delegate classes are as follows:

```
delegate void ContextChangeEventHandler(object sender,
    ContextChangeEventArgs e);
delegate void NodeInsertAndDeleteEventHandler(object sender,
    NodeInsertAndDeleteEventArgs e);
```

- When a node is inserted or deleted, it is often interesting to know whether the change is a result of the user inserting or deleting the element directly, or whether this is part of an undo or redo operation. This flag is therefore exposed on the event arguments class:

```
class NodeInsertAndDeleteEventArgs : EventArgs {
    NodeInsertAndDeleteEventArgs (bool inUndoRedo)
    bool InUndoRedo { get; }
}
```

- When a node is selected or deselected, the appropriate event is raised. A "context change" is a special kind of selection change in which the insertion point of the document moves from one XML node to another. Therefore, the event arguments for the ContextEnter and ContextLeave events specify the node that was until recently the home of the insertion point, and the new home.

```
class ContextChangeEventArgs : NodeSelectionEventArgs {
    ContextChangeEventArgs( Interop.Word.XMLNode oldXMLNode,
        Interop.Word.XMLNode newXMLNode, Interop.Word.Selection selection,
        int reason)
    Interop.Word.XMLNode OldXMLNode { get; }
    Interop.Word.XMLNode NewXMLNode { get; }
}
```

The XMLNode interface in the PIA has two parameterized properties, which are not supported in C#. Therefore, these properties have been redefined to return helper classes that implement parameterized indexers instead. The two methods are as follows:

```
_ValidationErrorTextType ValidationErrorText { get; }
_XMLType XML { get; }
```

Their helper classes are scoped to the XMLNode class itself. They are defined as follows:

```
class _ValidationErrorTextType : System.MarshalByRefObject {
    string this[bool Advanced] { get; }
}

class _XMLType : System.MarshalByRefObject {
    string this[bool DataOnly] { get; }
}
```

XMLNode objects also implement several convenient new methods for manipulating the XML bound to the document:

```
void LoadXml(string xml)
void LoadXml(System.Xml.XmlDocument document)
void LoadXml(System.Xml.XmlElement element)
void Load(string filename)
```

All of these take the contents of the XML in the argument and insert it into the given node and its children. However, the onus is on the caller to ensure both that the XML inserted into the node corresponds to the schematized type of the node, and that any child nodes exist and are mapped into the document appropriately. These methods will neither create nor delete child nodes.

As a further convenience for both view and data programming, the XMLNode object also provides a property that aggregates the Text property of the node's range:

```
string NodeText { get; set; }
```

Chapters 15, "Working with ActionsPane," 17, "VSTO Data Programming," and 22, "Working with XML in Word," cover data binding scenarios and actions pane scenarios for XMLNode and XMLNodes objects in detail. That sums up the VSTO extensions to the Word object model. The extensions to the Excel object models are similar but somewhat more extensive because of the larger number of host controls.

The Excel Workbook Host Item Class

The aggregating workbook class raises the same 29 events as the aggregated workbook class, with the same delegate types. Aside from renaming the Activate event to ActivateEvent, so as to avoid a collision with the method of the same name, there are no changes to the events raised by the Workbook object.

The Workbook object does have two new events raised when the customization starts up and shuts down:

```
event System.EventHandler Startup;
event System.EventHandler Shutdown;
```

The aggregated Workbook object also has two new methods, OnStartup and OnShutdown, which cause the workbook to raise the Startup and Shutdown events.

As with the Word document class, the Excel workbook class gains a ThisApplication property, which refers back to the Excel Application object; an ActionsPane property, which Chapter 15 covers; and a VstoSmartTags collection, which Chapter 16 covers. The Workbook object also has one additional new method, RemoveCustomization, which takes no arguments and has no return value. Calling this method on the aggregated Workbook object removes the customization information from the spreadsheet, so that after it is saved and reloaded, the customization code will no longer run.

There is only one other minor change to the view programming model of the workbook class. Because C# cannot use parameterized properties, the Colors property now returns a helper class (scoped to the host item class itself) that allows you to use a parameterized index:

```
_ColorsType Colors { get; }

class _ColorsType : System.MarshalByRefObject {
    object this[object Index] { get; set; }
```

The Excel Worksheet Host Item Class

Much like the workbook, the aggregating worksheet class does not have any major changes to its view programming model. The aggregating worksheet class raises the same eight events as the aggregated worksheet class, with the same delegate types.

Aside from renaming the Activate event to ActivateEvent, so as to avoid a collision with the method of the same name, there are no changes to the events raised by the Worksheet object.

The Worksheet object does have two new events raised when the customization starts up and shuts down:

```
event System.EventHandler Startup;
event System.EventHandler Shutdown;
```

The Worksheet object has two new methods, OnStartup and OnShutdown, which cause the worksheet to raise the Startup and Shutdown events. The worksheet also provides the Controls collection mentioned earlier in this chapter.

Worksheets classes can be customized by subclassing; the derived classes generated by the design have properties representing charts, named ranges, XML-mapped ranges, list objects, and other controls on each sheet.

There is only one other minor change to the view programming model of the worksheet class. Because C# cannot use parameterized properties, the Range property now returns a helper class (scoped to the worksheet class itself) that allows you to use a parameterized index:

```
_RangeType Range { get; }

class _RangeType : System.MarshalByRefObject {
  Interop.Excel.Range this[object Cell1, object Cell2] { get; }
}
```

The Excel Chart Sheet Host Item Class and Chart Host Control

Chart sheet host items and chart host controls are practically identical; the only difference between them as far as VSTO is concerned is that chart sheets are host items classes with their own designer and code-behind file. Charts, by contrast, are treated as controls embedded in a worksheet.

Both rename the Activate and Select events (to ActivateEvent and SelectEvent respectively) to avoid the name conflicts with the methods of the same name. The chart sheet host item class raises Startup and Shutdown events and has OnStartup and OnShutdown methods just as the worksheet class does.

Both the chart and the chart sheet have a parameterized HasAxis property that cannot be called from C#. The property therefore now returns an instance of a helper class that allows you to use a parameterized indexer instead:

```
_HasAxisType HasAxis { get; }

class _HasAxisType : System.MarshalByRefObject {
  object this[object Index1, object Index2] { get; set; }
}
```

The Excel NamedRange, XmlMappedRange, and ListObject Host Controls

All three of these are special kinds of Range objects. They raise the following new events shown in Table 13-4.

Table 13-4 New Events on VSTO's Aggregated NamedRange, XmlMappedRange, and ListObject Objects

Event Name	Delegate
BeforeDoubleClick	DocEvents_BeforeDoubleClickEventHandler
BeforeRightClick	DocEvents_BeforeRightClickEventHandler
Change	DocEvents_ChangeEventHandler
Deselected	DocEvents_SelectionChangeEventHandler
Selected	DocEvents_SelectionChangeEventHandler
SelectionChange	DocEvents_SelectionChangeEventHandler

All the event delegates are from the Microsoft.Office.Tools.Interop.Excel namespace in the Excel PIA.

The list object raises several more events in addition to those above, but because they all are primarily used to implement data binding functionality, Chapter 17 covers them.

There are many parameterized properties in both the NamedRange and XmlMappedRange interfaces that are not supported by C#. To make this functionality usable more easily from C#, these properties now return helper functions (scoped to the NamedRange or XmlMappedRange classes themselves) that expose parameterized indexers.

The NamedRange object only has one redefined property:

```
_EndType End { get; }
```

The _EndType helper class is defined as follows:

```
class _EndType : System.MarshalByRefObject {
  Interop.Excel.Range this[Interop.Excel XlDirection Direction] { get; }
}
```

The NamedRange aggregate also implements a parameterized indexer:

```
object this[object RowIndex, object ColumnIndex]
  { get; set; }
```

The following properties are redefined on both NamedRange and XmlMapped-Range aggregates:

```
_AddressLocalType AddressLocal { get; }
_AddressType Address { get; }
_CharactersType Characters { get; }
_ItemType Item { get; }
_OffsetType Offset { get; }
_ResizeType Resize { get; }
```

The corresponding helper classes are defined as follows:

```
class _AddressLocalType : System.MarshalByRefObject {
  string this[bool RowAbsolute, bool ColumnAbsolute,
    Interop.Excel.XlReferenceStyle ReferenceStyle, bool External,
    object RelativeTo] { get; }
}
class _AddressType : System.MarshalByRefObject {
  string this[bool RowAbsolute, bool ColumnAbsolute,
    Interop.Excel.XlReferenceStyle ReferenceStyle, bool External,
    object RelativeTo] { get; }
}
class _CharactersType : System.MarshalByRefObject {
  Interop.Excel.Characters this[int Start, int Length] { get; }
}
class _ItemType : System.MarshalByRefObject {
  object this[int RowIndex] { get; set; }
  object this[int RowIndex, int ColumnIndex] { get; set; }
}
```

```
class _OffsetType : System.MarshalByRefObject {
  Interop.Excel.Range this[int RowOffset, int ColumnOffset] { get; }
}
class _ResizeType : System.MarshalByRefObject {
  Interop.Excel.Range this[int RowSize, int ColumnSize] { get; }
}
```

As a convenience for both view and data programming, NamedRange host controls also expose directly all the methods of the associated Name object:

- string RefersTo { get; set; }
- string RefersToLocal { get; set; }
- string RefersToR1C1 { get; set; }
- string RefersToR1C1Local { get; set; }
- Interop.Excel.Range RefersToRange { get; }

If somehow the NamedRange object has been bound to a non-named range, these will throw NotSupportedException.

The NamedRange object also has a Name property that is somewhat confusing. The property getter returns the Name object associated with this named range. If you pass a Name object to the setter, it will set the Name property, just as you would expect. If you pass a string, however, it will attempt to set the Name property of the underlying Name object.

The NamedRange host control also slightly changes the exception semantics of the Name property in two ways. First, in the standard Excel object model, setting the Name property of the name object of a named range to the name of another named range deletes the range, oddly enough; doing the same to a VSTO NamedRange host control raises an ArgumentException and does not delete the offending range.

Second, in the standard Excel object model, setting the Name property to an invalid string fails silently. The VSTO NamedRange object throws an Argument-Exception if the supplied name is invalid.

> The XMLMappedRange and ListObject host controls do not aggregate the methods of the Name object or change the error handling semantics of the name setter. The changes to the Name property semantics only apply to the NamedRange object.

XML mapped ranges and list objects are the Excel equivalent of the XMLNode and XMLNodes controls in Word. The XML mapped range represents a mapped singleton element, and the list object represents a set of rows. We cover data binding scenarios in Chapter 17, "VSTO Data Programming," and other XML scenarios in Excel in Chapter 21, "Working with XML in Excel." In this chapter, we just discuss their use as host controls.

The list object host control has one new property:

```
bool IsSelected { get; }
```

This property is most useful for determining whether there is an "insert row." Excel does not display an insert row if the list object's range is not selected.

The list object host control also slightly changes the error handling semantics of these properties:

```
Interop.Excel.Range DataBodyRange { get; }
Interop.Excel.Range HeaderRowRange { get; }
Interop.Excel.Range InsertRowRange { get; }
Interop.Excel.Range TotalsRowRange { get; }
```

The only difference is that these properties now all return null rather than throwing an exception if you attempt to access the property on a list object that lacks a body, header, insert row, or totals row, respectively.

Chapter 17 discusses other new properties and methods added to the list object used for data binding.

Conclusion

VSTO brings the Word and Excel object models into the managed code world by aggregating key unmanaged objects onto managed base classes. Developers can then extend these base classes by using Word and Excel as designers in Visual Studio.

The next chapter takes a more detailed look at how to use Windows Forms controls in VSTO.

14

Using Windows Forms in VSTO

Introduction

O FFICE HAS A USER INTERFACE THAT has been designed to make it as easy as possible for an end user to access the functionality provided by each Office application. But the application that you are writing that is integrated with Office will have its own very specific user-interface requirements. The application you write will have user-interface needs that are not met by the default Office user interface.

In previous versions of Office, Visual Basic for Applications (VBA) provided the ability to show User Forms to meet your application user-interface requirements. You could also use custom ActiveX controls on the document surface. Visual Studio Tools for Office (VSTO) adds Windows Forms control support to Office to meet your user-interface needs.

Moving from ActiveX to Windows Forms

When we started designing VSTO, being able to build applications that extended the default Office user interface was one of our primary goals. We also wanted to ensure that developers writing managed code would not have to rely on ActiveX controls to do so—.NET developers want to use Windows Forms controls. To address these requirements, the team came up with a design to integrate Windows Forms deeply into Office. The vision was to allow you to use Windows Forms controls and forms in all the places you could use ActiveX controls and User Forms in previous versions of Office. We also wanted to make the design and coding experience similar to that of a traditional Windows Forms application.

This chapter covers how to use Windows Forms controls in your VSTO applications. You can use Windows Forms in VSTO in three basic ways:

1. You can put a Windows Forms control on the document or spreadsheet surface.

2. You can display a custom Windows Forms form as a modal or modeless dialog.

3. You can put Windows Forms controls in the Document Actions task pane using the ActionsPane feature of VSTO.

We cover the first two ways in this chapter. This chapter also covers how to create custom user controls that can be used to provide solutions to some of the shortcomings of the Windows Forms support in VSTO. The third way to use Windows Forms in VSTO—using controls in the Document Actions task pane—is covered in Chapter 15, "Working with Actions Pane."

When to Use Windows Forms Controls on the Document Surface

VSTO enables developers to put Windows Forms controls on the document surface. Just because you can put a control onto the document surface does not necessarily mean it is a good idea for your particular application. When should you use a control on a document as opposed to using a form, an intrinsic Office user-interface element such as a cell or a hyperlink, a custom menu command or toolbar button, a Smart Tag, or the actions pane?

Think about how you expect the document or spreadsheet to be used and how you want to extend the interface. Maybe you are going to use an Excel spreadsheet as a front end to corporate data. For example, many stockbrokers use Excel as their primary input and display mechanism when trading. In this scenario, the spreadsheet is very rarely e-mailed or printed, so changing the spreadsheet interface to meet the application requirements makes a lot of sense. Putting a Windows Forms button control on the surface of the document meets the requirement of making the spreadsheet more interactive and provides obvious actions that are available to the user of the spreadsheet. Figure 14-1 shows two Windows Forms buttons that have been placed on a spreadsheet—one that refreshes the stock quotes and the other that trades a particular stock.

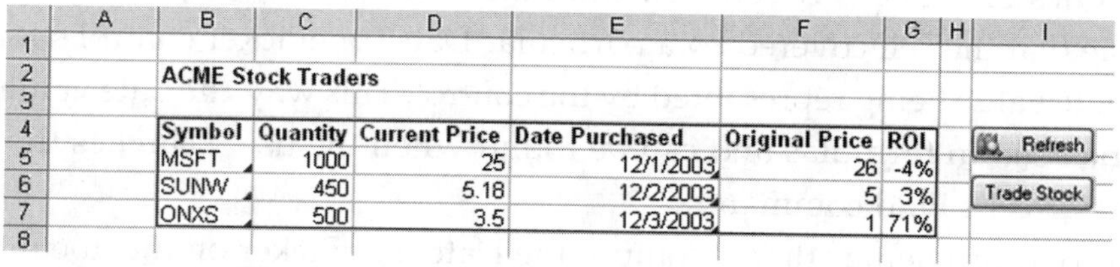

Figure 14-1 Two Windows Forms controls on a spreadsheet.

Sometimes you will have data that needs to be edited with a more effective user interface than Office provides. A good example of this is date input. Excel and Word provide a rich mechanism to display dates but do not provide an easy to use mechanism for entering dates other than basic text input. Windows Forms provides a DateTimePicker control that makes it easy for a user to enter a date. Combining the date entry interface provided by the DateTimePicker and the display capabilities of Excel or Word results in a more effective user interface.

You could integrate the DateTimePicker into your workbook, as shown in Figure 14-2. Here we have added a DateTimePicker control for each cell containing a date. The DateTimePicker provides a combo box drop-down that shows a calendar that the user can use to pick a different date.

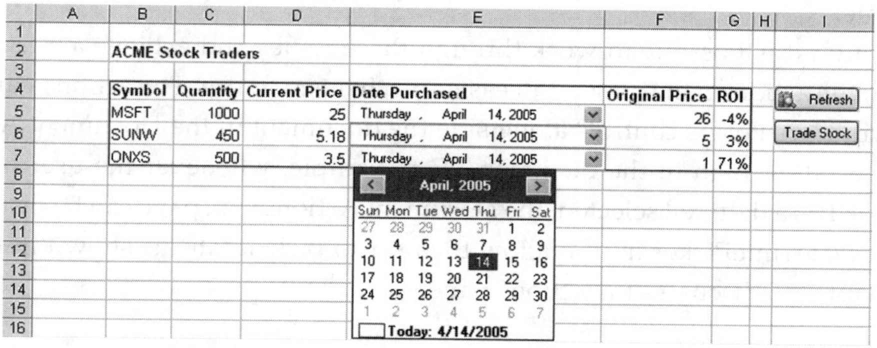

Figure 14-2 DateTimePicker controls on a spreadsheet.

However, the DateTimePicker may be better used in the Document Actions task pane than on the document surface. The first problem you will encounter with a solution such as the one shown in Figure 14-2 is what will you put in the spreadsheet for the values of the cells covered by the DateTimePicker controls? It would seem reasonable that the cell covered by a particular DateTimePicker control should contain the date value being represented by the control. This way, the date value for that cell can be used in formulas and can be found when the user searches the spreadsheet with Excel's Find command.

The second problem is that if you put the DateTimePicker on the document surface, the control does not automatically save its state into the Excel workbook when the document is saved. So if in a particular session the user selects several dates and then saves the document, the next time the user opens the workbook all the DateTimePickers will reset to today's date. You will lose the date the user picked in the last session unless you write code to synchronize the DateTimePicker with the cell value covered by it on startup of the Excel workbook and whenever the DateTimePicker or underlying cell value change.

A third problem is keeping the DateTimePicker controls looking like the rest of the workbook formatting. If the user changes the font of the workbook, the controls embedded in the document will not change their font. Printing is also an issue because the control replete with its drop-down combo widget will be printed. In addition, the user will likely want to add and remove rows to the list of stocks, which means that you will have to dynamically add and remove DateTimePicker controls at runtime.

Although it is possible to work through these issues and achieve a reasonable solution, the actions pane may be an easier mechanism to use. The actions pane can show Windows Forms controls along side the document in the Document Actions task pane rather than in the document. For example, whenever the user of your workbook has a date cell selected, the Document Actions task pane can be displayed with the DateTimePicker in it to allow the user to pick a date, as shown in Figure 14-3. Chapter 15 discusses the actions pane.

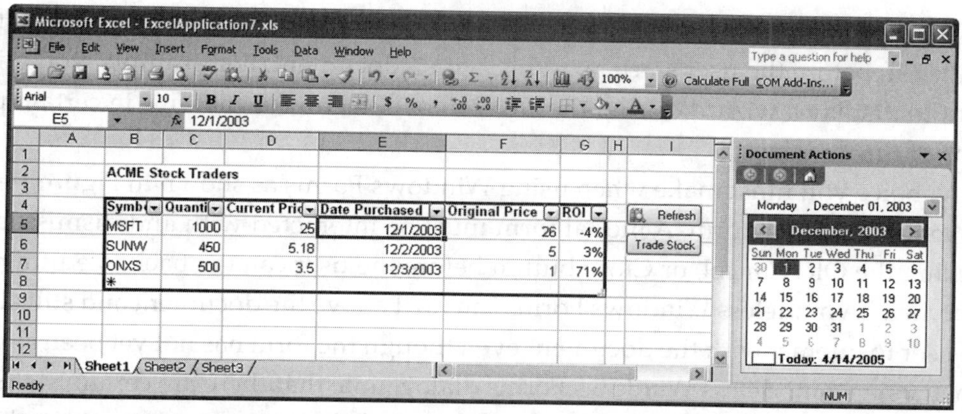

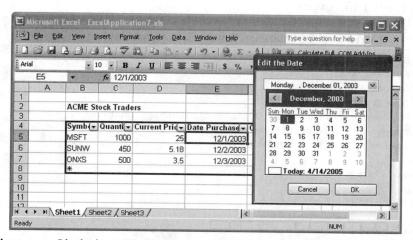

Figure 14-3 Using the DateTimePicker control in the Document Actions task pane.

When to Use a Modal or Modeless Windows Forms Form

Another way to use Windows Forms in an Office application is to use a standard Windows Forms form shown as a dialog. For example, you could handle the Before-DoubleClick event for the worksheet and if a cell containing a date is double-clicked, you could display a custom Windows Forms form, as shown in Figure 14-4.

Figure 14-4 Displaying a Windows Forms dialog when the user double-clicks a cell.

This approach is also quite useful if you want to ensure that certain information is filled in before the user starts working with a document. For example, you might want to display a wizard during the creation of a document that fills in certain portions of the document.

A choice you must make when using Windows Forms as shown in Figure 14-4 is the modality of the form. A modal form must be interacted with and dismissed by clicking the OK, Cancel, or Close button before the user can get back to editing the document. A modeless Windows Forms can float above the document and still allow the user to interact with the document even though the form has not yet been closed. When using a modeless Windows Forms dialog, note that there are certain states an Office application can enter where your modeless dialog cannot be activated. For example, if another modal dialog is displayed, users must dismiss the modal dialog before they can interact with the modeless dialog again. Cell editing mode in Excel also affects modeless dialogs. If the user is editing a cell value in Excel, the user cannot activate the modeless form until the user leaves cell editing mode.

Listing 14-1 shows a VSTO Excel customization that displays a simple modeless form. The modeless form has a button that when clicked shows the ID of the thread that the button handler is invoked on. The ID of the main Office UI thread is also shown in the Startup event.

Listing 14-1 A VSTO Excel Customization That Displays a Modeless Form

```
using System;
using System.Data;
using System.Drawing;
using System.Windows.Forms;
using Microsoft.VisualStudio.OfficeTools.Interop.Runtime;
using Excel = Microsoft.Office.Interop.Excel;
using Office = Microsoft.Office.Core;

namespace ExcelWorkbook1
{
  public partial class Sheet1
  {
    public Button btn1;
    public Form form1;

    private void Sheet1_Startup(object sender, EventArgs e)
    {
      MessageBox.Show(System.Threading.Thread.ManagedThreadID);
```

```
    btn1 = new Button();
    btn1.Click += new EventHandler(btn1_Click);

    form1 = new Form();
    form1.Controls.Add(btn1);
    form1.Show();

    Globals.ThisWorkbook.BeforeClose +=
      new Excel.WorkbookEvents_BeforeCloseEventHandler(
      ThisWorkbook_BeforeClose);
  }

void btn1_Click(object sender, EventArgs e)
{
  MessageBox.Show(System.Threading.Thread.ManagedThreadID);
}

void ThisWorkbook_BeforeClose(ref bool Cancel)
{
  form1.Close();
}

#region VSTO Designer generated code
private void InternalStartup()
{
  this.Startup += new System.EventHandler(this.Sheet1_Startup);
}
#endregion
  }
}
```

Note that using the ActionsPane feature of VSTO is often an easier way to achieve a modeless result because it provides all the benefits of a modeless form with the addition of the ability to dock within the Office window space.

Adding Windows Forms Controls to Your Document

One of the key design goals for VSTO was to keep the design experience as close to existing Windows Forms development as possible, and adding Windows Forms controls to the document is a key tenet of this goal. The great thing about adding controls to the document or spreadsheet is that you really do not have to think about it because most of the design experience is almost identical to that of creating a

Windows Forms form. However, there are some differences in the experience that we examine in this section.

When you create a new project based on an Excel workbook or Word document, VSTO creates a project and automatically loads the Excel or Word document surface into Visual Studio to provide a design surface for you to drag and drop controls onto. In the C# profile, the toolbox is set to auto hide by default. It is easier to pin the toolbox to make it dock to the side of Visual Studio window because it is difficult to drag and drop from the toolbox onto Word or Excel when it is in its default auto hide mode. Why? When the toolbox shows itself, it obscures quite a bit of the left side of the document or spreadsheet. When you drag and drop a control onto the document surface, the toolbox does not auto hide and get out of the way until the drag and drop is over.

Modes for Adding Controls

VSTO provides three modes for adding controls to the document surface:

- **Drag and drop**—This involves selecting the control from the toolbox and dragging it onto the document or worksheet. This method creates a default-sized control on the document and proves particularly useful for adding controls such as a button that tend to be a set size. Figure 14-5 shows this mode.

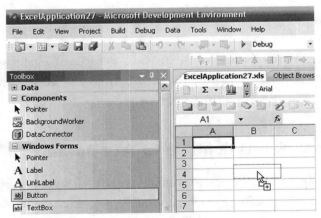

Figure 14-5 Drag and drop of a Button control from the toolbox to an Excel worksheet.

- **Drawing**—Clicking a control in the toolbox to select it and then moving your mouse pointer over the document or spreadsheet changes the cursor to the standard draw cursor. In this mode, you can click and drag a rectangle, thereby drawing the control onto the document or spreadsheet. Figure 14-6 shows this mode.

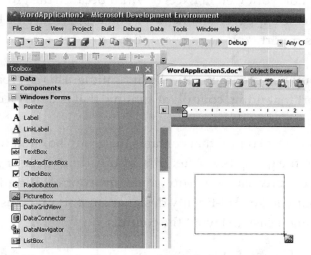

Figure 14-6   Drawing a PictureBox control on a Word document.

- **Double-click**—Double-clicking a control in the toolbox causes a control to be added at the current insertion point in the document or spreadsheet. The insertion point in Word behaves quite differently from Excel, not surprising given the flow-based nature of a document compared to the grid of a spreadsheet. Double-clicking a control in the toolbox in a Word VSTO project inserts the control at the cursor in the document. Double-clicking a control in the toolbox in an Excel VSTO project inserts the control at the center of the spreadsheet.

Controls That Are Not in the Control Toolbox

A number of Windows Forms controls do not show up in the controls toolbox for Excel and Word projects. These controls were purposely excluded because of known issues in using them on the document surface. Some of these issues are purely design-time related in that the design-time representation of the control does not work well. This does not mean that the control cannot be used, but it might mean that the only way that you can use it on a document is by adding it programmatically at runtime or by using the control in a user control that you then add to the document.

A good example of such a control is the group box. The design-time experience of the group box does not work well in Excel or Word because the group box designer requires the container to support container drag and drop, which the Excel and Word designer does not support. You have two options to work around this limitation:

- Create the group box programmatically at runtime. This approach uses VSTO's support for adding controls at runtime that is described later in this chapter.

- Create a custom user control that contains the group box and the contained controls within the group box. After this is built, drag the user control onto the document or spreadsheet as you would any control. The advantage to this approach is that you get full-fidelity designer support in the user control designer, making it easy to layout the controls.

Some other controls are excluded from the toolbox because of the following reasons.

- The control does not work with the VSTO control hosting architecture. For example, the DataNavigator control relies on a container model that is not supported in the VSTO control hosting architecture in order to communicate with other data components.

- The control relies heavily on being hosted in a Windows Forms form. For example, the MenuStrip control cannot be added to a document or spreadsheet, only to a form.

- The control has problems at design time. Because many controls were designed prior to the release of VSTO, some have bugs when hosted on a document or spreadsheet surface in the designer. For example, the Rich Edit control has considerable issues when running inside of Excel and Word at design time. In the interest of stability, it was removed from the controls toolbox, but you can add it to a document or spreadsheet programmatically at runtime.

Control Insertion Behavior in Word

A control added to Word is affected by the insertion settings set in Word's Options dialog. A control can be inserted "in line with text," which means the control is inserted into the text flow of the document and moves as the text flow changes. It can also be inserted "in front of text," which means that the control is positioned at an absolute position in the document that does not change when the text flow changes.

The default insertion behavior in Word can be changed to be exact-position based rather than flow based by changing the insert/paste pictures setting in Word's Option dialog from the default In line with text to In front of text. After you change this setting, all controls will be positioned where you want them instead of having to be in line with the text. To change this setting, choose Options from the Tools menu and click the Edit tab of the Options dialog. Figure 14-7 shows the Insert/paste pictures setting.

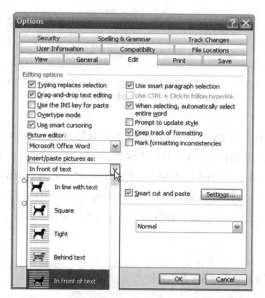

Figure 14-7 Changing the default insertion behavior
in Word's Options dialog.

You can also change the way a control in Word is wrapped with the text by right-clicking the control in the designer and selecting the Format Control menu option. Doing so brings up Word's Format Object dialog shown in Figure 14-8. Changing the wrapping style from in line with text to in front of text provides exact positioning.

Figure 14-8 Changing the wrapping style for a control with Word's Format Object dialog.

From the standpoint of the Word object model, a control whose wrapping style is set to In line with text, Square, or Tight is represented by the InlineShape object in Word's object model and found in the Document object's InlineShapes collection. A control whose wrapping style is set to Behind text or In front of text is represented by the Shape object in Word's object model and found in the Document object's Shapes collection.

Control Insertion Behavior in Excel

Excel also provides options for positioning a control on the worksheet surface, with the default being to move the control relative to the cell but not to size with the cell. This setting means that when you put a control onto the worksheet surface, it is linked to the cell that you dropped it on; so if you insert or delete cells around that cell, the control will stay positioned relative to the cell it was dropped on. However, if you resize the cell you dropped, the size of the control stays the same. This is usually the behavior that you would expect when adding a control. If you want your control to resize with the cell, you can either draw the control over the cell so that it exactly matches the size of the cell (not for the faint of heart) or right-click the control inside of Visual Studio and select Format Control, which brings up the Format Control dialog shown in Figure 14-9. Click the Properties tab and select one of three options:

- **Move and size with cells**—This option ensures that the control resizes and repositions relative to the cell resize. For example, if your control takes up half of the cell, it will continue to take up half of the cell when the cell is resized

- **Move but do not size with cells**—This is the default setting, which ensures that the control remains with the cell it was dropped on but does not resize.

- **Do not move or size with cells**—This setting provides you with exact positioning that does not change when the cell the control that was dropped on is moved or resized.

Figure 14-9 Setting object positioning options for a control in Excel.

Layout of Controls on the Document or Worksheet Surface

The Windows Forms editor in Visual Studio has some great alignment tools that make it much simpler to design professional-looking forms without having to resort to per-pixel tweaks on each control. Unfortunately, the alignment tools do not work on documents because the display surface is very different from a form. In the place of these tools, a new toolbar provides easy access to the alignment functionality in Word and Excel. Figure 14-10 shows the toolbar. To align controls, just select the controls you want to align, and then click the button that represents the alignment option you want.

Figure 14-10 The control positioning toolbar in VSTO.

Writing Code Behind a Control

Writing code behind a control on a document or spreadsheet is not much different from writing code behind a normal Windows Forms control. You can double-click a control and the designer will add a new event handler for the default event on the control in the partial class for the sheet or document you are working on. The only difference is where the event handler is hooked up in the code generated by the designer. In a standard Windows Forms form, the event handler is hooked up in the hidden generated code (form1.designer.cs). In a VSTO code item, the event hook up is generated into the visible user partial class (sheet1.cs rather than sheet1.designer.cs) in the InternalStartup method.

Event handlers can also be generated by using the Events view in the Properties window. In this view, you can double-click an event handler cell to add a default named event handler for an event. Alternatively, you can enter the name of the event handler function you want to use. The event handler hookup code is generated in the same place (InternalStartup) as if you double-clicked on the control. Listing 14-2 shows the code generated when you drop a button on a spreadsheet and then double-click the event handler cell for Click and SystemColorsChanged to generate default event handlers for these events.

Listing 14-2 Default Event Hookup and Handlers Generated by VSTO for a Button's Click and SystemColorsChanged Events

```
using System;
using System.Data;
using System.Drawing;
using System.Windows.Forms;
using Microsoft.VisualStudio.OfficeTools.Interop.Runtime;
using Excel = Microsoft.Office.Interop.Excel;
using Office = Microsoft.Office.Core;

namespace ExcelWorkbook1
{
  public partial class Sheet1
  {
    private void Sheet1_Startup(object sender, EventArgs e)
    {

    }

    private void Sheet1_Shutdown(object sender, EventArgs e)
    {
    }

    #region VSTO Designer generated code
    private void InternalStartup()
    {
      this.button1.Click +=
        new System.EventHandler(this.button1_Click);
      this.button1.SystemColorsChanged +=
        new System.EventHandler(this.button1_SystemColorsChanged);
      this.Shutdown += new System.EventHandler(this.Sheet1_Shutdown);
      this.Startup += new System.EventHandler(this.Sheet1_Startup);
    }
    #endregion

    private void button1_Click(object sender, EventArgs e)
    {

    }

    private void button1_SystemColorsChanged(object sender, EventArgs e)
    {

    }
  }
}
```

Events That Are Never Raised for a Control in an Office Document

Not all the events on a Windows Forms control are raised in an Office document. For example, the ResizeBegin and ResizeEnd events are common across all Windows Forms controls (these events are defined on the Control base class) but are never raised on controls on a document or worksheet because of the way the Windows Forms support in VSTO was designed.

The Windows Forms Control Hosting Architecture

Typically, the implementation details of a particular technology are interesting to know but not a prerequisite for using a feature. In the case of Windows Forms control hosting on an Office document, it is important to understand how the feature is implemented because you will be exposed to some implementation details as you create solutions using controls.

The Windows Forms Control Host ActiveX Control

Windows Forms control support in Office 2003 and VSTO is based on the capability of Word and Excel to host ActiveX controls on the document surface. When you add a Windows Forms control to a document, what actually is added is an ActiveX control called the Windows Forms control host. The Windows Forms control host acts as a host for each Windows Forms control added to the document. The Office application thinks that it is just hosting a basic ActiveX control because the Windows Forms control host implements all of the necessary ActiveX control interfaces.

When the customization assembly is loaded for the document or spreadsheet, the actual Windows Forms control instance is created in the same application domain and security context as the rest of the customization code. These Windows Forms control instances are then parented by a special parent Windows Forms control called the VSTOContainerControl that derives from UserControl. The VSTOContainerControl is then sited to the Windows Forms control host ActiveX control. Your control—for example, a Trade Stock button in a spreadsheet—is added as a child of the VSTOContainerControl. Figure 14-11 shows this "sandwich" architecture.

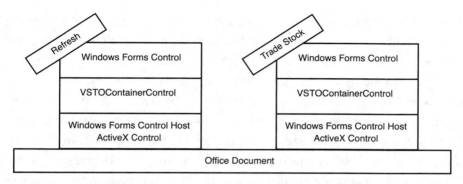

Figure 14-11 The basic hosting architecture for Windows Forms controls
on the document.

The fact that an ActiveX control is hosting the Windows Forms control on the document surface does peek through at times. One example is in the Excel design view. When you click a managed control that you have added to the Excel workbook surface, the formula bar shows that it is hosted by an embedded ActiveX control with ProgID "WinForms.Control.Host", as shown in Figure 14-12.

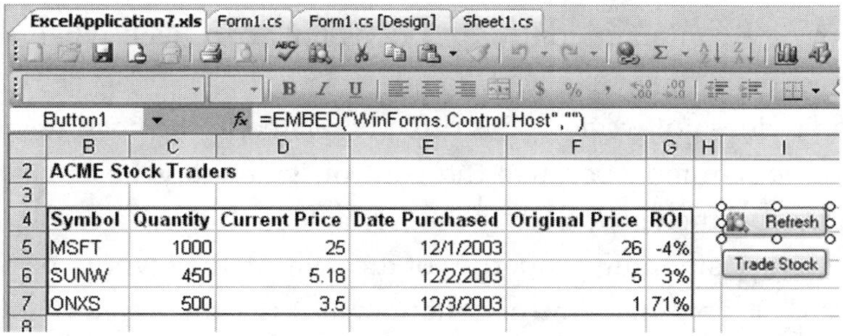

Figure 14-12 Excel shows the ProgID of the underlying ActiveX hosting
control.

Why Are VSTO Controls Derived from Windows Forms Controls?

The fact that an ActiveX control is hosting the Windows Forms control dragged onto the document surface does not show up immediately in your code. VSTO adds a member variable to the ThisDocument or Sheet1 class named something like Button1 that you can code against just as you would if you were working with a traditional Windows Forms form. At first glance, the experience appears to be identical to working with a Windows Forms form, but the type of the control that you added to the document is not quite what you would expect. If you drag a button from the Windows Forms toolbox, it would be natural to expect the type of the button created on the document to be System.Windows.Forms.Button. However, when you add a button to a spreadsheet, VSTO creates a button with type Microsoft.Office.Tools.Excel.Controls.Button that derives from System.Windows.Forms.Button. When you add a button to a Word document, VSTO creates a button with type Microsoft.Office.Tools.Word.Controls.Button that derives from System.Windows.Forms.Button. Understanding why a button in VSTO derives from the standard Windows Forms button requires some further digging into the details of how Windows Forms controls are hosted in a Word or Excel document.

Windows Forms controls, be it a control in the System.Windows.Forms namespace or a custom control written by a third party or you, were originally designed to be added to a Windows Forms form and not an Office document. Luckily, much of the Windows Forms control works just fine when used in an Office document. The main special case is around the positioning of the control. If you set the Left property of a Windows Forms control hosted in a form, it sets the distance in pixels between the left edge of the control and the left edge of its container's client area. This works fine in a form or a container control but does not work well when the control is placed in a document or spreadsheet.

The reason it does not work well is directly related to the hosting architecture of controls in the document, because the control is actually hosted by the VSTO-ContainerControl, which is hosted by the ActiveX control. As a result, if VSTO was to expose the raw positioning properties of the control, they would be relative to the area of the VSTOContainerControl container not the document. Setting the Left property of a control should actually move the ActiveX control within the document rather than the hosted Windows Forms control within the VSTOContainerControl.

Listing 14-3 illustrates this point. In Listing 14-3, we have a spreadsheet that we have added some Windows Forms buttons to, as shown in Figure 14-1. The Refresh button shown in Figure 14-1 is added to Sheet1 as a member variable called `refreshButton` of type Microsoft.Office.Tools.Excel.Controls.Button. We display that type in the Startup event. As mentioned earlier, Microsoft.Office.Tools.Excel.Controls.Button derives from System.Windows.Forms.Button. TheMicrosoft.Office.Tools.Excel.Controls.Button's override of Left sets the position of the ActiveX control hosting the Windows Forms control. The code in Listing 14-3 sets this Left to 0, which causes the control to move to the left edge of the worksheet. Casting refreshButton to a System.Windows.Forms.Button strips the override that VSTO adds for the Left property. Setting the Left property on refreshButton when cast to a System.Windows.Forms.Button sets the Left property of the control relative to the parent VSTOContainerControl. This listing when run gives the strange result in Figure 14-13, where the first call to Left moved the ActiveX control to the far-left edge of the worksheet but the subsequent calls to Left and Top on the base class System.Windows.Forms.Button moved the managed control relative to the VSTOContainerControl.

Listing 14-3 A VSTO Excel Customization That Exposes the Windows Forms Control Hosting Architecture

```
using System;
using System.Data;
using System.Drawing;
using System.Windows.Forms;
using Microsoft.VisualStudio.OfficeTools.Interop.Runtime;
using Excel = Microsoft.Office.Interop.Excel;
using Office = Microsoft.Office.Core;

namespace ExcelApplication7
{
  public partial class Sheet1
  {
    private void Sheet1_Startup(object sender, EventArgs e)
    {
      MessageBox.Show(refreshButton.GetType().ToString());

      // Cast to a System.Windows.Forms.Button
      // to set position on underived control
      System.Windows.Forms.Button refreshButtonBase =
        refreshButton as System.Windows.Forms.Button;

      MessageBox.Show(refreshButtonBase.Parent.GetType().ToString());
      MessageBox.Show(refreshButtonBase.Parent.GetType().
        BaseType.ToString());

      // Moving the control on Microsoft.Office.Tools.Button
      refreshButton.Left = 0;

      // Moving the control again on the base
      // System.Windows.Forms.Button
      refreshButtonBase.Left = 10;
```

```
        refreshButtonBase.Top = 10;
    }

    #region VSTO Designer generated code
    private void InternalStartup()
    {
        this.Startup += new System.EventHandler(this.Sheet1_Startup);
    }
    #endregion
}
}
```

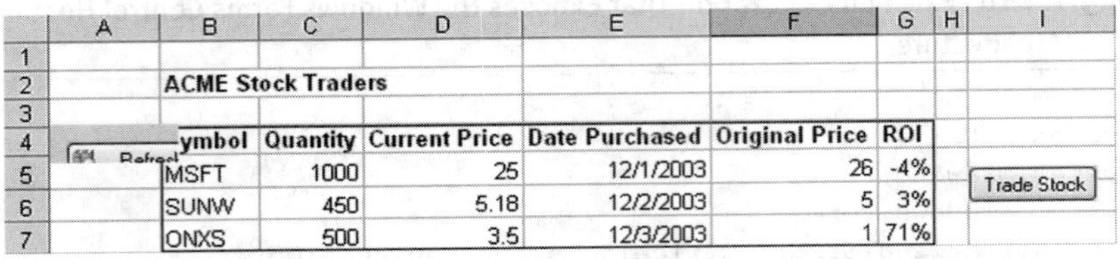

	A	B	C	D	E	F	G	H	I
1									
2		ACME Stock Traders							
3									
4		ymbol	Quantity	Current Price	Date Purchased	Original Price	ROI		
5		MSFT	1000	25	12/1/2003	26	-4%		Trade Stock
6		SUNW	450	5.18	12/2/2003	5	3%		
7		ONXS	500	3.5	12/3/2003	1	71%		

Figure 14-13 The result of running Listing 14-3—the Refresh button has been offset relative to the VSTOContainerControl in the VSTO hosting architecture.

To enable your code to set the position of the control relative to the document, VSTO creates a derived class for each control that extends the class of the original Windows Forms control and overrides the positional information with the positional information from the ActiveX control in the Office document. The object model object for Excel that provides the properties and methods to position the ActiveX control is called OLEObject, and for Word it is called OLEControl. The derived classes created for each VSTO Windows Forms control effectively merges together the original Windows Forms control class and the OLEObject object for Excel or the OLEControl object for Word.

If you create a Windows Forms control of your own or use a third-party control, when you drag and drop the control to a document or spreadsheet, VSTO automatically generates an extended class for you that merges your control with OLEObject or OLEControl. Because the ability to add custom Windows Forms controls onto a document requires the control to be extended, you can only use controls that are not sealed. The good news is that the vast majority of third-party controls are unsealed.

Security Implications of the VSTO Control Hosting Model

The security minded might be wondering about the implications of having to use an ActiveX control to host managed controls added to a document. This is something that we spent considerable time on to ensure that the ActiveX control did not provide a vulnerability to Office. The Windows Forms control host ActiveX control when initialized does not actually do anything and will not run any code until it is accessed by the customization assembly. This means that the control is safe for initialization, and the only way for it to do anything is for code with full trust (the customization) to call it. The control is marked safe for initialization to ensure that it will load in Office with the default security settings.

One strange side effect of our control hosting architecture is that Office requires Visual Basic for Applications (VBA) to be installed in order to add ActiveX controls to a document. Adding ActiveX controls to a document does not add VBA code to that document, but it does require the use of parts of the VBA engine. You therefore need to ensure that your Office installation has VBA installed to use managed controls in the document. VBA is installed by default in all versions of Office, so it is unusual for it not to be installed. VSTO also requires that the Trust access to Visual Basic Project check box be checked in the Macro security dialog box of Office on a development machine. This check box does not have to be checked on end-user machines unless you are adding dynamic worksheets at runtime as described in Chapter 13.

The macro security level in VBA can affect the loading of ActiveX controls and hence managed controls. If your user sets the VBA macro security settings to Very High (it is set to High by default), any ActiveX controls in the document will only be allowed to load in their inactive design mode state. In this state, Windows Forms controls in the document will not function properly. Luckily, the default macro security setting of High allows controls to be loaded assuming they are safe for initialization. Because all Windows Forms controls in the document are loaded by the Windows Forms control host ActiveX control, which is marked as safe for initialization, all managed controls can load in the High setting.

Limitations of the Control Hosting Model

Each Windows Forms control on the document is contained by an instance of the Windows Forms control host ActiveX control, which leads to some limitations. The most noticeable limitation that affects all controls is the lack of support for a control's TabIndex property. Tab order in a Windows Forms is determined by the containing form or control. This is not a problem with a traditional Windows Forms form because all controls on the form are contained by one container. In VSTO, each control placed onto a document or spreadsheet is contained by it is own container—by it is own unique instance of the Windows Forms control host. The net result of this is that the tab index of the control is scoped to its container and because there is a one-to-one relationship between control and container, the TabIndex property is of little use. This can have impact on the accessibility of your application because users would expect to be able to tab between fields, but nothing happens when they press the Tab key.

Another limitation is that controls such as radio buttons really require the control be contained within a container to make the controls mutually exclusive so that only one radio button within the container can be selected at a time. Without a common container, the radio button is not particularly useful. Adding each radio button directly onto a document or spreadsheet causes each radio button to be hosted in its own container. There is a simple way to work around this problem, however; you just create a user control that has a container (a group box, for example), and then add the radio buttons to the group box within the user control. The user control can then be added as a single control to the document.

Control State Is Not Saved in the Document

We already considered this limitation briefly in the introduction of this chapter—the limitation that the state of a Windows Forms control is not saved in the document. To illustrate, imagine a solution that generates customer service letters in Word. One of the key pieces of information in the document is the date the customer first called customer service. To aid with entering this date, the Word document contains a Date-TimePicker, as shown in Figure 14-14.

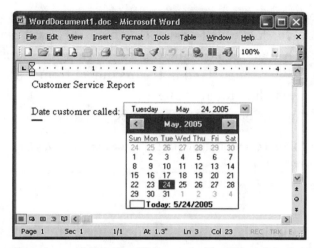

Figure 14-14 A DateTimePicker control in a Word document.

This is great functionality for your users, but where will the date that the user picks with the DateTimePicker be stored in the document? For example, consider the scenario where the user opens the document for the first time. The DateTimePicker defaults to show today's date. The user then picks a different date using the Date-TimePicker and saves the document. Now we have a problem: Windows Forms controls placed in a document do not save their state into the document when the document is saved. The next time the document is opened, the DateTimePicker will just show today's date again rather than the date picked by the user the last time the document was saved.

To get the DateTimePicker to remember the date picked by the user the last time the document was saved, you have to write code to detect when the user picks a new date by handling the DateTimePicker control's ValueChanged event. You need to store the date in the document somehow so that it will be saved when the document is saved. Some options you have for storing the date that was picked include inserting some hidden text in the document, adding a custom property to the document, or using the cached data feature of VSTO to cache the date in the data island of the document. Then you have to write some code in the Startup event handler to set DateTimePicker.Value to the saved date.

Listing 14-4 shows some VSTO code associated with the Word document shown in Figure 14-14. The code uses the cached data feature of VSTO described in

Chapter 18, "Server Data Scenarios," to save the date that was picked in the Date-TimePicker in a public field called `lastPickedDate` that has been marked with the `Cached` attribute. The `Cached` attribute causes the value of `lastPickedDate` to be automatically saved in a data island in the document from session to session. The Startup handler puts the stored value of `lastPickedDate` back in the DateTimePicker each time the document is reopened.

Listing 14-4 A VSTO Word Customization That Saves the Date That Was Picked Using the Cached Data Feature of VSTO

```
public partial class ThisDocument
{
  [Cached()]
  public DateTime lastPickedDate = DateTime.MinValue;

  private void ThisDocument_Startup(object sender, System.EventArgs e)
  {
    if (lastPickedDate != DateTime.MinValue)
    {
      this.dateTimePicker1.Value = lastPickedDate;
    }

    this.dateTimePicker1.ValueChanged += new EventHandler(
      DateTimePicker1_ValueChanged);
  }

  void DateTimePicker1_ValueChanged(object sender, EventArgs e)
  {
    lastPickedDate = dateTimePicker1.Value;
  }

  #region VSTO Designer generated code
  private void InternalStartup()
  {
    this.Startup += new System.EventHandler(ThisDocument_Startup);
  }
  #endregion
}
```

Why Are Controls Sometimes Slightly Blurry?

Have you noticed how sometimes a control in Word or Excel looks a little blurred when you are in the designer, but that it snaps back into focus when you run the project? This is because the Windows Forms control host ActiveX control stores a bitmap of the hosted Windows Forms control so that when Excel or Word first opens the document it can display the bitmap until the actual control is loaded. This was done because the actual control is not loaded until the customization assembly is fully loaded. If we did not do this, the control would have an attractive red *x* through it until the customization assembly loaded.

The reason it looks a bit out of focus is because Office anti-aliases the image when it stores it so it is not an exact copy of the original bitmap. So if you see a slightly out-of-focus control on your document, you know that your customization assembly has not loaded yet, did not load properly, or you have been up too late writing a book about Windows Forms controls on Office documents!

Properties Merged from OLEObject or OLEControl

After the control has been added to the document or spreadsheet, the experience of using the control on the design surface should be very close to that of working with a standard Windows Form. However, there are some differences. The biggest difference appears when you click a Windows Forms control in the document and use the categorized view in the Properties window. If you compare a Windows.Forms.Controls.Button with a Microsoft.Office.Tools.Excel.Controls.Button, you will see the extra properties merged in from the OLEObject. These properties are listed in the Misc category to denote that these properties are coming from OLEObject.

Excel Control Properties That Are Added from OLEObject

The OLEObject merge done for controls in the Microsoft.Office.Tools.Excel.Controls namespace adds several properties to VSTO extended controls that are not in the base Windows.Forms controls. Table 14-1 shows the most important properties that are added for controls in Excel.

Table 14-1 Additional Excel Control Properties

Name	Type	Access	Description
BottomRightCell	Excel.Range	Read-only	The Range object that represents the cell that lies under the lower-right corner of the control.
Enabled	bool	Read-write	Determines whether the control is enabled. If you set this to false, the control will show grayed-out in Excel. This enables you to control whether the control will accept input at runtime.
Height	double	Read-write	The height, in points, of the control.
Left	double	Read-write	The distance, in points, from the left edge of the control to the left edge of column A.
Placement	object	Read-write	Determines how the control will be placed. This can be one of three values: xlFreeFloating (equivalent to Do not move or size with cell setting in the placement dialog) xlMove (equivalent to Move but do not size with cell setting in the placement dialog) xlMoveAndSize (equivalent to Move and size with cell setting in the placement dialog)
PrintObject	bool	Read-write	Determines whether the control will print when the worksheet is printed. This can prove very useful if the control you are using is something like a button that should not be part of the final printed document.
Shadow	bool	Read-write	Determines whether Excel should provide a drop shadow for the control. When set to true, Excel will provide a simple black drop shadow around the control

Name	Type	Access	Description
TopLeftCell	Excel.Range	Read-only	The Range object that represents the cell that lies under the upper-left corner of the control.
Top	double	Read-write	The distance, in points, from the top edge of the control to the top edge of row 1.
Visible	bool	Read-write	Determines whether to hide the control at runtime.
Width	double	Read-write	The width, in points, of the control.

Word Control Properties Added from OLEControl

The OLEControl merge done for controls in the Microsoft.Office.Tools.Word.Controls namespace adds several properties to VSTO extended controls that are not in the base Windows.Forms controls. Table 14-2 shows the most important properties that are added for controls in Word.

Table 14-2 Additional Word Control Properties

Name	Type	Access	Description
Bottom	float	Read-only	The distance, in points, from the top edge of the first paragraph on the page to the bottom of the control
Height	float	Read-write	The height, in points, of the control
InlineShape	InlineShape	Read	Returns the InlineShape object in the Word object model corresponding to the control—returns null if the control is not inline
Shape	Shape	Read	Returns the Shape object in the Word object model corresponding to the control—returns null if the control is inline
Left	float	Read-write	The distance, in points, from the left edge of the control to the left edge of the first paragraph on the page

continues

Table 14-2 Continued

Name	Type	Access	Description
Name	string	Read-write	The name of the control
Right	float	Read-only	The distance, in points, from the right edge of the control to the left edge of the first paragraph on the page
Top	float	Read-write	The distance, in points, from the top edge of the control to the top edge of the first paragraph on the page
Width	float	Read-write	The width, in points, of the control

Many of the properties for controls running in Word are dependent on the wrapping style of the control. If the control is inline with text, the Left, Bottom, Right, Top, and Width properties will throw an exception. Why? Word represents ActiveX controls as either Shapes or InlineShapes depending on how the control is positioned on the document, and the positioning properties are only available on Shapes that are controls whose wrapping style is Behind text or In front of text.

Word controls also have an InlineShape and Shape property that provide you with access to the InlineShape or Shape object in the Word object model corresponding to the control.

Adding Controls at Runtime

So far this chapter has described how to add controls to the document or worksheet at design time with the Visual Studio control toolbox. Often the controls needed for your application need to be added (and deleted) at runtime. For example, consider the worksheet in Figure 14-1 again. Suppose you want to provide a trade button at the end of every row that shows a stock. This would be impossible to achieve by adding buttons at design time because the number of stock rows will vary at runtime as the workbook is edited. You would need to add a button to the end of the row dynamically as stock is added at runtime.

VSTO provides a mechanism to add controls at runtime via the Controls collection present on Word's Document class and Excel's Worksheet classes. This Controls collection works a bit differently than the Controls collection in Windows Forms. In the Controls collection associated with a Windows Forms form class, you can add controls at runtime by creating an instance of the control and adding it to the form's collection of controls. You can then set positioning on the control you created:

```
System.Windows.Forms.Button btn =
  new System.Windows.Forms.Button();

form1.Controls.Add(btn);

btn.Left = 100;
```

The VSTO Controls collection cannot take this approach because although the instance of the button could be added to the collection, there would be no way for the developer to change any positional properties on it because these are not available until the ActiveX control is created and connected to the Windows Forms control. There needs to be a way to return to the developer a wrapped control that has both the original control and the OLEObject or OLEControl. The VSTO Controls collection provides two mechanisms for adding controls:

- VSTO provides a generic AddControl method that can be used with any Windows Forms control. This method takes an instance of the Windows Forms control you want to add and returns to you the Microsoft.Office.Tools.Excel.OLEObject or Microsoft.Office.Tools.Word.OLE-Control that contains the control you passed in. So the equivalent of the Windows Forms code above in VSTO is shown here. The main difference is that you have to now track two objects: the Button object and the OLEObject object and remember to only set positioning on the OLEObject:

```
System.Windows.Forms.Button btn =
  new System.Windows.Forms.Button();

Microsoft.Office.Tools.Excel.OLEObject oleObject =
  this.Controls.Add(btn, 100, 100, 150, 100, "button1");

oleObject.Left = 100;
```

- For common Windows Forms controls, a set of helper methods on the Controls collection will return the VSTO extended control with positioning information merged in. For example, a method called AddButton is provided on Excel's Controls collection. This method returns a

Microsoft.Office.Tools.Excel.Controls.Button. The code below does the same thing as the code shown earlier, except it frees you from having to track two objects:

```
Microsoft.Office.Tools.Excel.Controls.Button btn =
  this.Controls.AddButton(100, 100, 150, 100, "button1");

btn.Left = 100;
```

Listing 14-5 shows code that dynamically adds a group box to an Excel worksheet using the AddControl mechanism. It doesn't even use the returned OLEObject because it sets the position as part of the initial call to AddControl. It then goes further and adds additional RadioButton controls to that group box.

Listing 14-5 A VSTO Excel Customization That Adds a Group Box to an Excel Worksheet at Runtime

```
using System;
using System.Data;
using System.Drawing;
using System.Windows.Forms;
using Microsoft.VisualStudio.OfficeTools.Interop.Runtime;
using Excel = Microsoft.Office.Interop.Excel;
using Office = Microsoft.Office.Core;

namespace ExcelWorkbook1
{
  public partial class Sheet1
  {
    System.Windows.Forms.GroupBox myGroupBox;

    private void Sheet1_Startup(object sender, EventArgs e)
    {
      myGroupBox = new System.Windows.Forms.GroupBox();

      // Add the group box to the controls collection on the sheet
      this.Controls.AddControl(
        myGroupBox, 100, 100, 150, 100, "groupbox");
      // Set the title of the group box
      myGroupBox.Text = "Insurance type";
      // Add the radio buttons to the groupbox
      myGroupBox.Controls.Add(new RadioButton());
      myGroupBox.Controls.Add(new RadioButton());
      // Set the text of the radio buttons
      myGroupBox.Controls[0].Text = "Life";
      myGroupBox.Controls[1].Text = "Term";
      // Arrange the radio buttons in the group box
```

```
myGroupBox.Controls[0].Top = myGroupBox.Top + 25;
myGroupBox.Controls[1].Top =
myGroupBox.Controls[0].Bottom + 20;
// iterate through each button in the controls collection
foreach (RadioButton rb in myGroupBox.Controls)
{
  rb.Left = myGroupBox.Left + 10;
}
}

#region VSTO Designer generated code
private void InternalStartup()
{
  this.Startup += new System.EventHandler(this.Sheet1_Startup);
}
#endregion
}
}
```

Working with the Controls Collection

The Controls collection provides a simple mechanism to add controls to your document or worksheet at runtime. Before we get into the details of the Controls collection, it is important to note that the implementation and methods exposed are different between Word and Excel. Although the behavior of the collection is the same in each application, it was necessary to have a different implementation to ensure that the collection takes advantage of the host application. For example, if you want to add a control to Excel, passing in an Excel.Range object for its position makes a lot of sense. If you want to add a control to Word, passing in a Word.Range object makes sense.

To illustrate using the collection, we start by looking at the helper methods available for all the supported Windows Forms controls that ship with the .NET Framework. The helper methods follow a common design pattern; call the method with positional arguments and an identifier and the method returns you the wrapped type for the control.

Word has two overloads for each helper method:

• A method that takes a Word Range object, a width and height for the control in points, and a string name for the control that uniquely identifies it within the controls collection:

```
Controls.AddButton(ActiveWindow.Selection.Range, 100, 50, "NewButton");
```

- A method that takes a left, top, width, and height for the control in points and a string name for the control that uniquely identifies it within the controls collection:

```
Controls.AddMonthCalendar(10, 50, 100, 100, "NewCalendar");
```

Excel also has two overloads for each helper method:

- A method that takes an Excel range object and a string name for the control that uniquely identifies it within the controls collection. The control will be sized to always match the size of the range passed to the method:

```
Controls.AddButton(Range["A1", missing], "NewButton");
```

- A method that takes a left, top, width, and height for the controls in points and a string name for the control that uniquely identifies it within the controls collection:

```
Controls.AddMonthCalendar(10, 50, 100, 100, "NewCalendar");
```

After the control has been added to the document or worksheet, you can program against it just as you do a control added at design time. Table 14-3 shows the complete list of helper methods to add controls on the Controls collection.

Table 14-3 Add Methods on the Controls Collection

Method Name	Return Type
AddButton	Microsoft.Office.Tools.Excel.Controls.Button
AddChart	Microsoft.Office.Tools.Excel.Chart
AddCheckBox	Microsoft.Office.Tools.Excel.Controls.CheckBox
AddCheckedListBox	Microsoft.Office.Tools.Excel.Controls.CheckedListBox AddComboBox
Microsoft.Office.Tools.	Excel.Controls.ComboBox
AddDataGridView	Microsoft.Office.Tools.Excel.Controls.DataGridView

Method Name	Return Type
AddDateTimePicker	Microsoft.Office.Tools.Excel.Controls.DateTimePicker
AddDomainUpDown	Microsoft.Office.Tools.Excel.Controls.DomainUpDown AddHScrollBar
Microsoft.Office.Tools. Excel.Controls.HScroll	Bar AddLabel
Microsoft.Office.Tools.	Excel.Controls.Label
AddLinkLabel	Microsoft.Office.Tools.Excel.Controls.LinkLabel AddListBox
Microsoft.Office.Tools.	Excel.Controls.ListBox
AddListView	Microsoft.Office.Tools.Excel.Controls.ListView
AddMonthCalendar	Microsoft.Office.Tools.Excel.Controls.MonthCalendar AddNumericUpDown
Microsoft.Office.Tools. Excel.Controls.Numeri	c-UpDown AddPictureBox
Microsoft.Office.Tools.	Excel.Controls.PictureBox
AddProgressBar	Microsoft.Office.Tools.Excel.Controls.
ProgressBar AddPropertyGrid	Microsoft.Office.Tools.Excel.Controls. PropertyGrid
AddRadioButton	Microsoft.Office.Tools.Excel.Controls.
RadioButton AddRichTextBox	Microsoft.Office.Tools.Excel.Controls.RichTextBox AddTextBox
Microsoft.Office.Tools.	Excel.Controls.TextBox
AddTrackBar	Microsoft.Office.Tools.Excel.Controls.TrackBar
AddTreeView	Microsoft.Office.Tools.Excel.Controls.TreeView
AddVScrollBar	Microsoft.Office.Tools.Excel.Controls.VScrollBar
AddWebBrowser	Microsoft.Office.Tools.Excel.Controls.WebBrowser

AddControl

Unfortunately, helper methods are not available for every control on your machine, so there needs to be a way to add controls outside the list in Table 14-3. To do this, the Controls collection provides an AddControl method that enables you to pass in an instance of any Windows Forms control, and it will return the OLEObject (for Excel) or the OLEControl (for Word) that can be used to position the control after it is added.

```
// Declare a OLEObject variable
Microsoft.Office.Interop.Excel.OLEObject myobj;

// Add the control to the A10 cell
myobj = Controls.AddControl(new UserControl1(),
  this.Range["A10", missing], "DynamicUserControl");

// Reposition it to the top of B15
myobj.Top = (double)this.Range["B15", missing].Top;
```

A common pitfall of using AddControl is forgetting to set the positioning on the OLEObject and setting it directly on the Windows Forms control itself. If you do this, the control will change its position relative to the container rather than move its position correctly in the document. For an example of this issue, consider Listing 14-3 and Figure 14-13.

Deleting Controls at Runtime

Now that we have some controls added to the document at runtime, it is important that there be a mechanism to delete controls from the collection. VSTO provides three ways to achieve this:

- Calling the Remove method on the Controls collection and passing in the instance or name of the control that you want to remove from the collection
- Calling the RemoveAt method on the Controls collection and passing in the index of the control to be removed
- Calling the Delete method on the control itself, which will in turn delete the control

You can only delete controls that have been added at runtime. If you try to remove controls that were added at design time, you will get an exception.

Why Are Controls Added at Runtime Not Saved in the Document?

We wanted to keep the behavior of the Controls collection as close to the Windows Forms development experience so that any control added at runtime is deleted from the document when the user saves the document. For example, if you add controls to a Windows Forms application at runtime, you do not expect those controls to just appear the next time you run the application without code being written to re-create those controls. We spent many hours debating the relative merits of this approach over the alternative, which was to allow Word or Excel to save the newly added control when the document was saved. The main deciding argument for not saving the newly added control was to make it easier to write dynamic control code in the document. If we had left the control in the document when the user saved the document, it would have been very difficult to write code that could hook up controls that had been added dynamically the last time the document was open. To understand why this was difficult really involves looking into how a control is added to the document at runtime.

When a control is added to the Controls collection, the VSTO runtime adds an instance of the ActiveX control that will host the control and then sets it to host the provided control. This works fine when the document is running but quickly becomes complicated when the user saves the document. If we were to save the control into the document, all that would be stored would be the ActiveX control itself but without any instance of the Windows Forms control because it must be provided by the code at runtime. The next time the document loaded up, the ActiveX control would load but would not get an instance of the control because the code that added the instance of the Windows Forms control would run again and add a new instance of the ActiveX control because it would have no link back to the saved ActiveX control. Extrapolate this situation out over a few hundred saves of a document and you quickly get a lot of "orphaned" ActiveX controls that will never be used.

The solution that was implemented in VSTO was to remove all ActiveX control instances that were added as a result of adding a control at runtime to the Controls collection. This way there will never be any "orphaned" ActiveX controls on the document, and it also makes your code simpler to write. Why is the code simpler to write? Imagine writing the code to add the buttons at the end of each row containing a stock:

```
foreach (StockRow stock in Stocks)
{
   // add stock information to row here
   this.Controls.AddButton(
      this.Range[currentrow, "12"], stock.Ticker + "btn");
}
```

If the control was persisted with the worksheet on save, the code would have to go through each control and ensure the buttons added in the last run were there, and quite possibly delete and add them again since the stock list changed. We believed it was more straightforward to just iterate through the stocks on every run of the workbook and add the buttons.

Why Are Controls in the Controls Collection Typed as Object Instead of Control?

VSTO documents and worksheets can have Windows Forms controls added to them at runtime via the Controls collection as well as host controls such as NamedRange and ListObject. Both these types of controls act like controls in the VSTO model. For example, you can click a NamedRange in VSTO and display a property window for it. You can establish data bindings to a NamedRange just as you can with a text box or any other Windows Forms control.

As a result, the VSTO model considers both NamedRange and a Windows Forms control to be a "control" associated with the worksheet or document. The Controls collection contains both host controls and Windows Forms controls. Although providing a strongly typed collection was something that we would have liked to do, there was no common type other than `object` that a host control and a Windows Forms control share.

Conclusion

The key to using Windows Forms controls in your Word or Excel solutions is to think about what user-interface options meet your requirements. VSTO provides you with considerable flexibility for extending the user interface of Word or Excel, and there is no one right answer as to which is the best way. Windows Forms controls allow you to extend the capabilities that ActiveX controls provided while leveraging the ever-growing Windows Forms controls ecosystem.

This chapter described how you can use Windows Forms controls to extend your Office solutions. In particular, the chapter examined how hosting controls on the document surface is a very powerful tool for developing applications. The chapter also covered the architecture of hosting controls on the document surface and the limitations and differences in this model compared to traditional Windows Forms development. Chapter 15 continues the discussion about Windows Forms and Office, specifically showing how to use Windows Forms controls on Office's Document Actions task pane.

15
Working with Actions Pane

Introduction to the Actions Pane

DEVELOPING A SOLUTION THAT RUNS within an Office application provides considerable benefits because you can take advantage of the functionality that already exists in Office. However, it is sometimes hard to design a user interface that meets your needs as most of the user interface space is controlled by the Office application. Office 2003 and VSTO introduce a number of new user interface capabilities, including the ability to use Windows Forms controls on the document. (See Chapter 14, "Using Windows Forms in VSTO," for more information on this capability.)

Placing a control on the document is not always the right paradigm for the user interface of your application. For example, putting a control onto the document can often lead to issues with layout when the controls are laid out relative to a range or paragraph. If you use a button on a Word document, by default it will be inline with the text. This means that when you reformat the document, the button will move with the text. Obviously, being able to move a control with the text is something that you would want if you are developing a flow-based user interface. But this model quickly becomes difficult when developing more traditional user interfaces. Things get even more complex if you start to consider what type of behavior you want when the user prints a document. For example, do you want your Windows Forms controls to be printed with the rest of the document?

To address these user interface challenges, Office 2003 introduced the ability to put your own custom user interface into the Document Actions task pane of Word and Excel. The task pane is designed to provide a contextual user interface that is complementary to the document. For example, Word provides a task pane that shows the styles and formats available in the current document and displays the style of the current selection in the document, as shown in Figure 15-1. To display the task pane, choose Task Pane in the View menu.

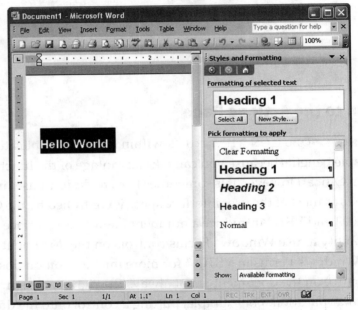

Figure 15-1 The Styles and Formatting task pane in Word.

The active task pane can be changed by dropping down the drop-down menu at the top of the task pane and selecting from the available task panes, as shown in Figure 15-2. The active task pane is a per-document setting. You can only have one task pane visible at a time per document. The drop-down menu shows several task panes that are built in to Office. The task pane acts like a toolbar when you drag it to move it to another location. It can float above the document. It can also be docked to the left, top, right, or bottom of the application window space.

Figure 15-2 Selecting a task pane in Word.

Figure 15-2 lists several of the built-in task panes available in Word, including the Getting Started task pane, Help, Clip Art, and so on. The task pane in the list that is customizable by your VSTO Word or Excel application is called the Document Actions task pane. In VSTO and in this book, we often refer to the Document Actions task pane as the actions pane, as kind of a contraction between the Document Actions and task pane. ActionsPane is the name of the control in the VSTO programming model that you will use to put your own content in the Document Actions task pane. Note that the Document Actions task pane is listed as an available task pane for a document that has a VSTO customization associated with it that uses the ActionsPane control.

Listing 15-1 shows a simple VSTO Excel customization that displays a Windows Forms button control in the Document Actions task pane. In Excel, the ActionsPane control is a member of the ThisWorkbook class. Because this code is written in Sheet1, we use the Globals object to access the ThisWorkbook class and from the ThisWorkbook class access the ActionsPane control. The ActionsPane control has a Controls collection that contains the controls that will be shown in the Document Actions task pane. We add to this collection of controls a Windows Forms button control we have previously created. Note that just the action of adding a control to the Controls collection causes the Document Actions task pane to be shown at startup.

Listing 15-1 A VSTO Excel Customization That Adds a Button to the Actions Pane

```
using System;
using System.Data;
using System.Drawing;
using System.Windows.Forms;
using Microsoft.VisualStudio.OfficeTools.Interop.Runtime;
using Excel = Microsoft.Office.Interop.Excel;
using Office = Microsoft.Office.Core;

namespace ExcelWorkbook1
{
  public partial class Sheet1
  {
    public Button myButton = new Button();

    private void Sheet1_Startup(object sender, EventArgs e)
    {
      myButton.Text = "Hello World";
      Globals.ThisWorkbook.ActionsPane.Controls.Add(myButton);
    }

    #region VSTO Designer generated code
    private void InternalStartup()
    {
      this.Startup += new EventHandler(Sheet1_Startup);
    }
    #endregion
  }
}
```

Figure 15-3 shows the result of running Listing 15-1. The Document Actions task pane is shown with a Windows Forms button displayed in the pane.

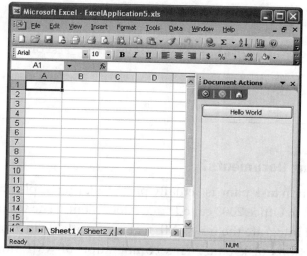

Figure 15-3 The result of running Listing 15-1.

Listing 15-2 shows a similar VSTO Word customization that displays a Windows Forms Button control in the Document Actions task pane. In Word, the ActionsPane control is a member of the ThisDocument class.

Listing 15-2 A VSTO Word Customization That Uses the Actions Pane

```
using System;
using System.Data;
using System.Drawing;
using System.Windows.Forms;
using Microsoft.VisualStudio.OfficeTools.Interop.Runtime;
using Word = Microsoft.Office.Interop.Word;
using Office = Microsoft.Office.Core;

namespace WordDocument1
{
  public partial class ThisDocument
  {
    public Button myButton = new Button();

    private void ThisDocument_Startup(object sender, EventArgs e)
    {
      myButton.Text = "Hello World";
      ActionsPane.Controls.Add(myButton);
    }
```

```
    #region VSTO Designer generated code
    private void InternalStartup()
    {
        this.Startup += new EventHandler(ThisDocument_Startup);
    }
    #endregion
    }
}
```

What About Smart Documents?

The Document Action task pane is actually part of a larger application development platform provided in Office 2003 called smart documents. The vision was that smart documents would integrate the new XML features available in Word and Excel and the Document Actions task pane. This combination of XML and the Document Actions task pane provides an application development platform that makes it easier to build documents that are "smart" about their content and provide the appropriate user interface.

Smart documents were primarily designed for the COM world. So although smart documents provided a powerful platform, it did not fit easily into the .NET development methodology. Why?

1. The way you create a smart document is by first creating a component that implements the ISmartDocument interface. This interface is rather COM-centric.

2. To use a smart document, you must have XML schema mapped in your document. Although XML mapping provides considerable functionality to your application programming (see Chapters 21, "Working with XML in Excel," and 22, "Working with XML in Word"), not all documents need or want to use XML mapping.

3. The Document Actions task pane only supports a small set of built-in controls and ActiveX controls. To use a Windows Forms control, you would have to register it as an ActiveX control and then attempt to get that to work within the Document Actions task pane. This requires COM registration and COM interop.

4. The smart documents infrastructure requires you to create an expansion pack, which includes the following:

Manifest.xml—contains links to all the components within the expansion pack

The document to be used

Schema for the smart document

Configuration XML file—contains the definition of the controls to be used

VSTO provides the ActionsPane control to enable you access to all the features provided by smart documents with a much more .NET development experience. You do not have to implement the ISmartDocument interface or use schema mapping in the document. You do not have to register Windows Forms controls in the registry so they can act as ActiveX controls. You do not have to create an expansion pack. Because using the ActionsPane control is so much simpler than smart documents and provides all the benefits, this book does not consider building smart documents in the old "COM" way.

The ActionsPane feature of VSTO is actually implemented under the covers as a specialized smart document solution—when you look at a customized VSTO document and examine the attached XML schemas, you will see a schema is automatically attached called ActionsPane. This schema provides the plumbing to connect VSTO's ActionsPane control to the smart document platform. When you install the VSTO runtime (see Chapter 20, "Deployment"), the ActionsPane schema is also installed and registered with Excel and Word, enabling the ActionsPane control to access the Document Actions task pane.

Working with the ActionsPane Control

A first step to understanding how VSTO's ActionsPane control works is delving a little into the architecture of VSTO's ActionsPane support.

The ActionsPane Architecture

The Document Actions task pane is a window provided by Office that can host ActiveX controls, as shown in Figure 15-4. VSTO places a special invisible ActiveX control in the Document Actions task pane that in turn hosts a single Windows Forms UserControl. This UserControl is represented in the VSTO programming model by the ActionsPane control—accessible in Word via Document.ActionsPane and accessible in Excel via Globals.ThisWorkbook.ActionsPane.

Although the Document Actions task pane can host multiple ActiveX controls, VSTO only needs to put a single ActiveX control and a single UserControl in the Document Actions task pane window because the UserControl can host multiple Windows Forms controls via its Controls collection (ActionsPane.Controls). You can add Windows Forms controls to the ActionsPane by using the ActionsPane.Controls.Add method.

The UserControl placed in the ActionsPane window is set to expand to fit the area provided by the ActionsPane window. If the area of the Document Actions task pane is not big enough to display all the controls hosted by the UserControl, it is possible to scroll the UserControl by setting the AutoScroll property of ActionsPane to `true`.

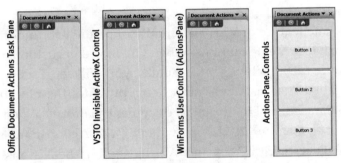

Figure 15-4 The four layers of the ActionsPane architecture.

The ActionsPane control is a wrapper around System.Windows.Forms.UserControl with most of the properties, methods, and events of a UserControl. It also adds some properties, events, and methods specific to ActionsPane. When you understand the architecture in Figure 15-4, you will not be too surprised to know that some properties from UserControl that are exposed by ActionsPane such as position-related properties, methods, and events do not do anything. For example, because the position of the ActionsPane UserControl is forced to fill the space provided by the ActionsPane window, you cannot reposition the UserControl to arbitrary positions within the Document Actions task pane window.

Adding Windows Forms Controls to the Actions Pane

The basic way you add your custom UI to the actions pane is by adding Windows Forms controls to the actions pane's Controls collection. Listing 15-1 illustrates this approach. It first declares and creates an instance of a System.Windows.Forms.Button control. This control is then added to the actions pane by calling the Add method of the Controls collection associated with the actions pane and passing the button instance as a parameter to the Add method.

The actions pane is smart about arranging controls within the ActionsPane. If multiple controls are added to the Controls collection, the actions pane can automatically stack and arrange the controls. The stacking order is controlled by the ActionsPane.StackOrder property, which is of type `Microsoft.Office.Tools.StackStyle`. It can be set to `None` for no automatic positioning or can be set to `FromTop`, `FromBottom`, `FromLeft`, or `FromRight`. Figure 15-5 shows the effect of the various StackOrder settings.

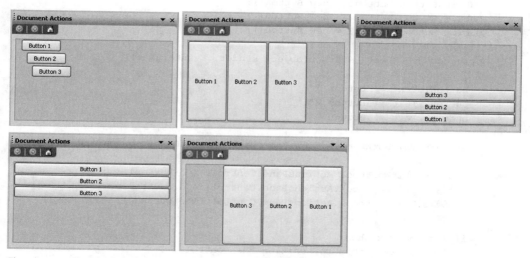

Figure 15-5 The result of changing the ActionsPane StackOrder setting from top left: `None`, `FromLeft`, `FromBottom`, `FromTop`, and `FromRight`.

Listing 15-3 shows some code that adds and positions controls in the actions pane when StackOrder is set to either `StackStyle.FromBottom` and automatically positioned or set to `StackStyle.None` and manually positioned.

Listing 15-3 A VSTO Excel Customization That Adds and Positions Controls with Either StackStyle.None or StackStyle.FromBottom

```csharp
using System;
using System.Data;
using System.Drawing;
using System.Windows.Forms;
using Microsoft.VisualStudio.OfficeTools.Interop.Runtime;
using Excel = Microsoft.Office.Interop.Excel;
using Office = Microsoft.Office.Core;

namespace ExcelWorkbook1
{
  public partial class Sheet1
  {

    public Button button1 = new Button();
    public Button button2 = new Button();
    public Button button3 = new Button();

    private void Sheet1_Startup(object sender, EventArgs e)
    {
      button1.Text = "Button 1";
      button2.Text = "Button 2";
      button3.Text = "Button 3";

      Globals.ThisWorkbook.ActionsPane.BackColor = Color.Aquamarine;

      Globals.ThisWorkbook.ActionsPane.Controls.Add(button1);
      Globals.ThisWorkbook.ActionsPane.Controls.Add(button2);
      Globals.ThisWorkbook.ActionsPane.Controls.Add(button3);

      if (MessageBox.Show(
        "Do you want to auto-position the controls?",
        "StackStyle",
        MessageBoxButtons.YesNo) == DialogResult.Yes)
      {
```

```
      Globals.ThisWorkbook.ActionsPane.StackOrder =
        Microsoft.Office.Tools.ActionsPane.StackStyle.FromBottom;
    }
    else
    {
      Globals.ThisWorkbook.ActionsPane.StackOrder =
        Microsoft.Office.Tools.ActionsPane.StackStyle.None;
      button1.Left = 10;
      button2.Left = 20;
      button3.Left = 30;

      button1.Top = 0;
      button2.Top = 25;
      button3.Top = 50;
    }
  }


  #region VSTO Designer generated code
  private void InternalStartup()
  {
    this.Startup += new System.EventHandler(Sheet1_Startup);
  }
  #endregion
  }
}
```

Adding a Custom User Control to the Actions Pane

A more visual way of designing your application's actions pane UI is by creating a user control and adding that user control to the ActionsPane's control collection. Visual Studio provides a rich design-time experience for creating a user control. To add a user control to your application, click the project node in the Solution Explorer and choose Add User Control from Visual Studio's Project menu. Visual Studio will prompt you to give the User Control a filename such as UserControl1.cs. Then Visual Studio will display the design view shown in Figure 15-6.

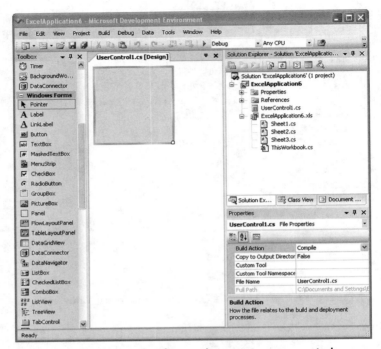

Figure 15-6 The design view for creating a custom user control.

The design area for the user control has a drag handle in the lower-right corner that you can drag to change the size of the user control. Controls from the toolbox can be dragged onto the user control design surface and positioned as desired. Figure 15-7 shows a completed user control that uses check boxes, text boxes, and labels.

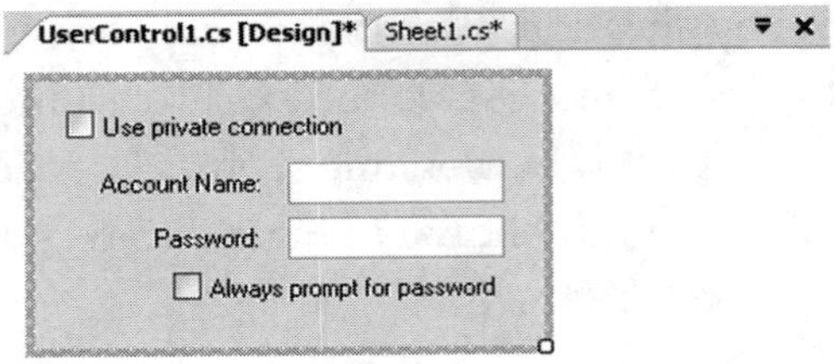

Figure 15-7 A custom user control.

Listing 15-4 shows a VSTO Excel customization that adds this custom user control to the Document Actions task pane. The user control created in Figure 15-7 is a class named UserControl1. Listing 15-4 creates an instance of UserControl1 and adds it to ActionPane's Controls collection using the Add method.

Listing 15-4 A VSTO Excel Customization That Adds a Custom User Control to the Task Pane

```
using System;
using System.Data;
using System.Drawing;
using System.Windows.Forms;
using Microsoft.VisualStudio.OfficeTools.Interop.Runtime;
using Excel = Microsoft.Office.Interop.Excel;
using Office = Microsoft.Office.Core;

namespace ExcelWorkbook1
{
  public partial class Sheet1
  {
    public UserControl1 myUserControl = new UserControl1();

    private void Sheet1_Startup(object sender, EventArgs e)
    {
      Globals.ThisWorkbook.ActionsPane.Controls.Add(myUserControl);
    }

    #region VSTO Designer generated code
    private void InternalStartup()
    {
      this.Startup += new EventHandler(Sheet1_Startup);
    }
    #endregion
  }
}
```

Figure 15-8 shows the resulting Document Actions task pane shown when Listing 15-4 is run.

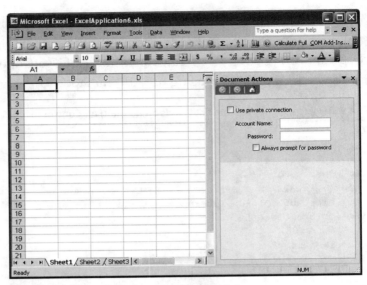

Figure 15-8 The result of running Listing 15-4.

Contextually Changing the Actions Pane

A common application of the ActionsPane is providing commands in the Document Actions task pane that are appropriate to the context of the document. For example, in an order form application, the Document Actions task pane might display a button for selecting a known customer when filling out the customer information section of the document. When the user is filling out the order part of the document, the Document Actions task pane might display a button for examining available inventory.

Listing 15-5 shows a VSTO Excel customization where two named ranges have been defined. One called orderInfo is a range of cells where the contents of an order are placed. The other called customerInfo is a range of cells specifying the customer information for the customer placing the order. Listing 15-5 contextually adds and removes an inventoryButton when the orderInfo range is selected and a customerButton when the customerInfo range is selected or deselected. It does this by handling NamedRange.Selected and NamedRange.Deselected events. When the Selected event indicating the customerInfo range of cells is selected, Listing 15-5 adds a customerButton that when clicked would allow the user to pick an existing customer. Listing 15-5 removes the `customerButton` when the customerInfo.Dese-lected event is raised. It calls ActionsPane.Controls.Remove to remove the `cus-tomerButton` from the actions pane.

Listing 15-5 is written in a way so that if both the `customerInfo` range and the `orderInfo` range are selected at the same time, both the `customerButton` and the `inventoryButton` would be visible in the document task pane.

Listing 15-5 A VSTO Excel Customization That Changes the Actions Pane Based on the Selection

```
using System;
using System.Data;
using System.Drawing;
using System.Windows.Forms;
using Microsoft.VisualStudio.OfficeTools.Interop.Runtime;
using Excel = Microsoft.Office.Interop.Excel;
using Office = Microsoft.Office.Core;

namespace ExcelWorkbook1
{
  public partial class Sheet1
  {
    public Button customerButton = new Button();
    public Button inventoryButton = new Button();

    private void Sheet1_Startup(object sender, EventArgs e)
    {
      customerButton.Text = "Select a customer...";
      inventoryButton.Text = "Check inventory...";

      this.orderInfo.Selected +=
        new Excel.DocEvents_SelectionChangeEventHandler(
        OrderInfo_Selected);

      this.orderInfo.Deselected +=
        new Excel.DocEvents_SelectionChangeEventHandler(
        OrderInfo_Deselected);

      this.customerInfo.Selected +=
        new Excel.DocEvents_SelectionChangeEventHandler(
        CustomerInfo_Selected);

      this.customerInfo.Deselected +=
        new Excel.DocEvents_SelectionChangeEventHandler(
        CustomerInfo_Deselected);
    }
```

```csharp
        #region VSTO Designer generated code
        private void InternalStartup()
        {
            this.Startup += new System.EventHandler(Sheet1_Startup);
        }
        #endregion

        void OrderInfo_Selected(Excel.Range target)
        {
            Globals.ThisWorkbook.ActionsPane.Controls.Add(inventoryButton);
        }

        void OrderInfo_Deselected(Excel.Range target)
        {
            Globals.ThisWorkbook.ActionsPane.Controls.Remove(inventoryButton);
        }

        void CustomerInfo_Selected(Excel.Range target)
        {
            Globals.ThisWorkbook.ActionsPane.Controls.Add(customerButton);
        }

        void CustomerInfo_Deselected(Excel.Range target)
        {
            Globals.ThisWorkbook.ActionsPane.Controls.Remove(customerButton);
        }
    }
}
```

You can also change the contents of the Document Actions task pane as the selection changes in a Word document. One approach is to use bookmarks and change the contents of the Document Actions task pane when a particular bookmark is selected. A second approach is to use the XML mapping features of Word and VSTO's XML-Node and XMLNodes controls described in Chapter 22, and change the contents of the Document Actions task pane when a particular XMLNode or XMLNodes is selected in the document.

Detecting the Orientation of the Actions Pane

In addition to the UserControl events documented in the .NET class libraries documentation, ActionsPane adds one additional event: OrientationChanged. This event is raised when the orientation of the actions pane is changed. The actions pane can be in either a horizontal or vertical orientation. Figure 15-3 shows an actions pane in a vertical orientation. Figure 15-9 shows a horizontal orientation.

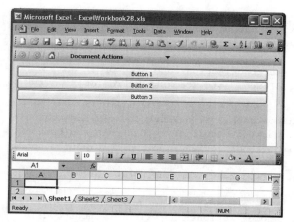

Figure 15-9 The actions pane in a horizontal orientation.

Listing 15-6 shows a VSTO Excel customization that adds several buttons to the ActionsPane's Controls collection. Listing 15-6 also handles the OrientationChanged event and displays the orientation of the ActionsPane in a dialog. It determines the orientation of the actions pane by checking the ActionsPane.Orientation property. The Orientation property returns a member of the System.Windows.Forms.Orientation enumeration: either Orientation.Horizontal or Orientation.Vertical.

Listing 15-6 A VSTO Excel Customization That Handles ActionsPane's OrientationChanged Event

```
using System;
using System.Data;
using System.Drawing;
using System.Windows.Forms;
using Microsoft.VisualStudio.Tools.Applications.Runtime;
using Excel = Microsoft.Office.Interop.Excel;
using Office = Microsoft.Office.Core;

namespace ExcelWorkbook1
{
  public partial class Sheet1
  {
    public Button button1 = new Button();
    public Button button2 = new Button();
```

```csharp
    public Button button3 = new Button();

    private void Sheet1_Startup(object sender, EventArgs e)
    {
      button1.Text = "Button 1";
      button2.Text = "Button 2";
      button3.Text = "Button 3";

      Globals.ThisWorkbook.ActionsPane.StackOrder =
        Microsoft.Office.Tools.StackStyle.FromTop;

      Globals.ThisWorkbook.ActionsPane.Controls.Add(button1);
      Globals.ThisWorkbook.ActionsPane.Controls.Add(button2);
      Globals.ThisWorkbook.ActionsPane.Controls.Add(button3);

      Globals.ThisWorkbook.ActionsPane.BackColor = Color.Aquamarine;

      Globals.ThisWorkbook.ActionsPane.OrientationChanged +=
        new EventHandler(ActionsPane_OrientationChanged);
    }

    void ActionsPane_OrientationChanged(object sender, EventArgs e)
    {
      Orientation orientation =
        Globals.ThisWorkbook.ActionsPane.Orientation;
      MessageBox.Show(String.Format(
        "Orientation is {0}.", orientation.ToString()));
    }

    #region VSTO Designer generated code
    private void InternalStartup()
    {
      this.Startup += new System.EventHandler(Sheet1_Startup);
    }
    #endregion
  }
}
```

Scrolling the Actions Pane

The AutoScroll property of the ActionPane gets or sets a `bool` value indicating whether the actions pane should display a scroll bar when the size of the Document Actions task pane is such that not all the controls can be shown. The default value of AutoScroll is `true`. Figure 15-10 shows a Document Actions task pane with 10 buttons added to it. Because AutoScroll is set to `true`, a scroll bar is shown when not all 10 buttons can be displayed given the size of the Document Actions task pane.

Figure 15-10 The actions pane when AutoScroll is set to true.

Showing and Hiding the Actions Pane

The actions pane is automatically shown when you add controls to ActionsPane's Controls collection using the Add method. To show and hide the actions pane programmatically, you need to use the Excel or Word object model. In Excel, set the Application.DisplayDocumentActionTaskPane property to `true` or `false`. In Word, set the property Application.TaskPanes[WdTaskPanes.wdTaskPaneDocumentActions].Visible property to `true` or `false`.

You might be tempted to call ActionsPane.Hide or set ActionsPane.Visible to `false` to hide the ActionsPane. These approaches do not work because you are actually hiding the UserControl shown in Figure 15-4 that is hosted by the Document Actions task pane rather than just the Document Actions task pane. You should use the object model of Excel and Word to show and hide the actions pane.

Listing 15-7 shows a VSTO Excel customization that shows and hides the actions pane on the BeforeDoubleClick event of the Worksheet by toggling the state of the Application.DisplayDocumentActionTaskPane property. Note that the DisplayDocumentActionTaskPane property is an application-level property that is only applicable when the active document has a Document Actions task pane associated with it. If the active document does not have a Document Actions task pane associated with it, accessing the DisplayDocumentActionTaskPane property will raise an exception.

Listing 15-7 A VSTO Excel Customization That Shows and Hides the Actions Pane When Handling the BeforeDoubleClick Event

```csharp
using System;
using System.Data;
using System.Drawing;
using System.Windows.Forms;
using Microsoft.VisualStudio.OfficeTools.Interop.Runtime;
using Excel = Microsoft.Office.Interop.Excel;
using Office = Microsoft.Office.Core;

namespace ExcelWorkbook1
{
  public partial class Sheet1
  {
    bool visible = true;

    private void Sheet1_Startup(object sender, System.EventArgs e)
    {
      for (int i = 1; i < 11; i++)
      {
        Button myButton = new Button();
        myButton.Text = String.Format("Button {0}", i);
        Globals.ThisWorkbook.ActionsPane.Controls.Add(myButton);
      }

      this.BeforeDoubleClick +=
        new Excel.DocEvents_BeforeDoubleClickEventHandler(
        Sheet1_BeforeDoubleClick);
    }

    #region VSTO Designer generated code
    private void InternalStartup()
    {
      this.Startup += new EventHandler(Sheet1_Startup);
    }
    #endregion

    void Sheet1_BeforeDoubleClick(Excel.Range target,
      ref bool cancel)
    {
      // Toggle the visibility of the ActionsPane on double-click.
      visible = !visible;
      this.Application.DisplayDocumentActionTaskPane = visible;
    }
  }
}
```

Listing 15-8 shows a VSTO Word application that shows and hides the actions pane on the BeforeDoubleClick event of the Document by toggling the state of the Application.TaskPanes[WdTaskPanes.wdTaskPaneDocumentActions].Visible property.

Listing 15-8 VSTO Word Customization That Shows and Hides the Actions Pane in the BeforeDoubleClick Event Handler

```
using System;
using System.Data;
using System.Drawing;
using System.Windows.Forms;
using Microsoft.VisualStudio.OfficeTools.Interop.Runtime;
using Word = Microsoft.Office.Interop.Word;
using Office = Microsoft.Office.Core;

namespace WordDocument1
{
  public partial class ThisDocument
  {

    private void ThisDocument_Startup(object sender, EventArgs e)
    {
      for (int i = 1; i < 11; i++)
      {
        Button myButton = new Button();
        myButton.Text = String.Format("Button {0}", i);
        ActionsPane.Controls.Add(myButton);
      }

      this.BeforeDoubleClick +=
        new Word.ClickEventHandler(
        ThisDocument_BeforeDoubleClick);
    }

    #region VSTO Designer generated code
    private void InternalStartup()
    {
      this.Startup += new EventHandler(ThisDocument_Startup);
    }
    #endregion

    void ThisDocument_BeforeDoubleClick(object sender,
      Word.ClickEventArgs e)
    {
      if (this.Application.TaskPanes[
        Word.WdTaskPanes.wdTaskPaneDocumentActions
        ].Visible == true)
```

```
        {
          this.Application.TaskPanes[
            Word.WdTaskPanes.wdTaskPaneDocumentActions
            ].Visible = false;
        }
        else
        {
          this.Application.TaskPanes[
            Word.WdTaskPanes.wdTaskPaneDocumentActions
            ].Visible = true;
        }
      }
    }
  }
```

Attaching and Detaching the Actions Pane

Sometimes you will want to go beyond just hiding the actions pane and actually detach the actions pane from the document or workbook. You might also want to control whether the user of your document is allowed to detach the actions pane from the document or workbook. Recall from earlier in this chapter that the actions pane is actually a smart document solution, and as such it can be attached or detached from the document or workbook via Excel and Word's built-in dialogs for managing attached smart document solutions.

When the actions pane is detached from the document, this means that the Document Actions task pane will not be in the list of available task panes when the user drops down the list of available task panes, as shown in Figure 15-2. To programmatically detach the actions pane from the document, call the ActionsPane.Clear method. Doing so detaches the actions pane solution from the document and hides the Document Actions pane. Calling ActionsPane.Show reattaches the actions pane and makes it available again in the list of available task panes. Note that in Word, when you call ActionsPane.Clear, you must follow the call with a second call to the Word object model: Document.XMLReferences["ActionsPane"].Delete.

If you want to allow the user of your document to detach the actions pane solution by using the Templates and Add-ins dialog in Word shown in Figure 15-11 or the XML Expansion Packs dialog in Excel shown in Figure 15-12, you must set the ActionsPane.AutoRecover property to false. By default, this property is set to true, which means that even when the user tries to detach the actions pane solution by deselecting it in these dialogs, VSTO will recover and automatically reattach the actions pane solution.

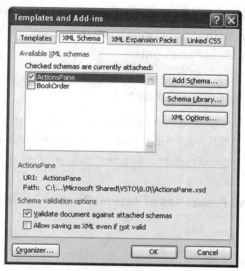

Figure 15-11 The actions pane solution attached to a Word document is visible in Word's Templates and Add-Ins dialog and can be removed if ActionsPane.AutoRecover is not set to true.

Figure 15-12 The actions pane solution attached to an Excel workbook is visible in Excel's XML Expansion Packs dialog and can be removed if ActionsPane.AutoRecover is not set to true.

After an actions pane solution is attached to the document and the user saves the document, the next time the user opens the document, the actions pane will be available and can be selected at any time during the session. If your code does not add controls to the actions pane until some time after startup, you might want to call the ActionsPane.Clear method in the Startup handler of your VSTO customization to prevent the user from showing the actions pane before your VSTO customization has added controls to the ActionsPane control.

Some Methods and Properties to Avoid

As mentioned earlier, the ActionsPane is a user control that has a fixed location and size that is controlled by VSTO. As such, you should avoid using a number of position-related properties and methods on the ActionsPane control, as listed in Table 15-1.

Table 15-1 Methods and Properties of ActionsPane to Avoid

Left	Top	Width
Height	Right	Location
Margin	MaximumSize	MinimumSize
Size	TabIndex	AutoScrollMargin
AutoScrollMinSIze		

Conclusion

The chapter covered the ActionsPane control in VSTO and how it enables custom UI in Office's Document Actions task pane. The chapter examined the properties, methods, and events unique to the ActionsPane control. You also learned the basic architecture of ActionPane and how ActionsPane has the properties, methods, and events found on a Windows Forms user control.

▪ 16 ▪

Working with Smart Tags in VSTO

Introduction to Smart Tags

THE SMART TAGS FEATURE OF WORD AND Excel enables you to display a pop-up menu with actions for a given piece of text in a document or spreadsheet. For example, a Smart Tag could recognize stock symbols (such as the MSFT stock symbol) and display a set of actions that can be taken for that symbol. When Word finds a piece of text that a Smart Tag has recognized, it displays a red dotted underline under the recognized text. If the user hovers over the text, a pop-up menu icon appears next to the cell, as shown in Figure 16-1. If the user clicks the pop-up menu icon, a menu of actions displays for the recognized piece of text, as shown in Figure 16-2. When an action is selected, Word calls back into the Smart Tag to execute the action.

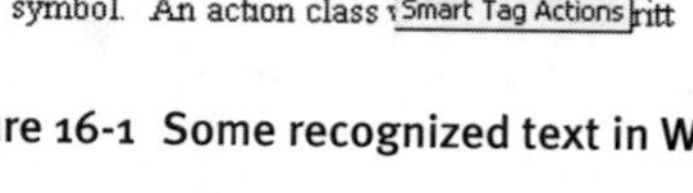

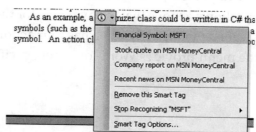

As an example, a ⓘ ▾ nizer class could
symbols (such as the MSFT stock symbol) a
symbol. An action class ⸝Smart Tag Actions⸜ritt

Figure 16-1 Some recognized text in Word.

Figure 16-2 Dropping down the Smart Tag menu in Word.

When Excel recognizes a Smart Tag, it displays a little triangle in the lower-right corner of the associated cell. If the user hovers over the cell, a pop-up menu icon appears next to the cell that the user can click to drop down a menu of actions for the recognized piece of text. Figure 16-3 shows an example menu. When an action is selected, Excel calls back into the Smart Tag to execute the action.

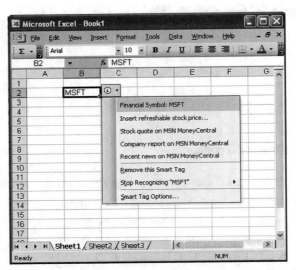

Figure 16-3 Dropping down the Smart Tag menu in Excel.

Figure 16-4 shows some additional detail about the drop-down menu that appears for recognized text. At the top of the drop-down menu, the name of the Smart Tag displays along with the text that was recognized. The next section of the menu shows actions that are available for the given Smart Tag. This particular Smart Tag, called Financial Symbol, has four actions associated with it. The bottom section of the menu provides Word- or Excel-specific options for the Smart Tag.

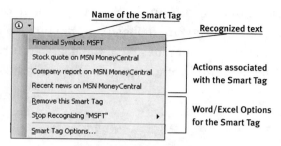

Figure 16-4 The Smart Tag menu.

Configuring Smart Tags in Word and Excel

Smart Tags in Word are managed from the Smart Tags page of the AutoCorrect Options dialog shown in Figure 16-5. The Smart Tags page can be displayed by choosing AutoCorrect Options from the Tools menu. Here the user can turn on and off individual Smart Tags as well as control other options relating to how Smart Tags display in the document.

Figure 16-5 Word's Smart Tags page in the AutoCorrect dialog.

Smart Tags in Excel are managed from the Smart Tags page of the AutoCorrect dialog, as shown in Figure 16-6. The Smart Tags page can be displayed by choosing AutoCorrect Options from the Tools menu. Here the user can turn on and off individual recognizers as well as control other options relating to how Smart Tags display in the workbook.

Figure 16-6 Excel's Smart Tags page in the AutoCorrect dialog.

The Persistent Tagging Generated by Smart Tags

To understand how Smart Tags work in Office, it is helpful to have a conceptual model in your mind. Otherwise, some of the behavior you will see when working with Smart Tags will be confusing.

A Smart Tag has a recognition engine that is passed text in the document or workbook. If the Smart Tag recognizes a segment of text, it can tell Word or Excel to tag the text as being recognized. This tagging is stored and saved in the document by Word or Excel. When text is tagged, it remains tagged until the user removes the tag by choosing Remove This Smart Tag from the Smart Tag menu. So even if a Smart Tag has stopped recognizing a particular term or is no longer active, the tagging in the document can remain.

Text that has been tagged by a Smart Tag has its tagged state saved into the document. You can see this tagging when you save into WordML format. A document with the stock symbol MSFT has been recognized in a Word document by a Smart

Tag with Smart Tag type name `customsmarttag`. This tag also can optionally store custom properties in the document when it recognizes a term—in this example, the Smart Tag stores the properties `LongStockName` and the current `StockValue`. You can see all this in the WordML markup:

```
<st1:customsmarttag LongStockName="Microsoft" StockValue="29"
w:st="on"><w:r><w:t>MSFT</w:t></w:r></st1:customsmarttag>
```

Creating Document-Level Smart Tags with VSTO

The simplest way to create a Smart Tag is by using VSTO's support for document-level Smart Tags. VSTO provides some classes that enable you to easily create a Smart Tag. First, VSTO provides a class called SmartTag in the Microsoft.Office.Tools.Word namespace and the Microsoft.Office.Tools.Excel namespace. You create an instance of this SmartTag class to define a new Smart Tag. The constructor of the SmartTag object takes two parameters: a unique identifier and the caption that will display in the Smart Tag menu. The unique identifier is constructed using a namespace URI such as "`http://vsto.aw.com`" and a tag type name such as "`mytagtypename`" separated by a number sign, resulting in "`http://vsto.aw.com#mytagtypename`".

The SmartTag object has several important properties and methods. The SmartTag object's Terms property returns a StringCollection to which you can add words you want to recognize. The SmartTag object's Actions property must be set to an array of Action objects representing the actions (the menu items) you want displayed for your Smart Tag. VSTO provides a class called Action in the Microsoft.Office.Tools.Word namespace and the Microsoft.Office.Tools.Excel namespace that you can instantiate. The constructor of the Action object takes one parameter—the caption that will display in the Smart Tag menu for the action. After you have created an Action object for each action you want to make available for your Smart Tag, you can set the SmartTag.Actions property to an array containing all the Action objects you want to provide. Finally, you can handle the Action.Click event for each Action to be called back by Word or Excel when the user selects that action from the Smart Tag menu.

After you have created a SmartTag object, set the SmartTag.Terms collection, created one or more Action objects, and set SmartTag.Actions, you must remember to add the newly created SmartTag to the VstoSmartTags collection on the VSTO Document object for Word and on the VSTO Workbook object for Excel.

Listing 16-1 shows a simple Word VSTO customization that illustrates these steps. It first creates a SmartTag instance passing `"http://vsto.aw.com#fish"` as the identifier and `"Fish Catcher"` as the caption. It then adds two terms to recognize using SmartTag.Terms: `"Mackerel"` and `"Halibut"`. Note that a term cannot contain a space—for example, a term such as "Eric Carter" could not be added to the terms collection.

Two actions are created, one with the caption `"&Fishing///&Catch a fish"` and the other with the caption `"&Fishing///&Throw it back"`. The ampersand (&) in these strings indicates which letter to use as an accelerator for the menu. The use of the three forward slashes tells Word to create a menu called Fishing with a child menu called Catch a fish and a second child menu called Throw it back. These actions are added to the SmartTag.Actions property by creating a new array of Actions containing both actions. Click events raised by the two actions are handled by the code. Finally, the SmartTag instance that was created is added to the Vsto-SmartTags collection associated with the document object.

Listing 16-1 A VSTO Word Customization That Adds a Smart Tag

```
using System;
using System.Windows.Forms;
using Microsoft.VisualStudio.Tools.Applications.Runtime;
using Word = Microsoft.Office.Interop.Word;
using Office = Microsoft.Office.Core;
using Microsoft.Office.Tools.Word;

namespace WordDocument1
{
  public partial class ThisDocument
  {
    private void ThisDocument_Startup(object sender, EventArgs e)
    {
      SmartTag mySmartTag = new SmartTag(
        "http://vsto.aw.com#fish", "Fish Catcher");
      mySmartTag.Terms.Add("Mackerel");
      mySmartTag.Terms.Add("Halibut");

      Action myAction =
        new Action("&Fishing///&Catch a fish...");
      Action myAction2 =
```

```
      new Action("&Fishing///&Throw it back...");
    mySmartTag.Actions =
      new Action[] { myAction, myAction2 };

    myAction.Click +=
      new ActionClickEventHandler(myAction_Click);
    myAction2.Click +=
      new ActionClickEventHandler(myAction2_Click);

    this.VstoSmartTags.Add(mySmartTag);
  }

  void myAction_Click(object sender, ActionEventArgs e)
  {
    MessageBox.Show(String.Format(
      "You caught a fish at position {0}.",
      e.Range.Start));
  }

  void myAction2_Click(object sender, ActionEventArgs e)
  {
    MessageBox.Show(String.Format(
      "You threw back a fish at position {0}.",
      e.Range.Start));
  }

  #region VSTO Designer generated code
  private void InternalStartup()
  {
    this.Startup += new EventHandler(ThisDocument_Startup);
  }
  #endregion
  }
}
```

The code to add a Smart Tag in Excel is very similar and is shown in Listing 16-2. The main changes are to use the SmartTag and Action classes from the Microsoft.Office.Tools.Excel namespace and to use the VstoSmartTags collection off of the Workbook object. Because the code in Listing 16-2 is written in Sheet1, the Workbook object is accessed using `Globals.ThisWorkbook`.

Listing 16-2 A VSTO Excel Customization That Adds a Smart Tag

```csharp
using System;
using System.Windows.Forms;
using Microsoft.VisualStudio.Tools.Applications.Runtime;
using Excel = Microsoft.Office.Interop.Excel;
using Microsoft.Office.Tools.Excel;

namespace ExcelWorkbook1
{
  public partial class Sheet1
  {
    private void Sheet1_Startup(object sender, EventArgs e)
    {
      SmartTag mySmartTag = new
        SmartTag("http://vsto.aw.com#fish", "Fish Catcher");
      mySmartTag.Terms.Add("Mackerel");
      mySmartTag.Terms.Add("Halibut");

      Action myAction = new Action("Catch a fish...");
      Action myAction2 = new Action("Throw it back...");
      mySmartTag.Actions =
        new Action[] { myAction, myAction2 };

      myAction.Click +=
        new ActionClickEventHandler(myAction_Click);
      myAction2.Click +=
        new ActionClickEventHandler(myAction2_Click);

      Globals.ThisWorkbook.VstoSmartTags.Add(mySmartTag);
    }

    void myAction2_Click(object sender, ActionEventArgs e)
    {
      MessageBox.Show(String.Format(
        "You threw back a fish at address {0}.",
        e.Range.get_Address(missing, missing,
        Excel.XlReferenceStyle.xlA1, missing, missing)));
    }

    void myAction_Click(object sender, ActionEventArgs e)
    {
      MessageBox.Show(String.Format(
        "You caught a fish at address {0}.",
        e.Range.get_Address(missing, missing,
        Excel.XlReferenceStyle.xlA1, missing, missing)));
    }
```

```
#region VSTO Designer generated code
private void InternalStartup()
{
    this.Startup += new EventHandler(Sheet1_Startup);
}
#endregion

    }
}
```

Action Events

In Listing 16-1 and Listing 16-2, we handled the click event of the Action object. The code that handled the click event used the ActionEventArgs argument e and accessed the ActionEventArgs.Range property to get a Word.Range object for Word and an Excel.Range object for Excel. The Range property allows you to access the range of text that was recognized in Word or the Excel cell that contains the recognized text.

The ActionEventArgs.Text property returns the text that was recognized. This proves useful when you are matching multiple string values with a single Smart Tag class.

The ActionEventArgs.Properties property allows you to access a property bag associated with the actions pane. This property bag can be used to store additional information about the text that was recognized. We consider this further in the "Creating a Custom Smart Tag Class" section.

The Action object also raises a BeforeCaptionShow event before the caption for an Action is shown in the actions pane menu. This event is also passed an ActionEventArgs argument e, which can be used to access information about what was recognized just as with the click event. You can use this event to change the caption of the action before it is shown.

Listing 16-3 shows a VSTO Excel customization that handles the Click and BeforeCaptionShow event. You must add a reference to the Microsoft Smart Tags 2.0 Type Library as shown in Figure 16-7 to access the types associated with the property bag.

Listing 16-3 A VSTO Excel Customization That Handles the Click and BeforeCaptionShow Events and Uses the ActionEventArgs Argument

```csharp
using System;
using System.Windows.Forms;
using Microsoft.VisualStudio.Tools.Applications.Runtime;
using Excel = Microsoft.Office.Interop.Excel;
using Microsoft.Office.Tools.Excel;

namespace ExcelWorkbook1
{
  public partial class Sheet1
  {
    Action myAction;
    Action myAction2;

    private void Sheet1_Startup(object sender, EventArgs e)
    {
      SmartTag mySmartTag = new SmartTag(
        "http://vsto.aw.com#fish", "Fish Catcher");
      mySmartTag.Terms.Add("Mackerel");
      mySmartTag.Terms.Add("Halibut");

      myAction = new Action("Catch a fish...");
      myAction2 = new Action("Throw it back...");
      mySmartTag.Actions =
        new Action[] { myAction, myAction2 };

      myAction.Click +=
        new ActionClickEventHandler(myAction_Click);

      myAction.BeforeCaptionShow +=
        new BeforeCaptionShowEventHandler(
        myAction_BeforeCaptionShow);

      myAction2.Click +=
        new ActionClickEventHandler(myAction2_Click);

      Globals.ThisWorkbook.VstoSmartTags.Add(mySmartTag);
    }

    void myAction_BeforeCaptionShow(object sender,
      ActionEventArgs e)
    {
      Random r = new Random();

      myAction.Caption = "Test caption " + r.NextDouble();
    }
```

```csharp
    void myAction2_Click(object sender, ActionEventArgs e)
    {
      MessageBox.Show(String.Format(
        "You threw back a fish at address {0}.",
        e.Range.get_Address(missing, missing,
        Excel.XlReferenceStyle.xlA1, missing, missing)));

      MessageBox.Show(e.Text);
      MessageBox.Show(e.Properties.Count.ToString());
      for (int i = 0; i < e.Properties.Count; i++)
      {
        MessageBox.Show(String.Format(
          "Prop({0},(1})",
          e.Properties.get_KeyFromIndex(i),
          e.Properties.get_ValueFromIndex(i)));
      }
    }

    void myAction_Click(object sender, ActionEventArgs e)
    {
      MessageBox.Show(String.Format(
        "You caught a fish at address {0}.",
        e.Range.get_Address(missing, missing,
        Excel.XlReferenceStyle.xlA1, missing, missing)));
    }

    #region VSTO Designer generated code
    private void InternalStartup()
    {
      this.Startup += new System.EventHandler(Sheet1_Startup);
    }
    #endregion
  }
}
```

Using Varying Numbers of Terms

It is possible to vary the number of terms recognized at runtime by adding and removing terms from the SmartTag.Terms collection. Listing 16-4 shows this approach. Note that instances of terms that have already been typed into the document and recognized will continue to be recognized even when you remove that term from the Terms collection. But new instances of the removed term that you type will no longer be recognized.

Listing 16-4 A VSTO Excel Customization That Varies the Number of Terms Recognized

```
using System;
using System.Windows.Forms;
using Microsoft.VisualStudio.Tools.Applications.Runtime;
using Excel = Microsoft.Office.Interop.Excel;
using Microsoft.Office.Tools.Excel;
using System.Text.RegularExpressions;

namespace ExcelWorkbook1
{
  public partial class Sheet1
  {
    Action myAction;
    SmartTag mySmartTag;

    private void Sheet1_Startup(object sender, EventArgs e)
    {
      mySmartTag = new SmartTag(
        "http://vsto.aw.com#variableterms",
        "Varying Number of Terms");

      mySmartTag.Terms.Add("Hello");

      myAction = new Action("Add a new term...");
      mySmartTag.Actions = new Action[] { myAction};

      myAction.Click +=
        new ActionClickEventHandler(myAction_Click);

      Globals.ThisWorkbook.VstoSmartTags.Add(mySmartTag);
    }

    void myAction_Click(object sender, ActionEventArgs e)
    {
      Random r = new Random();
      int numberOfActionsToShow = r.Next(5);

      if (mySmartTag.Terms.Contains(
        numberOfActionsToShow.ToString()) == true)
      {
        mySmartTag.Terms.Remove(
          numberOfActionsToShow.ToString());
        MessageBox.Show(String.Format(
          "Removed the term {0}.",
          numberOfActionsToShow));
      }
      else
      {
```

```
      mySmartTag.Terms.Add(
        numberOfActionsToShow.ToString());
      MessageBox.Show(String.Format(
      "Added the term {0}.",
      numberOfActionsToShow));
    }
  }

  #region VSTO Designer generated code
  private void InternalStartup()
  {
    this.Startup += new System.EventHandler(Sheet1_Startup);
  }
  #endregion
  }
}
```

Using Regular Expressions

Although the Terms collection provides a way to recognize specific words, you will inevitably want to have more power in the text patterns that are recognized. The SmartTag class allows you to use regular expressions to recognize text in a Word document or Excel spreadsheet. This book does not cover how to construct a regular expression—if regular expressions are new to you, try looking at the documentation in the .NET Framework for the Regex class.

We are going to construct a regular expression that will match stock symbols in a document. A stock symbol will be defined as any three- or four-letter combination that is in all caps, such as IBM or MSFT. The regular expression we will use is shown below and will match a word (`\b` indicates a word boundary) that is composed of three to four characters (specified by `{3,4}`) composed of capital letters from A to Z (`[A-Z]`):

```
\b[A-Z]{3,4}\b
```

This regular expression string is passed to the constructor of a Regex object. The Regex object is then added to the SmartTag.Expressions collection, as shown in Listing 16-5.

Listing 16-5 A VSTO Excel Customization That Adds a Smart Tag Using a Regular Expression

```
using System;
using System.Windows.Forms;
```

```csharp
using Microsoft.VisualStudio.Tools.Applications.Runtime;
using Excel = Microsoft.Office.Interop.Excel;
using Microsoft.Office.Tools.Excel;
using System.Text.RegularExpressions;

namespace ExcelWorkbook4
{
  public partial class Sheet1
  {
    Action myAction;

    private void Sheet1_Startup(object sender, EventArgs e)
    {
      SmartTag mySmartTag = new SmartTag(
        "http://vsto.aw.com#stock", "Stock Trader");
      Regex myRegex = new Regex(@"\b[A-Z]{3,4}\b");

      mySmartTag.Expressions.Add(myRegex);

      myAction = new Action("Trade this stock...");
      mySmartTag.Actions = new Action[] { myAction };

      myAction.Click +=
        new ActionClickEventHandler(myAction_Click);

      Globals.ThisWorkbook.VstoSmartTags.Add(mySmartTag);
    }

    void myAction_Click(object sender, ActionEventArgs e)
    {
      MessageBox.Show(String.Format(
        "The stock symbol you selected is {0}", e.Text));
    }

    #region VSTO Designer generated code
    private void InternalStartup()
    {
      this.Startup += new EventHandler(Sheet1_Startup);
    }
    #endregion
  }
}
```

Another great feature when you use regular expressions is VSTO's support for named groups in a regular expression. When you create a regular expression with a named group, VSTO creates a name value pair in the property bag for each recognized term with the name and value of each named group recognized by the regular expression. You can use the ActionEventArgs object's Properties object to retrieve the value of a named group by using the group name as a key.

Using Varying Numbers of Actions

You might have wondered why the SmartTag object has an Actions property that must be set to a fixed array of Actions. After all, wouldn't it be easier if you could write the code `mySmartTag.Actions.Add(myAction)`? The reason the Actions property was designed this way is to enforce the notion that the maximum number of actions for a given Smart Tag is fixed at the time you add the SmartTag object to the VstoSmartTags collection. This is a limitation of the Office Smart Tags architecture.

However, there is a way to have a varying number of actions. There is still the limitation that the maximum number of actions is fixed at the time you first add it to the VstoSmartTags collection. But you can then at runtime set actions within the array to `null` to vary the number of available actions up to the maximum number of actions. Listing 16-6 shows this approach. The maximum number of actions is set to be five actions by setting the initial array of actions to contain five actions. But each time an action is selected, the number of actions is changed by setting the items in the actions array to `null` or to an Action object.

Listing 16-6 A VSTO Excel Customization with a Varying Number of Actions

```
using System;
using System.Windows.Forms;
using Microsoft.VisualStudio.Tools.Applications.Runtime;
using Excel = Microsoft.Office.Interop.Excel;
using Microsoft.Office.Tools.Excel;
using System.Text.RegularExpressions;

namespace ExcelWorkbook4
{
  public partial class Sheet1
  {
    Action myAction;
    SmartTag mySmartTag;

    private void Sheet1_Startup(object sender, EventArgs e)
    {
      mySmartTag = new SmartTag(
        "http://vsto.aw.com#variableactions",
```

```
      "Varying Number of Actions");
    Regex myRegex = new Regex(@"\b[A-Z]{3,4}\b");

    mySmartTag.Expressions.Add(myRegex);

    myAction = new Action("Change Number of Actions...");
    mySmartTag.Actions = new Action[]
      { myAction, myAction, myAction, myAction, myAction};

    myAction.Click +=
      new ActionClickEventHandler(myAction_Click);

    Globals.ThisWorkbook.VstoSmartTags.Add(mySmartTag);
}

void myAction_Click(object sender, ActionEventArgs e)
{
    Random r = new Random();
    int numberOfActionsToShow = 1 + r.Next(4);

    MessageBox.Show(String.Format(
      "Changing to have {0} actions.",
      numberOfActionsToShow));

    for (int i = 0; i < numberOfActionsToShow; i++)
    {
      mySmartTag.Actions[i] = myAction;
    }

    for (int i = numberOfActionsToShow; i < 5; i++)
    {
      mySmartTag.Actions[i] = null;
    }

}

#region VSTO Designer generated code
private void InternalStartup()
{
  this.Startup += new EventHandler(Sheet1_Startup);
}
#endregion

  }
}
```

Creating a Custom Smart Tag Class

When the Terms collection and the Expressions collection are not sufficient to meet your Smart Tag recognition needs, you also have the option of creating your own custom Smart Tag class that derives from the Word or Excel SmartTag class. This gives you some additional capability. First of all, you get to write your own code to process text that Word or Excel passes to your Smart Tag class to recognize. Second, you can use the ISmartTagProperties collection to associate custom Smart Tag properties in the property bag associated with each instance of recognized text.

For example, suppose you are writing a Smart Tag that recognizes part numbers that are stored in a database. You know that part numbers are in a format such as PN1023, with a PN preface and four following digits. However, just because that pattern is found in the text does not mean it is a valid part number. It might be a part number that has been deleted or does not exist in the database. So after finding a match for the expected part number format, you also want to make a call into the database to make sure a row exists for the given part number. If the part number is not in the database, you do not want to tag it.

You can do this by writing your own custom Smart Tag class. Your class must derive from the Word or Excel SmartTag class in the Microsoft.Office.Tools.Word or Microsoft.Office.Tools.Excel namespaces. Your class must have a constructor that calls into the base class constructor passing the Smart Tag type name and the caption for the Smart Tag. The custom class must also override the Recognize method of the base class shown here:

```
protected override void Recognize(string text,
  Microsoft.Office.Interop.SmartTag.ISmartTagRecognizerSite site,
   Microsoft.Office.Interop.SmartTag.ISmartTagTokenList tokenList)
{
}
```

The Recognize method passes the text to recognize as a `string`, an ISmartTagRecognizerSite object that your code will use if it associates custom Smart Tag properties with an instance of recognized text, and a `tokenList` parameter. Your implementation of Recognize could find the basic part number format, and if a match is found it can then look up the part number in a database to verify it is a valid part number. If it is a valid part number, your implementation of Recognize must call into the base class's PersistTag method to specify the index within the text that the part number occurred, the length of the part number, and optionally specify custom Smart Tag properties to associate with the text that will be tagged.

Custom Smart Tag properties are useful when you need to cache additional information that was determined at recognize time that might be used later when an action associated with a tag is executed. In our example, we have talked to a database to get the row out of the database corresponding to the part number. Perhaps one of the actions available will be to display the price of the part. Because we have accessed the database row for the part, we have the price already. Rather than have to look up the price again in the database when the action displaying the price is invoked, you could choose to create custom Smart Tag properties and add the price as a custom property to the recognized text. A custom Smart Tag properties collection of type ISmartTagProperties can be created by calling the GetNewPropertyBag method on the ISmartTagRecognizerSite object passed into the Recognize method. To get the definition of ISmartTagProperties and ISmartTagRecognizerSite, you must add a reference to your project to the Microsoft Smart Tags 2.0 Type Library, as shown in Figure 16-7.

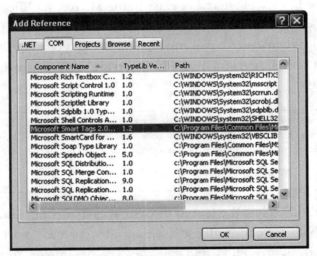

Figure 16-7 A reference to the Microsoft Smart Tags 2.0 Type Library is required to use the ISmartTagProperties and ISmart-TagRecognizerSite interfaces in your code.

The code in Listing 16-7 illustrates these ideas by defining a custom Smart Tag class that recognizes part numbers of the format PN1023 and uses ISmartTagRecognizerSite, ISmartTagProperties, and the PersistTag method to associate the custom property "Price" with a part number that has been recognized. Our class `Custom-SmartTag` derives from the SmartTag class in the Microsoft.Office.Tools.Word namespace because this custom Smart Tag will be used with Word. It implements a simple constructor that calls into the base constructor passing an identifier and caption. An action is created and added to the Smart Tag that will display the part cost already stored in the tagged text. It does this by accessing the ISmartTagProperties associated with the tagged text using the Properties property of the ActionEventArgs argument passed to the Action.Click event.

We override the Recognize method to write custom logic that looks for the part number and then calls `IsValidPart` to find out whether the part number is in the database and get the price for the part if available. The implementation of `IsValid-Part` does not actually connect to a database for this sample, but instead requires a part number be greater than 1000. To simulate getting a price from a database, it generates a random price that will be saved in the document when the text is tagged. You can easily imagine this function being rewritten to query a database instead.

Listing 16-7 A Custom Smart Tag Class for Word

```
using System;
using System.Collections.Generic;
using System.Text;
using Microsoft.Office.Tools.Word;
using System.Windows.Forms;
using SmartTag = Microsoft.Office.Interop.SmartTag;

namespace WordDocument1
{
  internal class CustomSmartTag : SmartTag
  {
    Action customAction;

    internal CustomSmartTag()
      : base(
      "http://www.aw-bc.com/VSTO#customsmarttag",
      "Custom Smart Tag")
    {
      customAction = new Action("Get Part Cost...");
      base.Actions = new Action[] { customAction };
```

```csharp
    customAction.Click +=
      new ActionClickEventHandler(customAction_Click);
}

  void customAction_Click(object sender, ActionEventArgs e)
  {
    ISmartTagProperties props = e.Properties;
    for (int i = 0; i < props.Count; i++)
    {
      MessageBox.Show(String.Format(
        "{0} - {1}", props.get_KeyFromIndex(i),
        props.get_ValueFromIndex(i)));
    }
  }

  protected override void Recognize(string text,
    ISmartTagRecognizerSite site,
    ISmartTagTokenList tokenList)
  {
    string textToFind = "PN";

    int startIndex = 0;
    int index = 0;

    while ((index = text.IndexOf(
      textToFind, startIndex)) >= 0)
    {
      if (index + 6 < text.Length)
      {
        string partNumber = text.Substring(index, 6);
        string price = "";
        if (IsValidPart(partNumber, out price))
        {
          ISmartTagProperties props =
            site.GetNewPropertyBag();
          props.Write("Price", price);
          base.PersistTag(index, 6, props);
        }
      }

      startIndex = index + textToFind.Length;
    }
  }

  private bool IsValidPart(string partNumber, out string price)
  {
    int numericPartNumber = 0;
    try
```

```
    {
      numericPartNumber = Convert.ToInt32(
        partNumber.Substring(2, 4));
    }
    catch { };

    // Only part numbers greater than 1000 are valid
    if (numericPartNumber > 1000)
    {
      Random rnd = new Random();
      price = rnd.Next(100).ToString();
      return true;
    }

    price = "N/A";
    return false;
  }
}
}
```

To add this custom Smart Tag to the document, you must put this code in the Startup method of your document:

```
private void ThisDocument_Startup(object sender, EventArgs e)
{
  this.VstoSmartTags.Add(new CustomSmartTag());
}
```

Using Smart Tag Properties Wisely

You must consider some other issues when using Smart Tag properties. These properties are serialized into the document, and the recognizer is not given a chance to re-recognize text that has already been recognized. For example, you might type in the part number on May 1 and the Recognize method runs. You then save the document and the price is saved with the document. When you reopen the document on May 31 and click the Smart Tag menu to select the Get Part Cost action, the action will go to the Smart Tag property created on May 1 and display the May 1 price. Therefore, if the price of parts frequently changes, the part price stored as a custom property may be out of date when the action is invoked at some time later than when the Recognize method was called.

Also, remember that any Smart Tag properties you put in the document for recognized text will be visible in the saved document file format. So be sure not to put Smart Tag properties in the document containing sensitive information. For example, you could have a document full of part numbers that you send to a competitor. If the custom Smart Tag in Listing 16-7 has recognized all the part numbers in the document before you save the document and send it to the competitor, the prices of all those parts will also be embedded in the document with each tagged part number.

Creating Application-Level Smart Tags

VSTO's document-level Smart Tags are great when you want to recognize a term in a particular document or a class of document created from a template. What are your options when you want to recognize a term in all open documents?

You can control the text that Word or Excel recognizes at an application level and the actions made available for that text by creating a Smart Tag DLL. A Smart Tag DLL contains two types of classes that are used by Office: a recognizer class and an action class. A recognizer class tells Office the text in the workbook to recognize. The recognizer class "tags" recognized text by creating a property bag—even an empty property bag—and attaching it to recognized text. An action class corresponds to an action displayed in the pop-up menu that Office displays when a user hovers over a recognized piece of text. Recognizer classes implement the ISmartTagRecognizer interface and optionally the ISmartTagRecognizer2 interface. Action classes implement the ISmartTagAction interface and optionally the ISmartTagAction2 interface.

Creating an Application-Level Smart Tag Class Library in Visual Studio

To create a Smart Tag class library DLL, start Visual Studio. Choose New Project from the File menu and create a new class library project as shown in Figure 16-8.

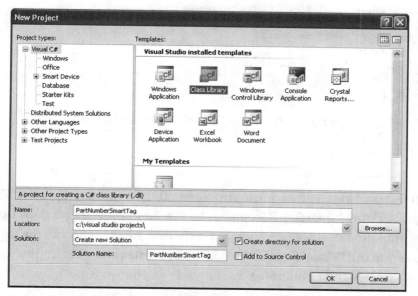

Figure 16-8 Creating a new class library project.

With the class library project created, right-click the References node in the Solution Explorer window and choose Add Reference. Click the COM tab and add a reference to the Microsoft Smart Tags 2.0 Type Library, as shown in Figure 16-7. Doing so gives you a definition for the two interfaces you have to implement—ISmartTag-Recognizer and ISmartTagAction.

Creating a Recognizer Class

Let us start by creating a class that implements ISmartTagRecognizer. Our class will be similar to the class we created in Listing 16-7 and will recognize part numbers in a document. In the newly created project, there is already a class created for you called Class1 in a file called Class1.cs. Add a `using SmartTag = Microsoft.Office.Interop.SmartTag` line to the `using` statements at the top of the class to bring the SmartTag interfaces into a namespace called SmartTag. Rename Class1 to be a class called `Recognizer`, and declare the class to implement Smart-Tag.ISmartTagRecognizer. The class now looks like this:

```
using System;
using System.Collections.Generic;
using System.Text;
using SmartTag = Microsoft.Office.Interop.SmartTag;

namespace PartNumberSmartTag
{
  public class Recognizer : SmartTag.ISmartTagRecognizer
  {
  }
}
```

Visual Studio provides a neat trick for implementing the ISmartTagRecognizer interface. Right-click the ISmartTagRecognizer text in the class. A menu pops up that displays an Implement Interface menu. From this menu, choose the Implement Interface command. Visual Studio automatically creates an initial implementation of the ISmartTagRecognizer interface, as shown in Listing 16-8

Listing 16-8 An Initial Stub Implementation of a Smart Tag Recognizer Class

```
using System;
using System.Collections.Generic;
using System.Text;
using SmartTag = Microsoft.Office.Interop.SmartTag;

namespace PartNumberSmartTag
{
  public class Recognizer : SmartTag.ISmartTagRecognizer
  {
    #region ISmartTagRecognizer Members

    public string ProgId
    {
      get { }
    }

    public void Recognize(string text,
      SmartTag.IF_TYPE dataType,
      int localeID,
      SmartTag.ISmartTagRecognizerSite site)
    {
    }

    public int SmartTagCount
    {
      get { }
```

```
        }

        public string get_Desc(int localeID)
        {
        }

        public string get_Name(int localeID)
        {
        }

        public string get_SmartTagDownloadURL(int smartTagID)
        {
        }

        public string get_SmartTagName(int smartTagID)
        {
        }

        #endregion
    }
```

There are two properties (ProgID and SmartTagCount) and five methods (Recognize, get_Desc, get_Name, get_SmartTagDownloadURL, and get_SmartTagName) that we must implement. Let's start by implementing the properties.

The ProgID property is only required for COM Smart Tags. For our Smart Tag, we will just return `null`.

```
public string ProgId
{
  get { return null; }
}
```

Now let's implement the SmartTagCount property. Normally, this property should just return the `int` value 1. This property does not affect how many terms our recognizer can recognize, it just affects how many unique recognizers our Smart Tag recognizer class provides. For simplicity, it is usually easiest to have one Smart Tag recognizer class expose one unique recognizer.

```
public int SmartTagCount
{
  get { return 1; }
}
```

The get_Desc method takes a locale ID as an `int` and returns a `string` representing the description of the Smart Tag recognizer. You can use the locale ID to provide localized descriptions if you want to. For our purposes, the code will just return a simple description `string` for all locales.

```
public string get_Desc(int localeID)
{
   return "Recognizes Part Numbers in PN#### format.";
}
```

The get_Name method takes a locale ID as an `int` and returns a `string` representing the name of the Smart Tag recognizer. When the Smart Tag is listed in an Office dialog, this name will display in parenthesis to the right of the string returned by get_SmartTagCaption in the Action class. get_Name should return a string no longer than 30 characters. We'll return the string `"English"` to indicate to the user that our Smart Tag is not localized into other locales:

```
public string get_Name (int localeID)
{
   return "English";
}
```

The get_SmartTagDownloadURL method takes a Smart Tag ID as an `int` and returns a URL as a `string` where Smart Tag actions associated with this recognizer can be downloaded from. For this example, we will be providing the Smart Tag action class in the same DLL, so we will always return `null`.

```
public string get_SmartTagDownloadURL(int smartTagID)
{
   return null;
}
```

This is the first method we have seen that is passed a `smartTagID` as a parameter. A Smart Tag ID is an `int` value that for this recognizer class will always be passed 1 because the code returns 1 for the SmartTagCount property. If the code returned some other number for SmartTagCount—say 5—all methods that are passed a Smart

Tag ID parameter in the recognizer class would be called five times, once with smart-TagID set to 1, then 2, then 3, and so forth. This lets one Smart Tag recognizer class provide multiple Smart Tags recognizers.

The get_SmartTagName method takes a Smart Tag ID as an `int` and returns a unique identifier as a `string` for the Smart Tag. The identifier must be in the form namespaceURI#tagname. A valid namespace URI would be something like a company Web site URL followed by a unique directory for the Smart Tag name. So in our case, we will use the URL http://www.aw-bc.com/VSTO. For the tag name, we will use our Smart Tag namespace PartNumberSmartTag. The critical thing when constructing your Smart Tag name is to make sure it will be unique and not conflict with Smart Tags released by other companies or by your company:

```
public string get_SmartTagName(int smartTagID)
{
    return @"http://www.aw-bc.com/VSTO#PartNumberSmartTag";
}
```

Now we have arrived at the method that does all the work of recognizing text in the document—the Recognize method. The method is passed parameters very similar to those passed to Recognize in Listing 16-7. The text to be looked at by our code is passed in as a `string`. The locale ID is passed in if our recognizer needs to recognize different text depending on the locale. An instance of the ISmartTagRecognizerSite interface is passed in as well. We will use this interface to associate a property bag with any text we recognize in the document.

Text that is recognized is marked with a property bag. The property bag can be empty—but for this example, we will stick a name value pair in the property bag to store a price. When we find some text we recognize, we must create a new property bag using ISmartTagRecognizerSite's GetNewPropertyBag method. This method returns an ISmartTagProperties object. We can use this object to write name value pairs into the property bag through ISmartTagProperties Write method that takes a key as a `string` and a value as a `string`. For this example, we will generate a property with key of `"Price"` and value being the price of the part identified by the part number we locate in the document.

To tell Office where recognized text is found, you must call ISmartTagRecognizerSite's CommitSmartTag method. This method takes the Smart Tag name as a string (we just call our existing implementation of get_SmartTagName to get this), the 1-based start position of the recognized text as an int, the length of the text we recognized as an int, and the ISmartTagProperties object we created using the Get-NewPropertyBag method. This is a little different from the document-level custom class we created in Listing 16-7 where the start position of the recognized text was 0-based.

Listing 16-9 shows the final implementation of our Recognizer class.

Listing 16-9 The Final Implementation of a Smart Tag Recognizer Class

```
using System;
using System.Collections.Generic;
using System.Text;
using SmartTag = Microsoft.Office.Interop.SmartTag;

namespace PartNumberSmartTag
{
  public class Recognizer : SmartTag.ISmartTagRecognizer
  {
    #region ISmartTagRecognizer Members

    public string ProgId
    {
      get { return null; }
    }

    public void Recognize(string text,
      SmartTag.IF_TYPE dataType,
      int localeID,
      SmartTag.ISmartTagRecognizerSite site)
    {
      string textToFind = "PN";
      const int length = 6; // Found part numbers will
                            // always be 6 characters long

      int startIndex = 0;
      int index = 0;

      while ((index =
        text.IndexOf(textToFind, startIndex)) >= 0)
      {
        if (index + length <= text.Length)
        {
          string partNumber = text.Substring(index, length);
          string price = "";
```

```
        if (IsValidPart(partNumber, out price))
        {
          SmartTag.ISmartTagProperties props =
            site.GetNewPropertyBag();

          props.Write("Price", price);
          site.CommitSmartTag(get_SmartTagName(1),
            index +1, // add 1 because this is 1-based
            length, props);
        }
      }

    startIndex = index + textToFind.Length;
  }
}

public int SmartTagCount
{
  get { return 1; }
}

public string get_Desc(int LocaleID)
{
  return "Recognizes Part Numbers in PN#### format.";
}

public string get_Name(int LocaleID)
{
  return "English";
}

public string get_SmartTagDownloadURL(int SmartTagID)
{
  return null;
}

public string get_SmartTagName(int SmartTagID)
{
  return @"http://www.aw-bc.com/VSTO#PartNumberSmartTag";
}

#endregion

private bool IsValidPart(string partNumber,
  out string price)
{
  int numericPartNumber = 0;
```

```
    try
    {
      numericPartNumber = Convert.ToInt32(
        partNumber.Substring(2, 4));
    }
    catch { }

    // Only part numbers greater than 1000 are valid
    if (numericPartNumber > 1000)
    {
      Random rnd = new Random();
      price = rnd.Next(100).ToString();
      return true;
    }

    price = "N/A";
    return false;
    }
  }
}
```

Creating an Action Class

Now that we have a complete Smart Tag recognizer class, we will create a Smart Tag action class. Right-click the class library project in Solution Explorer and choose Add and then Class to add a second class to the project. Visual Studio will create a class called Class2 by default. Add a `using SmartTag = Microsoft.Office.Interop.SmartTag` line to the using statements at the top of the class to bring the Smart Tag interfaces into a namespace called SmartTag. Rename Class2 to be a class called `Action` and declare the class to implement SmartTag.ISmartTagAction. The class now looks like this:

```
using System;
using System.Collections.Generic;
using System.Text;
using SmartTag = Microsoft.Office.Interop.SmartTag;

namespace PartNumberSmartTag
{
  class Action : SmartTag.ISmartTagAction
  {
  }
}
```

Use the "Implement Interface" trick again for implementing the ISmartTagAction interface. Right-click the ISmartTagAction text in the class. A menu pops up that displays an Implement Interface menu. From this menu, choose the Implement Interface command. Visual Studio automatically creates an initial implementation of the ISmartTagAction interface, as shown in Listing 16-10.

Listing 16-10 An Initial Stub Implementation of a Smart Tag Action Class

```
using System;
using System.Collections.Generic;
using System.Text;
using SmartTag = Microsoft.Office.Interop.SmartTag;

namespace PartNumberSmartTag
{
  class Action : SmartTag.ISmartTagAction
  {
    #region ISmartTagAction Members

    public string ProgId
    {
      get { }
    }

    public int SmartTagCount
    {
      get { }
    }

    public string get_Desc(int localeID)
    {
    }

    public string get_Name(int localeID)
    {
    }

    public string get_SmartTagCaption(int smartTagID, int localeID)
    {
    }

    public string get_SmartTagName(int smartTagID)
    {
    }

    public int get_VerbCount(string smartTagName)
    {
```

```
        }

        public int get_VerbID(string smartTagName, int verbIndex)
        {
        }

        public string get_VerbCaptionFromID(int verbID,
            string applicationName, int localeID)
        {
        }

        public string get_VerbNameFromID(int verbID)
        {
        }

        public void InvokeVerb(int verbID, string applicationName,
            object target, SmartTag.ISmartTagProperties properties,
            string text, string xml)
        {
        }

        #endregion
    }
}
```

There are two properties (ProgID and SmartTagCount) and nine methods (Invoke-Verb, get_Desc, get_Name, get_SmartTagCaption, get_SmartTagName, get_Verb-CaptionFromID, get_VerbCount, get_VerbID, and get_VerbNameFromID) that we must implement. Let's start by implementing the properties.

The ProgID property returns `null` because it is only used for COM Smart Tags:

```
public string ProgId
{
    get { return null; }
}
```

Now let's implement the SmartTagCount property. As described earlier, for simplicity, it is usually easiest to just return 1. This does not affect how many available "verbs" or menu commands we can provide for a recognized part number:

```
public int SmartTagCount
{
    get { return 1; }
}
```

The get_Desc method takes a locale ID as an `int` and returns a `string` representing the description of the Smart Tag action. You can use the locale ID to provide localized descriptions if you want to. For our purposes, the code will just return a simple description `string` for all locales:

```
public string get_Desc(int localeID)
{
  return "Provides actions for the part number Smart Tag.";
}
```

The get_Name method takes a locale ID as an `int` and returns a `string` representing the name of the Smart Tag action. The name should match what you returned for your Recognizer class:

```
public string get_Name (int localeID)
{
  return "PN####";
}
```

The get_SmartTagName method takes a Smart Tag ID as an `int` and returns a unique identifier as a `string` for the Smart Tag. The identifier should match what was returned in the Recognizer class implementation:

```
public string get_SmartTagName(int smartTagID)
{
  return @"http://www.aw-bc.com/VSTO#PartNumberSmartTag";
}
```

The get_SmartTagCaption method takes a Smart Tag ID as an `int` and a locale ID as an `int`. It returns a `string` that will be the caption used in the pop-up menu for the recognized text. It will also be used as the primary name of the Smart Tag in Office's Smart Tag dialogs:

```
public string get_SmartTagCaption(int smartTagID, int localeID)
{
  return "Part Number Smart Tag";
}
```

The get_VerbCount method returns as an `int` how many verbs or menu commands that this Action will provide to the Smart Tag menu. It passes as a parameter the

Smart Tag name for which the verb count is requested—you can ignore this parameter if you returned 1 for the SmartTagCount property. For this example, we provide two verbs or menu commands, one to display the price and the other to open a Web page to the price. So the implementation of get_VerbCount returns 2:

```
public int get_VerbCount(string SmartTagName)
{
  return 2;
}
```

The get_VerbID method gets a unique `int` identifier called a verb ID for each verb. This method is passed a verb index as an `int` that will be a number 1 through the number of verbs returned from the get_VerbCount implementation. For simplicity, we just reuse the verbIndex passed into this method as the verb ID:

```
public int get_VerbID(string smartTagName, int verbIndex)
{
  return verbIndex;
}
```

The get_VerbCaptionFromID method is passed a verb ID number as an `int`, the application name showing the Smart Tag as a `string`, and the locale ID as an `int`. Because we are just using the verb index as the verb ID because of how we implemented get_VerbID, the verb ID passed in will be 1 through the number of verbs returned from get_VerbCount. The method returns a `string` for the menu command caption to use for each verb supported by the action class.

Within the string, you can use three forward slashes in a row to create submenus and the ampersand (&) characters to tell Office what to use for accelerators in the menus. Here we have defined the return strings so we will have a Part Number menu with two submenus: Show part price and Show part Web page. We have also indicated that "N" should be the accelerator for the Part Number menu, "P" should be the accelerator for the Show part price sub menu, and "W" should be the accelerator for the Show part Web page sub menu.

```
public string get_VerbCaptionFromID(int verbID,
  string applicationName, int localeID)
{
  switch (verbID)
```

```
    {
      case 1:
        return "Part &Number///Show part &price...";
      case 2:
        return "Part &Number///Show part &web page...";
      default:
        return null;
    }
  }
```

The get_VerbNameFromID method take a verb ID as an `int` and returns an identifier `string` for each verb. We just return some unique strings for our two verbs:

```
public string get_VerbNameFromID(int verbID)
{
  switch (verbID)
  {
    case 1:
      return "ShowPartPrice";
    case 2:
      return "ShowPartWebPage";
    default:
      return null;
  }
}
```

Now we have arrived at the method that does all the work of handling a selected verb—the InvokeVerb method. This method takes the verb ID as an `int`, the name of the application the Smart Tag is being displayed in as a `string`, the property bag associated with the recognized text as an ISmartTagProperties object, the text that was recognized as a `string`, and the XML that was recognized as a `string`.

The implementation of InvokeVerb for this example first checks what verb is passed. Because the Smart Tag returned 2 for get_VerbCount, it will be passed a verb ID of 1 or 2. If the verb ID is 1, the code displays the price of the item by using the ISmartTagProperties object to read the price value the Recognizer class wrote to the property bag when it recognized the text. If the verb ID is 2, the code displays a dialog threatening to launch a Web page for the part number, which is passed in as the recognized text string. Listing 16-11 shows the complete implementation of our Action class. Because the Action class displays a message box, be sure to add a reference to the System.Windows.Forms library.

Listing 16-11 The Final Implementation of a Smart Tag Action Class

```
using System;
using System.Collections.Generic;
using System.Text;
using SmartTag = Microsoft.Office.Interop.SmartTag;
using System.Windows.Forms;

namespace PartNumberSmartTag
{
  class Action : SmartTag.ISmartTagAction
  {
    #region ISmartTagAction Members

    public string ProgId
    {
      get
      {
        return null;
      }
    }

    public int SmartTagCount
    {
      get
      {
        return 1;
      }
    }

    public string get_Desc(int LocaleID)
    {
      return "Provides actions for the part number Smart Tag.";
    }

    public string get_Name(int LocaleID)
    {
      return "The PN#### Smart Tag";
    }

    public string get_SmartTagCaption(int SmartTagID,
      int LocaleID)
    {
      return "Part Number Smart Tag";
    }

    public string get_SmartTagName(int SmartTagID)
    {
      return @"http://www.aw-bc.com/VSTO#PartNumberSmartTag";
    }
```

```
public int get_VerbCount(string smartTagName)
{
  return 2;
}

public int get_VerbID(string smartTagName, int verbIndex)
{
  return verbIndex;
}

public string get_VerbCaptionFromID(int verbID,
  string applicationName, int localeID)
{
  switch (verbID)
  {
    case 1:
      return "Part &Number///Show part &price...";
    case 2:
      return "Part &Number///Show part &web page...";
    default:
      return null;
  }
}

public string get_VerbNameFromID(int verbID)
{
  switch (verbID)
  {
    case 1:
      return "ShowPartPrice";
    case 2:
      return "ShowPartWebPage";
    default:
      return null;

  }
}

public void InvokeVerb(int verbID, string applicationName,
  object target, SmartTag.ISmartTagProperties properties,
  string text, string xml)
{
  switch (verbID)
  {
    case 1:
      string price = properties.get_Read("Price");
      MessageBox.Show(String.Format(
        "The price of the part is {0}.", price));
      break;
```

```
      case 2:
        MessageBox.Show(String.Format(
          "Launching web page for part {0}.", text));
        break;
    }
  }
  #endregion
}
}
```

Registering and Trusting an Application-Level Smart Tag Class Library

After you have completely implemented your Recognizer and Action class in your class library project, build the project to create a class library DLL. Then copy the class library DLL that was built to a convenient directory—in this example, we copy it to C:\PartNumberSmartTag\PartNumberSmartTag.dll.

Office can load the Smart Tag DLL we have created directly and without any of the problems associated with managed add-ins described in Chapter 23, "Developing COM Add-Ins for Word and Excel." Office will check the .NET 1.1 security policy to decide whether to trust the DLL. If there is policy in place to trust the Smart Tag DLL, Office will load the Smart Tag DLL into its own application domain.

We must do three things to get our Smart Tag to work:

1. We must register the Smart Tag recognizer class in the registry.
2. We must register the Smart Tag action class in the registry.
3. We must configure .NET 1.1 policy (not 2.0 policy) to trust the Smart Tag DLL.

The final requirement seems counterintuitive—why would we have to configure .NET 1.1 policy? After all, we built the Smart Tag with Visual Studio 2005 against .NET 2.0. The reason is that trust decisions for managed Smart Tags loaded by Office 2003 are made based on .NET 1.1 policy even when Office is running a newer version of .NET.

Registering the Smart Tag Recognizer Class in the Registry

To register the Smart Tag class library in the registry, we must add a registry entry for the Recognizer class and a registry entry for the Smart Tag Recognizer class. Recognizer classes are registered under this path in the registry:

```
HKEY_CURRENT_USER\Software\Microsoft\Office\Common\Smart Tag\Recognizers
```

Under this path, we must create a new key that has as its name the full name of the managed Recognizer class. In our case, we created a class called Recognizer in the namespace PartNumberSmartTag. Therefore, the full name of the managed Recognizer class is PartNumberSmartTag.Recognizer. We will create a new registry key named as follows:

```
HKEY_CURRENT_USER\Software\Microsoft\Office\Common\Smart Tag\
  Recognizers\PartNumberSmartTag.Recognizer
```

Under the new PartNumberSmartTag.Recognizer registry key, we will create a string value called Filename that is set to the full filename of the Smart Tag DLL (in our example, C:\PartNumberSmartTag\PartNumberSmartTag.dll).

We will also create under the new PartNumberSmartTag.Recognizer registry key a DWORD value called Managed that we will set to 1.

Listing 16-12 shows the final registry settings for registering the Recognizer class when exported to a .reg file.

Listing 16-12 Registry Entries to Register the Recognizer Class

```
[HKEY_CURRENT_USER\Software\Microsoft\Office\Common\Smart Tag\
Recognizers\PartNumberSmartTag.Recognizer]
"Filename"="c:\\PartNumberSmartTag\\PartNumberSmartTag.dll"
"Managed"=dword:00000001
```

Registering the Smart Tag Action Class in the Registry

With the Recognizer class registered, the next step is to register the Smart Tag Action class in the registry. Action classes are registered under this path in the registry:

```
HKEY_CURRENT_USER\Software\Microsoft\Office\Common\Smart Tag\Actions
```

Under this path, we must create a new key that has as its name the full name of the managed Action class. In our case, we created a class called Action in the namespace PartNumberSmartTag. Therefore, the full name of the managed Action class is Part-NumberSmartTag.Action. We will create a new registry key named as follows:

```
HKEY_CURRENT_USER\Software\Microsoft\Office\Common\Smart Tag\
  Actions\PartNumberSmartTag.Action
```

Under the new PartNumberSmartTag.Action registry key, we will create a string value called "Filename" that is set to the full filename of the Smart Tag DLL (in our example, C:\PartNumberSmartTag\PartNumberSmartTag.dll).

We will also create under the new PartNumberSmartTag.Action registry key a DWORD value called Managed that we will set to 1.

Listing 16-13 shows the final registry settings for registering the Action class when exported to a .reg file.

Listing 16-13 Registry Entries to Register the Action Class

```
[HKEY_CURRENT_USER\Software\Microsoft\Office\Common\Smart Tag\
Actions\PartNumberSmartTag.Action]
"Filename"="c:\\PartNumberSmartTag\\PartNumberSmartTag.dll"
"Managed"=dword:00000001
```

Setting Up .NET 1.1 Security Policy to Trust the Smart Tag Class Library

The final step is to set up .NET 1.1 security policy to trust the Smart Tag class library. We will consider how to configure .NET security policy in more detail in Chapter 19, ".NET Code Security." For now, we will use a command-line tool called caspol.exe that configures .NET security policy. From the command line, navigate to the version of caspol.exe that will be at a path such as C:\Windows\Microsoft.NET\Framework\v1.1.4322. In this directory, run the following command:

```
caspol -user -addgroup "All_Code" -url c:\PartNumberSmartTag\PartNumberSmart-
Tag.dll FullTrust -name "PartNumberSmartTag"
```

This command adds user-level security policy under the existing code group called All_Code, a new code group called PartNumberSmartTag that grants full trust to our DLL C:\PartNumberSmartTag\PartNumberSmartTag.dll.

Running and Testing the Application-Level Smart Tag

Now, launch Word or Excel to test the Smart Tag. Type text such as **PN1234** into Word or into an Excel cell. You will see that a Smart Tag appears. Click the Smart Tag indicator and the menu shown in Figure 16-9 will display. Note that because of the strings we returned from get_VerbCaptionFromID, a Part Number menu is shown with two submenus for our two verbs. Also note the accelerators (indicated by an underlined letter in the menu caption) that were created because of the use of the ampersand (&) character in the strings returned from get_VerbCaptionFromID.

In addition, you can see the Smart Tag listed in the Smart Tags page of the Auto-Correct dialog, as shown in Figure 16-10. To bring up this dialog in Word, choose AutoCorrect Options from the Tools menu. The part number Smart Tag is in the list of Recognizers with the string returned from the get_SmartTagCaption (Part Number Smart Tag) and in parenthesis the string returned from get_Name (English).

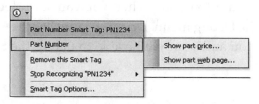

Figure 16-9 The two verbs for the part number Smart Tag.

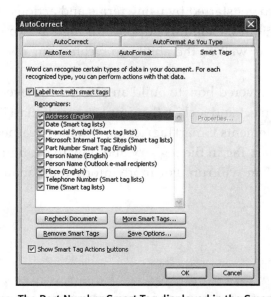

Figure 16-10 The Part Number Smart Tag displayed in the Smart Tags page.

Debugging an Application-Level Smart Tag

If you need to debug an application-level Smart Tag, make sure that the .pdb file that was built with your Smart Tag DLL is copied to the same location where you put your Smart Tag DLL. With your class library project open, use the Attach to Process command in the Debug menu of your project and attach to the Office application that has your Smart Tag loaded. Then set breakpoints in the methods you want to debug—most likely ISmartTagRecognizer.Recognize and ISmartTagAction.InvokeVerb.

If you need to attach the debugger earlier—for example, when the Smart Tag is first getting loaded—right-click the class library project node in the Solution Explorer window and choose Properties. In the Properties window, click the Debug tab. Change the Start Action to Start external program and enter the full path to the Office application you want to debug. Then you can start debugging by choosing Start debugging from the Debug menu. Doing so launches the Office application you entered in the start action and you will be able to debug the Smart Tag as it loads.

Conclusion

This chapter examined VSTO's support for document-level Smart Tags. VSTO provides a simple way to get started by using terms and actions. VSTO also supports more powerful techniques, including support for regular expressions and support for multiple actions as well as the ability to create your own custom Smart Tag classes.

This chapter also covered how to build an application-level Smart Tag by creating a class library project and a class that implements ISmartTagRecognizer along with a class that implements ISmartTagAction. You have learned how to register an application-level Smart Tag in the registry and how to configure .NET 1.1 security policy so the Smart Tag will run. For more information about .NET security and VSTO, see Chapter 19.

17

VSTO Data Programming

A FULL TREATMENT OF MICROSOFT'S ADO.NET data programming model could easily fill an entire book of its own. Therefore, this chapter starts with an example of how to use the VSTO designer to create a data-bound customized spreadsheet without writing a single line of code. After that, the chapter examines some ADO.NET features and then delves into the Word- and Excel-specific programming model.

To understand ADO.NET in all its complexity, read Shawn Wildermuth's *Pragmatic ADO.NET* (Addison-Wesley, 2002) and the data binding chapters of *Windows Forms Programming in C#* (Addison-Wesley, 2003) by Chris Sells.

Creating a Data-Bound Customized Spreadsheet with VSTO

Creating a no-frills data-bound customized document using the VSTO designer requires no coding but a whole lot of mouse clicking. What we are going to do is first tell Visual Studio about a data source—in this case, the Northwind sample database that comes with Office—and then drag and drop some data-bound controls onto the spreadsheet.

Defining a Data Source

Let's start up Visual Studio and create a new Excel project. From Visual Studio's Data menu, choose Show Data Sources to display the Data Sources pane. Click Add New Data Source to start the Data Source Wizard.

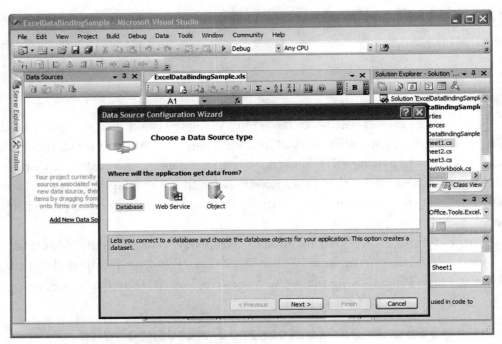

Figure 17-1 Starting up the Data Source Wizard.

Choose Database and click Next. Click New Connection. A second wizard will appear.

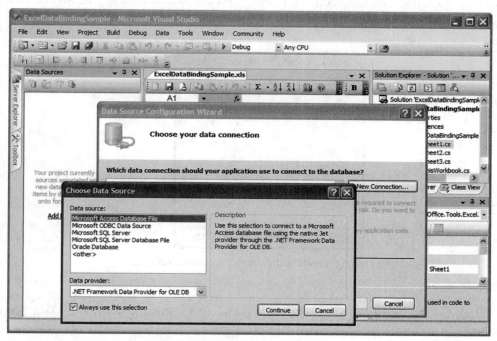

Figure 17-2 Starting up the Data Source Wizard.

Choose Microsoft Access Database File and click Continue to go on to the Connection dialog. The Northwind database file is typically in the Program Files\Microsoft Office\Office11\Samples directory. Click Browse and find the Northwind database. No security is enforced on this database file, so the default username Admin and a blank password are fine.

Figure 17-3 Creating the database connection.

Click OK to close the Connection Wizard and continue with the Data Source Wizard.

> In a real-world application with a secured database, it would be a very bad idea to have a blank administrator password. See the section "Data Sources and Security Best Practices" later in this chapter for more information.

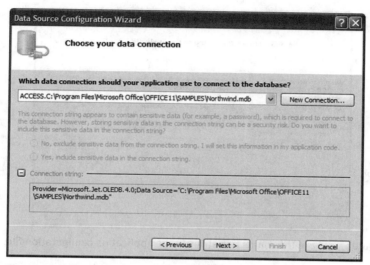

Figure 17-4 Viewing the connection string.

When you click Next, Visual Studio notes that you are creating a connection to a local database file that is not part of the current project. If you want this project to have its own copy of the database rather than modifying the original, you can do so and Visual Studio will automatically update the connection to point to the new location. In this first example, we do not have any reason to make a copy of the database, so click No.

As you can see, all the information about the database connection that you have just created is saved in a connection string. For both convenience and security, it is a good idea to save that connection string in a configuration file rather than hard-coding it into your program. Again, see the section below on security best practices for more details.

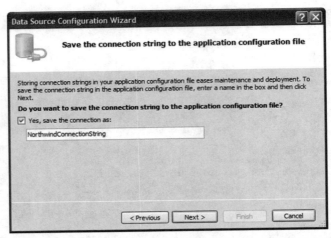

Figure 17-5 Save the connection string in the application configuration file.

The database to which we are connecting might have an enormous number of queries, tables, and columns within those tables and so on. To manage some of this complexity, Visual Studio enables you to choose which portions of the database will display in Visual Studio. Let's select the entire Suppliers table and the ProductName, SupplierId, QuantityPerUnit and UnitPrice columns from the Products table.

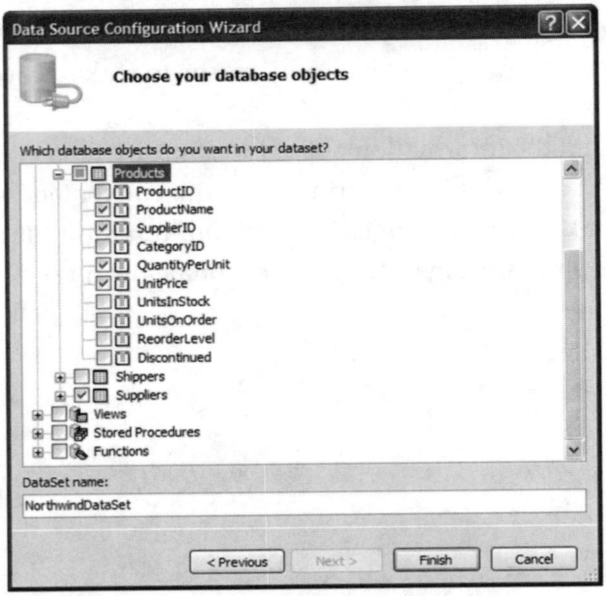

Figure 17-6 Choose your tables.

Finally, click Finish to exit the Data Source Wizard.

Creating Data-Bound Controls the Easy Way

The Data Sources window now contains an entry for the NorthwindDataSet. (Why *dataset* rather than *database*? We explain what exactly we mean by *dataset* later on in this chapter.) Expand the nodes in the tree view.

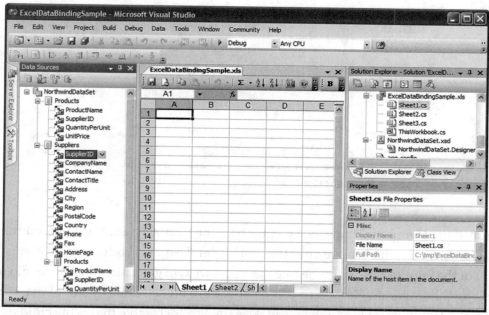

Figure 17-7 The Data Sources pane contains the dataset tree view.

Notice a few interesting things here. First, Visual Studio has discovered from the database that the Products table has a relationship with the Suppliers table; the Products table appears both as a table in its own right, and as a child node of the Suppliers table. This will allow us to more easily create master-detail views.

Second, notice that the icons for the columns have "named range" icons, indicating that if you drag and drop the icon onto the worksheet, you will get a data-bound named range to this column. The default for a column is a named range, and the default for an entire table is a list object, but you can choose other controls by clicking the item and selecting a drop-down. Suppose we want to have a combo box bound to the CompanyName, for instance. You can choose ComboBox from the drop-down as the control to use for CompanyName, as shown in Figure 17-8.

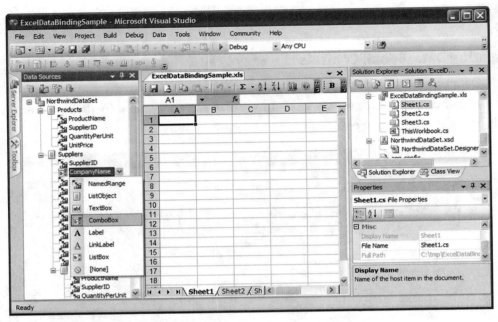

Figure 17-8 Choosing the control type.

Drag the CompanyName as a combo box, the ContactName as a named range, and the entire Products table onto the worksheet. Use the Products table that is the child of the Suppliers table in the tree view and we will get a nice master-detail view.

Drag the CompanyName as a combo box, the ContactName as a Bookmark, and the entire Products table as a data grid. Use the Products table that is the child of the Suppliers table in the tree view and we will get a nice master-detail view.

A whole lot of stuff has magically appeared in the component tray below the Excel designer: a dataset, two binding sources, and two table adapters. We get into the details of what these components are for later in this chapter. For now, compile and run the application. Without writing a single line of code, we have gotten a data-bound master-detail view on an Excel spreadsheet. As you select different items from the combo box, the named range and list object automatically update themselves.

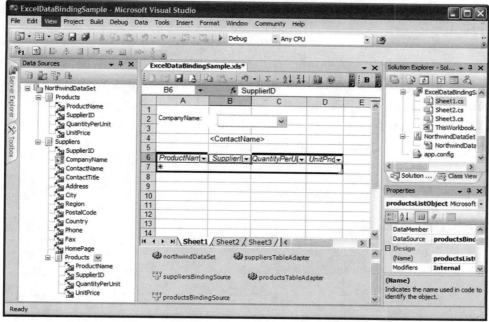

Figure 17-9 Creating the data-bound view.

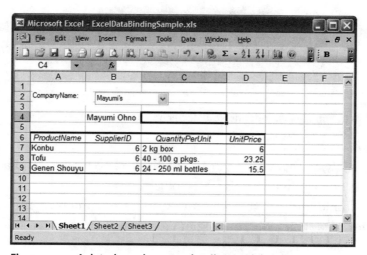

Figure 17-10 A data-bound master-detail spreadsheet.

Creating a Data-Bound Customized Word Document with VSTO

We can create a similar data-bound document in Word using bookmarks rather than named ranges and a data grid rather than an Excel List object. Create a new Word document project and again add the Northwind database as a data source to the Data Sources pane. Visual Studio should remember the connection string from last time, so you will not need to configure it again.

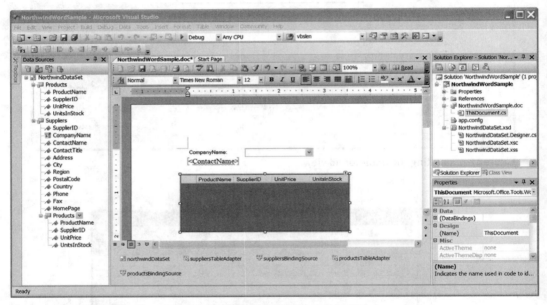

Figure 17-11 A data-bound master-detail Word document in the designer.

Unfortunately, in this version of VSTO, there is no way to bind a data table to a Word table as you can with an Excel list object.

When we build and run the customized Word document, again we have a master-detail view of a data table running in Word without writing a single line of code.

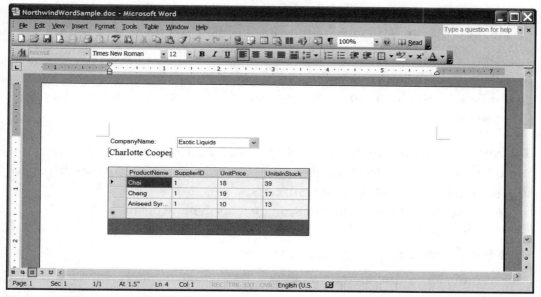

Figure 17-12   The master-detail view at runtime.

Datasets, Adapters, and Sources

Now that we have seen a couple no-coding-required examples, let's take a peek under the hood and see how data binding actually works. Several players make data binding work, many of which can be seen on the component tray or design surface:

- A **back-end data source**, such as an Access database, a remote SQL Server database, a Web service, or some other data storage and retrieval system, is where the data ultimately lives.
- A **dataset** is a disconnected local cache of some portion of the back-end data source.
- An **adapter** connects the dataset to the back-end data source, to both fill the dataset from the back-end source, and to update the back end with any changes. There is usually one adapter per table, which is why we saw two adapters in the preceding example.

- A **binding source** acts as the intermediary between the user interface control and the dataset. Although it is possible to bind a control directly to a dataset, as discussed later, it is usually more convenient to go through a dedicated binding source object.

- A **data-bindable control** provides a user interface element that enables the user to read or write the data.

The back-end data source is represented in a VSTO project by the connection string passed to the adapter; everything else is represented by a member of the customized host item (the worksheet or document) class.

Let's take a look at these different components in more detail.

Data Sources and Security Best Practices

As you probably noticed in the Connection Wizard, all the information required to connect to the back-end data source is stored in a "connection string" generated by the wizard. It typically looks something like this:

```
Server=MyDataServer; Database=Customers; Integrated Security=true;
```

That is, it says where the database is located, what it is called, and how the user should be authenticated. All this is potentially sensitive information! Use caution when embedding connection strings into your programs; remember, even without the source code, it is very easy to figure out which strings are embedded in a managed application. This particularly applies to connection strings where, instead of using Windows NT integrated security, you simply embed `UserID=eric; Password=BigSecret123` directly.

Furthermore, hard-coded embedded strings in your source code make it hard for developers, testers, end users, and database administrators to update your application should the database connection information change over time. As discussed previously, Visual Studio gives you the option of embedding the connection string in the configuration file. The automatically generated configuration file in our example above looks something like Listing 17-1.

Listing 17-1 A Typical Database Connection String in a Configuration File

```
<?xml version="1.0" encoding="utf-8" ?>
<configuration>
```

```
  <configSections>
  </configSections>
  <connectionStrings>
    <add name=
      "ExcelWorkbook11.Properties.Settings.NorthwindConnectionString"
      connectionString="Provider=Microsoft.Jet.OLEDB.4.0;Data
      Source=&quot;C:\Program Files\Microsoft
      Office\OFFICE11\SAMPLES\Northwind.mdb&quot;"
      providerName="System.Data.OleDb" />
  </connectionStrings>
</configuration>
```

It is also a good idea to use the "principle of least privilege." This is one of the fundamental principles of secure design: Grant exactly as much privilege as you need to get the job done, no more, no less. For example, if your user needs to be able to read from the database but not write to it, do not specify a connection string that gives the user administrator rights to the database. Instead, choose a connection string that specifies a username and password with read-only access. That way, if the username and password are ever compromised, at least the attacker does not get administrator access out of it.

Better still, do not use stored user IDs and passwords at all; some databases use integrated Windows authentication, so the logged-on user can seamlessly use his already authenticated credentials. Or, if your database system requires a username and password, make the user type them in rather than storing them. As you'll see later when we discuss adapters, you can manually change the connection string used by the adapter before it fills the dataset. That way you could ask the user to type in his user ID and password and then generate a new connection string from that information.

Datasets

The cornerstone of the VSTO 2005 data model, and of ADO.NET in general, is the dataset. We should motivate the existence of datasets by describing the old way of doing data access. Back in the twentieth century, you typically communicated with a database via "ADO Classic" something like this:

1. Create and open a connection to a database.
2. Create and execute a database command (such as SELECT partnumber FROM invoices WHERE price > 100).

3. Enumerate the resulting record set.

4. Close the connection.

This approach worked fairly well, but it has several drawbacks. The principle drawbacks are consequences of the fact that this model requires a live connection to a database. If there are going to be many live connections, the server needs to be scalable and robust, which can be expensive. Therefore, to minimize load upon the server, we want connections to be short-lived. But because the connection is open while the user is enumerating the record set, the connection is typically open for quite some time—as long as the user is working with the data.

Furthermore, even if the server-side expense of keeping connections open is unimportant, this model does not work well in a world where you want to be able to work with your data even if you temporarily lack network connectivity.

A Disconnected Strategy

Database connections are both expensive and necessary and therefore must be managed carefully. In a typical ADO application, much developer effort is expended writing code to ensure that the connection is open for as little time as possible while still meeting the needs of the application's users. ADO.NET addresses the problems of ADO by going straight to the root; if we cannot make connections inexpensive, we can at least make them less necessary. ADO.NET is therefore fundamentally a *disconnected* strategy. A typical ADO.NET scenario goes something like this:

1. Create a DataAdapter to manage the connection to a specific database or other data source.

2. Set properties on the adapter that tell it what query to execute against the database.

3. Create a dataset to be filled.

4. Invoke a method on the adapter to take care of the details of opening a connection, executing the query, saving the results in the dataset, and closing the connection as soon as possible.

5. Work with the data in the now-disconnected dataset.

6. When you have finished working with the data, invoke a method on the adapter to re-open the connection to the database and update it with any changes.

And indeed, as you will see later when we discuss adapters, VSTO does exactly this on your behalf.

Because the dataset acts much like the original database, the connection need be open only as long as it takes to fill the dataset. After the data has been copied to the dataset, you can query and manipulate the dataset for as long as you want without worrying that you are consuming a valuable database connection.

Furthermore, there is no reason why the data used to fill the dataset have to come from a connected database; you could fill the dataset from an XML file, or write a program to add tables and rows to build one "from scratch." Datasets have no knowledge of where the data they contain came from; if you need it, all that knowledge is encapsulated in the adapter.

> The foregoing is not to say that old-fashioned connected data access is impossible in ADO.NET, or even discouraged; the DataReader class allows for traditional always-connected access to a database. However, neither Windows Forms controls nor VSTO 2005 host items/host controls can use DataReaders for data binding, so we speak of them no more in this book.

Typed and Untyped Datasets

In the Solution Explorer of the Word or Excel projects we created earlier, you will find a NorthwindDataSet.xsd file containing the database schema. This is an XML document that describes the tables, columns, and relationships that make up the dataset. One of the child nodes in the Solution Explorer tree view is Northwind-DataSet.Designer.cs. This file contains the automatically generated code for the dataset and table adapters.

The first line of the declaration is interesting:

```
public partial class NorthwindDataSet : System.Data.DataSet {
```

The generated class is partial so that if you need to add your own extensions to it, you can do so in a separate file; it is a bad idea to edit automatically generated files. More importantly, this dataset extends the System.Data.DataSet class. A System.Data.DataSet consists of a collection of data tables. As you would expect, data tables consist of a collection of data columns and data rows. Each class exposes various collections as properties that allow you to navigate through the dataset.

System.Data.DataSet is not an abstract class; you can create instances and fill them from *any* back-end data source. But that would be an *untyped* dataset; the NorthwindDataSet is a *typed* dataset. Untyped datasets give you great flexibility but are so general that they are somewhat harder to use.

For example, if you were to fill an untyped dataset with data from the Northwind database file, you could access a particular datum with an expression such as this:

```
name = myDataSet.Tables["Products"].Rows[1]["ProductName"];
```

But that flexibility comes at a cost: You can accidentally pass in a bad table name, a bad column name, or make a bad assumption about the type of the data stored in a column. Because none of the structure of the tables or types of the columns is known at compile time, the compiler is unable to verify that the code will run without throwing exceptions. Also, the IntelliSense engine is unable to provide any hints about the dataset's structure while you are developing the code.

Typed datasets mitigate these problems. A typed dataset is a class that extends the dataset base class; it has all the flexible, untyped features of a regular untyped dataset, but also has compile-time strongly typed properties that expose the tables by name. A typed dataset also defines typed data table and data row subclasses, too.

As you can see from the NorthwindDataSet.Designer.cs file, the typed dataset has public properties that enable you to write much more straightforward code, such as this:

```
name = myDataSet.Products[1].ProductName;
```

Typed datasets extend untyped datasets in many ways; some of the most important are as follows:

- Tables are exposed as read-only properties typed as instances of typed data tables.
- Tables have read-only properties for each column.
- Tables have an indexer that returns a typed data row.

- Event delegates for row change events pass typed change event arguments. Each row type has a row-changing, row-changed, row-deleting, and row-deleted event. (You might be wondering where the row-adding and row-added events are. The changing/changed events pass a `DataRowAction` enumerated type to indicate whether the row in question was newly created.)
- Tables provide methods for adding and removing typed data rows.
- Rows provide getters, setters, and nullity testers for each column.

In short, it is almost always a good idea to use a typed dataset. Weakly typed code is harder to read, harder to reason about, and harder to maintain.

Adapters

Take a look at the Startup event handler in either the Word or Excel examples above. Visual Studio has automatically generated the code in Listing 17-2 on your behalf.

Listing 17-2 Auto-Generated Table-Filling Code

```
public partial class ThisDocument
{
  private void ThisDocument_Startup(object sender, System.EventArgs e)
  {
  // TODO: Delete this line of code to remove the default
  // AutoFill for 'northwindDataSet.Products'.
  if (this.NeedsFill("northwindDataSet"))
  {
    this.productsTableAdapter.Fill(this.northwindDataSet.Products);
  }
  // TODO: Delete this line of code to remove the default
  // AutoFill for 'northwindDataSet.Suppliers'.
  if (this.NeedsFill("northwindDataSet"))
  {
    this.suppliersTableAdapter.Fill(this.northwindDataSet.Suppliers);
  }
}
```

We discuss what exactly NeedsFill is for in more detail when we discuss data caching later in this chapter and in Chapter 18, "Server Data Scenarios." But for now, this should look fairly straightforward: If the two tables need to be filled from the back-end data source, the adapters fill the appropriate tables.

There are a number of reasons why you might want to not automatically fill the data tables in the Startup event, which is why the comment points out that you can remove the auto-generated code. For example, as mentioned earlier, you might want to require that the user enter a database password before attempting to fill the dataset. You can generate a new connection string and then set the adapter's Connection.ConnectionString property.

Or perhaps you want to give the user the option of whether to connect to the back end. If the user is on an expensive or slow connection, the user might want to skip downloading a large chunk of data. For any number of reasons, you might not want to connect right away or use the default connection string, so Visual Studio allows you to modify this startup code.

Visual Studio generates strongly typed custom adapters at the same time as it generates the typed dataset. If you read through the generated adapter code in NorthwindDataSet.Designers.cs, you will see that the generated adapter has been hard-coded to connect to the database specified by the connection string in the configuration file. The bulk of the generated adapter code consists of the query code to handle reading from the back-end data store into the typed dataset, and then taking any changes in the dataset and updating or deleting the appropriate rows in the store.

The adapter takes care of all the details of opening the connection, executing the query, copying the data into the dataset, and closing the connection. At this point, we have a local copy of the data, which we can use to our heart's content without worrying about taxing the server further.

When you are done editing the local copy of the data in the dataset, you can use the adapter to update the database with the changes by calling the Update method of the adapter. The adapter will then take care of making the additions, changes, and deletions to the back-end database.

By default, the adapter assumes that you want "optimistic concurrency." That is, other users will be able to update the database unless you are currently in the process of updating the database. Other concurrency models are possible but beyond the scope of this text. If you want either "pessimistic concurrency" (that is, the database remains locked during the whole time that you have the offline dataset) or "destructive concurrency" (that is, the database is never locked even when multiple people are writing at once), consult a reference on ADO.NET to see how to configure your adapter appropriately.

Using Binding Sources as Proxies

Why does Visual Studio bind the controls to a BindingSource "proxy" object, rather than binding controls directly to the data table?

The reason is because the control can bind to the proxy even if the data in the table is not currently available. For instance, perhaps the data table is going to be derived from a call to a Web service, which will not happen until long after the initialization is complete, or until the user types in his password or presses a button to start the database connection.

The proxy object is created when the customization starts up and controls can be bound to it even if there is no "real" data available. When the real data is available, the binding source updates the controls. It is essentially just a thin "shim" that makes it easier to set up bindings before the data is all available.

As you saw in the examples, multiple controls can share the same binding source and therefore have the same "currency." That is, when one control is updated, every other control linked to the same binding source is also updated automatically. Controls on different worksheets or even on the actions pane can share binding sources and thereby share currency. You will learn about currency management in more detail later in this chapter.

Data-Bindable Controls

The last piece of the data binding puzzle is the host control or Windows Forms control on the spreadsheet or document that actually displays the bound data. There are two flavors of data-bindable controls: "simple" and "complex." Controls that can bind a single datum to a particular property are "simple-data-bindable." Controls that can bind multiple rows and/or columns are "complex-data-bindable."

In the preceding examples, the list object in Excel and the combo box and data grid Windows Forms controls are complex-data-bindable; the list object and data grid display multiple rows and columns from a table, and the combo box displays multiple rows from a single column. The bookmark and named range controls by contrast are simple-data-bindable; only a single datum is bound to the Value property of the named range.

All the Windows Forms controls are simple-data-bindable, as are almost all of the Word and Excel host items and host controls. (There is one exception: Word XMLNodes host control is neither simple- nor complex-data-bindable.) Of the host items and host controls, only Excel's list object is complex-data-bindable.

The behind-the-scenes mechanisms by which controls implement data binding and manage currency are fairly complex; we cover them in more detail toward the end of this chapter. But first, now that we have gotten a little context as to what all these parts are and how they relate, let's take a look at a somewhat more labor-intensive way to do data binding in Excel. This time we are going to actually write a few lines of code.

Another Technique for Creating Data-Bound Spreadsheets

Unlike our previous example, in this case we do not define ahead of time where the back-end data store is located; you have to write a few lines of code to obtain the data.

Create a new Excel project and choose the Data > Microsoft Office Excel Data > XML > XML Source to display the XML Source pane. As you can see, no XML schemas are mapped into this document, so click the XML Maps button and add the schema file shown in Listing 17-3.

Listing 17-3 A Schema for a Two-Table Dataset

```
<?xml version="1.0"?>
<xs:schema
  id="OrderDataSet"
  targetNamespace="http://myschemas/Order.xsd"
  xmlns="http://myschemas/Order.xsd"
  xmlns:xs="http://www.w3.org/2001/XMLSchema">
  <xs:element name="Order">
```

```
<xs:complexType>
  <xs:sequence>
    <xs:element name="Customer" type="xs:string"
    minOccurs="0" maxOccurs="1" />
    <xs:element name="Book" minOccurs="0" maxOccurs="unbounded">
      <xs:complexType>
        <xs:sequence>
          <xs:element name="Title" type="xs:string" minOccurs="0" />
          <xs:element name="ISBN" type="xs:string" minOccurs="0" />
          <xs:element name="Price" type="xs:double" minOccurs="0" />
        </xs:sequence>
      </xs:complexType>
    </xs:element>
  </xs:sequence>
</xs:complexType>
</xs:element>
</xs:schema>
```

This is a dataset schema that defines an Order as consisting of a single Customer and any number of Books, where each book has a Title, ISBN, and Price. In a database, this would be organized as two related tables, as you will see.

The structure of the XML schema then appears in the XML Source pane, and you can drag and drop elements of the schema onto the spreadsheet. Try dragging the Customer node onto a cell. The single datum creates a named range host control. If you then drag over the Book node, you get a List object. Also, Visual Studio has again created a dataset source file. However, Visual Studio knows nothing about what the source of the data will be, so it does not generate any adapters.

Next, let's add a binding source. From the Toolbox, find the binding source component in the Data category. Drag it onto the spreadsheet. A binding source component appears in the component tray. Rename the binding source to OrderBook-BindingSource using the properties window. Then click on the list object you created by dragging the Book node onto the worksheet. In the properties window, set the DataSource of the list object to the OrderBookBindingSource you created.

If you compile and run the customization, not much will happen; the data binding source is just a "dummy"—there is no actual data in there. Also, there is no instance of the dataset on the components tray, so there is no chance that there will ever be data associated with this binding source as things stand now.

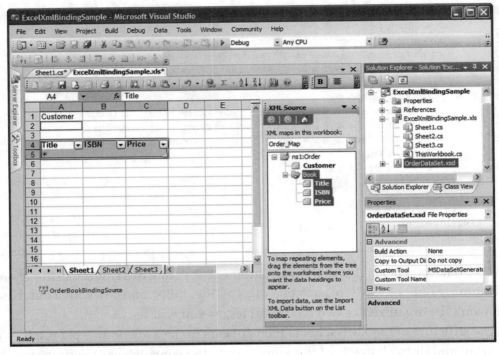

Figure 17-13 The XML Source pane.

Notice that the project system has automatically added the schema to the project; it will generate a typed dataset for this schema and add it to the project as well. But that class is just source code; the project system does not know yet what it is going to look like when compiled. Well then, let's compile it. Build the project, but do not run it.

Now if you pop open the toolbox, you will see a new set of tools under the name of the project. There should be an OrderDataSet item. Drag it over onto the spreadsheet's component tray and drop it; doing so adds an instance of the typed dataset to the customized worksheet class.

> Alternatively, you can add this typed dataset to your project *before* compiling if you open up the ToolBox tab on the left side of the designer and drag and drop the dataset component onto the design surface. When you drag and drop a dataset component, Visual Studio shows you a combo box that enables you to pick from all available typed datasets referenced by or in your project. This combo box shows you the new dataset even if you have not compiled your project.

We have gotten most of the parts we need: The binding source is hooked up to the list object, but the binding source does not yet know that the dataset we have just dropped onto the component tray is important.

Click the book binding source in the component tray and take a look at its Property pane. Start by clicking the DataSource drop-down, and navigate the tree view to select Other Data Sources > Sheet1 List Instances > OrderDataSet1. Then click the DataMember property drop-down and select the Book table.

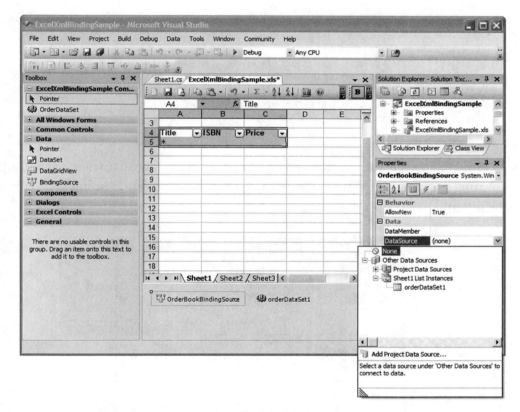

Figure 17-14 Setting the DataSource property of the binding source.

Do not forget to set the DataMember property when binding to a table. Without it, the binding data source will attempt to extract the columns for the table from the dataset itself, not from the Book table. This will then fail at runtime.

We have gotten almost everything we need; the only thing left is to put some data in the typed dataset instance we have added. Typically, we would fill the dataset by creating an adapter to talk to some external database; for this example, we just fill the typed dataset manually, using the code in Listing 17-4. (You could also fill it by loading XML out of a file or downloading XML from a Web service.)

Listing 17-4 Filling a Typed Dataset from "Scratch"

```
private void Sheet1_Startup(object sender, System.EventArgs e)
{
    // An order has a customer column
    this.orderDataSet1.Order.AddOrderRow("Vlad the Impaler");
    // A book has a title, ISBN and price, and is associated with
    // a particular order.
    this.orderDataSet1.Book.AddBookRow("Blood For Dracula",
        "0-123-45678-9", 34.95, this.orderDataSet1.Order[0]);
    this.orderDataSet1.Book.AddBookRow("Fang Attack!",
        "9-876-54321-0", 14.44, this.orderDataSet1.Order[0]);
}
```

Now build and execute the customized spreadsheet. You'll see that when the Startup event runs and creates the new row in the book table, the data binding layer automatically updates the list object.

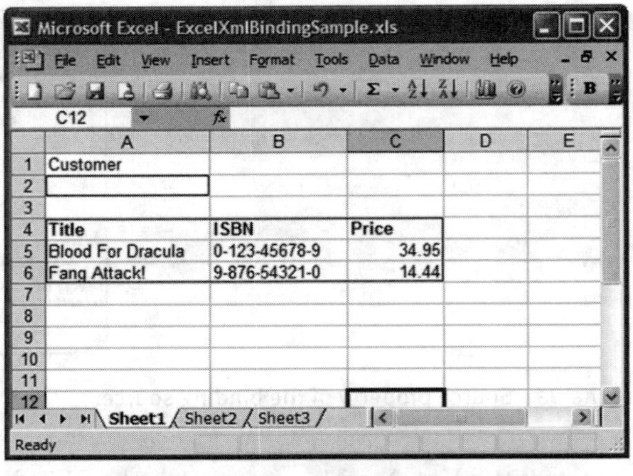

Figure 17-15 The List object is bound to the data table.

Furthermore, data binding to list objects goes both ways; updating the data in the host control propagates the changes back to the data table.

Complex and Simple Data Binding

What you have just seen is an example of "complex" data binding, so named not because it is particularly difficult but rather because many data are bound at once to a relatively complicated host control. Controls must be specially written to support complex data binding. By contrast, "simple" data binding binds a single datum to a single property of a host control.

Note that nothing happened to the Customer cell when we ran the code. Back in the designer, click the single-celled range you mapped to the Customer property earlier and take a look at its Properties pane. If you click the Advanced DataBinding property in the Properties pane, the dialog shown in Figure 17-16 displays.

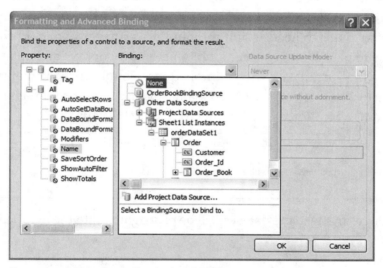

Figure 17-16 Creating a simple data binding.

Select the property you want to bind—Value—and in the Binding drop-down, you can select Other Data Sources > Sheet1 List Instances > OrderDataSet1 > Order > Customer. Now we have binding information that associates the Value property on the host control with the Customer field in the dataset. When we run the code, the value from the dataset is automatically copied into the host control, and when the dataset is changed, the binding manager keeps the host control up-to-date. Note in this example that we have not created a master-details relationship between the customer and the orders—the list object will show all orders created by all customers. For an example of creating a master-details relationship, see Chapter 21.

However, it does not work the other way; unlike our earlier list object example, changing the value in the cell does not automatically propagate that change back to the dataset. Why not?

In the Data Source Update Mode drop-down in the upper-left corner of the dialog we just looked at, there are three choices: Never, OnValidation, and OnPropertyChanged. The last choice certainly seems like a sensible choice; when a property on the control changes, update the data source to keep it in sync.

Unfortunately, that does not work with Excel host controls. Why? Because you can create a binding to any old property of a host control, but we cannot change the fact that the aggregated Range objects do not source any "some property just changed" event that the binding manager can listen to. Windows Forms Controls do source such an event, but Word and Excel host controls do not.

This means that we need to tell the binding manager explicitly that the data source needs to be updated, instead of relying on the control informing its binding manager for you. Fortunately, this is simply done. Double-click the mapped range in the designer to automatically create a Change event handler, and then fill it in with the line of code which forces the binding to update the source:

```
private void OrderCustomerCell_Change(Excel.Range Target)
{
  this.OrderCustomerCell.DataBindings["Value"].WriteValue();
}
```

Now all changes made to the dataset will be propagated into the mapped range, and vice versa.

Data Binding in Word Documents

Word also supports creating XML mapped documents. However, unlike the Excel designer, the Word designer does not automatically create typed datasets from mapped schemas. If you want to create a typed dataset from a schema mapped into Word, you have to add it to the project system yourself. Just add the schema XSD file to the project, and then ensure that in its Properties pane the Custom Tool property is set to MSDataSetGenerator; the build system will then create the typed dataset for you.

Because simple data binding in Word is essentially the same as in Excel, and Excel supports complex data binding in the list object host control, this chapter does not talk much more about data binding in Word.

Caching Data in the Data Island

When a customized document with data-bound controls starts up, the datasets have to be filled in somehow before the controls display the data. As you saw at the beginning of this chapter, if you use the Data Sources pane to create data-bound controls, Visual Studio automatically emits code to fill the datasets using custom-generated adapters:

```
private void ThisDocument_Startup(object sender, System.EventArgs e){
    if (this.NeedsFill("northwindDataSet"))
        this.productsTableAdapter.Fill(this.northwindDataSet.Products);
```

But under what circumstances would the dataset ever *not* need to be filled at startup? Consider, for example, a spreadsheet with a dataset containing a single table. One worksheet has a single datum bound to a named range. If you save that spreadsheet, only that one datum is going to be saved; all the other information in the dataset is just a structure in memory at runtime that will be lost when the workbook is closed. The data is potentially going to have to be fetched anew every time the worksheet host control starts up.

One of the key benefits of Word and Excel documents is that they are useful even on machines that are not connected to networks. (Working on a spreadsheet or document on a laptop on an airplane is the canonical scenario.) It would be unfortunate indeed if a data-bound customized document required your users to always be connected.

Fortunately, VSTO solves this problem. Click the icon for the typed dataset in the component tray, and then look at the Properties pane for this component. A Cached property defaults to `false`. If you set it to `true`, when you save the document the VSTO runtime will turn the dataset into XML and store the XML in a "data island" inside the document.

The next time the document starts up, the VSTO runtime detects that the data island contains a cached dataset and fills in the dataset from the cache. The call to NeedsFill in the Startup event will then return `false`, and the startup code will not attempt to fill in the data from the adapter. Essentially, the NeedsFill method returns `false` if the object was loaded from the cache automatically, `true` otherwise.

Caching Your Own Data Types

You can cache almost any kind of data in the XML data island, not just datasets. To be cacheable by the VSTO runtime, you must meet the following criteria:

- The data must be stored in a *public* member variable or property of a host item (a customized worksheet, workbook, chart sheet, or document class).
- If stored in a property, the property must have no parameters and be both readable and writable.
- The *runtime type* of the data must be either dataset (or a subclass), data table (or a subclass), or any type serializable by the System.Xml.Serialization. XmlSerializer object.

To tell Visual Studio that you would like to cache a member variable, just add the Cached attribute to its declaration. Make sure you check whether the member was already filled in from the cache; the first time the document is run there will be no data in the cache, so you have to fill in the data somehow. For example, you could use the code in Listing 17-5.

Listing 17-5 Auto-Generated Table-Filling Code

```
public partial class ThisDocument
{
  [Cached]
  public string CustomerName;

  private void ThisDocument_Startup(object sender, System.EventArgs e)
  {
    if (this.NeedsFill("CustomerName"))
      this.CustomerName = "Unknown Customer"
  }
}
```

Dynamically Adding and Removing Cached Members from the Data Island

Cached data can be large; what if you decide that at some point you want to stop caching a particular dataset in the data island? Or, conversely, what if you do not want to automatically fill in a dataset and store it in the cache on the first run of the document, but rather want to start caching a member based on some other criterion?

It would be unfortunate if the only way to tell VSTO to cache a member in the data island was to tag it with the `Cached` attribute at design time.

Therefore, all customized view item classes generated by a VSTO project expose four handy functions that you can call to query and manipulate the caching semantics, as follows:

- `bool NeedsFill(string memberName)`
- `bool IsCached(string memberName)`
- `void StartCaching(string memberName)`
- `void StopCaching(string memberName)`

NeedsFill we have already seen; if the named member was initialized from the data island by the VSTO runtime when the customization started up, this returns `false`. Otherwise, it returns `true`.

IsCached might seem like it is just the opposite of NeedsFill, but it is not. NeedsFill tells you whether the item in question was loaded out of the data island; IsCached tells you whether the item will be saved to the data island when the user saves the document.

StartCaching and StopCaching dynamically add and remove members from the set of members that will be saved to the data island. It is illegal to call StartCaching on a member already in the cache or StopCaching on a member not in the cache; use IsCached to double-check if you need to. The same rules that apply to cached members added to the cache by the `Cached` attribute apply to dynamically added members; only call StartCaching on public fields or public readable/writable properties.

> If a cached member is set to `null` at the time that the document is saved, the VSTO runtime assumes that you intended to call StopCaching on the member and it will be removed from the data island.

Advanced Topic: Using ICachedType

Suppose you have a large cached dataset that you loaded out of the data island when the customization started up. Serializing a dataset into XML can be a time- and memory-consuming process; so if there have been no changes to the dataset when the document is saved, the VSTO runtime is pretty smart about skipping the serialization.

This is also important if the user closes Word or Excel without saving the document. The host application needs to know whether to create the "Do you want to save changes?" dialog box. If the dataset is clean, there are no changes to save and the dialog should not be created.

How can VSTO tell whether a custom class added to the cached members is dirty? The VSTO runtime can track the Change events on a dataset or data table to tell whether they are dirty, but in general, any other types simply have to be written out every time. To prevent the "Do you want to save?" dialog, the VSTO runtime must pessimistically serialize the object and compare it to the state that it loaded; this is again potentially time-consuming.

If you require more finely grained control over the caching process for a particular member, you can implement the ICachedType interface. This interface enables you to not only hint to the VSTO runtime whether the item needs to be re-serialized, it also allows you to dynamically abort a save or load, and receive notification when the save or load is done. Listing 17-6 shows its members.

Listing 17-6 The ICachedType Inteface

```
namespace Microsoft.VisualStudio.Tools.Applications.Runtime
{
  public interface ICachedType
  {
    bool IsDirty { get; }
    bool BeforeLoad();
    void AfterLoad();
    bool BeforeSave();
    void AfterSave();
  }
}
```

If you implement this interface on a particular class and then add a member containing an instance to the class, the VSTO runtime will do the following:

- Call your BeforeLoad method when the item is loaded out of the cache. If you return `false`, the load will be aborted.
- Call your AfterLoad method when the XMLSerializer is done loading your object. (If you are tracking the dirty state of the object, this would be a good time to set it to clean.)

- Call IsDirty before saving the document; if the object has no changes since it was last loaded or saved, return `false` to avoid unnecessary expensive serializations.

- Call BeforeSave before saving the member to the data island. If for some reason you determine that the object is not in a state that can be saved, you can return `false` and the object will be removed from the cache.

- Call AfterSave when the XMLSerializer is done saving the document to the data island. (Again, this would be a good time to note that the object is clean.)

Manipulating the Serialized XML Directly

Chapter 18 discusses how to view and edit the contents of the data island, start and stop caching members, and so on, without actually starting Word or Excel.

Advanced ADO.NET Data Binding: Looking Behind the Scenes

The preceding section gave some of the flavor of ADO.NET data binding; we should more carefully describe what is happening behind the scenes here. After all, you might want to write your own code to set up data binding rather than relying on the code generated for you by the designer.

The first thing we need to do is describe what objects work together to bind data to controls. In the Excel data binding example, many objects are involved. There are the two controls—the list object and the XML mapped range—the dataset and the two data tables.

Each control implements IBindableComponent, so each control has a DataBindings property that returns an instance of ControlBindingsCollection. This object maintains a collection of Binding objects, one for each simple data binding. The collection is indexed by the name of the property, which has been simple-data-bound.

Each Binding object contains all the information necessary to describe the binding: what member of what data source is bound to what property of what control, how the data is to be formatted, and so on.

Binding Managers Manage Currency

One important member of the Binding object is the BindingManagerBase property. The binding manager is the object that actually does the work of the data binding: listening to changes in the data source and bound controls and ensuring that they stay synchronized.

The binding manager for data tables and other "list" data sources keeps track of the "currency" of the data source. If you bind a list to a control that displays a single datum, the control will display the current item as determined by the currency manager. (Because we'll almost always be talking about binding to list data sources, we use *binding manager* and *currency manager* interchangeably throughout.)

Most of the time, each binding source has exactly one currency manager associated with it; two controls bound to the same binding source share a currency manager and therefore share currency. In the event that you want to have two controls bound to a single binding source but with different currency, each control needs to have its own "binding context." A binding context is a collection that keeps track of pairs of binding sources and binding managers; within each context, every binding source has a unique binding manager, but two contexts can associate different managers with the same source, thereby keeping two or more currencies in one binding source.

In typical scenarios, there is only one binding context, so this point is largely moot. Even when you have only one, the binding context does have one use. When complex data binding, the binding context exposed by a list object lets you obtain the currency manager for the binding source.

Binding-Related Extensions to Host Items and Host Controls

All data-bindable host items and host controls allow you to bind any single datum to any writable property. These objects implement IBindableComponent, which defines two properties:

- BindingContext BindingContext { get; set; }
- ControlBindingsCollection DataBindings { get; }

Typically, you will have only one binding context; should you need to have two controls bound to the same list data source but with different currency for each, you can create new binding contexts and assign them to the controls as you want. Each host item and host control will raise a BindingContextChanged event if you do.

The ControlBindingsCollection object has many methods for adding and removing binding objects; there is one binding for each bound property on the control. It also has a read-only indexer that maps the name of a property to its binding object.

Extensions to the List Object Host Control in Excel

The list object aggregate in Excel has a large number of new properties, methods, and events added on to support complex data binding. We described the view extensions earlier; now that we have covered how data binding works, we can discuss the data model extensions.

New Data-Related List Object Host Control Properties and Methods

The two most important properties on the ListObject host control determine what data source is actually complex-data-bound to the control:

```
object DataSource { get; set; }
string DataMember { get; set; }
```

The reason that the list object divides this information up into two properties is because some data sources contain multiple lists, called "members." For example, you could set the DataSource property to a dataset and the DataMember property to the name of a data table contained by the dataset.

The properties can be set in any order, and binding will not commence until both are set to sensible values. However, it is usually easier to use one of the SetData-Binding methods to set both properties at once:

```
void SetDataBinding(object dataSource)
void SetDataBinding(object dataSource, string dataMember)
void SetDataBinding(object dataSource, string dataMember,
   params string[] mappedColumns)
```

Notice that in the last overload, you can specify which columns in the data table are to be bound. Doing so proves quite handy if you have a large, complicated table that you want to display only a portion of, or if you want to change the order in which the columns display.

In some cases, the data source needs no further qualification by a data member, so you can leave it blank. For instance, in the preceding example, the designer automatically generates code that creates a BindingSource proxy object, which needs no further qualification. The generated code looks something like the code in Listing 17-7.

Listing 17-7 Setting Up the Binding Source

```
this.OrderBookBindingSource = new System.Windows.Forms.BindingSource();
this.OrderBookBindingSource.DataMember = "Book";
this.OrderBookBindingSource.DataSource = this.orderDataSet1;
this.BookList.SetDataBinding(this.OrderBookBindingSource, "",
   "Title", "ISBN", "Price");
```

Because the binding source knows what table to proxy, the list object needs no further qualification.

> Unlike the DataGrid control, the list object does not allow you to set the bound columns using a column chooser in the list object's Properties pane. However, if you have a data-bound list object in the designer, you can simply delete columns at design time; Visual Studio will update the automatically generated code so that the deleted column is no longer bound when the code runs.

The information about which columns and tables are bound to which list objects is persisted in the document; you do not need to explicitly rebind the list objects every time the customization starts up. Should you want to ensure that all the persisted information about the data bindings is cleared from the document, you can call the ResetPersistedBindingInformation method:

```
void ResetPersistedBindingInformation()
```

The data source of the list object must implement either IList or IListSource. Should you pass an invalid object when trying to set the data source, the list object will throw a SetDataBindingFailedException (as described later in this chapter).

You can check whether the data source and data members have been set properly and the list object is presently complex-data-bound by checking the IsBinding property:

```
bool IsBinding { get; }
```

Complex-data-bound list objects keep the currency—the currently "selected" row in the currency manager for the data source—in sync with the currently selected row in the host. You can set or get the currency of the data source's binding manager with this property:

```
int SelectedIndex { get; set; }
```

Note that the selected index is one-based, not zero-based; −1 indicates that no row is selected. When the selected index changes, the list object raises the SelectedIndexChanged event. It raises IndexOutOfRangeException should you attempt to set an invalid index.

If the AutoSelectRows property is set to `true`, the view's selection is updated whenever the currency changes:

```
bool AutoSelectRows { get; set; }
```

Three other properties directly affect the appearance of data-bound list objects:

```
XlRangeAutoFormat DataBoundFormat { get; set; }
FormatSettings DataBoundFormatSettings { get; set; }
bool AutoSetDataBoundColumnHeaders { get; set; }
```

The DataBoundFormat property determines whether Excel does automatic reformatting of the list object cells when the data change. You have several dozen formats to choose from; the default is `xlRangeAutoFormatNone`. If you want no formatting at all, choose `xlRangeAutoFormatNone`. You can also pick and choose which aspects of the formatting you want applied by setting the bit flags in the DataBoundFormatSettings property. (By default, all the flags are turned on.)

```
enum FormatSettings
{
    Number      = 0x00000001,
    Font        = 0x00000010,
```

```
    Alignment   = 0x00000100,
    Border      = 0x00001000,
    Pattern     = 0x00010000,
    Width       = 0x00100000
}
```

The AutoSetDataBoundColumnHeaders property indicates whether the list object data binding should automatically create a header row in the list object that contains the column names. It is set to `false` by default.

New Data-Related List Object Events

Table 17-1 New Events Associated with List Object

Delegate Type	Event Name
EventHandler	DataSourceChanged
EventHandler	DataMemberChanged
EventHandler	SelectedIndexChanged
EventHandler	DataBindingFailure
BeforeAddDataBoundRowEventHandler	BeforeAddDataBoundRow
ErrorAddDataBoundRowEventHandler	ErrorAddDataBoundRow
OriginalDataRestoredEventHandler	OriginalDataRestored

The DataSource and DataMember properties on the list object aggregate determine to what data source the list object is complex-data-bound. The DataSourceChanged and DataMemberChanged events are raised when the corresponding properties are changed.

The SelectedIndexChanged event is primarily a "view" event; when the user clicks a different row, the event is raised. However, note that changing the selected row also changes the currency of the binding manager. This can be used to implement master-detail event binding.

If for any reason an edit to the list object fails—for instance, if the data binding layer attempts unsuccessfully to add a row or column to the list, or if a value typed into the list object cannot be copied back into the bound data source—the Data-BindingFailure event is raised.

The BeforeAddDataBoundRow event has two primary uses. Listing 17-8 shows its delegate.

Listing 17-8 The BeforeAddDataBoundRow Event Types

```
delegate void BeforeAddDataBoundRowEventHandler(object sender,
  BeforeAddDataBoundRowEventArgs e);
class BeforeAddDataBoundRowEventArgs : EventArgs
{
  Object Item { get; }
  bool Cancel { get; set; }
}
```

The item passed to the event handler is the row that is about to be added. The event can be used to either programmatically edit the row just before it is actually added, or to do data validation and cancel the addition should the data be somehow invalid.

After the BeforeAddDataBoundRow event is handled, the list object attempts to commit the new row into the data source. If that operation throws an exception for any reason, the list object deletes the offending row. Before it does so, however, it gives you one chance to fix the problem by raising the ErrorAddDataBoundRow event. Listing 17-9 shows its delegate.

Listing 17-9 The ErrorAddDataBoundRow Event Types

```
delegate void ErrorAddDataBoundRowEventHandler(object sender,
  ErrorAddDataBoundRowEventArgs e);
class ErrorAddDataBoundRowEventArgs : EventArgs
{
  object Item { get; }
  Exception InnerException { get; }
  bool Retry { get; set; }
}
```

The exception is copied into the event arguments; the handler can then analyze the exception, attempt to patch up the row, and retry the commit operation. Should it fail a second time, the row is deleted. The exception thrown in this case may be the new SetDataBindingFailedException, which is documented below.

A data source may have a fixed number of rows or a fixed number of columns. A data source can also contain read-only data or read-only column names. Therefore, attempting to edit cells, add rows, remove rows, add columns, or remove columns can all fail. In these cases, the list object disallows the change and restores the original shape. When it does so, it raises the OriginalDataRestored event. Listing 17-10 shows its delegate.

Listing 17-10 The OriginalDataRestored Event Types

```
delegate void OriginalDataRestoredEventHandler(object sender,
  OriginalDataRestoredEventArgs args)

class OriginalDataRestoredEventArgs : EventArgs
{
  ChangeType ChangeType { get; }
  ChangeReason ChangeReason { get; }
}
enum ChangeType
{
  RangeValueRestored,
  ColumnAdded,
  ColumnRemoved,
  RowAdded,
  RowRemoved,
  ColumnHeaderRestored
}

public enum ChangeReason
{
  ReadOnlyDataSource,
  FixedLengthDataSource,
  FixedNumberOfColumnsInDataBoundList,
  ErrorInCommit,
  Other,
  DataBoundColumnHeaderIsAutoSet
}
```

New Exception

Data binding can fail under many scenarios; the SetDataBindingFailedException is thrown in three of them:

- If the data source of the list object is not a list data source
- If the data source of the list object has no data-bound columns
- If the list object cannot be resized when the data change

The exception class has these public methods and a Reason property shown in Listing 17-11.

Listing 17-11 The SetDataBindingFailedException Types

```
[Serializable] class SetDataBindingFailedException : Exception
{
  SetDataBindingFailedException()
  SetDataBindingFailedException(string message)
  SetDataBindingFailedException(string message,
    Exception innerException)
  void GetObjectData(SerializationInfo info, StreamingContext context)
  FailureReason Reason { get; }
}

enum FailureReason
{
    CouldNotResizeListObject,
    InvalidDataSource,
    NoDataBoundColumnsSpecified
}
```

Conclusion

Using data binding effectively requires many objects to work well together: controls, datasets, data tables, binding sources, binding contexts, binding managers, and so on. This chapter, and indeed, this book, by no means descries all the data binding tools at your disposal. Fortunately, the designer generates many of the objects that you need and wires them up to each other sensibly. Still, having an understanding of what is happening behind the scenes helps considerably when designing data-driven applications.

The next chapter covers some more techniques for building data-driven applications—in particular, how to programmatically manipulate the data island without starting Word or Excel.

■ 18 ■

Server Data Scenarios

Populating a Document with Data on the Server

CONSIDER THE FOLLOWING PORTION OF an all-too-common server scenario. An authenticated user, perhaps a salesperson, requests an Excel spreadsheet from a server. The spreadsheet is an expense report, and the server is an ASP, ASP.NET, or SharePoint server. The server code looks up some information about the user from a database, Active Directory, or Web service. For example, perhaps the server has a list of recent corporate credit card activity that it will prepopulate into the expense list. The server starts up Excel but keeps it "invisible" because there is no interactive user on the server. It then uses the Excel object model to insert the data into the appropriate cells, saves the result, and serves up the resulting file to the user.

This is a very suboptimal document life cycle for two reasons. First, it is completely unsupported and strongly recommended against by Microsoft. Word and Excel were designed to be run interactively on client machines with perhaps a few instances of each running at the same time. They were not designed to be scalable and robust in the face of thousands of Web server hits creating many instances on "headless" servers that allow no graphical user interfaces.

Second, this process thoroughly conflates the "view" with the data. The server needs to know exactly how the document is laid out visually so that it can insert and remove the right fields in the right places. A simple change in the document format can necessitate many tricky changes in the server code.

But automatically serving up documents full of a user's data is such a compelling scenario that many organizations have ignored Microsoft's guidelines and build solutions around server-side manipulation of Word and Excel documents. Those solutions tend to have serious scalability and robustness problems.

What can we do to mitigate these two problems?

Data-Bound VSTO Documents

As discussed in Chapter 17, "VSTO Data Programming," one way to solve this problem is to move the processing onto the client. Just serve up a blank document that detects whether there is no cached data in its data island and fills its datasets from the database server if so. When the client is ready to send the data back to the database, it connects again and updates the database. No special document customization has to happen on the server at all, and the database server is doing exactly what it was designed to do.

This solution has a major drawback, however: It requires that every user have access to the database. From a security perspective, it might be smarter to only give the document server access to the database, thereby decreasing the "attack surface" exposed to malicious hackers. What we really want to do is have the document ready to go with the user data in it from the moment they obtain the document, but without having to start up Word or Excel on the server.

XML File Formats

Avoiding the necessity of starting up a client application on the server is key. Consider the first half of the scenario above: The server takes an existing on-disk document and uses Excel to produce a modified version of the document. Excel is just a means to an end; if you know what changes need to be made to the bits of the document and how to manipulate the file format, you have no need to start up the client application.

The Word and Excel binary file formats are "opaque," but Word and Excel now support persisting documents in a much more transparent XML format. It is not too hard to write a program that manipulates the XML document without ever starting up Word or Excel.

However, the XML file formats have some drawbacks. Although it is certainly faster and easier to manipulate the XML format directly, parsing large XML files is still not blazingly fast. XML files tend to be quite a bit larger than the corresponding binary files. And worst, although the Word XML format is "full fidelity," the Excel format is not. Excel loses information about the VSTO customization when it saves a document as XML.

Furthermore, unfortunately the Word XML file format does not store the data island in human-readable, editable XML. Rather, it serializes out the binary state that would have gone into the binary file format data island.

Also, we have not addressed the second problem that we identified earlier. Now we are not just manipulating the view, we are manipulating the *persisted state* of the view to insert or extract data. It would be much cleaner if we could simply get at the data island.

We need a way to solve these additional problems; we need a solution that works on binary non-human-readable files, works with VSTO-customized documents, and cleanly separates view from data.

Accessing the Data Island

Chapter 17 showed how to cache the state of public host item class members that contain data in a "data island" so that they could be persisted into the document as XML, independent of their user-interface representation. The VSTO 2005 runtime library comes with a class, ServerDocument, which can read and write the data island directly; it does not need to start up Word or Excel on the server. The Server-Document object can read and write Word documents in binary or XML format and Excel documents in binary format.

Let's re-create the above document life cycle using the data island. Then we describe the advanced features of the ServerDocument object model in more detail.

Using ServerDocument and ASP.NET

Many pieces must be put together here, but each one is fairly straightforward. Here is what we are going to do:

1. Create an ASP.NET Web site.

2. Create a simple VSTO customized expense report spreadsheet that has a cached dataset that is data bound to a list object and a cached string assigned to a named range in the Startup handler.

3. Publish the expense report template to the Web site.

4. Create an .aspx page that populates the data island (the cached dataset) before the document is served up.

5. As an added bonus, we adapt that page and turn into a custom file type handler.

In Visual Studio, select File > New > Web Site and create a new ASP.NET site. Suppose for the sake of this example that the server is http://accounting, and the Web site is http://accounting/expenses.

We come back to this Web site project later. For now, close it down and create a VSTO 2005 Excel spreadsheet project. Let's start by putting together a simple customization with one named range and one list object control bound to an untyped dataset. We will make the user's name and the expense dataset cached, so that the server can put the data in the data island when the document is served up. Figure 18-1 shows the spreadsheet with a named range and a list object. You can also see in Figure 18-1 the code behind Sheet1. The code defines a `string` called `EmpName` that is cached as well as a DataSet called `Expenses` that is cached. In the Startup handler for Sheet1, the code sets the Value2 property of the NamedRange called `EmployeeName` to the cached value `EmpName`. It also data binds the `Expenses` dataset to the ListObject called `List1`.

Choose the Build > Publish menu item and use the Publishing Wizard to build the spreadsheet and put it up on http://accounting/expenses. Doing so sets up the document so that it points to the customization on the Web server rather than the local machine. (Chapter 20, "Deployment," covers deployment scenarios in more detail.)

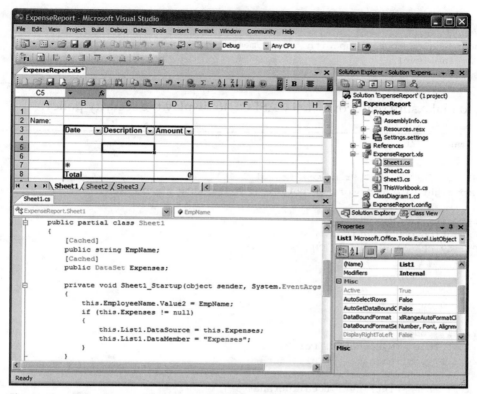

Figure 18-1 A simple expense report worksheet with two cached class members:
EmpName and Expenses.

For the customization to run on the client machine, you need to have a security policy set to trust the server. Chapter 19, ".NET Code Security," covers the whys and wherefores of security policy issues in detail; for now, just trust us that you need a security policy. On the client machine, you can use the command-line CASPOL.EXE tool or the MSCORCFG.MSC management tool to create a machine-level policy that grants full trust to the customization DLL. Here we use CASPOL.EXE to add a new policy that trusts content from a directory on the accounting Web server:

```
> caspol -ag 1.2 -url http://accounting/expenses/* FullTrust

Microsoft (R) .NET Framework CasPol 2.0
Copyright (C) Microsoft Corporation. All rights reserved.

The operation you are performing will alter security policy.
```

```
Are you sure you want to perform this operation? (yes/no)
yes
Added union code group with "-url" membership condition to the
Machine level.
Success
```

Just to make sure that works, tell CASPOL to display the security policy:

```
> caspol -lg


Microsoft (R) .NET Framework CasPol 2.0
Copyright (C) Microsoft Corporation. All rights reserved.

Security is ON
Execution checking is ON
Policy change prompt is ON


Level = Machine

Code Groups:

1. All code: Nothing
 1.1. Zone - MyComputer: FullTrust
    1.1.1. StrongName -: FullTrust
    1.1.2. StrongName -: FullTrust
 1.2. Zone - Intranet: LocalIntranet
    1.2.1. All code: Same site Web
    1.2.2. All code: Same directory FileIO - 'Read, PathDiscovery'
    1.2.3. Url - http://accounting/expenses/*: FullTrust
 1.3. Zone - Internet: Internet
    1.3.1. All code: Same site Web
 1.4. Zone - Untrusted: Nothing
 1.5. Zone - Trusted: Internet
    1.5.1. All code: Same site Web
Success
```

We have not set up the handler on the server yet, but do a quick sanity check on the client to make sure that the document can be downloaded and the customization run on the client machine. There will not be any data in it yet; let's take care of that next.

Setting Up the Server

Use Visual Studio to open the expenses Web site created earlier, and you will see that the deployed files for this customized spreadsheet have shown up. Now all we need to do is write a server-side page that loads the blank document into memory and fills in its data island before sending it out over the wire to the client. Right-click the Web site and choose Add New Item. Add a new .aspx Web form.

We need to add a reference to Microsoft.VisualStudio.Tools.Applications. Runtime.DLL to get at the ServerDocument class. After we do that, the code is fairly straightforward right up until the point where we set the serialized state. We discuss how that works in more detail later in this chapter.

Listing 18-1 An ASPX Web Form That Edits the Data Island on the Server

```
<%@ Page Language="C#" AutoEventWireup="true" %>
<%@ Import Namespace="System.Configuration" %>
<%@ Import Namespace="System.Web.Configuration" %>
<%@ Import Namespace="System.Data"%>
<%@ Import Namespace="System.Data.Common"%>
<%@ Import Namespace="System.Data.OleDb"%>
<%@ Import Namespace="System.IO"%>
<%@ Import Namespace= "Microsoft.VisualStudio.Tools.Applications.Runtime"%>

<script runat=server>

const int Forbidden = 403;

protected void Page_Load(object sender, EventArgs e)
{
  // If the user is not authenticated, then we do not want
  // to give the user any expense report at all.
  if (!User.Identity.IsAuthenticated)
  {
    Response.StatusCode = Forbidden;
    Response.End();
    return;
  }

  // If we do have a username, fetch the user's personal data from the
  // database (or Web service or other data source.)

  DataSet dataset = new DataSet();
  DataTable datatable = dataset.Tables.Add("Expenses");
  OleDbDataAdapter adapter = new OleDbDataAdapter();

  // Authenticated usernames are hard to malform. If there is a
  // chance that a string could be provided by a hostile caller,
  // do not use string concatenation without vetting the string
  // carefully. Better still, avoid SQL injection attacks entirely
```

```
// by using stored procedures.

adapter.SelectCommand = new OleDbCommand(
  "SELECT [Date], Description, Cost " +
  "FROM Expenses WHERE EmployeeName = \"" +
  User.Identity.Name + "\"");

// It's a good idea to store connection strings in the web.config
// file both for security — they can be encrypted in web.config —
// and for convenience — you can update the config file when the
// database server changes.

string connectionString = ConfigurationManager.
  ConnectionStrings["expenses"]. ConnectionString;
adapter.SelectCommand.Connection =
  new OleDbConnection(connectionString);
adapter.Fill(datatable);

// We do not want to modify the file on disk; instead, we'll read it
// into memory and add the user's information to the in-memory
// document before we serve it.

FileStream file = new FileStream(
  @"c:\INetPub\WWWRoot\expenses\ExpenseReport.XLS",
  FileMode.Open, FileAccess.Read);
byte[] template;
try {
  template = new byte[file.Length];
  file.Read(template, 0, (int)file.Length);
}
finally {
  file.Close();
}

// Finally, we'll create a ServerDocument object to manipulate the
// in-memory copy. Because it only has a raw array of bytes to work
// with, it needs to be told whether it is looking at an .XLS,
// .XLT, .DOC, or .DOT.

ServerDocument sd = new ServerDocument(template, ".XLS");
try {
  sd.CachedData.HostItems["ExpenseReport.Sheet1"].
    CachedData["EmpName"].SerializeDataInstance(User.Identity.Name);
  sd.CachedData.HostItems["ExpenseReport.Sheet1"].
    CachedData["Expenses"].SerializeDataInstance(dataset);
  sd.Save();

  // "template" still has the original bytes. Get the new bytes.
```

```
      template = sd.Document;
    }
    finally {
      sd.Close();
    }
    Response.ClearContent();
    Response.ClearHeaders();
    Response.ContentType = "application/vnd.ms-excel";
    Response.OutputStream.Write(template, 0, template.Length);
    Response.Flush();
    Response.Close();
  }
</script>
```

An Alternative Approach: Create a Custom Handler

It seems a little odd to go to an .aspx page to download a spreadsheet or document. An alternative approach to solving the problem of customizing documents on the server is to intercept requests for particular file extensions and customize the response before it goes out to the client.

This time, instead of creating a new .aspx Web form, create a new .ashx handler (see Figure 18-2).

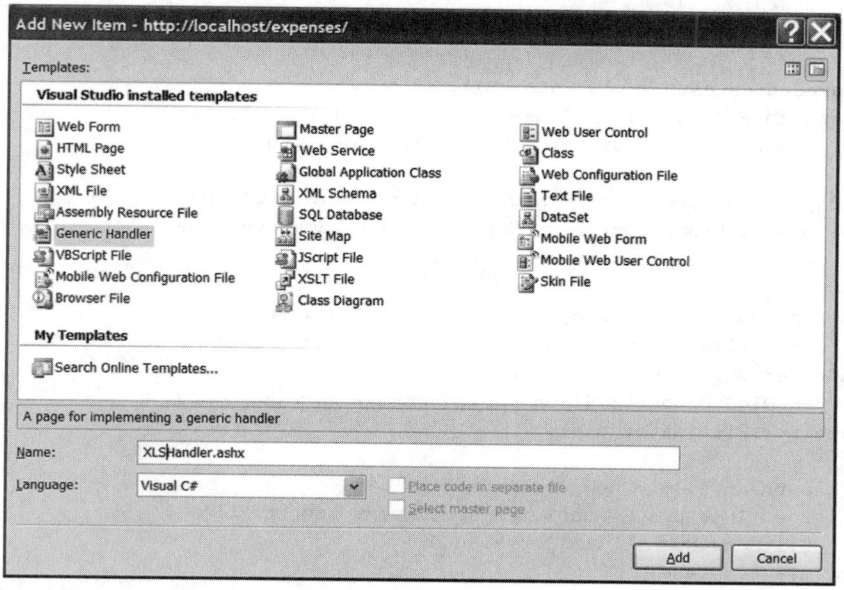

Figure 18-2 Creating a custom handler item.

The code is essentially identical; the only difference is that because a handler is not an instance of a Web page, we do not have any of the standard page objects such as Response, Request, User, and so on. Fortunately, the context of the page request is encapsulated in a special "context" object that is passed to the handler.

Listing 18-2 Creating a Custom Handler That Edits the Data Island

```
<%@ WebHandler Language="C#" Class="XLSHandler" %>

using System;
using System.Data;
using System.Data.Common;
using System.Data.OleDb;
using System.IO;
using System.Web;
using Microsoft.VisualStudio.Tools.Applications.Runtime;

public class XLSHandler : IHttpHandler {
  const int Forbidden = 403;
  public void ProcessRequest (HttpContext context) {

    if (!context.User.Identity.IsAuthenticated)
    {
      context.Response.StatusCode = Forbidden;
      context.Response.End();
      return;
    }

    DataSet dataset = new DataSet();
    DataTable datatable = dataset.Tables.Add("Expenses");
    OleDbDataAdapter adapter = new OleDbDataAdapter();

    adapter.SelectCommand = new OleDbCommand("SELECT [Date], " +
      "Description, Cost FROM Expenses WHERE EmployeeName = \"" +
      context.User.Identity.Name + "\"");

    string connectionString = ConfigurationManager.
      ConnectionStrings["expenses"].ConnectionString;
    adapter.SelectCommand.Connection =
      new OleDbConnection(connectionString);
    adapter.Fill(datatable);

    FileStream file = new FileStream(
      @"c:\INetPub\WWWRoot\expenses\ExpenseReport.XLS",
      FileMode.Open, FileAccess.Read);
    byte[] template;
```

```
  try
  {
    template = new byte[file.Length];
    file.Read(template, 0, (int)file.Length);
  }
  finally
  {
    file.Close();
  }

  ServerDocument sd = new ServerDocument(template, ".XLS");
  try
  {
    sd.CachedData.HostItems["ExpenseReport.Sheet1"].
      CachedData["EmpName"].SerializeDataInstance(
      context.User.Identity.Name);
    sd.CachedData.HostItems["ExpenseReport.Sheet1"].
      CachedData["Expenses"].SerializeDataInstance(dataset);
    sd.Save();

    // "template" still has the original bytes. Get the new bytes.
    template = sd.Document;
  }
  finally
  {
    sd.Close();
  }

  context.Response.ContentType = "application/vnd.ms-excel";
  context.Response.OutputStream.Write(template, 0, template.Length);
}
public bool IsReusable
{
  get { return false; }
}
}
```

Finally, to turn this on, add the information about the class and assembly name for the handler to your Web.config file in the application's virtual root. If you want to debug the server-side code, you can add debugging information in the configuration file, too.

Listing 18-3 A Web Configuration File to Turn on the Handler

```
<configuration>
  <system.web>
```

```
    <httpHandlers>
      <add verb="GET" path="ExpenseReport.xls"
        type="XLSHandler, XLSHandler"/>
    </httpHandlers>
    <compilation debug="true"/>
  </system.web>
</configuration>
```

Now when the client hits the server, the handler will intercept the request, load the requested file into memory, contact the database, create the appropriate dataset, and serialize the dataset into the data island in the expense report—all without starting Excel.

A Handy Client-Side ServerDocument Utility

The ServerDocument object was aptly named. It was primarily designed for exactly the scenario we have just explored: writing information into a document on a server. However, it can do a lot more, from reading the data back out of a document to updating the deployment information inside a document, to adding customizations to documents. We discuss the portions of the ServerDocument object model used in deployment scenarios in Chapter 20, and spend the rest of this chapter describing the data-manipulating tools in the ServerDocument in more detail.

Let's take a look at another illustrative use of the ServerDocument object, and then we give a more complete explanation of all its data properties and methods. Here is a handy C# console application that dumps out the "cached data manifest" and serialized cached data in a document.

Listing 18-4 Creating a Cache Viewer with ServerDocument

```
using Microsoft.VisualStudio.Tools.Applications.Runtime;
using System;
using System.IO;
using System.Text;

namespace VSTOViewer {
  public class MainClass {
    public static void Main(string[] args) {
      if (args.Length != 1) {
        Console.WriteLine("Usage:");
        Console.WriteLine("    CacheViewer.exe myfile.doc");
```

```csharp
        return;
      }

    string filename = args[0];
    ServerDocument doc = null;

    try {
      doc = new ServerDocument(filename, false, FileAccess.Read);
      Console.WriteLine("\nCached Data Manifest");
      Console.WriteLine(doc.CachedData.ToXml());

      foreach(CachedDataHostItem view in doc.CachedData.HostItems) {
        foreach(CachedDataItem item in view.CachedData) {
          if (item.Xml != null && item.Xml.Length != 0) {
            Console.WriteLine("\nCached Data: " + view.Id + "." +
              item.Id + " xml\n");
            Console.WriteLine(item.Xml);
          }
          if (item.Schema != null && item.Schema.Length != 0) {
            Console.WriteLine("\nCached Data: " + view.Id + "." +
              item.Id + " xsd\n");
            Console.WriteLine(item.Schema);
          }
        }
      }
    }
    catch (CannotLoadManifestException ex)
    {
      Console.WriteLine("Not a customized document:" + filename);
      Console.WriteLine(ex.Message);
    }
    catch (FileNotFoundException)
    {
      Console.WriteLine("File not found:" + filename);
    }
    catch (Exception ex)
    {
      Console.WriteLine("Unexpected Exception:" + filename);
      Console.WriteLine(ex.ToString());
    }
    finally
    {
      if (doc != null)
        doc.Close();
    }
  }
}
}
```

After you compile this into a console application, you can run the console application on the command line and pass the name of the document you want to view. The document must have a saved VSTO data island in it for anything interesting to happen.

Now that you have an idea of how the ServerDocument object model is used, we can talk about it in more detail.

The ServerDocument Object Model

The ServerDocument object model enables you to read and write all the deployment information and cached data stored inside a customized document. This section goes through all of the "data" properties and methods in this object model, describing what they do, their purpose, and why they look the way they do. Chapter 20 describes the "deployment" portions of the object model.

> Before we begin, note that the ServerDocument object model is what we like to call an "enough rope" object model. Because this object model enables you to modify all the information about the customization, it is quite possible to create documents with inconsistent cached data or nonsensical deployment information. The VSTO runtime engine does attempt to detect malformed customization information and throw the appropriate exceptions; but still, exercise caution when using this object model.

ServerDocument Class Constructors

The ServerDocument class has seven constructors, but five of them are mere "syntactic sugars" for these two:

```
ServerDocument(byte[] bytes, string fileType)
ServerDocument(string documentPath, bool onClient, FileAccess access)
```

These correspond to the two primary ServerDocument scenarios: Either you want to read/edit a document in memory, or on disk. Note that these two scenarios cannot be mixed; if you start off by opening a file on disk, you cannot treat it as an array of bytes in memory and vice versa.

The in-memory version of the constructor takes a string that indicates the type of the file. Because all you are giving it is the bytes of the file, as opposed to the name of the file, the constructor does not know whether this is an .XLS, .XLT, .DOC, .DOT, or .XML. Pass in one of those strings to indicate what kind of document this is. If you pass in .XML, the document you pass must be in the WordprocessingML (WordML) format supported by Word. ServerDocument cannot read documents saved in the Excel XML format.

The byte array passed in must be an image of a customized document. The ServerDocument object model does not support in-memory manipulation of not-yet-customized documents.

The on-disk version takes the document path, from which it can deduce the file type. The onClient flag indicates whether your code is presently running in a client scenario (such as the document viewer sample above) or a server scenario (such as the customized data island generation example at the beginning of this chapter).

Why does the ServerDocument care whether it is running on a client or a server? Most of the time it does not care. However, there is one important scenario: What if you pass in a document that does not yet have a customization?

In that case, the ServerDocument object attempts to add customization information to the uncustomized document. Adding the customization information requires the ServerDocument class to start up Word or Excel, load the document into the application, and manipulate it using the Office object model. Because doing that is a very bad idea in server scenarios, the ServerDocument throws an exception if given an uncustomized document on the server.

The file access parameter can be `FileAccess.Read` or `FileAccess.ReadWrite`. If it is "read-only," attempts to change the document will fail. (Opening an uncustomized document on the client in read-only mode is not a very good idea; the attempt to customize the document will fail.)

The other "in-memory" constructor is provided for convenience; it simply reads the entire stream into a byte array for you:

```
ServerDocument(Stream stream, string fileType)
```

Finally, the three remaining "on-disk" constructors act just like the three-argument constructor above with the onClient flag defaulting to `false` if omitted, and the file access defaulting to `ReadWrite` if omitted:

```
ServerDocument(string documentPath, bool onClient)
ServerDocument(string documentPath, FileAccess access)
ServerDocument(string documentPath)
```

Saving and Closing Documents

The ServerDocument object has two important methods and one property used to shut down a document:

```
void Save()
byte[] Document { get; }
void Close()
```

If you opened the ServerDocument object with an on-disk document, the Save method writes the changes you have made to the application manifest, cached data manifest, or data island to disk. If you opened the document using a byte array or stream, the changes are saved into a memory buffer that you can access with the Document property. Note that it is an error to read the Document property if the file was opened on disk.

It is a good programming practice to explicitly close the ServerDocument object when you have finished with it. Large byte arrays and file locks are both potentially expensive resources that will not be reclaimed by the operating system until the object is closed (or, equivalently, disposed by either the garbage collector or an explicit call to IDisposable.Dispose).

Server-side users of ServerDocument are cautioned to be particularly careful when opening on-disk documents for read-write access. It is a bad idea to have multiple writers (or a single writer and one or more readers) trying to access the same file at the same time. The ServerDocument class will do its best in this situation; it will make "shadow copy" backups of the file so that readers can continue to read the file without interference while writers write. However, making shadow copies of large files can prove time-consuming.

If you do find yourself in this situation, consider doing what we did in the first example in this chapter; read the file into memory, and edit it in memory rather than on disk. As long as the on-disk version is only read, it will never need to be shadow-copied and runs no risk of multiple writers overwriting each other's changes.

Static Helper Methods

Developers typically want to perform a few common scenarios with the ServerDocument object model; the class exposes some handy static helper methods so that you do not have to write the boring "boilerplate" code. All of these scenarios work only with "on-disk" files, not with "in-memory" files. The following static methods are associated with ServerDocument:

```
static string AddCustomization(
   string documentPath,
   string assemblyPath,
   string deploymentManifestPath,
   string applicationVersion,
   bool makePathRelative)
   out string[] nonpublicCachedDataMembers)
static void RemoveCustomization(string documentPath)
static bool IsCustomized(string documentPath)
static bool IsCacheEnabled(string documentPath)
```

AddCustomization

AddCustomization takes an uncustomized document and adds customization information to it. It creates a new application manifest and cached data manifest. If given an already customized document, the customization information is destroyed and replaced with the new information. This allows you to create new customized documents on a machine without Visual Studio; you could create the customization assemblies on a development box, and then apply the customizations to documents on a different machine.

> AddCustomization should only be called on client machines, never on servers, because it always starts up Word or Excel to embed the customization information in the uncustomized document.

The document and assembly paths are required; the deployment manifest path may be `null` or empty if you do not want to use a deployment manifest to manage updating your customization.

The application version string must be a standard version string of the form `"1.2.3.4"`. Note that this is the version number of the customization itself, not the version number of the assembly. (However, it might be wise to use the version number of the assembly as the version number of your customized document application.)

If the `makePathRelative` flag is set to `true`, the assembly location written into the customization information will be relative to the document location. For instance, if the document location is a UNC path such as \\accounting\documents\budget.doc, and the assembly location is \\accounting\documents\dlls\budget.dll, the assembly location written into the document will be dlls\budget.dll, not the full path. Otherwise, if `makePathRelative` is `false`, the assembly location is written exactly as it is passed in.

The AddCustomization method loads the assembly and scans it for document/worksheet classes that contain members marked with the `Cached` attribute so that it can emit information into the cached data manifest indicating that these members need to be filled when the customization starts up for the first time. Because the VSTO runtime will be unable to fill in nonpublic members of these classes, the AddCustomization method returns the names of such members to help you catch this mistake early.

RemoveCustomization

RemoveCustomization removes all customization information from a document, including *all* the cached data in the data island. It also starts up Word/Excel, so do not call it on a server. Calling RemoveCustomization on an uncustomized document results in an invalid operation exception.

IsCustomized and IsCacheEnabled

IsCustomized and IsCacheEnabled are similar but subtly different because of a somewhat obscure scenario. Suppose you have a customized document that contains cached data in the data island, and you use the ServerDocument object model to remove all information about what document/worksheet classes need to be started up. In this odd scenario, the document will not run any customization code when it starts up, and therefore there is no way for the document to access the data island at runtime. Essentially, the document has become an uncustomized document with no code behind it, but all the data is still sitting in the data island. The VSTO designers anticipated that someone might want to remove information about the code while keeping the data island intact for later extraction via the ServerDocument object model.

IsCustomized returns `true` if the document is customized *and* will attempt to run code when it starts up. IsCacheEnabled returns `true` if the document is customized at all, and therefore has a data island, *regardless* of whether the customization information says what classes to start up when the document is loaded. (Note that IsCacheEnabled says nothing about whether the data island actually contains any data, just whether the document supports caching.)

Cached Data Objects, Methods, and Properties

As you saw in our handy utility above, a customized document's data island contains a small XML document called the cached data manifest, which describes the classes and properties in the cache (or, if the document is being run for the first time, the properties that need to be filled). The cached data is organized hierarchically; the manifest consists of a collection of view class elements, each of which contains a collection of items corresponding to cached members of the class. For example, here is a cached data manifest that has one cached member of one view class. The cached data member contains a typed DataSet:

```
<cdm:cachedDataManifest cdm:revision="1">
  <cdm:view cdm:viewId="ExcelCached.Sheet1">
    <cdm:dataInstance cdm:dataId="NorthwindDataSet"
      cdm:dataType="ExcelCached.NorthwindDataSet,
      ExcelCached, Version=1.0.1854.30463, Culture=neutral,
      PublicKeyToken=null" />
  </cdm:view>
</cdm:cachedDataManifest>
```

Having a collection of collections is somewhat more complex than just having a collection of cached items. The cached data manifest was designed this way to avoid the ambiguity of having two host item classes (such as Sheet1 and Sheet2) each with a cached property named the same thing. Because each item is fully qualified by its class, there is no possibility of name collisions.

The actual serialized data is stored in the data island, not in the cached data manifest. However, in the object model it is more convenient to associate each data instance in the cached data manifest with its serialized state.

The Cached Data Object Model

To get at the cached data manifest and any serialized data in the data island, the place to start is the CachedData property of the ServerDocument class. The CachedData object returns the CachedDataHostItemCollection, which contains a CachedData-HostItem for each host item in your customized document. A CachedDataHostItem is a collection of CachedDataItem objects that correspond to each class member variable that has been marked with the `Cached` attribute. Figure 18-3 shows an object model diagram for the objects returned for the example in Figure 18-1.

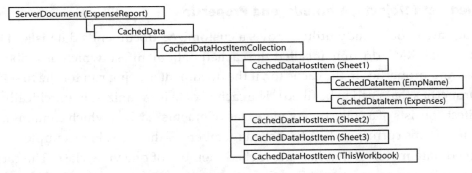

Figure 18-3 The cached data object model for the example in Figure 18-1.

To get to the CachedData object, use the ServerDocument object's CachedData property:

```
public CachedData CachedData { get; }
```

There are no constructors for any of the types we will be discussing. The CachedData class has four handy helper methods (Clear, FromXml, ToXml, and ClearData) and a collection of CachedDataHostItem:

```
void Clear()
void FromXml(string cachedDataManifest)
string ToXml()
```

```
void ClearData()
CachedDataHostItemCollection HostItems { get; }
```

Like the application manifest, the Clear method throws away all information in the cached data manifest, the FromXml method clears the manifest and repopulates it from the XML state, and the ToXml method serializes the manifest as an XML string.

The ClearData method throws away all information in the data island, but leaves all the entries in the cached data manifest. When the document is started up in the client, all the corresponding members will be marked as needing to be filled.

The CachedDataHostItem Collection

The HostItems collection is a straightforward extension of CollectionBase that provides a simple strongly typed collection of CachedDataHostItem objects. (It is called "host items" because these always correspond to items provided by the hosting application, such as Sheet1, Sheet2, or ThisDocument.)

```
CachedDataHostItem Add(string id)
bool Contains(string id)
int IndexOf(CachedDataHostItem item)
void Remove(CachedDataHostItem item)
void Remove(string id)
CachedDataHostItem this[string id] {get;}
CachedDataHostItem this[int index] {get;}
void CopyTo(CachedDataHostItem[] items, int index)
void Insert(int index, CachedDataHostItem value)
```

The id argument corresponds to the namespace-qualified name of the host item class. Be careful when creating new items to ensure that the class identifier is fully qualified.

The CachedDataHostItem Object

Each CachedDataHostItem object corresponds to a host item in your document and is a collection of CachedDataItem objects that correspond to cached members of the customized host item class:

```
CachedDataItem Add(string dataId, string dataType)
bool Contains(string dataId)
void Remove(CachedDataItem data)
```

```
int IndexOf(CachedDataItem data)
void Remove(string dataId)
CachedDataItem this[int index] {get;}
CachedDataItem this[string dataId] {get;}
void CopyTo(CachedDataItem[] items, int index)
void Insert(int index, CachedDataItem item)
```

You might wonder why it is that you must specify the type of the property when adding a new element via the Add method. If you have a host item class like this, surely the name of the class and property is sufficient to deduce the type, right?

```
class Sheet1 {
    [Cached] public NorthwindDataSet myData;
```

In this case, it would be sufficient to deduce the compile-time type, but it would not be if the compile-time type were object. When the document is run in the client and the cached members are deserialized and populated, the deserialization code in the VSTO runtime needs to know whether the runtime type of the member is a dataset, datatable, or other serializable type.

The CachedDataItem Object

The identifier of a CachedDataItem is the name of the property or field on the host item class that was marked with the Cached attribute. The CachedDataItem itself exposes the type and identifier properties:

```
string DataType { get; set; }
string Id { get; set; }
```

As well as two other interesting properties and a helper method:

```
string Xml { get; set; }
string Schema { get; set; }
void SerializeDataInstance(object value)
```

Setting the Xml and Schema properties correctly can be slightly tricky; the Serialize-DataInstance method takes an object and sets the Xml and Schema properties for you. However, if you do not have an instance of the object on the server and want to manipulate just the serialized XML strings, you must understand the rules for how to set these properties correctly.

The first thing to note is that the Schema property is ignored if the DataType is not a DataTable or DataSet (or subclass thereof). If you are serializing out another type via XML serialization, there is no schema, so just leave it blank. On the other hand, if you are writing out a DataSet or DataTable, you must specify the schema.

Second, the data island may contain DataSets and DataTables in either in regular "raw" XML form or in "diffgram" form. The regular format that you are probably used to seeing XML-serialized DataSets in looks something like this:

```
<DataSet1 xmlns="http://www.foocorp.org/schemas/customers.xsd">
  <dbo_Customers>
    <Name>Maria Anders</Name>
    <Address>Obere Str. 57</Address>
  </dbo_Customers>
  <dbo_Customers>
    <Name>Ana Trujillo</Name>
    <Address>Avda. de la Constitución 2222</Address>
  </dbo_Customers>
```

And so on. A similar DataSet in diffgram form looks different:

```
<diffgr:diffgram>
  <NorthwindDataSet
    xmlns="http://www.foocorp.org/schemas/NorthwindDataSet.xsd">
    <Customers diffgr:id="Customers1" msdata:rowOrder="0">
    <CustomerID>ALFKI</CustomerID>
    <CompanyName>Alfreds Futterkiste</CompanyName>
    <ContactName>Maria Anders</ContactName>
```

You can store cached DataSets and DataTables by setting the Xml property to either format. By default the VSTO runtime saves them in diffgram format. Why? Because the diffgram format not only captures the current state of the DataSet or DataTable, but also records how the object has changed because it was filled in by the data adapter. That means that when the object's data is poured back into the database, the adapter can update only the rows that have changed instead of having to update all of them.

Be Careful

One final caution about using the ServerDocument object model to manipulate the cache: The cache should be "all or nothing." Either the cached data manifest should have *no* data items with serialized XML, or they should *all* have XML. The VSTO runtime does not currently support scenarios where some cached data items need to be filled and others do not. If when the client runtime starts up it detects that the cache is filled inconsistently, it will assume that the data island is corrupted and start fresh, refilling everything. If you need to remove some cached data from a document, remove the entire data item from the host item collection; do not just set the XML property to an empty string.

Conclusion

The ServerDocument object model was primarily designed to enable server-side code to edit the contents of the data island before serving up a document, but it does much more. You can use it to read or write the data island, and to add customization assemblies to uncustomized documents. However, the latter requires ServerDocument to start up Word or Excel, so it is a bad idea to do this on a server. Chapter 20 examines another use for the ServerDocument: editing the deployment information inside a customized document.

The ServerDocument object model provides fine-grained control over the information stored in a document, and assumes that you know what you're doing. Be very careful, and test your scenarios thoroughly when using the ServerDocument object model.

■ 19 ■
.NET Code Security

N THE OLD DAYS—back in the twentieth century—the primary way that we got software onto our machines went something like this: Go to software store, buy a shrink-wrapped box containing disks, insert said disks into machine, install software. If that is the only way you put software on your machine, it is pretty hard to get a computer virus. Not impossible, but pretty hard.

That world is long gone; code in the twenty-first century is both highly mobile and highly componentized. Generally, "monolithic" applications such as Word and Excel now make extensive use of third-party components and store customized code behind documents. Many machines are constantly connected to the Internet, a worldwide network chock-full of evil hackers.

Ubiquitous networking and rich customization of everything from Web pages to spreadsheets are undoubtedly enabling technologies, but they come with the price of an enormous increase in the size of the "attack surface" available to malicious attackers. Anyone who has ever received a mass-mail virus e-mail or been infected by an Excel macro virus knows of what we speak!

Fortunately, the .NET Framework was designed from day one to provide tools to help mitigate the vulnerabilities inherent in modern software. This chapter starts with an overview of the .NET security system to explain some key concepts. Then the chapter takes a detailed look at how to use the .NET security system to keep yourself and your users productive while keeping attackers unproductive.

This discussion is especially relevant to VSTO because VSTO has the security model that *no* code is allowed to run by default. You will *always* have to configure the

.NET security system to trust a VSTO customization or add-in you build before it will run on a user's machine.

Code Access Security Versus Role-Based Security

The immediate and obvious example of a computer security system is the one most of us encounter the first thing in the morning: the login prompt. The purpose of the login prompt is to *authenticate* you, to somehow verify your identity. After your identity has been determined, you are then authorized to perform certain tasks: delete this file, run that application, and so on.

Determining identity is a hard problem, and many strategies exist for doing so. Each strategy, however, is based on consuming some *evidence* and making a decision based on it. Evidence might be based on the ability to produce a secret (such as a password), possession of an object (such as a smart card), biometrics (such as thumbprints or retinal scans), and so on.

After you have been authenticated, the security system knows of which groups you are a member and can enforce *policies* based on identity and group membership. For example, a policy might be "only members of the Administrators group can modify registry keys in the Local Machine hive." Policies are implemented by access control lists and other mechanisms in the operating system and administered by various application programming interfaces (APIs).

The system just described is a *role-based security* system. In a role-based security system, the fundamental question is "who is running the code?" After that has been determined, the code runs with all the privileges and restrictions of the user. A fundamental presumption of role-based security systems is that users run some code because they know what it does and want it to succeed. When you run format.exe, the operating system presumes that you really do want to format your hard disk, and checks to ensure that you have permission to do so.

But sometimes role-based security is not enough. Consider a Web page that runs a script that tries to format the hard disk. In that case, whether the *user* who started the Web browser has the right to destroy the disk in question is of secondary importance. What is more relevant is whether the user actually *intended* the Web page to format the hard disk! The fundamental presumption of role-based security no longer applies; in a world with mobile code that sits behind Web pages, e-mails, and documents, the user *does not necessarily know what the code is doing* and might not want it to succeed.

Internet Explorer therefore implements a *code access* security system. A code access security system consumes evidence not about the user running the code, but about the code itself. Where did it come from? Who wrote it? What is the user's trust relationship with the Web site? The browser can then enforce policies such as "Web pages in the Untrusted Sites zone are not allowed to run scripts at all," and users and administrators can set policies accordingly.

The .NET security system implements both role-based and code access security systems, but for our purposes this discussion examines only the code access security system; customized documents are much more like Web pages, where the user might not know exactly what the customization is doing.

Code Access Security in .NET

The .NET code access security system works like this: Every time an assembly is loaded into an application domain, the security system determines what *permission set* should be granted to that assembly. The .NET runtime does this by examining *evidence* about the assembly. Assemblies are categorized into one or more *code groups* based on their evidence. The policy evaluator then determines which permissions to grant based on which code groups the assembly belongs to (just as a role-based system determines which permissions to grant to users based on which user groups they belong to).

When the code runs, if it attempts to perform some task that requires a permission (such as deleting a file), the security system checks to ensure that the code was granted the appropriate permission. If not, it throws an exception and the attempt fails.

The Machine Policy Level

Let's take a look at the out-of-the-box policy. Go to your .NET Framework SDK directory and run the mscorcfg.msc file to pop up the management console shown in Figure 19-1.

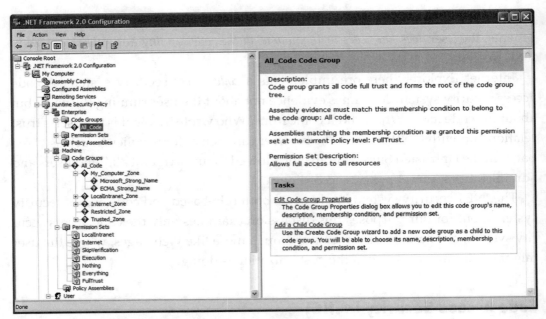

Figure 19-1 The .NET Runtime Security Policy management console.

As you can see, under Runtime Security Policy, there are three policy levels: Enterprise, Machine, and User. (There is also a fourth level, not shown, which is the Application policy level, which is discussed later in this chapter.) Open the Machine policy level, and you'll see that there is a tree of code groups. Each code group is associated with a particular permission set and evidence condition.

For example, code that has the My Computer Zone evidence is granted the Full-Trust permission set; code that is installed on your machine is granted permission to do anything. Code that has the LocalIntranet Zone evidence is granted the Local-Intranet permission set, which is rather more restrictive. If you run a managed assembly off of a share on your local intranet, it will be able to run, produce user-interface elements, and so on, but is not granted the right to modify your security settings or read or write to any file on your disk.

Notice that the root code group in the Machine policy level is All Code—every assembly is a member of this group irrespective of its evidence. If you look at the permission set granted by that group, however, it grants no permissions whatsoever. It denies the right to execute at all. What's up with that?

Within a policy level, the permission set granted to an assembly is (usually) the *least-restrictive union* of all the permission sets of all the applicable code groups. Code that belongs to the All Code group (which grants nothing) and the LocalIntranet Zone code group (which grants the LocalIntranet permission set) will be granted the permissions from the *less-restrictive* group.

> We say "usually" because there are ways of creating custom policies that enforce rules other than "take the least-restrictive union." For instance, you could create a policy tree with the rule "take the permission set granted by the first matching code group and ignore everything else." Policy trees can become quite complex.

Kinds of Evidence

So far we have seen the All Code group, which does not consider evidence at all, and various zone code groups that consider evidence about "where code comes from" in a broad sense. Zones describe whether the code comes from the local machine, the local intranet, an explicitly trusted Internet site, an explicitly untrusted Internet site, or an Internet site of unknown trustworthiness.

When we discuss the User policy level, you will see a much more specific kind of location-based evidence; you can create policies that grant permissions if the code is running from specific local or network directories or Web sites.

A close look at the Machine policy level shows two child code groups, subsets of the My Computer Zone code group, that grant full trust to assemblies in the My Computer Zone and are strong named with the Microsoft or ECMA keys. You will learn more about strong-name evidence, and why it should always be in a child code group, later in this chapter.

Finally, there is evidence associated with individual assemblies. Every assembly has a statistically unique "hash number" associated with it; it is possible to create policies that grant permissions to specific assemblies by checking their hash numbers. Assemblies can also be signed with a publisher certificate (such as a VeriSign code-signing certificate). When the loader attempts to load a publisher-signed assembly, it automatically creates evidence describing the certificate. You could create code groups that grant permissions to all assemblies signed with your internal corporate certificate, for instance.

Combining Policy Levels

Take a look at the Enterprise policy level shown in Figure 19-1. Unless your network administrator has set policy on your machine, this policy level should be much simpler than the Machine policy level. It consists of a single code group that matches all code and grants full trust.

But hold on a moment—if the Enterprise policy is "grant full trust to all code," how does this security system restrict anything whatsoever?

The .NET security system determines the grant set for each policy level—Enterprise, Machine, User, and Application—and actually grants the permission only if a permission is granted by all four levels.

Setting the Enterprise policy level to "everything gets full trust" cannot possibly weaken the restrictions of the other three groups. If the Machine policy level refuses to grant, say, permission to access the file system, it does not matter what the other three policy levels grant—that permission will not be granted to the assembly.

It works the other way, too: Suppose the Enterprise policy level states "grant full trust to all assemblies except for this known-to-be-hostile Trojan horse assembly." If you accidentally install the Trojan horse on your machine, the Machine policy level will grant full trust, but the Machine policy level cannot weaken the Enterprise policy level. Every policy level must agree to grant a permission for it to be granted, so the evil code will not run.

We discuss later in this chapter ways to get around the requirement that a permission must be granted by all four levels.

The User Policy Level

Take a look at your User policy level while logged in to a machine where you have been creating VSTO 2005 projects with Visual Studio. The contents of the User policy level as shown in Figure 19-2 might be a little bit surprising.

At the root, we have an All Code group that grants full trust, just like the Enterprise level. In keeping with the general rule that a policy level grants the least-restrictive union of permissions, it would seem that any further code groups in the policy tree for this level would be superfluous. And yet there is a child code group for VSTO projects—also an All Code group, although it grants no permissions. It in turn has a code group for every project you have created, which again is an All Code group that grants no permissions. (The code group is given a GUID as its name to ensure that the group is unique no matter how many projects you create.)

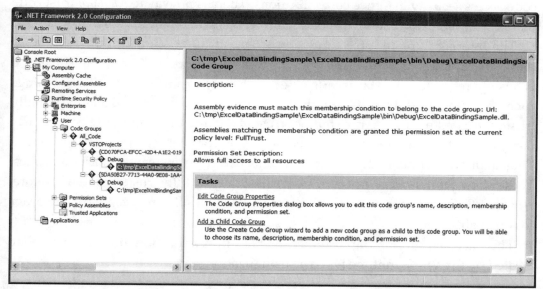

Figure 19-2 The User policy level—VSTO automatically creates policy so that VSTO projects are allowed to run on your development machine.

The project-level code groups have URL-based child groups for every build configuration you have built that grant only execution permission, nothing else, to all code in the named directory. And those have children that grant full trust to the specific customization assemblies.

What the heck is going on here? It looks like Visual Studio has gone to great lengths to ensure that the User policy level explicitly grants full trust to your customization assemblies. And yet the User policy level's root code group already grants full trust. How is this not redundant?

There is a good reason for this, but before we get to that, we should talk about full trust versus partial trust.

Full Trust and Partial Trust

As anyone who has ever been infected by a Word or Excel macro virus knows, the code behind a customized document does not always do what you want, and you do not always know what it does. Fortunately, that is exactly the scenario that code access security systems were invented to handle. However, there is a problem with code access security in Office customizations. There is no way to *partially* trust code that accesses the Word and Excel object models. Trust is all or nothing.

The Internet Explorer object model was specifically designed from day one so that code running inside the Web browser was in a "sandbox." Code can run, but it is heavily restricted. The browser's objects inherently cannot do dangerous things such as write an arbitrary file or change your registry settings. Code is partially trusted: trusted enough to run, but not trusted enough to do anything particularly dangerous. The Word and Excel object models by contrast are inherently powerful. They manipulate potentially sensitive data loaded from and saved to arbitrary files. These object models were designed to be called only by fully trusted code. Therefore, when a VSTO customization assembly is loaded, it *must be granted full trust* in order to run at all.

This fact has serious implications for the application domain security policy created by the VSTO runtime when a customization starts.

The VSTO Application Domain Policy Level

Before examining the details of VSTO security policy, let's take a step back and consider why anyone has any security policy at all.

It is the same reason why stores have merchandise exchange policy, governments have foreign policy, and parents have bedtime policy: Policy is a tool that enables us to make thoughtful decisions ahead of time instead of having to make decisions on a case-by-case basis. The Enterprise, Machine, and User policy levels allow network administrators, machine administrators, and machine users to independently make security decisions ahead of time so that the .NET runtime can enforce those decisions without user interaction.

Decisions about policy can also be made by application domains (or AppDomains, for short). Because only those permissions granted by all four policy levels are actually granted to the assembly, the AppDomain policy level can strengthen the overall security policy by requiring more stringent evidence than the other policy levels.

We know that VSTO customizations must be granted full trust. By default, the Enterprise and User policy levels grant full trust to all assemblies regardless of evidence. The Machine policy level grants full trust to all assemblies installed on the local machine. In the absence of an AppDomain policy level, a VSTO customization copied to your local machine is granted full trust.

That seems like a reasonable decision for an *application* that you have deliberately installed on your local machine. Users typically install applications that they trust, applications that perform as expected and do what users want them to do, so it makes sense to implicitly grant full trust to assemblies in the Local Machine Zone.

But spreadsheets are not usually thought of as applications. Do users realize that by copying a customized document to their machine, they are essentially installing an application that will then be fully trusted, capable of doing anything that the users themselves can do? Probably not! Users do not tend to think of customized documents as applications; they are much less careful about copying random spreadsheets to their machines than they are about copying random executables to their machines.

Good security policies take typical usage scenarios into account. Therefore, the VSTO runtime tightens up the overall security policy by creating an AppDomain policy level that grants all the permissions of the other three policy levels *except* for those permissions that would have been granted solely on the basis of membership in either an All Code code group or a zone code group. All other permissions granted because of URL evidence, certificates, strong names, and so on are honored.

Let's take a look at an example.

Resolving VSTO Policy

Consider a VSTO customization assembly that you have just built on your development machine that you want to run. The customization assembly must be granted full trust by all four policy levels; otherwise, it will not run. The Enterprise and User policy levels grant full trust to all code. The Machine policy level grants full trust to code from the My Computer Zone. Three of the four levels have granted full trust.

What about the AppDomain policy level? It grants the same permissions as the other three policy levels *except* for those permissions granted *solely* by All Code and zone code groups. The Enterprise policy level consists of a single All Code code group, so it is ignored by the AppDomain policy level. The Machine policy level consists only of zone code groups, plus two strong-name code groups for the Microsoft and ECMA strong names. Unless you happen to work for Microsoft and have access to the code-signing hardware, it is likely that those code groups do not apply; so effectively, the AppDomain policy level is going to ignore all of these, too. Things are not looking good; the AppDomain policy has found nothing it can use to grant full trust yet. If the User policy level also consists solely of an All Code code group, as it does on a clean machine, the customization will not run.

But the User policy level on your development machine has a code group that is *not* ignored by the AppDomain policy level; it has a URL code group that explicitly trusts the customization assembly based on its path. The AppDomain policy sees this and grants full trust to the assembly. Because all four policy levels have granted full trust, the code runs.

Now it should be clear why Visual Studio modified your User security policy and added a seemingly redundant code group for the assembly. The VSTO AppDomain policy level requires that the customization assembly not only be fully trusted, but be fully trusted for some better reason than "we trust all code" or "we trust all code installed on the local machine." Therefore, there has to be some Enterprise, Machine, or User code group that grants full trust on the basis of some stronger evidence.

Because the VSTO AppDomain policy level refuses to grant full trust on the basis of zone alone, you're pretty much forced to come up with a suitable policy to describe how you want the security system to treat VSTO customization assemblies. Take off your software developer hat for a moment and think like an administrator setting security policy for an enterprise. Let's go through a few typical security policies that you might use to ensure that customized Word and Excel documents work in your organization while still preventing potentially hostile customizations from attackers out on the Internet from running. After discussing the pros and cons of each, we talk about how to roll out security policy over an enterprise.

Location, Location, Location

One of the most straightforward ways to ensure that customized Word and Excel documents can run is to set a policy that states that customization assemblies that run from a particular place are fully trusted. You might have Web servers or file shares on your network where write access is restricted to trusted individuals; if the customization is there, that is pretty good evidence that it is trustworthy.

You can set an Enterprise-level policy that states that customization assemblies at a particular location are fully trusted by right-clicking the All Code code group in the Enterprise policy level and selecting New from the menu. Doing so causes the Create Code Group dialog to appear, as shown in Figure 19-3.

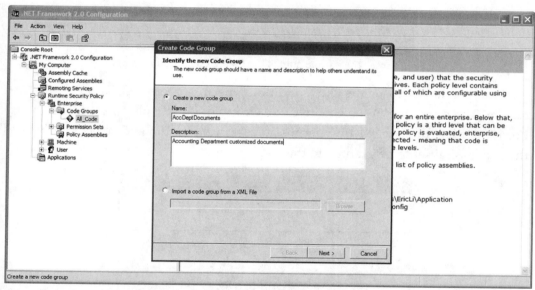

Figure 19-3 The first step of the Create Code Group dialog.

Enter a name for the code group and a description to help others understand what the code group is intended to do. Then click the Next button. The Create Code Group dialog shown in Figure 19-4 will appear. Choose a URL membership condition from the condition type drop-down box. For the URL, give the location to which the VSTO customization assembly will be deployed. In Figure 19-4, we are matching any customization assemblies in the Web folder http://accounting/customizations because we used the * wildcard in the URL.

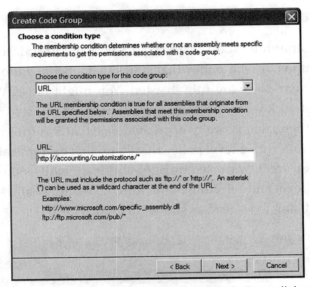

Figure 19-4 The second step of the Create Code Group dialog.

After you have chosen the URL condition type and entered a URL, click the Next button. The third step of the Create Code Group dialog displays, as shown in Figure 19-5. Select the Use existing permission set radio button and select FullTrust as the permission set to be granted to the code group.

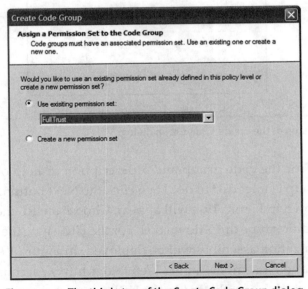

Figure 19-5 The third step of the Create Code Group dialog.

But hold on a moment. Clearly, this is not going to work. Remember, the policy evaluator only grants a permission if it is granted by *all four* code groups. When a user runs this customization, the Enterprise and User policy levels will grant full trust because of their root All Code code group. The AppDomain policy level will grant full trust because the Enterprise policy level contains a URL code group that grants full trust. But what about the Machine policy level? It will take one look at that thing, classify it as being from the LocalIntranet Zone, and grant it the LocalIntranet permission set. Because the customization assembly requires full trust, it will not run.

We have a problem here. You could, of course, solve this problem by setting the policy at the Machine level rather than the Enterprise level. Or you could set it at both levels. In the system described so far, however, policy levels can only add additional restrictions; it seems sensible that an enterprise administrator would be able to override the restrictions of a machine administrator. We need a way for a policy level to say "grant full trust even if another policy level disagrees."

Fortunately, we can tweak the code group to achieve this. Right-click the code group you just created, and choose Properties. Take a look at the check boxes at the bottom of the Properties dialog (see Figure 19-6).

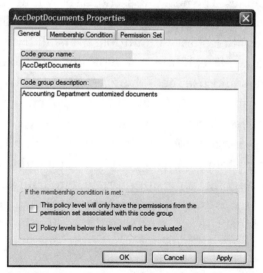

Figure 19-6 The Properties dialog for the AccDeptDocuments code group.

Checking the first check box makes this an "exclusive" code group; the regular rules about combining the permission sets of different code groups to determine the grant set for a particular policy level cease to apply. Checking the second check box makes this a "level-final" code group; policy levels from the "lower" code groups are ignored if the code's evidence matches the membership condition for this group.

What does "lower" mean? The Enterprise code group is the highest, then Machine, User, and finally Application Domain is the lowest.

> Creating a level-final code group considerably weakens your security policy because it prevents lower code groups from enforcing further restrictions. Always be careful when setting security policy, but be particularly careful when creating level-final groups.

Location-based policies are reasonably flexible. It is easy to deploy new documents to the trusted network locations and have them automatically be fully trusted by Enterprise policy. But there is always a tradeoff between ease of use and security; the drawback of location-based policies is that if some untrustworthy person does manage to install a hostile customization on a trusted server, it will run with full permissions on user machines. The next few sections show how to lock down the set of valid customizations even further to mitigate such vulnerabilities.

Some problems might also arise if multiple users all try to run the customized document from the same place. If users are typically going to download documents to their own computers and use them there, a more local URL policy might be in order. Instead of trusting a Web site in the policy, enter a URL such as file:///c:\MyCustomizedDocuments* or other local directory. Users can then download trusted customized documents to that folder and run them, while still preventing untrusted customizations copied to other locations from running.

In that scenario, it might be more appropriate to roll out User or Machine policy to allow individual users or machine administrators to change the location of their trusted documents folder.

Strong Names

Strong names allow you to grant full trust to only those assemblies that your organization (or other organizations that you trust) created. Confusion abounds about what exactly "strong names" are, what they are for, and how they work.

Back in the old days of "DLL hell," dynamically linked libraries were loaded based on filename and location. This approach has an inherent fundamental security problem: Attackers can name their evil DLLs system32.dll or oleaut32.dll, too. Attackers could try to trick you into loading their code rather than the code that you want to load by taking advantage of this weakness in the naming system.

The traditional DLL system also suffers from other technical problems, such as versioning. When you load oleaut32.dll, which version are you getting? Writing the code to figure it out is not rocket science, but it is not as easy as it could be.

Strong names mitigate these weaknesses. The purpose of a strong name is to provide every assembly with a unique, hard-to-forge name that clearly identifies its name, version, and author. When you load an assembly based on its strong name, you have extremely good evidence that you are actually loading the code you expect to be loading, not some hostile version that some other author managed to slip onto your machine.

Creating a Strong-Name Code Group

Because strong names identify the customization's author, you could set a policy that states that any code by a particular author is fully trusted. Suppose you have a strong-named assembly and you want to set a policy that says that all assemblies by this author are to be fully trusted. Again, create a new code group as *a child of the location code group* created before, but this time select the Strong Name membership condition shown in Figure 19-7.

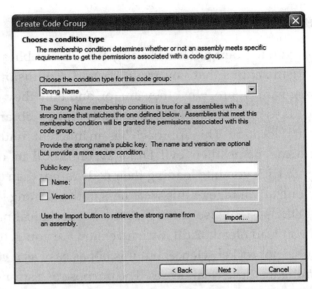

Figure 19-7 Creating a code group with a strong-name membership condition.

Import the public key from the strong-named assembly, and you have created a policy that trusts all assemblies by that author. (As the dialog notes, you can further strengthen the policy by trusting only certain names or even only certain versions.) But what exactly is a "public key" and what does it have to do with the code's author?

How Strong Names Are Implemented

Strong naming works by using public key cryptography. The mathematical details of how public key cryptosystems work would take us far off-topic, but briefly it goes something like this: An author generates two keys, appropriately called the public key and the private key. Assemblies can be signed with the private key, and the signature can be verified with the public key.

Therefore, if you have a public key and an assembly, you can determine whether the assembly was signed with the private key. You then know that the person who signed the assembly possessed the private key. If you believe that the author associated with that public key was not careless with the private key, you have good evidence that the assembly in question really was signed by the author.

The signing process is highly tamper-resistant. Changing so much as a single bit of the assembly invalidates the signature. Therefore, you also have good evidence that the assembly has not been changed post-release by hostile attackers out to get you.

Why Create a Child Code Group?

You might have wondered why we recommended that you create your Strong Name code group as a child code group of the location-based code group discussed earlier. And come to think of it, in the out-of-the-box Machine policy level, the Microsoft Strong Name code group is a child of the Local Machine Zone code group. Why is that? Surely if having a strong name is sufficient to grant full trust, it should be sufficient no matter where the code came from.

Code groups with membership conditions based on some fact about the assembly itself should *always* be children of location-based code groups. Here is why: Suppose you trust Foo Corporation. For the sake of argument, we assume that this trust is justified; Foo Corporation really is not hostile toward you. Consider what would happen if your Enterprise policy level grants assemblies signed with Foo Corporation's key full trust, period, with a level-final code group. You impose no additional location-based requirement whatsoever.

Foo Corporation releases version 1.0 of their FooSoft library, and no matter where foosoft.dll is located, all members of your enterprise fully trust it. Foo Corporation releases version 2.0, then version 3.0, and so on. Everything is fine for years.

But one day, some clever and evil person discovers a security hole in version 1.0. The security hole allows partially trusted code—say, code from a low-trust zone such as the Internet—to take advantage of FooSoft 1.0's fully trusted status to lure it into using its powers for evil.

Even if that flaw does not exist in the more recent versions, you are now vulnerable to it. Your policy says to trust this code *no matter where it is, no matter what version it is*. Evil people could put it up on Web sites from now until forever and write partially trusted code that takes advantage of the security hole, and you can do nothing about it short of rolling out new policy.

If, on the other hand, you predicate fully trusting FooSoft software upon the software being in a certain location, that scopes the potential attack surface to that location alone, not the entire Internet. All you have to do to mitigate the problem is remove the offending code from that location and you are done.

That explains why the Microsoft Strong Name code group is a child of the My Computer Zone code group. Should an assembly with Microsoft's strong name ever be found to contain a security flaw, the vulnerability could be mitigated by rolling out a patch to all affected users. If the out-of-the-box policy were "trust all code signed by Microsoft no matter where it is," there would be no way to mitigate this vulnerability at all; the flawed code would be trusted forever, no matter what dodgy Web site hosts it.

> This best practice for strong name code groups also applies to other membership conditions that consider only facts about the assembly itself, such as the hash and publisher certificate membership conditions.

Now that we have a child code group that grants full trust to code that is both strong-named and in a trusted location, we can reduce the permission set granted by the outer "location" code group to nothing. That way, only code that is both strong named and in the correct location will run.

Implementing Strong-Named Assemblies

So far we have been talking about the administrative problem of trusting a strong-named assembly after you have one. What about the development problem of creating the strong-named assembly in the first place? The process entails four steps:

1. Designate a signing authority (that is, some highly trusted and security-conscious person in your organization who can ensure the secrecy of the private key).

2. Create a key pair and extract the public key from the key pair. Publicize the public key, and keep the private key a secret.

3. Developers doing day-to-day work on the assembly should delay-sign it with the public key.

4. When you are ready to ship, the signing authority signs the assembly with the private key.

Let's take a look at each of these steps in detail.

Designate a Signing Authority

A strong name that matches a particular public key can be produced by anyone who has the private key. Therefore, the best way to ensure that only your organization can produce assemblies signed with your private key is to *keep the private key secret*. Create a small number (preferably one) of highly trusted people in your organization as signing authorities and make sure that they are the only people who have access to the private key file.

Create a Key Pair

When you need a key pair for your organization, the signing authority should create a private key file to keep to themselves, and a public key file for wide distribution. The strong-name key generation utility is sn.exe and it can be found in the bin directory of your .NET Framework SDK:

```
> sn.exe -k private.snk
Microsoft (R) .NET Framework Strong Name Utility Version 2.0
Copyright (C) Microsoft Corporation. All rights reserved.

Key pair written to private.snk

> sn.exe -p private.snk public.snk
Microsoft (R) .NET Framework Strong Name Utility Version 2.0
Copyright (C) Microsoft Corporation. All rights reserved.

Public key written to public.snk
```

The private.snk file contains both the public and private keys; the public.snk file contains only the public key. Do whatever is necessary to secure the private.snk file: burn it to a CD-ROM and put it in a safety deposit box, for example. The public.snk file is public. You can e-mail it to all your developers, publish it on the Internet, whatever you want. You want the public key to be widely known, because that is how people are going to identify your organization as the author of a given strong-named assembly.

Developers Delay-Sign the Assembly

Developers working on the customization in Visual Studio will automatically get their User policy level updated so that the assembly that they generate is fully trusted. But what if they want to test the assembly in a more realistic user scenario, where there is unlikely to be a User-level policy that grants full trust to this specific customization assembly? If users are going to trust the code because it is strong named, developers and testers need to make sure that they can run their tests in such an environment.

But you probably do not want to make every developer a signing authority; the more people you share a secret with, the more likely that one of them will be careless. And you do not want the signing authority to sign off on every build every single day, because pre-release code might contain security flaws. If signed-but-flawed code gets out into the wild, you might have a serious and expensive patching problem on your hands.

You can wriggle out of this dilemma in two ways. The first is to create a second key pair for a "testing purposes only" strong name for which every developer can be a signing authority. Your test team can trust the test strong name, making the tests more realistic. Because it is unlikely that customers ever will trust the test-only public key, there is no worry that signed-but-buggy pre-release versions that escape your control will need to be patched.

That is considerably better than real-signing every daily build, but we can do better still; another option is to *delay-sign* the assembly. When the signing authority signs the assembly, the public key and the private-key-produced signature are embedded into the assembly; the loader reads the public key and ensures that it verifies the signature. By contrast, when a developer delay-signs the assembly, the public key and a fake signature are embedded into the assembly; the developer does not have the private key, and therefore the signature is not valid.

To delay-sign a customization, right-click the project in the Solution Explorer and select Properties. In the Properties pane, click Signing, and then choose the public key file, as shown in Figure 19-8.

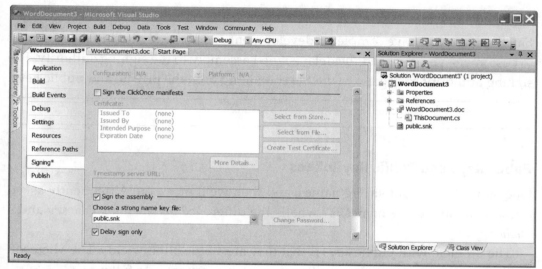

Figure 19-8 Delay-signing a customization.

If the signature is invalid, won't the loader detect that the strong name is invalid? Yes. Therefore, developers and testers can then set their development and test machines to have a special policy that says "skip signature validation on a particular assembly":

```
> sn.exe -Vr ExpenseReporting.DLL
```

Skipping signature validation on developer and test machines makes those machines vulnerable. If an attacker can deduce what the name of your customization is and somehow trick a developer into running that code, the hostile code will then be fully trusted. Developers and testers should be very careful to not expose themselves to potentially hostile code while they have signature verification turned off. Turn it back on as soon as testing is done.

You can turn signature validation back on with

```
> sn.exe -Vu ExpenseReporting.DLL
```

or use -Vx to delete all "skip validation" policies.

Really Sign the Assembly

Finally, when you have completed development and are ready to ship the assembly to customers, you can send the delay-signed assembly to the signing authority. The signing authority has access to the file containing both the private and public keys:

```
> sn.exe -R ExpenseReporting.DLL private.snk
```

Public Keys and Public Key Tokens

One more thing about strong names, and then we'll move on. A frequently asked question about strong names is "what's the difference between a *public key* and a *public key token*?"

　　The problem with public keys is that they are a little bit unwieldy. The Microsoft public key, for example, when written out in hexadecimal is as follows:

```
0024000004800000940000000602000000240000525341310004000001000100007D1FA
57C4AED9F0A32E84AA0FAEFD0DE9E8FD6AEC8F87FB03766C834C99921EB23BE79AD9D5
DCC1DD9AD236132102900B723CF980957FC4E177108FC607774F29E8320E92EA05ECE4
E821C0A5EFE8F1645C4C0C93C1AB99285D622CAA652C1DFAD63D745D6F2DE5F17E5EAF
0FC4963D261C8A12436518206DC093344D5AD293
```

That's a bit of a mouthful. It is easier to say, "I read *Hamlet* last Tuesday and quite enjoyed it," than "I read a play that goes like this. Bernardo says, 'Who's there?'" and finishing up four hours later with "'Go, bid the soldiers shoot,' last Tuesday and quite enjoyed it."

　　Similarly, if you want to talk *about* a public key without actually writing the whole thing out, you can use the public key token. The public key token corresponding to the public key above is b03f5f7f11d50a3a, which takes up a lot less space. Note, however, that just as the title *Hamlet* tells you nothing about the action of the play, the public key token tells you nothing about the contents of the public key. It is just a useful, statistically-guaranteed-unique 64-bit integer that identifies a particular public key.

　　Public key tokens are usually used when you write out a strong name. For example, the strong name for the VSTO 2005 runtime is this:

```
Microsoft.VisualStudio.Tools.Applications.Runtime, Version=8.0.1200.0,
Culture=neutral, PublicKeyToken=b03f5f7f11d50a3a, ProcessorArchitecture=MSIL
```

Publisher Certificates

Strong names, as just described, were invented to solve a particular problem. They provide strong evidence that the code you are loading is the code that you actually intended to load. Because the public key of the author is part of the strong name, you can use strong names as evidence to create policies that grant full trust to code authored by particular trusted individuals or groups.

But then what is a publisher certificate for? What is the difference between signing code with your organization's strong name private key and signing code with your organization's certificate?

You will note that by using strong names as evidence when setting security policy, we are essentially using strong names to do something that they were not designed to do. Strong names were designed to solve the naming problem, not to solve the more difficult problem of codifying trust relationships between code authors and code users.

This is not to say that strong names are not adequate; clearly, strong names are strong enough to use as evidence in security policy. But think about some of the shortcomings of the strong-name system:

- What if disaster strikes and the private key of a trusted author is revealed? There is no standard procedure in place to deal with this. There is no standard way to even publicize that a problem exists!

- The longer a strong name's public key has been public, the longer attackers have had to attempt to determine the corresponding private key through either brute-force or sophisticated cryptographic attacks. But strong name public keys have no standard mechanism for indicating expiry dates or updated keys.

- Suppose you want to add Foo Corporation's strong-name public key to your policy. How exactly do you know that you are adding Foo Corporation's key? If some evil hacker can convince you that his public key is actually Foo's key, you will write a policy that trusts the evil hacker.

Amateur cryptographers often think that coming up with the "unbreakable" algorithm is the hard part. That is hard, no doubt about it. But building a system to manage the keys effectively is often what makes or breaks an implementation. Clearly, strong names do not have a very sophisticated system for managing keys. By contrast, publisher certificates were designed for exactly these scenarios.

License to Code

An analogy might help. Imagine that you are reading a document, and you want to know whether it is factual or full of lies. If the author is trustworthy, you are more likely to believe the document's contents—provided, of course, that you have reason to believe that the document was in fact by the stated author. Perhaps the author has signed the document and you recognize the signature. The details of how you come to trust the author, how you learn to recognize the signature, and so on are left up to you.

Now suppose you have the signed document, you trust the author, but you do not know what the author's signature looks like. Therefore, you cannot tell whether this document is actually trustworthy—anyone could have signed it.

But if in addition you have a notarized statement from the editor-in-chief of the Encarta encyclopedia attesting to the accuracy of the document, that might be enough. The notarized, dated statement describes the document in question, identifies the author, and has a copy of the author's signature for comparison. You do recognize the signature of the editor-in-chief, and trust them to only put their imprimatur on trustworthy authors.

That's what a publisher certificate is like: It not only identifies the author, but it names a trusted authority who attests to the identity and trustworthiness of the author. It indicates details such as who everyone on the "chain of trust" is, when the various certificates identifying them were signed, and so on.

We use certificate-based evidence all the time in real life. A driver's license identifies the bearer by providing a description (name, age, height, weight, eye color, hair color), a photograph, and a signature. It also attests that the individual thereby identified has passed a driving test. To be useful as evidence, the description must match the bearer, and it must have actually been issued by the department of motor vehicles. Furthermore, it is only valid for a certain period of time, so that out-of-date licenses become invalid.

Various organizations that need to determine the trustworthiness of individuals they know nothing about use certificate-based evidence in their policies. If you are trying to get into a bar, any state-issued evidence that indicates your age is probably good enough. If you are trying to rent a car, odds are pretty good that you will need a driver's license, with its further evidence that you passed a driving test at some point. But either way, what is happening here is that organizations are leveraging their trust of one entity—the state—to obtain evidence about the identity and trustworthiness of an unknown individual.

Publisher certificates are essentially licenses to write code, not drive. A publisher certificate identifies a particular author and also identifies the certifying authority (CA), which vouches for the identity and trustworthiness of the author.

Of course, trusting the CA to make decisions for you once more trades convenience for risk. The CA might choose poorly, or fail to exercise due diligence in vetting its authors. You might not agree with the criteria that the CA uses to decide who is trustworthy. In such cases, do not trust the CA! You would not rent a car to a driver who presented a driver's license from Bob's Discount Driver's License Emporium, so only trust certifying authorities that you believe give out certificates to trustworthy people.

Code-signing certificates, like drivers' licenses, expire after a certain date. And, like drivers' licenses, they can be revoked by the CA due to bad behavior. Certifying authorities publish lists of revoked certificates; individuals can configure their computers to automatically download recent changes to the revocation lists so that they are less likely to be fooled by untrustworthy individuals who managed to obtain a certificate.

Obtaining Certificates

Suppose you decide that your customizations should have publisher certificate evidence. Where you get your publisher certificate from depends on how your customers' policies are likely to be configured; obtaining a certificate from a CA that your customers do not trust makes it unlikely that the .NET security system will actually grant full trust to your customization assembly. If you plan on distributing a customization widely to the public, you might consider getting a code-signing certificate from a widely trusted CA such as VeriSign or thawte.

On the other hand, if you are creating a customization to be rolled out inside an enterprise, you can be your own certifying authority by installing Microsoft Certificate Server and issuing your own code-signing certificates to your signing authority.

After you have a code-signing certificate from your CA, you can use the certmgr.exe utility to manage your certificates. Unfortunately, there is no GUI tool in Visual Studio to automatically sign a document with a publisher certificate. However, that's just as well; unlike strong names, there is no "delay-signing" option for publisher certificates; an assembly is either signed with a valid certificate or it is not. Use signcode.exe in the framework SDK directory to attach a publisher certificate to a customization assembly.

> If you want to provide *both* strong-name and publisher certificate evidence for your customization, make sure that the signing authority real-signs the *strong name first*, and then uses signcode.exe to apply your publisher certificate signature to the customization. Both are designed to detect tampering with the assembly; but because both strong-name signing and publisher certificate signing embed signature information in the document, you might wonder why they do not see each other as "tampering" with the document. Because the strong-name system was designed after the code-signing system already existed, the strong-name system takes this into account; adding a publisher certificate signature to a document does not invalidate the strong name.

Trusting the Document

So far we have been talking only about trusting the customization assembly. That makes sense—it is, after all, the container of the code that is going to run. However, there is something quite unusual about customized documents that makes them very different from traditional forms-based applications. Here is a silly but illustrative example. Suppose you write a customization for a budget spreadsheet that has two named ranges that have event handlers that handle their double-click events as shown in Figure 19-9.

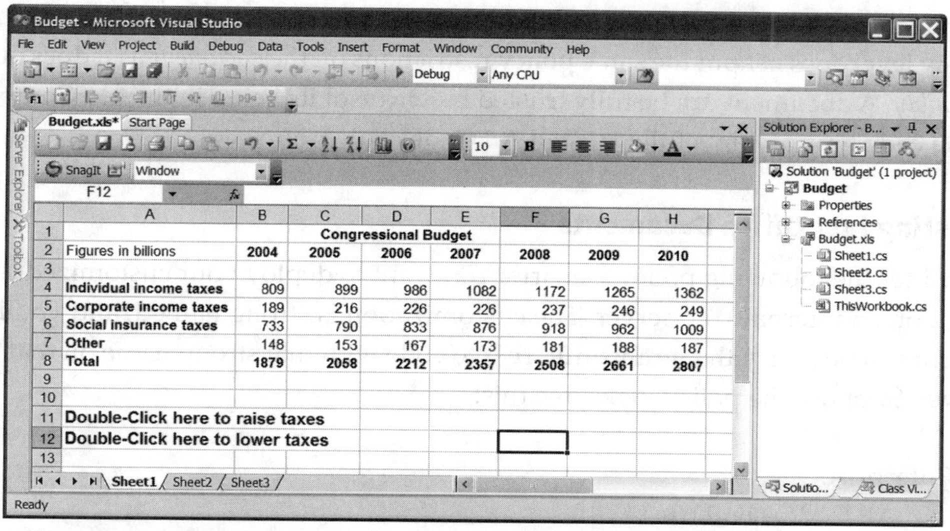

Figure 19-9 A budget spreadsheet that could be exploited by an attacker.

You build the customization, sign it with a strong name, ensure that company-wide security policy grants full trust to code with your strong name, and deploy the customization assembly and spreadsheet. But the text in the spreadsheet's named ranges is just *text*. What is to stop some unscrupulous person from changing the text in those ranges to whatever he wants? Anyone can swap the labels around, delete them entirely, change the size of the range, change the font to white letters on a white background, and so on. If the text in Figure 19-9's rows 11 and 12 is swapped, a double-click to raise taxes will actually invoke code that will lower taxes.

In most forms-based applications, the user interface is determined by the code. Not so with customized documents. The user interface is editable by end users and the customization is none the wiser. Therefore, it is not enough to trust only the customization; the document must be fully trusted as well. But how are we going to do that?

Unfortunately, all the techniques discussed thus far in this chapter for obtaining cryptographic evidence about the customization are not going to work well with the document. The whole point of cryptographic verification is to determine that not one bit of the assembly has been changed, but documents are edited all the time by their very nature.

For this reason, although the document must be fully trusted, the AppDomain policy level does *not* put the same policy restrictions on the *document* as it does on the *assembly*. A document can be fully trusted by virtue of its being in the My Computer Zone code group or in a fully trusted All Code code group.

Trusting Just Office Documents

Consider the following policy scenario: You want to deploy your customized document on an internal Web server. The customization is strong named, and you have an Enterprise policy that grants full trust to code with that strong name on that Web server. Suppose the policy looks like this:

```
Enterprise
    All Code—Full trust
            URL: http://MyServer/customizations/* —No permissions
                Foo Corporation Strong Name—Full trust, level-final
```

This will fully trust the customization assembly because the level-final attribute on the strong-name code group will prevent the other three policy levels from further restricting the assembly's granted permission set.

But what about the document? The document needs to be trusted, too. In this example, the Enterprise policy level will fully trust the document by virtue of that root All Code code group. But the out-of-the-box Machine policy level will only see that the document is in the LocalIntranet Zone code group, and not grant full trust.

We could fix up this policy by making the URL code group above also grant the full trust permission set and make it level-final. However, that represents a pretty serious weakening of the policy. That would then say that all documents *and code* on that Web site, regardless of whether it was associated with a customization or not, whether strong named or not, are fully trusted. Really what we want to say is "all code signed with the strong name on the server, and all *documents* on the server are fully trusted."

We need a new membership condition that only matches Word and Excel documents. Fortunately, there now is such a membership condition, the aptly named Office Document Membership Condition. Membership conditions are represented by objects in the .NET security policy, and the assembly containing those objects has to be in the Global Assembly Cache (GAC). If it is not already, use gacutil.exe to install msosec.dll into the GAC:

```
> Gacutil -i MSOSec.DLL
Microsoft (R) .NET Global Assembly Cache Utility. Version 2.0
Copyright (C) Microsoft Corporation. All rights reserved.
Assembly successfully added to the cache
```

You can now create a Custom security policy that trusts all Word and Excel documents on a particular server. Custom membership conditions are represented by XML files. The Office Document Membership Condition has a simple representation in XML; it contains just the name of the membership condition type and the strong name of the assembly containing it, as shown in Figure 19-10.

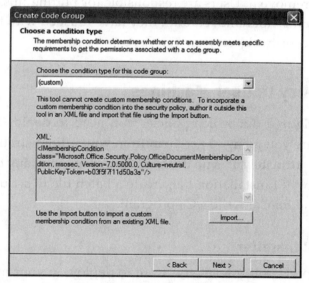

Figure 19-10 Creating a code group based on the Office Document Membership Condition.

Why Is MSOSec Not in the GAC by Default?

The other VSTO assemblies are put in the GAC for you automatically, so why not this one? There is a good reason.

A basic tenet of writing install/uninstall software is that you must uninstall what you install. If the VSTO installer installs msosec.dll into the GAC, the uninstaller must remove it. But consider what happens if the installer installs msosec.dll, a user creates a security policy that uses the Office Document Membership Condition, and then uninstalls VSTO. What happens the next time that user tries to run managed code with msosec.dll deleted?

The managed code loader will examine the security policy and discover that policy references a membership object that no longer exists. The policy engine has no idea which assemblies would match that membership condition, so the policy engine really has no idea what permissions ought to be granted to a given assembly! When faced with this situation, the policy engine simply bails out and refuses to grant any code permission to run until the situation is fixed. *All* managed code on the machine would cease to run.

But if you do not install msosec.dll into the GAC in the first place, the uninstaller does not have to remove it. Users are responsible for putting this code in the GAC and ensuring that it is not removed until they have finished with it. Be very careful when removing security objects from the GAC.

Deploying Policy to User Machines

After you have figured out which policies you need to deploy throughout your enterprise, how are you going to get them from your administration machine onto user machines? Fortunately, it is no different from deploying any other application: You can create an MSI installation file, create a batch file to set up security policy from the command line, or write a C# program.

Creating an MSI Installer

Create the Enterprise policy level you want to deploy on your machine using the mscorcfg.msc management tool. When you have a satisfactory policy, right-click the Runtime Security Policy node in the tree view and select Create Deployment Package. The dialog shown in Figure 19-11 will appear.

The wizard will then create an installation script that you can deploy the same way you deploy any other application throughout your enterprise, whether via System Management Server or Group Policy, to automatically update user machines, or simply putting the installation script up on a share and letting users click it themselves.

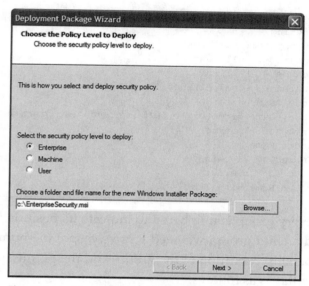

Figure 19-11 The policy Deployment Package Wizard.

Creating a Batch File

As discussed in Chapter 18, "Server Data Scenarios," you can use the caspol.exe utility to change security policy. Caspol.exe is usually found in the Windows\Microsoft.NET\Framework\v2.0 directory. Caspol.exe is extremely flexible and has many options, but for our purposes we just discuss how to view and edit a policy level.

To view a policy level, the syntax is as follows:

```
caspol.exe -<level> -listgroups
```

where <level> can be enterprise, machine or user. For example:

```
C:\> caspol -machine -listgroups

Microsoft (R) .NET Framework CasPol 2.0
Copyright (C) Microsoft Corporation. All rights reserved.
Security is ON
Execution checking is ON
Policy change prompt is ON
Level = Machine
```

```
Code Groups:
1. All code: Nothing
 1.1. Zone - MyComputer: FullTrust
  1.1.1. StrongName -: FullTrust
  1.1.2. StrongName -: FullTrust
 1.2. Zone - Intranet: LocalIntranet
  1.2.1. All code: Same site Web
  1.2.2. All code: Same directory FileIO - 'Read, PathDiscovery'
 1.3. Zone - Internet: Internet
  1.3.1. All code: Same site Web
 1.4. Zone - Untrusted: Nothing
 1.5. Zone - Trusted: Internet
  1.5.1. All code: Same site Web
```

As you can see, every group is numbered to indicate its position in the code group hierarchy. To add a child group, we need to give caspol the number of the parent group, the membership condition of the group, and the permission set granted by this group. The syntax is as follows:

```
caspol.exe -<level> -addgroup <parent> <condition> <permission set>
```

where `<permission set>` can be `Nothing`, `Execution`, `Internet`, `Local-Intranet`, or `FullTrust`. The `<condition>` is somewhat more complicated due to the number of possible membership conditions for a code group. Typically. you will want to pick one of the following:

- `-allcode` (The group grants full trust to all code.)
- `-strong` mycustomization.dll (The group grants full trust to the strong-named assembly; remember that strong name groups should be child groups of a location group.)
- `-url http://mysite/*` (URL groups can also refer to directories on the local machine.)
- `-zone <zone>` (`<zone>` is one of `MyComputer`, `Intranet`, `Trusted`, `Internet` or `Untrusted`.)
- `-custom customfile.xml` (To create a custom membership condition.)

To create a code group that includes all Office documents, use this customfile.xml:

```
<IMembershipCondition
class="Microsoft.Office.Security.Policy.
OfficeDocumentMembershipCondition, msosec, Version=7.0.5000.0,
Culture=neutral, PublicKeyToken=b03f5f7f11d50a3a"/>
```

To create a level-final or exclusive code group, add `-levelfinal` on or `-exclusive` on to the end of the command line.

For example, to create a policy in the Machine level that fully trusts all files on a particular intranet site, you could use caspol.exe like this:

```
caspol.exe -machine -addgroup 1.2 -url http://accounting/* FullTrust
```

Writing a C# Program

The System.Security namespace provides objects that enable you to manipulate all aspects of the security system programmatically. To set a security policy, we first obtain the three persisted policy levels (Enterprise, Machine and User are saved to disk; the Application policy is created dynamically whenever an application domain is created). We then create a new code group by associating a membership condition with a permission set. Finally, we search the Machine policy for the Intranet group and add a child group, as in Listing 19-1.

Listing 19-1 Programmatically Modifying Security Policy

```
using System.Collections;
using System.Security;
using System.Security.Policy;

public class ChangePolicy
{
  static public void Main()
  {
    PolicyLevel enterprisePolicyLevel;
    PolicyLevel machinePolicyLevel;
    PolicyLevel userPolicyLevel;
    ZoneMembershipCondition zone;
    CodeGroup accountingServerGroup;
    UrlMembershipCondition accountingServerCondition;
    PolicyStatement policyStatement;
    PermissionSet fullTrust;
    IList children;
```

```
// Obtain the three policy levels:

    IEnumerator policyEnumerator = SecurityManager.PolicyHierarchy();
    policyEnumerator.MoveNext();
    enterprisePolicyLevel = (PolicyLevel)policyEnumerator.Current;
    policyEnumerator.MoveNext();
    machinePolicyLevel = (PolicyLevel)policyEnumerator.Current;
    policyEnumerator.MoveNext();
    userPolicyLevel = (PolicyLevel)policyEnumerator.Current;

// Create a new group by combining a permission set with a
// membership condition:

    fullTrust = machinePolicyLevel.GetNamedPermissionSet("FullTrust");
    policyStatement = new PolicyStatement(fullTrust,
      PolicyStatementAttribute.Nothing);
    accountingServerCondition = new UrlMembershipCondition(
      @"http://accounting/*");
    accountingServerGroup = new UnionCodeGroup(
      accountingServerCondition, policyStatement);

// Search the Machine policy level for the parent group:

    children = machinePolicyLevel.RootCodeGroup.Children;
    // Note that this makes a _copy_ of the children, so we'll
    // have to copy it back when we're done editing it.
    foreach (CodeGroup codeGroup in children)
    {
      zone = codeGroup.MembershipCondition as ZoneMembershipCondition;
      if (zone != null && zone.SecurityZone == SecurityZone.Intranet)
      {
        codeGroup.AddChild(accountingServerGroup);
        machinePolicyLevel.RootCodeGroup.Children = children;
        SecurityManager.SavePolicy();
        break;
      }
    }
  }
}
```

This program just gives a good starting point for building a custom policy editor; a more sophisticated program would check to see whether the child group already existed, prompt the user before changing security policy, and so on.

Conclusion

That was a lot of information; security administration can be complex. The key take-aways from this chapter include the following:

- VSTO customization code will not run under the "out-of-the-box" security policy. Some additional policy must be applied that allows customizations to run. Choose your enterprise's security policies carefully.
- The AppDomain policy level will not consider zone-based evidence for the customization assembly.
- Both the customization and the document location must be fully trusted; there is no partial-trust scenario for calling the Word and Excel object models.
- Strong names and publisher certificates use similar technology but solve slightly different problems. It is possible to use both forms of evidence in the same assembly.
- A document that is opened from an intranet or Internet location must have additional policy to trust the document location; this policy is created using the Office Document Membership Condition.

20

Deployment

AFTER YOU HAVE BUILT A great VSTO 2005 solution by customizing a Word document or Excel spreadsheet, you have to get the final bits of the code to your users somehow. But how? There are two broad classifications of deployment scenarios: local install and network install. Each has pros and cons.

Consider how this problem has traditionally been solved in the application programming world. In the traditional "rich client" or "thick client" application, all the application logic is stored in files that somehow get copied to the local machine. There might be a single .exe file, or the solution might have a number of .dll files associated with it that also need to be installed. When installing a thick client application, often the administrator or end user needs to run some kind of setup program to ensure that everything is registered and in the right location.

Rich client applications can take advantage of the full power of the client environment and are always available. Install an application, unplug your laptop, hop on a plane, and your applications are still there. However, that very strength is also a potential weakness; you have whatever version you installed, which is not necessarily the latest version. If your organization has many applications installed on many machines, ensuring that every machine is up-to-date can be a full-time job.

Exactly the opposite is true for "thin client" applications, where the application logic is on a network server somewhere. When the client logic is in the form of HTML and script downloaded fresh every time you refresh the page in the browser, updating every client is easy; just put the latest version on the Web server and every client will get it the next time he or she navigates the browser to your site. But thin client applications often squander the power of modern desktop and laptop computers by targeting a lowest-common-denominator platform that assumes nothing more than a browser; JScript was not designed for manipulating huge datasets. Thin client applications also frequently work poorly in disconnected scenarios, particularly if much of the application logic is on the server.

VSTO is all about taking full advantage of the power of locally installed Office applications. Because the customization assembly need not be in the same location as the document itself, VSTO cleanly supports both local installs (for offline scenarios) and network installs (for always-up-to-date scenarios). Furthermore, advanced users can take advantage of local caching of network-installed customization assemblies to get the best of both worlds: offline access to a locally cached customization assembly, but a guarantee that you are always using the latest version when connected.

This chapter covers how to use the Publish Wizard in Visual Studio to deploy applications to servers, how to create a setup project for a Word or Excel project, and how to use the ServerDocument object model to edit the deployment information inside a Word or Excel document. The chapter finishes up with a discussion of some of the advanced offline-caching scenarios.

VSTO Prerequisites

No matter how your users are going to get the customized documents onto their machines, they will need some prerequisites, as follows:

- Microsoft Office Service Pack One, which can be found at http://www.microsoft.com/downloads/details.aspx?familyid=9C51D3A6-7CB1-4F61-837E-5F938254FC47
- The primary interop assemblies, which can be found at http://www.microsoft.com/downloads/details.aspx?familyid=3c9a983a-ac14-4125-8ba0-d36d67e0f4ad
- The .NET Framework 2.0
- The VSTO runtime

Those last two will also be available as standalone setup packages should you want to deploy them. The VSTO runtime redistribution setup package (VSTOR.EXE) is available on the VSTO installation CD-ROM, as is the .NET Framework 2.0 setup package (DOTNETFX.EXE). Unfortunately, the exact path to these files on the installation media was not yet finalized when this book went to press.

The .NET Framework 2.0 setup package will also be made available through Windows Update.

Deploying to an Intranet Shared Directory or Web Site

Suppose you are ready to roll out an expense reporting application using a customized Excel spreadsheet. You plan to put the application up on the http://accounting Web site. Users will download the spreadsheet to their local machines for editing, but the code will live up on the server.

As discussed in Chapter 19, ".NET Code Security," you need to ensure that users have policy that explicitly trusts the customization assembly. The policy should either explicitly trust the server, or the strong name of the assembly or, preferably, both. See the last section of Chapter 19 for tips on how to roll out security policy.

Deploying to a Server with the Publish Wizard

Choose Publish from the Build menu to start up the Publish Wizard and give the name of the intranet Web server or network share to which you want to publish the customization as shown in Figure 20-1.

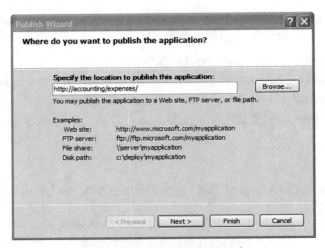

Figure 20-1 The Visual Studio Publish Wizard.

Click Finish. It is as simple as that; Visual Studio will build the customization and copy the document and customization assembly to the server. As you will see later in this chapter, Visual Studio also creates a deployment manifest for you. We discuss what exactly deployment manifests are for shortly, but first, what if you do not have write access to the server?

Some Security Questions

A few security questions may have just come to mind. What if your security-conscious administrators have not granted you write access to the Web site? What if the delay-signed assemblies must be properly strong-named by a signing authority, or signed with a publisher certificate before they are deployed?

The Publish Wizard creates a local copy of the files that it deploys up to the network site before it deploys them, but unfortunately there is no way to get the Publish Wizard to skip attempting to copy them up to the site. However, it is possible to do this from the command line, using the MSBuild.EXE utility. The syntax is as follows:

```
MSBuild.exe /target:Publish /property:PublishUrl=<PublishUrl> <ProjectFile>
```

This produces the files that would be deployed and puts them in the following directory:

```
<ProjectFolder>\<ProjectConfigurationOutputFolder>\<ProjectName>.publish
```

For example, the following would produce the files to be copied up to the Web server, but not actually copy them up there:

```
MSBuild.exe /target:Publish /property:PublishUrl=http://accounting/
ExpenseReport "c:\MyProjects\ExpenseReport\ExpenseReport.csproj"
```

Instead, they would be saved in the following:

```
c:\MyProjects\ExpenseReport\bin\Release\ExpenseReport.publish
```

After you have the files to be deployed on your local machine, you can get them strong-named by your signing authority, send them to the server administrator to be copied onto the Web server, or do whatever else needs to be done before the files become available on a live server.

Examining the Generated Files

Take a look at the contents of the network (or local) directory to which you just deployed the application. (This will typically be a subdirectory of the c:\inet-pub\wwwroot directory if you published to a Web site.) You should see a directory structure that looks something like this:

```
> dir /s /b
C:\Inetpub\wwwroot\ExpenseReport\ExpenseReport.application
C:\Inetpub\wwwroot\ExpenseReport\ExpenseReport.doc
C:\Inetpub\wwwroot\ExpenseReport\ExpenseReport_1.0.0.0
C:\Inetpub\wwwroot\ExpenseReport\ExpenseReport_1.0.0.0\ ExpenseReport.dll
C:\Inetpub\wwwroot\ExpenseReport\ExpenseReport_1.0.0.0\ ExpenseReport.dll.
manifest
C:\Inetpub\wwwroot\ExpenseReport\ExpenseReport_1.0.0.0\ ExpenseReport.doc
C:\Inetpub\wwwroot\ExpenseReport\ExpenseReport_1.0.0.0\ ExpenseReport.dll.
config
```

To understand what is going on here, we need to introduce some jargon. The ExpenseReport.application file is the "deployment manifest," and the Expense-Report.dll.manifest file is the "application manifest."

It is somewhat confusing that the ".application" file is not the application manifest; unfortunately we are stuck now with this poor choice of nomenclature.

The Deployment Manifest

The sole purpose of the deployment manifest is to point the VSTO runtime toward the most current version of the application manifest. The application manifest by contrast contains information about where the customization assembly is and which host item classes need to be created when the customization is started. There is always only one deployment manifest, but there can be many application manifests, one for each version of the customization.

A typical automatically generated deployment manifest looks something like this.

Listing 20-1 The Deployment Manifest

```
<?xml version="1.0" encoding="utf-8"?>
<asmv1:assembly
  xsi:schemaLocation=
  "urn:schemas-microsoft-com:asm.v1 assembly.adaptive.xsd"
  manifestVersion="1.0"
  xmlns:dsig="http://www.w3.org/2000/09/xmldsig#"
  xmlns="urn:schemas-microsoft-com:asm.v2"
  xmlns:asmv1="urn:schemas-microsoft-com:asm.v1"
  xmlns:asmv2="urn:schemas-microsoft-com:asm.v2"
  xmlns:xrml="urn:mpeg:mpeg21:2003:01-REL-R-NS"
  xmlns:xsi="http://www.w3.org/2001/XMLSchema-instance">
<assemblyIdentity
   name="ExpenseReport.application"
   version="1.0.0.0"
   publicKeyToken="0000000000000000"
   language="neutral"
   processorArchitecture="msil"
   xmlns="urn:schemas-microsoft-com:asm.v1" />
  <description
    asmv2:publisher="Microsoft"
    asmv2:product="ExpenseReport"
    xmlns="urn:schemas-microsoft-com:asm.v1" />
  <deployment install="true" />
  <dependency>
   <dependentAssembly
     dependencyType="install"
     codebase="ExpenseReport_1.0.0.0\ExpenseReport.dll.manifest"
     size="1460">
     <assemblyIdentity
       name="ExpenseReport.dll"
       version="1.0.0.0" />
     <hash>
```

```
    <dsig:Transforms>
      <dsig:Transform Algorithm=
      "urn:schemas-microsoft-com:HashTransforms.Identity" />
    </dsig:Transforms>
    <dsig:DigestMethod Algorithm=
      "http://www.w3.org/2000/09/xmldsig#sha1" />
    <dsig:DigestValue>8cQI8YsGgIUaSSysgK3Ad8do9t0=</dsig:DigestValue>
    </hash>
  </dependentAssembly>
  </dependency>
</asmv1:assembly>
```

We have emphasized the relevant portions of the deployment manifest. What is all of the rest of this stuff? There seems to be some confusing things in here. Why is the root element "assembly"? Why are there two inconsistent "assemblyIdentity" elements? And what's that digital signature?

VSTO uses the same deployment manifest format as "ClickOnce," a technology designed to facilitate deployment of entire applications, not single customizations; these oddities are a result of backward-compatibility factors from the ClickOnce world.

The oldest of these historical factors is the root element "assembly." Explaining that strange choice requires us to go back to a time before the version 1.0 .NET runtime shipped. When the .NET runtime was being designed, "assembly" referred to all of an application's files and configuration information. That is, all the bits described by what we now call a "manifest." The manifest file format above dates from that time, and its elements were not renamed when "assembly" came to mean "the smallest unit of versionable executable code."

That then explains why there are two inconsistent assemblyIdentity elements. The first assemblyIdentity identifies not a DLL but rather the *manifest itself*. Notice that the first assemblyIdentity element names the manifest. Manifests can have their own version numbers. Deployment manifests are usually versioned along with the customization assembly, but the deployment manifest can have its own version number distinct from that of the customization assembly if you so choose; as you will see later, it must be consistent with the application manifest, but need not be consistent with the customization assembly. VSTO considers only the name and version attributes in the first assemblyIdentity element.

The second assemblyIdentity element uses "assembly" in the modern sense, and identifies the customization code. Notice that the codebase attribute gives the relative path to the application manifest, and the assemblyIdentity identifies the name and version of the customization code. We discuss the meanings and interactions of the various codebase attributes later in this chapter.

Finally, ClickOnce supports digital signing security features in its manifests; unlike ClickOnce, VSTO does not do any kind of digital signature verification on its manifests. VSTO will ignore these elements.

The Application Manifest

As you have seen, the deployment manifest identifies the location and current version of the application manifest. The application manifest identifies the customization assembly and lists the classes that need to be created when the customization starts up. The application manifest looks somewhat similar to the deployment manifest.

Listing 20-2 The Application Manifest

```
<assembly xmlns="urn:schemas-microsoft-com:asm.v1"
  xmlns:asmv2="urn:schemas-microsoft-com:asm.v2">
  <assemblyIdentity name="ExpenseReport.dll" version="1.0.0.0" />
  <asmv2:entryPoint name="Startup" dependencyName="dependency0">
    <asmv2:clrClassInvocation class="ExpenseReport.ThisWorkbook"/>
  </asmv2:entryPoint>
  <asmv2:entryPoint name="Startup" dependencyName="dependency0">
    <asmv2:clrClassInvocation class="ExpenseReport.Sheet1"/>
  </asmv2:entryPoint>
  <asmv2:entryPoint name="Startup" dependencyName="dependency0">
    <asmv2:clrClassInvocation class="ExpenseReport.Sheet2"/>
  </asmv2:entryPoint>
  <asmv2:entryPoint name="Startup" dependencyName="dependency0">
    <asmv2:clrClassInvocation class="ExpenseReport.Sheet3"/>
  </asmv2:entryPoint>
  <asmv2:dependency asmv2:name="dependency0">
    <asmv2:dependentAssembly>
      <assemblyIdentity name="ExpenseReport"
        version="1.0.0.0" culture="neutral" />
      <asmv2:installFrom codebase="ExpenseReport_1.0.0.0\ExpenseReport.DLL" />
    </asmv2:dependentAssembly>
    <asmv2:installFrom codebase=
```

```
"http://accounting/ExpenseReport/ExpenseReport.application" />
  </asmv2:dependency>
</assembly>
```

Again, we have "assembly" used in the now-obsolete sense as the root element and an assemblyIdentity element that gives the version number of the application manifest. What is all the rest of the stuff in here?

Clearly, all the information we need to start up the customization is in here, but again the format is somewhat odd because it tries to be similar to the ClickOnce format. We have a collection of entryPoints listing the classes that are to be created when the customization starts up. We also have a single "dependency" (that is, the assembly containing the customization). Because a ClickOnce application manifest describes all the assemblies that make up an application, a ClickOnce manifest can have many dependent assemblies; a VSTO customization always consists of a single assembly, and therefore has only one dependency in the application manifest.

Notice that the application manifest also refers to the location of the deployment manifest. But is not the point of the deployment manifest to identify the location of the application manifest? What is going on here?

The Relationship Between Application and Deployment Manifests

The easiest way to explain this is to walk through a typical deployment scenario. Suppose you develop and publish version 1.0.0.0 of the expense reporting solution above. There are now four interesting files: the deployment manifest, the application manifest, the assembly, and the document. The deployment manifest points to the application manifest, the application manifest points to the assembly, and the document's data island contains a copy of the application manifest.

Now you e-mail the document, without the assembly, to a user. The user loads the document into Excel. The VSTO runtime reads the copy of the application manifest out of the document and notices a deployment manifest in the "installFrom" location. The VSTO runtime downloads the deployment manifest and discovers that both the application and deployment manifests are version 1.0.0.0. Therefore, the VSTO runtime knows that the document contains the most recent copy of the application manifest, and need not update it.

The deployment manifest's codebase refers to the location of the server's copy of the manifest and the customization DLL. The CLR assembly loader then downloads the assembly and configuration file, caches them locally, and loads the assembly into memory. (Although the file has been cached locally for convenience, the CLR assembly loader sets the evidence associated with the assembly to match its original location, not its temporary location on the local disk.) The VSTO runtime then starts up the classes named in the entryPoint elements, and the customization runs.

A few days later, you fix some bugs and roll out version 1.0.0.1 to the server using the Publish Wizard. The next time that the user starts the document while online, the VSTO runtime contacts the server to see whether there have been any changes in the deployment manifest.

This time the document's copy of the application manifest is 1.0.0.0, but the deployment manifest is 1.0.0.1. The VSTO runtime downloads the new application manifest from the server and caches a copy of it in the document. (Note that if the user quits Excel without saving the document, the change to the cached manifest will be lost with all of the other changes.)

The CLR loader detects that the assembly's codebase is different and downloads the new assembly. The user is now running the latest version without ever having to download or install anything manually.

Because the local copy of the application manifest knows where the deployment manifest is, and the deployment manifest knows where the latest application manifest is, the document can keep itself always up to date with the latest bits.

> A deployment manifest's version number must match the version number of the application manifest it refers to. If the deployment manifest's version attribute indicates that it is version 1.0.0.1, the referred-to application manifest must also be version 1.0.01. If the VSTO runtime detects that the deployment manifest refers to a mismatched application manifest, it assumes that the deployment server has been corrupted and refuses to load the customization.

Determining the Assembly Location from a Deployment Manifest

Did you notice that between the deployment manifest and the application manifest there were three codebase attributes? The application manifest says this:

```
<asmv2:dependency asmv2:name="dependency0">
  <asmv2:dependentAssembly>
    <assemblyIdentity name="ExpenseReport"
      version="1.0.0.0" culture="neutral" />
     <asmv2:installFrom codebase="ExpenseReport_1.0.0.0\ExpenseReport.DLL" />
  </asmv2:dependentAssembly>
  <asmv2:installFrom codebase=
"http://accounting/ExpenseReport/ExpenseReport.application" />
  </asmv2:dependency>
```

Whereas the deployment manifest says this:

```
codebase="ExpenseReport_1.0.0.0\ExpenseReport.dll.manifest"
```

How does the loader actually determine the codebase from which to load the customization assembly? In the preceding example, the application manifest has an absolute path to the deployment manifest, so the runtime starts there. The absolute path to the deployment manifest is combined with the codebase in the application manifest which is relative to the deployment manifest path for a published project. So the VSTO runtime looks for the assembly in http://accounting/ExpenseReport/ExpenseReport_1.0.0.0/

Had the application manifest contained an absolute path to the DLL, the VSTO runtime would ignore the deployment manifest information for the purposes of loading the customization, and just use the absolute path. You learn how to edit the codebase and other attributes in the application and deployment manifests later in this chapter.

Local Machine Deployment Without a Deployment Manifest

What if you choose to eschew the convenience of having customization assemblies deployed to centralized network locations? Perhaps there is no suitable location, or the number of users who will be using your customized document is sufficiently small that rolling out new assemblies to all of their machines is not particularly onerous. You could always stick with the default behavior, where the customization assembly must be in the same directory as the document it customizes.

As discussed at the beginning of this chapter, however, that leads to the inconvenience of having to copy around the associated files every time you move the document itself. The security system imposes an additional inconvenience; if the customization assembly is in the same location as the document, that location must be fully trusted for some reason other than it simply being in the local machine zone.

For these reasons, your users might want the convenience of having one location on their local machine for the customization. That way the customization need not be moved around with the document and only one location need be explicitly trusted.

If no deployment manifest is listed in the embedded application manifest, clearly the VSTO runtime will not be able to resolve the codebase relative to the nonexistent deployment manifest location. Instead, the VSTO runtime will resolve the codebase by taking the path relative to the current document location. Of course, having a relative path to the document again makes it difficult to move the document around without moving the assembly as well. Therefore, it is most likely that the assembly codebase will be an absolute path.

A particularly useful feature when setting the application codebase is that the VSTO runtime will expand any environment variables in the installFrom path. For example, you could set the installFrom path to this:

```
<asmv2:installFrom codebase=
"%ProgramFiles%\ExpenseReport\ExpenseReport.dll" />
```

The VSTO runtime would then replace the named environment variable with the appropriate path on the user's machine.

But how does one go about editing these paths? The application manifest in question is embedded in the document's data island. Fortunately, the VSTO runtime provides a convenient object model for manipulating embedded application manifests; the ServerDocument object which you saw used for manipulating a document's cached data in Chapter 18, "Server Data Scenarios," will come in handy again.

Editing Manifests

You can use several tools to edit deployment and application manifests.

Using MAGE to Edit Deployment Manifests

The Visual Studio Publish Wizard will automatically generate and update a deployment manifest for you, but should you want to edit the manifest yourself, you have two main options. First, the deployment manifest is nothing more than an XML file sitting on a server; you can use Notepad or any other editor of your choice.

If editing raw XML is not your idea of a good time, you can use the Manifest Generating and Editing tool, MAGE.EXE (see Figure 20-2). MAGE ships with Visual Studio, and provides a convenient graphical interface for editing deployment manifests. (Look in the SDK\v2.0\BIN directory of your Visual Studio installation.)

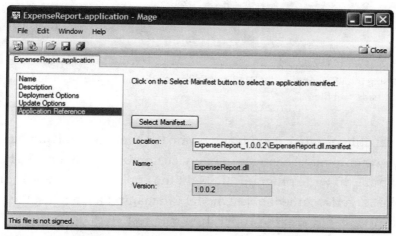

Figure 20-2 Using MAGE.EXE to manually update a deployment manifest to refer to a new version of the customization.

Unfortunately, the VSTO application manifest file format is sufficiently different from the ClickOnce file format that MAGE cannot be used to edit VSTO application manifests, only deployment manifests. To edit application manifests, you have a couple of options: You can use the VSTO Application Manifest Editor utility, or you can write your own tools using the ServerDocument object model.

Using the VSTO Application Manifest Editor

The VSTO SDK ships with a library of code samples, one of which is a graphical utility for editing application manifests. Load the ApplicationManifestEditor sample solution into Visual Studio and build it. You can then use this utility to edit the manifests inside of spreadsheets and documents (see Figure 20-3).

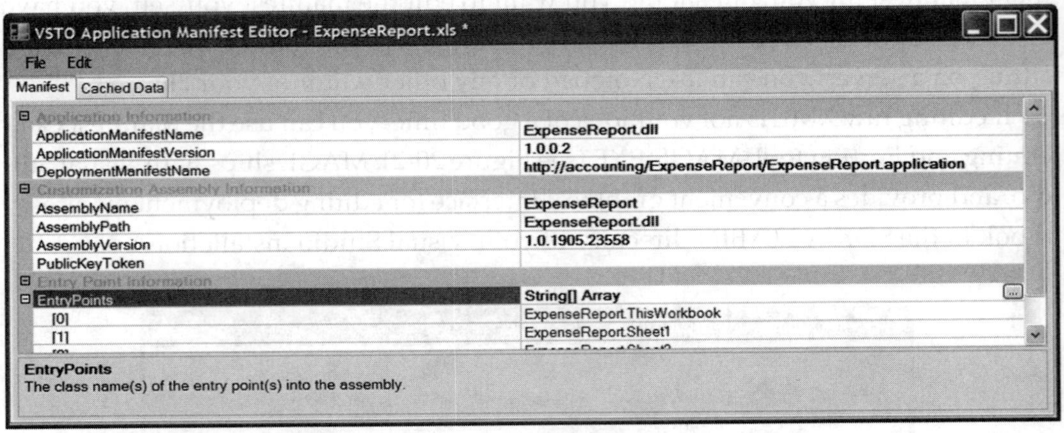

Figure 20-3 Using the VSTO Application Manifest Editor to edit the manifest embedded in a spreadsheet file.

Graphical utilities prove handy if you want to change a small number of files, but what if you want to make changes to many customizations at once? Then it would be nice to be able to write programs that edit the application manifests directly. Fortunately, the ServerDocument object model can manipulate not just the cached data inside a document, but also the application manifest.

Using the ServerDocument Object Model to Read and Edit Embedded Application Manifests

The ServerDocument object model, discussed in Chapter 18, was primarily designed to manipulate the cached data island on the server. However, you can also use it to read or edit the application manifest stored in a customized document. The Server-Document object can edit the application manifests stored in Word documents saved in either binary or XML format, and Excel documents saved in binary format only.

We can modify our cached data viewer from Chapter 18 to display the application manifest inside a document.

Listing 20-3 Creating an Application Manifest Viewer with ServerDocument

```csharp
using Microsoft.VisualStudio.Tools.Applications.Runtime;
using System;
using System.IO;
using System.Text;

namespace VSTOViewer {
  public class MainClass {
    public static void Main(string[] args) {
      if (args.Length != 1) {
        Console.WriteLine("Usage:");
        Console.WriteLine("   AppInfoViewer.exe myfile.doc");
        return;
      }

      string filename = args[0];
      ServerDocument doc = null;

      try {
        doc = new ServerDocument(filename, false, FileAccess.Read);
        Console.WriteLine("\nApplication Manifest");
        Console.WriteLine(doc.AppManifest.ToXml());
      }
      catch (CannotLoadManifestException ex)
      {
        Console.WriteLine("Not a customized document:" + filename);
        Console.WriteLine(ex.Message);
      }
      catch (FileNotFoundException)
      {
        Console.WriteLine("File not found:" + filename);
      }
      catch (Exception ex)
      {
        Console.WriteLine("Unexpected Exception:" + filename);
        Console.WriteLine(ex.ToString());
      }
      finally
      {
        if (doc != null)
          doc.Close();
      }
    }
  }
}
```

This section covers all the application-manifest-related properties and methods in the server document object model, describing what they do, their purpose, and why they look the way they do.

> As mentioned in Chapter 18, because this object model enables you to modify all the information about the customization, it is quite possible to create documents with nonsensical deployment information. The VSTO runtime engine does attempt to detect malformed customization information and throw the appropriate exceptions; but still, exercise caution when using this object model.

Application Manifest Objects, Methods, and Properties

The ServerDocument represents the application manifest as an object of type AppManifest:

```
AppManifest AppManifest { get; }
```

The AppManifest object has no public constructors; the only way to get an instance of an AppManifest is by opening a ServerDocument object. However, after you have one, there is an easy way to turn an XML manifest into the programmable object model:

```
void Clear()
void FromXml(string manifest)
string ToXml()
```

The ToXml method turns the current state of the object model into XML. The Clear method throws away *all* the information in the manifest, making it a blank slate. The FromXml method clears the present state of the document before loading the information from the passed-in XML string. The AppManifest object also has four properties:

```
string DeployManifestPath { get; set; }
EntryPointCollection EntryPoints { get; }
Dependency Dependency { get; }
AssemblyIdentity Identity { get; set; }
```

The AssemblyIdentity property is the "assembly" identity of the *manifest*, not of the *customization assembly*. This contains the application manifest's version number. If a deployment manifest is used, the VSTO runtime compares the application manifest and deployment manifest versions to see whether the application manifest is out-of-date.

The DeployManifestPath property gives the URL to the deployment manifest. This property sets the codebase attribute of the second installFrom element in the application manifest.

Using a deployment manifest is optional; if no deployment manifest path is set, the VSTO runtime assumes that the embedded application manifest is always up-to-date.

An EntryPointCollection is a straightforward strongly typed collection class that extends CollectionBase with these methods:

```
EntryPoint Add(string className)
int IndexOf(EntryPoint entryPoint)
void Remove(EntryPoint entryPoint)
EntryPoint this[int index] { get; }
void CopyTo(EntryPoint[] entryPoints, int index)
void Insert(int index, EntryPoint value)
bool Contains(EntryPoint value)
```

Like the AppManifest, the EntryPointCollection and EntryPoint objects have no public constructors. Use the Add method on the EntryPointCollection if you want to create a new EntryPoint. An EntryPoint has only one public property. It should be the namespace-qualified name of the view class:

```
string ClassName { get; set; }
```

The Dependency object has two properties:

```
string AssemblyPath { get; set; }
AssemblyIdentity AssemblyIdentity { get; set; }
```

To load the customization assembly, the runtime needs to know both the full name of the assembly and its location. The AssemblyPath corresponds to the codebase attribute of the first installFrom element in the application manifest. As mentioned previously, it may be either an absolute or relative URL. If absolute, the assembly is loaded from that location. If relative, the path is relative to the location of the deployment manifest's codebase, if there is one, or the document, if there is not.

The AssemblyIdentity object does have a public constructor, unlike every other object in the application manifest object model:

```
AssemblyIdentity(string name, FourPartVersion version,
   string publicKeyToken)
string Name { get; set; }
string PublicKeyToken { get; set; }
FourPartVersion Version {get; set; }
```

The Name property gives the name of the assembly, not the name of the file containing it; it should not end in .DLL.

The PublicKeyToken property is part of the strong name. A full public key encoded as a string is a rather long and unwieldy string. The public key token is a much shorter statistically guaranteed-unique key that identifies the public key used to verify a strong-named assembly. (See Chapter 19 for more details on what a strong name is and what the key token is for.) You can use `sn.exe -T myassembly.dll` to give the public key token of a strong-named assembly.

Finally, the FourPartVersion object is a value type that keeps track of `"1.2.3.4"`-formatted version numbers. It has the following properties and methods:

```
FourPartVersion(int major, int minor, int buildNumber, int revision)
int Major { get; set; }
int Minor{ get; set; }
int BuildNumber{ get; set; }
int Revision{ get; set; }
static FourPartVersion Parse(string value)
static FourPartVersion Empty
```

The FourPartVersion class also overrides all the comparison operators so that you can easily compare any two.

Creating Setup Packages

Creating a setup package to install a VSTO customized document on a user's local machine requires us to build a couple of custom installer classes. We need to update the application manifest stored in the document to refer to the location on the user's machine, and we need to update the user's security policy. Let's walk through all the steps required to add a setup package to a customized spreadsheet—say, an expense reporting application.

Open the solution for the customized document and right-click the solution (the root of the tree) in the Solution Explorer. Choose Add > New Project, and create a setup project as shown in Figure 20-4.

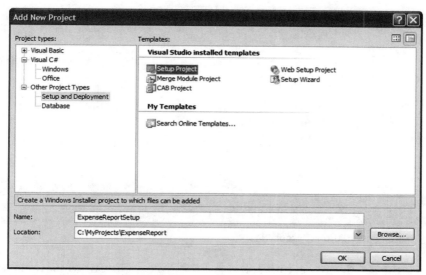

Figure 20-4 Creating a setup project.

This step is not necessary if you have created an Outlook Add-In VSTO project. Visual Studio will automatically create an installer project which installs the DLL, creates a manifest, and updates the Outlook add-in registry key for you. However, you will still need to ensure that the right security policy is rolled out and that the VSTO runtime assemblies are installed on the client machines.

Use the Properties pane for the setup project to customize strings such as the author, description, and so on, as shown in Figure 20-5.

We have not yet told the setup project what files it is going to be setting up. We want it to set up all the files produced by the expense report project in this solution.

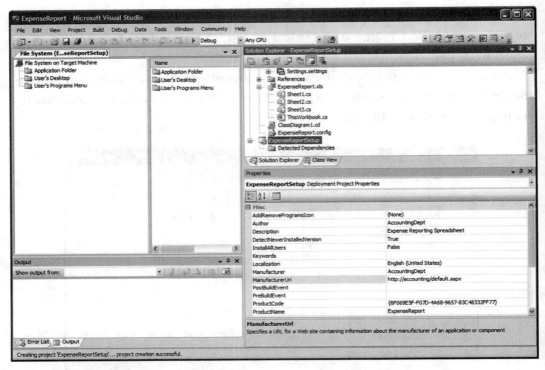

Figure 20-5 Setting setup project properties.

Right-click the setup project and select Add > Project Output to view the Add Project Output Group dialog shown in Figure 20-6.

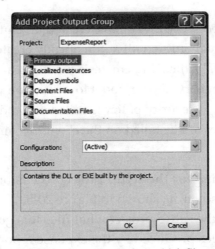

Figure 20-6 Telling the setup project which files to set up.

Select the Primary Output files associated with the Expense Report project and click OK.

At this point, if you want the users to take responsibility for installing the customization to a location that they trust, and do not care that that will have to copy around the customization assembly if they want to move the spreadsheet, you are done. You can build and execute the setup package, and it will copy the necessary files to the user's machine just as they are on the development machine.

However, you probably want to set the codebase in the application manifest so that it refers to the installation location rather than the current directory. You also probably want to set the user's security policy so that the customization location is fully trusted. That way the user can copy the document around without worrying about dragging the customization along with it.

To do that, we create yet another project in this solution. Right-click the solution in the Solution Explorer again and create a new, empty C# project (in the Visual C# > Windows branch of the tree view of the Add New Project dialog) called Custom-Setup. When you have the project, right-click it and select the Properties pane for the project. Change the output type to Class Library, as shown in Figure 20-7.

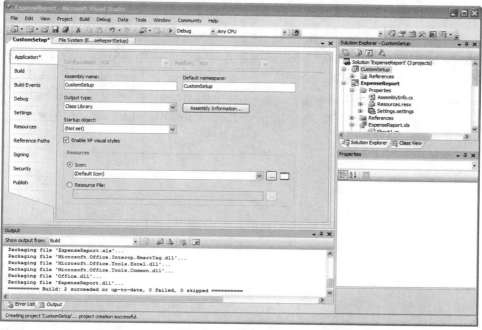

Figure 20-7 Setting the custom installer class project to build a class library.

Right-click the project again and choose Add > New Item. Add a new Installer Class, as shown in Figure 20-8. In fact, add two: one for the security change, and one for the application manifest change.

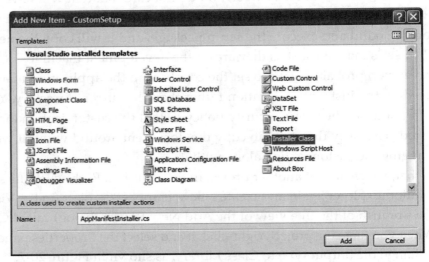

Figure 20-8 Adding custom installer classes.

Right-click the References node in the CustomSetup project's tree view and add a reference to Microsoft.VisualStudio.Tools.Applications.Runtime—we are going to need to create the ServerDocument class, so we need a reference to the VSTO runtime library. Finally, right-click the application manifest installer and select View Code. The Visual Studio IDE should now look something like Figure 20-9.

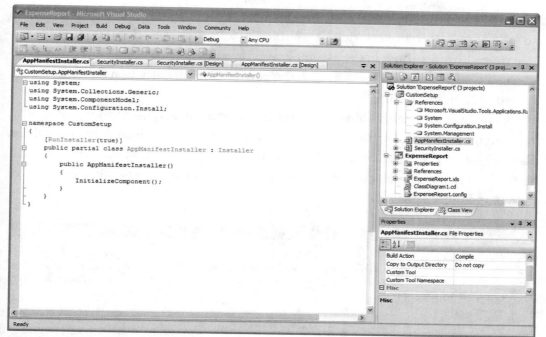

Figure 20-9 Editing the custom installer classes.

Before we get into adding code to these custom actions, however, let's tell the installer about them. Right-click the installer project in the Server Explorer and choose View > Custom Actions. In the Custom Actions viewer, right-click Install and choose Add Custom Action to view the custom action dialog shown in Figure 20-10.

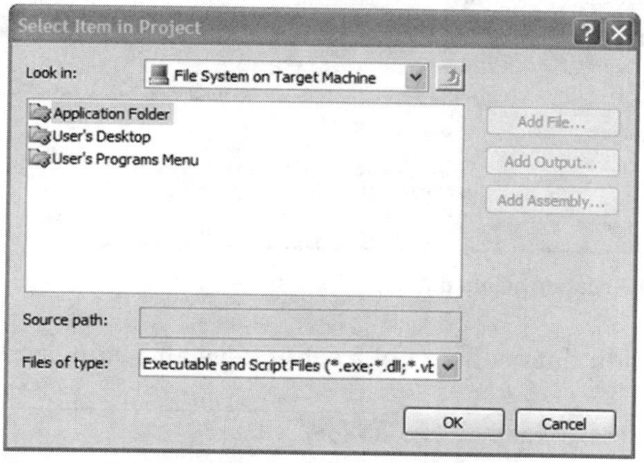

Figure 20-10 Selecting the custom install actions.

Click Application Folder and then Primary Output from CustomSetup. Doing so tells the setup project that it should look for classes decorated with the `RunInstaller` attribute in the assembly produced by the CustomSetup project. As you can see from the code editor, both the new custom install action classes are decorated with this attribute.

We must do one more thing to get the custom install actions working properly; they need to know the name of the assembly, the name of the document, and where they are located. To pass these strings from the installer to the custom action, we add the strings to the CustomActionData property of the custom action just created, as shown in Figure 20-11.

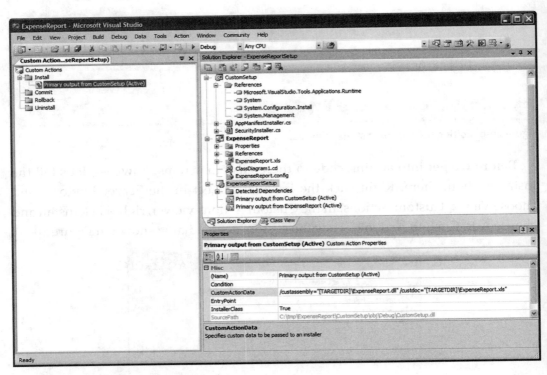

Figure 20-11 Setting the custom action data.

The custom action data consists of a set of keys and values:

```
/custassembly="[TARGETDIR]\ExpenseReport.dll"
/custdoc="[TARGETDIR]\ExpenseReport.xls"
```

Finally, we are all set up to write the custom installation actions. First, we write the application manifest editor shown in Listing 20-4. We get the strings passed by the main installer out of the installation context object, create a ServerDocument on the installed document, and set the assembly path to the absolute path. Finally, because this is a derived class, we make sure that we call the base class install method in case it does anything interesting (such as write a success message to a log file).

Listing 20-4 Creating an Application Manifest Editor Custom Install Action with Server Document

```
using System;
using System.Collections.Generic;
using System.ComponentModel;
using System.Configuration.Install;
using Microsoft.VisualStudio.Tools.Applications.Runtime;
namespace CustomSetup
{
  [RunInstaller(true)]
  public partial class AppManifestInstaller : Installer
  {
    public AppManifestInstaller()
    {
      InitializeComponent();
    }
    public override void Install(
      System.Collections.IDictionary stateSaver)
    {
      string assemblyPath = this.Context.Parameters["custassembly"];
      string documentPath = this.Context.Parameters["custdoc"];
      ServerDocument sd = new ServerDocument(documentPath,
        true, System.IO.FileAccess.ReadWrite);
      try
      {
        sd.AppManifest.Dependency.AssemblyPath = assemblyPath;
        sd.Save();
      }
      finally
      {
        sd.Close();
      }
      base.Install(stateSaver);
    }
  }
}
```

Second, we write code similar to the code we wrote in Chapter 19 to set the local security policy. This time, we set a user security policy that trusts the installation directory explicitly as shown in Listing 20-5.

Listing 20-5 A Custom Install Action Class to Set Local Security Policy

```
using System;
using System.Collections;
using System.Collections.Generic;
using System.ComponentModel;
using System.Configuration.Install;
using System.Security;
using System.Security.Policy;
namespace CustomSetup
{
  [RunInstaller(true)]
  public partial class SecurityInstaller : Installer
  {
    public SecurityInstaller()
    {
      InitializeComponent();
    }
    public override void Install(
      System.Collections.IDictionary stateSaver)
    {
      PolicyLevel enterprisePolicyLevel;
      PolicyLevel machinePolicyLevel;
      PolicyLevel userPolicyLevel;
      CodeGroup assemblyGroup;
      UrlMembershipCondition assemblyCondition;
      PolicyStatement policyStatement;
      PermissionSet fullTrust;
      string assemblyPath = this.Context.Parameters["custassembly"];

// Obtain the three policy levels:

      IEnumerator policyEnumerator = SecurityManager.PolicyHierarchy();
      policyEnumerator.MoveNext();
      enterprisePolicyLevel = (PolicyLevel)policyEnumerator.Current;
      policyEnumerator.MoveNext();
      machinePolicyLevel = (PolicyLevel)policyEnumerator.Current;
      policyEnumerator.MoveNext();
      userPolicyLevel = (PolicyLevel)policyEnumerator.Current;

// Create a new group by combining a permission set with a
// membership condition:
```

```
    fullTrust = userPolicyLevel.GetNamedPermissionSet("FullTrust");
    policyStatement = new PolicyStatement(fullTrust,
        PolicyStatementAttribute.Nothing);
    assemblyCondition = new UrlMembershipCondition(assemblyPath);
    assemblyGroup = new UnionCodeGroup(
        assemblyCondition, policyStatement);

// Add the new policy to the root:

    userPolicyLevel.RootCodeGroup.AddChild(assemblyGroup);
    SecurityManager.SavePolicy();

    base.Install(stateSaver);
        }
    }
}
```

If you build all three projects, right-click the installation project, and choose Install, you will see how the Installation Wizard allows the user to select the location, copies the files over, and then updates the user's security policy and sets the assembly code-base in the embedded application manifest.

Of course, this section has just given a bare-bones skeleton of a customized installation program. A more robust installer includes features such as custom logging, better error handling, user-interface elements, rollback/uninstall when things go wrong, and so on.

Advanced Topic: Deploying Network Solutions to Be Cached Locally

This chapter began by noting that VSTO supports two main deployment scenarios: Local install ensures that customizations always work even when the user is not connected to the network, and network installs ensure that the user always has the latest version. It would be nice to have the best of both worlds: the latest version whenever you are online plus the ability to work offline.

If your users need to be able to always run the latest version of the customization while online or offline and also want to have one centralized point at which the customization can be updated, there are two principle techniques for doing so: Deploy the customization to a Web server, and deploy it to an IntelliMirror shared directory.

IntelliMirror Versus Web Caching

If the customization is deployed to a Web server, the Visual Studio runtime loader keeps a local copy of the assembly and configuration file in the Internet Explorer cache so that the customization is available when Internet Explorer is offline. Similarly, a locally cached IntelliMirror share makes the network customization seamlessly available even when the network share is not available.

All other things being equal, the IntelliMirror technique is to be preferred over the Web server technique for several reasons. For example, suppose you deploy your customization assembly to http://accounting, a local intranet Web server. A user runs the customized document, which downloads the customization assembly from the intranet site and caches a copy in the Internet Explorer cache. The user then unplugs his laptop from the wall, heads to the local library, and connects to the library's free wireless networking service. Now when the user tries to run the customized document, the .NET Framework will not load the customization assembly out of the Internet Explorer cache because Internet Explorer *believes that it is connected to the network*. Instead, the .NET Framework attempts to connect to the intranet server, fails, and prompts the user to go offline to use the locally cached copy. The user is then faced with the unfortunate choice of either not running the customization or putting Internet Explorer into offline mode, negating the benefits of having wireless Internet access.

Also, because the Web server caching scenario puts the customization assembly into the Internet Explorer cache, anything that causes the cache to be cleared destroys the cached customization assembly along with everything else. Many users frequently clear their Web caches when the caches get too large, and it is very easy to accidentally delete a cached customization assembly when you do not intend to.

Finally, a further inconvenience of the Web caching scenario is that all customizations must have a configuration file associated with them for the offline scenario to work. The next section discusses why.

Therefore, all other things being equal, if you want a hybrid online/offline scenario, the IntelliMirror technique is the preferred one. IntelliMirror shares pay no attention to the state of the Internet Explorer cache or online status.

Why Do We Need a Configuration File?

One of the goals explicitly stated earlier was to be able to have code live up on a Web server, so that it was always up-to-date, and yet be able to also access the code when the machine is disconnected. To achieve this goal, the first time the remote code is run, it is downloaded into a local cache. If you run the code again while connected, VSTO checks to ensure that the latest version is downloaded; if offline, VSTO runs the cached code.

Consider this scenario: Suppose your customization assembly is on a Web server along with a configuration file. The customization assembly uses version 1.0.0.0 of a strong-named assembly containing some useful routines you have written. The first time the user runs the application, the customization assembly and configuration file are downloaded and cached. The user goes offline, but the customization continues to work because the cached assembly and configuration file are available.

So far everything is good. Unfortunately, one day you discover a serious security hole in your library. You fix it, and release version 1.0.1.0 of the library. Every customization, however, still attempts to load the old code because the customization assembly was built against the old version. You would rather not go to the trouble of recompiling what might be hundreds or thousands of customizations against the new library; instead, you just update their server-side configuration files to say that the new version should be loaded when the old version is requested. While the user is offline, of course, they will still be running the insecure code, but there's nothing anyone can do about that; when they go back online and run the code, the new configuration file can be downloaded, the new library installed, and everyone is happy again.

That scenario is reason enough to always use configuration files; it is very handy to be able to easily change the assembly loading policy. But why not create a configuration file only when you find yourself in this unfortunate situation? Why do we require you to always create a configuration file if you want to be able to run server-side code while offline?

Well, suppose you did not create a configuration file; let's go through that scenario again. Your customization assembly is on the Web, without a configuration file, and uses buggy version 1.0.0.0 of your library assembly. The user runs the application for the first time. The loader finds the customization assembly and caches it, and determines that there is no configuration file on the server. Then the user goes offline.

You discover your security hole and roll out a configuration file pointing the loader to version 1.0.1.0 of your library assembly. The disconnected user knows none of this, and attempts to run the customization again.

Look at this from the point of view of the CLR assembly loader: It has been asked to load a file off of an unavailable Web server. It tries to find a local copy of the assembly, and succeeds. It tries to find a local copy of the configuration file, but fails. If you had cached a local copy of the configuration file, the CLR can assume that you meant for it to use that configuration file and that you were fine with using potentially out-of-date configuration information. But because there is no cached file, the CLR has to assume the worst: that there is in fact a new and important configuration file available that it cannot find.

Therefore, if you want to ensure that users must always be online and using the latest version of your server-side customization, you should not create a configuration file on the server. On the other hand, if you want to allow users to use cached assemblies and configuration files when your server is inaccessible, ensure that you have a configuration file on the server.

To add a configuration file to your project, right-click the project in the Solution Explorer and choose Add > New Item > Application Configuration File. Name the configuration file after the customization assembly filename; if your assembly is ExpenseReport.dll, name the configuration file ExpenseReport.dll.config.

The configuration file need not have any loading policies in it; for now, stick with the bare minimum:

```xml
<?xml version="1.0" encoding="utf-8" ?>
<configuration>
</configuration>
```

Configuration files do not get any more straightforward than that. To ensure that this file is copied up to the deployment server, make sure that the Build Action is set to Content in the Properties pane for the configuration file.

Conclusion

VSTO's deployment system affords the ease of updating found traditionally in Web-based applications without squandering the power of the rich client or compromising the strong Office offline story. The key to understanding how the deployment system works is to understand the relationship between application manifests embedded in the document and deployment manifests stored on servers. The application manifest refers to the deployment manifest, which then points to the most recent copy of the application manifest, and hence the customization.

VSTO also supports local install scenarios without deployment manifests; by default, the customization loads out of the same directory as the document, but you can edit the embedded application manifest to point to a central machine location (such as the user's Program Files directory). Custom installation classes can use the ServerDocument object model to edit embedded application manifest information much as you would edit embedded cached data in the data island.

This chapter completes our look at the fundamentals of VSTO projects using Word and Excel. The final four chapters examine some advanced topics such as using XML data with Word and Excel and creating application-level managed add-ins for Word, Excel, and Outlook.

■Part Four ■

Advanced Office Programming

Part Four covers some advanced Office programming scenarios, including using the XML features of Excel and Word and building COM add-ins for Word and Excel and VSTO add-ins for Outlook.

- Chapter 21, "Working with XML in Excel," explores Excel's XML schema mapping capabilities and the features of VSTO that are enabled when you map a schema into the document.
- Chapter 22, "Working with XML in Word," explores Word's XML schema mapping capabilities and the features of VSTO that are enabled when you map a schema into the document. This chapter also covers VSTO's support for the WordML file format.
- Chapter 23, "Developing COM Add-ins for Word and Excel," describes how to create a managed COM add-in in .NET for Word and Excel. This chapter also explores the pitfalls to avoid when writing a managed COM add-in.
- Chapter 24, "Creating Outlook Add-ins with VSTO," covers add-in development for Outlook. In particular, this chapter examines the support for creating a VSTO Outlook add-in and the way that helps avoid the pitfalls with managed COM add-in development described in Chapter 23. This chapter also describes some Outlook-specific issues you might encounter when developing a managed COM add-in that you can avoid by building a VSTO Outlook add-in instead.

■21■

Working with XML in Excel

Introduction to Excel's XML Features

THE FIRST THING TO NOTE ABOUT THE XML features described in this chapter is that most of them are only available in Microsoft Office Professional Edition 2003 and the standalone Microsoft Office Excel 2003. If you work with other Office editions, such as Microsoft Office Standard Edition 2003, Microsoft Office Student and Teacher Edition 2003, or Microsoft Office Basic Edition 2003, the XML features described in this chapter are not available.

Many of the XML features of Excel are accessed via Excel's XML Source task pane. To bring up the XML Source task pane, display the task pane if it is not already displayed by choosing Task Pane from Excel's View menu. The task pane has a drop-down menu from which XML Source can be selected, as shown in Figure 21-1.

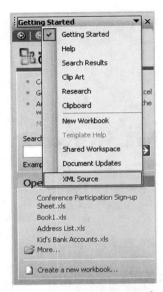

Figure 21-1 Selecting XML Source from the
task pane drop-down menu.

An alternative way of accessing the XML Source task pane is by using the XML menu in the Data menu. The XML menu has an XML Source command that will show the XML Source task pane. Figure 21-2 shows the XML menu. This chapter examines many of the commands in the XML menu.

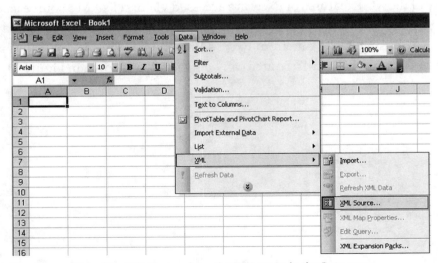

Figure 21-2 Selecting XML Source from the XML menu in the Data menu.

After you have made the XML Source task pane visible using one of these two methods, the XML Source task pane will appear as shown in Figure 21-3.

Figure 21-3 The XML Source task pane.

The XML Source task pane refers to something called an XML map. An XML map is a mapping from an XML schema to cells and/or lists in the workbook. Before you create an XML map, you must first have an XML schema to work with. The following section examines how to create an XML schema using Visual Studio 2005.

Introduction to XML Schema Creation in Visual Studio

Visual Studio 2005 has support for creating XML schemas. Launch Visual Studio 2005. Choose File from the New menu. The dialog shown in Figure 21-4 appears. Pick XML Schema from this dialog, and then click the Open button.

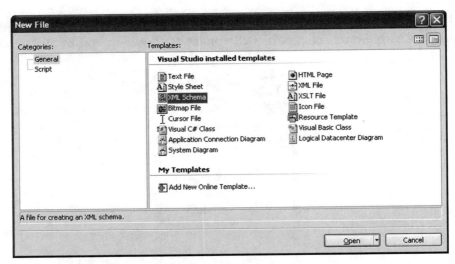

Figure 21-4 Creating a new XML schema file.

Visual Studio shows a design view for creating XML schema, as shown in Figure 21-5. The toolbox has XML schema objects that can be dragged onto the design surface for the new XML schema.

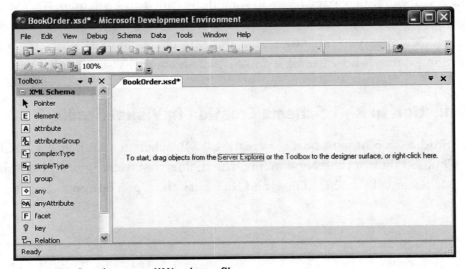

Figure 21-5 Creating a new XML schema file.

The schema object we will use most frequently in this example is element. An XML schema element defines an element in an XML file. For example, the simple XML file shown in Listing 21-1 has an element called Order in the namespace ns1. It also has an element called CustomerName in the namespace ns1. The Customer-Name element is parented by the Order element.

Listing 21-1 XML File Representing a Simple Order

```
<?xml version="1.0" encoding="UTF-8" standalone="yes"?>
<ns1:Order xmlns:ns1="http://tempuri.org/XMLSchema.xsd">
    <ns1:CustomerName>Eric Carter</ns1:CustomerName>
</ns1:Order>
```

The XML schema for this simple order XML file is created by following these steps:

1. Drag an element from the toolbox onto the schema design surface.
2. In the header row of the newly created element next to the E, type Order.
3. In the * row next to the asterisk (*), type CustomerName.

Figure 21-6 shows the resulting designer view.

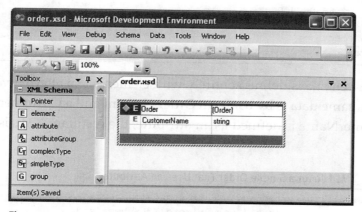

Figure 21-6 Design view of a simple Order schema.

When you save this schema, use the Save As command from the File menu to save it as order.xsd. You will have to pick XML Schema Files (*.xsd) from the Save as type drop-down in the Save As dialog. The order.xsd file will look like the one shown in Listing 21-2. You can see that an XML schema is just another XML file that defines what constitutes a valid Order XML file. It defines two elements—Order and CustomerName. Because the Order element contains other elements, it is defined as a complexType. It contains a sequence of CustomerName elements that are of type string. Sequence in this case is misleading—the way the XSD file is defined it will be a sequence of one and only one CustomerName elements. It is possible to define a sequence that has a varying number of elements in it using the maxOccurs and minOccurs settings, which we consider later in this chapter. For example, by setting minOccurs to 1 and maxOccurs to unbounded, you could allow one or more CustomerName elements to be associated with an order.

Listing 21-2 XSD Schema File for a Simple Order Schema

```
<?xml version="1.0" encoding="utf-8"?>
<xs:schema targetNamespace="http://tempuri.org/XMLSchema.xsd"
elementFormDefault="qualified" xmlns="http://tempuri.org/XMLSchema.xsd"
xmlns:mstns="http://tempuri.org/XMLSchema.xsd"
xmlns:xs="http://www.w3.org/2001/XMLSchema">
    <xs:element name="Order">
        <xs:complexType>
            <xs:sequence>
                <xs:element name="CustomerName" type="xs:string" />
            </xs:sequence>
        </xs:complexType>
    </xs:element>
</xs:schema>
```

Note that this schema is defined entirely with elements. An alternative way of representing this same data is by using an Order element and a CustomerName attribute. If CustomerName is defined as an attribute, the resultant XML is as shown in Listing 21-3.

Listing 21-3 XML File for a Simple Order That Uses an Attribute

```
<?xml version="1.0" encoding="UTF-8" standalone="yes"?>
<ns1:Order xmlns:ns1="http://tempuri.org/XMLSchema.xsd"
CustomerName="Eric Carter">
</ns1:Order>
```

The XML schema for an Order XML file that uses an attribute is created in Visual Studio by following these steps:

1. Drag an element from the toolbox onto the schema design surface.

2. In the header row of the newly created element next to the E, type **Order**.

3. In the * row next to the asterisk (*), type **CustomerName**.

4. Click the E next to CustomerName. A drop-down will appear. Select attribute from the drop-down to convert CustomerName to an attribute.

Figure 21-7 shows the resultant designer view.

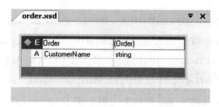

Figure 21-7 Design view of a simple Order schema that uses an attribute.

Listing 21-4 shows the schema for an order using an attribute. Because the Order element contains other attributes, it is defined as a complexType. It contains an empty sequence—this sequence can actually be removed without affecting the schema. It then defines CustomerName as an attribute of type `string`.

Listing 21-4 XSD Schema File for a Simple Order Schema That Uses an Attribute

```
<?xml version="1.0" encoding="utf-8"?>
<xs:schema targetNamespace="http://tempuri.org/XMLSchema.xsd"
elementFormDefault="qualified" xmlns="http://tempuri.org/XMLSchema.xsd"
xmlns:mstns="http://tempuri.org/XMLSchema.xsd"
xmlns:xs="http://www.w3.org/2001/XMLSchema">
    <xs:element name="Order">
        <xs:complexType>
            <xs:sequence />
            <xs:attribute name="CustomerName" type="xs:string" />
        </xs:complexType>
    </xs:element>
</xs:schema>
```

Excel works equally well with schemas that use attributes or elements. Word, however, does not work very well when you use attributes in a schema. If you are creating a schema that you need to use in Excel and Word, you should try to use elements instead of attributes. For more information, see Chapter 22, "Working with XML in Word."

An End-to-End Scenario

This section deals with a more complex end-to-end scenario that puts together the schema creation capabilities of Visual Studio and the schema mapping capabilities of Excel. When you take a schema and map it into Excel using the XML Source task pane, you enable the exporting and importing of XML data in the spreadsheet. We are going to create an Excel spreadsheet that can be used to record a customer's book order. The spreadsheet will support the import and export of XML that conforms to our book order schema. The spreadsheet will look like Figure 21-8.

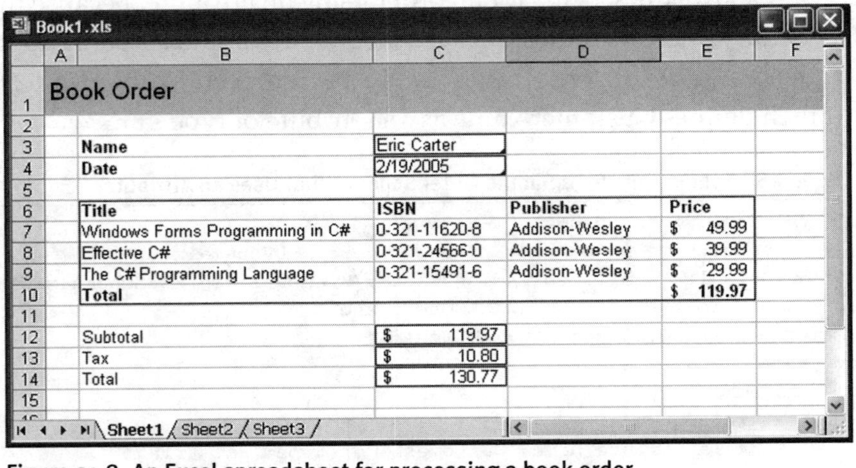

Figure 21-8 An Excel spreadsheet for processing a book order.

Listing 21-5 shows the XML that this spreadsheet will be able to import and export.

Listing 21-5 XML File Generated from Book Order Spreadsheet

```
<?xml version="1.0" encoding="UTF-8" standalone="yes"?>
<ns1:Order xmlns:ns1="http://tempuri.org/XMLSchema.xsd">
    <ns1:CustomerName>Eric Carter</ns1:CustomerName>
    <ns1:Date>2005-02-19</ns1:Date>
    <ns1:Book>
        <ns1:Title>Windows Forms Programming in C#</ns1:Title>
        <ns1:ISBN>0-321-11620-8</ns1:ISBN>
        <ns1:Publisher>Addison-Wesley</ns1:Publisher>
        <ns1:Price>49.99</ns1:Price>
    </ns1:Book>
    <ns1:Book>
        <ns1:Title>Effective C#</ns1:Title>
        <ns1:ISBN>0-321-24566-0</ns1:ISBN>
        <ns1:Publisher>Addison-Wesley</ns1:Publisher>
        <ns1:Price>39.99</ns1:Price>
    </ns1:Book>
    <ns1:Book>
        <ns1:Title>The C# Programming Language</ns1:Title>
        <ns1:ISBN>0-321-15491-6</ns1:ISBN>
        <ns1:Publisher>Addison-Wesley</ns1:Publisher>
        <ns1:Price>29.99</ns1:Price>
    </ns1:Book>
    <ns1:Subtotal>119.97</ns1:Subtotal>
    <ns1:Tax>10.7973</ns1:Tax>
    <ns1:Total>130.7673</ns1:Total>
</ns1:Order>
```

Creating the Schema Using Visual Studio

To create this schema using Visual Studio, follow these steps:

1. Start Visual Studio 2005.

2. Create a new XSD file by choosing File from the New menu of the File menu or by pressing Ctrl+N.

3. Choose XML Schema from the list of Visual Studio installed templates, as shown in Figure 21-4. Then click the Open button.

4. The Schema design view appears as shown in Figure 21-5. Drag an element object off of the toolbox onto the design surface.

5. Type **Order** and press the Enter key.

6. In the * row, type **CustomerName** and press the Enter key.

7. In the * row, type **Date** and press the Tab key, and then type **date** for the data type and press Enter.

8. In the * row, type **Subtotal** and press the Tab key, and then type **float** for the data type and press Enter.

9. In the * row, type **Tax** and press the Tab key, and then type **float** for the data type and press Enter.

10. In the * row, type **Total** and press the Tab key, and then type **float** for the data type and press Enter.

11. Now right-click the Order element box and choose New element from the Add menu.

12. Type **Book** and press the Enter key.

13. In the * row of the newly created Book element, type **Title** and press Enter.

14. In the * row of the newly created Book element, type **ISBN** and press Enter.

15. In the * row of the newly created Book element, type **Publisher** and press Enter.

16. In the * row of the newly created Book element, type **Price** and press the Tab key, and then type **float** for the data type and press Enter.

17. We now want to specify that multiple books can be included in an order. Click the Book row in the Order element box and show the Properties window by choosing Properties Window from the View menu. For the property maxOccurs, type **unbounded**. For the property minOccurs, type **1**.

18. Now save the schema using the Save As command from the File menu. In the Save File As dialog, drop down the Save as type combo box and pick XML Schema Files (*.xsd). For the filename, type BookOrder.xsd and save it to a convenient place such as the desktop.

WORKING WITH XML IN EXCEL

Figure 21-9 show what the final schema in Visual Studio should look like.

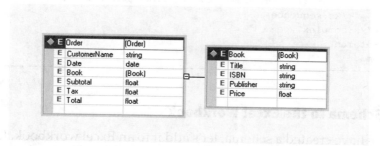

Figure 21-9 The book order schema in Visual Studio.

Listing 21-6 shows the generated XSD file. Note that the sequence of Book elements in an Order element is now a sequence with a minimum (minOccurs) of one Book elements and a maximum (maxOccurs) of unbounded Book elements. This will allow our schema to represent one or more Books in an Order. Also, having a sequence where maxOccurs is greater than one or unbounded will help Excel to know that it needs to represent the Books in an Order using an Excel list.

Listing 21-6 Book Order Schema XSD File

```xml
<?xml version="1.0" encoding="utf-8"?>
<xs:schema targetNamespace="http://tempuri.org/XMLSchema.xsd"
elementFormDefault="qualified" xmlns="http://tempuri.org/XMLSchema.xsd"
xmlns:mstns="http://tempuri.org/XMLSchema.xsd"
xmlns:xs="http://www.w3.org/2001/XMLSchema">
    <xs:element name="Order">
        <xs:complexType>
            <xs:sequence>
                <xs:element name="CustomerName" type="xs:string" />
                <xs:element name="Date" type="xs:date" />
                <xs:element name="Book" maxOccurs="unbounded" minOccurs="1">
                    <xs:complexType>
                        <xs:sequence>
                            <xs:element name="Title" type="xs:string" />
                            <xs:element name="ISBN" type="xs:string" />
                            <xs:element name="Publisher" type="xs:string" />
                            <xs:element name="Price" type="xs:float" />
                        </xs:sequence>
                    </xs:complexType>
                </xs:element>
```

```
              <xs:element name="Subtotal" type="xs:float" />
              <xs:element name="Tax" type="xs:float" />
              <xs:element name="Total" type="xs:float" />
          </xs:sequence>
      </xs:complexType>
    </xs:element>
</xs:schema>
```

Adding a Schema to the Excel Workbook

Now that we have created a schema, let's add it to an Excel workbook. Launch Excel and create a new empty workbook. Bring up the Excel XML Source task pane as described in the first section of this chapter. You should now see the XML Source task pane with no mappings as yet in the task pane. To add an XML map, click the XML Maps button in the XML Source task pane. Doing so brings up the dialog shown in Figure 21-10.

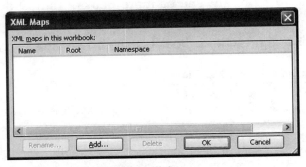

Figure 21-10 The XML Maps dialog.

Click the Add button and browse to wherever you saved your book order schema. Select the schema and click the Open button. The XML map now appears as a loaded XML map in the workbook. Using this dialog, you can delete and rename an XML map. For now, we will just click the OK button to exit this dialog.

The Excel XML Source task pane shows the XML map we just added, as shown in Figure 21-11.

Figure 21-11 The XML Source task pane with an XML map.

Mapping the Schema to the Excel Workbook

The XML Source task pane represents our book order schema in a tree view. The icon associated with Order indicates a required parent element. The icons associated with CustomerName, Date, Title, ISBN, Publisher, Price, Subtotal, Tax, and Total indicate required child elements. The icon associated with Book indicates a required repeating parent element. Excel also supports other schema constructs such as attributes and nonrequired elements and attributes. These constructs also have their own icons.

Let's try a few different ways of mapping the schema into the workbook. The first approach we will take is to click the root ns1:Order node in the XML Source task pane and drag it to cell A1 in the workbook. Excel creates one list to contain all the data, as shown in Figure 21-12.

Figure 21-12 The list created when ns1:Order is dragged to cell A1.

The XML Source task pane now indicates that all the elements have been mapped by bolding each element that has been mapped, as shown in Figure 21-13. Parent elements such as Order and Book are not mapped explicitly in the Workbook because these containing relationships do not need to be directly mapped to an Excel cell or list. You can remove a mapping by selecting the mapped cell or list in the Workbook and pressing the Delete key. You can also right-click the elements in the XML Source task pane that are in bold and choose Remove Element to remove the mapping.

Figure 21-13 Mapped elements are bolded in the
XML Source task pane.

At the very bottom of the XML Source task pane is a link that says Verify Map for Export. Click this link. Excel displays the dialog shown in Figure 21-14.

Figure 21-14 Mapping cannot be exported because of denormalized data.

To consider why this mapping cannot be exported, let's import the XML in Listing 21-5 into our current mapping. From the XML menu of Excel's Data menu, choose Import. Browse to an XML file containing the XML in Listing 21-5 and click the Import button. Because of the mapping we have established, Excel knows how to bring the XML into the list defined in the worksheet. Figure 21-15 shows the resulting worksheet.

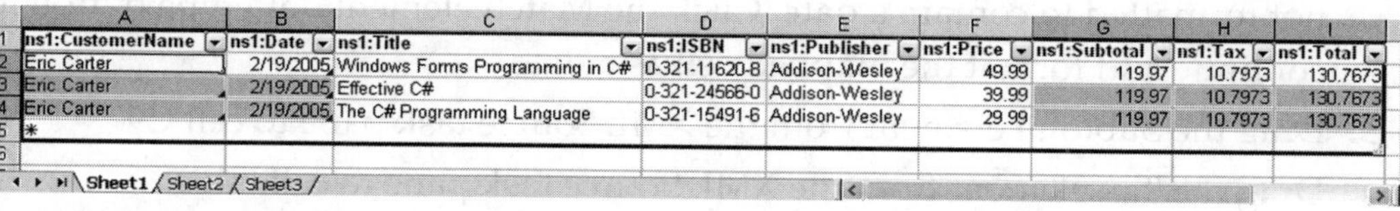

	A	B	C	D	E	F	G	H	I
1	ns1:CustomerName	ns1:Date	ns1:Title	ns1:ISBN	ns1:Publisher	ns1:Price	ns1:Subtotal	ns1:Tax	ns1:Total
2	Eric Carter	2/19/2005	Windows Forms Programming in C#	0-321-11620-8	Addison-Wesley	49.99	119.97	10.7973	130.7673
3	Eric Carter	2/19/2005	Effective C#	0-321-24566-0	Addison-Wesley	39.99	119.97	10.7973	130.7673
4	Eric Carter	2/19/2005	The C# Programming Language	0-321-15491-6	Addison-Wesley	29.99	119.97	10.7973	130.7673
5	*								
6									

Figure 21-15 Result of importing the XML in Listing 21-5.

The error we got when clicking Verify Map for Export was that the mapping contained denormalized data. In Figure 21-15, we have highlighted the data that is denormalized and redundant. If we were to try to export this list by selecting Export from the XML menu of Excel's Data menu, Excel would fail to export because it would not know how to deal with the redundant data.

Let's clear out this mapping and try to create a mapping that can be successfully exported as XML. Select the whole worksheet by pressing Ctrl+A, and then press the Delete button. This time, we are going to drag in CustomerName, Date, Subtotal, Tax, and Total as individual cell mappings, and we will map the Book element sequence as a list.

To prepare the spreadsheet for mapping, let's put in some labels in advance. Figure 21-16 shows the resulting spreadsheet.

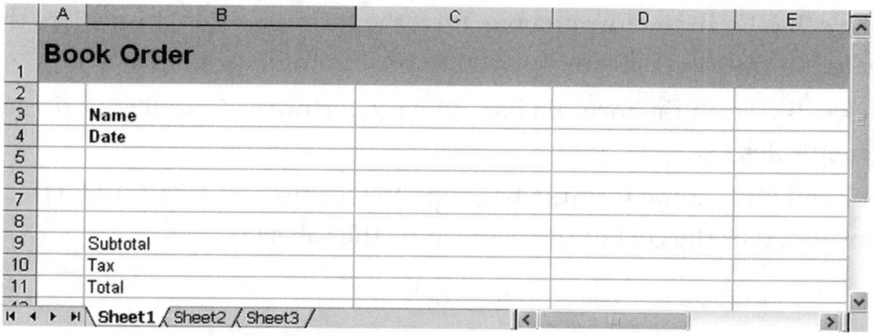

	A	B	C	D	E
1	**Book Order**				
2					
3		Name			
4		Date			
5					
6					
7					
8					
9		Subtotal			
10		Tax			
11		Total			

Figure 21-16 Preparing the spreadsheet for mapping.

Now, do the following to map the nonrepeating elements to cells in the spreadsheet:

1. Drag the CustomerName element from the XML Source task pane to cell C3.

2. Drag the Date element from the XML Source task pane to cell C4. You will be prompted that the formatting in the cell does not match the format of the data. This is Excel noticing that the format of the cell you are mapping to is not formatted to contain a date. Click the Match element data type button to continue and format the mapped cell as a date.

3. Drag the Subtotal element from the XML Source task pane to cell C9.

4. Drag the Tax element from the XML Source task pane to cell C10.

5. Drag the Total element from the XML Source task pane to cell C11.

Finally, let's map the repeating elements to a list:

1. Drag the Book element to cell B6. Because Book is a repeating element in a sequence with 1 to unbounded elements, this will create a list containing the elements Title, ISBN, Publisher, and Price as column headers in the list.

2. The column headers created by Excel have the format ns1:Title rather than Title. You can edit these columns in the spreadsheet without breaking the XML mapping.

We are also going to use some features of Excel in our spreadsheet:

1. Right-click the List object that was created and from the pop-up menu choose Totals Row from the List menu.

2. Click the lower-right cell of the List object in the total row (Cell E8). A drop-down menu appears next to the cell. Pick Sum from the drop-down menu.

3. Click cell C10. In the formula bar, type the formula =E8. This causes the total created in the total row to be saved in the Subtotal element as well.

4. Click cell C11. In the formula bar, type the formula =C10*.09 to calculate a 9 percent sales tax.

5. Click cell C12. In the formula bar, type the formula =SUM(C10:C11). This sums together the cost of the books plus the sales tax.

6. Let's also do some formatting. Click the cells C10 through C12 and click the $ button to format these cells as currency. Also click the column header for the Price column in the list and format this column as currency because it is the column where book prices will go.

The spreadsheet will now look like the one shown in Figure 21-17. Note the blue borders around all the mapped cells or lists. You can hide these blue borders by using the Options button in the XML Source task pane. Click the Options button, and then check the option from the pop-up menu that says Hide Border of Inactive Lists.

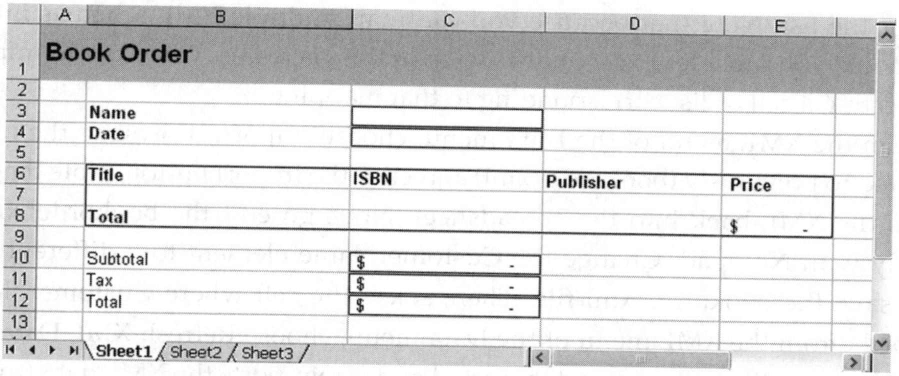

Figure 21-17 The final mapped spreadsheet.

Now, fill out the spreadsheet to make it look like Figure 21-8. Note that when you have the list selected, a new row marked with * displays, in which you can enter new items. Also note that as you type prices, the totals row sums up the prices in the list and the formulas in the spreadsheet calculate the Tax and Total.

Now, with the spreadsheet filled out, let's export the data in the spreadsheet as XML conforming to the schema we have mapped. We have assumed that this mapping will be exportable. To verify that, click the Verify Map for Export link in the XML Source task pane. A dialog should appear that says that our mapping is exportable.

From the XML menu of the Data menu, choose Export. Type the name of the XML file you want to export to, something like bookorder.xml. Then, after exporting the file, go open it in a text editor such as Notepad. You should see the XML very similar to that shown in Listing 21-5.

Advanced XML Features in Excel

We will use the mapped spreadsheet we have created to consider some other XML features in Excel.

Importing XML and Refresh XML Data

To import XML from an XML file into our mapped spreadsheet, follow these steps. First, clear out the rows in the Excel list and some of the mapped fields so that you can see that XML is being imported in subsequent steps. Select one of the mapped cells or the list. Note that because you can map multiple XML schemas into one workbook, you must let Excel know which of the mappings you want to import to by selecting a cell or list corresponding to that mapping.

From the XML menu of the Data menu, choose Import. Browse to the file you exported to previously (bookorder.xml) and click the Import button. Note that Excel brings the XML back into the spreadsheet. Now, go edit the bookorder.xml file directly with Notepad. Change the CustomerName element to a different value. Then save the bookorder.xml file. Then, select the cell where CustomerName is mapped. From the XML menu of the Data menu, choose Refresh XML Data. Excel remembers the XML file you last imported and it reimports the XML data from that file. Excel also stores this information in the document, so you can save, close, and then reopen the document at a later time and choose Refresh XML data. Note that Excel does not remember the XML file you last imported if you uncheck Save data source definition in Workbook in the XML Map Properties dialog (discussed next).

The XML Map Properties Dialog

Figure 21-18 shows the XML Map Properties dialog that can be shown by choosing XML Map Properties from the XML menu in the Data menu. Note that you must select a cell in the worksheet that is mapped to XML for this menu item and some of the other menu items in the XML menu to not be grayed out.

Figure 21-18 The XML Map Properties dialog.

XML Schema Validation

The first setting we consider in this dialog is the XML schema validation setting. With this setting unchecked, set the price of one of the books to a value such as cat. This is clearly not a valid floating-point number. From the XML menu in the Data menu, choose Export and export the XML to a file. No error will occur. Now check the Validate data against schema for import and export check box in the XML Map properties dialog. Export the XML again. This time you will get the error dialog shown in Figure 21-19 for using the value of cat in a place where a number was expected.

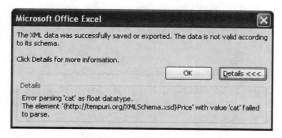

Figure 21-19 A schema validation error on export.

If you try to import XML that has the value cat for a floating-point number, you also get errors with the Validate data option checked. Figure 21-20 shows the first error dialog that appears.

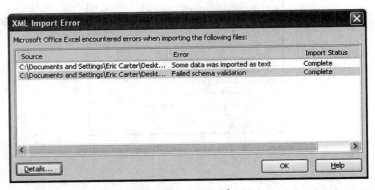

Figure 21-20 A schema validation error on import.

The first line warns that some data was imported as text—namely, the value cat was imported as text rather than as a floating-point number. When you click the second error line and click the Details button, the dialog shown in Figure 21-21 displays.

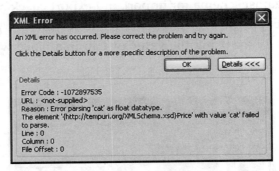

Figure 21-21 Details of the validation error on import.

Data Formatting and Layout

The XML Map Properties dialog provides settings for controlling the data formatting and layout of lists that are XML mapped. The Adjust column width check box when checked will make it so that an import of XML into a list will automatically adjust the column width to fit the data that is imported. Excel will make a column wider up to two thirds the width of the screen. To prevent automatically adjusting the column width of a list when XML is imported, uncheck this check box.

The Preserve column filter check box when checked will preserve the filtering settings for a list when XML is imported into the list. For example, if you have the list set to only show books whose publisher is Addison-Wesley, importing new XML will preserve that setting. If you uncheck this check box, whenever XML is imported into a list any existing filters will be cleared.

The preserve number formatting check box when checked will preserve any number formatting in the list that the XML is imported into. For example, if a column is set to display the book price in red if it is greater than $20, this setting will be preserved when XML data is imported into the list. If this check box is not checked, any number formatting in the list will be cleared when XML data is imported into the list.

Appending Data to Lists

The XML Map Properties dialog provides for two different behaviors when importing XML or refreshing XML and updating a mapped list. If you choose Overwrite existing data with new data, a mapped list will be cleared of its data before loading data from the XML data file on import or refresh. If you choose Append new data to existing XML lists, the data in the list will be preserved and the data from the XML data file will be appended on import or refresh. So with the Append setting set, importing the XML in Listing 21-5 into a blank list generates three book orders on the first import and on refresh it appends the three book orders to the list for a total of six book orders.

Excel-Friendly XML Schemas

Several characteristics make an XML schema more amenable to being mapped into Excel. First, an XML schema should have one root element. In our example in this chapter, the root element is Order. If a schema supports more than one root element, you must choose which element will be the root element when adding the XML map to the spreadsheet.

Unsupported XML Schema Constructs

Excel does not support several XML schema constructs. Table 21-1 lists these constructs.

Table 21-1 XML Schema Constructs That Are Not Supported by Excel

Construct	What It Does
<any>	Allows you to include arbitrary elements that are not declared by the schema.
<anyAttribute>	Allows you to include arbitrary attributes that are not declared by the schema.
recursion	A structure that refers to itself recursively.
abstract elements	Allows an element to be declared but never used—also uses substitution to substitute other elements for the abstract element.
<substitutionGroup>	Allows an element to be substituted for another element.
mixed content	When XML elements are intermixed with non XML. This proves to be very useful for Word XML mapping.

Constructs That Can Be Mapped But Not Exported

There are also several things that can be mapped but the generated mappings cannot be exported as XML. You have already seen that if an XML mapping is denormalized, it cannot be exported. You also cannot export a list of items containing a second list of items. Choice elements can also not be exported.

The other general class of issues that prevents exporting is when a mapped element's relationship with another element it is related to cannot be preserved by the mapping. For more information on these types of mapping issues, consult the Excel documentation.

VSTO-Friendly Schemas

VSTO puts some additional requirements on schema mapping if you want to use a schema mapped spreadsheet with VSTO. First, you need to have a schema mapping that can be exported. Second, the schema mapping must all be within a single worksheet. Although Excel will let you map some elements of the schema to Sheet1 and other elements to Sheet2, VSTO requires that all schema mapping for a given schema be on the same sheet.

How XML Schema Data Types Are Mapped to Excel Cell Formats

As you saw earlier in this book when mapping dates, Excel can automatically pick cell formatting based on the type in the schema. When we dragged a date into Excel, Excel prompted to change the cell formatting. Table 21-2 shows how Excel maps schema types to Excel cell formatting settings.

Table 21-2 XML Schema Types and Their Corresponding Excel Cell Formatting

XML Type	Excel Formatting	XML Type	Excel Formatting
anytype	Text	int	General
anyURI	Text	integer	General
base64Binary	Text	language	Text
boolean	Boolean	long	General
byte	General	Name	Text
date	Date *3/14/2001	NCName	Text
dateTime	m/d/yyyy h:mm	negativeInteger	General
decimal	General	NMTOKEN	Text
double	General	NMTOKENS	Text
duration	Text	nonNegativeInteger	General
ENTITIES	Text	nonPositiveInteger	General
ENTITY	Text	normalizedString	Text
float	General	NOTATION	Text
gDay	Number, no decimals	positiveInteger	General
		QName	Text
gMonth	Number, no decimals	short	General
		string	Text
gMonthDay	Custom d-mmm	time	h:mm:ss
gYear	Number, no decimals	token	Text
		unsignedByte	General
gYearMonth	Custom mmm-yy	unsignedInt	General
hexBinary	Text	unsignedLong	General
ID	Text	unsignedShort	General
IDREF	Text		
IDREFS	Text		

VSTO Support for Excel Schema Mapping

This section examines VSTO's support for Excel schema mapping. Let's create a new VSTO Excel project based on the book order spreadsheet we created in this chapter. Launch VSTO, and from the New menu in the File menu choose Project. In the New Project dialog, choose a C# Excel Application project. Give the project a name and location then click the OK button. A dialog then appears asking for a document to be used for the application. Click the Copy an existing document radio button. Then click the "..." button to browse to the spreadsheet you created in this chapter that has the book order schema mapped in it. Click the Finish button to create the project.

We want to consider several features of the generated VSTO project. First is the creation of XMLMappedRange controls. Second is the creation of ListObject controls. Third is the addition of the schema mapped to our spreadsheet to the VSTO project. Finally, we will consider how to use the controls that are created and the schema that is added to the VSTO project to hook up data binding in the project.

XMLMappedRange Controls

Use the class view to browse the members associated with Sheet1. Notice as you browse that the member variables listed in Table 21-3 have been created automatically based on the XML mapping in the spreadsheet to the book order schema.

Table 21-3 Sheet1 Member Variables Created from Schema Mapping

Name	Type
BookList	`Microsoft.Office.Tools.Excel.ListObject`
OrderCustomerNameCell	`Microsoft.Office.Tools.Excel.XmlMappedRange`
OrderDateCell	`Microsoft.Office.Tools.Excel.XmlMappedRange`
OrderSubtotalCell	`Microsoft.Office.Tools.Excel.XmlMappedRange`
OrderTaxCell	`Microsoft.Office.Tools.Excel.XmlMappedRange`
OrderTotalCell	`Microsoft.Office.Tools.Excel.XmlMappedRange`

For each nonrepeating element or attribute mapped to a cell in the Excel spreadsheet, VSTO creates an XMLMappedRange control. For example, we mapped the CustomerName element from the Order element into a cell. VSTO created an XMLMappedRange corresponding to this cell called OrderCustomerNameCell. An XMLMappedRanged control has all the properties and methods of an Excel Range object. In addition, it has several events that are not found on the Excel Range object:

- **XMLMappedRange.BeforeDoubleClick** is raised when the cell corresponding to the mapped element or attribute is double-clicked. Excel passes a `target` parameter of type Range for the range of cells that was double-clicked, and a `bool cancel` parameter passed by reference. The `cancel` parameter can be set to `true` by your event handler to prevent Excel from executing its default double-click behavior.

- **XMLMappedRange.BeforeRightClick** is raised when the cell corresponding to the mapped element or attribute is right-clicked. Excel passes a `target` parameter of type Range for the range of cells that was right-clicked. The `target` parameter is provided so you can determine whether multiple cells were selected when the right-click occurred. Excel also passes a `bool cancel` parameter by reference. The `cancel` parameter can be set to `true` by your event handler to prevent Excel from executing its default right-click behavior.

- **XMLMappedRange.Change** is raised when the cell corresponding to the mapped element or attribute is changed by a user editing the cell or when a cell is linked to external data and is changed as a result of refreshing the cell from the external data. Change events are not raised when a cell is changed as a result of a recalculation. They are also not raised when the user changes formatting of the cell without changing the value of the cell. Excel passes a `target` parameter of type Range for the range of cells that was changed. The `target` parameter is provided so you can determine whether multiple cells were changed at once—for example, if the user dragged the lower-right corner of a particular cell to drag that value across multiple cells.

- **XMLMappedRange.Deselected** is raised when the cell corresponding to the mapped element or attribute is deselected. Excel passes a `target` parameter of type Range for the range of cells that was deselected. The `target` parameter is provided so you can determine whether multiple cells were deselected at once.

- **XMLMappedRange.Selected** is raised when the cell corresponding to the mapped element or attribute is selected. Excel passes a `target` parameter of type Range for the range of cells that was selected. The `target` parameter is provided so you can determine whether multiple cells were selected at once.

- **XMLMappedRange.SelectionChange** is raised when the cell corresponding to the mapped element or attribute is deselected or selected. Excel passes a `target` parameter of type Range for the range of cells that was deselected or selected. The `target` parameter is provided so you can determine whether multiple cells were deselected or selected at once.

Listing 21-7 shows a VSTO customization that handles all the events associated with an XMLMappedRange. In this case, we choose to handle events associated with the XMLMappedRange called OrderCustomerNameCell, which corresponds to the CustomerName element from our book order schema that we mapped to Sheet1 in the Excel workbook.

Listing 21-7 A VSTO Excel Customization That Handles All Events Associated with an XMLMappedRange

```
using System;
using System.Data;
using System.Drawing;
using System.Windows.Forms;
using Microsoft.VisualStudio.OfficeTools.Interop.Runtime;
using Excel = Microsoft.Office.Interop.Excel;
using Office = Microsoft.Office.Core;

namespace ExcelWorkbook1
{
  public partial class Sheet1
  {
    private void Sheet1_Startup(object sender, EventArgs e)
    {
      this.OrderCustomerNameCell.BeforeDoubleClick += new
        Excel.DocEvents_BeforeDoubleClickEventHandler(
        OrderCustomerNameCell_BeforeDoubleClick);
```

```csharp
  this.OrderCustomerNameCell.BeforeRightClick += new
    Excel.DocEvents_BeforeRightClickEventHandler(
    OrderCustomerNameCell_BeforeRightClick);

  this.OrderCustomerNameCell.Change += new
    Excel.DocEvents_ChangeEventHandler(
    OrderCustomerNameCell_Change);

  this.OrderCustomerNameCell.Deselected += new
    Excel.DocEvents_SelectionChangeEventHandler(
    OrderCustomerNameCell_Deselected);

  this.OrderCustomerNameCell.Selected += new
    Excel.DocEvents_SelectionChangeEventHandler(
    OrderCustomerNameCell_Selected);

  this.OrderCustomerNameCell.SelectionChange += new
    Excel.DocEvents_SelectionChangeEventHandler(
    OrderCustomerNameCell_SelectionChange);
}

#region VSTO Designer generated code
private void InternalStartup ()
{
  this.Startup += new EventHandler(Sheet1_Startup);
}
#endregion

string GetAddress(Excel.Range target)
{
  return target.get_Address(missing, missing,
    Excel.XlReferenceStyle.xlA1, missing, missing);
}

void OrderCustomerNameCell_BeforeDoubleClick(
  Excel.Range target, ref bool cancel)
{
  MessageBox.Show(String.Format(
    "{0} BeforeDoubleClick.",
    GetAddress(target)));
}

void OrderCustomerNameCell_BeforeRightClick(
  Excel.Range target, ref bool cancel)
{
  MessageBox.Show(String.Format(
    "{0} BeforeRightClick.",
    GetAddress(target)));
```

```
    }

    void OrderCustomerNameCell_Change(Excel.Range target)
    {
      MessageBox.Show(String.Format(
        "{0} Change.",
        GetAddress(target)));
    }

    void OrderCustomerNameCell_Deselected(Excel.Range target)
    {
      MessageBox.Show(String.Format(
        "{0} Deselected.",
        GetAddress(target)));
    }

    void OrderCustomerNameCell_Selected(Excel.Range target)
    {
      MessageBox.Show(String.Format(
        "{0} Selected.",
        GetAddress(target)));
    }

    void OrderCustomerNameCell_SelectionChange(Excel.Range target)
    {
      MessageBox.Show(String.Format(
        "{0} SelectionChange.",
        GetAddress(target)));
    }
  }
}
```

ListObject Controls

As you saw in Table 21-3, a ListObject control was created for the repeating Book element in our mapped schema. A ListObject control is created for any repeating element. A ListObject control has all the properties and methods of an Excel ListObject
object. In addition, it has several events that are not found on the Excel ListObject
object:

- **ListObject.BeforeAddDataboundRow** is described in Chapter 17, "VSTO
Data Programming."

- **ListObject.BeforeDoubleClick** is raised when any cell contained by the ListObject is double-clicked. Excel passes a `target` parameter of type Range for the range of cells that was double-clicked, and a `bool cancel` parameter passed by reference. The `cancel` parameter can be set to `true` by your event handler to prevent Excel from executing its default double-click behavior.

- **ListObject.BeforeRightClick** is raised when any cell contained by the List-Object is right-clicked. Excel passes a `target` parameter of type Range for the range of cells that was right-clicked. The `target` parameter is provided so you can determine whether multiple cells were selected when the right-click occurred. Excel also passes a `bool cancel` parameter by reference. The `cancel` parameter can be set to `true` by your event handler to prevent Excel from executing its default right-click behavior.

- **ListObject.Change** is raised when any cell contained by the ListObject is changed by a user editing the cell or when a cell is linked to external data and is changed as a result of refreshing the cell from the external data. Change events are not raised when a cell is changed as a result of a recalculation. They are also not raised when the user changes formatting of the cell without changing the value of the cell. Excel passes a `target` parameter of type `range` for the range of cells that was changed. The `target` parameter is provided so you can determine whether multiple cells were changed at once—for example, if the user dragged the lower-right corner of a particular cell to drag that value across multiple cells.

- **ListObject.DataBindingFailure** is described in Chapter 17.

- **ListObject.DataMemberChanged** is described in Chapter 17.

- **ListObject.DataSourceChanged** is described in Chapter 17.

- **ListObject.Deselected** is raised when any cell contained by the ListObject is deselected. Excel passes a `target` parameter of type Range for the range of cells that was deselected. The `target` parameter is provided so you can determine whether multiple cells were deselected at once.

- **ListObject.ErrorAddDataboundRow** is described in Chapter 17.

- **ListObject.OriginalDataRestored** is described in Chapter 17.

- **ListObject.Selected** is raised when any cell contained by the ListObject is selected. Excel passes a `target` parameter of type `Range` for the range of cells that was selected. The `target` parameter is provided so you can determine whether multiple cells were selected at once.

- **ListObject.SelectedIndexChanged** is described in Chapter 17.
- **ListObject.SelectionChange** is raised when any cell contained by the List-Object is deselected or selected. Excel passes a `target` parameter of type Range for the range of cells that was deselected or selected. The `target` parameter is provided so you can determine whether multiple cells were deselected or selected at once.

Listing 21-8 shows a VSTO customization that handles all the events associated with a ListObject. In this case, we choose to handle events associated with the ListObject called BookList, which corresponds to the repeating Book element from our book order schema that we mapped to a list in Sheet1 in the Excel workbook.

Listing 21-8 A VSTO Excel Customization That Handles All Events Associated with a ListObject

```
using System;
using System.Data;
using System.Drawing;
using System.Windows.Forms;
using Microsoft.VisualStudio.OfficeTools.Interop.Runtime;
using Excel = Microsoft.Office.Interop.Excel;
using Office = Microsoft.Office.Core;

namespace ExcelWorkbook1
{
  public partial class Sheet1
  {
    private void Sheet1_Startup(object sender, EventArgs e)
    {
      this.BookList.BeforeAddDataboundRow += new
        Microsoft.Office.Tools.Excel.BeforeAddDataboundRowHandler(
        BookList_BeforeAddDataboundRow);

      this.BookList.BeforeDoubleClick += new
        Excel.DocEvents_BeforeDoubleClickEventHandler(
        BookList_BeforeDoubleClick);


      this.BookList.BeforeRightClick += new
        Excel.DocEvents_BeforeRightClickEventHandler(
        BookList_BeforeRightClick);
```

```csharp
    this.BookList.Change += new
      Microsoft.Office.Tools.Excel.ListObjectChangeHandler(
      BookList_Change);

    this.BookList.DataBindingFailure += new
      EventHandler(BookList_DataBindingFailure);

    this.BookList.DataMemberChanged += new
      EventHandler(BookList_DataMemberChanged);

    this.BookList.DataSourceChanged += new
      EventHandler(BookList_DataSourceChanged);

    this.BookList.Deselected += new
      Excel.DocEvents_SelectionChangeEventHandler(
      BookList_Deselected);

    this.BookList.ErrorAddDataboundRow += new
      Microsoft.Office.Tools.Excel.ErrorAddDataboundRowHandler(
      BookList_ErrorAddDataboundRow);

    this.BookList.OriginalDataRestored += new
      Microsoft.Office.Tools.Excel.OriginalDataRestoredEventHandler(
      BookList_OriginalDataRestored);

    this.BookList.Selected += new
      Excel.DocEvents_SelectionChangeEventHandler(
      BookList_Selected);

    this.BookList.SelectedIndexChanged += new
      EventHandler(BookList_SelectedIndexChanged);



    this.BookList.SelectionChange += new
      Excel.DocEvents_SelectionChangeEventHandler(
      BookList_SelectionChange);
}

#region VSTO Designer generated code
private void InsternalStartup()
{
  this.Startup += new EventHandler(Sheet1_Startup);
}

#endregion

string GetAddress(Excel.Range target, string event)
{
```

```
    return String.Format("{0} {1}.",
      target.get_Address(missing, missing,
      Excel.XlReferenceStyle.xlA1, missing, missing),
      event);
}

void BookList_BeforeAddDataboundRow(object sender,
  Microsoft.Office.Tools.Excel.BeforeAddDataboundRowEventArgs e)
{
  MessageBox.Show("BeforeAddDataboundRow");
}

void BookList_BeforeDoubleClick(Excel.Range target,
  ref bool cancel)
{
  MessageBox.Show(GetAddress(target, "BeforeDoubleClick"));
}

void BookList_BeforeRightClick(Excel.Range target,
  ref bool cancel)
{
  MessageBox.Show(GetAddress(target, "BeforeRightClick"));
}

void BookList_Change(Excel.Range targetRange,
  Microsoft.Office.Tools.Excel.ListRanges changedRanges)
{
  MessageBox.Show(GetAddress(targetRange, "Change"));
}

void BookList_DataBindingFailure(object sender, EventArgs e)
{
  MessageBox.Show("DataBindingFailure");
}

void BookList_DataMemberChanged(object sender, EventArgs e)
{
  MessageBox.Show("DataMemberChanged");
}

void BookList_DataSourceChanged(object sender, EventArgs e)
{
  MessageBox.Show("DataSourceChanged");
}

void BookList_Deselected(Excel.Range target)
{
```

```
      MessageBox.Show(GetAddress(target, "Deselected"));
    }

    void BookList_ErrorAddDataboundRow(object sender,
      Microsoft.Office.Tools.Excel.ErrorAddDataboundRowEventArgs e)
    {
      MessageBox.Show("ErrorAddDataboundRow");
    }

    void BookList_OriginalDataRestored(object sender,
      Microsoft.Office.Tools.Excel.OriginalDataRestoredEventArgs e)
    {
      MessageBox.Show("OriginalDataRestored");
    }

    void BookList_Selected(Excel.Range target)
    {
      MessageBox.Show(GetAddress(target, "Selected"));
    }

    void BookList_SelectedIndexChanged(object sender, EventArgs e)
    {
      MessageBox.Show("SelectedIndexChanged");
    }

    void BookList_SelectionChange(Excel.Range target)
    {
      MessageBox.Show(GetAddress(target, "SelectionChange"));
    }
  }
}
```

Schema Added to the VSTO Project

The final thing to notice about our generated VSTO project is that VSTO automatically adds the schema that was mapped into the workbook as a project item in the project, as shown in Figure 21-22. This schema is added to support the data binding features discussed in the next section. The schema is a copy of your original schema file that is copied to the project directory of the newly created project.

When you create an XML map, Excel grabs the schema you add and keeps a copy of it in the Excel workbook. If the schema file you created the XML map from is changed, Excel does not detect it. So if you edit the schema in Visual Studio, you then have to save the schema, remove the XML map corresponding to the schema from the Excel worksheet, re-add the XML map by browsing to the updated schema in your project directory, and then re-apply your XML mappings.

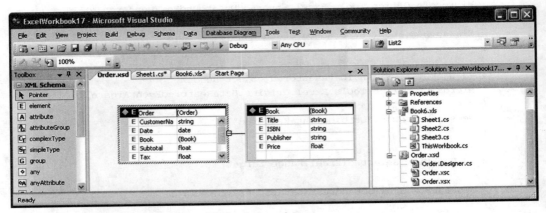

Figure 21-22 The VSTO Excel project with the Order schema.

To add and remove XML mappings without leaving Visual Studio, VSTO provides a toolbar button for quickly displaying the XML Source task pane as shown in Figure 21-23. The button that displays the XML Source task pane is the second button in the toolbar. As you map schemas using the XML Source task pane, VSTO automatically adds `XMLMappedRange` or `ListObject` member variables for new mappings.

Figure 21-23 The VSTO Excel toolbar with the
XML Source task pane button.

Combining XML Mapping with VSTO Data Binding

Given an XML mapping in a worksheet, you can programmatically import and export XML conforming to the schema associated with the mapping using the Excel object model. You may also want to combine this functionality with VSTO's support for data binding. Data binding will allow you to connect the worksheet to not just one book order, but to a database with many book orders. You can easily move a cursor in the database from row to row in the database and update the contents of the worksheet.

The first step is to build the project. This will result in a typed dataset being created for the order schema called NewDataSet. After you have built the project, make sure the toolbox is showing and expand the Data tab, as shown in Figure 21-24. Note the component tray in Figure 21-24—the empty area below the Excel worksheet. We will add one additional component to the component tray that we will use later to data bind the ListObject that was created when the schema was mapped into the workbook. From the Data tab, drag a BindingSource component to the component tray. Name this BindingSource OrderBookConnector. We are going to ignore this component for the time being because our initial goal is to data bind the XMLMappedRange controls in our worksheet.

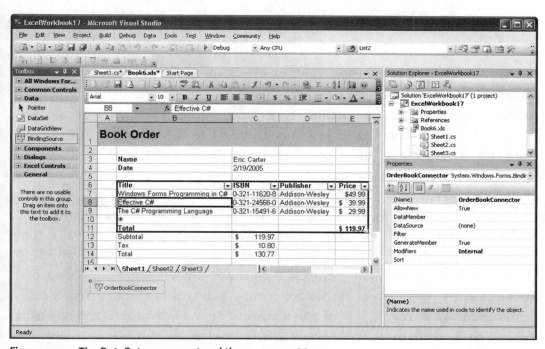

Figure 21-24 The DataSet component and the component tray.

Drag the DataSet component from the toolbox into the component tray—the empty area below the Excel worksheet. The dialog in Figure 21-25 will display. Pick the Typed dataset option. Then pick the NewDataSet. This is the dataset that was created from our Order schema. Finally, click the OK button.

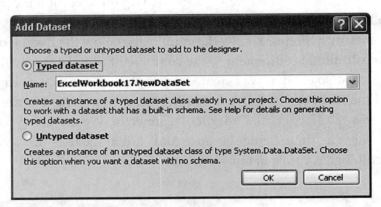

Figure 21-25 The Add Dataset dialog.

This will create a component called newDataSet1 in the component tray. Right-click the newly added component and choose Properties from the pop-up menu. Doing so will show and activate the Properties window. Let's change the name for the typed data set component from newDataSet1 to the more descriptive name BookOrderDataSet by typing this new name in the (Name) row in the Properties window and pressing the Enter key.

Because BookOrderDataSet is a typed dataset created from our Orders schema, as shown in Figure 21-22, we know that the dataset contains two tables. The two tables are the Order table and the Book table. We now want to connect the fields that come from the Order table to the corresponding XMLMappedRange controls in Sheet1. To do that, we must add a BindingSource component by dragging a BindingSource from the Data tab in the toolbox to the component tray. This creates a BindingSource called bindingSource1, which we will rename to OrderConnector because it will be used to connect the Order table from the BookOrderDataSet to the XMLMappedRange controls in the workbook.

Using the Properties window, set the DataSource property of OrderConnector to BookOrderDataSet. Figure 21-26 shows the drop-down that appears. Note that we have to expand out the Other Data Sources and Form List Instances nodes to find the BookOrderDataSet that we have already added to the component tray.

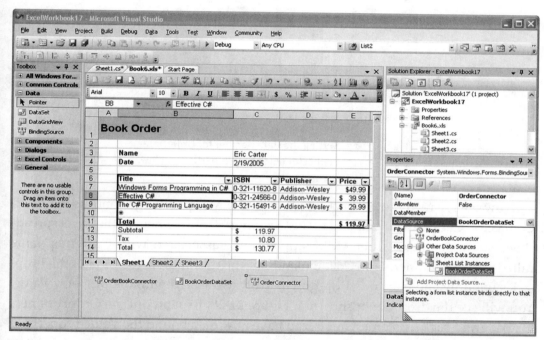

Figure 21-26 Setting a DataSource for OrderConnector using the Properties window.

With the DataSource property set to BookOrderDataSet, we now need to set the DataMember property to the Order table. Figure 21-27 shows the drop-down that appears. Note that the only options available are the Order table or the Book table. Pick the Order table.

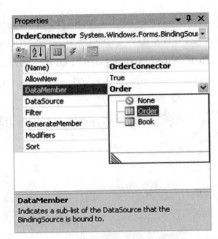

Figure 21-27 Setting the DataMember for OrderData-
Connector using the Properties window.

Now we are ready to connect individual XMLMappedRange controls to Order-
Connector. Click the cell mapped to the CustomerName element in the Excel spreadsheet—doing so selects the XMLMappedRange associated with CustomerName
called OrderCustomerNameCell. Expand out the (DataBindings) node in the Properties window and click the drop-down arrow associated with the property Value.
You will see the drop-down shown in Figure 21-28. Expand out the OrderConnector node and click CustomerName. You have now data bound the Value property of
OrderCustomerNameCell to OrderConnector's CustomerName.

Now click the cell associated with Date, expand out the (DataBindings) node in
the Properties window for the XMLMappedRange OrderDateCell, and data bind the
Value property to the Date field coming from OrderConnector. Continue to do this
for the cells associated with Subtotal, Tax, and Total.

Now let's connect the ListObject. Earlier, you created a BindingSource that you
named OrderBookConnector. Click on the ListObject in the spreadsheet, and in the
Properties window, set the ListObject's DataSource property to OrderBookConnector. We next need to connect the OrderBookConnector to our data. We could connect
OrderBookConnector directly to the Book table in BookOrderDataSet, but this would

not give us the behavior we want for this example. We want to allow BookOrder-DataSet to contain multiple book orders, and as we move from row to row in the Order table via OrderConnector, we want to only show the books for that particular order. If we connect OrderBookConnector to the Book table in BookOrderDataSet, this will result in all books in the books table being shown no matter what row is being shown from the Order table by OrderConnector. What we need is a way to tie OrderBookConnector to OrderConnector.

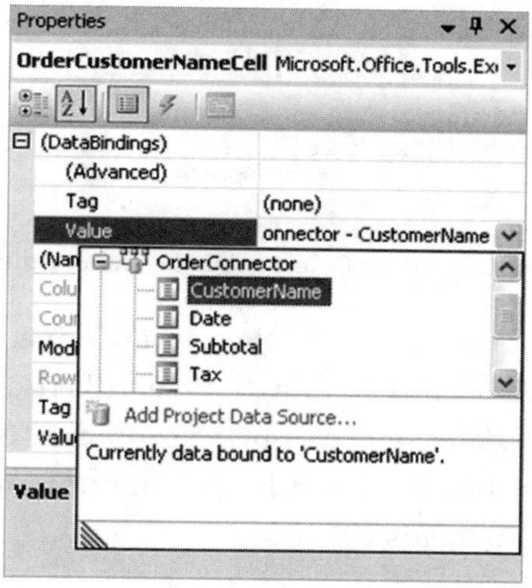

Figure 21-28 Setting a data binding connecting OrderCustomerNameCell.Value to OrderConnector.CustomerName.

Instead of connecting the OrderBookConnector to BookOrderDataSet, we connect it to the existing OrderConnector corresponding to our Order table. Doing so causes what is sometimes called a master-details relationship. As the OrderData-Connector moves from row to row in the Order table, our OrderBookConnector will display only the Books that correspond to the order row that OrderConnector is displaying. In the Properties window, set the DataSource property by expanding the OrderConnector node and selecting Order_Book, as shown in Figure 21-29.

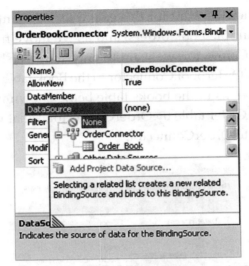

Figure 21-29 Connecting OrderBookConnector to OrderConnector.

To create this relationship between the OrderConnector and the OrderBook-Connector, VSTO creates a third BindingSource, called orderBookBindingSource, which acts as an intermediate connector between OrderConnector and OrderBook-Connector. Figure 21-30 shows the resulting configuration of the DataSet and the three BindingSource components.

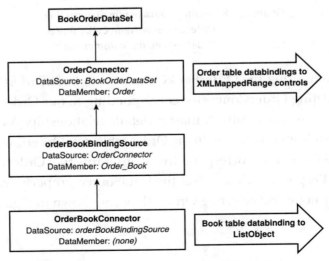

Figure 21-30 The relationship between the data set, binding sources, and data bindings.

Now let's add some code to Sheet1's Startup event so that this application does something interesting. We are going to populate our dataset with three orders. When the user double-clicks the Excel spreadsheet, we will call the MoveNext method on the OrderConnector to move to the next order or row in the Order table in the BookOrderDataSet.

Listing 21-9 A VSTO Excel Customization That Populates a Dataset and Uses the MoveNext Method

```
using System;
using System.Data;
using System.Drawing;
using System.Windows.Forms;
using Microsoft.VisualStudio.OfficeTools.Interop.Runtime;
using Excel = Microsoft.Office.Interop.Excel;
using Office = Microsoft.Office.Core;

namespace ExcelWorkbook1
{
  public partial class Sheet1
  {
    private void Sheet1_Startup(object sender, System.EventArgs e)
    {
      NewDataSet.OrderRow order1 = bookOrderDataSet.Order.
        AddOrderRow("Eric Carter", DateTime.Now,
        39.99f, 1.00f, 40.99f);

      NewDataSet.BookRow order1book1 = bookOrderDataSet.Book.
        AddBookRow("Effective C#", "0-321-24566-0",
        "Addison-Wesley", 39.99f, order1);

      NewDataSet.OrderRow order2 = bookOrderDataSet.Order.
        AddOrderRow("Andrew Clinick", DateTime.Now,
        49.99f, 1.00f, 50.99f);

      NewDataSet.BookRow order2book1 = bookOrderDataSet.Book.
        AddBookRow("Windows Forms Programming in C#",
        "0-321-11620-8", "Addison-Wesley", 49.99f, order2);

      NewDataSet.OrderRow order3 = bookOrderDataSet.Order.
        AddOrderRow("Eric Lippert", DateTime.Now,
        29.99f, 1.00f, 30.99f);

      NewDataSet.BookRow order3book1 = bookOrderDataSet.Book.
        AddBookRow("The C# Programming Language",
        "0-321-15491-6", "Addison-Wesley", 29.99f, order3);
```

```
        BeforeDoubleClick += new
            Excel.DocEvents_BeforeDoubleClickEventHandler(
            Sheet1_BeforeDoubleClick);
    }

    #region VSTO Designer generated code
    private void InternalStartup()
    {
        this.Startup += newEventHandler(Sheet1_Startup);
    }

    void Sheet1_BeforeDoubleClick(Excel.Range target,
        ref bool cancel)
    {
        OrderConnector.MoveNext();
    }
    }
}
```

Conclusion

This chapter explored the XML schema mapping feature of Excel. You have learned how to create a schema using Visual Studio that will work well with Excel's schema mapping features. This chapter also covered VSTO's support for Excel schema mapping and how to layer on top of an XML schema mapping VSTO's data binding features. The next chapter examines Word's model for XML, which is quite different from the Excel model.

22.

Working with XML in Word

Introduction to Word's XML Features

THE FIRST THING TO NOTE ABOUT THE XML features described in this chapter is that most of them are only available in Microsoft Office Professional Edition 2003 and the standalone version of Microsoft Office Word 2003. If you work with other Office Editions such as Microsoft Office Standard Edition 2003, Microsoft Office Student and Teacher Edition 2003, or Microsoft Office Basic Edition 2003, the XML features described in this chapter are not available.

Many of the XML features of Word are accessed via Word's XML Structure task pane. To show the XML Structure task pane, display the task pane if it is not already displayed by choosing Task Pane in Word's View menu. The task pane has a drop-down menu from which the XML Structure task pane can be selected, as shown in Figure 22-1.

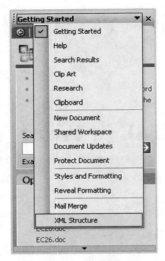

Figure 22-1 Selecting the XML Structure task pane
from the task pane drop-down menu.

The XML Structure task pane prompts you to go to the Templates and Add-Ins dialog to attach an XML schema to the document. To get to the Templates and Add-Ins dialog, you can click the Templates and Add-Ins hyperlink shown in the task pane in Figure 22-2 or choose Templates and Add-Ins from the Tools menu and then click the XML Schema tab.

Figure 22-2 The XML Structure task pane prompts you to go
to the Templates and Add-Ins dialog to add an
XML schema.

Figure 22-3 shows the Templates and Add-Ins dialog. This dialog shows available XML schemas that can be attached to the Word document by checking the check box next to an available schema. It also provides a button to add a new schema to the document.

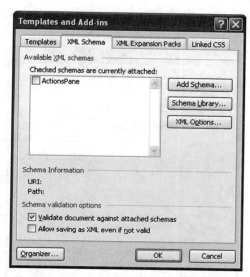

Figure 22-3 The Templates and Add-Ins dialog with the XML Schema page selected.

To add a new schema to the document, click the Add Schema button. When you click the Add Schema button, you are prompted to browse to the schema file you want to add to the document. Let's use the book order schema we created in Chapter 21, "Working with XML in Excel." After you select the schema, the Schema Settings dialog appears, as shown in Figure 22-4. Let's enter BookOrder as an alias or friendly name for the book order schema.

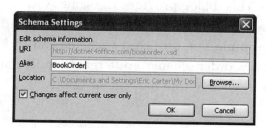

Figure 22-4 Picking an alias for a newly added schema in the Schema Settings dialog.

Click OK to dismiss the Schema Settings dialog. Doing so returns you to the Templates and Add-Ins dialog. The book order schema has been added, as shown in Figure 22-5, and is attached to the current document as shown by the checked check box next to the BookOrder schema. The BookOrder schema can be detached from the document by unchecking the check box.

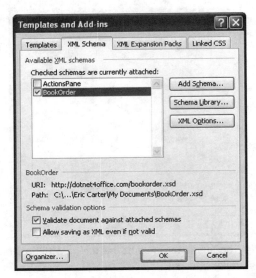

Figure 22-5 The BookOrder schema has been attached to the Word document.

Now that the BookOrder schema has been added, it will be available for attachment to other documents because Word automatically adds any added schemas to Word's schema library. To manage Word's schema library, click the Schema Library button in the Templates and Add-Ins dialog. The Schema Library dialog appears, as shown in Figure 22-6. This dialog provides the same Add Schema button that lets you add new schemas. It also can edit the schema settings dialog for an already added schema—for example, you can select a schema and click the Schema Settings button to assign the book order schema a different friendly name. A Delete Schema button lets you delete a schema from the schema library.

The bottom half of the Schema Library dialog provides options to associate smart document solutions with a document to which a particular schema is attached. In this book, we do not cover this part of Word's functionality because VSTO 2005 provides an easier way to build Word solutions through the ActionsPane mechanism described in Chapter 15, "Working with Actions Pane." However, we do cover the ability to use the Solutions section to associate an XSLT file with a particular schema.

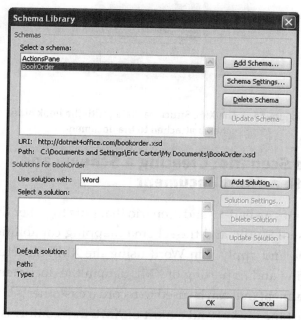

Figure 22-6 The Schema Library dialog.

When you close the Schema Library dialog and the Templates and Add-Ins dialog, the XML Structure pane is updated to show elements from the book order schema, as shown in Figure 22-7. With the book order schema attached to the document, you are now ready to start applying XML elements to the document.

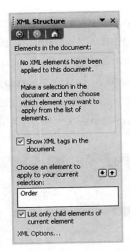

Figure 22-7 The XML Structure dialog with the book order schema attached to the document.

An End-to-End Scenario: Creating a Schema and Mapping It into a Word Document

This section examines an end-to-end scenario that puts together the schema creation capabilities of Visual Studio and the schema mapping capabilities of Word. When you take a schema and apply it in Word using the XML Structure task pane, you enable the exporting and importing of XML data in the document. We are going to create a Word document that can be used to record a customer's book order. The document will support the import and export of XML that conforms to our book order schema. The document will look like Figure 22-8.

ACME Book Sales

Customer Name:	John Doe
Date:	2005-09-30

Title	ISBN	Publisher	Price
Windows Forms Programming in C#	0-321-11620-8	Addison-Wesley	49.99
Effective C#	0-321-24566-0	Addison-Wesley	39.99
The C# Programming Language	0-321-15491-6	Addison Wesley	29.99

Subtotal:	119.97
Tax:	10.80
Total:	130.77

Figure 22-8 A Word document for processing a book order.

Listing 22-1 shows the XML that this document will be able to import and export.

Listing 22-1 XML File Generated from Book Order Document

```xml
<?xml version="1.0" encoding="UTF-8" standalone="no"?>
<Order xmlns=" http://dotnet4office.com/bookorder.xsd ">
     <CustomerName>John Doe</CustomerName>
     <Date>2005-09-30</Date>
     <Book>
          <Title>Windows Forms Programming in C#</Title>
          <ISBN>0-321-11620-8</ISBN>
          <Publisher>Addison-Wesley</Publisher>
          <Price>49.99</Price>
     </Book>
     <Book>
          <Title>Effective C#</Title>
          <ISBN>0-321-24566-0</ISBN>
          <Publisher>Addison-Wesley</Publisher>
          <Price>39.99</Price>
     </Book>
     <Book>
          <Title>The C# Programming Language</Title>
          <ISBN>0-321-15491-6</ISBN>
          <Publisher>Addison Wesley</Publisher>
          <Price>29.99</Price>
     </Book>
     <Subtotal>119.97</Subtotal>
     <Tax>10.80</Tax>
     <Total>130.77</Total>
</Order>
```

Creating the Schema Using Visual Studio

To create our schema using Visual Studio, follow these steps.

1. Start Visual Studio 2005.

2. Create a new XSD file by choosing File from the New menu of the File menu or by pressing Ctrl+N.

3. Choose XML Schema from the list of Visual Studio installed templates, as shown in Figure 22-4. Then click the Open button.

4. The Schema design view appears as shown in Figure 22-5. Drag an element object off of the toolbox onto the design surface.

5. Type **Order** and press the Enter key.

6. In the * row, type **CustomerName** and press the Enter key.

7. In the * row, type **Date** and press the Tab key, and then type **date** for the data type and press Enter.

8. In the * row, type **Subtotal** and press the Tab key, and then type **float** for the data type and press Enter.

9. In the * row, type **Tax** and press the Tab key, and then type **float** for the data type and press Enter.

10. In the * row, type **Total** and press the Tab key, and then type **float** for the data type and press Enter.

11. Now, right-click the Order element box and choose New element from the Add menu.

12. Type **Book** and press the Enter key.

13. In the * row of the newly created Book element, type **Title** and press Enter.

14. In the * row of the newly created Book element, type **ISBN** and press Enter.

15. In the * row of the newly created Book element, type **Publisher** and press Enter.

16. In the * row of the newly created Book element, type **Price** and press the Tab key, and then type **float** for the data type and press Enter.

17. We now want to specify that multiple books can be included in an order. Click the Book row in the Order element box and show the Properties window by choosing Properties Window from the View menu. For the property maxOccurs, type **unbounded**. For the property minOccurs, type **1**.

18. We also need to change the targetNamespace for the XML schema. Visual Studio defaults the namespace to be http://tempuri.org/XMLSchema.xsd. This needs to be changed to some other namespace name because if you create multiple schemas with this namespace and try to attach them to Word, Word will display an error because it expects the namespace from each attached schema to be unique. We will change it to http://dotnet4office.com/bookorder.xsd. To do this, show the Properties window if it is not already visible by choosing Properties Window from the View window. In the properties for the schema, you will see a row that says targetNamespace. Change the

targetNamespace from http://tempuri.org/XMLSchema.xsd to http://dotnet4office.com/bookorder.xsd.

19. Now save the schema using the Save As command from the File menu. In the Save File As dialog, drop down the Save as type combo box and pick XML Schema Files (*.xsd). For the filename, type **BookOrder.xsd** and save it to a convenient place such as the desktop.

Figure 22-9 shows the final schema as displayed by Visual Studio.

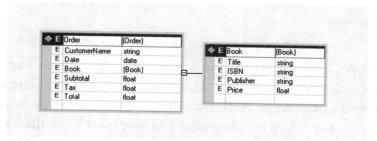

Figure 22-9 The book order schema in Visual Studio.

Listing 22-2 shows the generated XSD file. Note that the sequence of Book elements in an Order element is a sequence with a minimum (minOccurs) of one Book elements and a maximum (maxOccurs) of unbounded Book elements. This will allow our schema to represent one or more Books in an Order. Also, having a sequence where maxOccurs is greater than one or unbounded will allow Word to know that it can represent the Books in an Order using a Word table.

Listing 22-2 Book Order XSD Schema File

```
<?xml version="1.0" encoding="utf-8"?>
<xs:schema targetNamespace="http://dotnet4office.com/bookorder.xsd"
elementFormDefault="qualified" xmlns="http://dotnet4office.com/bookorder.xsd"
xmlns:mstns="http://dotnet4office.com/bookorder.xsd"
xmlns:xs="http://www.w3.org/2001/XMLSchema">
    <xs:element name="Order">
        <xs:complexType>
            <xs:sequence>
                <xs:element name="CustomerName" type="xs:string" />
                <xs:element name="Date" type="xs:date" />
                <xs:element name="Book" maxOccurs="unbounded" minOccurs="1">
                    <xs:complexType>
                        <xs:sequence>
```

```
                        <xs:element name="Title" type="xs:string" />
                        <xs:element name="ISBN" type="xs:string" />
                        <xs:element name="Publisher" type="xs:string" />
                        <xs:element name="Price" type="xs:float" />
                    </xs:sequence>
                </xs:complexType>
            </xs:element>
            <xs:element name="Subtotal" type="xs:float" />
            <xs:element name="Tax" type="xs:float" />
            <xs:element name="Total" type="xs:float" />
        </xs:sequence>
    </xs:complexType>
</xs:element>
</xs:schema>
```

An additional point to notice about our schema file is that it is element-centric—we use XML elements and do not use XML attributes at all in our schema. Although Word supports the mapping of XML attributes, it does so in a way that makes it difficult for the end user to edit the attributes. The user must show the XML tags in the document, right-click an XML tag, and use the Attributes dialog shown in Figure 22-10 to edit attributes. In this example, we have mapped a book order schema where Title, ISBN, and Publisher are attributes rather than elements. These attributes will not show directly in the document, so it is usually best to avoid having attributes in schemas you are going to use with Word and instead use only elements.

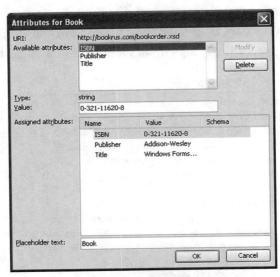

Figure 22-10 Word's attribute editing dialog.

Adding a Schema to the Word Document

Now that we have created a schema, let's add it to a Word document. Launch Word and create a new empty document. Bring up the Word XML Structure task pane as described in the first section of this chapter. You should now see the XML Structure task pane with no schema as yet associated with the document in the task pane. To add an XML schema to the document, click the Templates and Add-Ins hyperlink in the XML Structure task pane. Then, as shown in the first part of this chapter, click the Add Schema button shown in Figure 22-3 to add your book order schema to the document. Give your schema the friendly name or alias of BookOrder in the Schema Settings dialog shown in Figure 22-4. Then close the Templates and Add-Ins dialog by clicking the OK button. The XML Structure task pane should now look like Figure 22-7.

The XML Options Dialog and Mixed Content

Before we start to construct the document shown in Figure 22-8, we need to briefly consider one additional dialog—the XML Options dialog. In the XML Structure task pane, there is a hyperlink at the bottom of the pane with the text XML Options. Click this hyperlink to bring up the XML Options dialog. Alternatively, you can click the XML Options button in the Templates and Add-Ins dialog. Figure 22-11 shows the XML Options dialog.

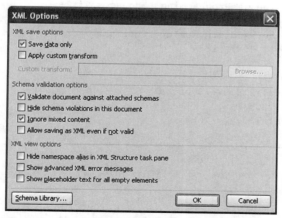

Figure 22-11 The XML Options dialog—Ignore mixed content should be checked.

For the purpose of this end-to-end scenario, we need to make sure that the check box next to Ignore mixed content is checked. By checking this check box, it will allow us to intersperse text that is not part of our customer order schema with text that is. Mixed content allows us to have a structure similar to that shown in Listing 22-3, where arbitrary text (in bold) is mixed with the tagged XML data text.

Listing 22-3 Book Order XML with Mixed Content in Bold

```
<?xml version="1.0" encoding="UTF-8" standalone="no"?>
<Order xmlns=" http://dotnet4office.com/bookorder.xsd ">
     Customer Name: <CustomerName>John Doe</CustomerName>
     Date: <Date>2005-09-30</Date>

     Books that were ordered:
<Book>
       <Title>Windows Forms Programming in C#</Title>
       <ISBN>0-321-11620-8</ISBN>
       <Publisher>Addison-Wesley</Publisher>
       <Price>49.99</Price>
</Book>
<Book>
       <Title>Effective C#</Title>
       <ISBN>0-321-24566-0</ISBN>
       <Publisher>Addison-Wesley</Publisher>
       <Price>39.99</Price>
</Book>
<Book>
       <Title>The C# Programming Language</Title>
       <ISBN>0-321-15491-6</ISBN>
       <Publisher>Addison Wesley</Publisher>
       <Price>29.99</Price>
</Book>

Subtotal: <Subtotal>119.97</Subtotal>
     Tax: <Tax>10.80</Tax>
     Total: <Total>130.77</Total>
</Order>
```

Creating a Document with Mapped XML Structure

To begin, let's construct a document with some text in it but no schema mapping. Create a document that looks like the one shown in Figure 22-12. Create a place to put a customer name, date, subtotal, tax, and total. Create a single table with four columns and two rows where we will put a book with a title, ISBN, publisher, and price.

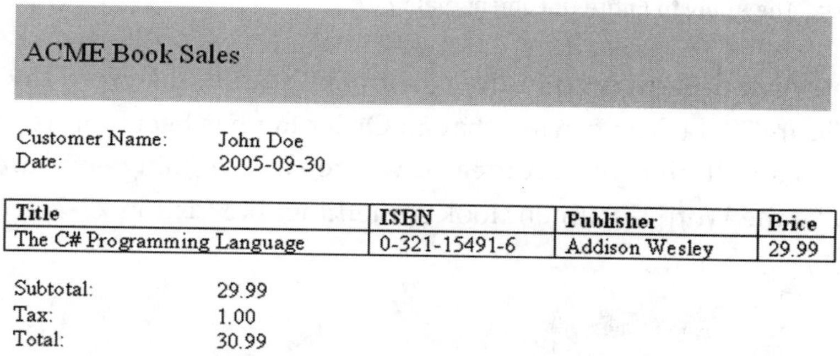

ACME Book Sales

Customer Name: John Doe
Date: 2005-09-30

Title	ISBN	Publisher	Price
The C# Programming Language	0-321-15491-6	Addison Wesley	29.99

Subtotal: 29.99
Tax: 1.00
Total: 30.99

Figure 22-12 A Word document with no schema mapping.

Now we can begin mapping our schema by inserting tags into the document. The experience of mapping schema into a Word document is quite different from mapping a schema into an Excel document. If you have ever edited an HTML page in a text editor, you will find that mapping a schema into a Word document feels somewhat similar to the way HTML tags are used to mark up text in an HTML page.

Make the XML Structure task pane visible and verify that the Show XML tags in the document check box is checked in the task pane. This will allow you to see the XML tags that Word is inserting into the document. Click anywhere in the Word document. Then in the bottom half of the XML structure task pane you will see an element list that is identified with the text "Choose an element to apply to your current selection." In that list is only one element, Order. Order is the root element of our schema, so it must be mapped first. Click Order in the element list. The dialog shown in Figure 22-13 will appear. For this example, we will choose Apply to Entire Document. It is possible to map multiple schemas into one document, but it is not possible to export valid XML from such a document. VSTO also does not support the mapping of multiple schemas into one document, so we will avoid constructing such a document.

Figure 22-13 The Apply to Entire Document dialog.

After you click the Apply to Entire Document button, the Word document now looks like Figure 22-14. You can see that an Order tag has been applied to the entire document. This will give you an idea of where we are going—we are effectively going to make the Word document look something like Listing 22-3.

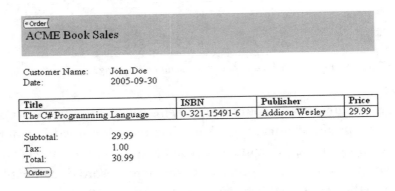

Figure 22-14 The Word document with an Order tag applied to the entire document.

The Order element has six child elements: CustomerName, Date, Book (which is a repeating element), Subtotal, Tax, and Total. Let's map these elements now. Select the text John Doe in the document. From the XML Structure pane, click Customer-Name in the element list, as shown in Figure 22-15. If CustomerName does not appear in the element list along with the other child elements of Order, toggle the List only child elements of the current element check box until it appears.

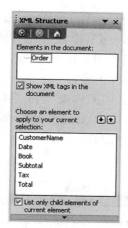

Figure 22-15 The element list shows child elements of Order.

Select the text 2005-09-30 and click the Date element in the element list. Select the text 29.99 and click the Subtotal element in the element list. Select the text 1.00 and click the Tax element in the element list. Select the text 30.99 and click the Total element in the element list. If you make a mistake and tag some text with the wrong element tag, right-click the element tag and choose the Remove tag menu option.

Figure 22-16 shows the document with the entire schema mapped except for the Book subelements. Note the pink squiggly line along the side of the document. This is Word's schema validation feature telling us that the mapped document has not yet been constructed in a way that conforms to the book order schema. This is because we have not yet mapped the Book subelements. You can right-click the squiggly line to get the exact error that is occurring that will prevent Word from exporting valid XML from this mapping.

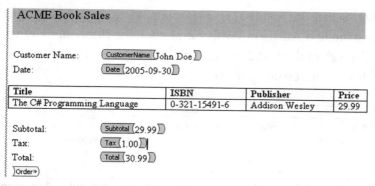

Figure 22-16 Mappings for all elements of the book order schema except for Book subelements.

We are going to map our repeating Book element into a table. If we map a Book element into a row of the table, Word will be smart about this and when additional rows are added to the table Word will automatically tag the newly inserted row as a new Book element with all related tags.

First, select the entire row with the book "The C# Programming Language" in it by clicking in the start of the row and dragging across the row. It is important that you do not select beyond the edge of the row—that you only select the current row, as shown in Figure 22-17.

Title	ISBN	Publisher	Price
The C# Programming Language	0-321-15491-6	Addison Wesley	29.99

Figure 22-17 Selecting the entire row but not beyond the entire row.

With the entire row selected, click the Book element in the element list. Figure 22-18 shows the resulting tagged row.

Title	ISBN	Publisher	Price
«Book«The C# Programming Language	0-321-15491-6	Addison Wesley	29.99 〕Book»

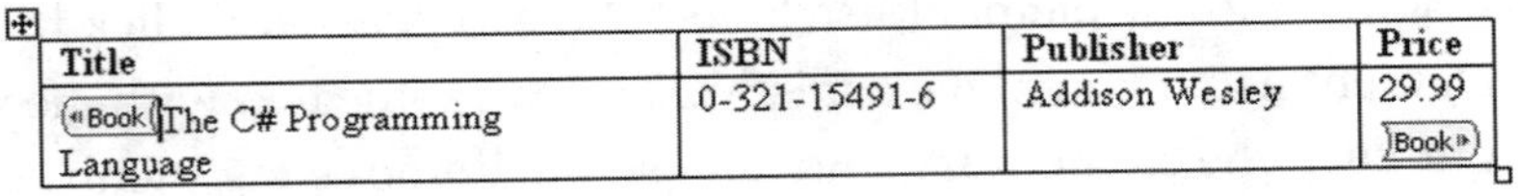

Figure 22-18 Tagging an entire row as a Book element.

Now we need to tag the column values to mark them with the child elements of the Book element. The Book element has four child elements: Title, ISBN, Publisher, and Price. Once again, if the elements do not appear in the element list, toggle the List only child elements of the current element check box to make the elements appear. Select the text The C# Programming Language and click the Title element in the element list. Select the text 0-321-15491-6 and click the ISBN element in the element list. Select the text Addison Wesley and click the Publisher element in the element list. Finally, select the text 29.99 and click the Price element in the element list. Figure 22-19 shows the resulting tagged row.

Title	ISBN	Publisher	Price
«Book«Title«The C# Programming Language 〕Title»	«ISBN«0-321-15491-6〕ISBN»	«Publisher«Addison Wesley〕Publisher»	«Price«29.99 〕Price» 〕Book»

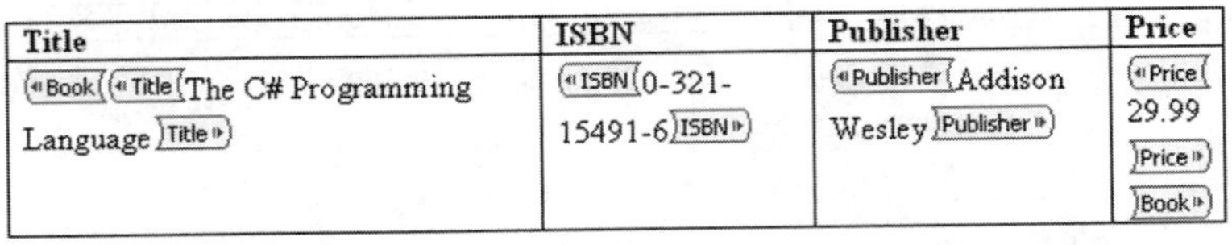

Figure 22-19 Completed tagging for a row in a table that represents a Book element.

Now let's verify that we have set up the table in a way that Word will automatically tag new rows as Book elements. Click somewhere in the table. From the Table menu, choose Insert and then Rows Below. As shown in Figure 22-20, Word automatically adds tags to the new row.

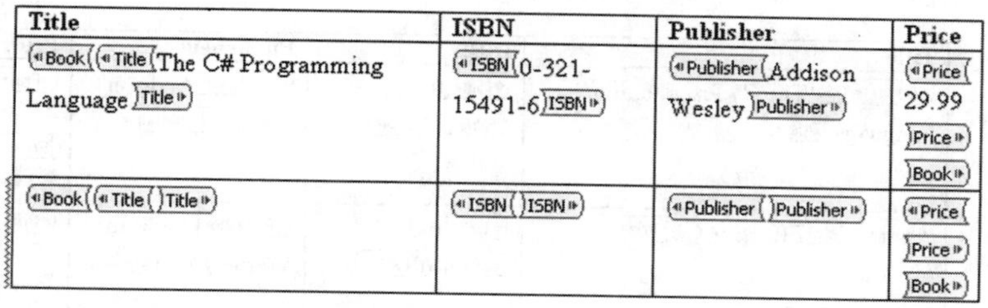

Title	ISBN	Publisher	Price
«Book(«Title(The C# Programming Language)Title »	«ISBN(0-321-15491-6)ISBN »	«Publisher(Addison Wesley)Publisher »	«Price(29.99)Price »)Book »
«Book(«Title( )Title »	«ISBN( )ISBN »	«Publisher( )Publisher »	«Price( )Price »)Book »

Figure 22-20 Word automatically tags new rows in the table with the Book element tags.

Now, fill out the remainder of the table to make it look like Figure 22-8. After you have filled out the table, you can hide the XML tags by unchecking the Show XML tags in the document check box in the XML structure pane or by pressing the keyboard accelerator Ctrl+Shift+X. Typically, when you deploy a document such as this to end users, you will not want to have the XML tags showing in the document. The only complication this causes is when a tag is empty—it is very hard for the user of your document to type text in the right place. To solve this issue, use the XML Options dialog box and check the Show placeholder text for all empty elements option. Figure 22-21 shows the final document with XML tags showing.

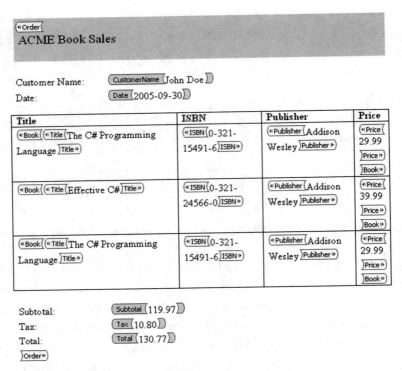

Figure 22-21 The final Word document with tags showing.

Also, note that the XML structure task pane shows the elements that have been mapped into the document in a tree view, as shown in Figure 22-22. You can right-click the elements in this tree view and a menu appears that allows you to unmap a particular element or edit attributes associated with a particular element.

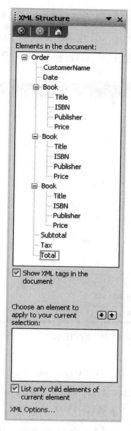

Figure 22-22 Elements mapped in the document are shown in
the document tree view.

Exporting the Mapped XML in the Document to an XML Data File

With the document mapped to our XML schema, let's save this document to XML
conforming to the book order schema we have used. First, make sure you save your
document as a .doc file so that you do not lose your work. After you have saved the
document, from the File menu choose the Save As command. From the Save as type
drop-down list, choose XML Document. Two check boxes appear in the dialog:
Apply transform and Save data only. Make sure the Save data only check box is
checked, as shown in Figure 22-23. Then Click the Save button. Word will warn you

that it is only going to save out XML and not any formatting. If you have already saved your document as a .doc file, click the Continue button to save as XML. When you open the saved XML, it will look like Listing 22-1.

Figure 22-23 Saving as an XML document with Save data only checked.

There are some other ways to save to XML that will not generate our book order XML. If save data only is not checked, Word will save the document in an XML format called WordprocessingML, or WordML for short. WordML is an XML file format that Word documents can be saved in that preserves all the formatting and features of a Word document. If you look at the WordML XML file that is generated for this example, you will notice that the WordML schema is used to represent Word content. The book order schema is also used in the saved WordML document to mark up any content that we schema mapped. In the snippet of the WordML file shown in Listing 22-4, you can see that the WordML file format uses the CustomerName element to mark up the customer name (John Doe), but what is marked up is the WordML representation of the customer name rather than just the simple text John Doe.

Listing 22-4 A Snippet of WordML Representing the Customer Name Label and XML Mapped Cus-
          tomerName

```
<w:p>
    <w:r>
        <w:t>Customer Name: </w:t>
    </w:r>
</w:p>
```

```
<w:r>
        <w:tab wx:wTab="555" wx:tlc="none" wx:cTlc="8"/>
    </w:r>
    <ns0:CustomerName>
        <w:r>
            <w:t>John Doe</w:t>
        </w:r>
    </ns0:CustomerName>
</w:p>
```

You can also use a transform when saving by checking the Apply transform box. A transform is an XSLT file that acts on the WordML XML file and transforms it to some other XML format. For example, you could create an XSLT transform that takes a WordML XML file and transforms it to XML conforming to the book order schema. This does not seem necessary because clicking the Save data only option already does this. There are compelling scenarios around a similar scenario: importing XML data and applying a transform to convert it to a nicely formatted document in WordML. The next section examines this scenario in more detail.

Importing an XML Data File into the Mapped Document

Let's consider the problem of how to get XML conforming to our customer order schema, such as the XML shown in Listing 22-1, imported into our formatted Word document shown in Figure 22-21. Word does not provide a menu command to import XML like Excel provides. Instead, Word relies on something called an XSLT file to transform XML conforming to our customer order schema to a formatted Word document in WordML format.

An XSLT file contains a set of instructions for transforming XML from one format to another format. Fortunately, you do not have to understand the XSLT language or WordML to create an XSLT file. Word provides a developer tool to help generate the XSLT file we need. The XSLT file can then be used to transform the customer order XML into the nicely formatted document shown in Figure 22-21. We will first provide a brief checklist of the steps to do this and then consider the steps in more detail.

To create the XSLT file, follow these steps:

1. Save the formatted and XML mapped Word document shown in Figure 22-21 to the WordML file format.

2. Run the WordprocessingML Tranform Inference Tool (WML2XSLT.EXE) on the WordML formatted file to generate an XSLT file. This XSLT file will transform XML conforming to the book order schema back to the formatted Word document in WordML format.

To manually convert the book order XML using the XSLT file, follow these steps:

1. Open an XML file conforming to the book order schema in Word.

2. Use the XML Data Views feature of Word to browse to the XSLT file and transform the XML data file back to the formatted Word document shown in Figure 22-21.

To automatically use the XSLT file when book order XML is opened, follow these steps:

1. Use the Schema Library dialog to add the XSLT file created by the WML2XSLT tool as a solution associated with the book order schema.

2. Whenever you open book order XML conforming to the book order schema, Word will automatically apply the XSLT transform to give back the formatted Word document shown in Figure 22-21.

Creating the XSLT File

The first step to creating an XSLT file is to take the document you created as shown in Figure 22-21 and save it in the WordML file format. To do this, choose Save As from the File menu. From the File Type drop-down, choose XML Document. Then make sure that the check boxes next to Apply transform and Save data only are not checked. Give the resulting WordML XML file a name such as Book Sales.xml. Save the file to a location where you can find it in the next step. Then click the Save button.

Book Sales.xml is a WordML format document. It can be used as input to the WordprocessingML Transform Inference Tool to create an XSLT file that can transform XML conforming to our book order schema back to the Book Sales formatted Word document. The WordprocessingML Transform Inference Tool is available for download at http://www.microsoft.com/downloads/details.aspx?Family ID=2cb5b04e-61d9-4f16-9b18-223ec626080e&DisplayLang=en. Download and install the tool on your machine. It will typically install to the directory C:\Program Files\Microsoft Office 2003 Developer Resources\Microsoft Office 2003 Wordprocessing ML Transform Inference Tool.

The transform inference tool is a console application called WML2XSLT.EXE. Open a command prompt and navigate to the directory where WML2XSLT.EXE is installed. For simplicity, we have copied the Book Sales.xml WordML file to the same directory where WML2XSLT.EXE is installed. At the command-line type this command:

```
WML2XSLT.EXE "book sales.xml" -o "book sales.xslt"
```

"book sales.xml" is the input WordML file. "book sales.xslt" is the output XSLT file that WML2XSLT.EXE creates. After running this command, Book Sales.xslt is created in the same directory where WML2XSLT.EXE is installed.

Manually Converting the Book Order XML File Using the XSLT File

Now, take the XML in Listing 22-1 and save it to a file called Book Order.xml. Edit the content of the file in some way so that it is different from the XML that was in Book Sales.xml. For example, change the customer name and some of the book titles. This will help convince you later that the XSLT file really works with arbitrary XML that conforms to the book order schema.

Now, from within Word, choose Open from the File menu. In the list of File Types, choose XML Files (*.xml). Browse to the Book Order.xml file and click Open. Word opens the XML file in a nice data-only view, as shown in Figure 22-24.

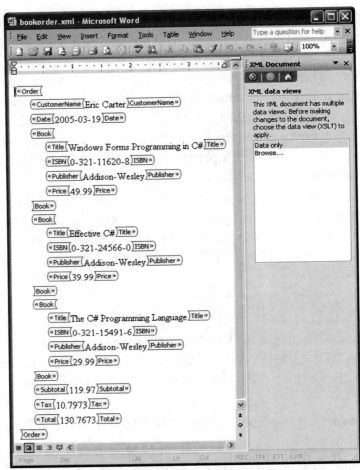

Figure 22-24 Opening Book Order.XML and displaying it in Word's XML data-only view.

This view of the XML is nice and all, but we would like to get it back to the formatted document in Figure 22-21. When you open the XML data file, the XML Document task pane automatically appears. This task pane is the key to converting back to the formatted document view. Click the Browse option in the task pane to browse to the Book Sales.xslt XSLT file you created using WML2XSLT.EXE. After you have located the XSLT file, click Open. Word will then transform the Book Order.xml to a formatted Word document that looks like the document in Figure 22-21 but has the specific data changes you made to the Book Order.xml file. If you go to the XML Structure pane and check the Show XML tags in the document option, you will see that the formatted Word document created by using the XSLT file on the Book Order.xml file still has the XML mapping applied properly to it.

Automatically Applying an XSLT File When XML Conforming to the Book Order Schema Is Opened

Word provides a way of bypassing the extra steps of browsing to the XSLT file whenever you open the XML data file. Using the Schema Library, we can associate an XSLT file with an XML schema so that whenever XML conforming to that schema is opened the XSLT file will be applied automatically to the XML.

Go to the Schema Library dialog by choosing Templates and Add-Ins from the Tools menu. Click the XML Schema tab in the Templates and Add-Ins dialog. Then, click the Schema Library button to display the Schema Library dialog shown in Figure 22-6. With the book order schema selected, click the Add Solution button in the lower half of the dialog to associate an XSLT file with the book order schema. You will be prompted to browse for an XSLT file. Browse to the XSLT file created by WML2XSLT.EXE called Book Sales.xslt. Then click the Open button. The dialog shown in Figure 22-25 will appear. Give the XSLT file an alias (friendly name) of Book Order View. Then click the OK button.

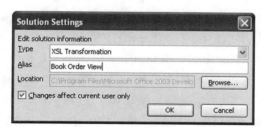

Figure 22-25 Adding an XSLT solution to the book order schema.

As shown in Figure 22-26, the XSLT file we created is now associated with the book order schema. This will cause Word to automatically apply the XSLT file when XML conforming to the book order schema is opened.

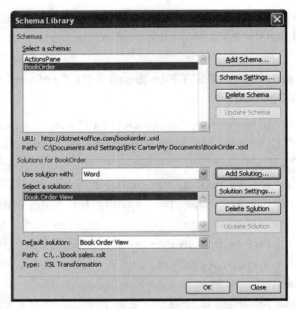

Figure 22-26 The book order view and XSLT is associated with the book order schema in the Schema Library.

Now let's verify that the XSLT we have associated with the book order schema will automatically be applied. From Word, choose Open from the File menu. In the list of File Types, choose XML Files (*.xml). Browse to the Book Order.xml file you created and click Open. Instead of defaulting to an XML-only view as shown in Figure 22-24, Word now opens the XML file and automatically applies the XSLT to display the formatted document, as shown in Figure 22-27. It also shows the XML Document task pane, which gives the user the option to go back to the data-only view or pick some other XSLT file that can transform XML conforming to the book order schema into a formatted document.

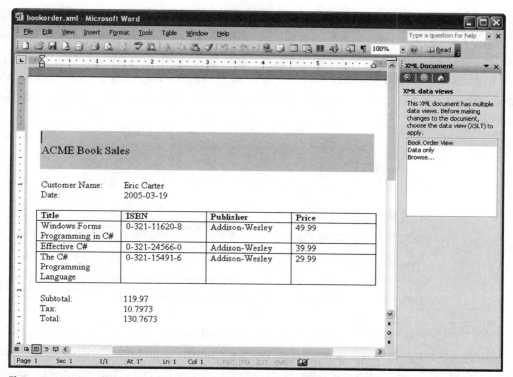

Figure 22-27 Word automatically applies the book order view solution and XSLT.

The XML Options Dialog

The XML Options dialog shown in Figure 22-11 has three categories of options: XML save options, Schema validation options, and XML view options. These options are applied and saved at the document level—different documents can have different sets of XML options. For XML save options, checking the Save data only option makes it so when you save the document as XML it will save the XML mapped into the document rather than saving the document in WordML format. The Apply custom transform option lets you specify an XSLT file to apply when you save the document. This feature is the inverse of the import XSLT file we considered earlier and is beyond the scope of this book.

The schema validation options let you control the way Word validates the document against the attached schema. With Validate document against attached schemas checked, Word validates the XML data in the document against the attached schema. If Hide schema violations in this document is not checked, Word displays squiggly lines under data that does not conform to the schema being used in the document. For example, in our book order document, consider what happens if we type an invalid date for the date of the order. Word displays a squiggly line under the date. If you right-click the squiggly line, you get a schema validation error, as shown in Figure 22-28.

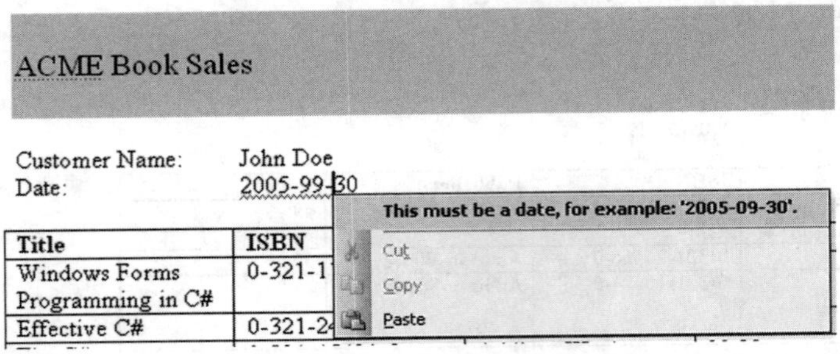

Figure 22-28 A schema validation error for an illegal date.

We have already considered the Ignore mixed content option and the necessity of turning this option on when you intermix formatting and labels with the XML that is mapped into the document. The Allow saving as XML even if not valid will let you save invalid XML—you typically should not check this option. Although Word will let you construct a document with multiple schemas attached that generate invalid XML, this prevents you from using features such as the XSLT feature and VSTO programming model features.

The XML view options section has some additional options for how Excel displays XML information. The Hide namespace alias in XML Structure task pane makes it so that the XML structure tree view does not display the namespace prefix before element names. For example, if the namespace is ns1 and the element is CustomerName, unchecking this option will result in Word displaying ns1:CustomerName in the tree view. Checking this option will result in Word displaying CustomerName.

Show advanced XML error messages shows advanced schema validation errors. This is useful during development of the document when you want to see the exact error message being returned by Word's XML validator. But these messages are not very friendly for end users, so you should be sure to turn this option off before you deploy your document. Figure 22-29 shows the error display for an illegal date when advanced XML error messages are turned on.

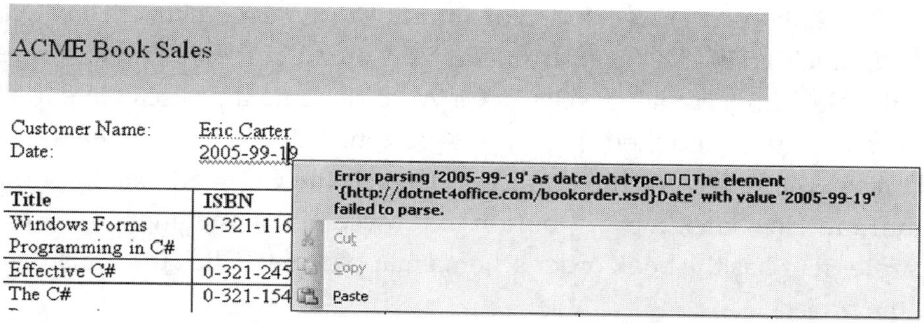

ACME Book Sales

| Customer Name: | Eric Carter | | |
| Date: | 2005-99-19 | | |

Error parsing '2005-99-19' as date datatype.□□The element '{http://dotnet4office.com/bookorder.xsd}Date' with value '2005-99-19' failed to parse.

Title	ISBN		
Windows Forms Programming in C#	0-321-116	Cut	
Effective C#	0-321-245	Copy	
The C#	0-321-154	Paste	

Figure 22-29 An "advanced" schema validation error for an illegal date.

Show placeholder text for all empty elements is an option you will almost always want to turn on before you deploy your document to end users. In a deployed document, you will typically not want to have the XML tags displayed because this is busy and confusing to the user of your document. But when the data within an XML tag is empty, it is impossible for the user of your document to know where to enter data. If you turn on the Show placeholder text for all empty elements, Word displays the name of the fields that need to be filled in so the user of the document can click the field name and type (see Figure 22-30). We have emptied out all the data between tags, but the placeholder text makes it clear to the user of the document where to enter data.

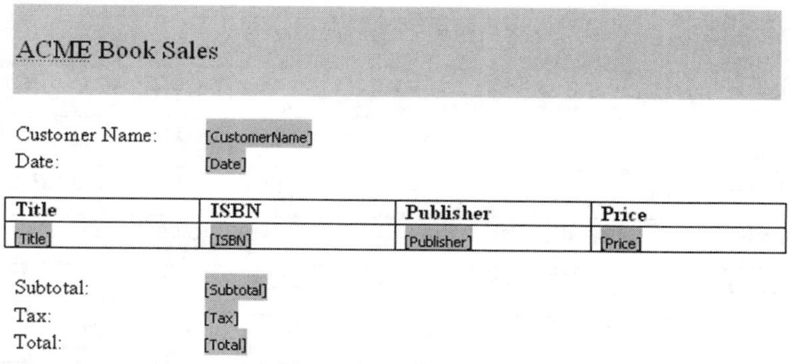

ACME Book Sales

| Customer Name: | [CustomerName] | | |
| Date: | [Date] | | |

Title	ISBN	Publisher	Price
[Title]	[ISBN]	[Publisher]	[Price]

Subtotal:	[Subtotal]
Tax:	[Tax]
Total:	[Total]

Figure 22-30 A document with Show placeholder text for all empty elements turned on.

VSTO Support for Word Schema Mapping

This section covers VSTO 2005's support for Word's schema mapping. Let's create a new VSTO 2005 Word project based on the book order document we created in this chapter. Launch VSTO 2005, and from the New menu in the File menu choose Project. In the New Project dialog, select a C# Word document project. Give the project a name and location, and then click the OK button. A dialog then appears asking for a document to be used for the application. Click the Copy an existing document radio button. Then click the "..." button to browse to the document you created in this chapter that has the book order schema mapped in it. Click the Finish button to create the project.

We want to consider several features of the generated VSTO project. First is the creation of XMLNode controls. Second is the creation of XMLNodes controls. Finally, we will consider how to use the UpdateXml methods on an XMLNode to load XML into our document without using an XSLT file.

Use the class view to browse the members associated with ThisDocument. Notice as you browse that the member variables listed in Table 22-1 have been created automatically based on the XML mapping in the document to the book order schema.

Table 22-1 ThisDocument Member Variables Added from Schema Mapping

Name	Type
OrderNode	Microsoft.Office.Tools.Word.XMLNode
OrderCustomerNameNode	Microsoft.Office.Tools.Word.XMLNode
OrderDateNode	Microsoft.Office.Tools.Word.XMLNode
OrderBookNodes	Microsoft.Office.Tools.Word.XMLNodes
BookTitleNodes	Microsoft.Office.Tools.Word.XMLNodes
BookISBNNodes	Microsoft.Office.Tools.Word.XMLNodes
BookPublisherNodes	Microsoft.Office.Tools.Word.XMLNodes
BookPriceNodes	Microsoft.Office.Tools.Word.XMLNodes
OrderSubtotalNode	Microsoft.Office.Tools.Word.XMLNode
OrderTaxNode	Microsoft.Office.Tools.Word.XMLNode
OrderTotalNode	Microsoft.Office.Tools.Word.XMLNode

The XMLNode Control

For each nonrepeating element mapped to the Word document, VSTO creates an XMLNode control. For example, by mapping the nonrepeating element Customer-Name from the Order element, VSTO created an XMLNode control called Order-CustomerNameNode. An XMLNode control has all the properties and methods of a Word XMLNode object. In addition, it has several events that are not found on the Word XMLNode object:

- **XMLNode.AfterInsert** is raised when a new XML element is added to the document.
- **XMLNode.BeforeDelete** is raised when an XML element is removed from the document.
- **XMLNode.ContextEnter** is raised when the XML node has focus.
- **XMLNode.ContextLeave** is raised when the XML node loses focus.
- **XMLNode.Select** is raised when text within the XML node is selected.
- **XMLNode.Deselect** is raised when text within the XML node is deselected.
- **XMLNode.ValidationError** is raised when a validation error occurs within the XML node.

Listing 22-5 shows a VSTO customization that handles all the events associated with an XMLNode. In this case, the code handles events associated with the XMLNode called OrderCustomerNameNode, which corresponds to the CustomerName element from the book order schema mapped into the Word document.

Listing 22-5 A VSTO Word Customization That Handles All Events Associated with an XMLNode Control

```
using System;
using System.Data;
using System.Drawing;
using System.Windows.Forms;
using Microsoft.VisualStudio.OfficeTools.Interop.Runtime;
using Word = Microsoft.Office.Interop.Word;
using Office = Microsoft.Office.Core;

namespace WordApplication1
{
```

```csharp
public partial class ThisDocument
{
  private System.Windows.Forms.ListBox list;

  private void ThisDocument_Startup(object sender, EventArgs e)
  {
    this.OrderDateNode.AfterInsert += new
      Microsoft.Office.Tools.Word.NodeInsertAndDeleteEventHandler(
      OrderDateNode_AfterInsert);

    this.OrderDateNode.BeforeDelete += new
      Microsoft.Office.Tools.Word.NodeInsertAndDeleteEventHandler(
      OrderDateNode_BeforeDelete);

    this.OrderDateNode.ContextEnter += new
      Microsoft.Office.Tools.Word.ContextChangeEventHandler(
      OrderDateNode_ContextEnter);

    this.OrderDateNode.ContextLeave += new
      Microsoft.Office.Tools.Word.ContextChangeEventHandler(
      OrderDateNode_ContextLeave);

    this.OrderDateNode.Select += new
      Microsoft.Office.Tools.Word.NodeSelectionEventHandler(
      OrderDateNode_Select);

    this.OrderDateNode.Deselect += new
      Microsoft.Office.Tools.Word.NodeSelectionEventHandler(
      OrderDateNode_Deselect);

    this.OrderDateNode.ValidationError += new
      EventHandler(OrderDateNode_ValidationError);

    list = new System.Windows.Forms.ListBox();
    ActionsPane.Controls.Add(list);
    ActionsPane.Show();
  }

  #region VSTO Designer generated code
  private void InternalStartup()
  {
    this.Startup += new EventHandler(ThisDocument_Startup);
  }
  #endregion

  private void Display(string text, string text2)
  {
```

```csharp
    list.Items.Add(String.Format("{0} {1}", text, text2));
  }

  void OrderDateNode_AfterInsert(object sender,
    Microsoft.Office.Tools.Word.NodeInsertAndDeleteEventArgs e)
  {
    Microsoft.Office.Interop.Word.XMLNode node = sender
      as Microsoft.Office.Interop.Word.XMLNode;
    Display("AfterInsert", node.BaseName);
  }

  void OrderDateNode_BeforeDelete(object sender,
    Microsoft.Office.Tools.Word.NodeInsertAndDeleteEventArgs e)
  {
    Microsoft.Office.Interop.Word.XMLNode node = sender
      as Microsoft.Office.Interop.Word.XMLNode;
    Display("BeforeDelete", node.BaseName);
  }

  void OrderDateNode_ContextEnter(object sender,
    Microsoft.Office.Tools.Word.ContextChangeEventArgs e)
  {
    Display("ContextEnter", e.NewXMLNode.BaseName);
  }

  void OrderDateNode_ContextLeave(object sender,
    Microsoft.Office.Tools.Word.ContextChangeEventArgs e)
  {
    Display("ContextLeave", e.NewXMLNode.BaseName);
  }

  void OrderDateNode_Select(object sender,
    Microsoft.Office.Tools.Word.ContextChangeEventArgs e)
  {
    Display("Select", e.Selection.Text);
  }

  void OrderDateNode_Deselect(object sender,
    Microsoft.Office.Tools.Word.ContextChangeEventArgs e)
  {
    Display("Deselect", e.Selection.Text);
  }
  }
}
```

The XMLNodes Control

For each repeating element mapped to the Word document, VSTO creates an XMLNodes control. For the repeating element Book from the Order element, VSTO created an XMLNodes control called OrderBookNodes. An XMLNodes control has all the properties and methods of a Word XMLNodes object. In addition, it has several events that are not found on the Word XMLNodes object:

- **XMLNodes.AfterInsert** is raised when a new XML element is added to the document.
- **XMLNodes.BeforeDelete** is raised when an XML element is removed from the document.
- **XMLNodes.ContextEnter** is raised when an element contained by the XMLNodes control gets focus.
- **XMLNodes.ContextLeave** is raised when the elements contained by the XMLNodes control loses focus.
- **XMLNodes.Select** is raised when text within the elements contained by the XMLNodes control is selected.
- **XMLNodes.Deselect** is raised when text within the elements contained by the XMLNodes control is deselected.
- **XMLNodes.ValidationError** is raised when a validation error occurs within the elements contained by the XMLNodes control.

Listing 22-6 shows a VSTO customization that handles all the events associated with an XMLNodes control. The code handles events associated with the XMLNodes control called OrderBooksNode, which corresponds to the repeating Book element from the book order schema that was mapped into the Word document.

Listing 22-6   A VSTO Word Customization That Handles All Events Associated with an XMLNodes Control

```
using System;
using System.Data;
using System.Drawing;
using System.Windows.Forms;
using Microsoft.VisualStudio.OfficeTools.Interop.Runtime;
using Word = Microsoft.Office.Interop.Word;
```

```csharp
using Office = Microsoft.Office.Core;

namespace WordApplication1
{
  public partial class ThisDocument
  {
    private System.Windows.Forms.ListBox list;

    private void ThisDocument_Startup(object sender, EventArgs e)
    {
      this.OrderBookNodes.AfterInsert += new
        Microsoft.Office.Tools.Word.NodeInsertAndDeleteEventHandler(
        OrderBookNodes_AfterInsert);

      this.OrderBookNodes.BeforeDelete += new
        Microsoft.Office.Tools.Word.NodeInsertAndDeleteEventHandler(
        OrderBookNodes_BeforeDelete);

      this.OrderBookNodes.ContextEnter += new
        Microsoft.Office.Tools.Word.ContextChangeEventHandler(
        OrderBookNodes_ContextEnter);

      this.OrderBookNodes.ContextLeave += new
        Microsoft.Office.Tools.Word.ContextChangeEventHandler(
        OrderBookNodes_ContextLeave);

      this.OrderBookNodes.Select += new
        Microsoft.Office.Tools.Word.NodeSelectionEventHandler(
        OrderBookNodes_Select);

      this.OrderBookNodes.Deselect += new
        Microsoft.Office.Tools.Word.NodeSelectionEventHandler(
        OrderBookNodes_Deselect);

      this.OrderBookNodes.ValidationError += new
        EventHandler(OrderBookNodes_ValidationError);

      list = new System.Windows.Forms.ListBox();
      ActionsPane.Controls.Add(list);
      ActionsPane.Show();
    }



    #region VSTO Designer generated code
    private void InternalStartup()
    {
```

```csharp
        this.Startup += new EventHandler(ThisDocument_Startup);
    }
    #endregion

    private void Display(string text, string text2)
    {
        list.Items.Add(String.Format("{0} {1}", text, text2));
    }

    void OrderBookNodes_AfterInsert(object sender,
        Microsoft.Office.Tools.Word.NodeInsertAndDeleteEventArgs e)
    {
        Microsoft.Office.Interop.Word.XMLNode node = sender as
            Microsoft.Office.Interop.Word.XMLNode;
        Display("AfterInsert", node.BaseName);
    }

    void OrderBookNodes_BeforeDelete(object sender,
        Microsoft.Office.Tools.Word.NodeInsertAndDeleteEventArgs e)
    {
        Microsoft.Office.Interop.Word.XMLNode node = sender as
            Microsoft.Office.Interop.Word.XMLNode;
        Display("BeforeDelete", node.BaseName);
    }

    void OrderBookNodes_ContextEnter(object sender,
        Microsoft.Office.Tools.Word.ContextChangeEventArgs e)
    {
        Display("ContextEnter", e.NewXMLNode.BaseName);
    }

    void OrderBookNodes_ContextLeave(object sender,
        Microsoft.Office.Tools.Word.ContextChangeEventArgs e)
    {
        Display("ContextLeave", e.NewXMLNode.BaseName);
    }

    void OrderBookNodes_Select(object sender,
        Microsoft.Office.Tools.Word.ContextChangeEventArgs e)
    {
        Display("Select", e.Selection.Text);
    }


    void OrderBookNodes_Deselect(object sender,
        Microsoft.Office.Tools.Word.ContextChangeEventArgs e)
```

```
    {
      Display("Deselect", e.Selection.Text);
    }

    void OrderBookNodes_ValidationError(object sender, EventArgs e)
    {
      Display("ValidationError", "");
    }
  }
}
```

Loading XML Programmatically with LoadXml

Another addition that VSTO makes to XMLNode is the LoadXml method. The Load-Xml method can be used to set the XML on the entire node tree of the XMLNode on which it is called. The LoadXml method has three overloads that take a `string` of XML, an XmlElement, or an XmlDocument.

LoadXml has one major limitation. It will not decrease or increase the number of XML elements in the document. So given the code in Listing 22-7 that has three book elements and given a document that has only one book in the table mapped to book elements, LoadXml will only transfer the first book to the document. To transfer the second and third book would require the addition of elements, which LoadXml does not do. As a second example, if you have a document that has three books in the table and you call LoadXml passing XML with only one book, LoadXml will update the first row of the table but will leave the two extra books there. The second and third books are left there because LoadXml does not remove elements.

Listing 22-7 The LoadXml Method on XMLNode Object

```
private void ThisDocument_Startup(object sender, EventArgs e)
{
  this.OrderNode.LoadXml(@"<?xml version=""1.0"" encoding=""UTF-8""
standalone=""no""?><Order
xmlns=""http://dotnet4office.com/bookorder.xsd""><CustomerName>
Lah Lah</CustomerName><Date>2005-03-19</Date><Book><Title>Windows Forms
Programming in C#</Title><ISBN>0-321-11620-8</ISBN><Publisher>Addison-
Wesley</Publisher><Price>49.99</Price></Book><Book><Title>Effective
C#</Title><ISBN>0-321-24566-0</ISBN><Publisher>Addison-
Wesley</Publisher><Price>39.99</Price></Book><Book><Title>The C# Programming
Language</Title><ISBN>0-321-15491-6</ISBN><Publisher>Addison-Wesley</
```

```
Publisher><Price>29.99</Price></Book><Subtotal>119.97</Subtotal><Tax>10.7973
</Tax><Total>130.7673</Total></Order>");
}
```

You will frequently want to get the XML from an XMLNode or XMLNodes. The way you do this is by using the get_XML method on the Range object returned by the Range property of an XMLNode or XMLNodes. The get_XML method takes a `bool` parameter to which you pass `true` to get the XML data. If you pass `false`, you will get the WordML for the XMLNode or XMLNodes instead. Listing 22-8 shows a simple VSTO application that displays the XML data in the document on startup using the root XMLNode called OrderNode.

Listing 22-8 Using the get_XML Method

```
private void ThisDocument_Startup(object sender, EventArgs e)
{
    MessageBox.Show(this.OrderNode.Range.get_XML(true));
}
```

VSTO Support for the WordML File Format

VSTO has several features that support the WordML file format. Although you cannot create a new VSTO Word project in the WordML format, you can take a Word document that has been customized in VSTO and save it as WordML. Because WordML preserves all the features of the Word document, the document continues to work and the VSTO customization will run even when saved in WordML format.

VSTO's ServerDocument object can open a file in the WordML file format without starting Word on the server and manipulate the cached data and application manifest inside the Word document. For more information on ServerDocument, see Chapter 18, "Server Data Scenarios" and Chapter 20, "Deployment."

VSTO also supports an easy way of attaching a VSTO customization to an uncustomized WordML document. If you add a document property to the Word document called _AssemblyName and set it to "*" and add a second property to the Word document called _AssemblyLocation and set it to the URL to a VSTO deploy manifest (as described in Chapter 20), Word will attach the customization specified in the deploy manifest when the document is opened on the client. This feature was added because it makes it much easier to attach a VSTO customization when using a WordML document or an XSLT transformation that transforms XML data to a WordML format document. When using this feature, make sure you start with a clean document that does not have a VSTO customization already associated with it. A document that is customized with a VSTO customization will already have its _AssemblyName and _AssemblyLocation properties set and it will have a hidden ActiveX control embedded in it that contains the data island. The whole point of using this feature is to not have to deal with the embedded ActiveX control in the document because it becomes unwieldy when generating WordML or writing an XSLT transform.

Conclusion

This chapter examined the XML schema mapping features in Word. You have learned how to create a schema using Visual Studio that will work well with Word's schema mapping features. This chapter also covered how to export XML from a Word document using Word's Save Data option when saving as XML. The chapter also addressed using XSLT files to effectively import XML into a Word document. You also learned how to work with VSTO's XMLNode and XMLNodes controls created for a mapped schema. The end of the chapter discussed VSTO's support for the WordML format.

23

Developing COM Add-Ins for Word and Excel

Introduction to Add-Ins

OFFICE PROVIDES A NUMBER OF PATTERNS to extend the functionality of Office applications. The most common patterns are these:

- Office automation executables
- Office add-ins
- Code behind an Office document or template

This chapter covers how to write COM add-ins in C# for Word and Excel. It also describes how COM add-ins are registered in the registry and why there is another step called "shimming" that must be taken before deploying a managed COM add-in.

Outlook Add-Ins

VSTO 2005 supports building a new kind of "VSTO-style" add-in for Outlook 2003. The VSTO Outlook add-in project is the preferred way to build Outlook add-ins for Outlook 2003 and is described in Chapter 24, "Creating Outlook Add-Ins with VSTO." The VSTO Outlook add-in project fixes many of the issues in COM add-in development discussed in this chapter as well as some additional Outlook-specific issues. The only reason to write a managed COM add-in for Outlook following the instructions in this chapter is if it must run in versions of Outlook older than Outlook 2003.

Scenarios for Using Add-Ins

Add-ins provide a mechanism to extend the core functionality of an application so that the new functionality will be available throughout the application. The key to writing effective add-ins in Office is to develop them so they look and feel like a natural extension to the Office application. A few examples of what add-ins can do in Office include the following:

- **Extending existing functionality**—If your users need to print to a color printer but they often find it difficult to find the color printer nearest to them, you could write an add-in to mitigate this issue. The add-in could add a Print to Color Printer command to their File menu and a Print to Color Printer button on their standard toolbar. When the user clicks the button or selects the menu item, your add-in can handle that event and print to the nearest color printer.
- **Integrating with data**—An add-in could be written that loads into Word and Excel that pulls data from a Web service and pastes it into the Office application. For example, the add-in could add a Paste Sales Information menu item. When the user selects the command from within Word, it would paste a table with the data from the Web service at the position your cursor is at in Word. In Excel, it would paste into the selected cells.

Functionality that only needs to be available for one particular document or template type is better written using the code behind a document pattern. For example, if sales information only needs to be retrieved when working with a Quarterly Report.doc file, it is better to put your code that retrieves the sales information into code behind the template or document for the quarterly report. This is an example of choosing the right context for your code. There is no reason to clutter up the application context with commands that are only used for a particular document or template.

How a COM Add-In Is Registered

A COM add-in from the standpoint of the Office application is a COM component registered in a particular place in the registry that implements the IDTExtensibility2 interface defined by Office and Visual Studio. From your standpoint as a C# developer, you are writing a C# class that you will compile into an assembly (DLL). Through .NET's' COM interop support, your C# class can be made to look like a COM component to the Office application. You will have to register your add-in just like any COM component to get the Office application to load it.

The registry settings and interface implementation described in this section are created for you automatically when you create an add-in project in Visual Studio. However, it is still important to understand the anatomy of an add-in should you have to troubleshoot add-in issues.

Registry Location of a COM Add-In: HKEY_CURRENT_USER or HKEY_LOCAL_MACHINE

Office determines which COM add-ins to load for a particular application by checking two places in the registry—either under HKEY_CURRENT_USER or under HKEY_LOCAL_MACHINE. To view the registry, choose Run from the Start menu of Windows and type `regedit.exe` and click the OK button.

The first place a COM add-in can be registered is in the registry under HKEY_CURRENT_USER\Software\Microsoft\Office\%appname%\Addins. This is where COM add-ins installed on a per-user basis are found, as shown in Figure 23-1. COM add-ins should typically be installed on a per-user basis so that the add-in user settings will move with the user should the user log on to a different machine.

Any COM add-ins registered in the registry under HKEY_CURRENT_USER will show up in the COM add-ins dialog for the relevant Office application. Finding the COM add-ins dialog in each Office application can be quite a challenge. In all Office

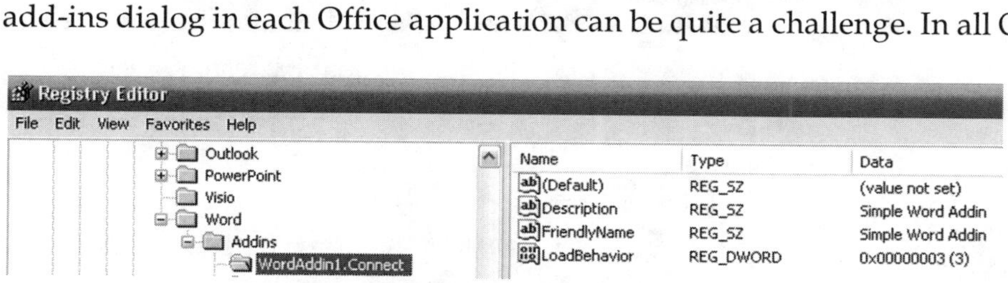

Figure 23-1 A registry entry for a COM add-in.

applications, the dialog is not available from a menu in the default install. To add a button to show the COM add-in dialog, you need to customize the toolbars in the Office application by right-clicking the command bar and selecting Customize. Doing so causes the Customize dialog to appear (see Figure 23-2). Click the Commands tab and select Tools from the Categories list. Then scroll through the list of available commands and find the COM Add-Ins command. Drag this command onto an existing toolbar.

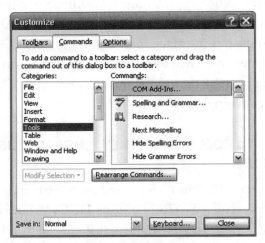

Figure 23-2 Locating the COM Add-Ins command in the Customize dialog box.

When you click the COM Add-Ins button that you have added to a toolbar, the COM Add-Ins dialog displays, as shown in Figure 23-3. This dialog shows you all the COM add-ins registered in the registry under HKEY_CURRENT_USER for the Office application you are using.

Figure 23-3 The COM Add-Ins dialog.

The second place a COM add-in can be registered is under HKEY_LOCAL_ MACHINE\Software\Microsoft\Office\%appname%\Addins. COM add-ins registered on a per-machine basis are available for all users but also are effectively hidden from the user within the Office application. If a COM add-in is registered under HKEY_LOCAL_MACHINE, it will never show up in the COM Add-Ins dialog. It is recommended that you register your COM add-in under HKEY_LOCAL_USER so that your COM add-in is visible to end users.

Registry Entries Required for a COM Add-In

Each COM add-in registered in the registry whether under HKEY_CURRENT_ USER or HKEY_LOCAL_MACHINE must be registered in the following way. First, there must be a key representing the COM add-in under the Addins key. This key is named with the ProgID of the COM add-in. A ProgID is an identifier for the COM add-in that is generated by Visual Studio. This identifier is used by COM to figure out how to create your COM add-in. The default ProgID for a Visual Studio COM add-in project is the name of the add-in project combined with the name of the class (Connect) generated in Visual Studio that implements IDTExtensibility2. So if you create a COM add-in project in Visual Studio called MyAddin2 for an Office application such as Outlook, the main key that Visual Studio creates in the registry for the COM add-in would be this:

```
HKEY_CURRENT_USER\Software\Microsoft\Office\Outlook\Addins\MyAddin2.Connect
```

Under the key for your COM add-in, several values are required. `FriendlyName` is a string value that contains the name of the COM add-in that will appear to the user in the COM Add-Ins dialog. `Description` is a string value that contains a more in depth description of the COM add-in. This description does not appear anywhere in the Office UI or COM Add-Ins dialog, but it is helpful when users or administrators are investigating by using regedit.exe what add-ins are installed on a machine and what they do. `LoadBehavior` is a DWORD value that describes the load behavior for the COM add-in. The values that `LoadBehavior` can be set to are a bitwise or of the values in Table 23-1. Typically, this should be set to the value of 3 to load and connect the COM add-in at startup. If the `LoadBehavior` is set to 2, the COM add-in is loaded but its IDTExtensibility.OnConnection method is never called, which effectively amounts to the COM add-in being disabled.

Table 23-1 Possible Values for LoadBehavior

Value	Description
0	Disconnected. The COM add-in is not loaded.
1	Connected. The COM add-in is loaded.
2	Load at startup. The COM add-in will be loaded and connected when the host application starts.
8	Load on demand. The COM add-in will be loaded and connected when the host application requires it, (for example, when a user clicks a button that uses functionality in the COM add-in).
16	Connect first time. The COM add-in will be loaded and connected the first time the user runs the host application after registering the COM add-in.

In addition to these keys, several entries under HKEY_CLASSES_ROOT\CLSID are made for the COM add-in, as shown in Figure 23-4. A unique ClassID (a GUID, which is a unique identifier that looks like {FEC2B9E7-9366-4AD2-AD05-4CF0167AC9C6}) is created by Visual Studio. This ClassID is added as a key under the HKEY_CLASSES_ROOT\CLSID path. This ClassID is registered so it corresponds to the ProgID for the COM add-in (MyAddin2.Connect in our example). The keys and values created under the ClassID key are described in more detail later in this chapter.

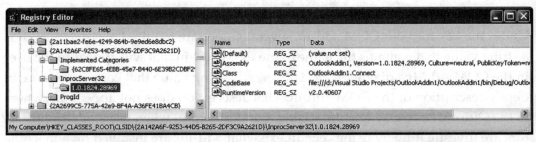

Figure 23-4 The registry entries for a COM add-in under the HKEY_CLASSES_ROOT\CLSID path.

Implementing IDTExtensibility2

The key to understanding COM add-in development is the IDTExensibility2 interface. This interface is used by all Office applications to communicate with a COM add-in. This ensures a common initialization mechanism and an ability to pass in the application's object model so that the COM add-in can communicate with the Office application. Listing 23-1 shows the IDTExtensibility2 interface.

Listing 23-1 The IDTExtensibility2 Interface

```
public interface IDTExtensibility2
{
  void OnAddInsUpdate(ref System.Array custom);
  void OnBeginShutdown(ref System.Array custom);
  void OnConnection(object Application,
    Extensibility.ext_ConnectMode ConnectMode,
    object AddInInst, ref System.Array custom);
  void OnDisconnection(Extensibility.ext_DisconnectMode RemoveMode,
    ref System.Array custom);
  void OnStartupComplete(ref System.Array custom);
}
```

Startup Order

IDTExtensibility2 is a simple interface, but it is important to note the loading order of the COM add-in and how that impacts where you write your code. Office instantiates your COM add-in, which causes your main Connect class to be created. But there is a key difference to normal programming practice in that the constructor of your Connect class cannot really be used to set up your class because the Office application context (typically the Application object from the Office application's object model) is not made available in the constructor. Instead, it is provided via the OnConnection method on the IDTExtensibility2 interface. Likewise, the shutdown behavior for an add-in is determined not by the destructor of the class but by when the OnDisconnection method is called.

Figure 23-5 illustrates the order in which these events occur for a COM add-in. First the COM add-in is loaded and the Connect class is created. This results in the Connect class's constructor being called. Then the Connect class's implementation of IDTExtensibility2.OnConnection is called, and the Office application's Application object is passed via this method. The Connect class's implementation of IDTExtensibility2.OnStartupComplete is called. The add-in is now loaded and connected Then, when the application exits or the user unloads the add-in, the Connect class's implementation of IDTExtensibility2.OnBeginShutdown is called followed by a call to IDTExtensibilty2.OnDisconnection.

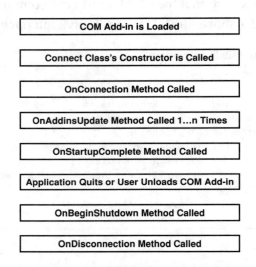

Figure 23-5 Order of COM add-in startup and shutdown.

The OnAddInsUpdate Method

The OnAddInsUpdate method is called when any COM add-in is loaded or unloaded in the Office application. This method is somewhat of an anomaly because the contents of the `custom` argument are never set by Office applications. As a result, this method can only really be used to tell you that a COM add-in has been loaded or unloaded, and you can then query the COMAddins collection in the application object model to see what has been loaded or unloaded. A good example of using this method is if your COM add-in relies on other COM add-ins to be running in order to work properly; so if one of the dependent COM add-ins is unloaded, your COM add-in can unload:

```
void OnAddInsUpdate(ref System.Array custom);
```

Parameter	Description
custom	An array of object that the host application can use to provide additional data. None of the Office applications set this value.

The OnBeginShutdown Method

The OnBeginShutdown method is called on a connected COM add-in when the Office application is being shut down:

```
void OnBeginShutdown(ref System.Array custom);
```

Parameter	Description
custom	An array of object that the host application can use to provide additional data. None of the Office applications set this value.

The OnConnection Method

The OnConnection method is called when a COM add-in is loaded into the environment. This method is the main entry point for the COM add-in because it provides the Application object from the Office application's object model that the add-in will use to communicate with the Office application:

```
void OnConnection(object Application,
    Extensibility.ext_ConnectMode ConnectMode,
    object AddInInst, ref System.Array custom)
```

Parameter	Description
Application	The application object of the Office application passed as an `object`. Because IDTExtensibility2 is a general-purpose interface, this has to be an `object` rather than a strongly typed parameter. This object can be cast to the Application object type of the Office application.
ConnectMode	The `ext_ConnectMode` constant specifying how the COM add-in was loaded. There are six possible values:

Constant	Value	Description
`ext_cm_After-Startup`	0	COM add-in was loaded after the application started. Typically this is if user has chosen to load an add-in from the COM Add-Ins dialog.
`ext_cm_Startup`	1	COM add-in was loaded at startup.
`ext_cm_External`	2	COM add-in was loaded externally by another program or component.
`ext_cm_Command-Line`	3	COM add-in was loaded through the application's command line.
`ext_cm_Solution`	4	COM add-in was loaded when user loaded a solution that required it.
`ext_cm_UISetup`	5	COM add-in was started for the first time since being installed.

Parameter	Description
AddInInst	An `object` representing the COM add-in. This can be cast to a COMAddIn object from the office.dll PIA in the Microsoft.Office.Core namespace.
custom	An array of `object` that the host application can use to provide additional data. None of the Office applications set this value.

The OnDisconnection Method

The OnDisconnection method is called when a COM add-in is unloaded from the application either because the application is shutting down or because the user disabled the COM add-in using the COM Add-Ins dialog:

```
void OnDisconnection(Extensibility.ext_DisconnectMode RemoveMode,
    ref System.Array custom);
```

Parameter	Description			
RemoveMode	The `ext_DisconnectMode` constant specifies why the COM add-in was unloaded.			
	Constant	**Value**	**Description**	
	`ext_dm_HostShut-down`	0	COM add-in was unloaded when the host application was closed.	
	`ext_dm_UserClosed`	1	COM add-in was unloaded when the user cleared its check box in the COM Add-Ins dialog box, or when the Connect property of the COMAddIn object corresponding to the COM add-in was set to `false`.	
	`ext_dm_UISetup-Complete`	2	COM add-in was unloaded after the environment setup completed and after the OnConnection method returns.	
	`ext_dm_Solution-Closed`	3	Only used with Visual Studio COM add-ins	
custom	An array of `object` that the host application can use to provide additional data. None of the Office applications set this value.			

The OnStartupComplete Method

The OnStartupComplete method is called when the Office application has completed starting up and has loaded all the COM add-ins that were registered to load on startup:

```
void OnStartupComplete(ref System.Array custom);
```

Parameter	Description
custom	An array of `object` that the host application can use to provide additional data. None of the Office applications set this value.

A Simple Implementation of IDTExtensibility2

Listing 23-2 shows a simple implementation of IDTExtensibility2 similar to what is generated when you create an add-in project in Visual Studio. This implementation displays several message boxes to give you information about the methods of IDTExtensibility2 that are being called on the Connect class. It is a COM add-in that loads into Excel, so it casts the application object to the Microsoft.Office.Interop.Excel. Application type. It also casts the addInInst object to the Microsoft.Office.Core. COMAddin type. Note also that the InteropServices namespace is used to add a GuidAttribute and ProgID attribute. The values of these attributes are used when registering the add-in, as described earlier in the chapter.

Listing 23-2 An Excel COM Add-In Connect Class That Implements IDTExtensibility2

```
namespace MyAddin1
{
  using System;
  using Extensibility;
  using System.Runtime.InteropServices;
  using System.Windows.Forms;
  using Excel = Microsoft.Office.Interop.Excel;
  using Office = Microsoft.Office.Core;

  [GuidAttribute("649D6562-F01F-4117-BF2C-198CDD3E11E4"),
    ProgId("MyAddin1.Connect")]
  public class Connect : Object, Extensibility.IDTExtensibility2
  {
    public Connect()
    {
      MessageBox.Show("Connect Constructor");
    }

    public void OnConnection(object application,
        Extensibility.ext_ConnectMode connectMode,
        object addInInst, ref System.Array custom)
    {
      MessageBox.Show("OnConnection");

      Office.COMAddIn addin = addInInst as Office.COMAddIn;
      MessageBox.Show("My add-in ProgID is " + addin.ProgId);

      Excel.Application app = application as Excel.Application;
      MessageBox.Show(String.Format(
        "The application this loaded into is called {0}.",
        app.Name));
```

```
      MessageBox.Show(String.Format(
        "Load mode was {0}.", connectMode.ToString()));
    }

    public void OnDisconnection(Extensibility.ext_DisconnectMode
      disconnectMode, ref System.Array custom)
    {
      MessageBox.Show("OnDisconnection");
      MessageBox.Show(String.Format(
        "Disconnect mode was {0}.", disconnectMode.ToString()));
    }

    public void OnAddInsUpdate(ref System.Array custom)
    {
      MessageBox.Show("OnAddinsUpdate");
    }

    public void OnStartupComplete(ref System.Array custom)
    {
      MessageBox.Show("OnStartupComplete");
    }

    public void OnBeginShutdown(ref System.Array custom)
    {
      MessageBox.Show("OnBeginShutdown");
    }
}
```

Writing a COM Add-In Using Visual Studio

Writing a class that implements IDTExtensibility2 is not particularly difficult, but setting up the registry settings for the application you are targeting and creating the setup package for the COM add-in can be tricky. Luckily, Visual Studio provides a wizard that makes writing COM add-ins considerably easier. The wizard creates two projects—one for implementing the COM add-in and a separate setup project for the COM add-in. The COM Add-In Wizard has actually been part of Visual Studio since version 7.0, but you might not have come across it because it is somewhat hidden in the project hierarchy and listed as a "Shared Add-in" project.

The wizard can be found under Other Project Types > Extensibility > Shared Add-in and is shown in Figure 23-6. The only clue that the Shared Add-in project might have something to do with Office is the Office icon included on the Shared Add-in icon.

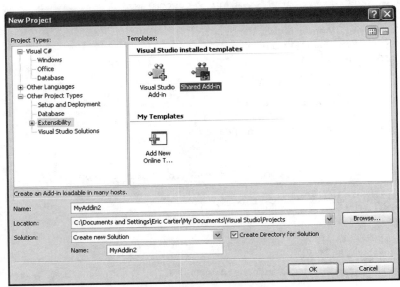

Figure 23-6 Creating a Shared Add-in project in Visual Studio.

The Shared Add-In Wizard steps you through the process of creating a COM add-in. One of the advantages of a generic interface such as IDTExensibility2 is that it can be used from just about any application that has a COM object model and as a result all the Office applications support loading IDTExtensibility2 COM add-ins. The wizard enables you to select the Office application that you want your COM add-in to load into, as shown in Figure 23-7. If you select the check box next to multiple Office applications, Visual Studio will register your COM add-in in a way that enables the same COM add-in to load in multiple Office applications.

Although it is possible to write a single COM add-in that works in all the Office applications, it actually is quite difficult to write and even more difficult to maintain because bug fixing different application behavior often leads to the code in the COM add-in becoming overcomplicated. If you want to be able to share code among COM add-ins, creating a common library called by an application-specific COM add-in provides a more manageable solution.

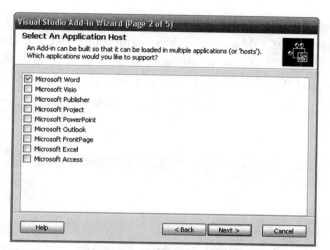

Figure 23-7 Selecting the application host.

In this example, the application host for the COM add-in will be Microsoft Word. Selecting Microsoft Word in the wizard will result in the setup project registering the COM add-in in the correct location for Word so that you do not have to worry about dealing with the registry when you run the project. The registry settings for the COM add-in require a name and description, and this is collected in the next step of the wizard, as shown in Figure 23-8.

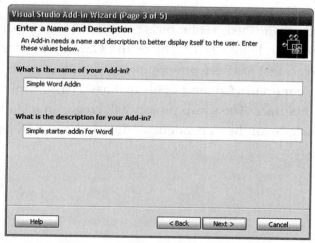

Figure 23-8 Setting a name and description for a COM add-in.

The final step of the wizard is used to determine the load behavior of the COM add-in and whether the COM add-in will be installed in HKEY_CURRENT_USER or HKEY_LOCAL_MACHINE. As mentioned before, it is preferable to register the COM add-in in HKEY_CURRENT_USER so that it will be visible in the COM add-ins dialog. Leaving the second check box unchecked in Figure 23-9 will ensure this behavior.

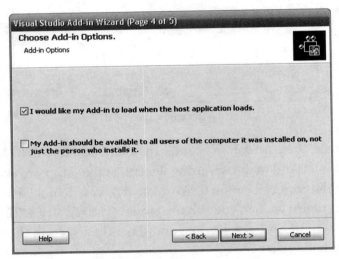

Figure 23-9 Setting load behavior for the COM add-in.

After the wizard has finished, a solution is created in Visual Studio containing the two projects, as shown in Figure 23-10. The main COM add-in project is a standard C# class library project that has been pre-populated with the core references required and a class called Connect in a Connect.cs file that has a basic implementation of the IDTExtensibility2 interface. The setup project will create an installer for the COM add-in that will include all the dependencies detected and will register the COM add-in in the registry.

Figure 23-10 The Solution Explorer view of a default COM
add-in solution.

Changing the COM Add-In Project to Be More Office-Specific

The COM Add-In Wizard will create a project for any application that supports
IDTExtensibility2, and as a result it creates a very generic project. The whole point of
writing a COM add-in is to integrate with a particular Office application, so the first
thing you need to do is add the appropriate primary interop assembly (PIA) for the
application the COM add-in is targeting. The COM add-in being built in this example will load into Microsoft Word, so it needs to have a reference to the Word PIA.
You will then be able to cast the `application` object passed in OnConnection to the
Microsoft.Office.Interop.Word.Application object defined in the Word PIA.

Adding the PIA for Word to a project is quite straightforward; it is just a matter
of adding the reference to the Microsoft Word 11 Object Library. Right-click the
WordAddin project node in the Solution Explorer tree view and choose Add Reference. Doing so brings up the Add Reference dialog shown in Figure 23-11. Click the
COM tab, and then select the Microsoft Word 11 Object Library from the list. Finally,
click OK to add a reference to the Word PIA to your Visual Studio project.

The Connect class that is created by the wizard contains untyped code, so a few
changes need to be made to make it more Word aware. By default, the project sets up
two member variables within the class that are of type object. The `addInInstance`
variable can be redeclared as type `Microsoft.Office.Core.COMAddin` object as
defined by the Microsoft Office 11.0 Object Library PIA. After you have typed the
`addInInstance` variable as a COMAddin object, you can use it to determine the

registry settings for the COM add-in, such as the GUID, the ProgID, and the description. It also has a Connect property of type `bool` that can be set to `false` to disconnect the COM add-in.

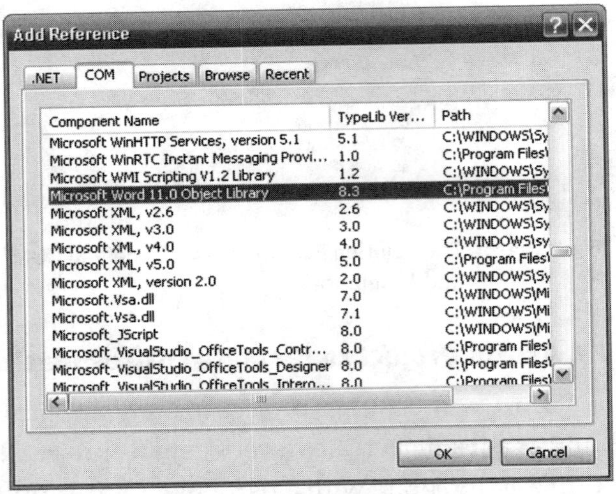

Figure 23-11 Adding a reference to the Word PIA.

The `applicationObject` member variable is also of type `object`. Because this COM add-in will only ever run inside of Word, it can be safely redeclared as type `Microsoft.Office.Interop.Word.Application`. Making this change will make developing considerably easier and safer. After changing the declaration of the `applicationObject` variable, all that remains is to change the assignment lines within the OnConnection method to cast the application argument from object to `Microsoft.Office.Interop.Word.Application` and the `addInInst` to `Microsoft.Office.Core.COMAddin`. Listing 23-3 shows the redeclaration of the `addInInstance` and `applicationObject` variables along with the new casts in OnConnection.

Listing 23-3 Strongly Typing applicationObject and addInInstance

```
public void OnConnection(object application,
    Extensibility.ext_ConnectMode connectMode,
    object addInInst, ref System.Array custom)
{
    applicationObject = application as
        Microsoft.Office.Interop.Word.Application;
```

```
addInInstance = addInInst as
    Microsoft.Office.Core.COMAddIn;
}

private Microsoft.Office.Interop.Word.Application applicationObject;

private Microsoft.Office.Core.COMAddIn addInInstance;
```

Setting the Start Action

The COM add-in is now almost ready to go. The last problem to solve is that the project is set to start up a new instance of Visual Studio rather than Word. This is easily solved by changing the debug settings for the project so that the project will start up winword.exe rather than devenv.exe. To do this, bring up the properties for the project by double-clicking the Properties project item in the Solution Explorer window, and then select the Debug tab. Doing so brings up the dialog with a Start Action section, as shown in Figure 23-12.

Start Action

○ Start project

◉ Start external program: `C:\Program Files\Microsoft Office\OFFICE11\WINWORD.EXE`   `...`

○ Start browser in URL:

Figure 23-12 The Start Action section of the Debug tab.

The start action for the project should be set to Start External Program. This value needs to change to the location of the Word process on your machine, typically C:\Program Files\Microsoft Office\Office11\winword.exe. Now when you run the project, Word will be started rather than a new instance of Visual Studio.

Word will reuse existing running instances of Word when you run the project. This can cause problems with COM add-in development. If an instance of Word is already running when you run the project, the debugger will attach to that running instance, but your COM add-in will not be loaded into that already running instance. A way to ensure that the COM add-in will always be loaded in a new instance of Word is to pass the command-line switch /w, which will cause Word to always start a new instance.

Excel automatically creates a new instance if you start it up at the command line, so there is no need to do this trick for Excel. Outlook is a single-instance application without the ability to override this behavior, so when programming against Outlook applications you need to shut down Outlook after every run of the project.

My COM Add-In Project Doesn't Work Anymore—What Happened?

A common issue that occurs in COM add-in development goes like this. "I just pressed F5 on my COM add-in project and nothing happens! My COM add-in doesn't appear to load. What's the deal?" Office has a system to protect itself from COM add-ins that fail. When you understand the system, you will better understand how to protect against your COM add-in not loading.

Office automatically disables a COM add-in if it detects that it crashed the host application while starting up. When the Office application loads and starts a COM add-in, it puts a sentinel in the registry associated with the COM add-in that it is loading. It then calls the COM add-in's OnConnection and OnStartupComplete methods. If the COM add-in successfully returns from these two methods, Office removes the sentinel in the registry and everything works fine. If the COM add-in crashes in OnConnection or OnStartupComplete or if you stop debugging and kill the Office process before OnConnection or OnStartupComplete return, the sentinel is still sitting in the registry. When you relaunch the Office application, Office detects that a sentinel got left in the registry on the last run and it disables your COM add-in.

It is very easy to have this happen during development—you might be stepping through code invoked by your OnConnection or OnStartupComplete entry point and you get to a line of code and say to yourself, "This line of code is completely wrong." You then stop debugging and change the code and press F5 to rerun the COM add-in. But on the second run the COM add-in does not work. Office detects the sentinel in the registry left over from the last run when you killed the process in the middle of OnConnection or OnStartupComplete and it disables your COM add-in.

The situation is even worse for unshimmed managed COM add-ins. The sentinel put in the registry for a managed COM add-in is the name of the DLL that bootstraps the COM add-in. In the case of a nonshimmed COM add-in, the bootstrap DLL is always mscoree.dll—a component of the CLR. Mscoree.dll acts as a class factory to create COM objects implemented in managed code for a host such as Office that expects a COM object that implements IDTExtensibility2. It bootstraps the CLR into the Office application process, loads the managed COM add-in registered in the registry, and gives the Office application the managed COM add-in class that implements IDTExtensibility2 and through interop makes that class looks like a COM object to Office.

So suppose you have two add-in projects—Addin1 and Addin2—both of which are unshimmed. You are debugging Addin1's OnConnection handler and you hit Stop Debugging in the middle of it. This leaves the sentinel in the registry saying not that Addin1.dll crashed Office but that mscoree.dll crashed Office. Now you open the Addin2 project and run it, and because Addin2 is also registered with mscoree.dll as its class factory both Addin1 and Addin2 (and any other unshimmed managed add-ins) will be disabled.

To un-disable a COM add-in that has been disabled, go to the Help > About box of the Office application and click the Disabled Items button. Doing so pops up a dialog that will let you re-enable mscoree.dll for an unshimmed COM add-in or for a shimmed COM add-in whatever your shim DLL name is.

There is a second way your COM add-in can get disabled. If your COM add-in throws an exception in OnConnection or OnStartupComplete code and does not catch it, that exception propagates out to Outlook and Outlook disables the COM add-in by setting the LoadBehavior key to 2 (HKEY_LOCAL_MACHINE\SOFTWARE\Microsoft\Office\<<Application Name>>\Addins\<<Add-in ProgID>>\LoadBehavior). There is an easy way to deal with this issue. Always put your code that handles OnConnection and OnStartupComplete inside a try..catch block. Do not leak any exceptions in OnConnection or OnStartupComplete back to Office. To un-disable a COM add-in that has been disabled in this way, you can change the LoadBehavior key back to 3 using regedit.exe or re-enable the COM add-in using the COM Add-ins dialog.

A Simple Word COM Add-In

To really understand what is possible with COM add-ins in Office applications, refer to chapters on the object models of Excel (Chapters 3–5), Word (Chapters 6–8) and Outlook (Chapters 9–11). To show that the COM add-in being developed actually works, let's add some code to the OnStartupComplete method of the COM add-in, as shown in Listing 23-4. The code will use the application object to add a button to the standard command bar in Word and show a message box when a user clicks the button.

Listing 23-4 A Simple Word COM Add-In

```
namespace WordAddin1
{
  using System;
  using Microsoft.Office.Core;
  using Extensibility;
  using System.Runtime.InteropServices;
  using System.Windows.Forms;
  using Word = Microsoft.Office.Interop.Word;

  [GuidAttribute("581C28BD-E701-4AC1-BD75-0979BCEEC91E"),
    ProgId("WordAddin1.Connect")]
  public class Connect : Object, Extensibility.IDTExtensibility2
  {
    private Microsoft.Office.Interop.Word.Application applicationObject;
    private Microsoft.Office.Core.COMAddIn addInInstance;
    private CommandBarButton simpleButton;
    private object missing = System.Reflection.Missing.Value;

    public void OnStartupComplete(ref System.Array custom)
    {
      CommandBars commandBars;
      CommandBar standardBar;
      commandBars = applicationObject.CommandBars;

      // Get the standard CommandBar from Word
      standardBar = commandBars["Standard"];

      try
      {
        // try to reuse the button is hasn't already been deleted
        simpleButton = (CommandBarButton)standardBar.Controls[
          "Word Addin"];
      }
      catch (System.Exception)
      {
        // If it's not there add a new button
        simpleButton = (CommandBarButton)standardBar.Controls
          .Add(1, missing, missing, missing, missing);
        simpleButton.Caption = "Word Addin";
```

```
        simpleButton.Style = MsoButtonStyle.msoButtonCaption;
    }

    // Make sure the button is visible
    simpleButton.Visible = true;
    simpleButton.Click += new
     CommandBarButtonEvents_ClickEventHandler(
     simpleButton_Click);

    standardBar = null;
    commandBars = null;
}

public void OnBeginShutdown(ref System.Array custom)
{
}

void simpleButton_Click(CommandBarButton ctrl,
  ref bool cancelDefault)
{
    MessageBox.Show("You clicked on the button");
}
    }
}
```

The Pitfalls of MsCoree.dll

The Visual Studio setup project created when you create a COM add-in using the Shared Add-In Wizard provides a setup package that you can use to deploy your COM add-in to your customers' machines. At first glance, the setup created by Visual Studio appears to cover all the deployment requirements for COM add-ins, but alas life is not quite that easy. A deployed COM add-in written in managed code really needs to be "shimmed." To understand what a shim is and why it is needed, we have to dig into how a COM add-in written in managed code is actually loaded into an Office application.

COM Interop and Regasm.exe

The mechanism for loading COM add-ins into Office was developed long before .NET existed and relies entirely on a technology called COM to instantiate the COM add-in. For a COM add-in written in C# to be used in Office, it must be registered as a COM component. The ability to register a C# class as a COM component is a core feature of the CLR called COM interop and can be achieved easily by running the regasm.exe tool on the assembly containing your Connect class or by selecting the Register setting for the primary output assembly in the setup project.

The regasm.exe tool works by reading the declaration of your class, and in particular the class-level attributes GuidAttribute and ProgID shown in Listing 23-5. These class-level attributes are defined in the System.Runtime.InteropServices namespace. The GuidAttribute tells the regasm.exe tool what CLSID to use in the registry for the class when registering it under HKEY_CLASSES_ROOT\CLSID. The ProgID tells the regasm.exe tool what ProgID to use when registering the class. The regasm.exe tool only writes the necessary keys under HKEY_CLASSES_ROOT\CLSID. The required key for the add-in with the ProgID name under HKEY_CURRENT_USER\Software\Microsoft\Office\%appname%\Addins and associated key values are *not* added by regasm.exe and must be added by custom install actions in the installer.

Listing 23-5 The Attributes in the Connect Class That Are Looked at by Regasm.exe

```
using System.Runtime.InteropServices;

[GuidAttribute("581C28BD-E701-4AC1-BD75-0979BCEEC91E"),
ProgId("WordAddin1.Connect")]
public class Connect : Object, Extensibility.IDTExtensibility2
{

}
```

Mscoree.dll and *Managed* Add-Ins

A managed component registered under HKEY_CLASSES_ROOT\CLSID differs from a typical unmanaged COM component primarily with regard to the InProcServer32 key in the registry for the component. An unmanaged component would set the InProcServer32 to be the DLL that implements the COM component. A managed component cannot set this value to the name of the managed DLL because to create an instance of the managed assembly the CLR needs to be loaded and there is no guarantee that the calling application will have already loaded the CLR into memory. In fact, it is almost certain that the calling application will not load have loaded the CLR because it is trying to load what it thinks is a COM component. To circumvent this chicken-and-egg situation, the CLR provides a DLL called mscoree.dll that loads the CLR, instantiates the class out of the managed assembly, and returns a COM Callable Wrapper for the managed class to the calling application.

When a managed class is registered by regasm.exe, the InProcServer32 key for the assembly always has a default value of `mscoree.dll` and an additional set of registry values are set that mscoree.dll uses to load the managed class. These additional keys provide information about the managed class and assembly that mscoree.dll will create and load. Figure 23-13 shows these values under a typical HKEY_CLASSES_ROOT\CLSID\{some guid}\InProcServer32 key for a managed add-in class called Connect in an assembly called WordAddin1.

Name	Type	Data
(Default)	REG_SZ	mscoree.dll
Assembly	REG_SZ	WordAddin1, Version=1.0.1759.37527, Culture=neutr...
Class	REG_SZ	WordAddin1.Connect
CodeBase	REG_SZ	file:///C:/Documents and Settings/andrewc/Desktop/vs...
RuntimeVersion	REG_SZ	v2.0.40430
ThreadingModel	REG_SZ	Both

Figure 23-13 The values under the InProcServer32 key for a typical managed COM add-in.

All managed COM add-ins created by the Shared Add-In Wizard use mscoree.dll to get loaded into the Office process. Unfortunately, this presents several problems for Office COM add-in development that have led to the need for replacing the mscoree.dll with a different custom loader—sometimes called a shim—when building COM add-ins for Office applications.

> If you are targeting Outlook 2003, you do not need to use a shim—you can use the new VSTO Outlook add-in project type that solves the problems associated with mscoree.dll.

Problems with Using Mscoree.dll to Load Your COM Add-In

Problem 1: Mscoree.dll Can Be Disabled, Causing All Managed COM Add-Ins to Stop Loading

Office is composed of some of the most widely used applications in the world, and ensuring that the Office applications remain as stable as possible is a key concern for the Office development team. Because Office is so widely used, a number of COM add-ins have been designed to run inside of Office applications. Unfortunately, not all of them are written well, and they crash. When a COM add-in crashes, the hosting Office application becomes unstable or often crashes itself, leaving the user with little or no way of knowing what on earth happened.

Office invested heavily in the crash detection and reporting system in Office XP to try to track down these crashes in Office. While doing this, they quickly realized that many crashes were a result of third-party COM add-ins that were crashing. Using this information, Office introduced the ability to detect when a COM add-in crashes during Office application startup. On the next run of the application, Office displays a dialog such as the one shown in Figure 23-14 offering to disable the COM add-in.

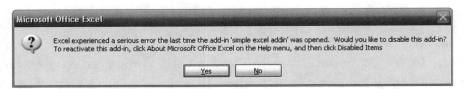

Figure 23-14 Office offers to disable a COM add-in.

If the user clicks the Yes button, Office will "black list" the COM add-in so that it will not be loaded into Office until an update has been received from the vendor. Although this is a great step forward for the reliability of Office applications, the way it was implemented does not work well with the default registration mechanism for managed COM add-ins because Office believes the offending DLL is mscoree.dll, which it blocks. Blocking mscoree.dll will not only block the crashing COM add-in but also every other managed COM add-in registered for that Office application.

Problem 2: Mscoree.dll Cannot Be Signed

In the late 1990s, Office was plagued with viruses such as the Melissa virus that took advantage of the ability to run code contained in an Office document. To defend against such attacks, Office introduced several security measures in Office XP primarily aimed at stopping malicious VBA code from running, but also to mitigate potential risks from COM add-ins. The primary defense against an add-in was to introduce the capability to only load COM add-ins signed by a trusted publisher. On the surface, this seems like a great idea, and indeed it is for unmanaged COM components. Unfortunately, it does not work well with the default registration mechanism for managed COM add-ins because Office checks the signature of the InProcServer32 binary, which is always mscoree.dll, and not the managed DLL started by mscoree.dll that contains the managed COM add-in. Mscoree.dll is a system DLL that is not signed and is installed by the CLR, so signing it with your own certificate is not possible. Mscoree.dll cannot be signed because it cannot vouch that the components it loads are safe.

Luckily, the default setting for Office is to trust all installed add-ins even if they are not signed, so this problem is not one that you will encounter on all Office installations. But it does mean if a company or individual is particularly security conscious and unchecks the Trust all installed add-ins and templates setting in the Security dialog shown in Figure 23-15, your COM add-in will not run. This dialog can be invoked by choosing the Security menu item from the Macros menu in the Tools menu of most Office applications.

Figure 23-15 The Trust all installed add-ins and templates option
in the Security dialog.

Problem 3: Mscoree.dll Loads All COM Add-Ins Into the Same AppDomain

Whenever managed code is loaded into an unmanaged application, the CLR must be hosted inside of the application in order to run the managed code. Hosting the CLR is something that can be achieved implicitly or explicitly. Implicit hosting of the CLR is achieved by the unmanaged application talking to mscoree.dll (which advertises itself as a COM object), which in turn starts up the CLR in the application and loads the managed code. Alternatively, the application can host the CLR directly by using the CLR hosting APIs, which provide considerable control over how the CLR gets loaded and in particular how assemblies get loaded. None of the Office 2003 applications host the CLR directly with respect to COM add-ins (although Word and Excel do host the CLR for document-based customizations created by Visual Studio Tools for Office), so all COM add-ins are loaded via their InProcServer32 setting.

When the CLR is running inside of a host application, it can load managed code into a unit of isolation called an AppDomain. You can think of an AppDomain as a little mini-process running inside of the Office application process. Each VSTO code-behind-document solution loads into its own AppDomain. So when you have three Excel workbooks loaded in the Excel process with VSTO code behind them, an AppDomain is created for each workbook. These AppDomains are isolated from one another—code in one AppDomain cannot adversely affect the other AppDomains.

Also, when the workbook is closed, the AppDomain corresponding to it can be stopped and unloaded without affecting the running code in other AppDomains.

By default mscoree.dll loads managed COM add-ins into the same App-Domain—an AppDomain known as the default AppDomain. This is bad because the COM add-ins are all running in the same AppDomain and can easily adversely affect each other. Also, there is no mechanism to unload managed code that was loaded when a COM add-in was connected but is no longer needed when the COM add-in is disconnected because the default AppDomain cannot be unloaded until the Office process exits. What you really want is for each COM add-in to load into its own App-Domain instead of loading all together into the default AppDomain.

Shimming: A Solution to the Problems with MsCoree.dll

Despite the gloomy picture painted for COM add-ins being loaded by mscoree.dll, a solution resolves these three problems. The solution involves writing a custom CLR host DLL called a shim DLL (written in C++) to be the loader for the CLR and the COM add-in instead of relying on mscoree.dll. A new shim DLL must be created for each COM add-in you are going to deploy. Using a shim DLL leads to a number of advantages:

- **Integration with the Office security system**—The shim DLL will now be the InProcServer32 for the COM add-in, allowing you to sign the shim and trust it on the users' machines that will guarantee that your COM add-in can load irrespective of whether Trust all installed add-ins and templates is checked. Of course, the COM add-in is only guaranteed to load if the user has trusted the certificate used to sign the custom shim DLL.

- **Reliability**—Because the shim DLL is now the InProcServer32 for the COM add-in, if something should go wrong with that COM add-in, the Office application will block only the shim DLL corresponding to that COM add-in, leaving other managed COM add-ins unblocked.

- **Isolation**—The shim DLL can create an AppDomain into which the COM add-in will be loaded instead of loading the COM add-in into the default AppDomain.

If you are building a managed COM add-in for Outlook 2003, consider using the new VSTO Outlook Add-in project. Building an add-in in this way resolves the problems with mscoree.dll as well as some other Outlook-specific issues with add-ins described in Chapter 24.

Microsoft has provided a Visual Studio COM add-in shim wizard project that works with Visual Studio 2003. It is available at http://msdn.microsoft.com/office/default.aspx?pull=/library/en-us/dno2k3ta/html/ODC_Office_COM_Shim_Wizards.asp. At the time this book was written, no wizards were available for Visual Studio 2005. However, you can use the C++ COM shim project generated by this wizard in Visual Studio 2003 and import it into Visual Studio 2005.

Conclusion

This chapter has examined the way a managed COM add-in can be created using Visual Studio. You also learned how a managed COM add-in is registered in the registry, and the pitfalls of mscoree.dll for loading a managed COM add-in. To solve the problems with mscoree.dll, we recommended using a shim DLL to load a managed COM add-in. If you are building a COM add-in for Outlook 2003, there is a much better story for add-in development—the VSTO Outlook Add-in project described in Chapter 24.

24

Creating Outlook Add-Ins with VSTO

Moving Away from COM Add-Ins

C HAPTER 23, "DEVELOPING COM ADD-INS for Word and Excel," examined several issues with building COM add-ins in C# for Office applications. In particular, the chapter considered several problems with using the default configuration of a COM add-in where mscoree.dll loads the COM add-in:

- Mscoree.dll can be disabled, causing all managed COM add-ins to stop loading.

- Mscoree.dll cannot be signed, which makes it so your COM add-in cannot be loaded when the Trust all installed add-ins and templates option is not checked.

- Mscoree.dll loads all COM add-ins into the same application domain, which allows COM add-ins to affect one another adversely.

VSTO add-ins for Outlook solves these issues. VSTO also fixes some other issues in Outlook COM add-in development that we consider here to motivate you to use the VSTO add-in technology rather than the COM add-in technology described in Chapter 23. This chapter describes the problems with the COM add-in technology in enough detail so that if you are forced to use a COM add-in approach, you will know how to work around these issues.

Getting Outlook to Shut Down Properly with a COM Add-In

The most troublesome issue in Outlook COM add-in development is that the OnDisconnection method you implement in a COM add-in sometimes is not called if you have variables such as a class member variable that is holding an Outlook object. The result is that when Outlook exits, all the Outlook windows go away but Outlook does not shut down—the outlook.exe process will continue running, waiting for the COM add-in to release the Outlook objects it is holding.

To get Outlook to shut down and call the COM add-in's OnDisconnection method, you must use a trick that involves listening to Outlook events to determine when the last window has been closed. Outlook windows are represented by two object model objects. The Explorer object in the Outlook object model represents the main Outlook window that consists of a view showing folders and items in folders. It is possible to open additional Explorer views by right-clicking an Outlook folder and choosing Open in New Window. The Inspector object in the Outlook object model represents the Outlook window that appears when you double-click an individual item in a folder such as a mail item, contact item, or other Outlook item.

The secret to getting OnDisconnection called and your COM add-in to unload is to listen to Explorer and Inspector Close events as well as the Application object's Quit event. When the last Explorer or Inspector has closed or when the Application object's Quit event is raised, you must make sure you set all the variables that are holding Outlook objects to `null`. You should then force a garbage collection after setting the variables to `null` to ensure that your add-in will not hold on to Outlook objects because objects are waiting to be garbage collected.

Listing 24-1 shows a helper class that you can create and use from your main `Connect` class in a COM add-in. The class takes as a parameter an Outlook Application object as well as a delegate to a `Shutdown` method that you would declare in your Connect class. The `Shutdown` method you declare in your `Connect` class would set all the class member variables in the `Connect` class that are holding Outlook objects to `null`, similar to what this helper class does in its `HandleShutdown` method. Note that you do not have to use this approach or this class in VSTO Outlook add-ins—only in COM add-ins. This is one of the strong arguments for switching to VSTO Outlook add-ins.

You might also notice that the helper class holds on to the Explorers and Inspectors collection objects, as well as an array of Explorer or Inspector objects. The helper class holds on to these things because if it does not, the event sinks it has established on these objects will not work. This is another variant of the classic "Why has my button stopped working" problem described in Chapter 1, "An Introduction to Office Programming."

Listing 24-1 A Helper Class That Helps an Outlook COM Add-In Shut Down Properly (This class is not necessary for VSTO Outlook add-ins.)

```
using System;
using Outlook = Microsoft.Office.Interop.Outlook;

namespace MyAddin
{
 public class EventListener
 {
  public delegate void Shutdown();

  private Outlook.Application application;
  private Outlook.Explorers explorers;
  private Outlook.Inspectors inspectors;
  private System.Collections.ArrayList eventSinks;
  private Shutdown shutdownHandlerDelegate;

  public EventListener(Outlook.Application application,
    Shutdown shutdownHandlerDelegate)
  {
   this.application = application;
   this.shutdownHandlerDelegate = shutdownHandlerDelegate;
   explorers = application.Explorers;
   inspectors = application.Inspectors;
   eventSinks = new System.Collections.ArrayList();


   explorers.NewExplorer += new
     Outlook.ExplorersEvents_NewExplorerEventHandler
     (Explorers_NewExplorer);

   inspectors.NewInspector += new
     Outlook.InspectorsEvents_NewInspectorEventHandler(
     Inspectors_NewInspector);

   ((Outlook.ApplicationEvents_10_Event)application).Quit +=
     new Outlook.ApplicationEvents_10_QuitEventHandler(
     Application_Quit);
```

```csharp
  foreach (Outlook.Explorer e in application.Explorers)
  {
   Explorers_NewExplorer(e);
  }

  foreach (Outlook.Inspector i in application.Inspectors)
  {
   Inspectors_NewInspector(i);
  }
}

public void Explorers_NewExplorer(Outlook.Explorer explorer)
{
 eventSinks.Add(explorer);
 Outlook.ExplorerEvents_Event explorerEvents =
   (Outlook.ExplorerEvents_Event)explorer;
 explorerEvents.Close += new
   Outlook.ExplorerEvents_CloseEventHandler(Explorer_Close);
}

public void Inspectors_NewInspector(Outlook.Inspector inspector)
{
 eventSinks.Add(inspector);
 Outlook.InspectorEvents_Event inspectorEvents =
   (Outlook.InspectorEvents_Event)inspector;
 inspectorEvents.Close += new
   Outlook.InspectorEvents_CloseEventHandler(Inspector_Close);
}

public void Explorer_Close()
{
 if (application.Explorers.Count <= 1 &&
   application.Inspectors.Count == 0)
 {
  HandleShutdown();
 }
}

public void Inspector_Close()
{
 if (application.Explorers.Count == 0 &&
   application.Inspectors.Count <= 1)
 {
  HandleShutdown();
 }
}
```

```
public void Application_Quit()
{
  HandleShutdown();
}

void HandleShutdown()
{
  // Release any outlook objects this class is holding
  application = null;
  explorers = null;
  inspectors = null;
  eventSinks.Clear();
  eventSinks = null;

  // call client provided shutdown handler delegate
  shutdownHandlerDelegate();

  // Force a garbage collection
  GC.Collect();
  GC.WaitForPendingFinalizers();
  GC.Collect();
  GC.WaitForPendingFinalizers();
  }
 }
}
```

Understanding RCWs, Application Domains, and Why to Avoid Calling ReleaseComObject

Some Outlook developers have used ReleaseComObject on class member variables holding Outlook objects instead of setting these variables to `null` and forcing a garbage collection as shown in Listing 24-1. ReleaseComObject is a function in the CLR that has some additional side effects if you misuse it that can adversely affect your code. It can also affect other COM add-ins if you are not using a COM add-in shim as described in Chapter 23. For this reason, we recommend against using ReleaseComObject. Because it has been recommended in the past, it is important to describe in more detail why calling ReleaseComObject is not advised. This will eventually lead us to VSTO Outlook add-ins and a description of why they do not have to do any of the tricks shown in Listing 24-1.

To understand ReleaseComObject, it is necessary to understand more of what is really happening when your code runs inside the Outlook process. The first thing you need to understand is the concept of an application domain, or AppDomain. An application domain is an isolated environment in which your code runs within a process—in this case within outlook.exe. You can think of an application domain as being a sort of process within a process. There can be one or more application domains running inside of a single process. There are several ways an application domain provides "process-like" isolation. An application domain can be stopped and unloaded without affecting another application domain. Individual application domains can be configured differently with different security policy, different settings for loading assemblies, and so on. Code running in one application domain cannot directly access code in another application domain. In addition, faults occurring in one application domain cannot affect other application domains.

With typical console applications or Windows Forms applications, you will usually have just one application domain where your code will run. There always is at least one application domain created automatically for any process running managed code. The application domain the CLR creates automatically is called the default application domain. The default application domain can only be unloaded when the process exits. This is often acceptable because you typically control all the code that loads into a console application or Windows Forms application that you have written.

In Office scenarios, you will want to have multiple application domains created in the same process where each add-in loads into its own application domain. This is desirable because if you load in the same application domain as another add-in, that add-in can adversely affect you, as discussed shortly. You also will not want to have an add-in or customization associated with a document load into the default application domain because the default application domain can only be unloaded and cleaned up when the process exits. A user might want to unload an add-in or close a document and the user will not want the customization to stick around in memory in the default application domain. Users will want the add-in to unload and free up that memory for other uses.

Figure 24-1 shows the most desirable situation for Outlook COM add-ins (and Office COM add-ins in general). If each COM add-in is shimmed as described in Chapter 23, each add-in will load into its own application domain, providing isolation so that one add-in cannot affect another. Note that no add-ins load into the default application domain in Figure 24-1. If you do not shim a COM add-in, mscoree.dll will load it into the default application domain. If we could rule the add-in world, no add-ins would ever load into the default application domain. You should avoid loading into the default application domain because a tested COM add-in that works fine on your developer machine might conflict with some other add-in loading into the default application machine on a user's machine and chaos will ensue.

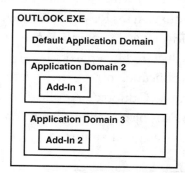

Figure 24-1 An ideal situation for add-ins—each add-in loads in its own application domain. No add-ins load into the default application domain.

If you do not use a shim to load a COM add-in and instead let mscoree.dll load your add-in, you will end up with a situation such as the one shown in Figure 24-2. COM add-ins that are not shimmed are loaded into the default application domain by default.

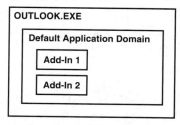

Figure 24-2 The undesirable situation that occurs when add-ins are not shimmed and loaded by mscoree.dll.

Given Figure 24-1 and Figure 24-2, we now consider what happens when you use a COM object in your customization. When you use a COM object in your customization such as Outlook's Application object, the CLR creates an object called a Runtime Callable Wrapper (RCW) for that COM object that your managed code talks to. The RCW in turn talks to the actual COM object. Any time your code talks to Outlook's Application object, your code is actually talking through the RCW.

RCWs are scoped to an application domain. The CLR creates one RCW that all code in a given application domain will use to talk to Outlook's Application object. Figure 24-3 shows the ideal situation for RCWs. With each add-in loaded into its own application domain, each add-in has its own RCWs. Figure 24-3 also illustrates that when multiple variables are declared in a particular application domain that are set to an instance of Outlook's Application object, they share the same RCW object. Note that the RCW is shared because Outlook's Application object is a singleton COM object. For nonsingleton COM objects, the RCW is not shared and the situation described below does not have as great an impact.

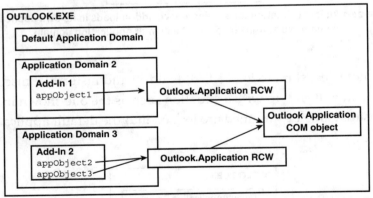

Figure 24-3 An ideal situation for add-ins—add-ins should not share RCWs.

Now we consider what ReleaseComObject does. Suppose you have a class variable in your add-in code called appObject1 that is set to an instance of Outlook's Application object. You also might have another class variable in another area of your add-in called appObject2 that is also set to an instance of Outlook's Application object. Even though you have two variables set to an instance of Outlook's

Application object, these two variables will both share one RCW that is at the application domain level.

Now suppose that appObject1 gets set to an instance of Outlook's Application object first. This causes Outlook's Application RCW to be created. The RCW is referenced counted—that is, a count is kept of each variable that is using the RCW. So the reference count of the RCW goes to 1. In addition, the RCW talks to the COM object for Outlook's Application object and adds a reference count to the COM object, too. Outlook now knows that there is some code that is "using" one of its objects. Later in the code, appObject2 gets set to an instance of Outlook's Application object. The CLR detects that an RCW is already available and so it increments the reference count on the RCW and has appObject2 share the RCW with appObject1. It does not increment the reference count on the COM object, however—the RCW will only take one reference count on the COM object and it will release that reference count when all the variables using the RCW are garbage collected.

Because Outlook is more strict about reference counts than the other Office applications, to get Outlook to shut down you need to release the reference count the RCW has made on any COM objects your managed code is using when the last Outlook window (either Explorer or Inspector) is closed or when Outlook's Application object raises the Quit event. The right way to do this is setting all the variables you have set to Outlook objects to null and then forcing two garbage collections. The quick and dirty way to do this is using ReleaseComObject. When you call ReleaseComObject on a variable, the CLR releases the reference count on the RCW associated with that variable type. So if you want to get rid of the RCW for Outlook's Application object and thereby release Outlook's COM object to get it to shut down properly, you could write the following code:

```
Runtime.InteropServices.Marshal.ReleaseComObject(appObject1);
Runtime.InteropServices.Marshal.ReleaseComObject(appObject2);
```

Note that this assumes that there are only two variables in the application domain that are using the RCW: appObject1 and appObject2. If you forgot about a variable that was set to Outlook's Application object or you are referencing a library that sets its own internal variables to Outlook's Application object, this code would not result in the RCW going away and releasing Outlook's COM object because the reference count on the RCW would be greater than 2.

ReleaseComObject also returns the number of reference counts left on the RCW. So armed with this knowledge, you could write this even scarier code:

```
int count;

do
{
   count = Runtime.InteropServices.Marshal.ReleaseComObject(appObject1);
}
while (count > 0);
```

This code keeps releasing the reference count on the RCW until it goes to 0, which then causes the RCW to be released and the COM object it is talking with to have its reference count released. This code would get rid of the RCW even in the case where you forgot about a variable that was set to Outlook's Application object or using a library that was using Outlook's Application object. The CLR also provides another method that is the equivalent to calling `ReleaseComObject` in a loop. This method is shown here:

```
Runtime.InteropServices.Marshal.FinalReleaseComObject(appObject1);
```

After the RCW has gone away because of calling `ReleaseComObject`, `ReleaseComObject` in a loop, or FinalReleaseComObject—if you attempt to use any of the properties or methods on any variables that were set to the Outlook Application object (for example you try to access `appObject1.Name`)—you will get the error dialog shown in Figure 24-4.

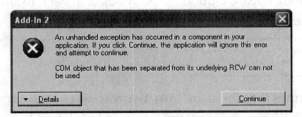

Figure 24-4 The error that occurs when you try to talk to a variable whose RCW has been released.

So you can probably see that *if* you load into your own application domain and *if* you are not using any referenced libraries that talk to Outlook's application object and *if* you can avoid talking to any properties or methods of Outlook's Application object after you have called `ReleaseComObject` in a loop or FinalReleaseComObject—you *could* get away with using this approach. This is only because you are in your own application domain and are presumably in control of all the code that might load there. If you shoot anyone in the foot by using `ReleaseComObject`, it will be yourself and not other developers.

Consider what happens if you are not using a shim and you load into the default application domain. Now you have great potential to adversely affect other add-ins that also are not shimmed and are loading into the default application domain. Figure 24-5 shows this situation. Suppose that Add-in 1 calls FinalReleaseComObject on its `appObject1` object. This will not only release the references that Add-in 1 has on the RCW, but because the RCW is shared at the application domain level and Add-in 2 is also loaded in the same application domain, it will release the references that Add-in 2 has on the RCW. Now, even if Add-in 1 is smart enough to not touch `appObject1` anymore, Add-in 2 has no way of knowing that when it talks to `appObject2` or `appObject3` it will get an exception due to the RCW going away.

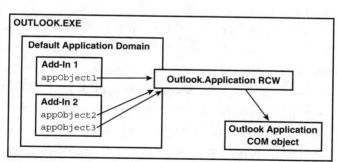

Figure 24-5   Worst-case situation for add-ins—add-ins share RCWs and one add-in calls ReleaseComObject in a loop or FinalReleaseComObject.

If instead, Add-in 1 sets `appObject1` to `null` and forces a garbage collection, .NET will make sure that the right number of reference counts are released on the RCW without affecting other users of the RCW. Also, with `appObject1` set to `null`, it will be clearer in your code that you are no longer allowed to talk to `appObject1`.

The CLR does not clean up the reference counts on the RCW until the variable you have set to `null` is garbage collected. In Listing 24-1, where we are trying to clean up the reference count immediately after the last window is closed, we force a garbage collection immediately after setting the variables referring to Outlook objects to `null`. To force the garbage collection, we call `GC.Collect()` followed by `GC.WaitForPendingFinalizers()`. Note that we then call `GC.Collect()` and `GC.WaitForPendingFinalizers()` a second time to ensure that any RCWs that were stored as members of objects with finalizers are properly cleaned up.

How Outlook Add-In Development Should Be—the VSTO Outlook Add-In Project

Outlook COM add-in development requires you to track any variables set to Outlook objects, sink the Close events of the Inspector and Explorer objects, set your variables set to Outlook objects to `null` when the last Inspector or Explorer closes or the Application object's Quit event is raised, and force two garbage collections. This complexity is not required when building add-ins for other Office applications, so do not apply these techniques to Excel or Word. Excel and Word are more robust to reference counts on their COM objects being held during the shutting down of the application. This situation also never occurs in VSTO 2005 customizations because of VSTO's better model for loading and unloading code.

If you use the VSTO Outlook add-in project, you will not have to worry about any of these Outlook-specific shutdown problems or any of the problems that we said required a shim in Chapter 23. The VSTO Outlook add-in project uses the VSTO model for loading and unloading an add-in. The VSTO model always loads a customization into its own application domain. When the add-in is unloaded or the application exits, VSTO raises a Shutdown event into the customization. The developer does not have to set any objects to `null` or force a garbage collection to clean up RCWs because once the Shutdown event handler has been run, VSTO unloads the application domain associated with the customization. When the application domain is unloaded, all the RCWs used by that application domain and customization are cleaned up automatically and the references on COM objects are released appropriately. After the application domain has been unloaded, memory used by the customization is freed, and the process can continue to run. Because VSTO Outlook add-ins apply this approach to add-ins, you never have to worry about setting variables to `null`, RCWs, or any of the complexity discussed in this section.

Creating an Outlook Add-In in VSTO

To create an Outlook add-in in VSTO, choose Project from the New menu of the File menu. The Outlook add-in project appears in the list of templates under the Visual C#/Office node in the tree of project types, as shown in Figure 24-6. Type a name for your new Outlook add-in project and pick a location for the project. Then click the OK button.

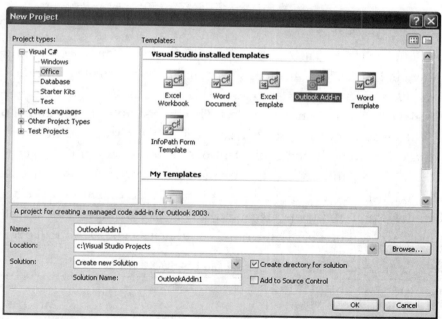

Figure 24-6 Creating a new Outlook add-in project.

A project is created with references to the Outlook 2003 PIA, the core Office PIA, and other needed references, as shown in Figure 24-7. One project item is created in the project called ThisApplication.cs.

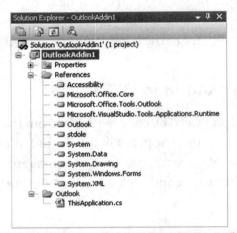

Figure 24-7 The Outlook add-in project in Solution Explorer.

If you double-click the ThisApplication.cs project item, you will see a simple code view, shown in Listing 24-2, that looks very similar to the ThisDocument.cs project item in the Word document or template VSTO project or the Sheet1.cs project item in the Excel workbook or template project. There is a simple Startup and Shutdown method where you can write code that executes on the startup and shutdown of the add-in. Startup is roughly the equivalent of OnConnection in IDTExtensibility2-based add-ins, and Shutdown is roughly the equivalent of OnDisconnection. Listing 24-2 also illustrates that the `ThisApplication` class derives from an aggregate of the Outlook Application object, enabling you to access properties and methods of the Outlook Application object by writing code such as `this.Inspectors.Count`.

Listing 24-2 ThisApplication.cs for an Outlook Add-In Project

```
using System;
using System.Windows.Forms;
using Microsoft.VisualStudio.Tools.Applications.Runtime;
```

```
using Office = Microsoft.Office.Core;
using Outlook = Microsoft.Office.Interop.Outlook;

namespace OutlookAddin1
{
  public partial class ThisApplication
  {
    private void ThisApplication_Startup(object sender, EventArgs e)
    {
      MessageBox.Show(String.Format(
        "There are {0} inspectors and {1} explorers open.",
        this.Inspectors.Count, this.Explorers.Count));
    }

    private void ThisApplication_Shutdown(object sender, EventArgs e)
    {
      MessageBox("Goodbye");
    }

    #region VSTO Designer generated code
    private void InternalStartup()
    {
      this.Startup += new EventHandler(ThisApplication_Startup);
      this.Shutdown += new EventHandler(ThisApplication_Shutdown);
    }
    #endregion
  }
}
```

When you run the project with the code shown in Listing 24-2, Outlook is launched and the add-in loads and displays a dialog box showing the count of the Inspectors and Explorers. Now go to Outlook's COM Add-In dialog by following these steps:

1. Choose Options from the Tools menu to bring up the Options dialog.
2. Click the Other tab of the Options dialog.
3. Click the Advanced Options button to bring up the Advanced Options dialog.
4. Click the COM Add-Ins button to bring up the COM Add-Ins dialog.

Figure 24-8 shows the COM Add-Ins dialog. The add-in you just created (OutlookAddin1) is displayed as if it were a COM add-in. If you look at the location of the add-in, it claims to be in the C:\program files\Common Files\Microsoft Shared\VSTO\8.0 directory.

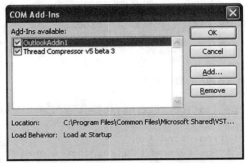

Figure 24-8 The COM Add-Ins dialog shows the VSTO Outlook add-in.

From the standpoint of Outlook, Outlook believes it is loading a COM add-in even though we know this is a VSTO Outlook add-in project. What is going on here? To answer that, let's do a little digging in the registry to understand how VSTO is hooking everything up. If we look under HKEY_CURRENT_USER\Software\Microsoft\Office\Outlook\Addins, we will find a registry key for the add-in we created in VSTO called OutlookAddin1 in our example, as shown in Figure 24-9. The registry entries look just like those for an IDTExtensibility2 add-in as described in Chapter 23. These registry entries make Outlook think it is just loading a COM add-in.

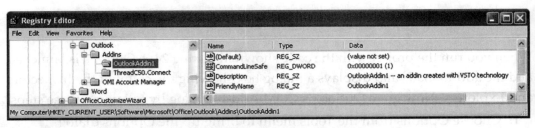

Figure 24-9 A VSTO Outlook Add-in registered under the Outlook Addins subkey.

If we search the registry under the HKEY_CLASSES_ROOT\CLSID key for the ProgID OutlookAddin1, we will find a key associated with the OutlookAddin1 ProgID. Looking under the InProcServer32 key for that ProgID, we see the entries in Figure 24-10.

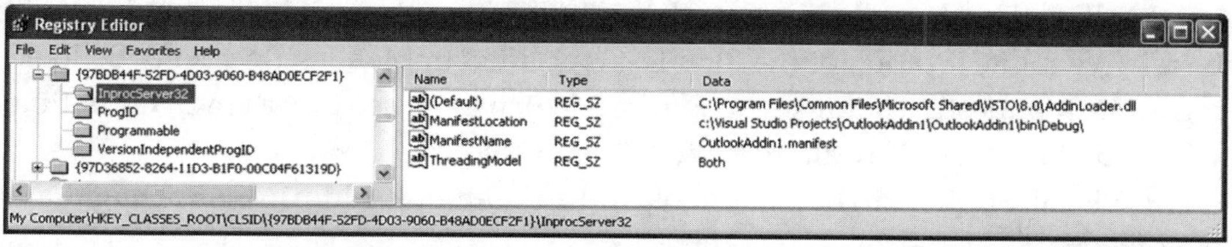

Figure 24-10 The InProcServer32 under the CLSID key associated with ProgID OutlookAddin1.

Under the InProcServer32 key are several important values. First, the (Default) value is the DLL that Outlook will start up to load the VSTO Outlook add-in we created. The DLL name is AddinLoader.dll. This is a VSTO-provided replacement for mscoree.dll that can load a managed add-in without the problems associated with mscoree.dll listed at the start of this chapter. This DLL also solves the Outlook shutdown problem, making it so that your add-in will always shut down cleanly and not leave Outlook running.

Second, we see a ManifestLocation key. Because the VSTO Outlook add-in project uses the VSTO runtime to load the add-in, a manifest is required to specify what to load. This manifest is identical to the manifest embedded in VSTO customized Word documents and Excel spreadsheets. The name of the manifest is stored in the ManifestName key. If we go to the ManifestLocation and open the file with the name ManifestName (OutlookAddin1.manifest), we will see the XML shown in Listing 24-3.

Listing 24-3 The OutlookAddin1.manifest File

```
<assembly xmlns="urn:schemas-microsoft-com:asm.v1"
xmlns:asmv2="urn:schemas-microsoft-com:asm.v2" manifestVersion="1.0">
  <assemblyIdentity name="OutlookAddin1.manifest" version="1.0.0.0" />
  <asmv2:entryPoint name="Startup" dependencyName="dependency0">
    <asmv2:clrClassInvocation class="OutlookAddin1.ThisApplication" />
  </asmv2:entryPoint>
  <asmv2:dependency asmv2:name="dependency0">
    <asmv2:dependentAssembly>
      <assemblyIdentity name="OutlookAddin1" version="1.0.0.0"
culture="neutral" />
```

```
      </asmv2:dependentAssembly>
      <asmv2:installFrom codebase="OutlookAddin1.dll" />
   </asmv2:dependency>
</assembly>
```

The manifest indicates that the actual managed add-in assembly that Addin-Loader.dll will load is called OutlookAddin1.dll. The path provided in codebase will be relative to the location of the manifest (specified in ManifestLocation). So looking at the ManifestLocation key in Figure 24-10, we can see that the VSTO runtime will load OutlookAddin1.dll from the full path below:

C:\Visual Studio Projects\OutlookAddin1\OutlookAddin1\bin\debug\OutlookAddin1.dll

Security

VSTO Outlook add-ins use the same security model that Word and Excel VSTO customizations use. That is, no Outlook add-in runs without .NET Framework security policy that trusts the Outlook add-in assembly and any dependent assemblies. When you create a new Outlook add-in project, Visual Studio automatically adds this policy to trust the bin directory for the project and any referenced assemblies that are copied locally to the project directory. When you deploy an Outlook add-in, however, you need to also create and install .NET policy that will trust the assemblies that are part of the Outlook add-in. Chapters 19, ".NET Code Security," and 20, "Deployment," cover this in more detail.

The VSTO security model is also the key to how the "Trust all installed templates and add-ins" problem is solved. When this check box in the Macro Security dialog is unchecked, Office requires the InProcServer32 registered for the add-in to be signed. Because VSTO's security model is that no add-in runs without .NET Framework security policy to trust it, VSTO can sign the AddinLoader.dll because it will only load code that has been trusted by .NET Framework security policy. This makes it so that your add-in will load even in environments where this check box is not checked.

Manifest Updating

VSTO Outlook add-ins use the same basic updating and publishing mechanism that Word and Excel VSTO customizations use to update the manifest in a document. You can publish a VSTO Outlook add-in that embeds in the manifest a URL to a deploy manifest. To publish an add-in, right-click the project node in Solution Explorer and choose Publish from the pop-up menu. The Publish Wizard shown in Figure 24-11 will appear. Here we choose to publish to a local directory called c:\myaddins.

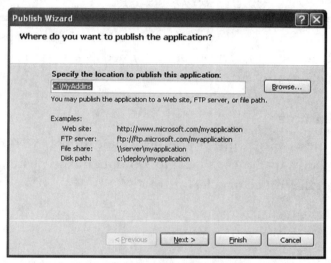

Figure 24-11 Publishing a VSTO Outlook add-in.

This causes a manifest to be generated that is slightly different from the manifest in Listing 24-3. The first difference is the manifest now points to a deploy manifest. Each time an Outlook add-in that has been published and has a deploy manifest location is loaded, the deploy manifest is checked to see whether a newer version of the manifest is available. If there is, a new version of the manifest is pulled down to the ManifestLocation specified in the registry, and it overwrites the old manifest. The second difference is that DLLs referred to in the application manifest are now located relative to the path to the deploy manifest instead of the application manifest. For more information on publishing and deploy manifests, see Chapter 20, "Deployment."

Installing

VSTO Outlook add-ins differ in one important way from Word and Excel VSTO customizations: They must be registered in the registry. This means that you will have to have an installer that installs your add-in onto a user's machine and puts the needed registry keys in the registry.

When you create a VSTO Outlook add-in project, a setup project for the add-in is automatically created for you. This setup project will generate an installer that puts the required registry keys in the registry and copies the manifest and add-in DLL to the desired location. It does not install the VSTO runtime redistributable (vstor.exe) or configure .NET security policy to trust the add-in. These steps must either be added manually to the setup project or performed as a separate step when rolling out VSTO to an enterprise. For more information, see Chapter 20.

Other VSTO Features

Although it would be nice, Outlook add-ins do not support VSTO's Smart Tags or ActionsPane features that are available to Word and Excel customizations. It also does not support the cached data feature of VSTO.

Conclusion

This chapter has examined the Outlook shutdown problem, the dangers of `ReleaseComObject`, and how application domains and RCWs are used by an add-in. This chapter also considered the VSTO Outlook add-in model as a solution to these problems.

Index

Microsoft .NET Development Series

0321154894

0321194454

0321113594

0321180593

0321334884

0321160770

0321246756

0321154916

032124673X

0201760401

0201760398

0321125193

0321169514

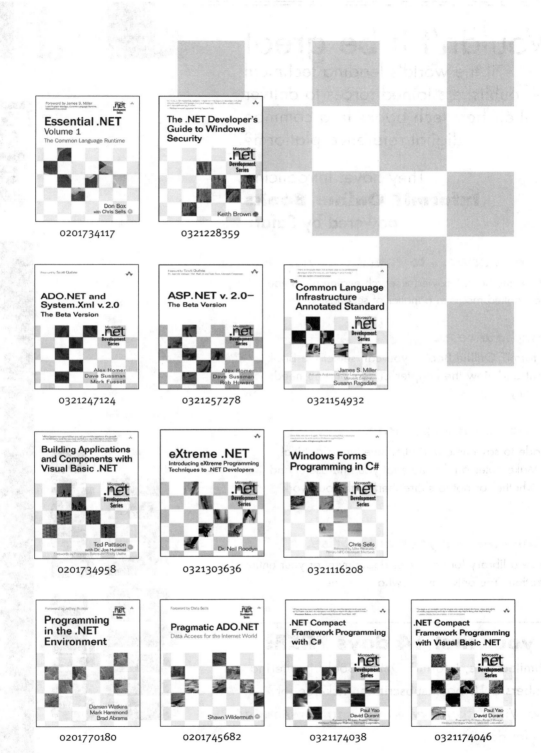

Essential .NET
Volume 1
The Common Language Runtime
Don Box
with Chris Sells
0201734117

The .NET Developer's
Guide to Windows
Security
Keith Brown
0321228359

ADO.NET and
System.Xml v. 2.0
The Beta Version
Alex Homer
Dave Sussman
Mark Fussell
0321247124

ASP.NET v. 2.0–
The Beta Version
Alex Homer
Dave Sussman
Rob Howard
0321257278

The Common Language
Infrastructure
Annotated Standard
James S. Miller
Susann Ragsdale
0321154932

Building Applications
and Components with
Visual Basic .NET
Ted Pattison
with Dr. Joe Hummel
0201734958

eXtreme .NET
Introducing eXtreme Programming
Techniques to .NET Developers
Dr. Neil Roodyn
0321303636

Windows Forms
Programming in C#
Chris Sells
0321116208

Programming
in the .NET
Environment
Damien Watkins
Mark Hammond
Brad Abrams
0201770180

Pragmatic ADO.NET
Data Access for the Internet World
Shawn Wildermuth
0201745682

.NET Compact
Framework Programming
with C#
Paul Yao
David Durant
0321174038

.NET Compact
Framework Programming
with Visual Basic .NET
Paul Yao
David Durant
0321174046

For more information go to www.awprofessional.com/msdotnetseries/